BE THE MEDIA

ENDORSEMENTS

"David Mathison's BE THE MEDIA offers the preposterous idea that broadcasting and publishing need not be exclusive to industrial titans. You (yes, he means you) can take the "big" out of "media" and return this most important feature of democracy to the people. The practical advice offered in this book are ideas whose time has come . . . and none too soon. For those who've come to understand that the "news" and what's hot in popular culture are decisions made by large corporations, this book is must reading. Here is the hand book for those Americans who want to join and help lead the revolution that is urgently returning to the people, the power of conveying information to a populace starved for new ideas from outside the box of big business commercialism." —**Phil Donahue**

"BE THE MEDIA is the 'Whole Earth Catalog' for independent media."
—**Steven Piersanti:** President, Berrett-Koehler Publishers

"BE THE MEDIA brings together a remarkable group of independent thinkers and media executives to create a provocative preview of the future of media."
—**Alexander Hungate:** Former Chief Marketing Officer, Reuters

"BE THE MEDIA is uplifting and empowering."
—**Tim Wu:** Columbia University Law Professor. Chairman, FreePress.net

"If BE THE MEDIA didn't exist, like Voltaire's God, it would have to be invented. David Mathison has assembled a mind-boggling collection of essays by people on the front lines of producing independent media. Since we are rapidly on our way to a point where that could include just about everyone, this is a book everyone needs to read."
—**Robert McChesney:** Co-founder, FreePress.net. Professor, University of Illinois at Urbana-Champaign. Author or editor of 12 award-winning books.

"If you are going to play the game, it helps to know the rules. If you want ink and airtime for your book, you need to know how the System works. David Mathison's BE THE MEDIA reveals the secrets."
—**Dan Poynter:** Author and Publisher, *The Self-Publishing Manual* (15th Edition)

"David Mathison's BE THE MEDIA is a text and bible on how modern methods permit every person and organization to reach an audience that only a few years ago was reserved for the multi-billion dollar media conglomerates. It is a reference for uninhibited and unlimited methods that use print, computers, and the whole spectrum of devices right at hand in almost every community and household. It shows how to spread ideas without the traditional massive presses, major networks and commercial studios." —**Ben H. Bagdikian:** Author, *The New Media Monopoly;* Pulitzer prize-winning journalist; Dean Emeritus, Graduate School of Journalism at the University of California, Berkeley

"David Mathison's BE THE MEDIA is the best overall resource available to help you build out your platform." —**Rick Frishman:** Founder, Planned Television Arts. Publisher, Morgan James Publishing

"Never has a book been better timed. This manifesto for the communications revolution is not New Media for Dummies. It's for smart, civically-engaged media producers and activists, and there are millions of us."
—**Jeff Cohen:** Park Center for Independent Media, Ithaca College

"This book should be called 'BE BETTER THAN THE MEDIA.' It tells readers how to realize that dream radio program, published book, or independent movie. It doesn't tell you how to break in — but how to break out. And it does it in the voices of those who have done it."
—**Adair Lara:** Award-winning columnist, San Francisco Chronicle. Author of five books, including "Hold Me Close, Let Me Go."

"BE THE MEDIA's chapter on Licensing alone is worth the price of the book."
—**Steven Ekstract:** Group Publisher, *License! Global* magazine

"Like the author himself, BE THE MEDIA is a unique and vital source of information, experience, and analysis that helps us to empower ourselves. Moving beyond the roles of media consumers who ingest what's dished out from on-high, those who take this book to heart and mind will gain essential tools and understanding for the struggles ahead—to create media that enliven and democratize instead of numbing and stultifying. If we can learn to "be the media," the process will move us far down the road toward a society where public discourse and governance is truly of, by, and for the people." —**Norman Solomon:** Author; nationally syndicated columnist; Executive Director, Institute for Public Accuracy

"David Mathison's BE THE MEDIA is a compendium of essential knowledge anyone trying to operate in the current media environment simply must have. It is smart, thorough and entertaining. I wish I had it when I started to plan the promotion of my first book."
—**Cliff Schecter:** Political Columnist, *The Guardian.* Author, *The Real McCain*

"Author-Publisher David Mathison has done his homework, and I expect BE THE MEDIA to sell very well." —**Al Canton:** President, Adams-Blake Company, Inc.

"BE THE MEDIA is one-stop shopping for any information you will need to publish your own book, produce your own radio show, or make your own film. At long last there is one comprehensive, state-of-the-art guide that includes all the information you will need to be an independent media producer by leaders in each media field. Thank you to David Mathison for this remarkable, enlightening and very timely book."
—**Kimberly Weichel:** Co-founder, Our Media Voice; Radio & TV producer; Author; Educator

"How can we the media 'consumers' BE THE MEDIA? Reading this remarkable collection of reports from the frontlines of the citizen media reform movement is an indispensable first step. Next, if you still don't like the news, make some yourself!"
—**Rory O'Connor:** President and CEO of Globalvision, Inc, an independent international media firm. Award-winning documentary filmmaker and journalist

"BE THE MEDIA is the everyman's guide on how to be a media creator/producer/distributor. No matter the medium, this compilation allows anyone and everyone to utilize new information technologies to overcome previous barriers to entry in a wide variety of media disciplines."—**Emanuel Stern:** President, Hartz Mountain Industries. The Stern family published *The Village Voice* from 1986–1999

"In a time of corporate media induced truth emergency, "BE THE MEDIA" is media democracy in action. It is the direction for grass roots bottom-up public truth telling in which we can all participate." —**Peter Phillips:** Director, Project Censored

BOOK REVIEWS

Getting Down to Business Books

By Al Caruba, *Bookviews*

"Since I have made my living in public relations after abandoning fulltime journalism decades ago, I will begin with a recommendation of BE THE MEDIA: How to Create and Accelerate Your Message . . . Your Way ($34.95) by David Mathison with more than sixty contributors. Why does it have a hefty price? Because it is over 500 pages of some of the smartest, best advice that authors, filmmakers, musicians, cartoonists, bloggers, and other creative types will find, but they are not alone. Policy makers, community organizers, educators and, just about anyone with a horn to blow will discover the power of podcasting, how to create and self-syndicate a radio show, how to promote your video using the Internet. There's a whole section on how to use the Internet for E-commerce, advice on how to license your ideas, and on and on and on! Crammed into this book is the kind of know-how it would otherwise take you a very long time to learn."

TESTIMONIALS

"I have my students read BE THE MEDIA for my class on Multimedia Journalism. The chapters on Blogs, Video, and Participatory Journalism are required reading." —**Steve Fox:** Lecturer/Multimedia Journalism Coordinator. University of Massachusetts, Amherst

"As we say in Massachusetts BE THE MEDIA is "wicked good." I keep it on my desk as a handy reference guide." —**Janet Spurr:** Author, Beach Chair Diaries

BE THE MEDIA

HOW TO CREATE AND ACCELERATE YOUR MESSAGE . . . *YOUR WAY*

COMPILED BY DAVID MATHISON

natural E creative

New York

BE THE MEDIA: How to Create And Accelerate Your Message . . . *Your Way.*
By David Mathison

Published by:

natural E creative

natural E creative group, LLC
1110 Jericho Turnpike
New Hyde Park, NY 11040
Tel: 516 488-1143
Fax: 516 488-4111
info@bethemedia.com
www.bethemedia.com

ISBN: 978-0-9760814-5-6
LCCN: 2004114734
Publisher SAN: 256-2804

Publisher's Cataloging-in-Publication Data available upon request:
Mathison, David
1. Business 2. Marketing 3. Internet

Printed and bound in Canada.
Cover design: Kathi Dunn, www.dunn-design.com
Interior design: Liz Tufte, Folio Bookworks and Dorie McClelland, Spring Book Design,
www.springbookdesign.com

IN MEMORIAM

My father, Walter Neil Mathison
March 9, 1932–June 4, 2005
Beloved son, brother, husband, father, and friend.
Rest in peace.

My grandmother, Louise ("Nanny")
January 12, 1900–May 12, 2002
My moral compass, my confidante, my nearest and dearest friend.
You reside in me always.

So live, that when thy summons comes to join
The innumerable caravan which moves
To that mysterious realm, where each shall take
His chamber in the silent halls of death,
Thou go not, like the quarry-slave at night,
Scourged to his dungeon,
but, sustained and soothed
By an unfaltering trust, approach thy grave
Like one who wraps the drapery of his couch
About him, and lies down to pleasant dreams.
—Thanatopsis, *William Cullen Bryant (1794–1878)*

DEDICATION

To my mother, Carolyn Elizabeth Mathison.
For keeping our family together,
for granting us existence,
for sustaining us,
and for supporting us
every step of the way.

The breath of life moves through a deathless valley
Of mysterious motherhood
Which conceives and bears the universal seed,
The seeming of a world never to end.
Breath for men to draw from as they will
And the more they take of it, the more remains.
—*Lao Tzu*

CONTENTS

PART ONE
THE PERSONAL MEDIA RENAISSANCE

FOREWORD: One Thousand True Fans   3
by Kevin Kelly

INTRODUCTION: Rebooting the American Dream   11
by David Mathison

1. BLOGS: How to Create and Promote Your Blog   25
by David Mathison

2. BOOKS: How to Self-Publish Your Book (and Promote the Hell Out of It)   39
by David Mathison
Teleseminar Secrets, by Alex Mandossian   63

3. MAKING MUSIC: How to Make Music With Just Three Chords and the Truth   67
The Medium Is the Music: Feel the Power of Creating Your Own, by Robert Laughlin   67
How to Play Guitar and Harmonica — The Easy Way, by David Mathison   80

4. THE MUSIC BUSINESS: The New Way to Promote and Sell Your Music   87
by David Mathison
What's Going on Here? The Artist Services Model, by Barry Bergman   95
The Home HD Studio: From Hobby to Small Business, by Jeff Mersman
    and Merlin Owens   117

5. PODCASTING: How to Create and Promote Your Podcast   127
by David Mathison
Lessons Learned from IT Conversations, by Doug Kaye, President, IT Conversations   139

6. RADIO: How to Create and Self-Syndicate Your Radio Show   143
by David Mathison
Skypecasts; Internet Radio; and Satellite Radio, by David Mathison   146

7. VIDEO: The Video Revolution   169
by David Mathison
How to Videoblog: Eleven Steps to Your First Vlog, by Jay Dedman   177

8. FILM: How to Produce and Distribute Your Ultra-Low Budget Digital Film   **189**
by Peter Broderick
The Revolution in Digital Movie Production and Distribution, by Peter Broderick   189
The Desktop Studio: Shooting Film vs Shooting Video, by Mark Stolaroff   202
House Parties, by Robert Greenwald   206
Addendum to House Party Sidebar, by Peter Broderick   208

9. INTERNET: How to Optimize Your Internet Presence for E-Commerce,   **211**
*or, how to get people to your web site and turn them into customers, subscribers,
    voters, or fans . . . even while you sleep*, by David Mathison   211

10. SYNDICATION: All About Syndication
by David Mathison   **233**
Illustrations by Lloyd Dangle and Keith Knight

11. LICENSING: How to License Your Ideas without Selling Your Soul
by David Mathison   **235**
Sesame Workshop, by Sherry Westin   246
National Wildlife Federation, by Jaime Berman Matyas   248

12. zines: Be a zinester: How and Why to Publish Your Own Periodical   **255**
by Anne Elizabeth Moore

PART TWO
THE COMMUNITY MEDIA RENAISSANCE

FOREWORD: The Opportunity for Renaissance   **273**
by Douglas Rushkoff

INTRODUCTION: We're All In This Together   **281**
by David Mathison

13. NEWSPAPERS: How to Create a High School, College, or Community Newspaper   **289**
Introduction: Don't Stop the Presses. Start Them, by David Mathison   289
Fault Lines: A Community Newspaper, by the Fault Lines Collective   292
How to Create a Great College Newspaper, by Rachele Kanigel   304
High School Journalism Matters, by Katharine Swan   306

14. WE MEDIA: Participatory Media, Online Community Newspapers, and Citizen Journalism   **311**
by David Mathison
craigslist, by Craig Newmark   326
Wikis: Platforms for Participation, by Adam Souzis and David Mathison   327

15. SOCIAL NETWORKS: How to Stay in Touch with your 1,000 True Fans   331
by David Mathison

**16. COMMUNITY RADIO: Put Your Hands on the Radio, People! A Hands-on Guide to
Starting a Community Radio Station**   343
by Pete triDish, Sakura Saunders, and Zach Schiller and the Prometheus
    Radio Project
Civil Disobedience, Legal Defense, and the Origin of Low Power FM, by Peter Franck   358

17. PUBLIC ACCESS: How to Create a Public Access TV Show   361
by David Mathison
Positive Spin, by Bill McCarthy   365
Mentors, by Robert Kubey   368
Homefront, by Dr. Jerold Starr   370

18. COMMUNITY MEDIA CENTERS: How to Create a Media Center for Your Own Community   377
by David Mathison, with thanks to Media Action Marin
How to Create an Award-Winning Public Access Station, by Susan Fleischmann   395

**19. COMMUNITY BROADBAND: How to Offer Your Community the "Triple Play"
of Voice, Video, and Internet Access**   401
by David Mathison
DIY Wireless Solution—CUWiN, by Sascha Meinrath   405

20. ((i))ndymedia: The Global Independent Media Center Network   413
by Dorothy Kidd
Open Publishing in a Nutshell, by Matthew Arnison   423

**21. CREATIVE COMMONS: Speaking about Your Creativity Legally: Copyright, Copyleft, and
Creative Commons**   427
by Mia Garlick
Did You Say "Intellectual Property"? It's a Seductive Mirage, by Richard M. Stallman   439

22. POLICY: Making Media Public Policy   443
by Ben Scott, Jeff Perlstein, and David Mathison

23. OPEN SOURCE: Making a New World   459
by Doc Searls

Author Biographies   463
Credits and Permissions   469
Disclaimer   471
Acknowledgments   473
Index   477

WHO SHOULD USE THIS BOOK, AND HOW:
BE-DO-HAVE

David Mathison

> "Give a man a fish and you feed him for a day.
> Teach him how to fish and you feed him for a lifetime."
> —*Lao Tzu*

Be the Media is for anyone who wants to harness technology to spread his or her message or products inexpensively, whether to a global or a local audience.

Notice we say *anyone*. Because of today's technology, almost anyone can be an author, musician, filmmaker, journalist, politician, blogger, cartoonist, podcaster, speaker, radio or TV host, or licensor. These entrepreneurial, independent do-it-yourselfers include the twenty-one million people who either are self-employed or own a small business.

Do they, perhaps, include you?

The strategies and digital products we propose in *Be the Media* can help you create multiple streams of income from diverse sources, while freeing you from the rising costs of fuel, ink, paper, and plastic. The tactics can be implemented on a part-time or full-time basis, from virtually anywhere—your office, den, or hotel room. And we teach you how to reach fans and other customers directly, bypassing the traditional gatekeepers entirely.

With many of our public and private institutions crumbling, the time has never been better to do it yourself. But be forewarned: Our strategies, ideas, and lessons do NOT amount to a get-rich-quick scheme. You will need to do a lot of hard work, and you will also face a lot of competition from people just as eager as you to exploit this explosion of global self-expression. Your exposure and success, though, are limited only by your creativity, hustle, ingenuity, and knowledge. A goodly amount of that knowledge, we believe, is contained in these pages.

Be the Media can be your new best friend.

To maximize the effectiveness of the book, we suggest that you first briefly skim it all, for these reasons:

- The book is progressive. Each chapter interrelates and builds upon the previous one.

- Reading the entire book allows for the cross-pollenization of marketing and promotional ideas. No matter what field you are in, you can learn from the techniques of people in other fields. Artists, to name only one group, need help promoting and selling their work, or finding people and resources that can assist them.

- Reading *all* the chapters also teaches you how to repurpose your content into various formats. This enables you to match your audience's media consumption habits and pocketbooks, so that they can get your message or product whenever, wherever, and however they want to.

After the skimming, we suggest that you focus on the specific chapters that relate to your particular field. But keep in mind always that these days, and in this book, no person or endeavor can afford to be one-dimensional. Like an octopus extending its tentacles, the idea is to expand yourself and your message into as many media nooks and crannies as possible.

In Part One (The Personal Media Renaissance), for example, if you are a writer considering the launch of a column or undertaking a book, you might want to start by creating a blog (Chapter 1), to measure audience interest. It's a way of testing the waters for free. If the reaction is negative, the project can be abandoned quickly, thus saving you a ton of money and headaches. If the reaction is positive, you can consolidate the blog posts into a newsletter, an E-book, or a standard book (Chapter 2).

Eventually, to amplify the print version, you might decide to host teleseminars to create audio versions of each chapter, or repurpose blog posts by recording them as a series of podcasts (Chapter 5) for mobile clients. The podcasts can be repurposed for a radio show, programmed using a free Internet radio station or BlogTalkRadio. Depending on demand, you might then repurpose this audio content either to self-syndicate your own radio show (Chapter 6) or to create a video book trailer that can be posted on a videoblog or on YouTube to increase the size and scope of your audience (Chapter 7).

In a similar manner, if you are a musician, you might want to start reading the blog, music (chapters 3 and 4), podcast, radio, and video chapters, while a filmmaker might zoom in on the chapters dealing with blogs, video, and film (chapter 8).

Everyone should read the Introductions and Forewords, as well as the chapters on Internet, Syndication, Licensing, and Social Networks (chapters 9, 10, 11, and 15). These all maximize the benefit from the other chapters. For example, the Internet chapter teaches you how to improve the effectiveness of your Web presence, such as accepting credit card payments, building your e-mail list, using autoresponders, and optimizing websites for search engines.

And that's just Part One of the book!

The Part Two chapters (The Community Media Renaissance) comprise the basic message that no one, but *no one,* makes it to the national stage without local experience. Not Oprah Winfrey, not Bruce Springsteen, not Mark Victor Hansen. Can't get on the news? Submit your content to a local community newspaper or indymedia.org site (chapters 13, 14, and 20). Can't get on radio or TV? Try your local radio station, public access TV station, or community media center (chapters 16, 17, and 18). Can't get attention on the giant social networks? We teach you how to create your own social network.

In Part Two, you will also find a chapter on community broadband (Chapter 19). After all, these days most of us rely on an open and affordable Internet to get our messages out, or to run our online businesses. There is a chapter on a creative, more flexible version of copyright (Chapter 21), and a chapter on media policy (Chapter 22). The Policy chapter is included because local, state, and federal legislation affects us all, regardless of which administration is in charge, and we need to be aware of and participate in the debate.

There's a lot you need to know, so we packed everything we could into a single volume. Technology changes fast, though. For updated advice and information, be sure to visit www. bethemedia.com.

What does this book *not* include? A "whining" approach to media. You will have neither excuses nor a reason to complain about the media, because now you will have myriad opportunities to **BE** *the Media.*

We encourage you to **BE** the media not only for the good of your enterprise and the people you touch, but also for your own mental health. Here's why:

Most of us operate under the misguided notion of *HAVE–DO–BE* (see sidebar). It goes something like this: "When I **HAVE** (more time, money), then I can **DO** the things (write a book, make music) that will enable me to **BE** (a successful author, musician)."

But in fact these three conditions are in reverse order: *Having* does not produce *being.* It's the other way around.

It all starts with BEING, or **BE–DO–HAVE.** Once you focus on who you want to **BE** (an author, musician), then you can **DO** things (write a book, blog, or make music), that will allow you to **HAVE** what you want. What you are *BEing*—whatever you give your attention to—will grow and manifest in your life. In thinking this way, your mind, body, and spirit become aligned in thought, word, and deed.

Consider "happiness" as an example. Happiness is not dependent on doing or having. It is a state of mind. Rather than hoping to achieve happiness at a future date (which may never come), why not *be* happy today, right now?

Or, as Walt Whitman wrote in *Carol of Occupations*, "Happiness, knowledge, not in another place, but this place—not for another hour, but this hour."

So, instead of making a to-do list, make a **TO-BE** list. Then, keep reading this book.

At the center of your being
You have the answer.
You know who you are
And what you want.

There is no need
To run outside for better seeing.
Nor to peer from a window.

Rather, abide at the center of your being . . .
Search your heart and see . . .
The way to do is to be.
—*Lao Tzu*

BE–DO–HAVE: The Three-Step Success Formula

By Bob Baker, author of the Guerilla Music Marketing Handbook *and www.TheBuzzFactor.com*

Last year I read the book *The One Minute Millionaire* by Mark Victor Hansen and Robert Allen. One of the book's prosperity principles is stated simply as "Be–Do–Have"—an approach to life that too few people take.

The best way to explain this formula is to show you how most creative people (and humans in general) do things: backwards. They set a material goal, such as "I want to write a best-selling book." Then they think, "If I could only HAVE a best-selling book, then I could DO the things a best-selling author does, then I would BE the successful author I want to be." You can easily insert "in-demand artist," "Grammy-winning songwriter" and more into this misguided Have–Do–Be equation.

Unfortunately, these people are working contrary to the laws of success and prosperity. First, you must BE the "successful artist" you want to be. And you must believe it and "know" it to the core. Success is not something you go and get; it's not a destination you reach. It's something that resides inside of you—a quality you bring to everything you do.

If you want to be a songwriter, BE a songwriter. If you want to be an actor, BE an actor…first. Then with that inner compass as a guide, DO the things that a successful songwriter (or artist, actor, etc.) does. BE and DO those things long enough and you will eventually HAVE (or manifest) the material symbols of success you desire.

This might sound like New Age babble to some, but I believe it's a solid philosophy—one that's helped propel most of my accomplishments in life.

Try this: Close your eyes and project yourself five years into the future. Imagine that your ideal artistic career has unfolded and that you've reached a stage that you consider extremely successful. Really visualize that you've arrived at this point.

If this high level of success was your reality, how would you act? How would you carry yourself? How would you treat others? How much energy would you pour into creating more art and satisfying your large and growing fan base? How confident would you be contacting other successful artists, producers, etc.? How much would you go out of your way to help good up-and-coming creative people? How content would you feel?

Now let me ask you: How does that vision compare to the way you act, feel and carry yourself now? If there's a drastic difference, look inward and realize that you're made of the same stuff as every successful person. You have as much right as anyone to embrace your own dreams.

So take that feeling of success you would feel five years from now and bring it to the present. Start having that sense of success now. Play the part, develop that all-important sense of knowing. **BE who you are**.

And . . . before you DO any more, and certainly before you HAVE what you want, focus on **BEing** the type of successful creative person you know you're destined to be!

PART I

THE PERSONAL MEDIA RENAISSANCE

"The way to do is to be."
—*Lao Tzu*

FOREWORD
ONE THOUSAND TRUE FANS

Kevin Kelly

*"When the sun comes up, have you noticed how some individual stars,
by which I mean human beings, begin to brighten?"*
—Rumi, "Energy You Can Spend"

The long tail is famously good news for two classes of people: a few lucky aggregators, such as Amazon and Netflix, and six billion consumers. Of those two, I think consumers earn the greater reward from the wealth hidden in infinite niches.

But the long tail is a decidedly mixed blessing for creators. Individual artists, producers, inventors, and makers are overlooked in the equation. The long tail does not raise the sales of creators much, but it does add massive competition and endless downward pressure on prices. Unless artists become a large aggregator of other artists' works, the long tail offers no path out of the quiet doldrums of minuscule sales.

Other than aim for a blockbuster hit, what can an artist do to escape the long tail?

One solution is to find 1,000 True Fans. While some artists have discovered this path without calling it that, I think it is worth trying to formalize. The gist of 1,000 True Fans can be stated simply: *A creator, such as an artist, musician, photographer, craftsperson, performer, animator, designer, videomaker, or author—in other words, anyone producing works of art—needs to acquire only 1,000 True Fans to make a living.*

A True Fan is defined as someone who will purchase anything and everything you produce. They will drive two hundred miles to see you sing. They will buy the super-deluxe reissued hi-res box set of your stuff even though they have the low-res version. They have a Google Alert set for your name. They bookmark the eBay page where your out-of-print editions show up. They come to your openings. They have you sign their copies. They buy the T-shirt, and the mug, and the hat. They can't wait till you issue your next work. They are true fans.

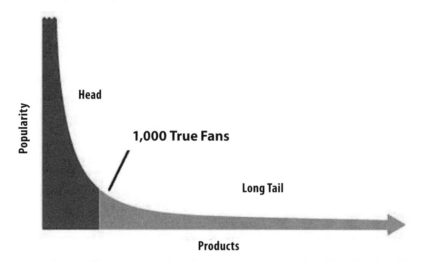

To raise your sales out of the flatline of the long tail, you need to connect directly with your True Fans. Another way to state this is, you need to convert a thousand Lesser Fans into a thousand *True* Fans.

Assume conservatively that your True Fans will each spend one day's wages per year in support of what you do. That "one-day-wage" is an average, because of course your truest fans will spend a lot more than that. Let's peg that per diem each True Fan spends at $100 per year. If you have a thousand fans, that sums up to $100,000 per year, which, minus some modest expenses, is a living for most folks.

One thousand is a feasible number. You could count to 1,000. If you started from nothing and added one fan a day, it would take only three years. True Fanship is doable. Pleasing a True Fan is pleasurable, and invigorating. It rewards the artist to remain true, to focus on the unique aspects of their work, the qualities that True Fans appreciate.

The key challenge is that you have to maintain direct contact with your 1,000 True Fans. They are giving you their support directly. Maybe they come to your house concerts, or they are buying your DVDs from your website, or they order your prints from Pictopia. As much as possible, you retain the full amount of their support. You also benefit from the direct feedback and love.

The technologies of connection and small-time manufacturing make this circle possible. Blogs and RSS feeds trickle out news, as well as notices of upcoming appearances or new works. Websites host galleries of your past work, archives of biographical information, and catalogs of paraphernalia. Diskmakers, Blurb, rapid prototyping shops, MySpace, Facebook, and the entire digital domain all conspire to make duplication and dissemination in small quantities fast, cheap, and easy. You don't need a million fans to justify producing something new. A mere thousand is sufficient.

This small circle of diehard fans, which can provide you with a living, is surrounded by concentric circles of Lesser Fans. These folks will not purchase everything you do, and may not seek out direct contact, but they will buy much of what you produce. The processes you develop to feed your True Fans will also nurture Lesser Fans. As you acquire new True Fans, you can also add many more Lesser Fans. If you keep going, you may indeed end up with millions of fans and reach a hit. I don't know of any creator who is not interested in having a million fans.

But the point of this strategy is to say that you don't need a hit to survive. You don't need to aim for the short head of best-sellerdom to escape the long tail. There is a place in the middle, not far away from the tail, where you can at least make a living. That midway haven is called 1,000 True Fans. It is an alternate destination an artist can aim for.

Young artists starting out in this digitally mediated world have another path other than stardom, a path made possible by the very technology that creates the long tail. Instead of trying to reach the narrow, unlikely peaks of platinum hits, best-seller blockbusters, and celebrity status, they can aim for direct connection with 1,000 True Fans. It's a much saner destination to hope for. You make a living instead of a fortune. You are surrounded not by fad and fashionable infatuation, but by True Fans. And you are much more likely to actually arrive there.

A few caveats. This formula—1,000 direct True Fans—is crafted for one person: the solo artist. What happens in a duet, a quartet, a movie crew? Obviously, you'll need more fans. But the additional fans you'll need are in direct geometric proportion to the increase of your creative group. In other words, if you increase your group size by 33 percent, you need add only 33 percent more fans.

A more important caveat: Not every artist is cut out, or willing, to be a nurturer of fans. Many musicians just want to play music, or photographers just want to shoot, or painters paint, and they temperamentally don't want to deal with fans, *especially* True Fans. For these creatives, they need a mediator, a manager, a handler, an agent, a galleryist—someone to manage their fans. Nonetheless, they can still aim for the same middle destination of 1,000 True Fans. They are just working as a duet.

A third caveat: Direct fans are best. The number of True Fans needed to make a living *indirectly* inflates fast, but not infinitely. Take blogging as an example. Because fan support for a blogger routes through advertising clicks (except in the occasional tip-jar), more fans are needed for a blogger to make a living. But while this moves the destination toward the left on the long tail curve, it is still far short of blockbuster territory. The same is true in book publishing. When you have corporations involved in taking the majority of the revenue for your work, then it takes many times more True Fans to support you. To the degree that an author cultivates direct contact with his or her fans, the smaller the number needed.

Lastly, the actual number may vary, depending on the media. Maybe it is 500 True Fans for a painter and 5,000 True Fans for a videomaker. The numbers must surely vary around the world. But in fact the actual number is not critical, because it cannot be determined except by attempting it. Once you are in that mode, the actual number will become evident. That will be the True Fan number that works for you. My formula may be off by an order of magnitude, but even so, it's far less than a million.

I've been scouring the literature for any references to the True Fan number. Suck.com cofounder Carl Steadman had a theory about microcelebrities. By his count, a microcelebrity was someone famous to 1,500 people. So those 1,500 would rave about you. Or, in the words of Danny O'Brien, "One person in every town in Britain likes your dumb online comic. That's enough to keep you in beers (or T-shirt sales) all year."

Others call this microcelebrity support "micropatronage," or distributed patronage.

In 1999 John Kelsey and Bruce Schneier published a model for this in First Monday, an online journal. They called it the Street Performer Protocol.

> Using the logic of a street performer, the author goes directly to the readers before the book is published; perhaps even before the book is written. The author bypasses the publisher and makes a public statement on the order of: "When I get $100,000 in donations, I will release the next novel in this series."
>
> Readers can go to the author's Web site, see how much money has already been donated, and donate money to the cause of getting his novel out. Note that the author doesn't care who pays to get the next chapter out; nor does he care how many people read the book that didn't pay for it. He just cares that his $100,000 pot gets filled. When it does, he publishes the next book. In this case "publish" simply means "make available," not "bind and distribute through bookstores." The book is made available, free of charge, to everyone: those who paid for it and those who did not.

In 2004 author Lawrence Watt-Evans used this model to publish his newest novel. He asked his True Fans to collectively pay him $100 per month. When he got $100 he posted the next chapter of the novel. The entire book was published online for his True Fans, and then later in paper for *all* his fans. He is now writing a second novel this way. He gets by on an estimated 200 True Fans because he also publishes in the traditional manner—with advances from a publisher, supported by thousands of Lesser Fans. Other authors who use fans to directly support their work are Diane Duane, Sharon Lee, and Steve Miller. Game designer Greg Stolze employed a similar True Fan model to launch two prefinanced games. Fifty of his True Fans contributed seed money for his development costs.

The genius of the True Fan model is that the fans are able to move an artist away from the edges of the long tail to a degree larger than their numbers indicate. They can do this in three ways: by purchasing more per person, by spending directly so the creator keeps more per sale, and by enabling new models of support.

New models of support include micropatronage. Another model is prefinancing the startup costs. Digital technology enables this fan support to take many shapes. Fundable.com is a Web-based enterprise that allows anyone to raise a fixed amount of money for a project, while reassuring the backers that the project will happen. Fundable withholds the money until the full amount is collected. They return the money if the minimum is not reached.

Here's an example from Fundable's site:

> Amelia, a twenty-year-old classical soprano singer, pre-sold her first CD before entering a recording studio. "If I get $400 in pre-orders, I will be able to afford the rest [of the studio costs]," she told potential contributors. Fundable's all-or-nothing model ensured that none of her customers would lose money if she fell short of her goal. Amelia sold over $940 in albums.

A thousand dollars won't keep even a starving artist alive long, but with serious attention, a dedicated artist can do better with their True Fans. Jill Sobule, a musician who has nurtured a sizeable following over many years of touring and recording, is doing well relying on her True Fans. Recently she decided to go to her fans to finance the $75,000 professional recording fees she needed for her next album. She has raised close to $50,000 so far. By directly supporting her via their patronage, the fans gain intimacy with their artist. According to the Associated Press:

> Contributors can choose a level of pledges ranging from the $10 "unpolished rock," which earns them a free digital download of her disc when it's made, to the $10,000 "weapons-grade plutonium level," where she promises "you get to come and sing on my CD. Don't worry if you can't sing—we can fix that on our end." For a $5,000 contribution, Sobule said she'll perform a concert in the donor's house. The lower levels are more popular, where donors can earn things like an advance copy of the CD, a mention in the liner notes and a T-shirt identifying them as a "junior executive producer" of the CD.

The usual alternative to making a living based on True Fans is poverty. A study done in 1995 showed that the accepted price of being an artist was large. Sociologist Ruth Towse surveyed artists in Britain and determined that on average they earned below-poverty-subsistence levels.

I am suggesting there is a home for creatives in between poverty and stardom. Somewhere lower than stratospheric best-sellerdom, but higher than the obscurity of the long tail. I don't know the actual true number, but I think a dedicated artist could cultivate 1,000 True Fans, and, by their direct support, and using new technology, make an honest living.

I'd love to hear from anyone who might have settled on such a path.

> **"A journey of a thousand miles starts under one's feet."**
> *—Lao Tzu*

INTRODUCTION
REBOOTING THE AMERICAN DREAM

David Mathison

"What this is really about is the American dream."
—Simon Cowell, American Idol

If you have any message at all, in any form, that you want to convey to the world, you now have a platform to do so. If you have something to say, or sing, or film, or write about, you have direct access to anyone who wants to hear, listen to, watch, or read it. "*You*" means not only "you" the writer, musician, filmmaker, journalist, blogger, podcaster, or talk show host, but you the activist, publicist, religious leader, cartoonist, businessperson, politician, or virtually anyone else.

Your fans and supporters are never more than a click or two away, and they're ready to help you make history—or change it.

Be the Media tells you—in detail—how to reach these fans. You'll not only find everything you need to spread your message, but you'll be able to do so without traditional publishers, music labels, broadcast networks, commercial film studios, and similar behemoths.

Our main message? **You can do it.** And you can do it *by yourself,* with a little help from your friends. Consider this book one of them.

THE AMERICAN DREAM, OR . . . DREAM ON?

The American dream—the belief that with talent, hard work, persistence, and perhaps a bit of luck, anyone can be successful—appears to be increasingly out of reach.

The gap between rich and poor Americans is wider than it has been since the Great Depression. The top 1 percent of Americans earns more income than the bottom 50 percent. The top 1 percent owns more wealth than the bottom 90 percent. Millions of Americans are working without a living wage or adequate health care. Their homes, pensions, and savings—all components of a traditional version of the American dream—are at risk under a trickle-down mentality that favors and rewards the wealthy few over the hardworking masses.

And what if the all-American dreamer happens to be an artist of any medium? Fat chance at quitting your day job, right? Or so it may have seemed lately. But take courage and read on.

These days, getting a deal from a major music label, book publisher, broadcast network, or movie studio lies far out of reach for more and more people. The major players in the entertainment industry mostly want bands that can move hundreds of thousands of CDs, authors who can sell tens of thousands of books, and filmmakers who can generate a hundred million dollars in ticket sales at the box office on opening night, plus DVDs later at retail and rental. They want artists who can be promoted with minimal development costs, a built-in audience hungry to buy whatever is offered, and an extensive platform—a roster of appearances on the *Today Show, Oprah,* and *Dr. Phil,* not to mention keynote speaking engagements, a newsletter, a popular web site, and a well-read blog.

In other words, the biggies mostly want you only *after* you too have become a biggie in your own right.

Those "lucky" few who do secure a contract from a major player typically are not so lucky, after all. They are "rewarded" by giving up their rights, forking over most of the royalties, and ceding control over the marketing, publicity, and distribution of their creations, or even their very identity. Nor do they receive much money for advances, promotion, touring, and support.

So much for luck.

"AMERICAN IDOL" . . . THE SMALL PRINT

A classic example of this expropriated version of the American dream is none other than the hugely popular show *American Idol.* Many consider winning *Idol* the ultimate sign of success. The show introduces the winner to an enormous audience of adoring fans, accompanied by international press coverage, an extensive distribution network, substantial revenues, and the freedom to create more products.

But in *Slaves of Celebrity*, journalist Eric Olsen argues that the *Idol* version of the American dream is an illusion:

"At first glance, [*Idol* winner] Kelly Clarkson would seem to have it made. But…Clarkson and the other finalists signed an unusually onerous contract with '19 Group,' headed by British pop entrepreneur Simon Fuller. These young performers are wrapped up for recording, management and merchandising under the most restrictive terms imaginable: ***Their careers are literally not their own.***" [emphasis added]

The one-sided terms in the contract from the first season revealed that Fuller and his company own the names, likenesses, and voices of *Idol* finalists, *forever,* anywhere in the cosmos:

> . . . I hereby grant to Producer the unconditional right throughout the universe in perpetuity to use, simulate or portray . . . my name, likeness, . . . voice, personality, personal identification or personal experiences, my life story, biographical data, incidents, situations, and events. I may reveal and/or relate . . . information about me of a personal, private, intimate, surprising, defamatory, disparaging, embarrassing or unfavorable nature, that may be factual and/or fictional.

American Idol is the fulfillment of a distorted version of the American dream—a dream, that is, for the rich Australian-born Rupert Murdoch, head of Fox and News Corp, the rich Briton Simon Fuller, and the rich Briton Simon Cowell, who recently signed a five-year contract worth $50 million—*every year.*

Idol is also fulfilling a dream for Freemantle Media, the company that produces the show. In 2007 alone, it earned $1.8 billion in revenues and $200 million *in profit.*

In an article titled "Idol Winners Aren't Singing All the Way to the Bank," Cox News Service's Rodney Ho wrote, "American Idol is a monstrous moneymaker—for creator Simon Fuller, for the judges, for Fox. *Except, perhaps, for the once-unknown singers*" [emphasis added].

And, perhaps, except for the show's writers and producers. Employees of Freemantle Media filed more than $250,000 in claims with the California Labor Commission, which cited the company for wage and hour violations. Employees work 15–20 hour days with "mandatory 6-day workweeks, no benefits, no health insurance, or pension contribution." The Writers Guild of America noted that writers "do not deserve to be cheated, abused and exploited…so that a few executives can rake in massive amounts of profits."

Such people and companies are not—mostly—playing illegally, just extremely well. If Simon Fuller, Simon Cowell, and Rupert Murdoch were to retire tomorrow, someone else would surely take their place. It's not the individuals or the corporations that are to blame; rather, it's the incentive and reward structure of the major label, publisher, and studio system that needs to change. And it *is* changing, thanks to the technological revolution, as well as to artists and transformed consumers, like us.

Meanwhile, the majors who rule this system and love their money-making stars have an unspoken message for independent musicians, writers, and filmmakers, not to mention new media creative people. It is this: "*You're on your own.*"

This leads us back to *our* major message: "Congratulations!" So you don't have a publisher wooing you, a record company knocking on your door, Hollywood begging to option your film. You may be much better off. If you are careful—that is, if you follow our advice—you'll maintain control over your content and keep most of the proceeds. You will, however, need to do a great deal of work.

The good news? **You are not alone.** Keep reading. We'll tell you how to work the new (and ever-evolving) innovations, and be your own media.

Let's face it. The past systems mostly sucked.

Before 2000, artists, media company executives, and consumers all had limited choices. The functions of recording, publishing, and distribution were controlled by media conglomerates that had vast resources to take the risks involved in creating, marketing, and selling potential blockbusters. They owned the plants that printed the books, pressed the albums, and processed and distributed the films. There were few other ways that creative artists could get their songs heard or their books published, and there were limited opportunities for them to develop a direct relationship with fans. With everybody competing for the elusive major deal, supplicants had no choice but to accept egregious contract terms.

High-quality, low-cost digital tools, along with the power and scope of the Internet, have changed everything.

Now anyone—this means you!—can have a global sales, marketing, distribution, and fulfillment infrastructure that rivals that of the majors. Furthermore, this digital media renaissance has made possible a flowering of creativity. Smart artists today don't chase publishers, labels, studios, and distributors. Like their progenitors in the punk movement in the 1970s, the cassette-culture boom of the '80s, and hip-hop entrepreneurs in the '90s, these new DIYers take their career into their *own* hands and forge direct relationships with their audience. They are not relying on a lucky break, becoming the next *American Idol,* or garnering an appearance on *Oprah.* They are building their own future themselves.

Before, the options were either stardom . . . or anonymity.

Today, there is a middle way, proposed by media futurists such as Brian Austin Whitney, Kevin Kelly, Jenny Toomey, Barry Bergman, Gerd Leonhard, Peter Broderick, and Janet Switzer.

In 2004, Brian Austin Whitney wrote, "I think a new definition of success will be the artist who has 5000 passionate fans who spend $20–$30 a year on [the artist's] creative output." That adds up to $100,000 per year, or more: enough to quit your day job, have health insurance, and own a car. In 2008, Kevin Kelly amplified this with his viral article *1,000 True Fans* (see Foreword). True fans, he wrote, are people who will purchase everything you produce. "You don't need a million fans to justify producing something new. A mere one thousand is sufficient. You don't need a hit to survive. You make a living instead of a fortune."

The very technology that enables this flowering of creativity, however, simultaneously holds the biggest challenge. How does an artist attract enough fans and create enough products to earn a respectable living, such as $100,000 a year?

With the help of fans like us.

In the past, conglomerates were enriched at the expense of consumers—yes, us—who unwittingly enabled and perpetuated a system rife with short-term greed, questionable accounting, and unequal rewards. The majority of revenues from our purchase of that $20 CD or book went to support executives, lawyers, accountants, distributors, retailers, and promoters—*everyone but the artist.*

It was not, and still is not, uncommon for even famous, talented artists to go without health care or a pension plan for a secure and dignified retirement, because at a young age they were exploited by abusive, one-sided *American Idol*–style contracts . . . and ended up with pennies on the dollar. Many consumers simply did not, and do not, realize that buying through a reseller (such as Wal-Mart or Amazon) gives 50 to 60 percent of the revenue to that *reseller,* instead of to the creator of the work.

So, what's different now? Today, you can rescue your favorite artists from the captive economics of the past. *You can reward them directly by buying from their websites, blogs, or widgets.* Peter Broderick refers to this as moving from "consumers of a product to patrons of an artist." Direct patronage ensures that your favorite artists have sufficient resources to create more products for your enjoyment. What could be more satisfying than that?

Today, fans or patrons—that's us again—act as publicists, distributors, affiliates, and even salespeople. Fans forward e-mails and links to friends and family of their favorite blog posts, books, music, and videos; they share music playlists at iTunes, eMusic, Internet radio stations, and music blogs; book selections at Amazon; photos on Flickr; favorite songs and films on social networks like MySpace and Facebook.

Fans—*not* corporate executives or focus groups backed by multimillion-dollar promotional campaigns—pick the hits. A fan's reward is not money, but the satisfaction of turning friends on to the hot new band, book, blog post, or film. (See chapters 4 and 15, music and social networks.)

Of course, today's technology also makes it easy to copy a CD or song and share it, but that's stealing, after all, and it means none of the revenue goes to the artist we love.

In other words, *when eating a fruit, think of the person who planted the tree.*

REBOOTING THE AMERICAN DREAM

It's indisputable. Over the past few decades, the American dream has been hijacked little by little and more and more by winner-take-all pirates and their intermediaries, who turned it into a nightmare of a system that benefitted only them and a few chosen "winners."

The effect of this cultural hijacking, on most entrepreneurs, artists, and society itself, has been unfair, unequal, exploitative, and—let's face it—in the products it presents to audiences, often boring.

Then, just when it looked like most creative people might as well let their dream die, rescue arrived in the form of a technological and populist revolution.

This ongoing revolution—some, like our contributing author Douglas Rushkoff, consider it a renaissance—is right now rebooting the American dream. It is giving it new life. It is bringing back the traditional *all*-American dream, one that is fair and just and that provides equality and opportunity to any and all dreamers, not merely corporate executives.

Together we can wrest the dream back and not only reboot it, but also upgrade it, so that the rightful owners—the artists and their fans—can use it democratically and benefit equally from it.

After all, every one of us dreams.

But how does a dream become reality? As the following chapters in *Be the Media* will make clear, in as few or as many details as you want, there are three basic steps:

1. Cultivate a Core Audience: Create a direct relationship with your fans, thus cutting out the intermediaries. This enhances the bond between you and the fans, while also increasing both opportunities and profits.

2. Own Your Rights: Control your material so that you have the freedom to create new products and to "repurpose" existing products differently. Artists should avoid exploitative agreements that take all rights exclusively and in perpetuity (which are truly a pact with the devil.)

3. Repurpose Your Work: Because you own the rights, you can constantly reconfigure your material and expertise into a range of progressively higher-value products and personalized experiences for your fans or your clientele.

A REPURPOSE-DRIVEN LIFE

Meet a leading light of repurposing, particularly in the field of publishing: Janet Switzer, the marketing guru behind some of the more successful publishing empires on the planet. She created no fewer than 327 new products for Jay Abraham, who had just a few products and a handful of special reports when they met. With Jack Canfield, she cowrote *The Success Principles,* which hit the best-seller lists of the *New York Times* and *USA Today.* She helped build the megaempire for Jack Canfield and Mark Victor Hansen's *Chicken Soup for the Soul.*

Switzer has since published the *Instant Income* series and *Publishing Mavericks: How Experts Build Empires,* which teach people to package their expertise into new products and services at higher prices.

The visualization of this model is the **Product Pricing Curve**,[1] which can be used by virtually anyone with something to, well, emote. According to Switzer, "As the sophistication of your buyer increases on the left (from book buyers up to corporations), the products they will buy also get more elaborate along the bottom (from digital ezines to corporate contracts)."

WHERE ARE YOU ON THE PRODUCT PRICING CURVE?

Most artists are in the lower left corner of the Curve—blithely giving away digital samples and offering a single product: a $20 book, or CD, or DVD. Once the patron makes a purchase, even directly from you, the artist, there is nothing else to buy. Offering more products enables you to

---

1 The Product Pricing Curve is printed by permission, courtesy of Janet Switzer's *Publishing Mavericks* series.

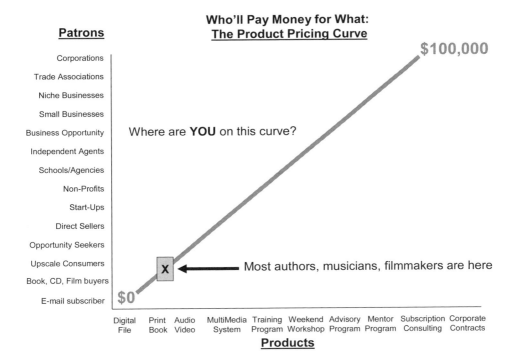

Who'll Pay Money for What:
The Product Pricing Curve

Patrons

Corporations
Trade Associations
Niche Businesses
Small Businesses
Business Opportunity
Independent Agents
Schools/Agencies
Non-Profits
Start-Ups
Direct Sellers
Opportunity Seekers
Upscale Consumers
Book, CD, Film buyers
E-mail subscriber

$100,000

Where are **YOU** on this curve?

Most authors, musicians, filmmakers are here

$0

Digital File | Print Book | Audio Video | MultiMedia System | Training Program | Weekend Workshop | Advisory Program | Mentor Program | Subscription Consulting | Corporate Contracts

Products

increase the potential lifetime value of each customer, which is worth vastly more than, say, a $20 book that will be read once.

Why is this important? As Switzer says, "Your book may never lead to a viable business model. Books are the lowest profit margined item in an information empire." The same can be said for sales of one-off songs, CDs, and DVDs.

Kevin Kelly agrees. Because multiple copies of *anything* have little or no value and are no longer the basis of wealth, he argues, "The key is to offer valuable intangibles that can not be reproduced at zero cost, and will thus be paid for. Such intangibles might include accessibility to the artist; authenticity; immediacy and priority access; patronage; curation; personalized products and experiences; support and guidance." (Think of the businesspeople, politicians, and journalists who get big money to consult or give keynote speeches; they know their way up the Curve.)

We all learn and experience things in different ways. Therefore, offering a variety of audio, video, print products, and live events will satisfy the unique needs of a larger audience, expand your opportunities and distribution outlets, and increase the likelihood of making sales that continue into your rosy future.

Media conglomerates know this well. They create multiple streams of income by selling products in various formats—print, audio, video, and digital products—as well as experiences such as conferences, concerts, and workshops. Why should conglomerates do all the conglomerating? By packaging your expertise into various media properties, you too can create multiple streams of income.

Let's summarize three scenarios for three different creative arenas.

EXAMPLE 1: AUTHORS, WRITERS, AND INTERNET ENTREPRENEURS

Experts at all levels—no matter whether they are just beginning their career, or already have a big following—can modify and leverage Switzer's Product Pricing Curve. "Ezine Queen" Alexandria "Ali" Brown went from struggling author "in tons of debt" (her own words) to a successful entrepreneur in just a few years. After having only one product to offer for two years, she packaged her expertise into information products and services, and now earns an average of $100,000—each month! Robert Kiyosaki, the ultrawealthy author of the *Rich Dad, Poor Dad* series (see chapter 2, books) is another person who has climbed the Curve.

Look closely at the chart and see where it starts. On the bottom-left, the focus should be on low-cost ways to get prospects into the marketing "funnel." In exchange for a prospect's e-mail address (which is crucial for building your "true patron" database), offer digital downloads that have no costs for shipping and handling, storage, fulfillment, or returns. For example, by giving away her free digital ezine, Brown grew her list to over thirty thousand subscribers. Other giveaways could include a special report, an MP3 file, a video trailer, or a digital course via autoresponder. You can also generate leads inexpensively by blogging, podcasting, optimizing search engines, and linking to affiliate programs. (See chapters 1, 5, and 9.)

As you move up and to the right on the Curve, you offer higher-value products such as your book, CD, or DVD for $30, or you provide a $40 teleseminar or audio book. Based on her subscriber's interests, Ali Brown created new products to satisfy their varying requests—a $19 book called *Power and Soul* and a six-CD audio series for $297 called *Think to Grow Rich*. It's easy to generate audio products by recording your concerts, lectures, training sessions, workshops, speaking engagements, seminars, phone calls, and radio interviews.

In the $497–$997 range, Brown offers a variety of full multimedia systems, which consist of print manuals, audio CDs, and video. Multimedia products improve the perceived value of a business and increase the likelihood of selling work through catalog companies such as Nightingale Conant. Kiyosaki augments his sales of print, audio, and video products with interactive software at $29.95, his $195 board game *Cashflow,* and annual subscriptions to his online community at $99.70 per year.

For those who prefer live training, Brown offers a three-day event for $3,995 called the *Online Success Blueprint* Workshop, as well as a $1,497 Home Study set, a recorded version of the Online Workshop on twenty-one CDs. At an average royalty of $1 per book sold, an author would need to sell fifteen hundred books to equal the income from just one sale of this CD audio series.

The most expensive offerings are personalized programs that provide greater access to the artist. Brown's *Silver MasterMind* has one hundred eighty superpatrons paying $560 per year (over $100,000) for monthly phone calls with her for ongoing advice. In 2006 she released a *Platinum MasterMind* inner-circle program, with just fifteen superpatrons paying $19,000 each ($280,000 per year). Members meet three times a year at luxury hotels.

It's easier to manage fifteen superpatrons paying $20,000 a year (or a hundred and eighty paying $560 per year) than three thousand patrons paying only $100. But these are not mutually exclusive. There is no reason you can't have them *all*.

And this is exactly how Ali Brown works the Curve to earn over $100,000—*every month*.

Why, you ask, would someone pay $20,000 for VIP consulting? Simple. It may be a wise investment. Say that you as an author use a traditional publisher and sell ten thousand books at $30 a book with a softcover royalty of 7.5 percent. Even if you earn the full percent royalty, which is most unlikely, you net only $22,500 of the $300,000 total revenue pool, some or all of which may be needed to pay back your advance.

By contrast, if you self-publish and sell ten thousand books at $30 per book, the entire $300,000 in revenue is yours, after covering costs. From this $300,000 in revenues, subtract the $20,000 fee plus the $22,500 you would have earned under the traditional publishing model, and you are still $257,500 ahead of the game! Engaging the right consultant may be well worth the investment. (See chapter 2, books.)

After all, as Janet Switzer says, ***"People buy results, not products."***

EXAMPLE 2: MUSICIANS

Like most authors, many musicians are stuck in the lower left corner of the Curve, giving away free digital song samples and selling CDs. But folks who buy CDs should not be their sole source of income. To paraphrase musician Robert Rich, "An animal that relies solely upon the fruit of one tree to survive is following a recipe for extinction."

If you're a musician trying to build an audience of repeat buyers, in exchange for a prospect's e-mail address (again, crucial for building a fan database) you can use free MP3 files as social discovery tools, or use digital artwork, posters, ringtones, or behind-the-scenes photos: whatever your imagination dreams up. As leads enter the funnel, you can start selling direct from your website or blog. Fans downloaded hundreds of thousands of free songs from musician Jonathan Coulton's website. He then sold songs both directly from his site and indirectly through Apples iTunes, earning a "reasonable middle class living—between $3,000 and $5,000 a month."

Selling this way lets you keep most of the income, amass the critical customer contact information, and also earn tip jar donations or advertising revenues from Google. Further on up the Curve, offers could include digital songs for as little as $0.99, albums for $20. Physical goods could include branded merchandise such as T-shirts and other apparel for $30–$40. Indirect sales can come through widgets, social networks, iTunes, eMusic, or affiliates. By using them, you'll give up a percentage of revenues, true; but you'll gain access to a wider potential audience, which is your long-term goal.

As you move to the right on the Curve, you'll see the lucrative option to license to other artists or corporations. ***Since you own the rights,*** you can also set the terms and conditions, *and* control all uses of your music. License it to TV shows, cell phones, ads, films, trailers, podcasts, retail, interactive applications, video games, ringtones, samples for other artists, and music libraries. As ex–Talking Head frontman David Byrne wrote in *Wired,* "I make very little from actual record sales. I make probably the most from licensing stuff; not to commercials, I license to films and television shows." (See chapters 4 and 11 for more.)

Music fans will gladly pay extra bucks to get as up-close and personal with musicians as they can, at least in the experience of Maria Schneider, Trent Reznor of Nine Inch Nails, and the German rockers Einstuerzende Neubauten. Their fans buy such items as printed scores, VIP tickets, autographed posters, "Deluxe Limited Edition" CD and DVD sets, and access to live webcasts of the band rehearsing, recording, and in concert.

Patrons will also gladly pay for that scarce commodity—the ability to interact live with the artist. Once you're a semi-big deal, consider offering premium concert tickets, "meet and greet" sessions, and personal backstage tours.

Many musicians augment earnings by helping other artists in a variety of ways, both artistic and technical. Singer-songwriter Bonnie Hayes consults with songwriters; produces other artists; has written hit songs for Cher, Santana, and Bonnie Raitt; and is a director and instructor at the Blue Bear School of Music in San Francisco.

Another way to earn recurring revenue streams is to start a fan club. Nine Inch Nails members get priority entrance and/or seating at concerts. Aerosmith's Aero Force One club offers a host of "flights," from a free basic membership in exchange for a fan's (all important) e-mail address; to a $29.99 Gold membership in exchange for an Aerosmith T-shirt, membership card, pin, and welcome letter; to a $59.99 Platinum membership that includes online video clips. Other perks could include decals, backstage passes, or preferred parking.

Today's fans are even funding new albums. Getting a quality recording with top-flight engineers, producers, musicians, and studio time used to mean securing a decent advance and a label contract (*which, as you know by now, meant losing rights to the songs*). Not anymore.

Instead of going to a label, singer Jill Sobule created JillsNextRecord.com to solicit donations, ranging from $10 to $10,000, from her fans. She wrote, "It would be sort of a patronage thing, where you guys are the Medici family" (referring to the dynasty of zillionaires who supported artists during the Renaissance). Her site features free music downloads, a discussion board, and funny, engaging, and authentic blog posts. Her fans feel like they are interacting with the "real" Jill, and meanwhile she is securing their loyalty by keeping them interested.

Here's Jill's bill of fare. "MicroPatrons" (mini-Medicis) who donate $10 get a free digital download of the album. For $100, they receive an advance copy of the CD and a T-shirt with Junior Executive Producer on it. $200 gets fans free admission to Jill's shows for a year. $250 gives fans membership to her "Secret Society Producer's Club," a website where she posts rough tracks. For $500, she will mention the patron's name at the end of the CD. "Macropatrons" shelling out $1,000 will have a theme song written for them by the grateful Jill, while $2,500 will get them Executive Producer credit on the album. Jill will perform a personal house concert for $5,000. And people parting with $10,000 get to sing on her CD. Brave Jill. Bravo, patrons!

Her goal was to raise $75,000 in online contributions; in two months, she raised $85,000. Furthermore, thanks to fan-financing, ***this is the first album that Jill fully owns and controls.***

EXAMPLE 3: FILMMAKERS

Any would-be filmmaker knows that creating a film of quality can be too expensive even to contemplate. And, as with music, filmgoers and film renters used to be consumers only: anonymous people who paid for their ticket with money that, for the most part, did *not* go to the filmmaker. That reel has changed.

Today, because filmgoers and film viewers are both identifiable and reachable, filmmakers can go the extra step by establishing a direct connection with them and thereby solicit donations.

Director Robert Greenwald sold twenty-three thousand DVDs of his film *Uncovered* through affiliate websites in just two days, and ultimately sold more than 120,000 copies. Armed with e-mail addresses from many of these purchasers, he now has a large, appreciative audience that can—and sometimes does—fund new films with donations in exchange for production credits. For his documentary *Iraq for Sale*, Greenwald raised $385,000 in online contributions in only ten days.

Kevin Smith, who directed *Clerks*, *Chasing Amy*, *Dogma*, *Jersey Girl*, also built a large fan base and has sold lots of merchandise from his website. If he makes a new film, he could easily generate enough sales on his website alone to cover a million-dollar budget.

You as a filmmaker could offer your supporters free video trailers. The e-mail addresses from that giveaway will help you build a mailing list of buyers who then might buy the $25 DVD direct from your website. Thus you reap as much as $20 in profit for each DVD. (According to Peter Broderick, a retail sale of the same DVD only nets $2.50 via a typical 20 percent royalty video deal.) If you sell an educational copy from the website directly to a college for $250 (a typical price), you can net up to $240. Higher-value items and "upsells" could include enhanced versions of the film, related products (books, posters, CDs), branded merchandise (apparel, and so on), soundtracks, limited editions, and previous work.

By owning and controlling your work, you also can create higher-value products by splitting up and selling various rights. That way, you can make separate or hybrid deals for theatrical distribution, nontheatrical, retail (Netflix, Amazon, and stores such as Blockbuster), home video, airlines, television, cable, advertising, educational, library, nonprofits, video-on-demand, digital (iTunes and others), and foreign sales. (See chapters 7 and 8 for more.)

THE CURVE APPLIES TO ANYONE . . .

As indicated earlier, the Product Pricing Curve model is not limited to artists, but works for anyone with a message and some marketing savvy. A stunning example is that of the Barack Obama 2008 presidential campaign. Senator Obama had almost two thousand free videos available on his site and on YouTube (viewed 110 million times), helping him to attract an audience to his message of change. He built an email list of 11 million names. Over a million people signed up on his website to work on his campaign. They held more than eighty thousand offline events, where they were given free buttons, decals, T-shirts, and bumper stickers to help market their main man. Then there were donations. Obama raised over $200 million from more than 1.5 million "micropatrons" who gave an average of $197 each.

As in any field, superpatrons are willing to give more to get more—in this case, a personal audience with the hot presidential candidate. Obama's higher-value offerings included backstage access to his speaking events, phone calls from him or his staff, autographed photos and copies of his book, a trip to the national convention, and VIP fund-raisers. In September 2008, he raised more than $9 million from superdonors willing to spend $28,500 each to spend an evening with the candidate at a California event. In October, twenty-five hundred people paid between $500 and $10,000 to attend a benefit concert in New York City featuring celebrity musicians Billy Joel and Bruce Springsteen.

THE OUTSOURCE OPTION; OR, READ THIS BEFORE GROANING

Obviously, not everyone possesses the skills, inclination, or patience to find and nurture patrons. Promotion can be a full-time job, and a wearying one. Most artists, in particular, just want to create art. Fortunately, an "artist services model" is emerging so artists can outsource the nonart activities, such as distribution, advertising, publicity, marketing, and booking. For instance, when consultant Peter Broderick helps filmmakers sell DVDs directly from their websites, the filmmakers earn up to nine times the profit per sale as compared to retail.

In other words, as you'll see in the outsourcing sections of the chapters on books (chapter 2), music (chapter 4), film (chapter 8), and the Internet (chapter 9), you are not alone. **We're all in this together.** Help is at hand and, in fact, *in* hand since you have this book to guide you.

FAIR AND BALANCED

The *Idol* version of the American Dream—the distorted, "winner-takes-all" model—is the ultimate version of an unfair system that continues to dominate the entertainment industry, as well as other areas of American life. The system relies on remote others' ownership and control of the creative output of some of our nation's most talented and beloved artists, as well as an upward redistribution of capital from hardworking consumers to a handful of already wealthy executives and corporations, which neither deserve it nor need it.

As *Be the Media* will point out in the following chapters, however, the hijacked American Dream, which too often lately has resembled a nightmare, is in the process of being rescued. The new, emerging model gives many, many artists and others the resources, freedom, and opportunity to succeed. Thanks to the participation and direct support of millions of people like you, unprecedented opportunities enable artists to control their own destiny.

The hope and promise of rebooting the American dream is to create a sustainable system that is more fair, balanced, and egalitarian; one that works for the people—from the bottom up—instead of enabling a few squillionaires to control the media (and the message) from the top down.

True, there are challenges and risks, and no guarantees of success. We face uncertain times in both the entertainment industry and the economy in general, making it even more critical for independents to repurpose their offerings to create multiple streams of income from diversified sources. Likewise, patrons should realize who benefits from every dollar they spend. Instead of supporting corporations and executives, a fan's hard-earned money should directly reward their favorite artists, so that those artists can keep a higher percentage of the revenues to grow, thrive, and prosper – and create more great products.

Our commitment is to stay on top of the changes and keep this book and website updated to help you, perhaps sooner than later, live your version of the classic American Dream—that is, to put in an honest day's work on your art or passion, earn a living wage from it, have adequate health care, provide a decent education for your children, save enough for a secure and dignified retirement, and leave this world a better place.

Send your feedback to us at info@bethemedia.com. Tell us how we're doing, and how *you're* doing.

If nothing else, I hope this book inspires, motivates, and empowers you to create and accelerate your own message, in your own way.

> "Rise like Lions after slumber
> In unvanquishable number—
> Shake your chains to earth like dew
> Which in sleep had fallen on you—
> Ye are many—they are few."
> —*"The Call to Freedom," Percy Bysshe Shelley (1819)*

1

BLOGS

HOW TO CREATE AND PROMOTE YOUR BLOG

David Mathison

"History will be kind to me, for I intend to write it."
— Winston Churchill

A blog, a portmanteau of Web log, is a personal publishing network. Blogs often start off as a one-person expression—a virtual letter in a virtual bottle, tossed into the sea of cyberspace. Yoo-hoo, is anyone out there?

If anyone is, blogs can build conversations, communities of interest, a fan base, a customer base, and more. Because blogs are participatory and interactive—picture someone sending back a note in the bottle—they help rally people to action, whether the action means getting a particular subject talked about (one not addressed by corporate media), organizing volunteers, or raising donations.

Blogs differ from traditional forms of media because they offer a conversation rather than a lecture. Feedback is interactive and instantaneous. One goal of the blogger is to start a public conversation that expands, contracts, analyzes, and perhaps reinterprets the original story.

Blogs are also virtually free. Without need for any expensive hardware, software, IT staff, or programmers, bloggers can make their little babies grow and grow and grow.

Some blogs now rival corporate publishers in reach and influence. The daily weekday circulation of New York's *Newsday* is around 450,000; the blog Daily Kos has 600,000 daily readers. A single review on Daily Kos pulled George Lakoff's book *Don't Think of an Elephant* from the cellar of Amazon sales ranking, and into the Top 10.

According to Daily Kos founder Markos "Kos" Moulitsas Zúniga, "People want to be part of the media. They don't want to sit there and listen anymore."

HISTORY

In December 1997, the term *Web log* was coined by Jorn Barger. Before blogs, Internet escribitionists (a term coined in June 1999 by Erin Venema) used what they called bulletin boards, chronicles, diaries, e-mail, ezines, and Usenet lists.

In early 1999, Infosift editor Jesse James Garrett sent links to the twenty-three blogs known at the time to Cameron Barrett, who published the list on Camworld. Meanwhile, Brigitte Eaton launched a searchable directory of blogs at eatonweb.com.

The tectonic shift occurred later in 1999, when San Francisco-based Pyra Labs offered free blog-creation software. That dramatically increased the number of blogs. Pyra became Blogger, which was eventually acquired by Google.

According to Internet information provider ComScore Networks, by the first three months of 2005, more than 30 percent of the total U.S. population (almost fifty million people) had visited a blog, a 45 percent increase over the same time period the previous year.

GROWTH OF THE BLOGOSPHERE

Among the boggling blogging statistics, the main one is this: In 1999 there were only around twenty-three known blogs, but in March of 2007 one hundred fifty thousand new blogs were being created every day. Two per second!

As of this writing, there are sixty-five million blogs and the blogosphere is doubling in size every five months, according to Technorati, a search engine that indexes blogs—in October 2007 it reported tracking 90.3 million blogs. There are 1.6 million new blog postings every day, or 18.6 posts per second.

SO, WHO ARE THESE BLOGGERS ANYWAY?

Before we show you how to join this growing group by teaching you how to make a blog, let us see some of the main ways in which blogs are used: for personal diaries, in politics, in business, and in participatory media/citizen journalism.

1. Personal diaries. Although most news coverage focuses on how blogs affect journalism (in articles written by journalists, naturally), the majority of bloggers aren't interested in becoming the next Woodward and Bernstein, or I. F. Stone. According to research firm Pew Internet, about 77 percent of bloggers say they post to express themselves creatively, rather than to get noticed or paid. Most just want to share their world through personal, unfiltered online diaries that reflect the personality and views of the author. The golden rule of blogs is that what you write is more important than who you are, what you do, or how much money you have.

For some well-written personal diaries, check out these blogs:

- wannabegirl.org   • dooce.com   • finslippy.typepad.com
- electrolicious.com   • smartypants.diaryland.com

2. Politics. Because blogs are participatory and interactive, they engage people in politics. Bloggers help rally people to action, organize volunteers, raise donations, and undertake intensive coverage of issues not addressed by corporate media.

In December 2002, at Strom Thurmond's one hundredth birthday party, Trent Lott referred glowingly to Thurmond's 1948 presidential run supporting racial segregation. Joshua Micah Marshall's journalistic Talking Points Memo blog and other blogs kept the story alive. Days later, the story was on *Meet the Press*. Lott subsequently apologized, and two weeks later he resigned his post as Senate majority leader. Talking Points Memo has one hundred thousand daily readers. Legendary broadcaster Bill Moyers, speaking with *Democracy Now!* in April 2007, noted that Talking Points Memo led coverage of the firings of federal prosecutors by Attorney General Alberto Gonzalez because "Josh Marshall has a team of reporters, but he also uses citizens out there to serve as his sources."

In March 2003, Howard Dean launched the first campaign blog by a U.S. presidential candidate. Almost $20 million of the $40 million Dean raised came from a wide base of small online contributions.

In the 2004 election, Daily Kos and Eschaton (aka Duncan Black) at atrios.blogspot.com raised from their blogs' readers hundreds of thousands of dollars in small increments for a dozen Democratic candidates.

In 2007, the perjury trial of former White House aide I. Lewis Libby Jr. represented the first federal case for which independent bloggers got official press credentials. According to reporter Scott Shane in the *New York Times*, Firedoglake's coverage was so strong that many mainstream journalists were drawn to the blog, whose audience during the trial grew to two hundred thousand daily visitors.

3. Business. According to a 2006 article by Matt Villano in the *New York Times*, "89 percent of corporations report that they are either blogging or plan to blog. Nearly 4,000 business blogs had linked to Robert Scoble's scobleizer.wordpress.com blog by the end of 2005." Technorati lists over forty-six thousand blogs tagged for the word *business*. Robert A. Lutz, the vice chairman of product development and chairman of General Motors North America, has a blog. More than three thousand of Sun Microsystem's thirty-seven thousand employees keep blogs.

This is a big change from the past, when a few key executives could control the corporate message and did so with relative ease. Today, blogs challenge this command-and-control hierarchy, offering both opportunities and risks for businesses of any size.

On the positive side, business-based blogs can help deliver accurate, reliable, and timely information. Customers and employees can ask questions, give and receive feedback, share thoughts and ideas, and exchange resources and information. For example, after Mike Kaltschnee of hackingnetflix.com requested information from Netflix in 2004 and was turned down, he posted the exchange on his blog. Soon, Netflix was battling a storm of criticism from his readers. Netflix now feeds information to Kaltschnee and other bloggers as part of its public relations mix.

On the other hand, anyone—employee, temp, intern, customer, or competitor—has the power to transmit information, including criticism, instantly and globally. Poorly managed internal corporate blogs can destroy a firm's reputation or result in a lawsuit over defamation. Employees have been fired for their blog posts, an occurrence so common that there is a name for it: *dooced.* The word evolved after dooce.com blogger Heather B. Armstrong was fired for posting satirical essays about her life at a dot-com start-up. Mark Jen was terminated by Google for allegedly publishing corporate secrets on his blog, 99zeros. Ellen Simonetti was fired for striking a suggestive pose in her Delta flight attendant's uniform and posting the photo on her blog, Diary of a Flight Attendant.

Businesses need to monitor the blogosphere not only for bad public relations but also for violations. In December 2004 Apple Inc. sued a site called Think Secret and three bloggers who may have illegally leaked some of Apple's trade secrets and information on upcoming products. You might want to automatically monitor the blogosphere by setting a Google or Yahoo! alert on your company or product name.

I would advise any business interested in blogging to set employee best-practice policies to protect the company from legal liabilities without infringing on its employees' rights. Follow legal guidelines and Securities and Exchange Commission laws, especially those that pertain to insider information. Do not release proprietary or confidential data such as sensitive product or corporate financial reports.

Six Apart, maker of the popular blog platforms Vox, LiveJournal, TypePad, and Movable Type, keeps in touch with its users through its blogs at sixapart.com/about/news/index, including blogs for each product. Even Six Apart cofounder Mena Trott occasionally stays in touch through both a corporate blog, Mena's Corner, on the Six Apart site, and a personal blog at dollarshort.org.

4. Participatory media/Citizen journalism. Anyone with a cell phone camera can share text, audio, photos, and video instantaneously and globally. (See chapter 14.) Individuals who happen to be at the right, or wrong, place can become bloggers, too. Consider the blogs during Hurricane Katrina, such as katrinacheck-in.org, which helped connect relatives of the storm's victims, and the blogs of Virginia Tech students such as silvertongue1, who used her LiveJournal blog to let her family and friends know she was okay.

Because blogs do, after all, state and report things that a newspaper or television network might miss, might not report, or might not follow up, they especially influence journalism. This has caused some tension between old and new media. Former CNN and MSNBC commentator Bill Press called bloggers people "with no credentials, no sources, no rules, no editors, and no accountability." On the contrary, journalist Jeff Jarvis of the blog BuzzMachine says, "No one owns journalism. It is not an official act, a certified act, an expert act, a proprietary act. Anyone can do journalism. Everyone does. Some do it better than others, of course."

No one is likely to disagree that blogs enable everyone, including consumers of traditional media, to respond quickly and to a lot more people than used to be the case. Blog readers are not limited to writing e-mails or letters to the editor to vent their agreement or disagreement (which may or may not get printed), or to trying to get through a television station's phone maze to leave a comment. Instead, they are empowered to engage the blog's author by posting their own comments on the blog. They can also get comments on their comments.

And they can get results. In just five months during 2004 and 2005, bloggers took down two prominent media careers and one questionable one. Conservative bloggers exposed flaws in Dan Rather's *CBS Evening News* report on George W. Bush's National Guard status. Mr. Rather, after a protracted investigation into the flaws, resigned as anchor. CNN President Eason Jordan resigned after conservative bloggers got angry about his alleged comment at the World Economic Forum in Davos, Switzerland, that journalists in Iraq were killed because the U.S. military deliberately targeted them, a comment he denied. And liberal bloggers exposed the male escort turned fake journalist James Guckert, who had been issued a White House press pass under the pseudonym Jeff Gannon.

With so much at stake, and in their own virtual backyards, some big media is now blogging. The news agency Reuters formed an alliance with a network of bloggers, called Global Voices Online, because according to cofounder Rebecca MacKinnon, "We believe that bloggers and journalists share a common goal of informing an engaged citizenry." The *New York Times* offers blogs such as The Lede (top stories), ArtsBeat (culture), Bats (baseball), On the Runway (fashion), The Pour (wine), and columnist Frank Bruni's Diner's Journal, among others.

SO, YOU WANT TO BE A BLOGGER?

Before writing a thing, search out and subscribe to blogs both inside and outside your field of interest. Blog contests such as the Koufax Awards and the Bloggies are ways to explore great blogs.

Understand your goals. What do you want to achieve with your blog—to convey information or to tell stories? Do you want to gain readers for yourself or win customers for your company? Do you want a professional look with no advertisements? Do you require multiple authors to be able to contribute from remote locations?

Also, know your intended audience. Do they want advice, humor, inspiration, gossip, or information? Goals will vary widely, from noncommercial to commercial.

Librarian in Black blogger Sarah Houghton started California's Marin County Free Library blog to do "what librarians do best, which is share information with as many people as possible."

The San Francisco DVD rental company GreenCine maintains a blog that reports on the world of independent film. It attracts about one hundred thousand visitors per month.

A blogger is not limited to the written word, in the ever expanding blogosphere. Graphic designer Sam Kuo of kuodesign.com has a blog that is mostly graphics, reflecting Sam's work, and his use of images for self-expression.

HOW TO GET STARTED

Having decided to be a brand-new blogger, or more appropriately, as someone who wants to use a blog as a way of communicating and connecting with others, you might start with a free service and progress from there. You are probably in one of two broad camps: "I want to get a blog, quickly and cheaply. I want features and flexibility, but I am not technical." Or, "I want to host the blog myself. I am technical or have access to technical support." Self-hosted systems are better solutions for intracompany blogs because they can be hosted inside corporate firewalls, where they can connect to enterprise-level systems and directories such as LDAP (see sidebar "For Propeller Heads").

For Propeller Heads

Corporations usually want to host the blog platform themselves so that they can put it securely behind corporate firewalls and manage it at the enterprise level. To host the blog platform yourself, you should make a list of your requirements and compare them to the functionality and service offered by each vendor. Evaluate applications such as Six Apart's Movable Type, or Manila, WordPress, Blosxom, and Blojsom. These products require knowledge of code, servers, and databases, and may need support from IT (information technology specialists) for installation, configuration, administration, upgrades, and maintenance.

Once you decide on a product, you will need a host for the blog. Be sure the host supports your platform and provides the required storage, bandwidth, data transfer, domains, e-mail accounts, setup, and administration, as well as the database support that your application will require, such as PHP calls to MySQL databases. Try BlueHost.com, AnHosting.com, DreamHost.com, and LaughingSquid.net.

Bottom line: If you have experience setting up a Microsoft IIS or an Apache server, know the ins and outs of a MySQL database, are familiar with some PHP, can deal with a little code, know FTP, and have a host that meets the requirements, you can probably handle this. If the previous sentence confused you, start with a Web-based hosted service, or send an e-mail to info@bethemedia.com and request a consultation.

For a fast and cheap (and free) hosted service for beginners, I recommend Vox, LiveJournal, or TypePad (all owned by Six Apart), Blogger (owned by Google), or Wordpress. These five are the most popular services, together dominating about 80 percent of the market.

To start your blog, follow these steps.

1. Go to blogger.com, vox.com, livejournal.com, or typepad.com.

   Create an account and name for your blog.

2. Type your text.

3. Select "Publish."

You are a blogger!

The benefit of a hosted service is that the people who run it handle installation, upgrades, support, and maintenance. They provide templates, too. You just type what you want to say. The service resides on the Internet, so you can post from any computer with a browser, or even from a phone (known as moblogging; see below).

KNOW YOUR INNER BLOG

The value of a blog is directly related to the writer's credibility. Even if readers disagree with you, the blogger, at least they are taking the time to read and comment on your posts, so consider them friends rather than foes.

Keep style in mind. A high-tech corporate blog will be more formal and analytical than a warm and friendly arts and crafts blog. Keep informed about your area of expertise and stick to the topic on the blog. Write naturally.

Keep your posts brief. It is better to write ten 1-paragraph posts than one 10-paragraph tome. Most bloggers present their most recent post first and update regularly, at least once per day. However, format, style, voice, updates, links, and content vary widely.

Schedule your posts so that they automatically go live on the blog at intervals throughout the day, weekend, or holiday. Drew Curtis, founder of fark.com, starts blogging at 7:30 a.m. and finishes by 9 a.m., scheduling his posts to appear to the site's five million daily viewers at various times throughout the day. To his audience, it seems that Drew is toiling away in front of his computer all day, when in fact Drew is the first to admit, "You'll find me in sports bars most of the day."

POSTS

A post is an entry in a blog. When you post, be sure to acknowledge copyrighted material and to properly attribute quotes from others. When you post entries that refer to other bloggers' posts, blog etiquette dictates that you link or add a TrackBack to that person's post rather than reposting their full entry in your post. To do this, refer to the post's permalink, which is a unique Internet address (URL) for every post. Permalinks enable bloggers to reference each post indefinitely—long after that post has disappeared from the front page and entered the archives. The cross-pollination that occurs by linking to other people's posts is one of the main goals of blogging.

Don't try to control the message. Instead, engage in conversation. You will learn from the audience. In your posts, ask readers to participate. Listen to their feedback, and respond to e-mails and comments.

COMMENTS

Your readers can use comments to become writers and to join the conversation. Most bloggers let readers leave comments on their posts. Comments are a great way to engage your audience in a conversation and to build community. Users may have more interesting comments than your original post. If readers have queries, turn the best question into the title of a new post that aims to answer the question. Huffingtonpost.com allows readers to vote for their favorite comments. The comment getting the most votes is then featured directly below the post.

Most blog platforms let you moderate comments, so you can approve comments before they appear on your blog. If you opt to allow public comments, it makes sense to include a policy statement such as the following:

Comments are welcome on any of the posts. We may edit comments, and we reserve the right to delete rude, insulting, or otherwise inappropriate comments. We ask that comments be appropriate, constructive, and civil. Links to blatantly commercial sites, advertisements, spam, and illegitimate TrackBacks will be removed.

SPREADING THE WORD: HOW TO GET MORE VISITORS TO YOUR BLOG

There are a number of ways to get more visitors to your blog, and the good news is, most of them are free. One of the most important is to post something every day, or at least a few times a week. Blog search engines specialize in tracking new, updated content. Engines also look for relevant keywords within the headline or title of each post. As you will see below, you can increase your audience by leveraging the power of syndication, by registering your blog with directories and search engines, and through reciprocal link exchanges with related blogs.

1. Syndicating your posts with feeds. Readers don't need to visit your blog every day to check on updates. Instead, they can subscribe to your feed by using an aggregator or newsreader.[2] All you have to do is publish ("syndicate") a feed of your blog, and updated posts will be delivered directly to your audience. Everyone who subscribes to the feed will automatically receive new posts into their newsreader.

Syndication is enabled by a standard protocol called Really Simple Syndication, or RSS. RSS allows for the automated creation, subscription, and management of feeds. (See chapter 10.) Most

---

2. Aggregators for RSS and blog feeds are called newsreaders; examples include Pluck and My Yahoo! (see Syndication chapter). Aggregators for audio feeds are called podcatchers; examples include Juice and iTunes (see Podcast chapter). Aggregators for both audio and video feeds include FireAnt and Mefeedia (see Video chapter).

blog hosts automatically create an RSS feed from every post. If your host does not provide syndication, you can create a feed by submitting posts to feedburner.com.

The big benefit of an RSS feed over e-mail is guaranteed delivery. For the blogger, RSS feeds are better than e-mail because posts go directly to your audience's newsreader. Your post won't get stuck in corporate or personal spam filters, firewalls, junk mail folders, or overflowing e-mail inboxes. Subscribers benefit from feeds because they do not have to give up their e-mail address and are therefore not susceptible to identity theft, phishing, spam, and viruses. The post goes straight into their newsreader.

To see what your blog's feed looks like to your audience, subscribe to it from a few newsreaders, such as My Yahoo!, Bloglines, Pluck, NewsGator, FeedDemon, Feedreader, Google Reader, Sharp Reader, NetNewsWire, or the new RSS reader in Microsoft Office 2007, or the most recent versions of web browsers from Internet Explorer, Firefox and Safari. Subscribe to the feed by right-clicking on the orange RSS button, copying the location, and pasting it into the newsreader.

2. Directories. Most blog software automatically notifies sites such as Technorati, weblogs.com, and blo.gs when you post a new entry. Weblogs.com automatically notifies subscribers when new content is posted to a blog. Blo.gs is a directory of recently updated Web logs and tools for tracking interesting blogs. Ping-O-Matic is a service that tells various search engines that you have updated your blog.

There are also community-focused directory sites for niche blogs, which can be alerted to your new entries. For example javablogs is a directory of blogs relating to the Java programming language. Find the directories that link your community of interest with the wider world, and alert them to your new posts.

3. Search Engines. Internet search engines such as Google—which the general public considers up to date—track Web pages that rarely change, returning roughly the same search results today as the engine did a month ago. By contrast, blog search engines are up to date; they track the current, live conversation in the blogosphere. For this reason, film studios use blog search engines to see which movies are hot. Advertisers use them to track responses to their campaigns.

It takes weeks to get a static Web page into Google's search engine. However, if the blog platform is set up to submit pings to Technorati, Google, and others, posts are usually indexed within hours. Blogger and all of Six Apart's blogs have services that submit pings to Google and Technorati.

To help your own blog make its way in the world, ensure that it is listed in Internet search engines such as Google, Yahoo!, Teoma, and Alltheweb, and some of the blog-specific engines listed in the sidebar—which are also places to learn about more blogs. Also check out Ari Paparow's Big List of Blog Search Engines at aripaparo.com/archive/000632.html.

Blog search engines

Technorati lets you see "what's hot" in the blogosphere. It tracks the top books, general news, and much, much more.

Feedster tracks thirty million sources throughout the blogosphere.

Icerocket searches the Internet, blogs, MySpace, and even cell phone pictures. It enables you to search for references *inside* a blog.

Blogstreet is a blog directory and search service that tracks 300,108 RSS feeds and 102,480 blogs.

Blogdex presents the most discussed memes in the blogosphere.

Blogsearchengine.com tracks ten million blogs in its search results.

BlogPulse is a blog search engine that also reports on daily blog activity.

Bloglines is a newsreader, search engine, and directory tracking one hundred thousand blogs.

4. Blogrolls. In contrast to links to other people's posts, as we discussed before, blogrolls are collections of links to other blogs. Blogrolls are usually reciprocal—you link to me, I link to you—and can usually be found in the side column of the blog or on a separate page. Get your coworkers, colleagues, and customers to link from their blog to yours. The reason for this is not only to spread news about your site but also because blog search engines rank the number of relevant inbound and outbound links to your site. The more relevant links are connected to your blog, the higher the blog search engines will rank your site.

Too many links can be hard to manage, however. If you are fortunate enough to have that problem, try blogrolling.com, a service that helps you manage your ever-evolving link list.

MOBLOGGING

Mobile + blog = moblog. A moblog is text, voice, photos, or video that is posted to a blog from a telephone or PDA. Anyone with a telephone can be a moblogger, from almost anywhere in the world. Call from a golf course, restaurant, party, trade show, conference, or your car. All that is required is to send an e-mail or call an access number provided by your host and then type, speak, or sing. Blogger, TypePad, and Audio-blogger are a few of the many hosts that provide this service.

Adam Seifer is a committed moblogger. For the past four years Seifer, chief executive of Fotolog Inc., has blogged photos of every meal he has eaten. He takes the photos with his camera phone and moblogs his meal from restaurants, the ball park, or wherever he is eating at the time.

On a somber note, mobile bloggers posted images from the December 2004 tsunami caused by the Indian Ocean earthquake, from the London subway attack in 2005, and from the Virginia Tech shootings in 2007.

SPLOGS AND FLOGS

Spam + blog = splog. Splogs are junk blogs filled mostly with keywords designed to increase a blog's search engine ranking, traffic, and therefore, ad revenue. Technorati estimates that between 2 and 8 percent of the one hundred fifty thousand new blogs created every day are splogs. Technorati will ban a splog from the system if it detects abuse. Similarly, SplogSpot is a splog search engine that offers a searchable database of splogs for consumer input and awareness. Splog Reporter enables users to report splogs. Don't splog.

Fake + blog = flog. Flogs are created by professional advertisers or corporate public relations and marketing departments to promote a company or product. For example, in March 2005 Captain Morgan created a fake blog to promote, or flog, its rum drinks.

REVENUE OPPORTUNITIES

Although most bloggers arguably do not enter the blogosphere to make money, there are nonetheless—I feel duty bound to report—several ways to make money blogging. You could write for niche blogs. For example, Sportsblogs.com splits ad revenue with site contributors. You could also write for corporate blogs. In 2004 Marqui paid a dozen bloggers $800 each to discuss its products. Or, you might want to find a sponsor. Audi was once the exclusive sponsor of the car blog jalopnik.com.

One of the easiest ways to earn revenue is from advertising, if you are ok with that. In 2008, Technorati surveyed 1,000 bloggers and found that the mean annual advertising revenue is $6,000, and that sites with over 100,000 or more unique visitors are generating over $75,000 in ad revenue.

In the past, advertising was the province of large media corporations that could afford an ad sales team. Now, however, just about anyone can have ads placed on their blog. The phenomenon is largely thanks to Google's AdSense, which lets bloggers earn money by allowing ads to be shown on their blogs. AdSense automatically inserts ads on a blog or in RSS feeds—and not just any old ad. Google uses its search technology to serve contextual ads based on the content in the blog. You write about Apple iPods, and suddenly your blog is advertising iPods. Bloggers get a share of the ad revenue on a per-click basis. (More about this in chapter 9.)

Blog readers are likely to be young, wealthy, online shoppers with high-speed Internet connections. It follows, therefore, that popular blogs can earn real money from sponsors trying to reach this affluent demographic. For example, according to its own survey, readers of the political blog Crooks and Liars had incomes in the $60,000 to $90,000 range; 76 percent of its viewers had a college or postgraduate degree; 71 percent were between twenty-one and fifty years old. In May 2007, a month-long premium ad on crooksandliars.com cost $7,500, and on dailykos.com it cost $30,000.

So if you start attracting a large audience, or if you are an influential voice in your field, you might be invited to join the select network of bloggers represented by ad placement companies like Blogads or Federated Media. Blogads represents blogs such as Atrios, Crooks and Liars, and Daily Kos. Advertisers include Paramount Pictures, the *Wall Street Journal,* Penguin Books, the *New Yorker,* Random House, and Oxford University Press. Blogads places ads on fifty to one hundred blogs a day, organized into categories such as music and film. In 2005 the music network of ten blogs had monthly traffic of over 1.6 million unique visitors. Sponsors can purchase a targeted ad-buy across the ten-blog music "hive." Average bloggers make up to $50 per month selling Blogads, with some earning up to $5,000 monthly. Blogads takes 30 percent. Bloggers can set their own prices, customize ad design, and write ad copy. Henry Copeland, CEO of Blogads, expects "more money to [flow to] more authors as smart advertisers bypass publishers and pay authors directly for their audience."

Like Blogads, the invitation-only Federated Media also sells ads on blogs. Federated's slogan is that "great voices attract great audiences." Highly selective, Federated represents only leaders of influential blogging conversations within their industries, communities, and peer groups, such as BoingBoing, Jeff Jarvis's BuzzMachine, Digg, SmartMobs, and wilwheaton.net. Federated get sponsors' ads in front of boatloads of readers—Federated sites generate more than 350 million page views every single month.

Not doing well enough to get an invitation, but still getting a decent sized audience for advertisers? Try OpenAds, which gives bloggers (and web site owners) free, open source adserver software, plus access to their network of advertisers.

BLOOKS

Attract a wide enough audience and your blog could turn into a blook. A term coined by librarian Mindell Dubansky in the 1990s, a blook is an online book published on a blog, or a print book based on a blog. To make a blook, all you need is a blog and a concept.

On his blog PostSecret, Frank Warren requested confessional postcards, resulting in more than seventy thousand submissions. He turned this into a spin-off book titled *My Secret.*

In 2004, Julie Powell of Queens, New York, spent a year trying to cook every recipe in Julia Child's book *Mastering the Art of French Cooking.* Powell's blogging of this adventure on Julie/Julia led to a book deal with Little, Brown and Company. The book, *Julie and Julia: 365 Days, 524 Recipes, 1 Tiny Apartment Kitchen,* sold more than one hundred thousand copies.

After Wil Wheaton (*Star Trek: The Next Generation*'s Wesley Crusher) inked a three-book deal, he used his blog to promote the book, *Dancing Barefoot,* selling three thousand copies in five months from his living room.

Diaryland.com, which has almost one million registered users and hosts over four hundred thousand live diaries from people all over the world, begot *The World According to Mimi Smartypants.*

If Mimi Smartypants can make a blook, so can you.

And you certainly can make a blog.

"Be yourself. Everyone else is already taken."

—*Oscar Wilde*

2

BOOKS

HOW TO SELF-PUBLISH YOUR BOOK (AND PROMOTE THE HELL OUT OF IT)

David Mathison

"If there's a book you really want to read but it hasn't been written yet, then you must write it."
— *Toni Morrison*

The publishing industry, in particular the self-publishing industry, is going through a change so revolutionary that the once-thrilling phenomena of getting agents, publishers, and distributors seem like, well, footnotes. The revolution is twofold. The first revolt from tradition is the explosion of do-it-yourself publishing in its many manifestations, including the one you are holding in your hands.

What does this mean? It means that *anyone* can publish a book.

The second uprising is the expansion of do-it-yourself promotion. It means that, yes, anyone can publish a book, but selling it and promoting it are entirely different battlefronts. If you already have a published book, but want to sell a few more zillion copies of it, this chapter is targeted at you, too. It just depends on when you're joining the revolution.

Before diving into the "how-to's," keep one thing in mind: No matter what new or old publishing or marketing avenue you choose, every one has both pros and cons. What pros? Great royalties, maybe. Or maybe enormous esteem. Not necessarily both. And what cons? Huge expenditures of time, maybe. Or maybe expensive and time-consuming production problems.

I can state unequivocally, however, that despite alarms about Americans' declining reading habits, and independent bookstores biting the dust, people are writing. Some 1.5 million titles are now in print in the United States. Traditional publishers, from corporate giants to university presses to tiny nonprofits, publish more than fifty thousand new titles annually. Add to that the number of self-published "other" books and the total is mind-boggling.

Today, you don't need an agent or giant publisher to print a book, but you *do* need to decide which option to take. You have four basic choices:

- Traditional publishing
- Vanity publishing
- Print on Demand (POD)
- And the option I am touting in these pages, Self-publishing

"What?" you may be thinking. "I thought there was just old-style publishing and new-style do-it-yourself publishing." Far from it. Let's look closer at what the choices entail.

TRADITIONAL PUBLISHING

This is old-fashioned publishing that goes back at least a century. You get an agent—no small feat nowadays—who carefully reviews your manuscript and then sends it to various publishers, who usually say "no, thanks" but maybe one says, "yes, we'll publish your book." That publisher then edits it, designs it inside and out, typesets and proofreads it, prints it, and finally sends it to bookstores or Internet resellers. This model is now defined by consolidated control, not only over the publishing of books, but also over their distribution and sales. In the last twenty years, more than three hundred publishers have merged. Seven multinational conglomerates,[1] four of which are not American, publish 80 percent of U.S. books. A handful of powerful distributors delivers most of the books to a few giant chain resellers.

The dream of many would-be authors is that getting a traditional publishing deal, especially with a corporate publisher, equals instant success. True, a major deal does bring prestige, if not necessarily sales. The publisher also handles most of the editorial work. Especially in university press nonfiction, the publisher arranges for experts to vet the material, meaning give it their expert appraisal and perhaps correct errors of fact. You, the author, are treated as a scholar. Tradi-

---

1. They are, according to size:
   - Bertelsmann AG (Germany), which includes imprints Random House: Bantam, Doubleday, and Fodor
   - Pearson PLC (UK), which includes Penguin, Putnam, Avery, and Viking
   - News Corporation (Australia), which includes HarperCollins, ReganBooks, William Morrow, and Zondervan
   - Von Holtzbrinck (Germany), which includes Henry Holt, St. Martin's, and Macmillan
   - Time Warner Book Group, which includes the Book of the Month Club and Warner Books
   - Viacom, which includes Simon & Schuster, MTV Books, Pocket, Scribner, and the Wall Street Journal books
   - Disney Publishing, which includes Hyperion, ESPN Books, and ABC Daytime Press

tional publishers also handle the design, layout, and printing, and have contacts with distributors and resellers. All great, but . . .

Fewer than 1 percent of books become best-sellers, and fewer than 1 percent of writers earn more than $50,000 a year from their writing alone. Only 6 percent of writers make a living as authors, according to noted literary agent Michael Larsen.

In sum, it is almost impossible for a new author to break into this constricted environment.

Without a large built-in audience, or what is sometimes now called a *platform*, the odds of getting a major publishing deal are low. For one thing, publishers rarely accept unagented book proposals or complete manuscripts; agents supply 90 percent of the books published by the major houses.[2] For another thing, agents and most publishers are increasingly risk-averse. They want blockbuster celebrity authors like John Grisham or J. K. Rowling, "repeaters" who regularly make the best-seller lists. Or, in the words of Frank Dane, "the great American novel has not only already been written, it has already been rejected."

Celebrity authors of both fiction and nonfiction get huge advances; $1.2 million was paid to Gail Sheehy after *Passages*, $3.2 million to Judith Krantz for paperback rights to *Princess Daisy*, and a world record (at the time) $15 million fee was paid to former President Bill Clinton for his 2004 autobiography *My Life*.

But the majority of authors get advances of less than $10,000, some considerably less than that. Most new writers are lucky to get anything at all. The "advance," as professional writers know too well, is not a gift but rather a loan that must be paid back by book sales before the author sees a penny in royalties.

And everyone gets a piece of the pie before the author earns those royalties. The standard author royalty from a traditional publisher is 7 to 15 percent of net sales. Before you, the author, can get your book into bookstores or on Amazon.com, you'll need a distributor. Distributors, often in a consortium, take 65 percent of the retail price, and give wholesalers and bookstores a discount of from 40 to 50 percent, leaving the distributor with about 15 percent. So the author's share is $10 of his or her $30 book. After the publisher takes its royalties of between 85 percent for hardcover and 93 percent for softcover of that $10, the author is left with around a buck a book. And don't forget the author's agent, who takes 15 percent of that, leaving the author with a few pennies to pay back the loan euphemistically known as an advance.

The fine print on most traditional contracts lets the publisher give discounts that reduce royalties even further. In 2007, five authors sued Eagle Publishing, parent company of the politically conservative Regnery Publishing, publishers of the 2004 book "*Unfit for Command*" that

---

2. If you can endure the process of finding an agent and a publisher, check the Association of Author's Representatives; Jeff Herman's *Guide to Book Editors, Publishers, and Literary Agents*, Author Link; and Publisher's Weekly. But be prepared: *The Godfather, Love Story,* and *The Celestine Prophecy* were all initially rejected. A total of 144 publishers turned down *Chicken Soup for the Soul,* whose agent actually fired the authors, thinking he would never sell the book to a publisher! The series went on to sell over 100 million books.

maligned Senator John Kerry, charging that it sells or gives away copies to book clubs and other organizations owned by Eagle "to avoid or substantially reduce royalty payments to authors."

What's worse, unless you are an author with clout, or have an especially aggressive agent, the publisher keeps most of the rights to your work, as well as subsequent editions of it and such subsidiary products as audio books, eBooks, and newsletters.

To rub even more salt into the wound of being a poorly paid first-time author, at checkout time the online and offline retailers own the customer contact and billing information, so the author rarely knows who his or her customers are and has no ready means of developing a relationship with them to sell future books.

VANITY PUBLISHING

Many people (incorrectly) think that all self-publishing is of the "vanity" type. Vanity publishing simply means that an author pays a publisher quite a lot of money to print a minimum number of books, which the author then buys. Most writers spend from $10,000 to $20,000 for production costs, then, being the owner of however many books, must find an audience to buy them, unless they give them away to family and colleagues. Vanity upon vanities! The steep upfront costs constitute one reason that traditional publishers have a dim view of vanity books. Distributors, retailers, bookstores, and reviewers alike generally shun vanity titles. Nevertheless, thousands of authors who need to express themselves end up writing big checks to vanity publishers. A leading vanity publisher, Vantage Press, which now refers to itself as a "subsidy" publisher, prints more than three hundred titles a year.

PRINT ON DEMAND

For the third form of publishing, print on demand, let's use the now-common abbreviation P.O.D., or just POD. The phrase, however, can mean two different things: print on demand *publishers,* such as iUniverse, or print on demand *printers,* like, say, your neighborhood Kinko's. In both cases, demand drives production; if just two copies of your manuscript are ordered, only two copies are printed. Good-bye, garage full of unsold books! Good-bye, the huge investment with little hope of return in vanity publishing. As with vanity presses, though, the author of a POD work pays to create the book, though POD is much less expensive, and also buys the book from the POD publisher, if at a steep discount. First-year sales for a new POD title rarely exceed a hundred to a hundred and fifty books, which is fine if that figure was all you planned on and hoped for. There are exceptions. The POD publisher Lulu had a top-seller, *Putting the Can in Cancer,* which sold forty thousand copies, but that is the rare exception. Other drawbacks: POD books do not use high-quality offset printing, and some POD companies do not check for errors. (Be sure to find out the specific publisher's policy.) Yet, the POD industry is thriving, thanks to its low cost, simplicity, and rapid turnaround.

Here are some of the POD leaders to consider doing business with:

iUniverse (49 percent owned by the bookstore chain Barnes & Noble). This is one of the best PODs, with low prices of $300–800 charged to the author, flexibility in design, and professional editing. Authors receive a royalty of 20 percent of the net sale. Your title becomes available, though is not sold aggressively, on Barnes & Noble.com, Amazon.com, and more than twenty-five thousand global resellers. iUniverse also attracts serious writers, such as ex-Reuters PR man Robert Crooke, whose novel *Sunrise* earned iUniverse's in-house designation as a "Publisher's Choice" selection.

AuthorHouse claims it has published twenty thousand titles, from 18,500 authors. It charges those authors more than other POD publishers, but with quality results. Book covers are created by in-house designers. The author sets the price of the book and receives a royalty of a heftier 30 percent of the cover price.

Xlibris (owned by Random House). This publisher charges the author more, typically $900–3,000, and offers fewer options than other POD vendors. Royalties range from 15 percent to 40 percent.

Lulu charges no set-up fees at all to the author. No money changes hands until the book is published. The author keeps all rights, sets the price, and receives a lulu of a royalty: 80 percent. Although the books may look shoddy, that hasn't stopped authors from printing more than 236,000 copies of their paperbacks since Lulu opened in 2002.

BookSurge (owned by Amazon.com). The author retains all rights to the book, sets the price, and controls the cover design. Because the book is available via Amazon.com, Amazon itself handles the fulfillment, which means orders get filled expeditiously and delivered to customers. The author royalty is 45 percent. See also Amazon's CreateSpace for POD CDs and DVDs.

Cafepress: This publisher's costs charged to the author is based on the type of binding and the number of pages. The author sets the price above the cost.

SELF-PUBLISHING

In my opinion, self-publishing is the mother of all publishing. But don't take only my word for it.

According to Dan Poynter, author of *How to Self-Publish Your Book,* "If you self-publish, you will get more money, get to press sooner, and keep control of your work."

Poynter, the leading expert in this ever-growing field, touts self-publishing because the author who self-publishes owns *everything*: rights (including related derivative works and subsidiary products), royalties, and even the ISBN number on the back of the title page. There is a minor stigma; the ISBNs (see page 48) for self-published books are coded to give away your "small fry" status, and book reviewers are among those who can tell the difference.

Thanks to the rise and power of home-based desktop computers, inexpensive but sophisticated digital tools for publication, and the ubiquitous and ever-expanding Internet for promotion and distribution, self-publishing has grown dramatically; it's virtually the Big Bang of publishing. In 1947, there were only 357 publishers; in 1973, some three thousand. Today, there are almost eighty thousand. Like Starbucks, there's a self-publisher on virtually every block.

Self-publishing, furthermore, has a rich tradition. If you follow that star you are, in some ways, in the splendid company of T. S. Eliot, Benjamin Franklin, Ernest Hemingway, Anaïs Nin, Beatrix Potter, Upton Sinclair, Gertrude Stein, Leo Tolstoy, Mark Twain, Walt Whitman, and Virginia Woolf. All initially published their own words.

Nowadays, relatively little fiction or poetry is self-published, as opposed to P.O.D., simply because so much effort is involved. Self-publishing, though, is especially attractive for people in the field of business nonfiction, and it has the potential to be very lucrative.

To wit:

- *The One Minute Manager* (twelve million copies sold), by Ken Blanchard and Spencer Johnson, sold over twenty thousand copies before publisher William Morrow picked it up.
- *What Color Is Your Parachute?* (eight million), by an Episcopal clergyman, Richard Nelson Bolles, landed for 288 weeks on the *New York Times* best-seller list.
- *The Celestine Prophecy* (5.5 million), by James Redfield, started off with the author's selling an astonishing hundred thousand copies of it from the trunk of his Honda. He then sold the rights to Warner Books for $800,000.

The writer who self-publishes pays a few thousand dollars for a cover and layout, and prints books digitally, meaning directly from a computer to a high-speed laser printer, without the need and expense of film for printing presses. Without an advance to pay out, the entire investment can be recouped after just a few hundred or thousand books are sold. So any additional sales—as well as subsidiary opportunities such as foreign rights, licensing, and merchandising—are pure profit. The audience may be smaller, but so are your costs. You can likelier make a living on sales of a few thousand books than you could with a traditional publisher.

Meanwhile, duh, you need a book. The best way to get started is to write a book proposal. Do this for your own sake—to organize your thoughts, not to attract an agent or solicit a publisher. Refer to *Write the Perfect Book Proposal,* by Jeff Herman, or Michael Larsen's book, *How to Write a Book Proposal.* The proposal should be around fifty double-spaced pages, with a title that can "tell and sell." Author and award-winning professional speaker Sam Horn relates that the title can be as simple as everyday dialogue, like *Don't Make Me Stop This Car*, or a play on words such as *Goal Models* or *Dalai Mama*, or her own book titles *ConZentrate* or *Tongue Fu!*

For nonfiction, it is also important to create a *hook*, the most exciting, compelling aspect of the book, which can be expressed in one sentence. Best-selling author, speaker, and publicist Rick Frishman says that a good hook should solve a problem—for example, *The Five Ways to Lose Ten Pounds by Next Week.*

Self-publishing is a business

Repeat after me, and post on your bathroom mirror: "Self-publishing is a business. Self-publishing is a business. Self-publishing . . ."
Are you convinced you want to self-publish? Fine, but there is a lot to know about the process, and a lot you will have to do to make your book (let's dream big: *books!*) successful.

Don't quit your day job. Keep a steady income, and get advance sales to cover printing costs. Ask yourself whether you can afford to pay for, and have time to manage, the following aspects of self-publishing: advertising, artwork, binding, copyediting, cover design and production, design (inside), distribution, editorial, fulfillment, indexing, layout, marketing, order processing, page proofs, printing, promotion, publicity, sales, shipping, and storage. Oh, yes, and writing.

Fortunately, today there are reasonably priced services available to make the entire process easier and help your books appear more professional, which I will describe below. Nonetheless, you should treat your enterprise as your own publishing company, because it is.

Outline your working capital, expenses, and schedule. Set up a business checking account, and get an Employee Identification Number (EIN) from the Secretary of State of your own state. Register a Web domain and set up a business e-mail account. No more AOL or free e-mail addresses or wacky e-mail nicknames. You have to be reached at something professional, like myfirstname@mybusiness. com. Check to see whether your book title is already taken on Amazon.com, and follow up by using the library (ask a reference librarian for help) and Google for research. Titles cannot be copyrighted—you could name your memoirs Adventures of Huckleberry Finn, but why would you?—but your life will be a whole lot easier if your title is yours alone. Organize your files carefully on the computer, and be sure to back up every day, safely, preferably to a CD or an on-site service, which you may already have with your Internet Service Provider, or ISP.

Also, at some point along the way, because you have neither a traditional agent nor a traditional contract, you need to get legal advice. Make certain that your business is set up as one, that you pay appropriate taxes, and so on. Have a lawyer look over any contracts you sign with anyone connected to your business.

The proposal should include an overview of no more than a page, a table of contents, descriptions of all chapters, two complete sample chapters, and a list of competitive and complementary books. List any celebrities who have agreed to pen your foreword, write a chapter, or give endorsements (the more grandiose word for "blurbs").

Most important, define as many potential subsidiary products from the work as you can envision at this early stage, and make your marketing and promotional plans for the book and for those products. This is where you describe your audience and how you plan to address it and sell to it. Mention any bulk or advance purchases you have secured.

You can write the book yourself (what a concept!) or, these days, you can get experts to write it for you. For the latter, try your local writer's workshop, or Matchwriters.com, or find freelancers on websites like eLance.com, which connects some hundred thousand collaborators with projects. According to Rick Frishman, up to 70 percent of nonfiction books use ghostwriters, including books by many, perhaps most, celebrities and political leaders. One such ghost is Mark Steisel, who worked with Jay Conrad Levinson on the Guerilla Marketing guides. Hiring a writer is an expensive but time-saving option. Plan on spending from $20,000 to $50,000, depending on the subject and the word count; the average nonfiction book runs fifty to sixty thousand words.

To manage your project, a book shepherd can help guide you through the overall maze of editing, copyediting, cover creation, design, and print options. Google "book shepherd" for references. Costs will vary, depending on the scope of work.

Whoever writes your book, whether it's you yourself, you and your best friend, or you and your new best friend (a terrific ghostwriter), be sure that you control the rights to the final product. Otherwise, why self-publish?

Let's go through the publishing process, step by step, page by page.

EDITORIAL

"Spare the reader, not the writer," or, as Ernest Hemingway once said, "The first draft of anything is shit." Successful books are professionally edited to improve the manuscript. For an average-sized book, whether fiction or nonfiction, over sixty hours are spent editing. Even best-selling authors have valued and hard-nosed editors. The authors of the wildly successful series *Chicken Soup for the Soul* had every single story edited six times. If you pick up any book you like and check the acknowledgments section, you will find that the author often thanks the editor, along with Mom, Dad, spouse, and siblings. To find a freelance editor, you can start by asking friends in publishing to share with you the name of their own editor. Also, check out writers' conferences in person or online, or contact anyone involved with a book that you find well-edited (e-mail or write to them in care of the publisher), or check out Literary Market Place, Editcetera, *Editor and Publisher,* and Media-Alliance.org. Some of us find editors by unusual routes. My own editor, Alison Owings, was recommended to me by the pastors of my church, Doug Huneke and Barb Rowe, who know her.

When you get a few recommendations, make sure you also check out their references, and call the editor's former clients. Editorial can cost up to $100 and more an hour.

After editing, sometimes called developmental or principal editing, comes copyediting, also called line editing, which is more than just checking grammar, spelling, and punctuation. Copyeditors help create a unifying language for the book as a whole. The path to a good copyeditor can be along the same route to a good editor. I found one of my copyeditors through Steve Piersanti, the president of Berrett-Koehler Publishers in San Francisco; and Mark Woodworth through Editcetera, a long-time nonprofit association of freelance professionals. Copyediting can cost around $40 per hour, more for technical or specialty editing.

Fortunately today, both editing and copy editing can be done on a computer and drafts and final versions simply e-mailed back and forth. No more waiting for UPS or FedEx, a slow and unreadable fax, or snail mail via the Postal Service.

At some point, though not necessarily after editors have worked their will on your prose, you need peer reviews. A staple of serious publishing, especially among university presses, peer reviewers are experts in the field about which you or your hired hand are writing. They are invaluable not only for enhancing the work, and thus improving its credibility, but also for spotting factual errors or misinterpretations and even omissions for which you later might be pilloried, thus damaging your chances for a future work.

In at least one case, peer reviewing merged into marketing. The *Chicken Soup for the Soul* authors, for example, asked forty people to review and grade each story on a scale of one to ten, and included only the highest-rated stories in the book. In this case, the "focus group" method produced astoundingly good results.

COVER

Like your own face, your book's cover is your most important sales and marketing tool. You get a first impression only once, on the street or at a bookstore. According to cover designer Kathi Dunn of Dunn & Associates from Hayward, Wisconsin, book browsers spend an average of eight seconds looking at the front cover, and fifteen seconds skimming the text and art on the back cover.

The front cover copy and design should grab a browser's attention, while the back cover copy closes the deal with a statement of the book's promise, plus an arresting headline addressed directly to buyers. *The Self-Publishing Manual*'s back-cover headline is catchy and short: *Why Not Publish Yourself?* The back cover copy also typically includes a brief author bio, advance reader testimonials, and celebrity endorsements. Graham Van Dixhorn of Write to Your Market helped tremendously with the front and back cover copy for *Be the Media*.

Finally, to a bookseller, as well as potential buyers, the book's spine, which shows the title and author name and sometimes a publisher's logo, is another sales tool, unless, of course, you are buying the book online or see it face up on a friend's table. But in a bookstore, 99 percent of books are shelved spine out, with only that sliver of the book showing. Make sure you arrange the title and image on the spine so they are easy to read and catch your eye, too.

To start the process of getting a good design for front and back covers and the spine, find a book cover you like and then contact the designer. I met book cover designer Kathi Dunn at one of Mark Victor Hansen's Mega Book Marketing conferences, and she introduced me to graphic designer Sam Kuo of KuoDesign.com in Brooklyn, New York, who created *Be the Media*'s "hand" images. If you Google "book designers," you can find someone of related experience, perhaps in your area, who understands the market you are trying to reach. Steer clear of ad or brochure designers, who may not understand the particulars of book cover design. Plan on spending between $1,500 and $7,500 for a cover design that can sit on the same shelf as a book from Random House.

LAYOUT

The person who designs your cover may or may not be the person who designs your book's interior layout. To get an idea of the look you want your designer to follow or at least consider, find books that not only fit your design ideas and aesthetic tastes but also encourage the consistent rhythm of reading. Homemade-looking books using word processing programs do not look good or sell well, and so are shunned by reviewers, distributors, and retailers. Brian Taylor of Pneuma Books warns, "Don't use Microsoft Word for layout. It is *not* a typesetting or layout tool and renders shabby, poorly structured, and ugly designs." Work with a professional who understands book design and its language: *appendices, binding, bullets, Sidebars, charts, endnotes, fonts, glossaries, gutters, orphans, stacks, headers and footers . . .* oh, my!

For laying out the book you are either holding in your hands or viewing online, *Be the Media,* I solicited five bids, which averaged $2,500. That included the design, flowing my word processor files into the page layout software, making the initial page proofs, and three rounds of corrections. The supercapable Liz Tufte of Folio Bookworks and Dorie McClelland of Spring Book Design laid out this very book.

As your own publisher, you should be sure to include the following digits within the opening pages, called "front matter":

ISBN. The International Standard Book Number is attached to each title, so that industry and retail outlets can track the book's movements from printer to customer. The traditional place to register for an ISBN is the firm of R.R. Bowker, "the official U.S. agency for providing ISBNs," found at bowker.com. When I last checked, $225 got you a block of ten 13-digit ISBN numbers. Why ten? You'll need a separate ISBN for each edition of whatever you print, and for each subsidiary product. Also go to Bowker for your **ABI,** or advanced book information, which gets your book listed in the publications *Forthcoming Books in Print* and *Books In Print*.

SAN. The Standard Address Number is used to identify all buying and selling transactions between publishers, distributors, retailers, and customers. See ISBN.org.

LCCN and PCN. The first is the Library of Congress Catalog Number; the second is the Preassigned Control Number, which adds your book to the Library's collections. See LOC.gov to start the process.

Barcodes. Also called OCR-readable code (optical character recognition), a bar code is now typically printed on books, for the inventory convenience of retailers and distributors. Your ISBN and retail price are coded into the bar. Use the "Bookland EAN/13" bar code, and print the bar code on the lower part of the outside back cover of your book.

PRICING

Start considering your pricing options while you are getting your tracking information and designing your cover, because the price will be embedded in the bar code. Your decision will rest on countless variables: page count, size, whether you are printing a hardcover or paperback, whether you seek a consumer or an academic market, and costs for printing, binding, storage, management, and fulfillment.

You as a self-publisher can stop right here. You can save your book as a PDF file, in the portable document format created by Adobe, and sell it online as an **eBook.** Or you can opt for traditional features, such as an index.

INDEX

Schools, libraries, and some bookstores want an index for books they buy. Nancy Humphreys, an indexer since 1985, says, "An index enables the reader to find information they seek. Imagine the *Joy of Cooking* with no index to ingredients or recipes." My editor, Alison Owings, was dissuaded by her publisher from including an index in one of her books, titled *Hey, Waitress! The USA from the Other Side of the Tray*, and has regretted it ever since. Anyone researching the civil rights sit-in at the Woolworth's lunch counter in Greensboro, North Carolina, for example, would have to come upon her interviewee's eye-witness account of it almost by accident.

Microsoft Word can create a rough index, but the reasoning and judgment of a human indexer is critical. For example, if you are publishing an anthology or compilation, your indexer can standardize terms, vocabulary, and concepts. For indexing, budget one week for every two to three hundred pages, at $3 to $4 per indexable page. Check the website of the American Society of Indexers to find a pro, and even a sample contract.

ADVANCE SALES

Try to lock in sufficient advance sales to cover your first print run. Believe me, it is easier to sell one order for a thousand books than to sell a thousand books individually, like an itinerant peddler selling trinkets door-to-door. Bulk buyers might use the books as training for their employees, as a thank-you to clients, or as incentives to buy products. Jerry Jenkins, founder of the publisher The Jenkins Group, notes that a medical ad agency needed to buy 187,000 copies of *Fit to Cook,* but within four weeks! Other boons about bulk buyers are that they pay for shipping, and the books are nonreturnable.

With big sales, you can afford to be generous. Because you are self-publishing, you more likely will earn enough royalties to give back to causes that you support. Richard Blair and Kathleen Goodwin of Marin County, California, self-published a book called *Point Reyes Visions.* Over the course of four years, it became the best-seller at the local Point Reyes bookstore, to the tune of $50,000 worth of copies, or about a tenth of its eventual sales. From their royalties, Blair and Goodwin donated $20,000 to the Point Reyes Seashore Association. If the authors had used a traditional publisher, they might have netted just $37,500 (for example, 7.5 percent royalty on $500,000 gross), leaving them less likely to donate $20,000 (more than 50 percent of their $37,500 net) to the association.

For additional bulk sales, try universities, some of the twenty-six thousand associations in the U.S. (many specialty directories are available in a good reference library and online), or the more than hundred thousand foundations (it's not just Bill and Melinda Gates). Book clubs are another great resource. Check out BookSpan, which operates over thirty clubs, including the long-lived Book-of-the-Month Club, the Literary Guild, and the History Book Club. Catalogs sell in bulk, too, and over sixteen thousand of them (whether a monthly, a quarterly, or an annual) are printed in the U.S. and Canada, six hundred of which carry books. *Plow and Hearth* catalog, for example, sold sixty thousand copies of *How to Keep Squirrels Out of Your Bird Feeder.*

PRINTING

Be conservative. Print only the number of copies you can count on selling. But have your printer run off a couple of hundred more covers than books to use for promotional purposes.

The self-publisher today has three printing choices:

POD printing: This method is good for printing a few hundred books, but the cost is relatively high and the quality relatively low. Try Ingram's Lightning Source or AdiBooks. For even fewer books, try the local Kinko's or other chain copy shop.

Digital printing: This is a good choice for a few hundred to a few thousand books, although the quality is not tops.

Offset printing: For a major job, of more than a few thousand books, and good quality, this is the traditional way to go. Paper and labor will be 50 percent of total printing costs. Choose one of your printer's in-house paper stocks to save money. First-timers might want someone experienced as a guide through the offset print process, such as your layout person or a book "shepherd," because the maze of offset printing has its own lingo. According to Michele DeFilippo of 1106 Design, based in Phoenix, "It's much easier (and less expensive) to submit your job with the correct file formats, halftone adjustments, fonts, trim sizes, bleeds, and more, than to ask your printer's prepress department to fix problems at the last moment and delay production." It's also worth the effort to be on-site when proofs of the book are run off, especially if color is involved. I was not present when my *Be the Media* business cards were printed, and the golden-sunshine yellow background I counted on turned out to be a 1970s mustard. I give away a lot of those cards. You can be sure I did not make the same mistake of inattention with my much more expensive book covers.

FULFILLMENT

As indicated above, fulfillment means packing up the book, sending it to the customer, and dealing with returns. Obviously, if you have low volume, you can save money and increase your profit margins by doing the work yourself, perhaps with a family member or a young neighbor who could use a few bucks. Or, if you sell a few hundred books a month, you can hire someone to do the work, for $4 to $5 per individual book. A third option, however, is online fulfillment services, which make this process much easier and less expensive. (See the Fulfillment section in chapter 9.)

RIGHTS

Know your rights, and guard them. Your book is a huge financial asset, possibly with lucrative subsidiary opportunities capable of generating multiple streams of income—into print, audio, and video products, which can in turn be sold at higher price points. Your primary and subsidiary rights, in fact, are considered capital on your company's balance sheet. Ownership of these rights is the best reason to self-publish, especially if you are planning on a series. Completing your first title will get you valuable experience, a team of professional partners, and, with luck and the right planning, an eager audience. The remaining books in the series will be easier and more lucrative. Why give all those benefits to a publisher?

Copyright: Once your original thought or expression is fixed in tangible form, you are automatically granted a copyright. This copyright is good for the life of the author plus seventy years. As the copyright owner, you have exclusive rights to reproduce the work, create derivative works from it, distribute copies for sale, and perform the work publicly. While copyright is automatically granted, you should absolutely play it safe and register your work by filing two copies of the book, with a $35 fee, to the U.S. Copyright Office at copyright.gov.

Owning the copyright entitles you to the book's *primary* and *subsidiary rights.*

Primary rights include: hardcover versions, paperback, excerpts, book clubs, first serial rights, electronic (online books, databases, print-on-demand), large type, Braille, and direct-response marketing, such as direct mail, TV commercials, infomercials, Home Shopping Network, and so on.

Subsidiary rights include: foreign rights, audio and video versions, performance rights (as for feature films and TV movies, videos, plays, and radio programs), electronic rights (software, CD-ROMs, DVDs), and licensing/merchandising (T-shirts, coffee mugs, calendars bearing quotes, and the like). See chapter 11 for more on Licensing.

A traditional publisher's boilerplate (meaning "off the shelf," though usually then customized) contract grants *all* these rights to the publisher for a specified term. Yes, all! In self-publishing, however, you the author own all such rights yourself. The opportunity and challenge, then, is how to make the most of them. For more on this, be sure to check the other chapters in this book, especially chapters 9, 10, and 11.

Creative Commons. As discussed in chapter 21, Creative Commons licenses are an alternative to copyright, and have a number of advantages. Many chapters in this book use the flexible "some rights reserved" Creative Commons licenses, instead of copyright's restrictive "all rights reserved" regime. In 2003, popular Boing Boing blogger Corey Doctorow published his first novel, *Down and Out in the Magic Kingdom,* for free online. It was downloaded more than 750,000 times from his site alone. He used a Creative Commons license, which treats copying as a feature, not a theft, and which offers opportunities for collaboration, all without needing a team of lawyers. According to Doctorow, "Creative Commons turns my books from nouns into verbs. My books 'do stuff,' get passed around. . . . Creative Commons lets me be financially successful, but it also lets me attain artistic and ethical success."

PROMOTING AND SELLING THE HELL OUT OF YOUR BOOK

You will need to devise a number of strategies for marketing and selling your book, as well as getting it talked about everywhere you can. First, you should do your best to sell as many copies of your book as you can. Don't wait to get publicity, which may be hard to come, or come only in dribbles. Start early by lining up reviewers four to six weeks before your publication date, called the *pub date*. Send them finished if uncorrected layouts of the book, or the bound book itself. Rio-Reviewers.com enables authors to target reviewers by name, genre, and the list of publications for which they write. Check the submission guidelines before you submit your book to the industry heavies: Kirkus, Publishers Weekly, Booklist, and Library Journal. You won't want to waste money by not following the rules to the letter.

However well the book sells, that is only part of the challenge. Because you own all rights possible, you have the opportunity not only to sell the book, but, perhaps even better, to *repurpose* it. With rights in hand, many smart self-published authors go beyond their book. They repackage the book, and may have had a vision for doing so all along, into lucrative derivative products, such as audiobooks, board games, boot camps, calendars, CDs, coaching, conferences, consulting, eBooks, home study programs, mentoring, newsletters, special reports, speeches, teleclasses, training, and material for websites.

A Repurpose-Driven Life

Pastor Rick Warren's book *The Purpose-Driven Life* sold twenty million copies, five million of them directly from his website. More than thirty thousand churches bought copies in bulk. His daily e-mail program, "40 Days of Purpose," enhances the book, as does his new "40 Days of Community" program. He sends a weekly e-mail sermon to 125,000 pastors, has a "Daily Devotional" e-newsletter, and offers a free daily Bible study eBooklet called "First Steps to Spiritual Growth."

In another example, in 1997, Robert Kiyosaki self-published *Rich Dad, Poor Dad* as a $15.95 brochure to "upsell" customers to Cashflow, his $195 board game. Today his *Rich Dad* series consists of twenty-six books. His website, richdad.com, sells print books and guides at $16.95, software at $29.95, audio and video packages at from $39.95 to $219.80, and annual subscriptions to an online community at $99.70 per year. He even sells products en español, such as *Padre Rico, Padre Pobre*. In 2006, Kiyosaki told Fortune Small Business magazine, "We're approaching $1 billion at retail worldwide. I've sold 25 million copies of my books, 350,000 games. Running it with 20 people, no debt, and 70% margins."

You could repurpose your book by summarizing each chapter into sections to resell as print articles to newspapers and magazines, which often motivates readers to buy the book, often also grabbing several more copies as gifts for likeminded friends or colleagues. Or you can create an audiobook, a teleseminar, or an eBook. Customers perceive multimedia products to have a higher value than print products, so you can charge more for audio, video, and interactive versions.

Audiobooks are quick and inexpensive to produce. And millions of commuters who spend hours each workday in cars and on buses, planes, and trains and might find it more convenient to listen to your book than read it. Sell direct from your website, or via Audible.com, SimplyAudiobooks, Jiggerbug, SoundsGood, iTunes, and the Audio Publishers Association.

Teleseminars are quickly replacing book signings and related author events. You as the author/expert can lead teleseminars from your home, office, or hotel, and reach thousands of people. Alex Mandossian sold 1,782 books in a single teleseminar. (See his sidebar on teleseminars.) Tom Antion made $60,000 in two days, from home, just by speaking three to six hours on the phone. His seminar was recorded to create a CD that could generate another forty to sixty thousand dollars. "It's the easiest money I ever made. No airplanes, no three days out of the office to do one speech, no power suit, no schlepping props and handouts, and no great risk and expense." Teleseminar services you can use include Dan Janal's GreatTeleseminars.com, or free services for up to ninety-nine participants from MyFreeTeleconference.com, FreeConference.com, and Skype's Skypecasts.

eBooks, as I mentioned earlier, can be written in Word, saved as a PDF, and you are done! eBook authors can charge the same price as a print book at, say, $29, yet they keep nearly 100 percent of the sale price. The digital product costs nothing to make or ship, so the author faces no costs for print, storage, distribution, returns, or employees. Going "all digital" also saves trees and fuel. *And,* you keep the customer contact information to reach potential customers again, repurposing them, so to speak. Stephen King's *Riding the Bullet* eBook had hundreds of thousands of downloads. According to the International Digital Publishing Forum, eBook sales rose from $6 million in 2002 to $33 million in 2007, but comprise less than one percent of the $35 billion publishing industry. Top eBook Sites are Fictionwise, eReader, and Book Locker.

POUR YOUR BOOK INTO A FUNNEL
The goal is to get all your book's possible products and prospects into what is called a "funnel." At the widest end of your metaphoric funnel, you give away something of value, such as an eZine, report, newsletter, chapter, audio, or video, in exchange for the prospect's e-mail address. This builds your customer contact database.

In the middle of the funnel, you upsell higher-value knowledge, basically pieces of your book repackaged in multimedia formats. These could include reports and manuals for $19; books, workbooks, seminars, and eBooks for $29; audiobooks or programs, and teleseminars (via MP3 download/streaming, or on CD) for $39; videobooks or programs (via download/streaming, or on DVD or VHS tapes) for $49; and, moving right up there, workbooks, self-study courses, and complete "Systems" for $89 to $159 or more.

The narrow end of the funnel is used to upsell customers to interactive and VIP gold- or platinum-level, personalized "inner-circle" experiences. These might include larger home-study workshops from $159 to $499. For up to $999, offer workshop and product combinations, or a one-hour private consultation. Want to squeeze more from your funnel? Charge up to $2,999 for a personal coaching plus product bundle, or for a two-day weekend retreat/workshop. More more more? Charge $3,000 to $20,000 for an in-person speaking engagement, consulting plus product offer, or a VIP private mentoring program. If you are worth it, you can get it.

In other words, the life-time value (LTV) of your customer is vastly more than a single $30 book that soon might be gathering dust on a shelf. For you as an author to earn $100,000, you will need, for example, to sell ten thousand books at a net of $10 per book. To make the same $100,000, you only have to sell twenty personal coaching programs at $5,000. It's far easier dealing with twenty people than ten thousand. Or let's say you have a $50 product promotion, you send it to your list of twenty thousand names, and 10 percent of them buy it. Now you have generated $100,000 in sales, all from a single mass-distributed e-mail.

You may be asking, "Why would someone want to pay up to $20,000 for VIP consulting?" Simple: It may be a wise investment. Let us say an author uses a traditional publisher and sells ten thousand books at $30 a book with a softcover royalty of 7.5 percent. Even if the author earns the full 7.5 percent royalty, which is most unlikely, she nets only $22,500 of the $300,000 total revenue pool, or a measly $2.25 per book, some or all of which may be needed to pay back the advance.

By contrast, if that same author self-publishes and sells ten thousand books at $30 per book, the entire $300,000 in revenue is hers to use however she likes, after costs for cover design, editing, layout, printing, and so forth. The author has plenty of revenue to engage expert consultants for à la carte marketing or promotion services (no contract, no retainer), who may in turn help generate far more than ten thousand sales. This way, the author does significantly less work, owns the rights, and ends up hundreds of thousands of dollars ahead of the traditional publishing game. Convinced yet?

TO MARKET, TO MARKET . . .

There are countless paths to follow that will get you to market. Some will lead you into the brambles, some onto the rocks. Here are the most effective.

Websites. First, let's drive all those people wading in the wide end of your funnel—the ones who got the freebie or whatever—to your website, and then turn on the heat and turn them into customers. By selling directly to customers via your website, not only will you achieve higher margins than by going down the Amazon, but you also will forever own the customer contact information for future upsells. Affiliates and special-interest groups are another great way to generate sales. Got a book on fishing? E-mail every fishing enthusiast, blog, website, chat room, and bulletin board on fishing you know of to become an affiliate and thus help drive fishing enthusiasts to your site to buy the book. Many such sites are starving for fresh articles and information, which you can provide. See chapter 9 for more on how to optimize your site for ecommerce and sign on affiliates.

Always be promoting. Do five things every day to market your book. One "thing" would be to create twelve articles from the book, six hundred words apiece, one for every month of the next year. Or, just order the articles from a freelancer you find on Elance, where quotes are as low as $250 for fifty articles, or just $5 per article. Tie the articles in with a holiday, movie, TV show, celebrity, award, or event. Chase's Calendar of Events lists more than twelve thousand entries. Send the articles to blogs, ezines, magazines, and newspapers (get contact information from Bacon's Publicity Checker), adding a personalized pitch letter. At the bottom of each article, the most important thing is to leverage your "About the Author" Resource Box, which has room for a photo of you or your book cover, some brief biographical details, and a link back to your website. The anchor text link should be the name of your book or website, not "*click here.*" Internet search engines look for keyword-rich sentences with fresh content, so try to post/publish one article per month, and then track and analyze the results.

Before distributing the articles, use E-filtrate.com, which checks the text of the article to be sure it can get past the sp*am filters. E-filtrate will be looking for obvious words like *Viagra* and *casino,* as well as not-so-obvious words like *free, investment, discount,* and *money,* so try to keep those out of your article. Google "free article directory" and submit your articles to the top twenty resulting sites, such as article99.com, articlemarketer; bookcatcher; expertarticles; ezinearticles; ezinetrendz; isnare; prleap; prweb; and theopenpress. The sites act as matchmakers. They want content, indeed they live by it, and you want customers! Now your article can appear on thousands of websites, to no cost to you.

Blogs. Post these articles, or other sections of your book, to your own blog, and comment on related blogs, always with a link back to your site, which will increase your search engine rank. Add influential bloggers to your press release list. According to Joe Garofoli in the *San Francisco Chronicle* in 2006, bloggers helped Glenn Greenwald's book, *How Would a Patriot Act?,* get "a virtually overnight advance sales bump—and a second printing of 20,000 copies." It topped the Amazon chart before it was even published. A promotional video came out before the bound copies, and its "circulation was more valuable than kudos from book critics."

Don't forget the blogs that review books. These include Ex Libris Book Reviews at elise.com/books/el and Book Slut at bookslut.com/blog, as well as book-blog.com, blogcritics.org, paperfrigate.blogspot.com, and jollyblogger.typepad.com.

Podcasts. You can distribute your whole book or one audio chapter at a time via podcast, which differ from audiobooks in that listeners can subscribe to a podcast to get updated chapters or shows delivered automatically to a variety of devices at home or on the go. Author Scott Sigler's podcast-only novel, *EarthCore,* grew by eight thousand fans in just a few months. "Many of my fans listen to their chapters while driving or working out," he commented. Mignon Fogarty's podcast helps more than two million listeners with tips on grammar. It tops iTunes in the Education category with over five million downloads. Audio Renaissance will publish Fogarty's first audio book, and the venerable Henry Holt will publish her hardback in 2008. Fogarty rules her Quick and Dirty Tips empire at QDNow.com.

Be sure that you promote your podcast in the following directories, but also listen to what else they are podcasting and learn from their success.

- **Apple iTunes Store.** Its podcasts include Disney's *Last Minute Book Reports.*

- **Podcast.net** offers one hundred and thirteen book podcasts, including *The Literate Loser, The Secrets of Harry Potter, Book Snark,* and KCRW's *Bookworm.*

- **Podcastalley** has one hundred and six book podcasts, including *Page Turners, The Comic Geeks,* and *Rabbit Hole.*

- **Odeo** has thirty-five book channels, such as KCRW's *Bookworm, Words for the Week, Writer's Voice, Book Voyages,* and *Books & Writing.*

Radio. About five thousand radio, broadcast TV, and cable talk shows need guests like you, each and every day, to fill their air 24/7. Do your research by checking the website of a particular station, or Burrelle's and Bacon's Media Directories. Steve Harrison's Radio and Television Interview Report (RTIR) is snail-mailed to six thousand radio and TV producers, who use it to book guests. Authors and speakers pay for an ad to be included in the report. RTIR comes up with a *hook,* or show idea, and even writes your ad for you.

The publicity firm Planned Television Arts (PTA) offers "follow the sun" satellite radio tours. The author sits in one spot, such as a favorite chair at home, and becomes a guest on a different radio station across the country every hour. PTA founder Rick Frishman has hints for such authors. Do not say the words "in my book" during interviews, or you come off as pushy and self-promoting. Instead, teach people three things from the book, and then direct them to your website to get a free chapter download or a report—not (supposedly) to buy the book. Wink, wink.

Once you've been selected to be on a show, you can do the interview from the comfort of your home or office. It is best to use a land line, not a speaker phone or cell phone, and always disable call-waiting. Of course, turn off all alarms, beepers, and ringers and send the baby out with the nanny. To open the interview, it is suggested you sum up your book into a ten-second sound bite, not unlike the so-called Hollywood or Silicon Valley "elevator pitch," a pithy phrase you can say to someone while riding up to the third floor. The sound bite should be the most interesting, memorable, or unusual thing about your book. You might compare the book to something people can relate to. The memorable elevator pitch for the movie *Alien* was "It's like Jaws in Outer Space."

Have your five talking points handy, preferably memorized. Answer the interviewer's first question with your most important point or a passage from the book. If you opt to give away books on the air, the host will mention the title more frequently. Have a strong close, with a call-to-action on how and where listeners can buy the book. Make sure to mention your website or toll-free number. Afterward, send a brief thank-you letter to the host and producer. Ask if they will post your name, number, and a few (kind) words about your appearance on radio bulletin boards and prep services like BitBoard.com or New Radio Star at nrs.blogtronix.net.

Television. David Bach, the best-selling author of *Start Late, Finish Rich,* advises authors to do their homework before even attempting to appear on television. Research prior shows, monitor the show's message boards, and check for related upcoming shows. Bach even studied the transcripts from the Oprah Winfrey and Suze Orman shows, and did approximately three hundred local TV shows before he finally got on ABC's *The View.* It took him another five years to get on CNN. When such opportunities did knock, Bach was prepared.

To win a slot on any TV program, you need to demonstrate that your appearance will help the host have a great show and increase the audience. Customize each pitch to the right producer; know the correct name, specialties, and segments he or she produced. Never blindly blast out generic pitches, which will go straight into the recycle bin. Give producers numerous ways to contact you. Then, when you are called for a preshow telephone interview, do not sit, but stand up straight as if you are meeting someone face to face. Smile, be energetic, and give quick answers. You have already memorized your talking points, of course, but have them near you just in case. This is show business, so even though you're on the phone, try to create an exciting, visual experience. David Bach's telephone interview for Oprah's producer lasted fifty-two minutes. But he got the gig. After all his work, the segment hook used to introduce him was only six words: "How to be an Instant Millionaire," followed by, of course, " . . . next, on Oprah."

After the show, thank the producer, copiously! An appearance on Oprah's Book Club can result in sales of more than a million copies.

Video. If you can't get on *Oprah, be* Oprah! Create a viral video or book trailer, and post it on YouTube. Scott Stratten helped the husband and wife who both got cancer and founded The Cancer Crusade create *The Survivor Movie.* It got over a hundred and fifty thousand views and four thousand e-mails. Ian McEwan, a Man Booker Prize winner for a work of fiction, screened his short film in bookstores in fifty-four cities instead of a book tour for his tenth novel, *On Chesil Beach.* Other good book trailers include Alan Davidson's *Body Brilliance* and Naomi Klein's *The Shock Doctrine.*

Et Cetera. Use the wonderful **craigslist** to promote your book, your product, and yourself, locally. Edit a **wikipedia** entry to drive people to your site, or create a wikipedia entry on your own. Online social networks such as Library Thing, Good Reads (which lists over ten million books), Amazon's and Shelfari's bookshelf let you demonstrate your own tastes, by rating and sharing books you've read, and also help you discover books that have been popular with your friends. We'll be starting our own social network at bethemedia.com. Join list serves such as Pub-Forum.net, Publish-L.com, and Ind-E-Pubs.com (which covers eBooks), and post comments, where appropriate, to make yourself known to other members. To find your way among blogs, wikis, podcasts, and syndication, see the relevant chapters.

Book Tour. The way the world used to work, and in part still does, authors gave readings and did signings in bookstores to promote their work. In my opinion, it is more sensible to make such appearances only where you have an audience. Who wants to travel across the country to speak to empty chairs? To promote your event, use websites such as Eventful.com and BookTour.com, which enable authors to post their upcoming tours and connect with interested audiences. Eventful permits audiences to "demand" that an artist come to their town, and some rabid fans even book the venues for the author. (See chapter 4.) Meetup.com has local book discussion groups for writers. The site enables you to search by city and zip code, so you can find out where they meet, how often, and how many members they have.

Coordinate local TV and radio interviews with appearances at local bookstores, conferences, libraries, and schools.

Bookstores. I suggest bypassing giant corporate bookstores, at the beginning of your career,[3] because you would need to pay a distributor, fight for shelf space, and deal with shipping and returns. But do support local independent bookstores, such as, in Marin County, California, Book Passage and Book Depot, by scheduling talks or classes there, and by dropping in and signing books, even if you're not speaking. Request, in return, that the bookstore provide an ad budget and big signs.

Conferences. For conferences, Google "book conferences," and see where you might fit. The biggest book conference in the United States is Book Expo America (BEA), which brings together over thirty thousand book buyers and sellers from around the world. At the conference, pay visits to your distributors, fulfillment houses, partners, printers, and resellers. Sneak up on the competition as well. But at this point, advises marketing expert Mark Victor Hansen, marketer of the *Chicken Soup* series, skip going to writing conferences, and instead go to marketing conferences. Your book is done and it is time to change hats. I suggest attending Hansen's Mega Book Marketing conference.

Libraries. The library market for adult books is $2 billion a year and for children's books $800 million a year. If you can get reviewed in library periodicals such as *Booklist, Kirkus Reviews, Library Journal,* or the *School Library Journal,* you are partway there—with a good review, of course. For library sales, hook up with a proven wholesaler like Baker & Taylor, or a distributor like Ingram. Speak at libraries, too. Since you self-published, you can afford to donate a percentage of book sales to them, either during a signing at the library or later. Authors earning just pennies a book can't afford to be so generous, especially if they need to repay a publisher's advance.

Schools. If you have an academic title, or are an expert in a subject being taught at a college or university, or continuing education class, you could likely arrange to speak on campus, or place articles or ads in the college newspaper about your book. Colleges have budgets for authors, speakers, and performers. Make sure your book is on sale in the college bookstore, which is generally a separate operation from other bookstores. The authors of *Chicken Soup for Teacher's Soul* created a 5x5 Matrix Marketing Plan that identified five audiences that would read the book, plus five ways to reach each one. To get teachers, they targeted administrator conferences, mailings to superintendents and principals, ads in magazines to students, and lists of school board association members.

Distribution. If you *do* undertake a book tour, in part to get national radio and TV exposure, you'll need a lot of books. Your car trunk or carry-on luggage allotment will not be sufficient. So, you'll need to hire a distributor to ensure that your books are available through online retailers, wholesalers, and chain and independent bookstores. Distributors do not come cheap (remember, they

---

3. **Chains:** Barnes & Noble; B. Dalton; Books-A-Million; Borders; Coles; Crown Books; Walden; WH Smith. **Specialty wholesalers:** Sam's Club; Costco; BJ's Wholesale Club; Staples; Office Max; Office Depot; WalMart.

take 65 percent of your sales price), but they do the work you probably do not want to. Wholesalers, on the other hand, fulfill orders but don't promote books.

Dan Poynter says, "Distributors have sales reps that visit the stores, bring back the orders, ship the books and collect the money due. They give the wholesalers 50 to 55 percent and the stores 40 percent or a little more. Distributors earn their money."

For example, Ingram provides distribution, sales, marketing, and inventory management from four warehouses that can reach 86 percent of retail customers within a short two days. Its in-house sales team represents clients' titles to Amazon, Borders, and many others. It also handles returns, which can be very high. New titles have a 30 to 60 percent return rate; returns from the chains are worse.

How can you become allied with a distributor?[4] It is not easy, and in fact is quite as difficult as getting an agent or a traditional publisher. Having a best-selling series, or the potential for one, is better than just one title, hence more appealing to a distributor, who needs to know that people are ordering your books. *Chicken Soup*'s Mark Victor Hansen met his distributor personally and even bought breakfast for some of the employees. An author should work six months in advance of a release date, send a cover letter announcing the title or series, and prove to the distributor that there are already thousands of prepublication orders.

If even that fails to get you a distributor, John Kremer, author of *1001 Ways to Market Your Books,* has a new eBook called *Choosing a Book Distribution System,* which covers thirty book distributors, four library distributors, eighty-nine book publishers who also distribute, three sales reps to the chains, twenty-seven bookstore wholesalers, thirty-four library wholesalers, and even twenty-three Spanish-language wholesalers. This eBook could prove invaluable.

Alternative distribution channels are out there as well. Rick Warren didn't do a book tour or send out review copies. As pastor of one of the five largest megachurches in the United States, he didn't have to. "I created a new distribution channel," he remarks. "I went direct to these pastors who have loved me and trusted me for years." 'Nuff said. Talk about alliances!

Another alternative channel is "bypass" marketing through salons, medical offices, sporting goods stores, and gift shops, to name only a few types. Nutri-Books distributes books to six thousand natural-food stores. Whole Foods Markets has 175 natural-foods stores with books on cooking, health and wellness, gardening, and nutrition. Diamond Comic Distributors offers books on film, pop culture, and music. Don Tubesing, author of *The Quiltmaker's Gift,* targeted twenty-four hundred quilt shops. "Not only were there no returns, but they paid their bills."

If all else fails, here are two more distribution ideas. Ever try "reverse shoplifting"? You put

---

4. Major distributors include: Ingram, Baker and Taylor, Biblio, Consortium Book Sales, Independent Publishers Group (IPG), Lightning Source, Midpoint Trade Books, National Book Network, and AtlasBooks Distribution (BookMasters). Be careful! Advanced Marketing Services and Bookworld went bankrupt in 2006, owing publishers hundreds of millions of dollars, and leaving them without warehousing and distribution.

your book on a shelf in Barnes & Noble and arrange to have a friend try to buy it. The clerk, who always wants to serve the customer, then places an order for more through the distributor. How about Bookcrossing? You leave a copy of your book in a public place, such as a hotel lobby or an executive board room. Then, you can track your bookcrossed titles as they travel around the globe by using the bookcrossing.com website.

WHAT ABOUT AMAZON?

There certainly are pros and cons about this behemoth. The biggest con is that Amazon.com owns the customer contact information. In fact, you have no idea who your customer is, which is another reason to sell directly from your website. And until very recently, Amazon kept 55 percent of the price. Now, however, authors can create an Amazon "Storefront," which gives authors an 80 percent royalty.

One "pro" or advantage to using Amazon is that by doing so your titles become available on other sites, such as Borders, CDnow, and Target. If you go for Amazon, your book will need an ISBN (or a UPC for a CD/DVD; see chapter 4). Next, register with Amazon Advantage for $30 per year, and ship Amazon two copies of your book with your bar code and a scan of the cover. Now you can be among the authors who promote and sell books on its site, with Amazon handling the distribution and fulfillment.

To improve your book's visibility on Amazon, fill out the "About You" area, and write short, two-hundred-character reviews for your own book and related books. Sign all reviews with "by ME, publisher of MY BOOK" (insert the correct names, of course) and add a link to your funnel, er, website.

Another good reason to sell on Amazon is to achieve "best-seller" status, which gives you credibility, more shelf space, increased speaking and consulting fees, and better deals from publishers and distributors. To "game" the system and attain best-seller status, your goal is to drive huge numbers of buyers to Amazon over a short period of time. The website PromoteABook.com helps drive books up the best-seller list. Also, infomarketers Randy Gilbert and Peggy McColl offer an online program called *How to Make Your Book an Amazon Bestseller in 38 Days at Almost No Cost.* One author sold 6,828 copies for $27 each, for a total of $184,000 in sales, and spent not one dollar on advertising.

The best-seller program in a nutshell: Write up a great offer with loads of free bonuses. Pick a day and time when your book won't compete with blockbuster launches, such as *Harry Potter and the Deathly Hallows,* which sold 8.3 million copies on its first day of sale. Next, find people and groups with large e-mail lists who are willing to promote your book sale through Amazon at the predetermined day and time. Don't know anyone with big e-mail lists? Gilbert and McColl devote time to approaching big list owners, and Randy will e-mail his list of thirty thousand to help promote your book.

Other best-seller lists can be ascended, too. Bryan and Jeffry Eisenberg wanted to make *Call to Action* a *Wall Street Journal* "Business" section best-seller. They set a goal of ten thousand copies and funneled all orders through any of the three approved *WSJ* sites: Amazon, Barnes & Noble, and 800-CEO-READ. They beat their goal by 70 percent, selling seventeen thousand copies in a single week.

After selling that many books in one week and making the *Wall Street Journal* "Business" best-seller list, guess what? Literary agents, traditional publishers, distributors, and resellers all fought and clawed to contact the authors, instead of the other way around.

It can happen to you, too. Once your self-published book is a best-seller, traditional publishers may come acallin'. Maybe you'll be interested. Maybe not. It's your choice.

"A professional writer is an amateur who didn't quit."
—Richard Bach

Teleseminar Secrets

Alex Mandossian

I was so excited my hands were shaking.

It was the evening of August 25, 2004, and I had just conducted a 70-minute teleseminar interview with personal development and goal achievement guru Brian Tracy. Three hundred forty-two participants had paid the $29.95 tuition without raising an eyebrow and 83% of them opted to pay $10 more to get unlimited download and replay access to the online release of the audio files and transcripts.

If you do the math, you'll discover my 70-minute call generated $13,082 in revenue.

But the story doesn't end there. Fifty-eight of the tele-participants decided to pay $30 more to acquire a binder of the printed transcripts and an audio CD of the seminar. Chalk-up another $1,740.

All told, we racked-up nearly $15,000 for just a few hours of work!

Since 2001, I've trained entrepreneurs, independent professionals, and small business owners—some 14,100 people in all—how to use teleseminars in combination with the Internet to boost and accelerate their business profits. Teleseminars have changed my life. Sixteen times in 2006, I earned in one hour what had taken me a year to earn in 2001.

The key that makes teleseminars work so well is "marketing intimacy" (in other words, live access to the speakers), coupled with a new use of the Socratic Method.

I use three steps.

Step 1: Ask Your Market. I first ask members of my market what they want, and then ask them to pay for it. For the seminar with Brian Tracy, this meant posting a worldwide online survey, called JustAskBrian.com, three weeks prior to the actual call. I then put 860 responses captured from the survey into a special database I've developed, called the Ask Database. (See AskDatabase.com.)

Step 2: Promote to Your Market. Your "market" collectively is the marketing genius. That's why after getting the survey responses, I was ready to post an online sales letter not written by me (the "marketer") but ostensibly by my "market." The sales copy simply turned the 12 most popular results of the survey into topics for the teleseminar, such as Closing Techniques, Follow-up, Referrals, and Fear of Rejection.

Step 3: Repurpose Your Content. Because teleseminars produce audio content, it makes sense to "repurpose" that content and monetize it beyond the money you make from your live event. Put the recording on a CD and sell it. Sell transcripts of the audio. Make MP3 downloads available online so your listeners can listen anywhere, anytime. [See chapters 2 and 4 for how to "repurpose" original works into other products.] Step 3, furthermore, requires almost no human effort.

It's that easy.

Besides Brian Tracy, I've conducted teleseminars with other "thought leaders" such as Ken Blanchard, Jack Canfield, Stephen Covey, Barbara DeAngelis, Joe Vitale, Mark Victor Hansen, Jay Conrad Levinson, Zig Ziglar, and Donald Trump, to name a few.

But you don't have to be famous to become a successful teleseminar marketer. Like me, you can interview famous people in your business niche and share the profits and create many ultra-fruitful strategic alliances along the way.

All from the comfort of your home or office.

3

MAKING MUSIC

HOW TO MAKE MUSIC WITH JUST THREE CHORDS AND THE TRUTH

THE MEDIUM IS THE MUSIC: FEEL THE POWER OF CREATING YOUR OWN

Robert Laughlin

"Music in the soul can be heard by the universe."
—Lao Tzu

The First Amendment guarantees Americans the right to speak our minds and protects us from repercussions if we put our ideas into print. However, that same First Amendment does not necessarily give every citizen equal footing. One catchphrase that I first heard in the 1960s puts a cynical spin on this most celebrated item in the Bill of Rights: "Freedom of the press belongs to those who own one."

That slogan rings awkwardly out of date in the technology-laced twenty-first century, thanks in part to the Internet. Now, one doesn't need a press in order to publish. Just create a website, blog, or wiki.

If every citizen has the inalienable right to publish on the Internet, we may think we now have not only freedom of the press but also equality of the press. Of course, it's not that simple. What about the rights of the citizen who never learned to write? Moot point, perhaps. In the developed world illiteracy is nearly extinct, so theoretically, universal literacy puts First Amendment freedoms within the grasp of the everyday person.

However, universal literacy is really not that universal. Throughout the course of my work over the past twenty-five years, I have dealt with a type of illiteracy on a daily basis.

I'm a piano teacher. I teach thousands of adults a year, many of whom come to me because they want to taste the freedom and power that come from playing a musical instrument. They tell me they feel deprived of the freedom to create, because of their musical illiteracy. They reason that because they can't read music, they cannot play the piano, and thus their right to express themselves musically has been abridged.

They may be right. The fact is, as a nation we are musically illiterate. Most of those who took piano lessons as children, who played recitals, who marched in the high school band, and even those who studied music in college, end up musically illiterate. Why? Because they stop playing music recreationally and lose their skills. Today's rate of musical literacy is probably not even measured. If it were, I would venture that it would be minuscule.

True musical literacy is the domain of an educated few, a tightly knit priesthood of rhythmic shamans who would like to think they have an exclusive stranglehold on musical culture. Like the rituals of a secret, medieval sect, those who hold the keys to musical literacy pass along a legacy of beliefs that has not changed since the days of Bach. Neophytes are shown the rules, but few have the fortitude to complete the studies that enable them to enter the musical priesthood.

Sound crazy? It is. However, such is the belief system of most of the people who come to my seminars looking for musical answers. Unfortunately—no, make that *fortunately*—their belief system is all wrong. They just don't know it yet. They don't realize that thanks to the Great Liberator, aka Thomas Alva Edison, the freedom and power to create music is already in their hands (or it soon will be). Actually, Edison did not put musical literacy into the hands of the masses; he merely made musical literacy unnecessary. And he probably didn't even realize it when he did it.

For anyone who enjoys popular music of any kind, February 19 should be a national holiday. On February 19, 1878, Edison invented the phonograph, a device that was able to freeze time—a veritable time machine. And although Edison didn't know it at the time, his invention would make musical literacy a mere option for musicians—not a requirement—and in doing so it helped launch what might have been the biggest cultural renaissance in history.

Without Edison's time machine, musical culture today would be nearly unrecognizable. There would be no widespread dissemination of jazz, rock and roll, rhythm and blues, country and western, or gospel. Music as we know it wouldn't exist. It would still be mostly classical, practiced only by the exclusive musical priesthood that was put into place centuries ago.

Without Edison we would likely never have known the likes of Louis Armstrong, Duke Ellington, Charlie Parker, Jimmie Rogers, Bob Wills, Ray Charles, Elvis, or the Beatles. Without Edison's invention, you might as well erase all those icons from our cultural slate, as well as everyone else who followed in their footsteps. Their music thrives without depending on music notation. In fact, their music challenges and defies the ability of music notation to capture it. Edison's time machine made it possible for music to be taken from a notation-based system to a chord-based system. Suddenly, music literacy—the ability to read and write notation—was no longer necessary to create music.

It was Edison's invention of the phonograph that enabled humans to capture actual sound, to freeze sound in time. At last we could preserve music itself, not just a paper-and-ink approximation of it. And how much later could it have been that people started learning to *play* music from recordings instead of from music notation?

Prior to the phonograph, we relied on a type of written symbolism to preserve a composer's creations. This type of written language—standard music notation—worked pretty well for the preservation of the music of its time. But it was a poor system for preserving certain musical nuances that fell outside the realm of the classical music paradigm. Composers could be creative, but their palette was limited. They had to create within the narrow limits that formal music notation dictates, otherwise there would be no way to preserve their creations.

For me, Edison's invention, the sound recording device, made the following possible: In 1972, at the age of twenty-three, I started to learn to play the piano, using the chord-based system. I honed my skills by listening to records, not by reading notation. In 1977 I started playing piano professionally.

In 1981 I devised a three-hour workshop that provided students with the tools to play piano themselves. After the three-hour course they could play any song, any style of music, any key, with both hands. Some twenty-five years later I have taught this workshop to more than thirty-five thousand people, and my method has been used by scores of other teachers to reach hundreds of thousands of people in the three-hour workshop.

Only through the use of recordings of music, as opposed to printed sheet music, was any of this possible.

Do my students really learn to play the piano in one three-hour course? Absolutely. The common assumption is that learning to play the piano (or any other musical instrument) takes hours of daily practice over a period of many years. It used to be that way, but not anymore. What makes it possible? Edison's time machine, the recording device.

TWO WAYS TO LEARN

Despite Edison's breakthrough invention, piano is still mostly taught the old way—the hard way. You take weekly lessons for a number of years, you learn all your scales and basic exercises. You come to understand key signatures, time signatures, and the rhythm of note values. After several years you possibly become proficient at reading music notation and playing it on the piano.

But even with all those musical skills, there's a big piece missing. Sure, you can play a few classical pieces, but if you try to play music that isn't classical, you're completely lost. You can't improvise, you can't memorize all that well, your attempts at sight reading pop music don't sound authentic, and most importantly, you can't play piano without the note-for-note music notation in front of you.

You eventually realize that it's not you that's making the music. You are just regurgitating what someone else has already written. You become just a kind of typist, converting arcane symbols on a page into finger twitches. Finally, you give up. I don't have the exact figures, but I would guess the classical piano lesson dropout rate is close to 100 percent. Think about it: How many people do you know who have ever had piano lessons? Now, how many of those people play the piano at least once a week?

In my seminars students learn to play with both hands, to accompany singers, to improvise, to transpose, to play by ear, and to master various styles of popular music—all without the tedium and complexities of learning how to read music. How is it done? Well, first they need to disregard almost everything they have already learned, musically. They start with a clean slate.

You can do it, too. If for the next few pages you are willing to suspend whatever musical belief system you currently have, you will learn the secret. It starts with understanding how music works. It has little to do with little dots on lines and spaces. It's actually pretty simple.

HOW MUSIC WORKS

In music there are really only two things going on at any given time: a melody and an accompaniment to the melody. That's it. A melody is a succession of individual musical notes (or tones) played or sung one at a time. For most people the melody is the most prominent and easily the most identifiable element of music. In addition to the melody, the listener also hears other notes in the music. These other notes support the notes of the melody and are played simultaneously with them. These extra notes form the accompaniment to the melody. Sometimes these accompaniment notes are referred to as the harmony; we prefer to call them chords.

This principle applies to both classical and popular music. No matter how different pop music sounds from classical, the structure is the same. One of the instruments (often the human voice) expresses the melody at any given time, while all the other instruments (or voices) collectively supply the accompaniment. It's the same for big bands, Dixieland bands, folk singers, jazz combos, rock bands, gospel groups, country bands, Latin bands, everything.

SOLO INSTRUMENTS VS. ACCOMPANIMENT INSTRUMENTS

Some instruments are considered solo instruments (or melody instruments), whereas others are exclusively accompaniment instruments. A few do both. Any instrument that is limited to playing one note at a time is a solo or melody instrument. Such instruments either play the melody or they must act in ensemble with other solo instruments to create the accompaniment. They can't play the accompaniment by themselves. Examples of such instruments are violins, trumpets, flutes, tubas, trombones, and saxophones. One rarely, if ever, hears any of these types of instruments performing alone. Bare melody without accompaniment tends to sound unpleasant to the Western ear.

On the other hand, there are a few instruments that are exclusively or primarily accompaniment instruments. The autoharp (you might remember it from grade school) is an example of an accompaniment instrument. Its role is to provide accompaniment for singing. The autoharp is popular in the elementary schools primarily because it's relatively easy to play. But its versatility is very limited. Other instruments in the accompaniment category include guitar, banjo, mandolin—the basic strum instruments. Although the guitar can be used for playing melody, its usual role is one of accompaniment. Guitar strumming by itself sounds tedious without a melody to go along with it. Thus, guitars are usually strummed in tandem with a singer or some other instrument capable of providing a melody.

THE PIANO DOES IT ALL

Few musical instruments are capable of doing what the piano can do. Other instruments are classified as either solo (melody) or chord (harmony) instruments. The piano plays both parts; thus, the piano operator is responsible for playing both the melody and the accompaniment, simultaneously. This is why you often hear single pianos in hotels, restaurants, lounges, and shopping malls.

Sounds difficult, doesn't it? But it's not, if you know the secret.

The truth is, the piano is an inherently easy instrument to play compared to any other instrument (with the possible exception of the kazoo).

What makes the piano so easy? The student learns to play a melody (just one note at a time) with the right hand, while playing the chord accompaniment with the left. Chords are very easy to play on a piano. Playing the piano becomes essentially a matter of pushing buttons. Push the right buttons at the right time, and you're playing correctly.

Still, questions remain. For example, isn't it difficult for the piano player to do two things at once—to play the melody and the accompaniment, too? Well, yes and no. Playing piano is something of a balancing act between melody and accompaniment. But it becomes much simpler when one understands the simple system that is the foundation underlying all music. Classical pianists seldom gain this understanding.

Some traditional teachers are in denial about the chord system. I've actually received late-night irate phone calls from traditional piano teachers demanding to know how I dare teach the piano this way. Thus more questions are born: How do piano teachers get this angry? What would it be like to be a child taking lessons from these people?

THE OLD WAY VS. THE NEW WAY

Many traditional piano teachers use a one-dimensional approach to teaching students to play the piano. It's a process based on learning how to sight-read music notation. If your goal is to learn how to hit the right notes at the right time on the piano, irrespective of whether you understand what's going on musically, this system works. Most classical students learn to play exactly this way, whether they want to or not. They read and play notes without having the slightest idea of what is happening musically when they do.

Think of it as a system based not on understanding but on stimulus and response. It's a translation of written symbols into motor functions. Notation-based piano playing emphasizes precision over creativity.

To get an idea of this musical process, imagine yourself to be an expert typist given the job of typing a manuscript written in some foreign language you don't understand. Is this a possible task? Of course. As a typist you are trained to react reflexively to symbols, whether or not those symbols have any meaning to you. Even if you don't understand a single word of what you are typing, you can still type accurately because you learned to type reflexively. Your eyes register the symbols on the page and your fingers tap the keys accordingly.

Your brain, of course, makes this process happen, but it's a passive facilitator. The brain is neutral. It doesn't judge. In this situation the brain can't make adjustments or corrections for spelling, punctuation, syntax, or semantics because it doesn't understand the symbols. As long as you type the letters of the words and the punctuation exactly as you see it, you don't have to understand the meaning of a single word. With practice you can actually learn to excel at typing in foreign languages. Your success is measured by how fast you recreate the symbols on the page with your typewriter.

But it's a lot of work, and it's not much fun, is it? Because you don't understand the meanings of the words or the syntax you're writing, you won't be able to catch any mistakes in the original, nor will you be able to do any kind of editing. You won't be able to change words to make them sound better or to make their meaning clearer. You become a mindless processor of words and phrases that may have significance to some people but that are totally meaningless to you. You're simply a drone, a robot.

Now, isn't that close to the way notation-based classical piano is taught? You learn to follow the music notation, and your fingers learn to press down all the right buttons according to the written music, but aren't you missing something? How much of the music do you really know? Do you understand why the accompaniment is the way it is? Do you understand what went through the composer's mind? Would you be able to recreate the song without the written music? Would you be able to improve on it? Chances are you wouldn't.

Nonetheless, this highly restrictive and noncreative system of regurgitating music notation is how music is taught to almost all students of music—regardless of age and musical preference.

After years of such unfulfilling piano study, students want to know when the fun begins. After all, isn't that the ultimate purpose of music, to create a sense of fun?

The traditional method of teaching music notation may indeed be the best way to approach classical music, but because of its involvement with detail, precision, and regimentation, it falls short as a means of learning nonclassical musical forms (in other words, popular music).

Here's the problem with the way music—especially piano music—is being taught today:

1. Most piano teachers are trained to teach classical technique only.

2. Most adults wish to learn to play pop music.

3. These two concepts are 100 percent incompatible.

So where does that leave you?

Our teaching methods offer you an alternative to typewriter-style music playing. You learn how music works, right from the start. You learn that playing the piano means you play a melody with the right hand and the accompanying harmony (chords) with the left hand. Because a melody, by definition, can include only one note at a time, you need only play one note at a time with the right hand. Meanwhile, you learn to play three- and four-note chords with the left hand, using a fast and easy method based on simple logic.

You still might use written music, but it's a much different type of written music. Instead of traditional music notation in which you precisely play every single note that's written on the page, you now will be following a lead (rhymes with *need*) sheet. A lead sheet gives you the chords and the single-note melody line. No longer will you struggle to read and respond to every individual note on the page. Instead, you will use this lead sheet as a kind of a guide or outline. Piano "fake books" are just compilations of different lead sheets.

This approach to playing is a little like referring to a few notes on three-by-five index cards when giving a speech. You use the cards as a reference, to keep important facts handy and to remind you of the points you wish to cover in your speech and in what order you wish to cover them. But you give the speech in your own words and in your own speaking style.

The classically based method of reading music notation is more like reading a speech from a text, word for word. It's regimented and can sound stilted. On the other hand, playing pop music from a lead sheet is more natural and flowing. The lead sheet method gives you room to breathe. To goal is no longer to recreate precisely the music that a total stranger has written. Rather, it's intended to empower you with some basic musical tools that let you express music in your own way.

But there's still something missing. What ultimately makes it possible for you to breathe life into the music you create with your fingertips? It's Edison's time machine. It would hardly be possible to make music without it. We'll get back to that a little later. Now it's time for you to get involved with the music.

WELCOME TO YOUR INSTANT PIANO LESSON

As we've implied, learning to play the piano is a two-step process: learning to play the melody and learning to play the accompanying chords. Let's start with the melody.

There are two ways to learn melodies: by reading simple notation or "by ear." Most adults are already experienced to some extent with both methods, whether they realize it or not. Care to give it a try? Okay, let's try it through notation first. Melodies by themselves are not difficult, because they consist of just one note at a time. Here's what the first few melody notes of "Mary Had a Little Lamb" look like in music notation:

Starting with the E note near the middle part of the keyboard, play the first seven notes of "Mary Had a Little Lamb." If you've had even the barest musical background already, you should be able to do at least this much. If not, you may be able to apply basic logic and figure out the notation system on your own. It's really not that difficult to understand; however, we won't attempt to explain it here. (We have some free learning aids available at our website, pianofun.com/mini-lesson.html, if you would like to explore further). Give it a try, but try not to think about it too much. If it comes to you readily, great. If not, you can just skip to method two—learning by ear.

The other (and no less effective) way to learn to play a melody is by ear. Start on the E note closest to the middle of the keyboard. If you don't know which note is E, here is what it looks like.

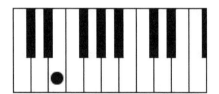

After you find the first melody note (E), you're on your own. From here on out it's just experimentation on your part. Play the first E note and then doodle around until you hear the melody start to take shape. It's nothing more than a system of trial and error. Keep repeating this trial-and-error process until you work your way through the entire song—or at least through the first seven notes.

There you have the two methods for learning melodies. One is scientific; the other is intuitive. Neither method is necessarily better or more appropriate than the other. Eventually, you will be well served if you understand and use both methods. Just remember, a melody is a sequence of single notes played with the right hand.

If you think about it, it's pretty simple, isn't it?

Playing the accompaniment isn't any more difficult than playing the melody, if you learn it properly. In fact, many people think it's a lot easier. Let's start by trying to understand exactly what an accompaniment is. Simply put, basic accompaniment is what many music students have come to know as harmony or chords.

If we think of the melody as being a sequence of single notes, harmony can be considered a sequence of a group of notes (usually three or four) played simultaneously. On a keyboard instrument the right hand plays the melody and the left hand plays the harmony (accompaniment).

We distill harmony into discrete units called chords. Chords consist of a group of notes (usually three or four) played simultaneously. These groupings of notes have names, similar to the names used for the notes themselves. The chord we call C major, for example, contains the notes C, E, and G.

On a piano, the white keys are lettered A through G, and repeat in octaves. The C chord on a piano (notes C, E, and G) would be played like this:

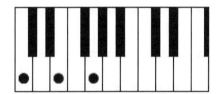

Go ahead and play the C, E, and G notes simultaneously with your left hand. You are now playing the C chord, a strategic building block of accompaniment.

I told you it was easy.

We never need to use standard music notation to write out chords, but if we did, the notation for a C chord would look like this:

We use the bass clef here, because that's the one that's usually associated with the piano player's left hand. If this confuses you a little right now, don't worry. Just take a deep breath and marvel at the needless complexity of it all, because we're about to make it much simpler.

Let's go back to our "Mary Had a Little Lamb" example and add the harmony. In the old-fashioned two-line notation it looks like this.

The right hand plays the single note melody while the left hand plays and holds a C chord at the beginning of each measure. But in pop music we make all this much simpler by using a notation system that looks like this.

Believe it or not, this simple single-clef example has all the information contained in the complicated two-clef example shown above it. This simpler example is actually the correct notation system for playing all popular music.

The letter C above the first note means to play the full C major chord—all three notes, C, E, and G—with the left hand. By convention we play the chord once at the beginning of every measure and hold it down for the duration of each measure. (A measure is a musical unit of time that's represented on music paper by the vertical lines that run perpendicular to the five lines of the staff. For example, the musical segment in the above example comprises two measures.)

The written music of a lead sheet will tell you what chord to play with the left hand for every measure of music. Add the appropriate left-hand chords to the right-hand melody at the appropriate time and you've got complete music.

Notice the C symbol is not written again over the second measure in this example. By convention, however, you must repeat that chord with your left hand at the beginning of every measure until the music specifies that you switch to another chord.

HOW DO WE KNOW IT'S RIGHT?

Play these two measures of the song now, using both hands. Keep playing it until it sounds right. Once it sounds right, it's correct. That's the new criteria for musical perfection, by the way. The music has to *sound* right. That's all. No one is concerned with whether you are performing the notes written on the page with strict precision. That's the classical paradigm. The pop music paradigm tells us to work on the music until it sounds good to the ear, regardless of what's written on the page. The information on the page is just a guide, a map, an outline, a suggestion. The information is useful in that it helps you locate melody notes and harmony chords more quickly than if you were just working it out by ear. It's not to be taken literally.

This is how pop music works, this is how it is written, and this is what goes through the mind of the pop pianist when playing. Yes, this is basically the system used by professional pianists for more than a century, and this is how I have taught it in my seminars since 1982.

Unlike the classical notation approach, in this approach music is not reduced to a blur of notes on a page. As we've seen, music is really just two elements: the melody and the chords. Chords are pretty simple. One nice thing about chords is they don't move as fast as melody notes. Chords will seldom change more than once or twice per measure, so the left hand can be more relaxed than the right. As a bonus, chords on a piano are much easier to play than the corresponding chords on the guitar. And rest assured, it's 100 percent musically correct to play music this way.

I don't mean to imply this is all there is to playing music. In fact, it's just a start. The typical professional pianist knows and uses thousands of different chords and never stops learning. However, with just three chords—C, F, and something called G seventh—there are hundreds of thousands of songs you can play.

THE SECRET OF THE TIME MACHINE

After you learn the basic melody and chord progression of a song, you can improve upon it by listening to a recording of it and imitating what you hear. Edison's phonograph, his time machine, paved the way for pop music to exist. The same machine also makes music relatively easy to learn. The phonograph freezes time and preserves moments. Before Edison, there was no way to preserve actual sound, and thus no way to capture and save a musical moment in time. The invention of music notation or writing was a step in the right direction, but it was a halfway measure. With music notation we have a way to recreate the symphonies of Beethoven but we have no way to hear what Beethoven's own orchestra sounded like. Thanks to Edison, we can live here in the twenty-first century and still listen to the voice of Caruso, preserved forever. Not only does the time machine preserve music but also it enables us to learn how to play it more efficiently.

We can learn music directly through our ears, bypassing the awkward visual interface of printed music notation.

Thanks to Edison, music no longer had to be confined to the narrow restrictions imposed by music notation. His invention liberated music. The beat was released. Jazz was born. New forms of popular music emerged. This music never needed to be written down; it just needed to be recorded.

No longer were freedom and creativity hampered by the restrictive nature of music notation. At last, music could be preserved and stored exactly as it had been performed. The new breed of musician uses recordings to learn not only songs but also subtle musical styles and nuances of performance.

Thanks to recordings, anyone can listen to Art Tatum play the piano on demand, 24/7. Just as important, Art Tatum can be every aspiring jazz pianist's teacher and mentor. His ghost is present wherever jazz piano is played. Had his performances not been preserved by the time machine, there is no telling what jazz piano would sound like today. But very few living jazz pianists have ever met Tatum. Most of us weren't even alive during his lifetime. Had it not been for the time machine and the recorded media that followed, it could be argued that the type of music we loosely refer to as jazz could not exist. The same goes for country and western, rock and roll, rhythm and blues, gospel, and many other forms of popular music. That body of music that is time machine-dependent is at least 95 percent of what is heard on radios and sold to consumers worldwide.

ONE STUDENT'S MUSICAL JOURNEY

I began my serious piano studies at the age of twenty-three. I took weekly lessons and I brought a tape recorder to my lessons to preserve what I was being taught. There was no other way to do it. After a year I figured out I didn't need weekly lessons. Instead, I sought out piano players I thought could teach me something. When I found such people, I tried to convince them to sell me an hour of their time so that I could essentially interview them at the piano. I brought my portable time machine to record the encounters, and I didn't return for another session until I had mastered the previous one. I listened to the tape of the lesson/interview and practiced what I had learned until I sounded somewhat like the teacher on the tape. Only then would I make an appointment for another lesson. Very little was ever written down on music paper, and I've still got recordings from at least ten of these informants.

Less than five years after I started, I figured out I could play piano in bands. I played in all kinds of bands, playing all kinds of music: rock, jazz, country, swing, oldies, you name it. The common thread was that all these bands learned their repertoire not from printed music but from Edison's time machine. Rarely if ever would we purchase sheet music.

A few years later I tired of my crazy life as a performer and decided to do something even crazier: I planned to develop a seminar in which students could learn to play the piano from me, from scratch, in a single three-hour course. I packaged what amounted to a lot of the same information about playing piano that I myself had learned just a few years earlier.

But would my students see results? Would they walk away from the seminar with all the information needed to play the piano? And would it stick?

To ensure good results, I provided each student with the magic ingredient that made their success at the piano possible—a prerecorded cassette tape of all the musical examples they had heard me play in the seminar. There it was, frozen in time and easily accessible, a little piece of plastic and acetate they could listen to, emulate, and learn from. After they abandoned the old piano-lesson paradigm of note reading, they were free to learn they way I had learned—by listening to actual music. It worked.

Almost a quarter century after the day of the first one-day workshop, some two hundred thousand people have taken the seminar and have the essential information frozen in time for review whenever they choose. I now have trained and certified piano workshop leaders all over North American to give this workshop essentially the way it was originally taught some twenty-five years ago. I have also seen the demand for follow-up information, and I have created about a dozen follow-up programs to meet these needs. What makes the programs work is that every one of them, without exception, comes with its own time machine—currently either a CD recording or a video DVD—as the media that fuels the learning process.

Resources

About Instant Piano: For general information about the Instant Piano method, visit pianofun.com. For information about attending a seminar, visit pianofun.com/seminars.html. Courseware available only at website: pianofun.com/catalog/product_list.html. Music Reading for Hopelessly Busy People (CD and eight-page booklet). Preparation for Instant Piano (basic beginning course) (book, DVD, CD, 25 songs).

About how to become a certified Instant Piano Workshop Leader
The New School of American Music
309 Wall St.
Chico, CA 95928
800-726-7654
questions@pianofun.com

Sources for Lead Sheets (Fake Books)
Hal Leonard Publications (halleonard.com). Amazon.com (search for "fake books"). Your local library. An Internet search on "fake book" or "lead sheet" will yield numerous leads. Issues regarding copyrights have not been resolved, so use caution.

"Use what talent you possess: The woods would be very silent
if no birds sang except those that sang best."
—*Henry Van Dyke*

How to Play Guitar and Harmonica—The Easy Way

David Mathison

Dedicated to Ray Charles Robinson (September 23, 1930–June 10, 2004)

All you need for the blues is three chords and the truth.

Consider this now-you-really-have-no-excuses factoid: Ninety percent of popular music consists of three chords. To be precise, three simple chords. By learning only them, you can play thousands of songs in almost every genre—rock, jazz, soul, country, pop, rhythm and blues, hip-hop, blues, punk, and heavy metal. That is, you can because I could.

Inspired by the music at church, I decided to teach myself how to play music (Thanks to Brandon Brack and Bethany Nelson of Westminster Presbyterian Church and Cindy Cohen of music-makers.org.) Fast forward three years, and I can now play thousands of songs on the guitar and harmonica. And, thanks to Robert Laughlin, I can even play a couple of songs on the piano. Because all these songs were among my favorites, I enjoy them even more now that I can play them.

Traditional Music Education: Read First, Play Later

For six hundred years, traditional music education has been based on teaching students how to read complex notation, originally intended to record classical music. Beginners had to master complex chords, practice scales, and learn to read sheet music—all before they could play the songs they loved. This "read first, play later" method is tedious, slow, and frustrating. As self-taught guitar virtuoso Frank Zappa said, "Standard method of notation is very difficult." People start to believe that music is complicated—for professionals only—and lose the desire to play. The result? Many instruments gather dust, unloved, untuned, and unplayed.

Shorthand Notation: Play Now, Have Fun Now

That was then. Now, it is possible to demystify old-school music education by learning simple shorthand music notation known as "tabs" (short for tablature). This learn-by-doing approach focuses on the fun of playing and produces astounding and fast results.

Expecting students to read music before they learn to play is like expecting toddlers to read before they have learned to talk!

—Neil Moore, founder, simplymusic.com

Let's start with learning how to play guitar—easily.

Step 1: Tune it. Tuning a guitar has never been simpler. Small, inexpensive, battery-operated chromatic tuners such as the Korg CA-30 (under $20) can be found in most music shops. Or you can tune your guitar online at totaltabs. com, which hosts a free online guitar tuner. Or type "How to tune a guitar" into Google and follow the directions in the first few links.

Step 2: Learn some chords, using tabs. Now that your guitar is tuned up, learn the fingering in the illustrations below for three easy, basic, open chords (G, C, and D), so you can play the song at the end of this chapter. These three chords will give you a solid foundation to play most popular and familiar songs.

In the old days, learning to play popular songs meant that you needed to work out the chords yourself, have someone teach you, or go to the local music store to buy sheet music. But today, you can learn to play almost all modern music by going to websites that offer tabs for most songs. Tabs simplify writing and reading music by eliminating complex notation. Tabs are more or less signposts showing you the way along the song. They are analogous to lead sheets for simplified piano instruction, which are sometimes compiled into cheat books.

In guitar tabs, chords are written using six lines, each line representing a string on the guitar. The neck of the guitar has numbered ridges called frets. The closest to the guitar headstock is fret 1, the next is fret 2, etc.

The tab for a G chord, written as 320003, is

```
e || --- 3 ------- ||
B || --- 0 ------- ||
G || --- 0 ------- ||
D || --- 0 ------- ||
A || --- 2 ------- ||
E || --- 3 ------- ||
```

Notice that tabs are written upside down in relation to the neck of the guitar. The top string in the diagram is actually the bottom string on your guitar, closest to your pinkie. Also, notice that there are two E strings. The one closest to your pinkie is written with a lowercase e to distinguish it from the other E, close to your thumb.

To play the 320003 chord (G), put your first finger on the second fret of the A string. Put your middle finger on the third fret of the E string. Finally, put your ring finger on the third fret of the first string (the lowercase e). Curl your fingers so that you leave the remaining strings untouched. Keeping your fingers in this position, strum all six strings. You can now play the G chord.

Here are two more chords for you to master. An X indicates that the string is not played/strummed.

The tab for a C chord, written as X32010, is

```
e || --- 0 ------- ||
B || --- 1 ------- ||
G || --- 0 ------- ||
D || --- 2 ------- ||
A || --- 3 ------- ||
E || --- X------- ||
```

The tab for a D chord, written as XX0232, is

```
e || --- 2 ------- ||
B || --- 3 ------- ||
G || --- 2 ------- ||
D || --- 0 ------- ||
A || --- X------- ||
E || --- X------- ||
```

Step 3: Go to tab sites to find songs that you enjoy, and use the three chords that you know. Now, using the word *tabs*, use Google to find your favorite artist (for example, search for "U2 tabs") or song ("U2 'One' tabs"). Google will point you to sites that provide free chords and tabs, such as ultimate-guitar.com, guitaretab. com, azchords.com, thetabworld.com, 911tabs.com, or countrytabs.com. Some tabs teach you how to play chords, and you will also find tabs that show you how to play lead guitar riffs (where just one note/string is played at a time).

You can also go to these sites directly to look up the songs and/or artists. One popular tab site is e-chords.com, which has more than 12,000 artists and over two hundred thousand tabs. It even allows you to change the key to match your vocal range by simply clicking on the desired key. The chords automatically change to reflect the new key. Hover your mouse over the chord and a pop-up box appears with the correct fingering. Some tabs have MIDI files, allowing surfers to play along with the MIDI version of the song, right on the site.

Another site, chordfind.com, visually represents which strings and frets on the instrument are being played. If you've been trying to figure out how to play that special A sharp/B flat chord, this is the place for you! A premium membership ($1.99 per month) gives you access to hundreds of video guitar lessons for artists like The Police and popular songs like Jack Johnson's *Posters*.

Be wary of quality control. Because tab sites are mostly free, and because tabs are contributed by users with varying levels of experience, you will sometimes find multiple versions of a tab for a popular (or tricky) song. Also, because most sites allow users to rate tabs according to accuracy, you'll soon find both trusted tabbers and their tabs.

To create tabs, tabbers can use any word processor or Notepad, or the free Power Tab Editor (power-tab.net), a tablature authoring tool that allows beginners and experienced musicians to easily transcribe and play back their own music or lessons.

Can't find a tab to your favorite song? Create your own. I partially tabbed a favorite Pete Yorn song and submitted it to a tab site, where other fans corrected and finished it.

Optional Step 3a: Free Video Lessons. Some people learn faster by watching other people play, in the same way that they learn a new language by listening and mimicking. A great site for video lessons is none other than YouTube.com. Search for "How to play guitar" and you'll find free guitar lessons for many popular songs. Many other video sharing sites offer free lessons, as well as the aforementioned e-chords.com.

Some cable subscribers receive a channel called Mag Rack, which airs a program called *Guitar Xpress* that provides free video guitar lessons of favorite songs. Viewers can pause, fast-forward, and rewind the episodes, and learn at their own pace. Thanks to *Guitar Xpress*, my brother Eric can now play songs such as "Born to Be Wild," "Sweet Home Alabama," "Takin' Care of Business," and ZZ Top's "Tush," much to his wife's and family's delight.

Step 4: Play along with the music you love! Find a song that you like and can play along to. For example, Billy Bragg's "There Is Power in a Union" consists of the three guitar chords described above: G, C, and D. Play the song on your CD or tape. Or, if you want access to the wide range of Bragg's songs, log on to your Rhapsody or iTunes account. Listen a few times first, to get the pattern, a basic G, C, G, D, as follows:

```
G                          C
There is power in a factory, power in the land,

G                              D
Power in the hand of the worker,

G                          C
But it all amounts to nothing if together we don't stand.

G               D G
There is power in a Union.[1]
```

That's all there is to it.

The Caveat: Takedown Notices

Unfortunately, some tab sites, such as the Online Guitar Archive (olga.net) and guitartabs.com, have received "takedown" letters from the National Music Publishers' Association and the Music Publishers' Association of the United States, claiming that sharing tablature constitutes copyright infringement under the 1998 Digital Millennium Copyright Act's takedown provisions. Site owners claim tabs are fair use because friends jamming together have always helped each other in the same way, and nobody is getting paid.

To get around these takedown provisions, artists, bands, and music schools are putting up free tabs. Thanks to John Caspar and Terry McDermott for pointing me to a great tab site of one of my favorite songwriters, the John Prine shrine (jpshrine.org/chords/index.htm). Also, since 1995 guitarist Roger McGuinn has been posting tabs and lyrics to songs at Roger McGuinn's Folk Den (ibiblio.org/jimmy/folkden-wp). The Berklee College of Music, with alumni that include Quincy Jones, Diana Krall, and John Mayer, have posted free music lessons at berkleeshares.com. Both McGuinn and Berklee use Creative Commons licenses. (See chapter 21.)

---

1. "There Is Power in a Union," words and music by Billy Bragg (from *Talking with the Taxman About Poetry* 1986). Copyright ©1986 Chrysalis Music. All rights reserved. Used by permission. All rights in the U.S. and Canada administered by Chrysalis Music. Adapted from *The Battle Cry of Freedom* by George F. Root (1862).

How to Play the Harmonica
David Mathison

How to play the harmonica in three steps:

Step 1: Buy it.
You can buy inexpensive harmonicas of good quality at most music stores or online. For example, a "Suzuki Easy Rider" costs just $5.50, while a "Hohner Blues Harp" retails for under $20.

Step 2: Learn harmonica tabs.
Harmonica tabs are incredibly simple. A standard harmonica has ten numbered holes. Harmonica tabs are numbered to match the holes. A positive number means you "blow" into the corresponding hole, and a negative number means you inhale or "draw" from that hole.

For example, the harmonica tab notation "5 –4 5" means to blow into the fifth hole, draw (or inhale) from the fourth hole, then blow into the fifth hole. When learning a new tune, it's best to listen to a song a few times first to get the feel of it. Then try to play along with the tabs.

Step 3: Search harmonica tab websites.
To find the tabs for songs you like, either type "harmonica tabs" into your brower, or point it to these sites:
- harmonicacountry.com. Jack Earl's site offers free harmonica lessons and tabs.
- bluesrevue.com. Dave Barrett offers blues harmonica courses online in Real Audio.
- harpinanawhinin.com. Mark Purinton's site lists thousands of popular songs.
- modempool.com/dking/blues%20harp%20tabs/index.htm.

The motto of this harmonica site is: "If you don't blow, you suck."

That's good advice.

4

THE MUSIC BUSINESS

THE NEW WAY TO PROMOTE AND SELL YOUR MUSIC

David Mathison

"Music is spiritual. The music business is not."
—*Van Morrison*

I f you write or play music, this chapter is for you. Who are "you"? Megastars, emerging artists, guitar heroes, indies, local celebrities who never broke nationally, retired rockers with families or responsibilities who can't afford to tour (you know—"too old to rock and roll, too young to die")—all of you.

Advisory: You will like this chapter more if you have even the slightest aversion to the recording industry, corporate radio ownership, or traditional retail sales.

My major theme is simple: Hang in there. Despite all the doom and gloom about the demise of the music "industry," there has never been a better time than today for independent music, musicians, and the fans who support them. According to Jenny Toomey, cofounder of the Future

Thanks to Barry Bergman, Peter and Mushi Jenner, Future of Music Coalition (Jenny Toomey, Kristin Thomson, Brian Zisk, and Michael Bracy), Downhill Battle, Don Henley, Federal Communications Commissioners Michael Copps and Jonathan Adelstein, U.S. Senator Russ Feingold, American Association for Independent Music (Peter Gordon and Don Rose), Eric Boehlert, Shana Morrison, Bonnie Hayes, Susan Zelinsky, and David Rubinson.

of Music Coalition, today we may be witnessing the emergence of a "musician's middle class." Now anyone—yes, this truly means you!—can record a song with inexpensive equipment and distribute it over the Internet to a global audience. Furthermore, your fans can, and will, help you promote and sell it. The question is, how exactly does your music get heard above the Fray, and possibly even earn you a living?

Before we explain, and get to the good news, though, let's take a cold, hard look at the challenges. Traditionally, or at least in most of the twentieth century before the Internet, musicians had two options. The first was to sign with a major label and get exploited, to gain access to the means of production, airplay, and distribution—and perhaps to become a superstar. The second was to remain independent, suffer through the sounds of silence, and all but certainly not be able to quit your day job.

One reason for the two options was the concentrated "triple play" of major record labels, radio conglomerates, and retail mass merchandisers. All conspired to distort the American sound system.

MAJOR RECORD LABELS

In 2007, the big four music labels accounted for more than 80 percent of the $12 billion in music sales: Vivendi's Universal Music Group got 32 percent of sales, Sony BMG Music got 25 percent, Warner Music Group 15 percent, and EMI 9 percent. Independent labels accounted for the remaining 19 percent, which was their biggest share of the market in five years, according to Nielsen SoundScan.

The majors, like virtually all businesses, are risk averse and treat music as a product. They emphasize quarterly results and favor superstar acts—the top 1 percent of mainstream bands that can sell half a million CDs to already established fan bases. The music from the majors gets blasted into the public conscience through expensive publicity campaigns and various forms of payola. (Yes, payola is still alive and well. More on that later.) Major label records cost millions to create and promote, from making music videos to paying executive salaries and running ad campaigns, so to break even, big labels need blockbuster artists and sales.

The floors of the entertainment industry are littered with examples of one-sided contracts.[1] In "The Problem with Music," Nirvana *In Utero* producer Steve Albini writes that whenever he talks to an artist or band considering a major label deal, he imagines a "trench filled with runny, decaying shit," with the artists at one end, and "a faceless industry lackey at the other end holding a fountain pen and a contract waiting to be signed." With a thousand artists willing to sign, songwriters traditionally had little choice but to hold their nose and dive into the trench themselves.

If they are lucky, the artist gets a loan euphemistically known as an "advance," which the artist

---

1. Among many examples, see Steve Albini, "The Problem with Music." Salon.com, June 14, 2000. Wendy Day, "Artists Don't Make Money from Record Deals." Don Passman, *All You Need to Know About the Music Business.*

has to pay back through royalties. A 15 percent artist royalty ends up being from just twenty cents to $1 for every $20 retail CD sold, after "standard industry deductions" take their toll (returns, credits, free goods, packaging, breakage, new media, and reserves). The artist only gets paid on "royalty bearing units," so markdowns, record clubs (think Columbia House, where consumers buy ten CDs for a dollar), and other promotional goods often net the artist no royalties at all.

Everyone gets paid before the band: accountant, agent, engineer, lawyer, manager, producer, record label, and studio. The IRS takes its share later. The artist doesn't get a *penny* until enough royalties are earned to pay back the advance, and only after the label recoups its expenses, if that ever occurs. Expenses include the costs for advertising, distribution, indie promotion (aka payola), manufacturing, onstage outfits, overhead, packaging, production, publicity, shipping, touring, unions, and videos. Don't even get me started on the Caligula-like album release parties. Oh, and the label keeps track of accounting, of course!

Most contracts are "cross-collateralized," so if the label fails to recoup expenses on the first album, the money is paid back from the artist's *subsequent* earnings. Well-known, platinum-selling acts often end up owing their record label lots of money. By 1998, five-time Grammy-winning R&B singer Toni Braxton sold $188 million of CDs for the music industry, but filed for chapter 7 bankruptcy protection partly because of a contract that paid her less than 35 cents per album.

The label earns millions in profits off a musician's hard work, while, as Courtney Love aptly put it, "the band may as well be working at a 7-Eleven."

Despite an artist's hard work, labels may decline to release the album, and worse, refuse to give or sell the unreleased album back to the artist. Singer-songwriter Bonnie Hayes has written songs for Cher, Robert Cray, Santana, Natalie Cole, and Bonnie Raitt, including the hit songs "Love Letter" and "Have a Heart" on Raitt's triple Grammy-winning album, *Nick of Time*. According to Hayes, Warner Brothers "passed on distributing my debut album *Good Clean Fun* when Slash released it in 1982 because it was too 'edgy,' effectively killing the record." In 1995, Hayes tried to buy the masters back, but Slash had been absorbed many times, and nobody knew where the masters were. In late 2007, Hayes learned that the *Good Clean Fun* CD was available online, licensed from none other than—wait for it—Warner Brothers. This actually pleased Hayes, who expected to receive some portion of the licensing fee, but nothing ever showed up on her statement from Universal, the company that ate the company that originally published the songs, Almo-Irving. Repeated attempts to contact both Warner and Universal failed to garner even a return call. According to Hayes, "The company that refused to release my record is now profiting from the sale of the same record. I still have never received a penny from Warner or Universal from the sale of this very popular record—even with the re-release."

Many artists get locked into long-term contracts that require the production of new albums every year. On the opposite side of the spectrum, Prince insisted on releasing *more* music—on double and triple CDs—a strategy his label, Warner, disagreed with. In protest, Prince changed his name to an unpronounceable symbol, wrote the word *slave* on his cheek, and finally created his own label, NPG. Singer LeAnn Rimes signed a twenty-one-album contract with Curb Records, a deal that even the most prolific artist would find difficult to fulfill, when she was just twelve years old. In September 2001, she testified to the California State Senate, "at that age, I didn't understand everything that was in my contract."

Even worse, the label owns the copyright to the song, even after the band repays the advance. As Barenaked Ladies lead vocalist Ed Robertson told Jeff Howe of *Wired* magazine, "It's as if you received a loan for a house, but when you finish paying off the loan, the label says thank you and keeps the house."

MAJOR RADIO GROUPS

Radio airplay can make or break a music career. According to Edison Media Research, 75 percent of music buyers say their CD purchases are influenced by songs heard on the radio. Howie Klein, a former president of Reprise Records, agrees, saying, "Radio is still the biggest single factor to get something going."

Part of the trouble today, fellow Radioheads, is one word: consolidation. Prior to the Telecommunications Act of 1996, no single company could own more than twenty AM and twenty FM stations. The Act got rid of such limits, thereby allowing tsunamis of consolidation. Before long, Clear Channel owned twelve hundred stations, followed by Cumulus with four hundred and four and Citadel Broadcasting with two hundred twenty-four, with EMMIS Communications, Entercom Communications, and Viacom's Infinity vying for the few local, independent stations that remained.

Individuality and localism were tuned out. Content was piped in to stations from remote corporate headquarters, completely removed from the community the local station purported to serve. Consolidation led to strict formats (or genres, such as R&B, pop, rock) and playlist (song) homogeneity. A Future of Music Coalition study released in 2006 reported that "just 15 formats make up three-quarters of all commercial programming. The playlists of stations in the same format owned by the same company can overlap by up to 97%."[2] In October 2006, REM's Mike Mills testified at a Federal Communications Commission hearing that "playlists have been corporatized, nationalized, and sanitized. Airplay for local and new artists is a virtual impossibility."

The most enthusiastic consolidator was Clear Channel Communications. Its monopolistic control gives it tremendous power in determining which performers succeed, how much they are paid, and where and when they play. By 2006, the company owned not only twelve hundred U.S. radio stations, but also forty TV stations, 824,000 billboards, and one hundred fifty concert halls, amphitheaters, venues, and clubs, concert promotions, and ticket sales. It owns Premiere

---

2. Future of Music Coalition: "False Premises, False Promises: A Quantitative History of Ownership Consolidation in the Radio Industry." futureofmusic.org/research/radiostudy06.cfm

Radio Networks, which syndicates seventy radio programs such as extremists Rush Limbaugh and Glenn Beck to more than five thousand affiliates, reaching over 190 million listeners weekly.[3] In 2005, Clear Channel changed the name of its Chicago music operations to Elevated Concerts. A more appropriate name might be "Elevated Ticket Prices," since concert ticket prices increased 50 percentage points higher than the consumer price index over the past decade. That same year, Clear Channel spun off its concerts and venues businesses into a stand-alone company called Live Nation, the world's largest concert promoter, with $1.3 billion in concert box-office receipts in the United States alone. In 2006 Live Nation bought the number three music promoter, House of Blues, for $350 million, thereby reducing the number of national promoters from three to two.

In 2005, then-New York Attorney General Eliot Spitzer uncovered a massive payola scandal involving bribes to radio programmers in exchange for airplay.[4] Spitzer's office subpoenaed five major labels, seven radio broadcast groups, and two independent promoters. According to Spitzer, "Payola is nationwide and industry-wide in scope." A study by Columbia University sociology professor Duncan J. Watts published in *Science* found that people select a song if they think others like it, too. "The [study] results are certainly consistent with the motivations for payola . . . getting it on people's radar screens increases its likelihood of it becoming popular."

Payola violates federal statutes, FCC regulations, and state bribery laws. The payola bribes were inventive, and included vacations, laptops, plasma TVs, airfare, electronics, tickets, and, of course, money. Lots of money. For example, in 2001, Shania Twain's record label, Mercury Nashville, spent $1.5 million on independent promotion. Epic (Sony BMG) paid epic money for Jennifer Lopez's songs to get "spins" (radio airtime); a November 2002 rate card stated that radio stations in small markets would get $500 per spin, midmarkets $800, and large-market stations $1,000. In the biggest markets, stations got five grand per song.

---

3. In November 2007, Clear Channel sold thirty-five full-power TV stations to private equity firm Providence Equity Partners for $1.2 billion, giving Providence eighty-six TV and ninety-nine radio stations. It also has shares in MGM studios and Warner Music Group. The Providence board includes former FCC Chairman Michael Powell, whose push for yet more consolidation in 2003 was soundly defeated. Clear Channel also sold one hundred sixty-one radio stations for $331 million to a number of parties, including Thomas H. Lee Partners LP and Bain Capital Partners LLC, which was cofounded by former Republican presidential candidate Mitt Romney in 1984. It remains to be seen how the privatization of our airwaves by private equity companies with opaque management structures will serve the public interest and localism requirements of broadcast radio licensees.

4. In 1960, disc jockey Alan Freed's radio career was ruined because of a payola scandal. In 1981, it was found that independent promoters cost record companies hundreds of millions of dollars each year. In 1986, NBC investigative journalist Brian Ross reported a connection linking independent promoters with organized crime. Fredric Dannen's exposé *Hit Men* showed that it cost $5,000 per song for airplay in the biggest radio markets, $1,000 for midsize markets, and $800 in small markets. Rudy Giuliani, when he was New York's Attorney General, began a federal grand jury investigation into indie promotion. Then Senator Al Gore (D-Tenn.) launched a Senate probe. But payola reemerged, and by 2001 pay-to-play fees were as high as during the 1980s.

So now we know. We are not crazy. We hear the same inane songs over and over again—and don't hear great music—because commercial radio stations collude with major labels to promote their own acts. Radio airtime is not allocated based on songs' popularity or merit, but instead is meted out to those who can afford to pay the bribes.

Ownership consolidation has enabled radio conglomerates to directly benefit from payola's ill-gotten gains. According to Lorne Manley's 2005 *New York Times* article "How Payola Went Corporate," Clear Channel "shook up the promotion world by directing independent promoters to cut future deals with executives at corporate headquarters, not with individual station programmers."

Who really pays the payola? The musicians themselves. The costs of independent promotion are deducted from artist's royalties. As Don Henley testified in front of the Senate Commerce Committee in 2004, "I know there's payola, because I get billed for it."

MAJOR RETAILERS

Mass merchandisers Best Buy, Wal-Mart, and Target are the three largest music retailers, controlling 65 percent of music sales. These big-box outlets are not music stores. To them, music is a commodity that must compete with other products in terms of sales per square foot of shelf space. The stores stock only music from the major labels, backed by huge promotional campaigns with prime display space in windows or on shelf end-caps. As with commercial radio, you won't hear, or buy, some of the best music at Best Buy.

One result of limited choice and consumers forced to buy music they don't want? CD sales are down, way down. According to the June 2007 issue of *Rolling Stone,* in 2006 CD sales fell 16 percent. The ten top-selling albums in the United States sold a combined 25 million copies, less than half the 60 million copies sold in 2000.

Another reason for the sales decline, as Dixie Chicks manager Simon Renshaw said in *Rolling Stone,* "With digital technology, everyone's figured out that a business built only on the manufacture, distribution and sale of CDs has ended." Alain Levy, the CEO of EMI, was more direct: "The CD, as it is now, is dead."

The reason is that the CD is a container for music, and in today's digital world CDs are almost as outmoded as any other physical container, such as 33⅓, 78, or 45 rpm vinyl records, or eight-track tapes, or cassettes. Retailers are not selling music; they are selling containers—albums, tapes, or CDs—formats that most customers no longer want to own. Shelf space is limited. Retailers compete with online stores like Apple's iTunes and peer-to-peer file sharing sites that require no physical storage or shipping. Wherehouse had $378 million in inventory and $155 million in plant and equipment when it filed for Chapter 11 bankruptcy reorganization. Retailers that have survived have moved away from music, or use rock-bottom prices to lure customers into stores to sell higher-margin items such as MP3 players and audio equipment.

The result? Some 2,700 U.S. record stores (36 percent of the total) have gone bankrupt or closed since 2003. Tower Records, the number two music retailer, closed all eighty-nine stores; Musicland Group, which operated eight hundred stores under the Sam Goody brand, is gone, as is the hundred and forty-eight-store Wherehouse chain and National Record Mart. TransWorld Entertainment Corp (which operates the Coconuts chain), closed one hundred thirty-four of its 1,087 stores.

This "triple play" of the three consolidated majors—labels, radio stations, and retailers—made it easy for a handful of executives to decide which artists get produced and promoted, which radio stations get paid for airplay, and which bins to stack with plastic.

The consolidation/greed/mess (choose your term) also led, to no one's surprise, to massive layoffs. According to the January 2008 *Rolling Stone,* major labels have shrunk by one quarter since 2000, and more than five thousand music industry employees have lost their jobs. In July 2005, as part of Spitzer's payola settlement, Sony BMG paid $10 million and Warner later settled for $5 million. The FCC got radio station owners to voluntarily agree to set aside 4,200 hours of airtime for local independent artists. As for the retail side, in addition to store bankruptcies, the five largest U.S. record labels and three major retail chains admitted to cheating consumers by conspiring to boost the prices of CDs from 1995 to 2000. In a landmark settlement, they refunded $143 million to music CD consumers in 2002.

This collusion hurt the two groups that should benefit the most from music: artists and their fans. Musicians who can't pay-to-play are simply left off commercial radio. Fans get less choice on the air, and pay higher prices at retail and concerts. The consumer's money benefits label executives, indie promoters, radio owners—everyone but the artists the fans want to support.

One musician who spoke out about this abusive system eight years ago was Courtney Love. In her address to the Digital Hollywood conference, which was reprinted in Salon magazine ("Courtney Love Does the Math," June 14, 2000), Love lucidly outlined the significance to artists:

> "Of the 32,000 new releases each year, only 250 sell more than 10,000 copies. And less than 30 go platinum. The 273,000 working musicians in America make about $30,000 a year. Only 15 percent of American Federation of Musicians members work steadily in music. But the music industry is a $40 billion-a-year business. The annual sales of cassettes, CDs, and video are larger than the gross national product of 80 countries. Americans have more CD players, radios and VCRs than we have bathtubs. There are hundreds of stories about artists in their 60s and 70s who are broke because they never made a dime from their hit records, living in total poverty, never having been paid anything. Not even having access to a union or to basic health care. Artists who have generated billions of dollars for an industry die broke and un-cared for."

The times, though, they are a changin'. And both musicians and their fans are reaping the rewards, sometimes big time.

THE NEW WAY

Musicians now can perform a triple bypass around the gatekeepers and connect directly with their audience. It's not always easy, and you'll probably need help (more on that below), but it *is* increasingly possible and has become the preferred option of artists, both known and undiscovered. This emerging "Artist Services Model" is a combination of industry-savvy partners, consultants, and tools that enable musicians to earn a living from their passion. The model lets fans directly support the musicians they love. (See Sidebar "What's Going on Here? The Artist Services Model: An Interview with Barry Bergman.")

Let's look first at what record labels historically did for musicians. They put up the money to produce an album, promoted it on the radio, and got the container into retail bins. But a musician no longer needs this top-down gatekeeper model of labels, radio, and retail.

For one thing, high-quality, low-cost computers and digital editing software means that artists don't need $100,000 from a label to create music or videos, and don't need to sell half a million CDs just to pay back the advance. Recording music is no longer expensive.

As for promotion, sure, radio play is nice, but the Internet gives artists a direct relationship with their audience. Fans discover and buy music themselves, from the bottom up. They promote music to each other, through viral "word-of-mouse," by forwarding website URLs and MP3 files, and by blog postings, podcasts, social network profiles, their cell phone ringtones, videogames, and shared playlists on iTunes, Rhapsody, and Pandora.

This digital distribution is almost free. Call it "free." Since tunes are online, there is no need to manufacture, store, and distribute physical albums, tapes, or discs to retail outlets.

It's a virtual viral meritocracy in which almost anyone can succeed. *Rolling Stone* reported that the indie label bands Arcade Fire, Interpol, and Bright Eyes sold more than three hundred thousand copies each, without the majors. Hawthorne Heights' *The Silence in Black and White* sold 560,000 albums, without radio play. Radiohead's *In Rainbows* was initially offered to fans (who even named their own price) direct from the group's website, without retail distribution.

No major label! No radio! No retail!

And no payola. At least, not yet. (See Sidebar "Rock the Net Neutrality.")

In a December 2007 *Wired* article titled "David Byrne's Survival Strategies for Emerging Artists—and Megastars," the ex-Talking Head front man outlined six models:

1. The 360 (or Equity) Deal: The 360-degree deal enables major labels, whose earnings from CD sales are declining, to control a broader array of rights and get a percentage of revenues from anything

What's Going on Here? The Artist Services Model
An Interview with Barry Bergman
Bob Grossweiner and *Jane Cohen*
from an interview in CelebrityAccess/Encore (March 14, 2003)

What is the future of the music business from your perspective?
The near future of the music business is going to be about a radical, irrevocable change in the way that people connect to and consume music. The collapse of the traditional music retail sector is imminent and that retail collapse will inevitably be followed by the collapse of the physical distribution network presently owned by the major labels. And while radio will continue to be around for a long time to come, it will continue to diminish in importance with respect to marketing music.

In order to survive, the record industry will have to move away from relying upon the traditional mass marketing approach of introducing new music and move toward serving sustainable micro markets—away from radio toward word of mouth communities of like-minded consumers.

The future of music is about consumer empowerment and choice—getting what you want, when and how you want it. The future of the industry really is a sea of change in the entire relationship between creators and consumers. This change is overdue and inevitable.

The good news is that there are very clear indications that people continue to love music as much or more than they ever have. For all the doom and gloom in the record business, the concert industry is extremely healthy and the use of music in movies and video games seems to increase each year. It's the method of marketing and distributing pre-recorded music that has become outmoded.

Who are the winners and losers in the future industry you depict?
The two principal winners in the future music business are consumers and the artists. The consumers will get whatever they want, and the artists won't need to rely as much upon the industry machine in order to reach and serve their audience. It will be possible for the artist to own and control a much larger part of their traditional business by communicating directly to the consumer. As a result, the artists will be able to participate in a myriad of completely new revenue streams by garnering a higher share of their existing customer. Of course, the artists will need partners that are savvy in the ways and means associated with this new style of business. I am quite sure that those artist services will start to rapidly emerge over the next few years.

and everything connected to an artist: publishing, touring, videos, merchandise, and licensing. According to Byrne, "The artist becomes a brand, owned and operated by the label." Examples include recent deals with Robbie Williams, Korn, U2, Madonna, and the Pussycat Dolls, whose Interscope deal covers everything from toys to a Las Vegas strip club. In April 2008, rapper Jay-Z concluded the biggest 360 deal yet: a reported ten-year, $150 million deal with Live Nation. Manager Barry Bergman called the equity deal "a desperate last-ditch attempt to grab replacement revenue for declining sales. At this point, the record labels do not have the ability to add any value to the concert or merchandising business. They aren't in that business at all."

Madonna's 360

The 360 does makes sense, however, for Madonna and Live Nation. In October 2007, she left her label, Warner Music Group, for concert promoter Live Nation in a $120 million, ten-year, 360 deal. Because Madonna earned $200 million in touring (second only to the Rolling Stones), and since Live Nation is the nation's biggest concert promoter, this 360 deal is a match made in heaven. Live Nation now has exclusive rights to promote Madonna's future concerts, DVDs, fan club, films, merchandise, music, television, and website. The *Wall Street Journal* estimated that Madonna would keep "90% of touring revenue, 70% of merchandise revenue, and 50% of licensing sales." Wisely, the "Material Girl" also took actual stock in Live Nation. Another downside of the 360 is that artists lose creative control . . . unless you are Madonna, who has always had a firm grip on her brand.

2. Standard Distribution: In this typically exploitative deal (described at the beginning of this chapter), the label pays for recording, manufacturing, distribution, and publicity, and also pays the artist a royalty after expenses are recouped and the advance is paid back. The label owns the copyright forever. According to Byrne, "The typical pop star often lives in debt to their record company. If they hit a dry spell they can go broke. Michael Jackson, MC Hammer, TLC—the danger of debt and overextension is an old story."

3. License: This is a better deal for the artist, who retains ownership of the song's copyrights and master recordings and gives the label the right to exploit the music for a specified term, usually seven years. After the term, rights revert to the artist. Byrne writes, "If the Talking Heads held the master rights to our catalog today, we'd earn twice as much in licensing as we do now—and that's where artists like me derive much of our income."

4. Profit-Sharing: This is an even better deal for the artist. For Byrne's 2003 album, *Lead Us Not Into Temptation*, he received a small advance from the label, paid for recording costs himself (using

Rock the Net Neutrality

(With thanks to FreePress.net. See Chapter 22.)

Recently, giant cable and phone companies feel that they have a right to charge higher prices to use the Internet. Those who can't pay will experience discrimination — their websites won't load as fast, or their music downloads won't be given priority. This goes against the long-standing principle of "Network Neutrality," the idea that the Internet should be open, free, and unrestricted, and that every website, every feature, and every service should be treated exactly the same. That's how up-and-coming (or established) musicians — like you — can build and connect directly with your audience.

If these self-appointed gatekeepers have their way, the ability for independent musicians to reach millions through the Internet will be restricted and controlled. The carriers would have the power to pick and choose which artists get distribution, as well as the quality and the cost of that distribution. Exclusive deals between phone and cable companies could give the fast-lane option to preferred content providers such as big record labels which can afford to pay bribes. Smaller artists and sites would get kicked to the virtual curb.

Future of Music Coalition writes, "What would happen if Sony paid Comcast so that sonymusic.com would run faster than iTunes, or, more important, faster than CD Baby, where over 135,000 indie artists sell their music? Would a new form of Internet payola emerge? Would it shut down the burgeoning new economy and replace it with one that looks a lot like our closed media market?"[1]

In March 2008, OK Go lead singer Damian Kulash visited Capitol Hill to urge Congress to support Net Neutrality. On April 5 of that year, Kulash wrote an op-ed piece in the *New York Times*, stating, "The Internet shouldn't be harnessed for the profit of a few, rather than the good of the many; value should come from the quality of information, not the control of access to it. If network providers are allowed to build the next generation of the Net as a pay-to-play system, we will all pay the price."

OK Go, along with eight hundred other bands and musicians, is a member of Future of Music Coalition's Rock the Net campaign (futureofmusic.org/rockthenet), a nationwide coalition of independent artists and labels that support the principal of Net Neutrality.

For more, read Chapter 22 to see how legislation affects musicians, and how musicians can affect legislation. Also visit savetheinternet.org and freepress.net.

---

1. "Indie-Rock Revolution, Fueled by Net Neutrality," by Jenny Toomey and Michael Bracy (Future of Music Coalition). The Hill.com, June 13, 2006.

money from a movie soundtrack budget), and shared the profits. Byrne also retained ownership of the master.

5. Manufacturing and Distribution: This is a rare case, in which the label handles solely the manufacturing and distribution. Large labels generally sign manufacturing and distribution deals only with artists who can guarantee payment for CD-pressing costs, regardless of projected income from music sales.

6. Self-Distribution: This is the DIY (do-it-yourself) model, in which the artist (or artist plus consultant) nets the highest percentage of potential revenues. The musician writes, produces, promotes, and sells his or her music, while maintaining complete creative control, and also keeping ownership of the copyright, master, and publishing rights. Byrne writes, "The more the artist takes control, the more they can make per unit sold. The artist stands to receive the largest percentage of income from sales per unit—sales of anything. A larger percentage of fewer sales, most likely, but not always. Artists doing it for themselves can actually make more money than the massive pop star, even though the sales numbers may seem minuscule by comparison."

In my opinion, Byrne's sixth survival strategy is the best option, and thus is the focus of the rest of the chapter. Why? Unknown artists will have a tough time getting *any* of the first five choices. But more important, self-distribution is potentially the most lucrative route for everyone, whether they be emerging artists; ticked-off veterans of the music scene who have left or lost their label; or even megastars, as they become free agents and realize the benefits of owning their own work, earning higher royalties, and using consultants to handle the work that the labels did (or didn't) do.

Prince is a pioneer of the DIY model, having founded his own label, NPG, in 1996. Because he owns the rights to his work, has a higher net royalty, and has a large built-in fan base, he can afford to give away free CDs at concerts, insert three million free copies of his new album inside the British Sunday paper *The Mail,* and give away songs via Verizon phones.

In March 2003, Natalie Merchant followed Prince and launched her own label, Myth America Records. Then she self-released her album *The House Carpenter's Daughter.* According to Jon Pareles in the *New York Times,* Merchant only needed to sell fifty thousand copies to break even, less than 15 percent of what her previous album, *Motherland,* sold. "When we sell 200,000 copies, we'll be standing on our chairs, hollering. At Elektra, if you just sell 1.5 million, everyone goes around with their heads down."

It took a few years for existing contracts to expire, but in October 2007 three megastar artists ditched their labels, too. Trent Reznor of Nine Inch Nails, Madonna (see the 360 deal, above), and Radiohead all leaped over the fence, breaking from their labels for greener pastures.

After Reznor fulfilled his contract with Interscope Records, he wrote on his website: "Nine Inch Nails is a totally free agent, free of any recording contract with any label . . . it gives me great pleasure to be able to finally have a direct relationship with the audience as I see fit and appropriate." A few months later, in March 2008, Reznor released *Ghosts*. According to journalist Glenn Gamboa in *Newsday,* Reznor "racked up a minimum of $750,000 in one week when he sold out 2,500 copies of his *Ghosts I-IV* project at $300 apiece through his web site." The "*I-IV*" refers to Reznor's simultaneous release of four albums with different instrumental song versions. According to Gamboa, "depending on their interest, fans could get nine tracks for free, get them all for a $5 download, a $10 double CD and a $75 deluxe package that provides a Blu-ray disc high quality version and all the songs in multitrack format that can be remixed to their heart's content."

In 2003 Radiohead fulfilled its six-album contract with EMI with *Hail to the Thief* (the title perhaps an ironic dig). For the band's seventh studio album, in 2007, *In Rainbows,* Yorke told *Time,* "I like the people at our record company, but the time is at hand when you have to ask why anyone needs one. And, yes, it probably would give us some perverse pleasure to say 'Fuck you' to this decaying business model."

With *In Rainbows,* Radiohead retained ownership both of the songs and of the master—a first for the band. Since the band owns the rights, it could put its songs online and let fans "name their own price" to pay for downloads, or not pay, in exchange for their e-mail address. With no middlemen or costs for materials or shipping, it was estimated that the band earned millions of dollars after paying typical expenses such as recording, engineers, managers, accountants, as well as website construction, maintenance, and bandwidth. They kept 100 percent of the royalties and gained worldwide publicity from the strategy, plus reportedly millions of e-mail addresses for future marketing and sales. A traditional label may not have allowed such online distribution, and if it did, the band would have only earned 10 percent of the royalties (minus recoupable expenses, and the advance).

As Thom Yorke told David Byrne in *Wired,* "In terms of digital income, we've made more money out of this record than out of all the other Radiohead albums put together, forever. EMI wasn't giving us any money for digital sales."

Putting songs online beats the pirates at their own game. Before 2000, Radiohead, a British group, never had a Top 20 hit in the United States, and got little radio airplay. Then, in July 2000, songs from its album *Kid A* were made available for free on Napster. Millions were downloaded. Three months later, the *Kid A* CD was number one in its debut week on the Billboard 200. Napster served as a major promotional tool, and actually increased, rather than hurt, CD sales of *Kid A*. This contradicts the music industry view that file sharing is a major cause of declining CD sales, an argument the Recording Industry Association of America uses when suing music fans. The RIAA also conveniently ignores a study by Harvard Business School professor Felix Oberholzer-Gee and University of North Carolina researcher Koleman Strumpf, who concluded that file sharing actually increases CD sales. Their study found that every hundred fifty downloads of a song meant album sales increased by one copy.[5]

TIP-JAR REVOLUTION?

Radiohead manager Bryce Edge thinks that digital technology has reintroduced the age of the troubadour. He was quoted in the *New York Times* as saying, "You are worth what people are prepared to give you in the digital age because they can get it for nothing."

Loyal fans will buy your music, lap up your merchandise, and see you in concert, then rave about it afterward. If they are *not* loyal, they'll steal what they can and diss you, besides.

Like *Kid A*, the *In Rainbows* album is a case in point. In the last week of 2007, three months after the digital downloads were made available, Radiohead released the *In Rainbows* CD through traditional retailers. For this, the band used Dave Matthews' label ATO in the United States and the British label XL Recordings for overseas. In its first week, *In Rainbows* was the top-selling album in America, with 122,000 copies sold (Nielsen SoundScan), once again challenging the notion that music fans won't buy CDs if songs are available for free online.

Radiohead plans to perform in twenty U.S. cities in 2008. Promoting these concerts could be easier if the band leverages the millions of e-mail addresses received from the online download campaign, which netted fans willing to pay more for the scarce commodity of a personal experience seeing the band perform in the flesh. And fans willing, possibly, to buy some merchandise at the concert.

Critics argue that the Radiohead example can't be replicated, and even manager Edge feels this model "is not a prescription for the industry."

An emerging middle class of musicians begs to differ. Jonathan Coulton is one such musician. Starting in September 2005, Coulton, who was label-less and relatively unknown at the time, wrote, recorded, and posted a song to his blog each week for one entire year. Even though he gave away his music free online, fans bought, and still buy, his songs to support him. According to Clive Thompson's article "Sex, Drugs and Updating Your Blog" in the *New York Times*, "His most popular songs were being downloaded as many as 500,000 times; he was making what he described as 'a reasonable middle class living'—between $3,000 and $5,000 a month—by selling CDs and digital downloads of his work on iTunes and on his own site." Some 41 percent of Coulton's income came from digital sales, 29 percent from CDs (through CD Baby), 18 percent from concerts, and 12 percent from selling T-shirts.

The message: Instead of chasing labels, DJs, and distributors, launch your career by chasing an *audience*. You might start with DIY, using online promotion and local gigs, and change as circumstances evolve. Without a doubt, DIY is hard work and can be expensive, but the rewards are

5. "Study: File-Sharing No Threat to Music Sales," by David McGuire. *Washington Post,* March 29, 2004.

much greater. You, the artist, pay for production costs, accounting, design, distribution, licensing, marketing, sales, and touring. You may have a smaller audience, but by keeping costs low, owning all the rights, repurposing your assets, and diversifying income streams, your net revenues will be higher. As the audience and revenues increase, you can spend more to broaden the tour, enhance recordings, or hire consultants at key milestones.

Here are some suggested steps to follow.

STEP ONE: CREATE GREAT MUSIC

According to Tim Westergren, founder of Pandora, "Your music is the one investment you can reliably know will have a big return." The goal is to keep production values high and costs low. Inexpensive, professional digital studio gear includes Digidesign's ProTools, MOTU's Digital Performer, Cakewalk, and even the free Audacity. And check out the "Home HD Studio" sidebar, at the end of this chapter, on how to create a high-definition recording studio in your spare room.

As a role model, take singer-songwriter Bonnie Hayes, who wrote all the songs for her recent album *Love in the Ruins*, recorded it in her Marin County, California, home studio with Digidesign's Pro Tools, and released it on Bondage Records, a label she co-owns with Steve Savage. As Hayes told the *San Francisco Chronicle*'s David Armstrong, "It doesn't have to cost $300,000 to make a new record, and records don't have to cost $18." With lower costs, Savage added, "Five thousand CDs would be a success. Ten thousand CDs would be a hit."

Or take Lorrie Line, who works from home in Orono on the shores of Lake Minnetonka, Minnesota. According to *Fortune Small Business,* Line cashed in her husband's 401(k) plan and spent the $2,000 to record her first record, which generated more than $1 million in sales within three years from a local department store (a gigantic return on investment). She recorded her next album in two days of studio time for just $9,558. By 2004, her independent label, Lorie Line Music, had revenues of more than $5 million: $3.8 million in concerts, $800,000 in CDs, and $400,000 from printed songbooks.

Outside of betting your spouse's retirement money on your music career, another funding alternative is the emerging patronage system, in which fans support their favorite bands directly through microcontributions. In 1998, two thousand fans or patrons of Todd Rundgren donated $60 each ($120,000 total) directly to Rundgren through his website, Patronet.com, to record his album, *One Long Year.*

For its 2002 independent release, *A Little Voodoo*, the Philly-based band Grey Eye Glances raised several hundred thousand dollars through a private offering from fans who became investors. Another patronage effort involved brothers Dean and Gene Ween, who told Neil Strauss of the *New York Times,* "On Elecktra, our best-selling record sold 200,000 copies or more, but we still owe all this money to the label. Then we sold just five [thousand] or 10,000 CDs through our Website (ween.com) and raised $100,000 to make our new album."

Another patronage system that enables fans to support their favorite artists is ArtistShare.com. Maria Schneider was the first musician to sign with ArtistShare for her 2004 album *Concert in the Garden,* which subsequently won a Grammy. According to Fred Kaplan in the *New York Times,* Schneider "previously had made three albums on the Enja record label. Each sold about 20,000 copies. She didn't make a dime off any of them. On two of them, she lost money." Through Artist-Share, by contrast, the day before *Concert in the Garden* was even released, online advance sales orders totaled $33,700. In 2008, Schneider won her second Grammy award, in conjunction with ArtistShare, for her album *Sky Blue.*

ArtistShare is proof that fans will pay more to have a personal experience with their idols. According to the *Times,* Schneider's CD sells for $16.95, but her online customers "are spending an average of $53, nearly three times the price of the CD" to take part in the creative process, from buying printed scores or paying to listen to rehearsal sessions and interviews, to purchasing limited edition recordings, autographed CDs and posters, and VIP tickets. Some even pony up cash to get production credit listings on the record—and why not? Jazz singer Allan Harris solicited $15,000 from a fan in exchange for executive producer status on his next album (looks good on a résumé).

Money sings.

Want some even better news? In today's world, you don't even need to create a whole CD worth of material, let alone a physical CD. No more stress or pressure to come up with roughly twelve so-so songs to fill out an album. One song is all you need to post on your website, or wherever you're posting it (more on that below). Digital single sales are the "new black." Even labels get it. One of them, Universal/Republic Records, signed the band Candy Hill to record just two singles instead of an entire album. According to *Rolling Stone,* sales of digital singles are up 2,930 percent since 2003. In the last week of 2005, digital single sales outsold CDs for the first time. In 2006, fans bought 582 million digital singles. Buyers of digital music purchased singles over albums by a margin of 19 to 1.

There has never been a better time than *now* to make a one-hit wonder, then use the windfall to fund your next song or tour. It took six years and eight albums for Pink Floyd to top the charts with *Dark Side of the Moon.* Today, you don't need to wait that long. After all, when you're singing in the shower, you're singing a song, not an album, right?

Not only are digital singles inexpensive to produce, they also can be distributed for free. Because there is no CD, there are no packaging deductions, and no costs for manufacturing, distribution, storage, fulfillment, or returns. Digital is cheaper for fans, too. About 50 percent of traditional CD sales goes to overhead, with the buyer paying indirectly for the plastic, trucks, warehouses, fuel, a dozen songs, and payola . . . uh, I mean, independent promotion.

STEP TWO: CONTROL YOUR RIGHTS

Copyright is an exclusive right owned by the author of a work. Once you pen a song and your work is fixed in a tangible means of expression, copyright is automatically granted. But to be safe, you should absolutely register songs with the government's Copyright Office by sending a $35 registration fee and two copies of the work to it. You can get more information at copyright.gov.

According to copyright law (specifically Title 17, Section 106, paragraphs 1–6), the owner has the exclusive rights to: reproduce the copyrighted work; prepare derivative works; distribute copies of the copyrighted work to the public by sale, rental, or lease; perform the copyrighted work publicly (in the case of musical and other works); display the copyrighted work publicly; and perform the copyrighted work publicly (in the case of sound recordings). Who would want to give any of that up?

Owning the rights is crucial. Chuck Berry's song *Maybellene* listed DJs Alan Freed and Russ Fratto as cowriters, along with Berry, though Berry wrote it himself. This arrangement, typical of the bad old days, reduced Berry's royalty payments by two thirds. In exchange, his "cowriters" played the song on their radio shows. Berry is widely known for his pioneering 1950s rock and roll classics, such as *Roll Over, Beethoven; Johnny B Goode;* and *Sweet Little Sixteen*. However, most of the loot from his hits went to his label, not to him. Berry's 1972 novelty song *My Ding-A-Ling* earned him the most money, not because it was his only number one hit but because all rights to the song were wholly owned by his publishing company, Isalee.

John Fogerty of the band Creedence Clearwater Revival made the Top 10 from 1969 to 1972 with nine singles, and even outsold the Beatles in 1969. His songs earned a fortune for the label, Fantasy Records, and its owner, Saul Zaentz. But not Fogerty. "Even though," according to Fogerty, who was lead singer, guitarist, and songwriter, "I am the main inventor of the property that generates all that wealth. I'm the guy that wrote and sang all those songs, and arranged and produced the records."

A flexible supplement to copyright is Creative Commons, which has put together licenses so important, and useful, that we dedicated an entire chapter to them. (See chapter 21.) More than a million creations, from movies to songs and blog posts, have used these licenses. Creative Commons, or "some rights reserved," licenses are more flexible than copyright's restrictive "all rights reserved" regime. Hip-hop musicians and rappers, for example, can allow other musicians to copy, share, sample, and create derivative works, without needing to get a team of lawyers involved. The Berkeley-based label Magnatune (its motto: "We are not evil") uses Creative Commons licenses. The label splits royalties with artists 50/50, and lets them keep the rights to their music. Magnatune's contracts are nonexclusive; artists can sell their own CDs and even sign with another label. No long-term commitment is required.

STEP THREE: BUILD YOUR CORE AUDIENCE AND SELL TO IT DIRECTLY

Your current and future success depends on your ability to build and maintain a core audience and have a direct relationship with them. For example, Fall Out Boy amassed a large fan base through the Web, and those fans helped keep the band's debut album, *From Under the Cork Tree,* on Billboard's Top 200 chart for almost one full year.

You should first offer your digital music via your website or blog, since that way you will keep almost 100 percent of the revenues (minus a few points for credit card transaction fees). For information on optimizing your website for e-commerce, see chapter 9. Be sure to register your domain as www.YourBandName.com. True fans will find a way to support you. Those who consider it a hassle to buy music directly from you are not part of your core audience. For more about true fans and your core audience, see the Foreword, the Introduction, and chapter 8.

You should also maintain (and regularly update) profiles on social networks with a large audience, such as MySpace, Facebook, or Second Life, and sell via widgets (we'll get to those in a minute). In 2006, New York singer-songwriter Ingrid Michaelson uploaded her self-produced album *Girls and Boys* to her MySpace page, where L.A.-based artist manager and music licensor Lynn Grossman discovered the songs. Grossman helped place a number of her songs on the ABC television series *Grey's Anatomy,* and Old Navy chose her song "The Way I Am" for its Fair Isle sweater TV commercial campaign. The twenty-eight-year-old Michaelson subsequently made the January 2008 cover of *Billboard* after selling more than 175,000 copies of the album, earning the number two spot on the iTunes pop chart, and becoming the first unsigned artist ever to appear on VH1—all from one MySpace page!

Another benefit of social networks, according to guitarist Frogg Marlowe, who promotes himself on Second Life, is that "You're actually reaching a far wider audience than if you were jamming in your local area. I don't have to pay for gas to get to and from the gig, and the gear's already set up." For more on social networks, see chapter 15.

The downside of sites like MySpace, however, is that you lose control of YourSpace. Rupert Murdoch's News Corporation, which is the new owner of MySpace, could go bankrupt (wishful thinking), or, more likely, could allow the site to be overrun with ads, spam, or pornbots posing as humans. At one point, MySpace actually claimed the rights to anything posted on its site. Musician and songwriter Billy Bragg has tried to keep the copyrights to most of his recordings, licensing them to companies that released his albums. In May 2006 Bragg removed his songs from MySpace, complaining that the terms and conditions gave MySpace ownership of music posted on the site. Bragg's vocal advocacy forced MySpace to revise its terms of service so that musicians retain ownership of their music on the site.

Your own website is the key to maintaining control of your identity, your music, and your fans, and possibly your financial future. The goal is to create a community where you can communicate personally with fans, and allow them to connect with each other. You might offer a chat room, bulletin board, blog, e-mail list, and newsgroup. List your upcoming concerts and events. Provide links to your artwork, songs, videos, liner notes, lyrics, tabs, mashups, memberships, merchandise (T-shirts, posters, calendars), original scores, and photos. To keep fans (and search engines) coming back, update the content regularly, give away exclusive tracks, or hold a contest. The rock band Thursday held an online scavenger hunt complete with prizes, which helped the band sell 46,000 copies of *A City by the Light Divided* in its first week, with no support from radio or MTV.

For future success, build your e-mail list and contact database. Use ethical "bribes" to get e-mail addresses. Like Radiohead or Jonathan Coulton, regularly upload a new song, video, PDF file, guide, newsletter, or exclusive track, something personal that fans cannot get elsewhere. Fans want an intimate connection, so behind-the-scenes takes, backstage videos, and even sound checks become desirable properties. When you offer digital song downloads, be sure to use high-quality music that is free of viruses, interoperable with any MP3 player or iPod, and delivered from a secure, trusted site that accepts major credit cards and PayPal.

WIDGET WONDERS

Besides your website and blog, you can also use widgets, or Flash-based MP3 players that enable artists to promote and sell music, videos, merchandise, and concerts direct to fans. Widgets can be placed on any website, blog, or social network profile. Bands can put this mobile store wherever their fans are. No longer do fans have to navigate to your website; they're delivered by virtual limo.

Into the widget, bands can upload songs, artwork, photos, video, and a bio; sell individual songs or entire albums; and collect fans' e-mail addresses. Fans use the widget to hear streamed music, buy tracks, chat, and—how is this for a concept?—earn commissions from selling the band's songs and merchandise to their friends. Widgets do have a downside: cost. When you sell through your website, you get 100 percent of the revenues (minus service fees by credit card companies). When you use a widget, though, you have to give up a percentage of the sale. Sometimes, to broaden your audience, the percentage is worth it.

Some sales widgets, as of this writing (in order of personal preference), are:

- **Hooka:** Artists keep 80 percent of the revenue, at a fixed price of $0.99 per song. Hooka's big feature: fans can sell songs through an affiliate program, and earn a 10 percent commission. In this case, the artist earns 70 percent, Hooka 20 percent, and the fan 10 percent. Hooka also offers a chat feature.

- **Nimbit OMT:** Artists can sell not just digital songs, but physical merchandise and CDs as well. One unique feature lets artists give away tracks, in exchange for e-mail addresses—just like Radiohead did—only, in this case, through a widget, not a website. Artists set their own price (minimum of $0.49 per song) and get 80 percent of the revenues.

- **SNOCAP:** This widget integrates directly into MySpace. Artists set their own wholesale price, to which SNOCAP adds a flat $0.39 fee, plus a $30 annual fee. Artists can monitor sales daily. It accepts PayPal and credit cards, and offers WMA and Windows DRM versions. Recording rights are registered through SNOCAP's digital directory, protecting artist's ownership rights. (Note: In late 2007, SNO-CAP laid off 60 percent of its staff, and is now being phased out of MySpace.)

- **Musicane:** Artists can sell music, video, and ringtones. Musicane also offers Windows Media DRM protection. Artists set their own price, and get 60 percent of the revenue. Alternatively, by paying a fee of $20 per month, the artist gets 80 percent of the sale price.

- **Blast My Music:** All songs are $0.99, and the artist gets 65 percent of the sale price.

- **Project Opus Folio:** This widget offers multiple media formats, such as Ogg and AAC. All songs sell for $1, of which the artist gets $0.50.

- **Sproutbuilder and Gydget:** These viral promotional tools don't offer sales features yet, but they do enable artists to create their own personalized widgets to spread the word across social networks.

Watch for PayPal and eBay to enter the sales widget scene, along with the popular iLike and ReverbNation, which offer widgets for promotions, but not sales—yet. iLike's free social music discovery widget has over 20 million web users, and half a million Facebook users. It enables artists to build viral music communities, and it helps fans discover and share playlists, new music, and concerts that match their tastes. ReverbNation is used by 200,000 artists and bands, 6,000 labels and managers, and 2,500 venues and clubs. They provide promotional widgets for viral distribution across social networks, websites, and blogs. One of their most popular is TuneWidget, which is five widgets in one: *Music Player*, *Info*, *Tour Dates*, *Video*, and *FanCollector*, the last of which gathers e-mail addresses and demographic information such as zip code, gender, and age. This enables artists to prove to venue owners and promoters in Ohio, for example, that they have enough fans in Akron to add that city to the tour.

LET FANS DEMAND YOU

In the past, you, the artist, needed to find an audience. Today, the audience finds *you*. Services like ReverbNation help artists decide where to tour, based on listener demographics and fan demand. Their GigFinder tool enables artists to locate venues and clubs that fit their characteristics, style, and capacity requirements. Be sure to explore Gigfinder's "similar venues" and "similar artists" search feature. In addition to Reverb, try Eventful, upcoming.yahoo.com, and Jambase, which has more than half a million music fans and over forty thousand artists performing in fifty thousand venues. Another popular service is MusicIP, which helps artists decide where to tour, determined by listener habits.

The touring business is thriving, earning a record $437 million in 2005, according to NPD Group. There is nothing better than the energy of a live show, and artists can't beat the margins by selling music and merchandise directly to a supportive and appreciative audience. No percentage. No commissions. But it makes no sense to travel the country and play to empty venues. Take Jenny Toomey's sage advice: "If you have a following, tour. If you don't have a following, don't tour."

Eventful, one of the biggest services to help artists tour, has millions of users in one hundred and eighty countries. Its site lets fans create grassroots campaigns, known as *Demands*, or appearances, for performers. Not only do artists get a performer page that shows the cities where fans are demanding them, but fans can even book the venue for the performer. In July 2006 one of Eventful's first demands was for author and actor Wil Wheaton, who portrayed Wesley Crusher in the TV series *Star Trek: The Next Generation* and Gordie LaChance in the film *Stand By Me.* Some hundred and twenty fans mounted a grassroots campaign and "demanded" his presence at the Booksmith bookstore in Brookline, Massachusetts. The crowd of three hundred was so large they had to rent the theater across the street, where Wheaton read from his book, *Just a Geek,* and screened *Stand By Me.* Eight out of ten visitors had never heard of the bookstore before. Since then, more than 2,800 people in one hundred thirty-eight cities have "demanded" that Wheaton appear in their town.

STEP FOUR: LEVERAGE ONLINE SALES CHANNELS . . . FOR A PRICE

At this point in your growth, you might want to put your music on third-party sites to expand your true fans and core audience to a wider, more general one. The widest of all is Apple's iTunes. Since Apple released the iPod in 2001, more than 140 million have been sold. Apple has locked up 74 percent of the worldwide market for digital music players. In 2003, the iTunes online store opened, and sold one million $0.99 songs within the first five days. iTunes accounts for 80 percent of the worldwide digital music market, helping make Apple the second largest U.S. music retailer, behind Wal-Mart and ahead of Best Buy and Amazon. iTunes has sold more than 2.5 billion songs and fifty million TV shows. It also sells ringtones, music videos, audio books, podcasts, and games.

The boon for artists, says musician Thomas Dolby in an interview with the AlwaysOn-Network, is that "the line connecting the musician and the fans has been shortened. Three o'clock in the morning, that sounds pretty good, hit a button, boom, it's on iTunes. Get some sleep, wake up in the morning. I've got 399 sales on iTunes. That's fantastic; to live like that is a dream for an artist."

However, unlike selling from your site where you keep virtually 100 percent of the revenues and set your own price, iTunes keeps approximately 30 percent of the royalties, at a set price of $0.99 per song and $9.99 per album.

Another service, eMusic, is the world's second-largest digital music retailer, and the largest service to sell songs in MP3 format. Its subscription-based service has 1.4 million tracks from more than four thousand independent labels.

Artists don't have to decide which online store, iTunes or eMusic, to choose. Instead, they can use aggregators to get their songs and albums into hundreds of digital stores at once, sometimes with better royalty rates. Artists sign up, and aggregators then process, encode, and deliver their digital songs to online stores and collect payments. The hundreds of digital sites include subscription services such as Rhapsody, Napster, and eMusic, as well as online stores such as Amazon, iTunes, Hear Music (Starbucks), Napster, Sony Connect, MusicNow (Circuit City), MusicMatch (Yahoo), MusicNet (AOL/Virgin), MSN Music, Real Networks, and MP3.com.

Aggregators that work with labels (not individual artists) include the Digital Rights Agency (bought by Digital Music Group), the Orchard, and the Independent Online Distribution Alliance (IODA).

Aggregators that work with individual artists include Digital Music Marketing, TuneCore, and CD Baby. TuneCore lets artists keep their copyrights, masters, and 100 percent of the royalties. Their deals are nonexclusive, and artists can opt out at any time. In one week in January 2008, TuneCore delivered 622 albums to iTunes, and in that week, artists earned $116,428.30 in music sales. TuneCore charges $0.99 per track, or $0.99 per store per album, and $19.98 per album for one year of storage and maintenance. They have no setup fee, and pay artists quarterly.

Another great service is CD Baby. Since 1998 it has helped more than 150,000 musicians sell over $65 million in digital songs and CDs. For digital songs, CD Baby charges a one-time setup fee of $35 and takes 9 percent of the revenue, so the artist keeps 91 percent. You are alerted when a song sale is made, and, unlike Amazon (which takes half of your revenues), CD Baby tells you who your customers are. Remember, the customer contact information is *critical* for your future success! Every week, CD Baby pays over $300,000 directly to its musician clients.

And if you decide to sell CDs, CD Baby is your answer. It warehouses your discs, sells them, processes credit card transactions, and ships them to customers. In a traditional label deal, as we have seen, musicians make less than $1 per CD, if they ever get paid. With CD Baby, you set the price, CD Baby keeps $4 per disc sold, and you get paid weekly. The deal is nonexclusive, and you can cancel at any time. Simply sign up and send them five CDs to get started. CD Baby also acts as a distributor, making your CD available to more than 2,400 retail stores across the United States. That's big news for small bands, as traditional distributors only want to deal with major-label artists who move hundreds of thousands of CDs.

To sell CDs via CD Baby (or any other legitimate middleman), you'll need to obtain a Universal Product Code (aka a "barcode") and register it with Soundscan, the service used to track record sales. This way, when the CD flies off the shelves, your sales numbers will show up in the charts, catching the eye of record labels, radio programmers, and industry magazines. To get a barcode, you can register as a company with the GS1 US organization, and pay it $750 to be a member. Or, go to CD Baby, which already paid the $750 for you. CD Baby will give you your own unique UPC barcode, which is yours, forever, for $20 (plus your one-time $35 CD Baby setup fee). According to CD Baby's website, "When your barcode on your CD is scanned by a retail store, it will show up on the register as YOUR album, YOUR band, YOUR record company. Not CD Baby."

STEP FIVE: REPURPOSE AND LICENSE

The music business until quite recently counted success in CDs sold, but that is no more considered success than the sales of eight-tracks, cassettes, 78s, 45s, LPs, or player piano rolls. Today, smart artists earn multiple streams of income from many sources—including touring, selling branded merchandise (T-shirts, hats, and hoodies), and licensing music (in ads, films, TV shows, retail, and ringtones). As we have seen from Nine Inch Nails and Maria Schneider, successful acts continually repurpose their music and sell it in all possible forms. For example, Barenaked Ladies wrote twenty-nine new songs, then repackaged them into almost two hundred "assets," including ringtones and multiple digital and acoustic versions.

To sell branded merchandise (see chapter 11 for details), artists license their band logo, name, or album cover images onto everything imaginable, from lighters, bottle openers, magnets, and matchbooks to calendars, posters, and "wallpaper" for computers or cell phones. Guitarist Les Paul famously licensed his name to Gibson guitars. Madonna's H&M fashion line is said to have earned $20 million in its first year. Fashion licensing can include watches, footwear, belts, wallets, and jewelry. *American Idol* licensed its lucrative name to everyone and everything, to Sony for the $19.95 American Idol Jam Trax recording studio for kids, to Dreyer's ice cream. Flavors such as American Idol Soulful Sundae and American Idol Triple Talent are just as valuable to the Idol franchise as Ben and Jerry's Cherry Garcia is to the heirs of the estate of rock legend Jerry Garcia (if not quite as tasteful).

Merchandising your band's name on a magnet is one thing, but licensing sales of your music—into ads, retail, TV shows, films, videogames, cell phones, ringtones, and music libraries—is the focus here. Licensing can be extremely lucrative, *if* you own the rights. Artist manager Michael Hausman told attendees at the 2007 Future of Music Policy Summit that "Aimee Mann, against great odds, retained ownership of all her masters and songs. That's the best position to be in." Starbucks licensed a single song from Mann that earned her $42,000 ($0.12 per record with a guarantee of 350,000 units). That one deal practically covered the entire cost ($50,000) of her most recent album. "And," says Hausman, "you get a check within weeks of doing the license." Hausman urges musicians to "hold on to every right possible."

As David Byrne wrote in *Wired,* "I make very little from actual record sales. I make probably the most from licensing stuff; not to commercials, I license to films and television shows. I would personally advise artists to hold on to their publishing rights. This, for a songwriter, is your pension plan."

He is right. It is crucial to protect your rights, and your publishing income. As we've said before, when you write a song, you own the copyright and you keep 100 percent of the publishing income—both the writer's share (50 percent), which stays with you, the writer, for life (even if you don't end up owning the copyright), and the publisher's share (the other 50 percent).

Yes, you can and *should* do everything possible to publish your songs yourself and keep 100 percent of the income. However, this means you have more work ahead of you—that is, if you want to maximize your song's income from licensing opportunities like getting your music into ads, films, ringtones, videogames, and TV shows. You'll need the experience, time, connections, and patience required to deal with sales administration, agreements, audits, copyright registration, infringement suits, legal issues, licensing, and negotiating fees and settlements, among other things not musical.

Let's face it: Most bands just want to make music. They prefer not having to deal with the frustrating and time-consuming aspects of licensing and sales. Options exist today for independents who seek to retain all or a higher portion of their publishing income, without dealing with the messy sales, administrative, and legal work.

One option is a **copublishing agreement,** which enables the writer to co-own a percentage of the copyright along with the publisher. The writer may also negotiate an advance. Legendary music producer and Automatt founder David Rubinson argues against this option, stating flatly that it is "better to borrow from a bank, or work a day job, than to give up one speck of copyright for a song."

Then there is the **administration agreement,** by which, for a specified term, the administrator collects the royalties and may help promote the songwriter's catalog. Fees are around 10 percent of the gross proceeds. Generally no advance is paid, but an administration agreement gives the writer more control (the writer keeps the copyright) and a higher net (90 percent of gross revenues).

Either way, remember that if you wrote the song, you will always get your 50 percent (the writer's share), even if you trade away the publisher's share. That's why Paul McCartney and John Lennon's estate still get paid for uses of the songs they wrote some four decades ago, even though Michael Jackson subsequently bought (and still partly owns) the publisher's share of the Lennon-McCartney song catalog.

Repeat after me: *It is good to be the writer!*

There are four types of publishing income for writers and publishers (today, you may be both):

1. Synchronization fee (aka synch fee): This is a one-time fee paid up front to the song's writer and publisher for the rights to use the song as audio to accompany visual images. The fee is determined by the music budget and the negotiating power of the artist. Advertising, for example, pays anywhere from a few thousand dollars to six figures and higher for superstar acts. Indie films and trailers pay less than studio feature films. Television synch fees are determined by the number of estimated viewers, so broadcast network TV generally pays more than cable. A prime-time network TV show might pay a fee of $500 to $5,000 for a song by an emerging artist. Well-known artists get up to tens of thousands of dollars for a song on a successful TV show, such as *Grey's Anatomy*. At the other end of the spectrum, songs used in podcasts or wedding videos earn $25 to $100 in synch fees.

2. Performance royalties: Royalties are supposed to be paid to writers and publishers each time the song gets played on the radio, on TV, or in an elevator or other public venue, such as clubs, concerts, or events. Performing Rights Organizations (or PROs, such as BMI, ASCAP, and SESAC in the United States) collect and distribute payments to member songwriters and publishers. If your tune is used as the theme song for a TV show that goes into syndication, performance royalties can earn the writer and publisher a lot of money. Songs in films that are shown in U.S. theaters don't pay performance royalties, but songs in films shown in some European and Asian countries do.

3. Mechanical royalties: These are royalty payments from music sales, based on the number of units sold. The mechanical royalty rate (known as the "statutory rate") is set by law, and is currently $0.091 per song. The label pays mechanical royalties to the publisher, who pays the writer (again, the publisher and writer may be the same person). Many music publishers are represented by the Harry Fox Agency, which issues licenses and collects, distributes, and audits royalties on the publisher's behalf.

4. Print royalties: This is money earned from the sale of sheet music.

Here are a few places to consider licensing your music:

Ads: You might not want to be known as "the band with the song from that coffee ad," but as the administrator of the rights to your work, now *you* have a choice where your music ends up, not some publishing or label executive. From high schlock to ultra cool, from "no way will I sell out" to "I'm laughing all the way to the bank, so who cares?" Just be careful not to trade short-term income at the expense of your long-term career. The Pittsburgh-based Voo Doo Babies became nationally known due to a song on TrimSpa TV commercials. Apple Computer featured a Jet song on an iPod TV commercial.

In 2005, manager Barry Bergman's client Marc Ribler wrote, produced, and sang the thirty-second spot titled "This Life" in a national television commercial for Trojan condoms. According to Bergman, "In the months that followed, several thousand people sent us e-mails wanting to know how they can buy the entire song. Based on my over thirty years in the entertainment industry I have never seen a response like this—especially from a thirty-second spot with no artist or song identification." Ribler has since written and produced songs for Dannon Activia Yogurt; produced, arranged, and sung on a spot for Office Depot; and sung on a V8 juice commercial. Ribler is one of the artists who ran laughing, and singing, all the way to the bank.

Music libraries: Music libraries are middlemen. They match your music with clients such as ad agencies, film directors, corporations, and game companies, all looking for the perfect piece of music for the moment. For their trouble, they take the publisher's share (50 percent) of income. Music libraries carry all genres, from hip-hop, jazz, rock, and pop to R&B, Latin, and so on. Bob Mould of the 1980s punk band Husker Du struck a low-five-figure deal for his song "Circles" on the (since cancelled) Fox show *The OC*. Music libraries offer great opportunities for independent artists, since many television and cable shows crave "unknown" bands and new sounds. *Grey's Anatomy* helped new bands such as Snow Patrol and The Fray gain national attention.

Check out music libraries such as Associated Production Music (apmmusic.com), KillerTracks.com, Megatrax.com, Opus1 Music Library (opus1musiclibrary.com), and PumpAudio. Be aware, however, that music libraries usually require an exclusive contract. Rumblefish also offers a 50/50 split with the writer but, more important, it offers nonexclusive contracts. For smaller deals ($500 and less), Rumblefish has even streamlined the licensing process with its online Music Licensing Store, which *Billboard* called "the iTunes of licensing." Someone looking for, say, a song for a podcast or an anniversary video can search this online catalog. An online rate calculator shows what the song would cost for different circumstances, and users simply enter a credit card number to license the song.

Retail: Getting your songs into retail exposes your music to a targeted audience, like teens in one of Hot Topic's 650 clothing stores, or customers in retail stores, hotels, restaurants, spas, or health clubs. Whenever businesses play your music in public, you get paid a performance royalty. There are licensors that deliver packages of atmospheric programs to retail businesses via satellite, DVD, cable, or the Internet. Try licensors Playnetwork, DMX, and Gray V. And yes, there is Muzak, which offers eighty-five programs of music content to four hundred thousand locations, reaching millions of listeners . . . whether they want to listen or not. But who am *I* to suggest how a wildly successful musician earns cash?

Videogames: The market for video consoles and games is $9 billion per year. On average, videogames pay artists less than TV commercials do, but they are a great way to expose your music to a young, and usually male, fan base. Game maker Electronic Arts even started a label to exploit the music in its games, such as a wrestling game for teens called *Vendetta*. It features hip-hop music from Island Def Jam artists, including DMX, Scarface, and Method Man. Tony Hawk's *American Wasteland* videogame features punk classics played by current bands such as My Chemical Romance and Fall Out Boy. Videogames *Halo3* and *Guitar Hero,* addictive combinations of music and gaming, are sprouting entire communities of kids and adults alike, giving artists a way for their new music to be discovered, or have their old songs reinvigorated and aimed to a young market.

Cell phones: The cell phone market is ideal for getting your music, and your message, to an increasingly mobile and fragmented audience. With over two billion wireless phones worldwide, more people own handsets than computers or MP3 players. The Sprint Music Store has half a million songs in its catalog. Verizon's V CAST music store reaches 150 million people. In addition to licensing, musicians are also leveraging cell phones' SMS text messaging capability. Text messages are popular with teens, and have a 100 percent open rate, meaning you can be sure kids are reading your message. According to Jeff Leeds in the *New York Times,* during a Gwen Stefani tour, 20 percent of the audience "agreed to pay $0.99 cents for text messages and the chance to win better seats." On its Family Values tour, the band Korn let fans enter an SMS text contest for $1.99 "to win an expense-paid trip to a coming show in California." Popular acts could earn up to $100,000 a tour. The benefit to bands goes beyond these new revenues. The artist gets thousands of fans' cell phone numbers for future sales opportunities, as well as a continuing dialog.

Ringtones: About 21 percent of U.S. cell phone subscribers have downloaded a ringtone. According to *Rolling Stone,* $600 million worth of ringtones were bought in 2006. When cell phones play a ringtone, the song is being virally marketed to everyone within earshot. Doors drummer John Densmore agrees, saying, "What could be a better ring tone than 'Hello, I love you'?"

Since you own the rights, you are free to sell the tunes, uh, tones. As Terry McBride told Jeff Howe in *Wired,* "It used to take months to sell a frickin' ringtone to Bell Canada. With Barenaked Ladies, one phone call gets the job done." Plenty of examples come to mind. AC/DC's *Back in Black* sold over 1 million ringtones, reinvigorating the twenty-year-old song. T-Mobile ranked the song as the number one rock ringtone in the Top 10. Janet Jackson's *All for U* ringtone was included within the song of the same name, and sent people scrambling for their cell phones every time the song came on the radio. Madonna's *Hung Up* debuted as a $2.99 ringtone a month before the full song was available. Coldplay debuted *Speed of Sound* as a ringtone product placement in an episode of *CSI: Miami.*

Dividing Up The Ringtone Pie

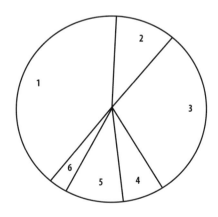

1 **Owner of Master Recording**
   [Record Label]: 40% ($1.20)

2 **Owner of Copyright in Composition**
   [Publisher]: 10% ($0.30)

3 **Mobile Carrier: 30% ($0.90)**

4 **Ringtone Aggregator**
   [e.g., Moderati, Thumbplay]: 7% ($0.21)

5 **Cost of Network Delivery**
   [e.g., mQube, mBlox]: 10% ($0.30)

6 **Performance Rights Societies**
   [ASCAP, BMI, SESAC]: 3% ($0.09)

Possible scenario for a "master tone"
(sample from master recording) selling for $3.00
copyright2008MasurLaw

For artists, ringtones can be lucrative. If a songwriter owns the copyright, masters, and pub-lishing rights, and if fans buy the ringtone direct from a musician's website, that musician can earn almost 100 percent of a $2.50, twenty-second ringtone clip, versus getting just 70 percent of $0.99 for the entire song from iTunes. If a songwriter sells ringtones indirectly, third parties can take up to 50 percent of the revenues. As you can see by the chart, "Dividing Up the Ringtone Pie," mobile carriers take roughly 30 percent of the sales price, network deliverers such as mQube or mBlox may take 10 percent, and aggregators such as Moderati, Thumbplay, or Zingy can take around 7 percent.

Sure, anyone with some technical chops can make a ringtone by clipping the sound file using the free Audacity editing software. And Xingtone's $15 application automatically transforms sound files into ringtones. But if the point is to have your fans support you, why not encourage them to buy direct from your website?

STEP SIX: BUZZ, OR LET YOUR FANS PROMOTE YOU

Forget radio play, MTV, and *Rolling Stone*. When it comes to music, films, and entertainment, nothing is more powerful than a personal referral. According to Tim Quirk of Rhapsody, "Fans are dictating. It's no longer about a big behemoth beaming something at a mass audience." Songs get rated and recommended through word of mouth and shared playlists from AOL Instant Mes-senger, Internet radio stations, iTunes, and iLike. Fans pass along links to MP3 songs on blogs, social networks, and websites, and they virally market ringtones through cell phones. Sites such as GarageBand let the user community rank contributed songs. Listeners pick the hits, not some label or radio executive. Since it was founded in 1999, more than fourteen bands have signed with major music labels. (Not that we're pushing major labels, of course.)

The traditional, passive fan club has evolved into the hip, active street team. Members of street teams are a band's most devoted fans, family, friends, and groupies, er, followers. The artist gives the street team incentives to carry out a variety of missions to promote the band, from posting comments on blogs and social networks, to putting up flyers in stores and bars, to requesting songs on the radio. The North Mississippi Allstars band has a street team called 51 Phantoms that distributes handbills for shows, and uses the web, SMS, and chat to build audiences in colleges, record stores, coffee shops, and bars. In exchange, Phantoms get rewards and prizes, such as free tickets, backstage tours, posters, or CDs.

Fancorps, echoStreet, and ReverbNation have software to help bands build, organize, main-tain, and manage a grassroots street team.

Video is another massive promotional device where fans are doing the work. (See chapter 7.) Jonathan Coulton's fans make music videos using his music, and upload them to YouTube. Bare-naked Ladies held an online video contest for its song "Wind It Up." Fans played air guitar, and the band spliced the best takes to make a "Wind It Up" music video.

Artists who do make videos themselves no longer need to spend millions of dollars on an MTV-worthy joint directed by Spike Jonze. The Gym Class Heroes MySpace-spoofing *New Friend Request* cost only $5,000, and ended up being one of the most-viewed music videos on YouTube. Chicago band Ok Go's video, *A Million Ways,* was made in just five takes, and had millions of views on YouTube. The follow-up, *Here it Goes Again* (aka the Treadmill Dance) cost $5,000, and got more than fifteen million views. Even better, both videos spawned hundreds of spoofs, which spread their music like viral wildfire. Users aren't merely watching videos anymore, they're responding to videos with videos of their own, using the original video as a cultural springboard to yet more video expression.

Video, videas, videat.

STEP SEVEN: THE FIFTH BEATLE—HELP!

As you've been reading about the brave new world of music, you've been thinking, *yeah, great, yeah, sure, makes sense, don't let them rip me off, man, but how the &%@$ do I find time to learn how to do all this stuff that has nothing to do with my riffs?!* Right?

The answer is basic. Just like the "fab four" Beatles did, appoint a fifth Beatle for the stuff you don't see on stage or hear in the music.

You don't need someone to help you say "no" to signing away your rights, for you can handle that yourself. Yet once you start promoting your band online, you may well need help. The helper initially can be the techie in your band, or whoever you can convince, or pay, to navigate the countless sites and services for you. There is an opportunity cost to spending time and effort on sites that offer little in return. When it comes to online promotion, an artist should be a late adopter, engaging only those sites, social networks, communities, and Internet radio stations that the fifth Beatle has figured out really "give back" to the artist. The give-back can be in fans or sales, with services such as free MP3 hosting, easy-to-create profile pages, gig calendars, fan club tools, gig promotion tools, audio and video streaming and downloads, messaging, photo galleries, blogs, e-mail lists, and sometimes even storefronts to sell songs.

The choices are overwhelming, with communities like MusicBrainz, UBL (Ultimate Band List), MP3.com, MOG, AmpCast, ArtistServer, BeatMaka, SoundSlam, Blastro, iMeem, Garage-Band, PureVolume, Lala, CDfuse, and Psychobaby. And there are thousands of Internet radio stations, such as Pandora, SomaFM.com, Music.Yahoo.com, VirtualRadio, ShoutCast, Live365.com, Last.FM, blip.FM, muxtape, and Mercora.

How does an artist decide which sites and services will be here next year, and which will disappear? This is where your fifth Beatle comes in. At a panel moderated by Brian Zisk at the Future of Music Policy Summit in 2007, Pandora's CEO Tim Westergren wisely advised the audience, "Every band should have one person that focuses on getting their content online, and on social networks and blogs. Half these tools and social networks aren't going to be around a year from now, so as an artist don't waste your valuable time. Find an enthusiastic, online savvy person and make them part of the band. The fifth Beatle must be an online one. The key word for artists is 'outsource.'"

One thing musicians traditionally outsourced was publicity, but a decent campaign could cost up to $20,000 a month. Today, consultants provide great PR for significantly less. One such fifth Beatle is publicist Ariel Hyatt, who has seventy-five musical clients. Hyatt gave up promoting through traditional media such as newspapers, radio, TV, magazines, MTV, and *Rolling Stone,* realizing they are no longer the road to success. Instead she focuses her promotional efforts on bloggers, podcasters, Internet radio, fanzines, and social networks. Hyatt also creates and updates profiles for bands. She charges $500 to $1,000 for a three-month campaign. Even platinum level campaigns run a reasonable $2,500.

Hyatt's services are well worth it, as she keeps in touch with the latest hip sites so you don't have to. Staying in touch with bloggers alone is a full-time PR job. For example, Dan Bierne's Saidthegramophone.com helped launch the bands Clap Your Hands, Say Yeah, and Arcade Fire. Then there's music.for-robots.com, gorillavsbear.blogspot.com, the Hype Machine (hype.non-standard.net), Largehearted Boy (blog.largeheartedboy.com), Stereogum.com, Sixeyes (sixeyes. blogspot.com), Tofu Hut (tofuhut.blogspot.com), Fluxblog.org, and Obscuresound.org.

For more grassroots buzz, check out the Word of Mouth Marketing Association at womma.org, and GuerrillaPR.com, a company whose handy logo we at Be the Media adore.

So you see, the fifth (or sixth, or seventh) Beatle doesn't have to be a member of the band or even carry a tune. But they should be able to carry publicity, promotion, technology, management, and licensing. These are precisely the things smart artists should outsource to expert members of the emerging Artist Services model predicted in 2003 by manager Barry Bergman.

For more information related to the music business, be sure to read chapter 11 (licensing), chapter 5 (podcasting), and chapter 6 (radio, including sections on Internet radio, satellite radio, and low power FM). Also read chapter 15 (social networks), chapter 1 (blogs), chapter 7 (video), and chapter 21 (Creative Commons). And be sure to read chapter 2 (books) for publicity tips.

Or check out bethemedia.com or bethemedia.org. You can also send an e-mail to info@bethemedia.com. We're gearing up to have a fifth Beatle available to *Help!* you.

In the meantime, in the words of David Byrne, "The totally DIY model is certainly not for everyone—but that's the point. Now there's choice. For existing and emerging artists . . . this is actually a great time, full of options and possibilities."

"The future of music as a career is wide open."
—*David Byrne*

Home HD Studio: From Hobby to Small Business

Jeff Mersman and Merlin Owens

It is well known that producing high-quality audio and video in a home studio is much more possible these days than it was even a few years ago. Not being a technophile or having much music production experience, I've learned that the tricky part is confronting the beauty and frustration in the myriad choices facilitating production in a relatively inexpensive way that provides lots of room for talent and aspiration to grow.

Following are some of the challenges and solutions we contemplated in our pursuit of high-definition (HD) broadcast quality on a relatively small budget and within a small space.

- High Definition Video is a 10bit conversion sampled at 720-line (1280x720) resolution or 1080-line (1920x1080) resolution uncompressed.
- High Definition Audio is a 24bit conversion sampled at 96kHz or 192kHz.

Any sized project can adapt the following ideas to build a more efficient studio. Our discussion considers the two important factors of deciding on desired functionality and technology, and designing a comfortable space in which to work.

START SMALL THINK GROWTH

OMM HD is a three-person partnership that began with a desire to get half a dozen friends over to a 255-square-foot spare bedroom in my flat in San Francisco to play and capture music on a basic "home studio in a box." This was accomplished with a digital audio workstation (DAW) that records, mixes, and burns onto a CD up to eight live inputs and sixteen tracks, a six-channel headphone amplifier and the typical odds and ends. Being a hobbyist musician and having no professional aspirations, I was ready to have some fun, but my soon-to-be-partner Merlin had bigger ideas.

Merlin's experience working with Stevie Wonder and others at Wonderland Studios during the 1980s and 1990s helped him hatch a blueprint to build a broadcast-quality HD audio/video suite targeting independent production for the advent of HD broadcasting. The demand for HD production is strong and getting stronger, with companies like Mark Cuban's HDNet already distributing 100 percent HD programming. The 2005 FCC digital tuner mandate paves the road to a Hi Def future by requiring equipment manufacturers to include both analog (NTSC) and digital (ATSC) tuners.

Goals

Considering our limited budget and space, we have somewhat sophisticated goals:

- a hybrid MIDI/live audio studio with at least sixty-four automated tracks/channels, at 96-192kHz HD, using the ADAT S/MUX protocol
- the ability to edit uncompressed HD video
- the ability to use a live drummer in our MIDI scenario
- a growth path to a virtual, collaborative network environment.

However, not all of this would be feasible—given our space and budget limitations—if we went with legacy solutions like analog recording and copper cabling.

Merlin sought to create a production suite that has everything a professional music and/or video producer needs for broadcast-quality content. And looking further into the future, he felt that it made no sense to build for broadcast quality without providing for HD capability in both the audio and video realms. Unfortunately, the sticker price on a ready-to-go, turnkey system for what we wanted is beyond the budget of almost every do-it-yourselfer.

So what's the point? The point is this: There are many ways to put together a home HD studio that can achieve the more advanced functionality of turnkey solutions costing considerably more. In other words, start small and plan for growth.

PLATFORM

Our first decision was which operating system to work with, the two main choices being Microsoft versus Apple. We chose Apple OSX, despite the higher cost, partly because of performance and partly because of compatibility with a majority of other independent A/V professionals.

The important thing to know about HD production is the requirement for faster processing, greater storage capacity and lots of RAM. Integration of audio and video production requires a networking solution that is also designed to scale for growth.

POORMAN'S 64 TRACK HD AUDIO

Our studio is designed to be audio-centric, with the ability to edit uncompressed HD video, not the other way around. To compete effectively in higher quality audio production, especially for highly orchestrated TV and film compositions, we wanted 64 automated HD tracks/channels. An integrated studio class solution for that is over our budget, so we're building a 32 track system on less expensive yet highly functional "pro-sumer" class hardware that, with some coaxing, should get us similar results. With one 32 track system in place we can then set up a duplicate system in a primary/secondary (aka master-slave) scenario to achieve our desired 64 tracks. The growth path is dependent on the hardware chosen, and there's tons to choose from, so having the path mapped out in detail is crucial.

OPTICAL vs. COPPER

Besides which operating system, another decision that will influence subsequent hardware choices is that of using the ADAT audio optical protocol. A copper hardwired patchbay for a 64 track studio is complicated, not particularly cheap, nor easily put into small confines. More importantly, copper does not permit use of the ADAT/SMUX II or IV protocols, which increase the ADAT sample rate of 44.1-48khz to either 96khz or 192khz respectively. Using S/MUX, the eight channels transmitted through each ADAT/TOSLink cable are reduced to four channels when sampled at 96khz, or two channels when sampled at 192khz. ADAT allows the use of an optical patchbay, which with its very simple track routing and 99 recallable patch options, is key to making this system easy to use.

HARDWARE CHOICES

We chose ProTools and M-Audio interface equipment (ProFire Lightbridge), putting us clearly on the 32 track path. Functionality, a small footprint, and cost pushed us towards using Behringer's DDX3216 and their optional ADAT ADT1616 interfaces for our automated console. Other affordable software and hardware solutions include Cubase, Digital Performer, Apogee, RME, PreSonus, Yamaha, Tascam and Mackie.

We get 16 pretty good mic pres capable of A/D conversion at 192khz from eight M-Audio 1814's (used only for input in our scenario). This is a fraction of the cost of a bank of sixteen studio class mic preamps from Neve, SSL, Harrison and others. These devices are patched via our 16 channel snake into the DDX console and out through its ADT1616 interfaces to the Lightbridge. The processed digital signal is passed to the hard drives via firewire 800 ports.

FINAL MIX AND MASTER

Because our Pro Tools sessions are set at the highest sample rate, we have the option to mix compositions in our facility or, depending on complexity, take the composite mix to a more sophisticated facility for final mix and mastering. Such a facility would have Pro Tools HD|3 Accel with at least 4 Digidesign 192kHz Audio Interfaces and a customized Digidesign automated console, all of which our system attempts to emulate as closely as our budget will allow.

STUDIO REFERENCE MONITORS

High resolution audio requires high quality monitors for accurate reproduction. A PreSonus Central Station ensures the quality of the audio signal received by our Dynaudio Acoustics BM15A reference monitors. An M-Audio Audiophile 192 PCI soundcard plays back the resolution we've gone to the trouble to create. To our surprise we preferred the BM15A monitors at the lower price to the more popular Genelec 1032A we initially wanted (See the OMM shopping wish list below, for the $30,000 pair we dream about)

STORAGE

Uncompressed HD video/cinema capture uses terabytes of storage, requiring a RAID Array which combines multiple hard drives into a single logical unit facilitating high levels of throughput, storage space, redundancy and data integrity. Read and write speeds, dual/quadcore processing platforms, and lots of RAM are critical factors in uncompressed HD editing. We found we could build a more efficient and less expensive RAID Array than Apple's (Ultra ATA) drive option at the same price point when we purchased it, offering older technology with more storage but less speed. We purchased eight of Western Digital's Raptor (Serial ATA) 150GB, 10,000 RPM drives, and found California based Adjile Systems to configure them for us in their enclosure. When our needs and the technology mature, we plan to handle storage on the Blu-ray DVD disc arrays rather than expensive legacy SCSI or Fibre Channel hard drives.

STUDIO DESIGN

The design and furnishing of the available space was our other top priority as our concept evolved from home hobby audio studio to home "professional" HD audio/video suite. To keep domestic peace in the home part of home studio, the room must double as my home theater, be presentable for clients, and most importantly, serve as a functional room that can host up to six musicians for playing and recording. This means that we can't have the nest of cables, equipment stacks, and egg carton "wallpaper" that musicians on a budget frequently deal with.

FOLLOWING A DIFFERENT DRUMMER

Our goal of combining aspects of both a MIDI recording studio with one that facilitates live players—including the notorious problem instrument, drums—challenges us in terms of function and cost. In our hybrid studio, the solution for drums has been to capture onto a sequencer a live drum performance that triggers sound modules from our Yamaha electronic drum set, allowing for manipulation of both the structure and the sound of the recorded MIDI data later. We can sample a drummer's own acoustic set, providing him or her with the drum sounds they're used to hearing while playing in our room. We didn't spring for the most expensive option, but knowing the difficulty of enticing good drummers onto an electronic set, we did upgrade to Yamaha's more advanced cymbal technology.

SOUNDPROOF ENCLOSURES

You cannot get that live guitar and bass sound without an amplified performance, and who has neighbors who will put up with that? Our standard approach is to custom-build things we need, which in this instance is a soundproof enclosure (with mic'ing capabilities) to house the guitar or bass amplifier we're recording with at the time. A&S Case Company will build out a custom enclosure to your specifications, or provide a 'build it yourself' kit. Because of our space restrictions, the trick for us is creating a design that allows for swapping out amplifiers without disturbing equipment residing on top of the enclosure.

CUSTOM MOBILE WORKSTATION

We called on our designer/artist friend Christo Braun to build a cockpit to house our mixing consoles and provide maximum rack space on each side, right at our fingertips. This was no small task, considering that the console had to be big enough for its use yet small enough, in modular units, to fit through the door. And like everything in the studio, it needed to be mobile so we could roll it to accommodate our various musician configurations and provide easier access for wiring. It ended up being a relatively inexpensive work of art itself, coming straight from our imaginations and that of a skilled friend. I handled light construction of things like two rolling synthesizer/controller stands with pullout trays for our wireless keyboard/mouse, thereby allowing control from all three stations, thanks to a 50-inch plasma monitor at the front of the room.

REDUCE CABLES—MAKE A SNAKE

Reducing cables is critical in our small space, so beyond using the ADAT/TOSLink protocol, we commissioned a custom-built snake for static patching of instruments and mic's into our mixing board. By building direct input (DI) circuitry into six of the snake's sixteen channels, we've avoided cables crossing the room from instruments to the board. Musicians have what they need, without the hardware and cabling of standard direct input setups, such as the Countryman DI. It wasn't easy to find someone to make our snake, but at $750, it was less expensive than the individual components it replaced, and it's worth twice that in manageability and comfort when working with a full complement of players.

ROOM ACOUSTICS

It is our good fortune to be using an L-shaped bedroom with ten-foot ceilings and hardwood floors. The room sounded like a gymnasium but had the potential to offer good acoustics and versatility. We custom-built sound baffling panels of various dimensions, which now hang over 80 percent of the six walls, but we disguised them as framed decorative pieces. They're easily brought down to change the room's dynamic or to help silence the amplifiers (in the event it goes beyond the enclosure's ability) for that metal guitar solo the neighbors never even heard. These were built with two hundred square feet of 2.5-inch acoustic foam, recycled and new wood, and recycled quarter-inch foam board. Cheap cloth from the local discount fabric store covers the foam and nicely complements the room's existing color scheme. Because they were having a sale, we also bought material to upholster the console cockpit, adding a more professional look.

THE WALLS HAVE BOOTHS

There was a dire need, but no room, for some sort of vocal booth. So perhaps our craftiest space-saving idea was to design and construct three 7-by-4-foot and two 4-by-4-foot sound panels that come off the walls and fit together to make a vocal booth that goes right back onto the walls when the recording is finished. It was almost accidental how the design and materials came together (frames of 1.5-inch holed angle iron, acoustic foam on backing of 7-by-4-foot, three-quarter-inch recycled foam board, all covered with cloth material held by, oddly enough, automotive spire nut fasteners).

In the end, the panels turned out to be very sturdy yet lightweight, easy for one person to take off the wall, and have a nice aesthetic. Also, we're designing a floating floor for the booth to sit on. This involves separating the bottom of the booth from the main flooring by using rubberized sound- and vibration-dampening materials, which will get us closer to the techniques professional studios use to isolate sensitive vocal microphones.

A PICTURE IS WORTH A THOUSAND NOTES

To view the configuration and equipment and see the studio, visit bethemedia. com/ommstudio.htm.

CLOSING WITH A DREAM

We've had to be creative in every facet of our studio, from figuring how to use current technology to how to finance it. The bulk of the money we saved was in our solutions for mixing boards, the RAID array, and I/O interfacing, with the space being saved by customization and fiber optics. Although we are making the most of our space and budget, our dream is to do well enough to purchase the turnkey solutions for a studio class HD recording and uncompressed HD video postproduction suite. When that day comes, our current setup will provide a great 64 track HD mobile rig and extra digital audio workstations.

Because of the wide variety of equipment and price ranges, there were, and are, many options for configuring a Hi-Def studio. Some specific requirements led us to our particular choices below. Your choices will depend on your own personal preferences, requirements, infrastructure, and budget.

A rule of thumb? Research. Design. Research. Purchase.

"Harmony is his who can hear beyond sound"
—*Lao Tzu*

OMM HD Shopping Wish List

AUDIO

Audio Server: Apple Quadcore 64bit XServe with 4GB RAM and three 750GB SATA Apple Drive Modules (ADMs)	$ 6,000
Digidesign ICON D-Control ES 64-Fader Custom Bundle PCI-X/e (referenced in Final Mix and Master section above)	$155,000
Meyer Sound X-10: High-Resolution Linear Control Room Monitor (pair)	$ 30,000
Microphone complement	$ 45,000
AMS Neve 88R Remote Microphone Rack—12 Slot	$ 10,000
Miscellaneous effects processing	variable

VIDEO

Video Server: Apple Quadcore 64-bit Xserve with 16 (4x4) GB RAM and three 300GB SAS 15K rpm ADMs	$ 20,000
Final Cut Studio 2/Server software and support applications	$ 3,500
BlackMagic Multibridge Eclipse™	$ 3,495
Adjile 12-bay Fibre Channel to SAS RAID enclosure with 12 Seagate 300GB SAS 15K rpm hard drives	$ 15,000
50" Panasonic TH-50PZ750U HDTV Plasma Monitor	$ 3,995
HP 30" HD Cinema LCD monitors —capture and edit (2 x $1,700)	$ 3,400
Cinemage CT-2142 24" HD Cinema LCD Monitor (color correction)	$ 20,000
Sony PDW-700 XDCam	$ 30,000
Sony PDW-HD1500 Mastering and Authoring Deck	$ 22,000
AJA Video Systems KONA^3 HD 4:4:4 video capture cards (2 x $1,400)	$ 2,800
QLogic SANbox 5602 8-port Fiber Channel Switch	$ 4,000
Apple Xsan	$ 1,000
Atto CTFC-42XS-0R0 Fibre Channel PCI X/e 4 Gbps Host Bus Adapter	$ 975
Miscellaneous equipment	variable

5

PODCASTING

HOW TO CREATE AND PROMOTE YOUR PODCAST
David Mathison

"The common people love a sound man because he does not talk above them."
—Lao Tzu

Because you are reading this, you may already know that the word *podcast* is a combination of *iPod* and *broadcast,* and that an iPod is not required. It just gets free product placement.

Do you also know that podcasting statistics (let us call them podstats) are astonishing? And that the potential for regular people, not (only) titans of industry, to reach squillions of people via a podcast is but a few clicks and sounds away?

But before we teach you how to make your own podcast and—or the absolute beginner—how to receive and subscribe to one or many, here is a little background about podcasting and a look at who is involved in receiving and sending podcasts today.

A BRIEF HISTORY OF PODCASTING

On January 11, 2001, programmer and blogger Dave Winer enclosed a Grateful Dead song in his Scripting News weblog and into his weblog product, Radio Userland.

In 2003, Winer and Christopher Lydon distributed Chris's audio interviews using Really Simple Syndication (RSS), a standard protocol for content syndication.[1] The protocol delivers new episodes to subscribers automatically, so users don't need to surf the Web for updates. In other words, RSS delivers the pizza so you don't have to pick it up.

---

1. RSS allows for the automated creation, subscription, and management of feeds. Feeds are published by content providers (bloggers, podcasters, video bloggers, and the like) and are subscribed to by users. On the Internet, this publish/subscribe model is known as syndication and aggregation.

In fall 2004, former MTV veejay Adam Curry wrote a software script that delivered the audio file to an iPod. His RSS-to-iPod script became the popular audio aggregator[2] iPodder, now known as Juice. With that, podcasting was born. It freed the content from the platform. And podcasting freed the audience from the desktop, and from radio programmers and their "day part" time slots.

WHAT'S IN A NAME?

On February 12, 2004, the term *podcasting* was proposed by Ben Hammersley in the *Guardian*. On September 28, 2004, Doc Searls began tracking references to the term in Google. That day, there were twenty-four hits for the word *podcasts;* within a month, there were one hundred thousand (see chapter 23).

On September 28, 2005, just one year later, Google found more than one hundred million hits on the word *podcasts. The New Oxford American Dictionary* named *podcast* the word of the year for 2005.

GROWTH IN PODCASTS AND SUBSCRIBERS

Podcast, however, proved to be much more than just a word. In November 2004, FeedBurner, which promotes and measures podcast, blog, and video blog feeds, found 505 actual podcasts; by June 2005 there were 6,000.

People were listening, and subscribing. The average number of subscribers to podcasts on FeedBurner was 15 in 2004, doubling to 33 in 2005.

Now, reports FeedBurner CEO Dick Costolo, "Our top twenty highly popular shows have thousands of subscribers, and a couple of top podcasts have tens of thousands." In June 2005, *Behind the Scenes,* a podcast about podcasting, had five thousand subscribers, and Adam Curry's program *Daily Source Code* had fifty thousand.

On June 28, 2005, Apple Inc. made podcasts available through its iTunes music directory. Within three weeks, iTunes users subscribed to more than five million podcasts from tens of thousands of podcasters.

On October 12, 2005, Apple CEO Steve Jobs unveiled the first video iPod and demonstrated a video podcast from Rocketboom. (This chapter concentrates on audio. For more about video podcasts and videoblogs, see chapter 7 (video).

Today, Yahoo!, AOL, and even TiVo offer podcast directories where users can rate, rank, and review shows and can search or browse through a directory that lists tens of thousands of podcasts by topic, author, subject, or keyword. In April 2007, Apple sold its one hundred millionth iPod, a large potential listening audience for audio creators.

---

2. Aggregators for audio feeds, like iTunes and Juice, are called podcatchers. Aggregators for both audio and video feeds include FireAnt and Mefeedia (see *Video* chapter). Aggregators for RSS and blog feeds, like Pluck and My Yahoo!, are called newsreaders (see *Blog* chapter).

WHO IS LISTENING?

A 2006 report by Arbitron found that podcast listeners are tech savvy, smart, wealthy (22 percent earn more than $100,000 per year), and young—from teens to middle age. Twenty-seven million Americans (11 percent) have listened to an audio podcast. More than half of all American teenagers own an iPod or similar portable music device. One out of five 18- to 24-year-olds has purchased downloadable music online.

WHO IS PODCASTING?

Not as many people make and send podcasts as listen to them, but podcasters represent a vast number of people and professions . . . and income levels. A great advantage to being a podcaster, as opposed to being a radio host, is that it is cheap. Podcasters, for their part, do not need to buy expensive transmitters, receivers, licenses, or equipment. They can work from the road, using just a phone or a laptop with a headset. Nor do they need to purchase expensive airtime or duplicate and ship thousands of cassettes and CDs worldwide to reach their listeners.

Podcasts are coming from DJs, musicians, authors, filmmakers, bands, radio show hosts, salespeople, business owners, coaches, speakers, trainers, consultants, teachers, students, politicans, publicists, insurance/real estate/travel agents, journalists, and reporters—all of whom can reach a global audience on a less than global budget.

Successful podcast formats include speeches, comedy, audiobook excerpts, original music, reviews (restaurants, travel, recipes, TV, and film), and audio walking tours of cities or museums.

Podcasts are being published by noncommercial shows like *Democracy Now!* and by independent broadcasters such as KPFA (a Pacifica Radio station in Berkeley, California). National Public Radio offers podcasts of episodes from *All Songs Considered, On the Media,* and *Science Friday.*

San Francisco's KYOU Radio (1550 AM), the world's first all-podcast radio station, lets listener/participants contribute shows. The station's first show was a six-minute version of software guru Dave Winer's *Morning Coffee Notes.*

Educational podcasts are extremely popular, enabling teachers, students, and parents to share classes, tutorials, and assignments. Sebastien Babolat's *FrenchPodClass* attracts over ten thousand listeners who want to learn French.

Religious podcasts (or "godcasts") are up from just 177 in July 2005 to 2,511 in December 2007 on podcastalley.com's directory alone. Jeff Mills, a youth pastor in Minnesota, created his own podcast and wrote an ebook about it, which supplements his income and helps pay down his seminary student loans. According to the Reverend Mark Batterson of National Community Church in Washington, D.C. (theaterchurch.com), "Basically every church can have its own radio show."

CORPORATE PODCASTERS

Podcasting is so popular, guess who's coming to the airwaves—er, podwaves? Corporate media! The big music labels like BMG (obviously) and columnists from newspapers such as the *New York Times* (not so obviously) are on the scene, and even Paris Hilton promoted her film *House of Wax* via podcast. Podcasts draw audiences away from traditional TV and radio, so broadcasters are now offering podcasts of such productions as ABC's *Lost*. Yes, the TV show also can be heard on an audio podcast. Large publishers such as Simon & Schuster podcast audiobooks featuring celebrities such as Steve Martin, who read an excerpt from his book *Shopgirl*. Even a strictly corporate interest such as Purina has a podcast for pet lovers, with tips on pet care.

Now, for the Lessons . . .

HOW TO HEAR A PODCAST

Listening to a podcast is easy. Go to a website like itconversations.com, find an interesting podcast, and select "Play." But there is no need to visit websites every day to get updates. Just subscribe to the podcasts you want and let RSS automatically deliver the new episodes to you.

SUBSCRIBING TO PODCASTS

Here is how to subscribe to a podcast:

1. Download and install your podcatcher, such as Apple's iTunes, or Juice. (See "Podcatchers," below.)

2. Find the podcast feed you want, usually marked with an orange button labeled "RSS 2.0."

3. Right-click (PC) or Control-click (Mac) on the feed you want and select "Copy Link Location" or "Copy Shortcut."

4. In iTunes, choose "Advanced" from the menu and choose "Subscribe to Podcast." Using Juice, click the "Add Feed" button in the program's toolbar, a green circle with a plus (+) sign.

5. Paste the URL of the feed into the URL text area of the dialog box by pressing Control-V (PC) or Command-V (Mac). It may take time to download the feed.

6. Save the entry and you are done. You should see a list of episodes.

7. iTunes and Juice can be set to automatically update and download new episodes.

8. Download the MP3 file to your player by using the software that syncs your portable device with your computer. The audio can be played on any MP3-compatible device—a computer, iPod, PDA, cell phone, or even your car stereo (with adaptor).

Podcatchers: Subscribing to Podcasts

Not only can you subscribe to podcasts using aggregators such as *iTunes,* you can also have your own personal aggregator. *Podcatchers* are applications that run on your computer or mobile phone that let you subscribe to audio podcasts.

The most popular podcatcher, *Juice* (juicereceiver.sourceforge.net), has been downloaded more than 1.8 million times. It offers a directory that lists thousands of podcasts. The software is free and licensed under GPL (open source).

Other podcatchers to consider include *DopplerRadio* (dopplerradio.net); *NIMIQ* (nimiq.nl); and *ziePOD* (ziepod.com). Linux users can try *PenguinTV* (penguintv.sourceforge.net) and *Liferea* (liferea.sourceforge.net).

Mobile podcatchers let you subscribe to podcasts and deliver them to your mobile phone. Try *Voiceindigo.com* or *MobilCastNetwork.com.*

THE ADVANTAGES OF MOBILITY

All this mobility means that you the listener are not tethered to your radio or computer to hear the podcast you want. You can time-shift (listen anytime, start, stop, and rewind); location-shift (listen anywhere—at the gym, in the car, or on the subway); and listen on any MP3 player (a computer, an iPod, or a cell phone).

Podcasting puts the audience in control. Instead of being restricted to the lineup and time slots determined by programmers at radio stations, the listener controls the program schedule. You get to subscribe to favorite shows, create the program lineup, listen wherever and whenever you want, and get new episodes delivered automatically, without having to surf daily through dozens of sites for updates.

HOW TO CREATE A PODCAST

So, you want to make podcasts yourself? As you already know as a podcast listener, they can be any length and there are no hard-and-fast rules.

Before recording a thing, listen to as many podcasts as possible to see what good (and bad) shows are like. Start with Adam Curry's podfinder.podshow.com, which evaluates and recommends exceptional podcasts.

You might want to plan your show with a whiteboard, script, or handwritten notes and to practice with dress rehearsals, but you'd be in the minority. Some podcasts are formally structured, but most are not. However, if you are industrious, efficient, and well-organized (read: a Virgo), then feel free to run through your lines, stick to the clock, and check that your recording equipment is operating properly.

Because most podcasters rely on his or her own voice in their podcasts—whether interviewing someone else or speaking solo—you will want to prepare your voice. Warm up with vocal stretches like humming or scales, and make sure you drink enough water to keep your pipes hydrated. Although your voice should be clear and articulate, the important thing is to be yourself and "just do it."

PODCASTING THE EASY WAY: FREE PHONE PODCASTING

Recording a podcast can be as easy as making a phone call from wherever you are in the world, whenever you want. No need to worry about equipment, file formats, or even recording software. These solutions are perfect for talk show hosts, interviewers, authors, public speakers, teachers, pastors, or rabbis—anyone that has something to say.

TALKSHOE.COM

A great place to start for beginner—or expert—podcasters is talkshoe.com. This is a free service that lets anyone easily create live, interactive podcasts. The host chooses a topic and starts the show from his or her phone or computer. People then join the show, also via telephone or computer. Everyone is able to listen, talk, and chat during the show. After the show, Talkshoe automatically records the show as a podcast, hosts it, and lists it in its directory. Talkshoe's widget enables you to post the podcast on your website, blog, social network, iTunes, or other podcast directories. You don't need any equipment or software to create your podcast. Talkshoe provides a complete package—conferencing, chat, storage, bandwidth, ads, statistics, and directory listing—all for free. Another free service to consider is BlogTalkRadio.com (see Radio chapter, page 147).

If you insist on paying, and some do, try hipcast.com ($4.95 per month) or BYOAudio at byoaudio.com ($19.95 per month), which lets you record phone messages, seminars, or whatever you want for up to sixty minutes (conference calls up to two hours), with no surcharges and unlimited call-in lines. Simply dial a phone number provided by the host, enter a personal code, and record your voice, song, or other audio clip. An MP3 podcast of your message will be immediately posted to your blog or saved for later manipulation and publishing.

WEB-BASED RECORDING

Web-based solutions let you create and distribute your radio show or podcast right from your browser—for free.

Clickcaster.com: A free, Internet-based service that hosts a global directory where you can broadcast your show, subscribe to other people's shows, and track who is listening. The site offers unlimited storage, and you can sync your iPod straight from the Internet.

Studio.odeo.com: Enables you not only to create a podcast with your browser but also to record podcasts from your telephone. There are over 230,000 accounts at Odeo Studio, whose directory hosts over two million MP3s. You can use Odeo's directory to share your show with a global audience and discover new podcasts.

GETTING SERIOUS: RECORDING EQUIPMENT

Now that you have tried podcasting the easy, cheap, and quick way, you might want to get serious and record with your own equipment. Free phone and Web podcasts are an inexpensive and ubiquitous way to help you maintain contact with your fans, even from the road. You can upload live clips from a recent show, jokes, tour updates, or a few teaser chords from that new song you've been working on. But serious DJs, musicians, and bands will want to use recording software to create quality podcasts complete with edits, sound effects, and music.

For this method, you will need a computer with Internet access, a microphone, and sound-recording software. You can find gear at podcastacademy.com/pcr-index, podcastgear.com, or industrialaudiosoftware.com, and even professional-sounding narration from radiodaddy.com, a free service that provides professional voiceovers from 2,700 members.

Sound quality is one of the most important aspects of a podcast. Be selective about your choice of recorder, microphone, mixer, and software. Yes, you can record on the road with the Griffin iTalk microphone ($40) attached to your iPod, but the sound will be very poor. A much better choice is the Samson Zoom H4 ($480 new, $300 used) or the Marantz PMD670 digital recorder ($599). To further improve sound quality, couple the recorder with a quality microphone such as the Shure SM57 ($99) or, even better if you can afford it, the Electrovoice RE20 ($400).

Use a mixer to connect high-end mikes and digital devices to the PC. The Behringer Eurorack UB802 mixer is an inexpensive solution at $50, but you might regret not spending a bit more for higher quality equipment. Mackie's ONYX 1220 12-channel mixer at $500 is a fine system but could be overkill and out of budget range for the average podcaster. Doug Kaye of IT Conversations (see the section "Lessons Learned from IT Conversations") recommends the Alesis Multi-Mix 8 USB 2.0 mixer ($299). Experiment with the sound quality and balance out the recording levels by adjusting the gain control.

SOFTWARE RECORDING TOOLS

Audacity (free): Lets you record, edit, play, import, and export audio file types. You can add intros, music, effects, and ads, and normalize balance and levels.

Feedforall.com ($39.95): Enables you to create a professional-sounding podcast in just ten minutes. The company offers a free thirty-day trial.

Apple iLife ($79): Enables you to create podcasts using GarageBand, iMovie, or QuickTime Pro. Captures sounds from instruments or a microphone and offers a wide range of music and sounds, such as instruments, samples, and loops (a repeated sample).

Adobe Audition (formerly Cool Edit Pro) ($249): Lets you record, edit, mix, add effects, burn CDs, or post on a website. Converts multiple file formats.

Also try WireTap Pro ($19), Audio Hijack Pro ($32), Propaganda ($50), and ePodcast Creator ($89.95).

AUDIO FILE FORMATS

Your computer should have a built-in sound card that plays, records, and processes sound files from a microphone, CD player, or radio. Sound files include both audio and metadata—data about the data—such as size, duration, sample size, sampling rate in kilohertz, compression type, text, and graphics.

There are many different audio file formats, both uncompressed, such as Apple's Audio Interchange File Format (.aiff) and Microsoft's Waveform (.wav), and compressed, including MP3, RealAudio (.ram), Windows media (.wma), QuickTime (.qt or .mov), and Ogg Vorbis for Linux (.ogg).

Always use uncompressed formats while working on a show. When you are ready to release your podcast to the world, save it in MP3 format as the last step, so it can be distributed and played on any MP3-compatible device.

READY, SET, RECORD

Find a quiet place to record your show. Put a note on the door so no one knocks, turn off your cell phone, set your landline to go straight to voice mail, and put the pit bull outside. (See chapter 6 for more tips on recording.)

PODSAFE MUSIC

Now that you've recorded your audio, let's add some music as a theme for your intro and outro and to use as background music. Because podcasts can be downloaded and saved to portable devices, copyright law prohibits the use of other people's music without their permission. Here is the chance for independent musicians and bands to promote and market their music. Use your own original tunes, license music from a friend, or use "podsafe" music, which is any audio or musical content that can be legally used in a podcast.

Sites offering podsafe music include archive.org, dmusic.com, garageband.com, iodapromo-net.com, magnatune.com, music.podshow.com, music.download.com, ourmedia.org, and the Flash developer resource site flashkit.com/loops, which also offers thousands of royalty-free music loops categorized into techno, funk, rhythm and blues, sound effects, etc.

Using Audacity, select "Project/Import Audio" and import your .wav or MP3 sound files. GarageBand users can add audio files or use the copyright-cleared Apple Loops and optional Jam Packs, which include thousands of professional-sounding loops.

COVER ART

If you plan to make more than one episode and develop an audience, use an eye-catching logo, image, artwork, or photo as the "album cover" that will be displayed in iTunes and other directories. Use images that illustrate your topic.

Check out Audio Lite from Gigavox at cms.gigavox.com. After you have your MP3 file, Audio Lite can help you with cover art, filling out ID3 tags, and other important podcast features.

FILL OUT ID3 TAG

It is critical to fill out an ID3 tag. This tag stays with the audio file when it is distributed to your subscribers. Be sure to include the name of your podcast, the artist, the album, and the year. This way, when listeners play the file the name of the track and artist is displayed. In the comments field, put your company name, contact information, Internet URL, e-mail address, and phone number.

Audacity users are prompted to edit ID3 tags upon saving.

GarageBand users select "File > Get Info." Click on the "Info" tab. Click "OK."

SAVE THE FILE AND BACK UP

Save your work regularly—every day is best—both to your hard drive and to external sources. You'll probably want to get a portable external hard drive or storage unit. You also should back up onto DVD or CD and keep a copy off-site, preferably in a safe deposit box at your bank.

Save the recording as an MP3 file for compatibility with most players.

To save your file as an MP3 in Audacity, select "File/Export as an MP3."

In GarageBand, select "File > Export to iTunes."

In the case of audiobooks, sermons, and other forms of talk, save the material as a 64 kbps mono file. For quality podcasts with music and stereo, save the file as 128 kbps stereo. The higher the bit rate, the better the quality, but the podcast will be larger in size. Reducing the size of the file will reduce the quality of the sound.

Because you likely will have multiple episodes over time, use a standard naming convention with logical names and dates, such as "BeTheMedia-podcast_episode1_04-1-2008.mp3".

LISTEN TO YOUR RECORDING

Listen to your show one last time before submitting it. Michael Geoghegan, who podcasts movie reviews at reelreviewsradio.com, suggests testing your show using the iPod's earbuds, because this is the device your listeners will most likely use. For quality headphones at a reasonable price, Doug Kaye recommends the Sony Pro MDR-7506 ($100).

CREATE THE PODCAST AND FEED

The top blog providers offer instant podcasting. Use TypePad, Blogger, or another platform to insert the audio file into your blog post and publish it. Your host does all the work, adding your audio file as an enclosure to your blog's RSS feed. Add descriptive text about the podcast on your blog to ensure that search engines such as Google will index it.

That's it. You've created a podcast.

VALIDATE THE FEED

Before publishing to the Web, use feed validator software that supports all versions of RSS and Atom, such as feedvalidator.org. Enter the URL of the feed and select "Validate." If your feed is valid, which means it can be understood by other computers, you can post it to the Web. If not, the validator will let you know where your problems are so you can correct them before publication.

HOSTING YOUR PODCAST

If you don't have a blog to host your podcast, ourmedia.org and archive.org host content for free, indefinitely. If you insist on paying, libsyn.com offers $5-per-month basic hosting, which includes storage, a blog, an RSS feed, and a directory. Other paid hosts include podshowcreator.com, mediablog.ilaugh.com, mypodcasts.net, genetichosting.com, podomatic.com, and switchpod.com.

SYNDICATE YOUR PODCAST

Most blogs automate the process of syndication. (See chapter 10.) For hosted podcast services that don't offer syndication, submit your podcast feed to FeedBurner at feedburner.com. As of September 2007, more than half a million publishers used FeedBurner to burn over one hundred and forty thousand podcast and video feeds. And, as mentioned earlier, it also lets your subscribers receive updates through e-mail.

PUBLISHING YOUR PODCAST TO AGGREGATORS AND DIRECTORIES

If you want to get your podcast in front of millions of potential subscribers, you can promote your podcast through aggregators and directories. Most provide statistics, such as the Top 10 shows per month. Here are some to consider:

- iTunes.com: Apple's iTunes directory lists thousands of podcasts. To submit your podcast to the Apple iTunes directory, go to their podcast directory, and click the "Submit a Podcast" link on the left column.

- podcastalley.com: Lists more than 5,000 podcasts and 80,000 episodes.

- podcast.net: Offers tens of thousands of podcasts organized into categories.

- podcastpickle.com: Contains 12,000 podcasts comprising 215,000 episodes.

- podnova.com: A distributed directory of 75,000 podcasts, maintained by volunteers.

- podfeed.net: Publishes a directory with 8,156 podcasts comprising 466,820 episodes.

- odeo.com: Offers a podcast directory, software, and tools, and has 237,000 subscribers. Acquired in September 2007 by SonicMountain.

- More: podcastingnews.com: podcasts.yahoo.com, clickcaster.com, google.com/base, ipodder.org, podshow.com

REVENUE OPPORTUNITIES FOR PODCASTERS

Most podcasts are free right now. Some podcasters earn money by charging for memberships or subscriptions to podcast or archival/premium content; through sponsorships or donations from individuals, corporations, foundations, organizations, and nonprofits; or through pay-on-demand or barter. (See chapter 6.)

If you are a podcaster, you also can repurpose audio clips for sale on CD, on DVD, or via your website as streaming or downloadable files. Programs also can be sold to other websites, traditional broadcast, HD, or satellite radio stations.

Another thought is to promote something you are passionate about. The coffee-loving Adam Curry earned thousands of dollars by selling coffee machines through an affiliate partnership with amazon.com. (See chapter 9 .)

ADVERTISING

According to eMarketer, $80 million was spent on podcast advertising in 2006, and this number is expected to grow to $300 million by 2010. Some podcasts have enough subscribers to engage sponsors or advertisers, whereas others have small but extremely targeted audiences that are valuable to retailers. IT Conversations includes in its podcasts ads targeted to a high-tech audience—a desirable demographic for sponsors.

There are other commercial services that can help you. Wordcast.audible.com can dynamically insert and rotate advertisements in your podcasts, accurately measure your audience, and provide your podcasts over cellular networks to wireless listeners. It also lets producers create subscription services and enables sales of archival episodes.

Fruitcast.com automates the process of ad insertion, payments, and reporting for both podcasters and advertisers. Other podcast ad networks include radiotail.com, podtrac.com, and blastpodcast.com.

However, as Mark Cuban points out, making money from podcasting won't be easy. "For those who are trying to jump on the podcasting bandwagon and create a "hit" podcast that you plan on selling advertising in, it's cheap and easy to do, but even with Google AdSense for RSS it's going to be really tough to do it as a full-time job and make minimum wage back."

And as Dave Winer reminds us, it's not all about making money. "The power of RSS lies in its democratizing potential, not in its "over-hyped" business promise." Making podcasts is supposed to be fun. Enjoy the process. A bigger audience will bring new challenges and more responsibility—which may change your favorite pastime into a (gasp!) job. (For more on that, see chapter 6.)

**"A bird doesn't sing because it has an answer,
it sings because it has a song."**
—*Maya Angelou*

Lessons Learned from IT Conversations
Doug Kaye

While researching a book I was writing, I decided to record my interviews so I wouldn't have to take notes. Then I began to realize that the recordings might actually be a better way to communicate the experts' ideas, in their own words, to my readers. I began IT Conversations in 2003 by re-recording some of those interviews, editing them, and posting them on the Internet as downloadable MP3 files. Prior to my twenty-six-year career in IT, I had worked as a recording engineer and sound editor in the motion-picture business, so this was a chance to brush off those rusty skills.

We now produce an average of ten new programs each week for IT Conversations (itconversations.com); they are heard by tens of thousands of listeners each day. In addition to my own interviews, which I no longer have time to do as often as I'd like, we produce programs from many of the leading information-technology conferences, as well as produce the *podcasts* of a number of popular series hosted by others, such as the public-radio Tech Nation show hosted by Dr. Moira Gunn.

It has long been possible to download MP3 files from the Internet manually, just like any other files. But in 2003, Dave Winer, the inventor of RSS, or Really Simple Syndication, got together with Christopher Lydon, a terrific public radio host, to distribute Chris's interviews over the Internet as MP3 audio files using the RSS protocol. RSS allows you to *subscribe* to a *feed*—in effect to say, "Automatically check for any new MP3 files, and download them to my computer." It's a great way to receive the latest posts to blogs, meaning weblogs, or audio or video series.

In summer 2004, *podcasting* became the rage when Adam Curry wrote a simple script that completed the "last yard" of MP3 delivery by copying the received MP3 files all the way to an Apple iPod. As of early 2005, there were already eight thousand podcasts, ranging from personal diaries recorded on built-in laptop microphones to high-quality programs recorded and produced in expensive radio-station facilities. Because of my addiction to high-end audio equipment, IT Conversations falls into the latter category, but I've also learned many shortcuts that will help you get your own podcast up and running with as little effort or expense as possible. I could fill this entire book with the things I've learned over the past two years, but here are some highlights that should help you get started with your own podcast.

Face-to-Face Interviews

For my first face-to-face interview, I purchased a pair of $30 lavalier microphones (the kind you hang around your neck or clip to your lapel) and a $60 mixer, then fed the output into a Windows laptop running an early release of Audacity, a free, open-source program, available at audacity.com. I tested everything at home and was confident in my setup, but after exactly one hour of recording that hard-to-get interview, the computer crashed and I lost the whole thing. "Never again!" I swore.

For a more reliable but still somewhat portable device, I opted for a direct-to-CD recorder (Marantz CDR300). It met the requirement for reliability, but as I branched out to record live conference presentations in addition to interviews, I encountered another problem: You can't record more than 80 minutes on a CD, and many conference sessions run 90 minutes or more. (No, you can't quickly change discs. You lose about a minute of audio in the process.)

My search for a long-format medium ended with a solution I never would have guessed: the old VHS recorder from my living room. The HiFi audio found on late-model VHS recorders is of excellent quality, and not only can you get a good VHS recorder for less than $100, there's the added benefit that you can record up to six hours on a single tape. When shopping for a VHS recorder, look for three things: (1) that you can record from the audio auxiliary input without having a video signal present, (2) that you can control the recorder (via the remote or front panel) without having to hook up a television, and (3) that it has a good AGC (automatic gain control) to keep the audio levels consistent with wide variations in input levels. You'll probably have to take it home to test it, so make sure you can exchange it for another model if necessary. I've had particularly good luck with some of the Sony recorders.

In my current studio configuration, the primary recorder is Sony's SoundForge software running on a Windows XP computer. My backups are the CD and VHS recorders. Yes, I run *three* recorders, and twice out of about five hundred recordings I've had to go all the way to number three. The long-tape format of VHS also helps me avoid "pilot error." With all the excitement at the start of an interview, I have the nasty habit of forgetting to hit the Record button. Now I start the VHS recorder ten minutes or more before the interview, just in case.

For remote recordings, I use either a Compact Flash recorder—a Sansom Zoom H4 ($480 new, $300 used) or a Marantz PMD671 ($900)—or a Sony MiniDisc recorder (model MZ-NHF800, $250), either as backups for a laptop, or if I need to be ultraportable, as sole recorders. The Marantz is a professional-quality device, which means I don't have to worry about microphone plugs that make noise or fall out. But while the new HD minidisc recorders have less-reliable "minijacks" and a truly awful user interface, they hold nearly eight hours on a single reusable disk, so I can record an all-day event by pressing the Record button in the morning and the Stop button at the end of the day. Like Sony's VHS recorders, their MD recorders have excellent AGC.

Recording interviews via telephone is an entirely different matter. I used to recommend all sorts of techniques that were complex, or expensive, or both. But now there are some terrific online services that will record a conference call and create an MP3 file without the need for any more equipment than a standard telephone. I'd start with TalkShoe.com, and I'd think carefully before taking the next step to a more sophisticated setup. It's a big step.

The Tools

As for the Mac versus PC question, you can use either platform. I find things are somewhat easier on a PC, and for the same cost a PC is faster. That doesn't matter when you're working with three-minute songs, but if you're mixing or encoding a ninety-minute interview or lecture, a high-performance PC can help a lot.

Regarding software, I do most of my one- and two-track editing and processing using Sony's SoundForge (mediasoftware.sonypictures.com/Products/ShowProduct. asp?PID=961). Once you learn the interface, it's fast and efficient. Accurate editing is a breeze using SoundForge, and with it I've never lost or corrupted a file. For multitrack work—for example, when I need to mixdown separate tracks or add music under an introduction—I use n-Track Studio from Flavio Antonioli at FASoft (fasoft.com/what_is.shtm). SoundForge and n-Track use the same DX plug-ins (software audio processors), so if I buy a tool to use with one application, I can use it with the other as well.

One of the most important tools in my toolbox is the Levelator from GigaVox Media (gigavox.com). It's free software that smooths out all those uneven sections where one speaker is louder or quieter than the others.

When it comes time to turn your recordings into podcasts, you can use virtually any audio software to encode your tracks into MP3 files. Encode at a bit rate of 64 kbps for spoken-word programs and 128 kbps for those with a significant amount of music. That will give you good-enough quality, and your files won't be too large to download or store.

Whether you want to record live with microphones or via the telephone, you'll find it's easy to become a podcaster.

6

RADIO

HOW TO CREATE AND SELF-SYNDICATE YOUR RADIO SHOW

David Mathison

"Radio is the theater of the mind; television is the theater of the mindless."
—*Steve Allen*

WHY START YOUR OWN RADIO SHOW?

The short answer is, Why not? These days, almost anyone can create and host a radio show. For most readers of this book, the goal is to reach as wide an audience as possible. A radio show is a great way to attract people to whatever it is you do, make, or think. All you need are some basics: an idea, time to devote to the idea, start-up money, and a modicum of technical know-how. That's it. Okay . . . some business sense, a passable voice, talent, and patience won't hurt.

In radio, there is only one thing better than being interviewed on a show, and that is hosting your own show. It is easier to gain credibility as a host than as a guest. You establish yourself as a recognized authority in your field—that is, if you have a field. Or you might want to start a show for enjoyment, intellectual stimulation, or pique. If you build up a big enough audience, however, you will be able to attract professionals and celebrities in your field as guests, new sales leads for your products or services, and advertisers who might want to reach your listeners.

In other words, be forewarned: Your show could pay off financially. I'll get to that later.

You might want to host your own radio show if you are:

- an author, musician, or filmmaker trying to build a platform for your new book, CD, DVD, or film;

- passionate or expert in anything, such as finance, health, snowboarding, wine, arts, publishing, sports, empowerment, cooking, or pet care;

- an attorney, a real estate agent, or an insurance agent looking for new customers;

- a professor (or student) with expertise in a particular field, such as media, law, public affairs, or business;

- a member of a community activist group, religious organization, or labor union; or

- a public speaker, entrepreneur, coach, consultant, or elected official trying to reach a wider audience.

TOPIC, OR WHAT'S THE BIG IDEA?

The topic or idea should be something you care a lot about. There are two general rules of thumb: know yourself and know the audience. This will help you identify the type and content of the show, its length, the most likely day and time that the show will air (its "daypart"), potential sponsors and advertisers, rates, costs, and affiliates. For example, Warren Eckstein is passionate about pets. *Parents* magazine calls him the "Dr. Spock of the pet world." Eckstein is host of *The Pet Show* (thepetshow.com), a nationally syndicated radio show broadcast on Saturdays from 4 to 6 p.m. by WOR (710 AM) in New York City. Eckstein trained and deployed the K9 corps in Vietnam and is pet advisor to stars such as David Letterman and Al Pacino. Naturally, he aims at the 60 percent of Americans who own pets and support the $23 billion pet products marketplace.

Because my passion is independent media, I might create a show called "*Be the Media.*" Let us say it will be a weekly, one-hour, taped radio show about the independent media community and will include guests. There are other types of formats, of course. You have to decide what format will your show take—talk, advice, sports, call-in, music, etc.

If you are a celebrity with a recognized voice, vignettes are best. Vignettes are one- to two-minute segments such as John Madden's "Football Minute" or Paul Harvey's "The Rest of the Story." This short form is easy to sell to affiliates because vignettes are so short they don't threaten to replace existing programs, and they can enter almost any daypart—the lucrative morning or afternoon drive, middays, and evenings. Also, production costs are minimal: a few months' worth of edited segments can be created in just a few hours. Vignettes are not for newcomers, but neither are live, call-in shows, because these are expensive to produce and are most prone to technical failure.

For our purposes, we will focus on a one-hour, pretaped talk-and-interview format. Simply substitute the name of your show over mine, go through the same exercises, and by the end of the chapter, you too will have created a radio show.

After you have decided on a topic—your idea—and on a format, create a list of subtopics to see how broad the scope of the show could be. You need to be certain that your idea is broad enough to ensure you have enough material for a few years.

A few years?

Yes. If you go to the effort and expense of launching your own radio show, you must think long term, not short term. The stations ("affiliates") that pick up your show need to be sure you are serious and that your topic is broad enough to last at least that long. Affiliate stations are run by professionals who don't want to waste time with shows that last only a few seasons.

Subtopics and show ideas for *Be the Media* could include:

- Musicians, bands, and labels: What can independent musicians learn from Prince, Radiohead, and Nine Inch Nails?

- Filmmakers and movies: Festival news. Meet no-budget film school founder Mark Stolaroff, and indie producer Peter Broderick.

- Television and cable: Learn which stations support independent producers.

- Publishing: How did M.J. Rose go it alone? Learn about print-on-demand and eBooks.

- Agents/representation: Which agents represent independents? Are they worth it?

- Audio and video: Hear the latest independent audio mashups and meet the artists.

- Satellite, HD, and Internet radio: Is satellite radio Sirius? How to leverage Internet and HD radio.

- Musical instruments: Celebrate the Fender Strat with Hendrix, Zappa, and Clapton.

- Instruction: The five-minute guitar school. The five-minute piano school. Tips from pros.

- Repair: Where to get your groove back on. Self-help for do-it-yourselfers. Tips from pros.

- Computers, hardware, and software: A review of tools for audio and video editing.

- Funding: How and where to get funding for your independent media production.

- Venues, clubs, concerts, and galleries: Get your kicks—Where to see and be scene.

TIME

Don't quit your day job. You should plan on not making money for at least a year. However, because only a few hours each week are needed to start a radio program, the effort can easily start as a part-time project. You might want to start slowly with a simple podcast, Skypecast, or Internet radio show to see how you fare (see Sidebars).

Skypecasts

Founded in 2003, Skype is an Internet telephony network created by the founders of the file-sharing application Kazaa. Skype offers a wide range of services, including its own popular free and paid Internet voice (VOIP) and video conferencing programs. The Skype Group was acquired by eBay in October 2005 for $2.6 billion.

With more than one hundred million global users, Skype is a great, free way to attract more listeners to your radio show or podcast, more visitors to your website, and more readers to your blog or book. One of its features, the Skypecast, is akin to having your own personal online radio station. As host and moderator of the "show," you can talk, interview guests, play music, and take live calls from up to one hundred people.

Skypecasts are completely free to join and host. All you need is a computer, a microphone or headset, and software: Skype version 1.4 or later. The host can choose to "mute all" while speaking and can then "unmute" and invite people to speak in turn. Participants can ask questions through the "request mic" feature. The host also can mute or eject people who are being noisy or disruptive.

You can promote a Skypecast by simply cutting and pasting HTML code into blog posts or websites. Although the Skype application itself does not have recording capability, you can use third-party software to record the conversation.

For more information, visit skype.com.

Internet Radio

Internet radio is programming broadcast via the Internet. Many companies now provide easy-to-use (and sometimes free) production tools, enabling anyone with a computer and an Internet connection to create his or her own Internet radio station. This gives individuals, authors, musicians, communities, and organizations a voice that can be heard by a huge, global audience—from anywhere and at any time. Listeners—34.5 million in the United States and 49.5 million in Europe—get an unparalleled variety of globally produced programming, such as talk, music, sports, entertainment, news, and weather.

BlogTalkRadio is an all-in-one platform that integrates Internet radio with a blog, podcast, social network, and chat feature. Their site makes it simple - and free—for anyone to create and host their own live call-in talk show, with no need for expensive equipment or software downloads. Hosts can have up to five simultaneous call-in guests, and the audience can participate in the show via the live chat feature. Shows are archived and made available as podcasts so listeners can subscribe via iTunes or RSS readers. A widget allows the host to promote the show on their own blog, social network, website or other directory. Be The Media has a BlogTalkRadio program here: blogtalkradio.com/Be-The-Media..

The most popular Internet radio networks for music are Yahoo! Music (with 23 percent of the market's listeners), music.aol.com, the free Pandora (with 8.5 million registered listeners), Live365, SHOUTcast, SomaFM, and the open source Icecast. Musicians and bands can leverage Internet radio stations to promote their music to thousands of DJs and millions of new listeners. Pandora alone has 8.5 million registered users.

Live365 has more than four million listeners per month. For just $3.65 per month, Live365 lets listeners browse thousands of unique music, sports, talk, comedy, and political radio programs. Individuals can start a personal radio station for just $9.95 per month and professionals can build an Internet radio business starting at $24.95 per month. Live365 has tools to let musicians send tracks to DJs (free), create an official band or label station ($75 per month), or add tracks to its virtual record store for DJs to preview ($200 per month), in addition to artist and label promotions that offer targeted song placement opportunities (over $1,000). Live365 adheres to rules set forth in the Digital Millennium Copyright Act, so it is completely legal to create, broadcast, and listen to its stations. And according to its website, Live365 pays royalties to labels, artists, songwriters, and publishers.

On March 2, 2007, the United States Copyright Royalty Board proposed increasing royalty rates payable to performers broadcasting on the Internet from a percentage of revenue to a per-song, per-listener fee, effectively raising the rates between 300 and 1,200 percent. According to Pandora founder Tim Westergren, "If this rate does not change, it will wipe out the majority of Web radio."

This new fee only affects Internet radio, not AM or FM, because broadcast stations only pay royalties on song compositions, which are then paid to songwriters through ASCAP and BMI. In 1995 the Recording Industry Association of America pushed Congress to pass a law requiring a "performance fee" on digital music, forcing Internet radio stations to pay royalties on both composition and performance.

Many performers are opposed to the increase, arguing that the hike could threaten the business models of the Internet radio stations that give them valuable exposure. Although the performers support the digital performance royalty, they feel a one-size-fits-all rate calculation is harmful to small, hobby Webcasters who must compete with wealthier, large commercial Webcasters.

According to the Future of Music Coalition, "The new rates could mean less music and more advertising or, even worse, stations going off the air altogether because they can't afford to pay the new rates. FMC hopes that the Webcasters and SoundExchange can work together to strike a balance that recognizes the value of Webcasting to creators and listeners but also compensates artists, performers, and labels for uses of their work."

In May 2007, Senators Sam Brownback (R-KS) and Ron Wyden (D-OR) cosponsored legislation (the Internet Radio Equality Act) that would overturn the Copyright Royalty Board's decision.

For more information, visit live365.com, shoutcast.com, pandora.com, icecast. org, voiceamerica.com, futureofmusic.org, or savenetradio.org.

Satellite Radio

Satellite radio is a digital signal broadcast from a communications satellite. Satellite radio channels provide a wide variety of commercial-free talk, sports, and music programming. Subscribers require a special receiver and pay around $12.95 per month for the service.

North America has two satellite radio companies with a combined total of about 14 million subscribers. Sirius Satellite Radio has six million subscribers and XM Satellite Radio has almost eight million. By comparison, terrestrial radio has two hundred and eighty million listeners per month, while seventy two million people listen to Internet radio per month (see above), and about one hundred and forty million people own Apple iPods (see chapter 5).

To attract subscribers, satellite radio companies have inked deals to broadcast events such as Major League Baseball and NASCAR. They also are in competition to sign up famous people to gain more subscribers. For instance, Sirius will pay former broadcast radio jock Howard Stern $500 million over the life of his five-year contract. Recently, Stern was awarded an additional $300 million in Sirius stock for meeting subscriber growth goals. Oprah Winfrey and Bob Dylan are some of the marquee stars for XM.

In July 2008, Sirius acquired XM for $3.3 billion dollars. At the time of the merger, they had a combined audience of 19 million satellite customers.

For more information, visit sirius.com or xmradio.com.

This is what you need to do with those few dedicated hours a week. First, check the availability of the tentative name of your show (*Car Talk,* for instance, is taken) by registering it as a URL/domain name. If your show's name is available, there probably isn't a radio show with the same name. Second, research your potential market. If you are serious about profiting from your radio show, think of it as you would any other business. This includes preparing a detailed business plan with a thorough market analysis (see details below).

Meanwhile, get some experience; spend time working at a local community or college radio station, even as a volunteer. This provides firsthand industry knowledge and contacts with key personnel who will be valuable later. They may even give you late-night or weekend airtime to practice broadcasting live. Study the local, regional and national markets to find out which shows are popular and which stations might be interested in your personality, content, and format. Jim Hightower's liberal talk radio show did poorly when affiliates "cleared" his program on stations with the wrong audience; it was sandwiched between conservative programs. Naturally, his show does much better with affiliates that cater to liberal shows and audiences. Be sure—or as sure as you can be—that your proposed program is unique and desirable, with an easily accessible audience and potential sponsors.

The next step is to make a sample demo CD of your program and to gather all the bells and whistles (such as technical data) you have to include with it. There is no point in marketing your idea to any stations until you have at least a few solid shows in the can. If a station wants to buy your show immediately, you'll need some program samples and auxiliary information to send them.

START-UP MONEY

To get started, you probably need to invest about $2,000.

APPEARANCES COUNT

For just a few hundred dollars you can and should acquire a professional-looking logo, business cards, some marketing materials, dedicated telephone/fax lines, and a simple yet functional Internet presence. These materials and your demo CDs will act as a virtual sales team. Consider them your ambassadors to the business world. Station managers want to work with people and companies that take programming seriously. After all, they have a business to run. So don't skimp on appearance.

ALL YOU NEED IS . . . A COMPUTER

A personal computer (PC or Mac) and color printer are the main pieces of equipment you need to get started. I use a 2006 Dell PC running Windows XP Professional, with a 250 GB hard drive, 1 GB of RAM, and read/write CD and DVD drives to burn finished shows to disc. I also have a few external hard drives for storage and backup. Storage is cheap today. You can purchase a 500 GB Western Digital or Maxtor external drive for under $250. This is plenty of space to store and back up many full-length, digitized shows.

As for software, you'll need a word processor for creating marketing and promotional materials, and Pro Tools or Adobe Audition (or the free Audacity) for audio editing. I also purchased a royalty-free library comprising four CDs of sound effects for $19.95. It was well worth it, although Adobe Audition has a sound library included.

Total cost for hardware and software? Around $1,500. Later, I may opt for a CD/DVD duplicator to quickly make multiple copies of the show for distribution to affiliates and interested radio stations.

IS THIS THING ON?

The most important piece of audio equipment you will need is a quality microphone, preferably with stand and cables. You can pick up this gear at your neighborhood Radio Shack. Although high-end mikes to record music can run over $2,000, you should be prepared to spend a minimum of $100 on the microphone for your talk radio program. It is your most important investment in the quality of your finished show. Prometheus Radio Project Board member Sakura Saunders says, "It is better to have a tape recorder with a great mike than a Minidisc with a lousy one."

Other costs include soundproofing material, a stash of blank CDs, copying costs, and postage. These aren't for broadcasting your program but for marketing and selling it.

BROADCASTING LIVE! . . . FROM YOUR CLOSET

Then there is the matter of a studio. Many radio programs are created at in-home studios. Big, expensive production facilities are not required. A studio can be built in a spare bedroom or even a closet, at practically no cost. The room simply needs to be as quiet as possible. If you are using a spare room, you should cover your windows with heavy drapes. For avid readers with limited budgets, bookshelves filled with books can be used to absorb sound. I recommend using the most common sound-absorption material—two-inch-thick strips of Auralex acoustic foam—and covering all exposed walls and windows with it.

Be sure that your studio is free from audio interruptions, such as family, phones, doorbells, and barking dogs. When I lived in New York City, my main noise problems were police and fire sirens, traffic, shouts, whistles, and gunshots. Now I live on a bay where I hear birds singing and frogs belching, but even these beautiful sounds need to be edited out of a professional broadcast.

Let's say you have decided on your topic and your format, you have audioproofed your closet, you have set up your computer and microphone, and you have a guest scrunched into the closet with you, or accessible via the telephone, whom you are about to interview. Now you are ready to make your first demo.

FOUR KEYS TO PRODUCING A GREAT RADIO SHOW

1. Maintain excellent audio quality. Audio is the most important technical component of your program. It needs to be of the highest quality or people will tune out—and affiliates will not buy the program in the first place. Before making a demo or going on the air, be sure to check all your connections, wires, jacks, and microphones.

By now, you have listened carefully to other broadcasts and analyzed their audio and sound effects. Notice that you don't hear dogs barking, babies crying, or dishes being washed. Even if you are working from home, your show shouldn't sound that way. Also listen to how some popular hosts use ambient noise to sound authentic. For example, some hosts rustle the newspaper as they are reading the news, and morning drive-time talk show hosts eat breakfast during the show. This helps them come across as real people.

Today's powerful editing tools make it easy to equalize sound levels, to add special effects, theme music, intros, and outros, and to rejoin bumpers. Bumpers are five to ten seconds of distinctive music that make it clear to listeners that your show has returned from commercial breaks. During this bumper music fade-out, the host will normally welcome the audience back, mentioning the names of the host, show, and any guests on the phone or in the studio.

2. Be entertaining. With today's many distractions, you must keep your listeners' attention. Promotions, contests, on-air giveaways, call-ins, polls, quizzes, Top 10 lists, concert tie-ins, and even countdowns are a good way to keep your audience listening to your show. When Casey Kasem debuted *American Top 40* on July 4, 1970, the concept of counting down the forty biggest hits off Billboard's Hot 100 singles charts was new. No one was sure if the show would be a success. Yet by the early 1980s, the show was heard on over five hundred radio stations in the United States alone. Later, the show expanded to four hours and spawned a variety of yearend countdowns and books.

3. Be informative. People must derive value from your show or they will not come back after the break, let alone next week. Regular, informative features encourage listeners to return. Even purely entertainment-driven radio programs have some informational value, such as revealing where George Clooney eats lunch, and with whom.

4. Practice, practice, practice. Listen to the CD demos of your first few sample shows over and over and over before even attempting to go on the air. Redo them again and again. Your delivery, timing, and inflection will improve with experience.

THREE PARTS OF A GREAT SHOW

1. In the beginning. . . . You need to outline your show with a defined beginning, middle, and end—usually by using sound effects or music. Begin with a siren, foghorn, or a whisper. Anything loud—or soft—will get people's attention. Remember that each show must draw people in within the first minute. You might want to open and close with signature theme music. It should be identifiable, professional, and entertaining. Think about the memorable music of *Cheers, Seinfeld,* or *Friends.*

2. The middle: Be fully scripted. During the show, be completely scripted for a full forty-eight minutes (Why forty-eight minutes? Stay tuned.), and do dress rehearsals. The best hosts in the business may *sound* as if they are improvising, but rest assured, they have an outline of the show prepared well in advance. Many hosts hire professional writers and journalists or have comedians join them to add sparkle to their programs. Some hosts use "cheat sheets" and showprep (material pre-prepared for the show) to stay focused and on target. Most importantly, you need to tell a great story, provide a unique perspective, and push the envelope. Basically, you must be *different.*

3. Finally, have a strong close. Be sure to have an intriguing close that will entice people to tune in again next week. After the threat of a large indecency fine from the Federal Communications Commission (FCC), Howard Stern told his audience that his final show was imminent. His ratings shot up! Why? People tuned in because they wanted to hear his "last" broadcast.

The beginning, middle, and end are just rough guides for the listener, though. For the broadcast technicians at the affiliate station, for the affiliate, and for the FCC, you need to be much more exact. You need to work in specific segments, counted to the second, as the table and charts below will demonstrate.

SHOW SEGMENTS

For a one-hour broadcast, a typical run time will be about 47:50, calculated as sixty minutes minus twelve minutes of commercials and a ten-second FCC-mandated identification break at 59:50. This identification break must be taken each hour at every U.S. station, whether it is commercial or noncommercial. For commercial stations, standard commercial time allotted per program hour is twelve minutes. For the example that follows, I want to hit each commercial break at twenty minutes, forty minutes, and fifty minutes past the hour. Approximately 60 percent of talk-format stations play news at the top of the hour, for about six minutes. Then comes two seconds of complete silence to alert the board operator (or computer, if the station is automated) to bring in commercials.

Let us say that our *Be the Media* show will offer two opens (one open for the 60 percent of stations that play top-of-the-hour news, one open for the 40 percent of stations that do not), three segments, and a close, as follows:

SEGMENT	TIME
SHOW OPEN 1: Theme music. Why listeners should stay tuned.	6:00
SHOW OPEN 2: Theme music. Why stay tuned? Introduction to Segment 1.	2:00
SEGMENT 1: News, events, clubs, venues, acts.	14:00
SEGMENT 2: Main interview.	16:00
SEGMENT 3: Equipment, instruction, repairs, tips.	6:00
COMING ATTRACTIONS: Why listeners should tune in next time.	3:00
SHOW CLOSE. Theme music fade to show close.	1:30 to 3:00
TOTAL	48:30

THE PROGRAM CLOCK

The program clock is a simple diagram used by every station to define a programming hour. It enables control board operators at the local radio affiliate to understand any show in virtually one glance. You can plot the information above onto the clock using a word processor, a graphics program, or by hand. See the clock with added details, in figure 1.

The board operator must pay attention to the timing of the show, so these terms are very technical and precise. Here is a translation of what the clock figure tells the board operator at the station.

ELEMENT	INDICATES
0:02 pause	Two seconds of complete silence. This is an identifier so that the control board operator can lower station volume and bring in commercials.
0:02 sting out	A two-second-long distinct sound or tone that indicates you are entering commercials.
0:10 fade-in to rejoin	Allows the station to identify itself. Must always be ten seconds.
Network 2:00	The two-minute commercial spots you sold to your sponsors—your compensation. (More about that farther along.)
Local 2:00	The two-minute commercial spots the local station sells to sponsors—its compensation. (More about that farther along, too.)
Music out	The bed of music that closes the show and tells the DJ at the local station that they should enter into commercials. The music bed should be long enough to cover gaps.
Name of show and producer	Include on the page of the program clock your phone, fax, e-mail, and mailing address in case the station has any problems with the show, or if a listener wants to contact you.
Hard out at 29:00 and 59:50	Stations in the United States air an identification at twenty-nine minutes after the hour, and all stations are required to air a legal identification at 59:50, so you must keep this time reserved.
All other breaks float	This alerts the board operator that commercials can come at any time after the sting. In other words, the sting indicates an upcoming commercial.
Relay 0 and Relay 1	Indicates there will be distinct tones indicating local versus network commercial breaks.
Due to time constraints	Indicates the show schedule is flexible and subject to change.

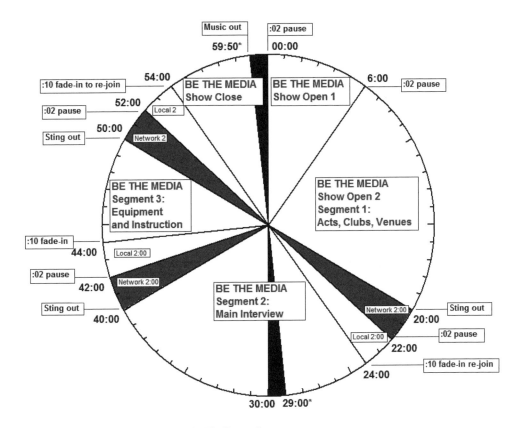

Figure 1: Sample program clock for *Be the Media,* with added details.

MARKETING YOUR PROGRAM WITH AN INFO KIT

Let's say that your program clock is in order, that you like what you hear of yourself and your guests so far on your sample CD, and that you have several more shows ready to go and ideas for years. The next step is to find someone to put your show on the air. In other words, it's time to go to market.

The best way to promote your show is through the use of "info kits." Info kits, which you will make yourself at this stage, are your virtual sales team. Each kit should include a one sheet (see below), a sample demo CD (not a whole show), your bio/résumé, and press clippings or reviews from previous endeavors, all placed in the right-hand pocket of a high-quality folder. In the left-hand pocket, you have placed a cover letter addressed to the program director (by name) and have inserted your business card in the tab. Make sure the kits look professional. Again, don't skimp on quality.

THE ONE SHEET

The one sheet is a single page that will be your show's main selling tool. It should contain the following elements: a description of the show's contents; technical details, including how and when you'll deliver the shows you are creating; and your full contact information. It should grab the reader's attention, be informative yet easy to read, and enable the station to contact you to get more information or to order the show. Put it on your website (see figure 2). You do have a website, don't you? (See chapter 9.)

THE DEMO CD

The demo CD is your virtual salesperson. It is a "best of" that provides samples of your program. Never include a full show. The demo should be no longer than five minutes of several of your show's best bits and clips. Include on the CD your own verbal description of the show, then samples of it, a brief explanation of the segments and features, theme music, thirty-second edits from each of the features mentioned, and the close. End the disc with the show's format, availability, and your contact information. Periodically change the disc's content, because new shows may provide better samples.

Make at least fifty copies of your info kit and demo CDs to have available for potential affiliates. These days, you can also point interested affiliates to the electronic version of the kit on your website.

WHICH STATIONS SHOULD YOU TARGET?

Research and approach local, small-market stations first, or stations where you may have personal contacts. Do your homework—check the station's format and lineup of shows and see where yours might fit in. Check trade publications such as *Radio Ink* and *Current* to see which

BE THE MEDIA
America's First Radio Program for Independent Media
~ Where the Audience Makes the Show ~

Be The Media is a one-hour, weekly radio program about local independent media. It features:

- **Celebrity Interviews:**
    Robert Greenwald, Craig Newmark, Douglas Rushkoff, Doc Searls
- **Tips From The Pros — And The Audience:**
    Tips from authors, filmmakers, cartoonists, producers, musicians, artists
- **Recording, Production, and Print Facilities:**
    Where to make independent media — cheaply!
- **Independent Distributors, Venues, Outlets, and Galleries:**
    How to get your creations to market — where to see and be scene
- **Independent Labels:**
    The best artist-friendly labels around town
- **Equipment And Instruments:**
    Reviews of digital video cameras, audio tools, equipment, instruments
- **Hardware And Software:**
    Reviews of Macs, iPods, PCs, scanners, Adobe Premiere, Photoshop, Final Cut
- **Independent Media Instruction:**
    The 5-Minute Film School, The 5 Minute Piano and Guitar Schools

Affiliates get the following:
- A one-hour, weekly show, complete with 25-35 Hz sting tones.
- Free weekly delivery on CD or cassette or digitally via Satellite or the Internet.
- Six minutes of local advertising time to sell. 100% barter.
- Large, interactive, up-scale audience with tremendous purchasing power.

For demo CD and information package, fax the following to **(800) BE-MEDIA**:

Name _____

Radio Station _____

Address _____

_____

City _____ Zip _____

Phone _____

Fax _____

Figure 2

programs are being picked up or canceled, and what stations are looking for in each of their day-parts. New hourly programs are usually introduced in weekend or overnight dayparts to gauge audience response.

WHICH PEOPLE (IN THE STATIONS) SHOULD YOU TARGET?

To begin your marketing campaign, target the program director at small-market stations that have formats fitting your show's profile. At small stations, the program director has the authority to sign new shows and to cancel existing ones. It is important to contact the program director directly and by name. Never send an info kit to "Anonymous," or worse, using the wrong person's name. That kit will be discarded. Radio station personnel move around a lot, from territory to territory, and from small to medium to large markets as they gain experience.

At larger stations, there is more hierarchy. At midsized stations, the program director may report to an operations manager, who runs the daily operation of the station. At large stations, the operations manager reports to the general manager, who focuses more on the sales aspects of the station.

JUST THE FAX, MA'AM—AND E-MAIL

Save money and time. Don't mail the entire info kit to every station you know about. You will need to contact some stations repeatedly before they respond to say whether they even want to look at a kit. Many stations will probably throw the kits away if they arrive unsolicited.

Instead, first do the market research, identify appropriate stations, and then fax or e-mail the one sheet (or the URL of the one sheet on your website) to the attention of the program director. If, after a few weeks, there is no response from the program director, try the operations manager, then the general manager. Still no response? Try the sales department. If someone there expresses interest, mail the full kit with demo CD to the attention of the respondent. Follow up a few days later with a phone call to close the sale. Be persistent. It may be a good idea to offer market exclusivity, meaning that you agree not to air your show at another station in your potential affiliate's listening area.

BUYING TIME—ANOTHER WAY TO CLOSE YOUR FIRST STATION

Avoid the Catch-22. Few stations will want to broadcast a show that is not already on the air. An alternative way to get your first station is to buy what's called brokered time. Yes, you pay to put your own show on somebody's radio station.

This is how that works: You call the sales managers from your list of local stations to learn their rates. An hour of weekend airtime in most small and medium markets is just a few hundred dollars, and even this is highly negotiable. After a few calls, you will have learned competitive rates to lock in the best deal. Compare prices for weekdays, evenings, weekends, and overnights, which are always the cheapest. Note that winter and summer offer better bargains than spring and fall. Then swallow hard and write the check. Now, because you own the time, you can make money by selling commercials within the show to advertisers.

CLOSING THE DEAL

Congratulations on getting your first affiliate! Even if you bought the time slot to put your show on the air in the first place, your listeners can't tell the difference. They think you are a professional broadcaster; after all, they hear your voice coming out of their radio. The next step is to sign a contract, one that locks the affiliate into broadcasting your show and that stipulates what, how, and when you need to deliver the program. There are standard, boilerplate contracts out there, but at this stage I recommend having an experienced attorney review the contract. Be sure to define the start date (as soon as possible), term (aim for one year), and cancellation terms (aim for ninety days minimum, in writing).

After the contract has been signed, mail the station a new affiliate welcome kit that comprises the show's program clock, a welcome letter from you to the new affiliate, contact information, trouble-shooting guide, and the first program on CD.

BUILDING AN AFFILIATE NETWORK IS EASY—SORT OF

With your first station as a reference, even before your program has aired, continue targeting small-market stations. Set a goal to fax or e-mail 10 one sheets per day to the desired stations. Remember that people move around a lot and stations regularly change formats and ownership. So send to the program director first. Then, if you have not received a response, send to the operations manager, then the general manager, and then sales. At this point, you should be getting responses and possibly have a few active affiliates.

Work with small-market groups for at least a year before approaching the midmarket groups. As your midmarket affiliates grow, you can start to target the major-market stations. This is the big time, and of course, extremely competitive. You might consider buying or brokering time on a flagship large-market station. Avoid large-market stations that have existing syndication feeds and ownership groups that bring feeds with them, such as Clear Channel and Viacom. These groups are very difficult for new shows to break into, because they already have programming and it is hard to get them to switch.

MEDIA OWNERSHIP CONCENTRATION

The passage of the Telecommunications Act in 1996 led to an unprecedented concentration of radio station ownership. Fewer owners means fewer independent stations to buy your program. Before 1996, no single radio owner was allowed to own more than forty stations (twenty AM and twenty FM). Since 1996, however, Clear Channel Communications alone at one point owned more than 1,200 stations. They fired "redundant" employees, disc jockeys, hosts, and program directors, and some observers say they gutted localism by piping in canned content from remote locations or their own syndicates.

For example, Clear Channel owns Premiere Radio Networks, which syndicates programming to over five thousand radio stations worldwide, including conservatives Rush Limbaugh and Glenn Beck. Viacom/CBS owns Westwood One Inc., which syndicates more than one hundred and fifty radio programs to over 7,700 U.S. stations. Its stable includes Bill O'Reilly's "The Radio Factor,"[1] and Don Imus, who famously was fired in April 2007 for making a racist, sexist comment on the air about members of a women's college basketball team. The termination of Imus, who was carried on sixty-one CBS affiliates, will cost CBS $15 million in lost annual advertising and syndication revenue. Imus was hired by CBS rival Citadel Broadcasting just eight months after being fired.

Conservative talk dominates the daytime talk radio airwaves. A June 2007 report from FreePress.net, titled "The Structural Imbalance of Political Talk Radio," found that 91 percent of weekday talk radio programming is conservative and just 9 percent progressive. The report stated: "Ownership diversity is perhaps the single most important variable contributing to the structural imbalance. Quantitative analysis of all 10,506 licensed commercial radio stations reveals that stations owned by women, minorities, or local owners are statistically *less* likely to air conservative hosts or shows." (For more, see chapter 22.)

DISTRIBUTING YOUR PROGRAM TO AFFILIATES

Be sure to distribute your show to affiliates in a professional and timely manner. The most expedient method is to send it as audio files over the Internet. This costs virtually nothing and involves fewer distribution and administrative hassles for you (the producer) and your affiliates. The simplest way to send a program via the Internet is to point potential affiliates to your website, where they can archive downloadable versions of your shows.

Alternatively, you can mail each CD first class (under $1), to arrive at least three days prior to the broadcast date. Put yourself on the mailing list to see how long delivery takes, and what the package will look like when it arrives. Alternatively, use a local tape/CD/DVD duplicator that will copy and mail the show for a nominal fee. It costs more than doing it alone, but it may be worthwhile, depending on the number of affiliates. Remember, though, the way to end worries about a lost or malfunctioning CD, or postage or delivery mishaps, is to use the Internet.

---

1. O'Reilly condoned a terrorist strike on San Francisco's Coit Tower, a monument to fallen firefighters (bethemedia.org/2005/11/san_francisco_t.html). Indiana University media researchers found that "O'Reilly called a person or a group a derogatory name once every 6.8 seconds, on average, or nearly nine times every minute during the editorials that open his program each night," and that "O'Reilly employed six of the seven propaganda devices 13 times each minute in his editorials." (newsinfo.iu.edu/news/page/normal/5535.html).

If you should you get sick or need to take a vacation, don't bother the stations with details. They just want to receive a professional show, on time, every week. Have a few extra shows on hand (or send a repeat, if you and the stations have agreed to that), in case you need some time off.

AFFILIATE RELATIONS: SERVICE, SERVICE, SERVICE

Solid affiliate relations start with maintaining dedicated, high-quality service. Affiliates are lost for many reasons: change of ownership, format, management, or personnel; lack of sponsorship; complaints. Some of these can be helped, some can't. The best way to keep a show on the air is to have listeners tell the station how much they love it. (Sure, have your friends call in.) Actively solicit regular feedback by making occasional visits to the station to meet the executive and operational team, and visit with local advertisers and sponsors. Keep in touch. The program director for your small-market affiliate may some day take over a large-market station and might want to pick up your show at his or her new, bigger location.

THE MONEY PART—SMALL CHANGE

After you have your show on the air, you can start earning some money. There are a few ways to make money in radio. One is to get paid cash for a show, but this is very rare and usually only applies to work-for-hire people at a syndication company.

Another option is through "per-inquiry" ads. These involve companies that provide prerecorded, professional-sounding advertisements for various services such as life insurance and real estate. You simply sign up to use this service and then run the company's ad inventory during your program. For every call that comes into their switchboard from your listeners, the company pays you a fee. The ads make your show sound professional, but you certainly won't get rich this way.

You might want to repurpose the shows. This means taking some of the content and reworking it into audio clips that can be downloaded or put on CD, perhaps to use as teleclasses, seminars, or training. Another way to make money is to sell show-related merchandise such as branded T-shirts, mouse pads, coffee mugs, or copies of past shows and books. However, this is all small change when compared to barter.

BARTER ADVERTISING: THE ROAD TO RICHES

The exchange of ad minutes for programming is called barter. Barter advertising is commercial radio's road to riches. Radio stations get almost all syndicated shows for free, in exchange for broadcasting the show in its entirety, including advertisements—its own and yours. Leveraging barter and syndication, you could end up owning many minutes on lots of different radio stations. Depending on the number of affiliates you have (and their audience size), this can be extremely valuable. For example, Rush Limbaugh makes over $20 million per year due to his control over this advertising time.

As we saw in the previous section, for an hour-long program, the affiliate station will have six minutes of local time to sell. You will usually own the same amount of network advertising time to sell.

Even though the affiliate and not you will be getting local ad income from its six minutes does not mean you just stand by. You can help the station's sales department by identifying a sample list of potential local sponsors who might be interested in reaching your audience. For *Be the Media,* these sponsors might include photo developers, concert venues, or stores that sell music, computers, or audio/video equipment (see figure 3).

HOW TO SELL YOUR SHOW TO NETWORK SPONSORS

Syndication sales firms—that is, firms that deal with "network" ad sales—won't represent shows with fewer than fifty affiliates, the point at which they can viably sell commercials in the national spot market. Until then, it's up to you to get your own sponsors. Network sponsors for *Be the Media* might include photo companies like Kodak, instrument makers like Casio, software providers like Adobe, computer manufacturers like Intel, video camera producers like Sony, cell phone providers like Nokia, or home electronics manufacturers like Phillips.

Before calling potential advertisers, you should have landed (or paid for) at least a few affiliates and should have a decent audience estimate. Call the target company, like Kodak, and ask for the person in charge of national advertising. First, though, rehearse your sales pitch before trying it out on a new advertiser. Prepare answers to standard questions such as "Why should we sponsor your show?", "How many listeners do you have?", and "What affiliates air the show, where, and when?"

Be professional, courteous, convincing, and persistent. If the people with the advertising dollars indicate interest, send them a complete sponsor kit with a cover letter, a one sheet with audience size, a list of affiliates and advertising rates, a program clock, and a demo CD (see figure 4).

Stations must sign a certificate to prove that they have played your program in its entirety, including advertisements. This is called a certificate of performance (see figure 5).

BE THE MEDIA
~ Where the Audience Makes the Show ~
POTENTIAL LOCAL SPONSORS

Agents/Representation	Music Halls/Venues
Art Supply Stores	Photographic Equipment/Supplies
Art Galleries	Photo Developing
Audio Stores	Phone Companies
Audio-Visual Equipment	Printers/Copiers
Accountants/Attorneys/CPAs	Publishers
Computer Resellers	Radio/Stereo/TV Stores
Computer Manufacturers	Radio Equipment/Supplies
Computer Repair Stores	Recording Studios
Computer Training	Restaurants
Concert Halls	Satellite TV Systems
Education	Software Providers and Resellers
Electrical Equipment/Supplies	Sound Systems/Equipment
Graphic Designers	Stationery Stores
Hardware Stores	Television Dealers/Service
Home Theater Manufacturers	Telecommunications Dealers/Service
Independent Bookstores	Theatrical Venues
Internet Service Providers	Theatrical Equipment
Instrument Resellers	Ticket Sales/Services
Instrument Tuning/Repair	Trade Shows/Expositions/Fairs
Instrument Manufacturers	Video Stores/Rentals
Movie Theaters	Video Production Services
Motion Picture Production/Studios	Video Equipment/Dealers
Music Stores and Schools	Video Tape Editing

Figure 3

BE THE MEDIA
~ Where the Audience Makes the Show ~

Current Estimated Listeners: 5,250,300

Be The Media is a one-hour, weekly radio program about local media. It features:

- **Celebrity Interviews:**
  Robert Greenwald, Craig Newmark, Douglas Rushkoff, Doc Searls
- **Tips from the Pros—and the Audience:**
  Tips from authors, filmmakers, cartoonists, producers, musicians, and artists
- **Recording, Production, and Print Facilities:**
  Where to make independent media—cheap!
- **Independent Distributors, Venues, Outlets, and Galleries:**
  How to get your creations to market—where to see and "be scene"
- **Independent Labels:**
  The best artist-friendly labels in town
- **Equipment and Instruments:**
  Reviews of digital video cameras, audio tools, equipment, and instruments
- **Hardware and Software:**
  Reviews of Macs, PCs, iPods, scanners, Premiere, Photoshop, and Final Cut

Current Affiliates Include:

WTFL Tampa, FL, WHEM Hempstead NY, KEUR Eureka CA, WMIN Minneapolis MN, KMAD Madison WI, WNEW New Orleans LA

Rate Card:
- **Package One: Media Gold $2,000**
- One 60-second commercial
- One segment sponsorship
- Three-month commitment
- **Package Two: Media Platinum $2,500**
- Two 60-second commercials
- Two segment sponsorships
- Three-month commitment

Figure 4

BE THE MEDIA
Certificate of Performance
For the Month of _____/_____

NATIONAL SPOTS AIRED WITHIN THE PROGRAM:

	DATE	TIME	A.M./P.M.
1) :30 Adobe :30 Kodak	_____	_____	_____
2) :30 Yamaha :30 Steinway	_____	_____	_____
3) :30 Intel :30 Sony	_____	_____	_____
4) :30 Gateway :30 AT&T	_____	_____	_____
5) :30 Phillips :30 Apple	_____	_____	_____
6) :30 Nokia :30 Fujitsu	_____	_____	_____

I hereby acknowledge and attest that the above national commercial spots aired unedited in the Be The Media show on the dates and times indicated.

Authorized Signature _____
Print Name _____
Station Call Letters/Date _____/_____
Please return this form by _____/_____/_____ (date)

Figure 5

DOING THE MATH

The revenue from bartered advertising time on a syndicated show is based on audience size. In 1999, advertisers spent over $1 billion on nationally syndicated radio advertisements. The formula used to calculate the value of these ads is called cost per point, or CPP. The cost is what advertisers pay, and the point is the show's audience size—one point equals 1 percent of the U.S. population. For example, in 2000 the CPP was $3,000, meaning that advertisers were willing to pay $3,000 for a one-time, thirty-second ad that reached 1 percent of the U.S. population. A show with a 4.0 audience share, like Rush Limbaugh's, means that advertisers are willing to pay $12,000 for a thirty-second ad.

THE ROAD TO RICHES

How can we make our $2,000 investment in a radio program called *Be the Media* worth millions? In a typical division, we give the local station six minutes of ad time in our hour-long show to sell to its sponsors, and we control the other six minutes. Let's assume that we have successfully sold the show to fifty stations, mostly small-market stations but including a couple of midmarket stations, too. Our audience reaches just one tenth of 1 percent of the U.S. national radio audience— the bottom rung of the syndication sales ladder. Take the CPP of $3,000 for a thirty-second ad, divide by ten, and we can charge $300 per thirty-second spot. Multiply $300 by twelve spots (six minutes total) and we will gross $3,600 each week. Multiply $3,600 by fifty-two weeks per year and we can gross up to $188,000 for a one-hour weekly show.

The more stations that air our show, the more money we can potentially earn. As our audience grows, our income grows. If the audience doubles from a 0.1 share to a 0.2 share, our gross income doubles to $376,000. Grow ten times, from a 0.1 to a 1.0 share, and that $188,000 per year becomes $1.8 million.

That is not bad for an upfront cost of $2,000 and a few hours of work each week.

"A hero is no braver than an ordinary person,
but he is braver five minutes longer."
—*Ralph Waldo Emerson*

7

VIDEO

THE VIDEO REVOLUTION

David Mathison

"Television is for appearing on—not for looking at."
—Noel Coward

In little more than five years, the choke hold that the corporate media have had on us, whether we're a video producer or a viewer, has been obliterated.

The people who ruled what we saw and heard, such as broadcast and cable TV executives, film studio heads, theater owners, resellers, and distributors, among others, formerly determined exactly what video content was created, who created it and how, and when and where any of it was distributed.

Oh, and—surprise!—they more or less also got the lion's share of the revenues.

Within a short period of time, all that has changed. Low-cost digital tools now enable almost anyone to create high-quality video. And thanks to the Internet and high-speed broadband connections, the choke hold over distribution has been removed from our collective throats.

Populist Web-savvy inventors, which we'll get to in a bit, and business renegades such as YouTube, Apple, and Brightcove, among others, helped bust through the old ways of doing things. A new wave of millions upon millions of individuals—viewers, creators, or both in one—took up the charge, relished the new freedom they found, and helped spark this video revolution.

If you have not yet joined in, but want to, and if you want to reap the audiences and possibly revenues that follow, then this chapter is especially for you. You'll find the how-to's are really easy.

But first, a little background on how this came about, for what is freedom without context?

BEFORE THE REVOLUTION

Of all the forms of media, video used to be the most challenging and expensive form there was to produce and distribute. Now video is, or *can* be, one of the simplest and least expensive.

A person witnessing a disaster like the train bombings in London with no more than a mobile phone as a camera can record video one minute, upload the video to YouTube the next, and in five minutes attract millions of global viewers. Make that *tens* of millions. The current YouTube video champ is motivational speaker Judson Laipply from Cleveland. His six-minute video, "Evolution of Dance," has been watched more than eighty million times.

Those numbers have been, well, inspiring. Bands are now using YouTube as the "new" MTV to promote their songs. Pop singer Avril Lavigne's music video of her song "Girlfriend" is in second place, with seventy-six million views, followed by two music videos from the band My Chemical Romance, "Famous Last Words" (fifty million views) and "Teenagers" (forty-five million). Another widely known example of an extensively watched music video is OK Go's "Treadmill Dance," showing the Chicago band dancing over eight moving treadmills to the song "Here It Goes Again": thirty-five million views.

This popularity can be translated into financial success. The rock band called "Panic! At the Disco" won over a huge fan base and even got a record deal after one of its music videos on YouTube was viewed five million times. Los Angeles-based Terra Naomi went from struggling singer-songwriter to being signed by Island Records, all a result of her YouTube exposure.

FACING (BEYOND) THE MUSIC

The higher rungs on the media ladder—that is, film and television—have long been, and in ways still are, extremely costly propositions. A studio movie, for example, on average costs nearly $100 million. Such huge expenses require a big box office opening for a film to be considered a "success," even leaving aside the matter of studio "creative accounting." Few titles ever receive theatrical distribution, so to generate more revenue quickly while cutting down on piracy, many films are now opening simultaneously in theaters, on home video/DVD, over cable TV, on pay-per-view, on airplanes, on-demand, via downloads over the Internet, and even on mobile phones. But it is still difficult for independent films to secure retail shelf space and be exposed to interested eyes. More than a third of all DVDs are sold at Wal-Mart, which is stocked almost exclusively with titles from the major studios.

Television in its heyday was no better. Network executives generally did not accept unsolicited pitches from unknown producers. Independent producers needed an agent, connections, experience, a track record, and lots of luck. Shows needed to appeal to millions of people to recoup production costs and satisfy sponsors. In recent years, however, younger audiences and the advertisers who cater to them have been leaving to spend more time on the Internet, on social networks like MySpace, on video-sharing sites such as YouTube, on Apple's iTunes directory, and on video iPods.

And for the parent who simply wanted to record and broadcast a baby's first words and send the video to eager grandparents, or for activists who wanted to tape and broadcast a speech, conference, or rally, such video files were too bulky to e-mail. The advent of DVDs improved distribution, but costs for discs, envelopes, and postage limited widespread dissemination.

That was yesterday, though, and yesterday's gone. Today, the means of video production and distribution is literally in your hands.

VIDEO POWER TO THE PEOPLE

A major change in the motion picture landscape was the introduction of inexpensive, high-quality recording devices such as digital cameras, webcams (small cameras, typically for video only), and millions of video-enabled cell phones. They are now ubiquitous, creating what *Time* magazine called "a culture of Zapruders," a reference to the man who filmed the assassination of President John F. Kennedy. *Time* offered as evidence the camera phone that caught *Seinfeld* actor Michael Richards at a comedy club "spewing racial slurs at African-American hecklers."

Today's video producers, whether pros or amateurs, don't need millions or even thousands of dollars worth of video, audio, editing, and production equipment. Nor do they need to know about standards, encoders, decoders, bit rates, compression, editing, hosting, storage, display, or formats.

Video producers do, however, need to know about distribution, and, in particular, need to know that it is now easier than ever. Distribution had been the final frontier. Distributing a video is now more significant than making it, whether it's of a garage band, a cottage for sale, a boffo speech to an alumni association, or a bowling team's most embarrassing moments. Yes, it has come to this: Today, Now anyone can create his or her own video distribution network; so when you update your business card you can call yourself a "video producer."

You record what you want to, then upload the results to your website, a blog, or a video-sharing site like YouTube or blip.tv. Exposure can be instantaneous and global. If people fail to salute or get excited about your work, you, the videographer, move on, all without much risk, without losing a big investment, without sticking around for the ratings. Because costs are low, you and other producers can afford to create niche channels focused on topics like hiking, surfing, sailing, or the latest cooking or exercise craze, which don't require large audiences for advertisers. As Dan Myrick, codirector of *The Blair Witch Project,* which became an overnight movie sensation, said in a *New York Times* interview about his Internet TV series, called *The Strand: Venice, CA,* "We can get by with 100,000 subscribers. Networks are canceling shows on 3 million viewers."

Today, even the TV networks are using this model as a low-cost pilot system, testing out short, low budget, online video serials such as *Duder, The Burg,* and *Floaters.*

A record ten billion videos were viewed online by more than 141 million Americans in December 2007 alone, according to research firm comScore. This brave new world of video distribution has been enabled by increased broadband speeds, home and office networks, portable video players, and devices that attach televisions, or stream TV feeds, to Internet-connected computers, laptops, or smart phones (Sling Media and Akimbo are two companies that make them).

So now there is no need to get a movie into theaters, Blockbuster, or Wal-Mart. No need to beg a corporate suit to put your TV program, or even an entire channel, onto a broadcast or cable network. No need to buy and burn DVDs, or pay for envelopes and postage.

The cost of distribution is now *zero.*

The implications of this are well-understood by the people who create the films and TV shows: the writers. In November 2007, the Writers Guild of America, a labor union representing some thirteen thousand writers in the film, television, and radio industries, went on strike against the Alliance of Motion Picture and Television Producers (AMPTP).

The writers demanded residuals for programs streamed or downloaded over the Internet. Currently, writers get nothing for these uses. The writers requested a residual of eight cents per DVD, up from the current four cents. AMPTP refused the increase. According to Jennifer Pozner of Women in Media and News, "It's the height of nickel and diming. They're not even asking for a dime, and they don't want to give them a nickel." According to National Public Radio, the strike cost the economy of Los Angeles $1.5 billion.

Before we go to the how of producing and releasing your own video, though, let's explore the who and the why a bit more.

WHO USES VIDEO, AND WHY?

Ask yourself why you use video in your own life. The reasons are endless. You do so not just to showcase your piano-playing kitten or skateboarding dog or cute new gurgling baby. Video can be virtually all things to almost all people. For example, motivational speakers can get their message out, or pundits gunning for exposure can show conference planners and TV producers how they look and sound and smile. Musicians can promote their music videos to potential and actual fans, as well as communicate with them from the road. Authors can discuss their book, interview guests, and take Q&A from audiences and readers. Filmmakers can show trailers and excerpts from their film, or interviews with various participants, such as the director and the stars. Students can subscribe to videos of seminars, and teachers can post video homework and assignments for remote viewing by homebound students or those studying at night. Real estate agents can give impressive, virtual video tours of residential or commercial properties. Businesses can air video testimonials from satisfied customers or celebrity endorsers, or infomercials to showcase their products to a global audience.

And, finally, family members can create video greeting cards, such as scenes from weddings, announcements of births, and, of course, baby's first words, which well may be "My mommy's a video producer!"

THE AUDIENCE TAKES CONTROL

Audiences now control what, when, how, and where they watch. Because the viewers use a host of digital platforms, such as mobile devices, YouTube, Xboxes, and PlayStations, successful distribution requires producers to think "outside the box" (office).

Thanks to flexible time-shifting devices such as VHS taping and personal video recorders like TiVo, audiences are no longer confined by program slots chosen by corporate decision-makers. With millions of programming choices, the online TV lineup looks more like a Google search than *TV Guide*. The concept of channels, networks, and even "prime time" disappears. Who cares what network, channel, or time a show is on, or who sponsored it? And, thanks to video iPods, smart phones, and devices from companies like Sling Media, members of the audience are no longer tethered to the TV or movie theater. They can placeshift, meaning watch downloaded video clips anywhere in the world, while commuting on the train, flying to the other side of the globe, pedaling at the gym, or even sitting by the pool at home.

How in the world did the world of online video change so radically? Here's a brief timeline.

1995: GETTING REAL

Apple's QuickTime was released in December 1991, with Microsoft delivering its competing product, Video for Windows, a year later, in November 1992. In April 1995, Progressive Networks (renamed RealNetworks in 1997) was founded by ex-Microsoft executive Rob Glaser, whose aim was to provide distribution for politically progressive content. His company created the RealAudio and RealVideo compressed audio and video formats, which enabled producers to stream rich media, meaning audio or video or both, to audiences through the Internet. Viewers used the free RealPlayer media player application to listen and watch. However, production remained limited to deep-pocketed organizations that could afford the cost of hosting the files, buying Real's software, and hiring the technical experts required for installation and deployment.

1999: NAPSTER

In 1999, Shawn Fanning's Napster truly democratized rich media distribution. Napster was a file-sharing service that offered a searchable catalog of content, enabling users to find, retrieve, and share their own and others' media, notably audio and images. At its peak in early 2001, Napster had over 24 million users. But because users could obtain songs without paying royalties to the copyright holder, guess what? Record labels and the Recording Industry Association of America sued. In 2001, they won. The Ninth Circuit Court ruled that Napster could not trade copyrighted content on its network. Many independents argued that Napster was an important promotional tool for artists who lacked the backing of major labels, but nevertheless in 2002 Napster was forced to liquidate its assets under U.S. bankruptcy law. Later, the company Roxio Inc. bought the Napster brand and reintroduced Napster as Napster 2.0, this time, to sell *legal* content.

2002: BITTORRENT

In 2002, Bram Cohen launched the BitTorrent peer-to-peer file-sharing communications protocol. (For nontechies: A protocol is a set of rules enabling communications between systems, such as HTTP, or Hypertext Transfer Protocol, which Web browsers such as Firefox use to transfer information over the World Wide Web). Cohen's BitTorrent enables users to distribute very large files such as music, audio, video, images, software, and games, without incurring the associated costs for hardware, hosting, and bandwidth. By 2003, CacheLogic estimated that BitTorrent accounted for up to 35 percent of all Internet traffic; as of this writing, it accounts for 60 percent. And in June 2004, for the first time, the volume of video traffic on the Internet surpassed that of audio traffic.

What made BitTorrent so special? By comparison, serving up video the "old," pre-BitTorrent way would translate into huge expenses, due to increased equipment and bandwidth requirements. For example, in October 2004, in the heat of the U.S. presidential election, over seventy million people watched the Jib Jab animation of candidates John Kerry and George Bush singing the Woody Guthrie song *This Land Is Your Land*. "Swarming," or a rapid and large collection of viewers, resulted, and the video's popularity quickly became its downfall. Jib Jab faced an enormous bill from its Internet service provider for hosting the popular file.

With BitTorrent, by contrast, popularity is a virtue; the more popular a large audio or video clip is, the faster, easier, and cheaper that it can be downloaded. BitTorrent spreads the task of downloading the file across the entire network of people who want it. The key, according to the company's website, is cooperation among BitTorrent users. "Cooperative distribution can grow almost without limit, because each new participant brings not only demand, but also supply. Popularity creates a virtuous circle . . . there is limitless scalability for a nearly fixed cost."

In his May 2004 article "Redefining Television," Mark Pesce, author, researcher, teacher, and co-inventor of the Virtual Reality Modeling Language (VRML), argued that because anyone with a digital video recorder such as TiVo, a computer, a BitTorrent client, and a broadband Internet connection can now be a "broadcaster," the mass media are finished, done, dead as a doornail. "I'm not telling you broadcasting is *going* to be obsolete. I'm telling you that it's *already* obsolete," he wrote.

A year later, in his piece titled "The Audience Takes Control," Pesce added, "With BitTorrent, the audience has taken control of distribution. The days of the mass media, as we have understood them, are already over. Through behavioral and commercial inertia, they will continue to exist, in some form, for several more years."

BitTorrent users can upload and download not only their *own* content, but *licensed* content as well, including TV shows, films, and music, or episodes of *The Sopranos,* or the latest *Star Wars* film. Not wanting to repeat the Napster debacle and get sued out of existence, in February 2007 BitTorrent introduced a legal video service to the 150 million who use the BitTorrent clients. The bittorrent.com site is now a popular destination where users can buy video from a catalog of licensed films from major studios and network TV shows, as well as music, games, and even software.

Try BitTorrent yourself by downloading its free client software. It is offered in several versions, distributed by a number of different groups and companies, and runs on a variety of computer operating systems:

- vuze.com

- BitTorrent, bittorrent.com/download (Windows, Mac OS X, Linux)

- Miro, getmiro.com

2004: VIDEOBLOGS

The next stage of the revolution occurred in 2004, with the introduction of videoblogs, sometimes called vlogs, which is more fun to say.

A videoblog is, well, a blog (see chapter 1) with video as the main content. The video usually is accompanied by graphics, text, and metadata, or data about data. For a video clip, metadata might include the producer's web site URL, the title of the clip, date, author, director, and episode number. It is important for creators to include metadata, so that when the video is distributed across the Internet, viewers can find out who created it and how to get in touch.

Videoblogs are like podcasts, in that viewers can subscribe to them, and can have new shows automatically delivered to their computer or transferred to a portable player, such as a video iPod.

On January 1, 2004, blogger and video producer Steve Garfield created his first videoblog, after making a new years resolution to figure out how to put video on a blog. Later that year, Jay Dedman left a comment on one of Steve's videoblog posts, alerting Steve to the Yahoo videoblog group.

Jay Dedman was there at the creation of videoblogging, in part by helping create it himself. The coauthor of *Videoblogging*, he previously worked with CNN International in Atlanta, then became a freelance journalist in the Democratic Republic of Congo and later worked at Manhattan Neighborhood Network, a public access TV station.

In June 2004, Dedman and Peter Van Dijck started the Yahoo Videoblogging group at tech.groups.yahoo.com/group/videoblogging. There were only about a dozen known vlogs at the time. A year later, the list expanded to a thousand members. In late 2004, Peter launched mefeedia.com, the first vlog directory, and now also provides video search and navigation features.

According to Dedman, "We realized that blogging was the perfect way to easily publish and distribute video. We formed an online community where we taught people how to videoblog for free. People from around the world were using inexpensive digital cameras to record their lives for each other. Pretty quickly, there was too much video to watch on individual web pages. So in January 2005 we released a tool called *FireAnt* that lets you find, subscribe, watch, and share videoblogs."

Before this chapter teaches you how to create a videoblog, check out a few of the founding vlogger's vlogs to see some examples:

- Jay Dedman: momentshowing.net

- Peter Van Dijck: poorbuthappy.com/ease

- Ryanne Hodson: ryanedit.blogspot.com

- Josh Kinberg: joshkinberg.com

- Michael Verdi: michaelverdi.com

- Steve Garfield: stevegarfield.com

There are also some popular vlog series, such as *Rocketboom* and *Tiki Bar TV*. The latter (tikibartv.com), which started in 2005, features five-minute-long episodes and currently has around 200,000 viewers. The low-budget episodes revolve around a tiki bar in an otherwise generic-looking bachelor apartment, plus, of course, the show's namesake cocktails. Tiki Bar's audience numbers got a boost when Apple stores aired the program during a six-month promotion for video iPods in 2006.

Perhaps the best-known vlog series is *Rocketboom* (rocketboom.com). The series, launched in October 2004, is a daily three-minute videoblog newsmagazine, shot with a consumer-grade digital camera and edited on a laptop, in Andrew Michael Baron's one-bedroom apartment on Manhattan's Upper West Side. Baron initially spent $20 per show on production costs, $15 per month for hosting, and zero dollars on marketing and promotion, relying mostly on word of mouth. Amanda Congdon became the popular hostess of the show after she answered an ad on craigslist in 2004, but left in late 2006 after a dispute with partner Baron, who owned 51 percent of the show, to her 49 percent. In April 2007, she launched a videoblog on the ABC News website. The show, called *Starring Amanda Congdon,* is on blip.tv, MySpace, and iTunes, and is sponsored by Unilever's Dove Cream Oil Body Wash.

Rocketboom programs are released every weekday at 9 a.m. Eastern time. Around three hundred thousand people download the show daily, making it one of the most popular videoblogs, with an audience as large as CNN's old *Crossfire* show. On February 2, 2006, Rocketboom was included in an episode of *CSI: Crime Scene Investigation*, which led to a further jump in viewership.

You now know the history of videoblogging, or some of it, and its implications, or some of them. So, are you ready to make a vlog of your own?

How to Videoblog: Eleven Steps to Your First Vlog

Jay Dedman

The founding vloggers are a wonderful, helpful group, and they can show you how easy it is to vlog. They offer many free resources to get new vloggers started. For example, Michael Verdi's and Ryanne Hodson's freevlog.org offers a step-by-step vlog tutorial that uses vlogs (what else?) to teach both Mac and PC users how to vlog. They also wrote a book on the topic, called *Secrets of Videoblogging*. I highly recommend going to their site directly for information and resources. Meanwhile, their eleven steps to vlogdom can be summarized as follows:

1. Shoot the video: Use a cell phone, a digital camera, or a PDA, meaning a personal digital assistant, such as a Palm Treo. Keep it short, no more than five minutes total.

2. Import: Import (transfer) the video from your camera or phone to your computer, using Windows Movie Maker or Apple's iMovie, usually via USB cable.

3. Edit: Include transitions, music, or narration to improve the piece. You don't even need editing software, as you can edit online. Eyespot, Itiva, Jumpcut, and VideoEgg let you edit a movie right in your browser.

4. Compress: Find a compromise between quality and file size. The higher the quality, the larger the file. It is best to publish a compressed file of no more than five minutes of video, which will result in a file size of around 10 MB. To achieve that, vloggers suggest saving the file as "video for broadband," at 512 kbps.

5. Screen grab: Save an image from the video to use as a screen shot, which is like a virtual book jacket or album cover art.

6. Save: Name the video clip, and save it. At this stage, you should also decide how you want to license the clip. You can use Creative Commons licenses, which lets others share and remix the clip, or you can opt for the more restrictive copyright (see Chapter 21).

7. Find a host: Depending on the size of your clips, or files, storage and bandwidth costs for hosting could be high. Some hosts might include:

    a. Blogs: Typepad and Blogger automatically link your video to blog entries. Blogger, for example, offers free hosting.

    b. Free hosting: BlipTV, Internet Archive/OurMedia will host your content for free, forever, and have an artist-friendly Terms of Service (more on that below).

c. Paid hosting: Some reliable hosts include 1and1.com, content-type.com, and dreamhost.com.

8. Publish the video: Post the video to your blog, blip.tv, OurMedia/Internet Archive, or your paid host.

9. Enter text on your blog: Type as much information as possible about the video, so that search engines can read the text and alert searchers to your video.

10. Promote: Get an RSS 2.0 feed. RSS encloses the video into your feed, and enables viewers to subscribe to the feed and get automatic updates each time you create a new video. Without an RSS 2.0 feed, you are just inserting video into a Web page, and nobody will know about your new video unless they go to the trouble of checking the Web page for updates. Also try FeedBurner.com, which automates this process. (See Chapter 10 for more.)

11. Subscribe to vlog: Now, subscribe to your vlog using an aggregator, so that you can see what it looks like, as opposed to what you *thought* it would look like. It is also a good idea to subscribe to others' vlogs, to see what the competition is doing.

    What is an aggregator? Put simply, an aggregator is software that searches out and collects, in this case, videoblogs and sends you the ones that you have told it interest you. It is, in effect, your mother mailing you newspaper and magazine clippings about the Arctic because she knows you love that region. Today's aggregators are faster and more far-reaching, but less loving than your mom.[1]

    Aggregators include:

- Mefeedia: MeFeedia.com

- Miro: getmiro.com

- PenguinTV: penguintv.sourceforge.net (Linux)

- FireANT: getfireant.com (acquired by Odeo/Sonic Mountain in late 2007)

Distribution, Distribution, Distribution

As soon as it is up and available, and you are satisfied that your vlog is vloffo, you can promote it to millions of potential viewers via free directories such as MeFeedia.com, VlogMap.org, VlogDir.com, Videoblogging.info, and iTunes at apple.com/itunes.

---

1. Aggregators for RSS and blog feeds are called newsreaders; examples include Pluck and My Yahoo! (See *Blog* chapter). Aggregators for audio feeds are called podcatchers; examples include Juice and iTunes (see *Podcast* chapter). Aggregators for both audio and video feeds include FireAnt and Mefeedia.

2005: INTERNET TV

YouTube and the many other video-sharing sites are part of a phenomenon called Internet TV. Whenever you send your videos out into the world, or watch, via the internet, you are participating in Internet TV.

It is now big business. Once YouTube and other free video-sharing sites started attracting huge audiences in early 2005, advertisers soon followed.

Before you jump into these ad-filled waters, however, you should know the downsides, at least as compared to videoblogging. Most free video-sharing sites use Adobe's proprietary Flash format, which only offers low-resolution video and does not support RSS feeds. Worse, when creators upload a popular program to YouTube, YouTube gets the audience, and, therefore, the advertisers. Vlogging, on the other hand, supports RSS for distribution, and vloggers have full control of the video's quality, resolution, and format. Finally, the vlogger, not YouTube, owns the audience, and possible revenues.

YouTube is the squillion-pound gorilla in Internet TV, but other popular video-sharing sites abound. They include Yahoo, Microsoft (video.msn.com), AOL (uncutvideo.aol.com), MySpace, blip.tv, Grouper (now Crackle, which is part of Sony Pictures), Vimeo, Dailymotion, Veoh Networks, Metacafe, Youare.tv, ClipShack, Heavy, GUBA, Lulu.tv, Dave.tv, Kyte.tv, and Vidiac, among hundreds of others. Each offers varying levels of service, audience, functionality, and security. These sites offer quick and easy video uploads, as well as a large potential audience of viewers.

And what an audience! YouTube, for example, is huge. *Huge.*

The site offered three million videos at its debut in February 2005. Today, one hundred million videos are watched each day by an estimated twenty million viewers. Half of their audience is under thirty-four. YouTube's site enables you to buy and sell videos, and submit your own content for others to watch for free or a fee. Anyone can easily upload and share videos, and then integrate the videos into websites, blogs, or profiles on MySpace and Facebook, by simply copying and pasting the "embed" code. YouTube did so well that, Google bought it in November 2006 for $1.65 billion. Check out Be The Media's YouTube channel here: youtube.com/BeTheMedia..

But we are jumping the timeline.

OCTOBER 2005: APPLE'S VIDEO IPOD

On October 12, 2005, TV networks and film studios got another wake-up call that life as they knew it was changing. That was the day Apple launched the video iPod. It plays not only music and podcasts, but also video, and all on a 2.5-inch screen.

This move, coupled with Apple's enabling RSS on the iTunes online store earlier in 2005, legitimized and expanded the market, making it possible for podcasters and videobloggers to distribute their works through the iTunes directory. And by setting a price on videos, Apple's move also created a nice revenue stream for independent TV, film, and video producers. They can earn up to 70 percent of the revenue through iTunes, netting $1.39 on a $1.99 video after Apple takes its 30 percent cut.

By September 2006, the online iTunes directory had sold more than forty-five million TV programs such as *Lost;* movies from Walt Disney, Pixar Animation Studios, Touchstone Pictures, and Miramax; and 1.5 billion songs and music videos.

One presumably happy customer of Apple's iTunes is San Francisco filmmaker Tiffany Shlain. Her eighteen-minute award-winning film *The Tribe* was released on iTunes in fall 2007 for $1.99 a download. Within a few months it had become the number one most-downloaded film on iTunes.

In an October 2007 article by Joe Garofoli in the *San Francisco Chronicle,* David Straus, CEO and cofounder of Withoutabox.com, an eight-year-old Los Angeles outfit that has helped 150,000 independent filmmakers market their films using the Internet, said, "We are at the beginning of a transitional moment. It's not just that people can download them and see films online, it's that filmmakers are learning what they can do to reach out to audiences themselves."

WE INTERRUPT THIS PROGRAM . . . FOR AN EXPLANATION

Beware: Internet TV is not *IPTV,* even though IPTV's full name, Internet Protocol Television, sounds like it.

IPTV is corporate. It is a model driven by satellite, cable, and telecommunications companies. IPTV services are IP in name only. AT&T, for example, uses its own private infrastructure, not Internet IP addresses. The IPTV model is finite, top-down, closed, and proprietary. The proprietors, or carriers, control the network from end to end, including the devices attached to the network, the programming, and the price. The infrastructure is bound geographically to communities, homes, and offices and is regulated by local, state, and national policies such as cable franchise agreements. (To learn more about the nefarious dealings of cable companies, see chapter 18.) IPTV is good for the established media because it gives them total control over the content, and limits the potential for theft and piracy. IPTV subscribers are offered a range of programs determined solely by the carrier. The programs are mostly professionally produced and of relatively high quality, such as ESPN or MTV. Today, there are about half a million IPTV subscribers in North America, the majority being Verizon FiOS subscribers.

Internet TV, by contrast, is operator and device independent; there is no need for a satellite dish, cable carrier, or set-top box. Internet TV is driven by you, me, and millions of others on the Internet, and it offers limitless capacity and gazillions of "shows" from all over the globe. This includes everything from low budget shorts produced on a camcorder to expensive, professionally produced programs such as Joel Comm's *The Next Internet Millionaire,* an Internet TV reality series. Internet TV is ad hoc, bottoms-up, infinite, free, à la carte, open, and standards-based, like the Internet. Anyone, whether "professional" or "amateur," can publish, access, develop, and distribute content to a global audience. Nobody needs permission, or needs to pay a carrier to get into the cable lineup, nor is a producer geographically bound by local cable company restrictions.

INTERNET TV: TALKING BACK TO THE TUBE

Another big difference between the old broadcast/cable TV model and the new Internet TV platform is that the former is exclusive and one-directional, while the latter is inclusive and participatory. Internet TV audiences are not satisfied with simply downloading and consuming, but want to upload and participate. On YouTube, for example, video posts encourage responses, by text or video or both, from other YouTube members. This is like the "comments" feature at the bottom of blog entries, and a far-distant cousin to letters written to the station manager or network president.

One prominent YouTube "first responder" is Renetto, *nom de video* of Paul Robinett, who has tens of thousands of subscribers and millions of views. Renetto's responses encourage yet more video responses from other members. As with blogging, the original video post is just the beginning of a public conversation that expands, contracts, analyzes, and reinterprets the original entry.

Broadcasters and cable/satellite carriers, of course, don't like competing with all these videos uploaded from the unwashed masses, to even more unwashed masses. Broadcasters want you to buy and consume their content, not produce and freely distribute your own. Hence the disdain by cable, and now telecommunications, companies for public access TV stations and community media centers, and their desire to replace local cable franchises with state and national ones. This attitude is also why cable modem and satellite upload speeds are significantly slower than download speeds; companies like Comcast don't want your free home movies or public access programs to compete with their for-profit cable TV programming (see chapters 17 and 18).

Nor does Comcast want to compete with folks who use BitTorrent to distribute content. In October 2007, Peter Svensson of the Associated Press reported that "Comcast actively interfered with attempts by some of its high-speed Internet subscribers to share files online" using the BitTorrent protocol. In a number of experiments, the AP tried to use the BitTorrent protocol to upload a digital version of the King James Bible, a book that is obviously in the public domain. Comcast blocked the transmission by inserting "reset" commands; this is the same technique used by government censors in China that causes connections between transmitter and receiver to drop. As Professor Susan Crawford explained, "it's as if someone else that sounded like you got on the phone as you were talking to your mother and said, 'We need to hang up right now.'"

The upshot? Comcast made it impossible to distribute The Good Book via a Comcast cable modem connection using the BitTorrent protocol, an act that is counter to the tradition of treating all data equally. The Associated Press called Comcast's move "the most drastic example yet of data discrimination by a U.S. Internet service provider." In August 2008, the FCC ruled that Comcast violated federal policy by interfering with data traffic.

To find out more about data discrimination, and what you can do about it, see the Net Neutrality section in chapter 22.

We now return to our regularly scheduled program.

HOW TO MAKE INTERNET TV

Making Internet TV is simple. In many ways it is similar to making a video for a videoblog. (See the checklist in the vlog section above.) There are some differences, however, and to address them, as well as help people start from scratch, the best guide I know of comes from the Knight Citizen News Network and the Participatory Culture Foundation, which created a self-help portal. The guide, called "Make Internet TV," teaches citizens, journalists, and even you how to shoot, edit, publish, and promote video. The site is at kcnn.org/mitv.

Also try Ustream.tv, which enables anyone with a camera and an Internet connection to broadcast to a global audience. Your fans can paste the "embed" code into their blogs to promote the video, thus increasing the likelihood of a viral hit. Also check out seesmic, kyte, and stickam.

Tips for a Successful Video, or a Series

1. Post your text transcriptions and contextual information about your video on your blog so that search engines can properly spider and index the video, and so that users can follow along.

2. Use captions. For example, show URLs for companies profiled or when giving instructions, such as "Mac users Ctrl+click."

3. Include your company's logo. The video may be distributed around the Internet without the accompanying text. You want viewers to know who created the show.

4. Use a snappy intro and "outro" as an audiovisual identifier for your program.

5. Adjust volume levels in your final edit, especially if you used multiple takes over many days with different recording equipment and background noises.

6. Listen to the show before broadcast to ensure that the sound quality is good on both high-quality headphones as well as iPod ear buds.

7. Use meta tags. Include your name, contact information, web URL, and key words to describe the show for search engines, such as comedy, drama, silent, whatever. Be sure you spel rite! Use your most important key words in the title, and use descriptors that people will likely search for, helping search engines to find it. Your video will rank high not just in Google's video search results, but in the main Google search engine results, too.

SUBMITTING YOUR VIDEO TO MULTIPLE SITES

Once you have created your video, be sure to enter your metadata, such as producer, title, date, and episode. Put your URL first in the description field, to make it visible. Then enter your top keywords, such as your name, company, and contact info. Search engines are giving video sensationally high rankings, often within hours of the video's being posted, but you must enter keywords in the description field in order for the search engines to pay attention, and index it.

Now, you send it out into the world. There are hundreds of free online video-sharing sites you can post to, but don't forget to post to your own blog or website, too! I advise posting to the top ten or twenty sites with the largest audience, like YouTube. But because your video may get "lost" on them, you might also post to a few small sites, so that the video stands out or gets featured. Also, try a few sites specific to your niche, such as music, comedy, or drama. More equals more. I suggest putting your video on many sites, which enables you to reach a wider audience and increases your chances of having a viral video hit.

Posting your videos to all these sites individually, though, is time consuming and takes time away from creating the video itself. Enter *Tubemogul.com,* a free tool that uploads your video to multiple sites from one single interface. Once your video is published, Tubemogul's technology shows how many times your video has been watched. This tool is great for content producers, record labels, film studios, and advertisers, helping them track trends and marketing efforts. Similarly, *Traffic-geyser.com* lets you upload up to twenty-five videos a month to the top fifteen video sharing sites, all for $47 a month. Or try *PowerUploads.com*, which charges $0.99 for each video uploaded to over fifty sites.

CAVEAT VIDEOGRAPHER! TERMS OF SERVICE

Before you send your video to any site, let alone many, be sure to read the fine print on its Terms of Service, or TOS. (For more, see chapters 14 and 15). Some sites take over the rights to your work with impunity, and ruthless exclusivity. Knowitallvideo has a TOS that grants the company a perpetual, nonrevocable, nonexclusive, sublicenseable, royalty-free worldwide license to use your content as well as your name, voice, and likeness. Perhaps the company should be called "Ownitallvideo." College humor is no joke, either. "Every item you submit becomes the property of CollegeHumor.com for any use whatsoever." Other bad Terms of Service include those of Bofunk, Break, Vidilife, Ugoto, Sharkle, and Putfile, to name a few.

On the other end of the spectrum, artist-friendly TOS can be found at Open Media Network (omn.org) and Ourmedia.org, a nonprofit site started in 2004, built and staffed by volunteers using open-source code. Courtesy of a relationship with the Internet Archive, a nonprofit whose mission is the long-standing preservation of digital material, Ourmedia provides free storage space and bandwidth for people to share audio, video, text, and software. One condition is that contributors must share their work, using licenses from Creative Commons. See chapter 21.

From Ourmedia's Terms of Service: "YOU OWN YOUR OWN MATERIAL. Ourmedia claims no intellectual property rights on the material you provide to our service." Nice.

MAKING MONEY MAKING MOVIES

Be warned, little pictures can make you big bucks, if you build a large enough audience. For example, United Talent Agency created UTA Online to discover and promote creators of Internet TV. They recently partnered with video-sharing site Veoh Networks to create the Breakthrough Channel, a site that encourages digital artists to submit their work and be considered for representation. NBC signed YouTube stars Joe Beretta, twenty-three, and Luke Baratz, twenty-two, of Spokane, Washington, to write a pilot in a deal valued at about half a million dollars. The Ask a Ninja series earns $100,000 a month in ads, licensing, and merchandise. Atom films has paid video creators more than $3 million to date. Metacafe pays creators $5 for every thousand views, with popular acts earning tens of thousands of dollars. Magnify and Kyte also share ad revenue with producers. In part because of the defection of some of its "stars" to these other sites, YouTube announced it will start sharing advertising revenues with successful producers.

According to former WB network CEO Jordan Levin, "Production and distribution are the barriers to entry that have kept studios and networks in power. But those barriers are continuing to come down…maybe now you can make a little money. It's not Hollywood money, but $35,000–50,000, which is what some content generators are starting to make. For a kid in Nebraska in his garage, that's probably pretty good."

2006: BRIGHTCOVE, A COMPLETE PLATFORM FOR PRODUCERS

Brightcove is the most recent addition to the reinvention of television. It offers a complete system that gives producers an open, self-service Internet TV platform for editing, publishing, hosting, and distributing video. It is, in effect, a self-contained network in a box, but without the box. Smaller video producers now have a low-cost, low-risk way to compete with big broadcasters. Producers can create and distribute video, or an entire series, and charge viewers through any of three methods: by subscriptions to channels of programming, by à la carte downloads, or by advertising inserted into the video stream. Advertising revenues are increased by syndicating the video to sites that have large audiences. For example, anyone can add the Brightcove video player to their blogs, websites, and personal profile pages on social networks like MySpace or Facebook. Of the resulting ad revenues from those sites, Brightcove gives 50 percent to the original content creators, and gives up to 20 percent of the revenues to the owners of the websites and blogs that display the videos. It pockets the rest.

According to Brightcove founder and Chairman Jeremy Allaire, "We are working toward a world where television and video production and distribution are much more democratized and where a creative spark, a camera, and a computer are all it takes to put television programming before the eyes of the consumer."

TOMORROW: GOING MOBILE

As broadcasting and cable company executives know, the typical viewer is no longer the all-American couch potato flipping through channels with a remote. Video audiences now have access to three different, and vastly different-sized, screens: televisions (from petite to humongous), computers, and handheld devices. The handhelds range from cell phones to Blackberries and Palm Treos to Apple's iPhone and video iPods.

The screens are small, but the numbers are ginormous. Some twenty-five million Americans can watch, or send, video on their phones. That's out of approximately two hundred million total cell phones in United States, and more than two billion mobile phone subscribers worldwide. If you want to make videos to work on handhelds, that is the size of your potential audience. And services like qik.com and kyte.tv enable you to stream live video from your cell phone to a global audience via social networks and blogs, so you need not worry about the limited storage capacity on the phone.

Mobile minicasters should keep a few things in mind, however.

MOBILE THEATER TIPS: "TWO-MINUTE TV"

Before you film anything for mobile devices, watch and listen to professional and amateur mobile clips on various makes and models of phones to see what kinds of video clips do and do not work. Watch videos in communal settings such as airports, ballparks, bars, and restaurants, since viewers may be interrupted or on-the-go. Your program needs to grab their attention quickly and hold it.

Filming: Because mobile screens are about 2x2 inches, it is best to shoot only close-ups. Use scenes that don't change much. TV uses thirty frames per second, but most cell phones deliver only half that, which creates a blurry result. Don't use wide-angle, panoramic, or group shots, either. Limit special effects, transitions, zooms, and pans. Avoid quick, jerky movements. Keep your small screen video personal, with talking heads saying, "I am talking to YOU!"

Sound: You can't count on the listener's environment, so lighten up on heavy dialogue. Unless the listener is alone or wearing an earpod, the device's speaker will likely be meager. Use simple titles or captions to tell the story, keeping them to less than a few words per screen. The clip should be three to five minutes, max. Some minicasters say that no video should last more than thirty seconds.

Lighting: The brightest light should come from behind the camera operator, illuminating the subject, naturally if possible. If filming at night, in low light, or indoors, shed more light on the subject by opening a shade or directing a light at it.

Programming: Stand-up comedy and talking head shows like the *Colbert Report* and the *Daily Show* work well on handheld devices. NASCAR's cars racing around a track at high (blurry) speeds do not. Funny is more likely to be successful than sad. Think comedy clips, weather reports, sports updates. TIP: Before posting, view your clip on multiple cell phones, to test the user experience.

MOBILE FESTIVALS

Today, entire film festivals are devoted to mobile video shot entirely on cell phones. For example, Motorola sponsored a mobile category at the Toronto International Film Festival.

Here are a few more festivals, for the next mobile Martin Scorsese:

- zoiefilms.com/cellularcinema.html: Zoie offers an annual cell-phone film festival.

- festivalpocketfilms.fr: The French Forum des Images's sponsors une "Pocket Film Festival."

- cellflixfestival.org: Ithaca College offers a $5,000 prize to American High School and college students for the best thirty-second movie shot entirely with a cell phone.

- cellfest.org: The Marin County Fair (California) held a cell-phone festival with $1,500 in prizes. The length could not exceed thirty seconds.

- mobifest.ca: Canada's first mobile film festival had more than sixty-five thousand entries.

So, whatever you want to record, whether it's a videoblog about your trip to Argentina, a seminar about learning string theory, or a cell-phone-sized ode to a tulip opening up, consider this: Billions of customers may be waiting. Or even just a really special one.

As the French film director Francois Truffaut predicted in 1957,

> "The film of tomorrow appears to me as even more personal than an individual and autobiographic novel, like a confession, or a diary. The young filmmakers will express themselves in the first person and will relate what has happened to them. It may be the story of their first love or their most recent; of their political awakening, the story of a trip, a sickness, their military service, their marriage, their last vacation . . . and it will be enjoyable because it will be true, and new."

"The film of tomorrow will be an act of love."
—Francois Truffaut, 1957

8

FILM

HOW TO PRODUCE AND DISTRIBUTE YOUR ULTRA-LOW BUDGET DIGITAL FILM

THE REVOLUTION IN DIGITAL MOVIE PRODUCTION AND DISTRIBUTION

Peter Broderick

"The film of tomorrow will resemble the person who made it, and the number of spectators will be proportional to the number of friends the director has."
—*Francois Truffaut, 1957*

The digital revolution in moviemaking is well underway. New digital tools—from cameras to editing software—have changed not only how movies are made but also which movies are made and who makes them.

So far, the digital revolution has had the greatest effect on independent productions. Operating without the infrastructure and inertia of the major Hollywood studios, independent producers have the flexibility to embrace new opportunities quickly. And because they lack the ample financial resources of studios, independent producers are highly motivated to find ways to reduce production costs.

The earliest adopters of digital production technologies were the filmmakers with the least money. Seeking to make their first movies, they had little to lose and everything to gain. Digital cameras and postproduction editing software empowered them to make features they could not afford to shoot on film.

No previous development in film production technology has so dramatically lowered the overall cost of moviemaking. Some successful digital features have been made for under $1,000. The thriller *The Last Broadcast,* for example, was shot and edited for $900. It had a limited theatrical release, was shown on cable television, and is available on home video in the United States and abroad.

Moviemaking was previously one of the most expensive art forms. Unlike a poet or a painter, a filmmaker needed substantial financial resources and expensive equipment. Now, for the first time, independent filmmakers can afford to own both the means of production and the means of postproduction. When asked by aspiring filmmakers how much money they need to make a digital movie, it is now possible to say, "Whatever you have is probably enough." Independents with digital cameras have the freedom of novelists to be spontaneous, to improvise, to strike out in new directions, and to start over.

The spectrum of budgets for digital movies is very wide. The last two *Star Wars* films, *Sin City,* and each of the three *Spy Kids* films were shot on budgets in the $30 million to $100+ million range. Lars Von Trier's digital feature *Dancer in the Dark* cost about $15 million. Other established directors have made digital features in the $2 million to $8 million range, including Mike Figgis (*Time Code*), Spike Lee (*Bamboozled*), and Wayne Wang (*Center of the World*). The films made by InDigEnt, which include *Pieces of April* and *Tadpole,* had budgets in the $300,000 range.

Many novice filmmakers have directed first features for less than $10,000. The feature *Boxes,* for example, was made on a budget of $280 and was aired nationally on the Independent Film Channel. In general, the lower the budget, the greater the financial impact of deciding to shoot a feature digitally instead of on film. The cost of film stock and processing can eat up a high percentage of an independent producer's budget.

A NEW APPROACH TO FINANCING

Although higher budget digital movies are likely to follow the traditional model of production, a new model has emerged at the lowest budget levels for digital video (DV) features.

In the traditional model, a writer first creates a script. Then the search begins for third parties willing to provide the money to make the script into a movie. This search often requires a great deal of time and effort, with no guarantees of success. After two or three years, the supplicants usually give up if they haven't raised the money. If they do find financing, they probably have to trade off substantial creative control to get it. This often involves giving the financing entity—whether a Hollywood studio or an independent distributor—final approval of the script, key cast, and ultimately, of the film itself. If the financiers are not satisfied with script revisions and the cast, they are unlikely to green-light production.

In the most radical new model of low budget digital moviemaking, filmmakers conduct a no-nonsense resource assessment even before writing the script. The goal is to determine exactly what resources are available—how much money the filmmakers have to make the movie (or how much they can be sure of getting from family, friends, and possibly some private investors), what equipment they own or have access to, what locations they can use, what vendor deals they can make, and so forth. After this assessment, a script is written for a movie that can be made within the framework of available resources. Instead of wasting months and possibly years seeking money, filmmakers can spend their time writing, rehearsing, shooting, and editing, and they do not have to give creative control to a financier.

The concept of making films with available resources was central to the ultra-low budget feature movement that began in the early 1990s. Shot on film before the advent of digital video, influential micro-budget features maximized the use of available resources. For *El Mariachi*, Robert Rodriguez had free access to a dog and a school bus, which are both prominently featured in the film; for *Clerks,* Kevin Smith set his film in the convenience store where he worked and he shot it there in the middle of the night, when the store was closed; and Ed Burns filmed much of *The Brothers McMullen* in his parents' house, where his mother cooked for the cast and crew. These features inspired filmmakers across the United States and overseas to make films for under $100,000 rather than spending years trying to raise millions.

Then digital tools arrived. These not only dramatically lowered the budgets of first features but also provided filmmakers with more creative options.

NEW CREATIVE OPTIONS ON THE DIGITAL SET

Digital tools expand a filmmaker's creative opportunities in many important ways. Replacing costly film stock with inexpensive videotape changes fundamental production dynamics. On a film set, the camera is rolling a small percentage of the time, given the expense of stock, processing, and the amount of time required to light and set up each shot. On a digital set, the camera can be recording a much greater percentage of the time, simply because videotape costs so little and doesn't need to be processed. Because the costs of digital cameras are so minimal, directors often use two cameras simultaneously, something that is unaffordable on most lower budget film shoots.

Directors usually shoot much more footage for a digital movie. On some very low budget features shot on film, the ratio of footage shot to footage used in the final cut is as low as 5:1 or even 3:1. On comparable digital features, the shooting ratio could be as high as 30:1 or even 100:1. This enables filmmakers to work with actors in ways that would be impossible if they were shooting on film. For instance, directors can now shoot rehearsals, capturing inspired moments that would otherwise be lost. Instead of only being able to afford to film a few takes of a scene, a director can shoot as many takes as needed to achieve the highest level of performance. On a digital set, the actors usually don't have to stand around for hours between scenes waiting for the lights to be rigged; digital features often are shot with available light or with minimal lighting.

The opportunity to immediately view what has been shot (rather than waiting one or two days to see film dailies) fosters more risk-taking. The director can try many variations on a scene and use the immediate feedback of video playback to see what is working best and is worth pursuing further. Playback also provides greater creative latitude to other members of the production team, such as the director of photography, who can explore different visual paths and textures.

The goal on many film sets is to execute efficiently the carefully planned shots from a fixed script. Many digital sets, in contrast, allow for some degree of improvisation by the actors. Experimentation is affordable and inspiration is encouraged.

One source of inspiration on digital shoots is the real world. Using an inconspicuous digital camera and a small crew, it is possible to shoot a fictional story in a nonfiction environment. Michael Rehfield, the director and star of *Big Monday,* shot his feature on the streets and in the subways of New York. Unlike studio films shot on location in Manhattan using carefully choreographed extras in diligently policed cocoons, *Big Monday* incorporated real life into the frame, giving it the authenticity of a documentary.

Director Paul Wagner used a small digital camera to shoot key scenes in Tibet for his feature *Windhorse.* The Tibetan authorities would never have permitted such a movie to be shot there, but they mistook the filmmakers for tourists making a home video. Extremely critical of the Chinese occupation of Tibet, *Windhorse* was distributed in theaters in the United States and overseas.

Digital tools also have enabled directors to transform the production process. Film features are normally made in three stages. During pre-production, filmmakers make all the necessary preparations. They shoot the film during the production phase. They then edit and mix the film during postproduction. They often begin editing during production, and sometimes do a few additional days of filming during postproduction. Otherwise, these three stages are discrete and sequential.

The digital production process is more fluid. Directors have much greater flexibility. They can shoot, edit, and evaluate what worked and what did not. Then they can write new scenes and shoot them. This allows the movie to evolve in an organic way. Moviemakers can abandon the worst material and build on the best. If they own the digital camera and are working with a small crew and dedicated actors, they can take advantage of unpredictable factors. I once asked a director when he was going to finish shooting his first digital feature. He replied, "Tonight, if it rains."

Economics play a significant role in shaping the production process. The higher the budget of a digital movie, the more its production stages will resemble those of a movie shot on film. Digital auteurs have the greatest creative freedom at the lowest budget levels. If filmmakers own the camera, then production costs and constraints can be minimal. If they own the computer and editing software, postproduction costs also can be kept to a minimum, at least during initial editing.

The new economics of digital production have given filmmakers "affordable time"—more time for production and postproduction. They are not struggling to shoot and cut their film on a fixed and very tight schedule. If they can find a committed but flexible cast and crew, they can shoot, edit, write, shoot, edit, and write until they are satisfied. If they decide their project isn't working, they can abandon it at any point and start shooting something new.

In addition to eliminating the need to pay for film stock and processing and to rent equipment for editing, digital production also avoids the high cost of creating optical effects on film. The power to create spectacular or subtle effects on desktop computers is increasing by leaps and bounds. It is now possible to make an ultra-low budget science fiction film with amazing desktop effects that would previously have cost at least $1 million or $2 million if a special effects house had made it.

NINE RULES OF ULTRA-LOW BUDGET DIGITAL PRODUCTION

In my 1993 *Filmmaker* magazine article "Learning from Low Budgets" I listed nine rules of thumb for micro-budget production. These rules have evolved from the early 1990s, when low budget features were being shot on film, to today, when the vast majority of ultra-low budget features are made digitally.

Hell or high water commitment: A committed core group, determined to make a movie come hell or high water, is essential.

No-nonsense resource assessment: Filmmakers start by assessing the resources they have and those they are certain they can find. It is important to determine accurately the money, equipment, locations, crew, and postproduction facilities that will be available to the production. For any digital production (especially one designed to be transferred to film), it is critically important to research technical issues (e.g., the best format in which to shoot) to determine how the necessary image and sound quality can be achieved.

Realistic scripting: The script is often written after the resource assessment is done. But whenever it is written or modified, it must be possible to make the scripted movie with the resources available. Shooting digitally rather than on film usually reduces the budget, thus lowering the risk of running out of money during production.

Imaginative financing: Every conceivable method is used to minimize and postpone expenditures. Digital makes both easier. It reduces the cost of production by eliminating the cost of film stock and processing, and camera rental. Digital also postpones and in some cases eliminates the cost of making film prints if filmmakers use digital projection at festivals. If theatrical distribution is not an option, a film print may never be needed. The video master will be sufficient for cable and broadcast television, as well as satellite, home video, and Internet distribution.

Recruiting cast and crew: It is crucial to find a capable cast and crew who will work for little or no compensation while enduring the rigors of ultra-low budget production. Shooting digitally may make it easier to attract actors who want the opportunity to give their best performances. For digital productions, it is important to find a talented director of photography who either is experienced in digital cinematography or is committed to learning the fundamentals.

Pragmatic planning: Budgeting, scheduling, and other planning must be done carefully to maximize the use of limited resources and to minimize problems. This is especially true for digital production. As part of the extra technical research required, lab tests should be done prior to production in order to select the right format and the best lab. After a lab is chosen, footage should be shot using the designated camera under anticipated lighting conditions. If theatrical distribution is a goal, the lab should then transfer this footage to 35 mm film and project it for the director and the director of photography. This makes it possible to optimize the camera settings in advance and enables the director and the director of photography to know exactly how their digital images will look on film. When shooting digitally, it is also necessary to have a realistic plan for your postproduction workflow.

Guerrilla production: Ultra-low budget production on film is usually short and intense because only a small shooting ratio is affordable. When shooting digitally, the camera (or cameras) can be on most of the time. Using small digital cameras and a small crew enables inconspicuous production in real-world locations, making it possible to capture reality rather than faking it. Owning a digital camera allows greater scheduling flexibility. When shooting with a small crew (unpaid or deferred), digital production can also be much longer, with more shooting days spread over an extended schedule.

Extended postproduction: Postproduction on film can require significant amounts of cash for equipment rental, lab work, negative cutting, etc. This money is often raised in bits and pieces, which can extend postproduction. Digital postproduction is less resource intensive because more steps can be done on a desktop computer. The length of digital postproduction is usually determined by creative rather than financial needs. In fact, because digital allows relatively quick and inexpensive recuts, it can be a challenge to stop re-editing and decide that the movie is finally done.

Boundless opportunism: Ultra-low budget filmmakers have to be able to create and take advantage of opportunities. Digital production allows more opportunities for creative choices throughout the process.

Digital moviemaking has rapidly gained momentum in the independent sector. While I was president of Next Wave Films, a company that provided finishing funds to emerging filmmakers, the percentage of films shot on video skyrocketed from 13 percent in 1997 to over 70 percent in 2002.

THE DISTRIBUTION CRISIS

Although the barriers to production have fallen for independent filmmakers, the barriers to distribution have risen. The overall state of independent feature distribution is grim. Studio franchise films with theme park ride potential are doing exceptionally well. As the costs of marketing and distribution have risen, studios have increased their dominance over theatrical distribution. The advances paid to distribute independent films have declined, along with the willingness of distributors to take risks on independent features without stars or other presold elements. And when such films have found distribution, their fate is often determined by the size of the audience during their first weekend in theaters. Unless a substantial crowd appears, their theatrical life is usually short, undercutting their ancillary possibilities. Although a handful of independent features succeed in distribution each year, these are aberrations that belie the fate of the hundreds of films that find little or no distribution. Most indie features never find distribution.

These days it is much harder for independents to usher a movie out into the world than to create one in the first place. The traditional system for distributing independent films is in critical condition. But as old distribution paths have become more treacherous, promising new ones are opening up. The challenge for every independent is to understand the current distribution crisis, to assess older and newer options, and to design distribution strategies that will maximize chances of reaching the widest possible audience.

For decades independents have dreamed of selling their films to distributors that can get them into theaters and video stores across America. Independents have hoped to make overall distribution deals. Today, a part of such deals, distributors are insisting on acquiring all North American rights for fifteen to twenty-five years. Although distributors sometimes pay substantial advances for such rights, these days a token advance is more common. Sometimes there is no advance.

The possible benefits of making an overall deal are alluring: a distribution company (with expertise, experience, a full staff, and relationships with exhibitors and press) will handle and finance the distribution of your film. This could mean a wide release, press enthusiasm, awards, substantial financial returns, and opportunities to make more movies. It is essential, however, that filmmakers also understand the potential problems with such deals.

Loss of control: You are giving away control of your film's North American distribution for at least fifteen years. Although you may have some input, contractually the distributor will have the power to make all decisions about the marketing and distribution of your film. If the trailer, poster, and overall campaign are misconceived, there is little you can do about it, and your film may be irreparably harmed.

Loss of faith: If your distributor loses faith in your film before its theatrical release and keeps postponing it, there may be little you can do. If your distributor gives up on your film after its opening weekend, there also may be very little you can do. Attempting to force the distributor to meet contractual commitments to open the film in a certain number of cities or to spend a certain amount on prints and advertising may be counterproductive.

Loss of video opportunities: Your distributor will determine who will handle every ancillary distribution avenue, from cable, satellite, and broadcast television to non-theatrical distribution. In most cases the ancillary area with the greatest revenue potential is video. But the choice of which company will have the video rights will *not* be based on which company could do the best job with your film. It will be determined by corporate structures and relationships. Your overall distributor may have a video subsidiary or affiliate, or it may have selected a company to release all its films on video.

Loss of revenues: It is common in overall deals for distributors to receive substantial revenues from distribution fees and to have a substantial portion of their expenses reimbursed, without any money being returned to the filmmakers. When filmmakers do receive revenues, they often are insufficient to pay their deferments and repay their investors. Distributors are usually paid distribution fees off the top and then will have their expenses (and the advance, if any) reimbursed. All revenue streams and expenses are normally cross-collateralized. This is a mysterious process in which revenues seem to melt away.

Loss of independence: You become totally dependent on your distributor. You must rely on the company's continuing commitment to your film, its ability to execute the distribution plan successfully, its overall financial viability, the honesty of its accounting, and the timeliness of its payments.

SPLITTING UP THE RIGHTS

Filmmakers unwilling or unable to make a traditional overall deal can split up the distribution rights, dividing some among different companies and keeping others. When considering splitting up rights, the first question to explore is how to handle theatrical distribution. Unless a filmmaker decides to skip theaters entirely and to premiere on television or video, the best approach to theatrical distribution requires careful consideration. The basic alternatives are a service deal or self-distribution. In both cases, the filmmaker must find the resources to cover the costs of advertising, marketing, and distribution.

THE SERVICE DEAL

A filmmaker hires a company or an individual to provide a range of distribution services: supervising the creation of the ad campaign, press kit, and marketing materials; booking theaters; hiring publicists; shipping prints; and collecting revenues. Service deal companies are given the monies to cover distribution expenses and are paid a fee (typically $50,000 or more), usually against a percentage of revenues (10 to 25 percent). By retaining control of the film's theatrical distribution rights, the filmmakers can participate in key decisions on spending, the trailer, the poster, positioning, publicity efforts, and timing, because the service company is working for them. The filmmakers can decide whether to change the distribution strategy and whether additional expenditures are justified.

While retaining control, the filmmakers also have the benefit of the expertise and relationships of the service deal company. But service deals are expensive. In an overall distribution deal, the distributor covers the distribution costs and also has more leverage in booking theaters and collecting revenues—because they supply the theaters with a steady stream of product.

Notable recent service deals include *My Big Fat Greek Wedding,* which grossed $241 million in theaters; *The Passion of the Christ,* which took in $370 million; and *Fahrenheit 9/11,* which grossed $119 million.

SELF-DISTRIBUTION

Distributing their films themselves may be the only option for filmmakers who cannot afford to make a service deal. Using this approach, the filmmakers themselves handle as many aspects of distribution as possible. Although they may pay for some help (with the trailer or poster, for example), they will try to do everything as cost-effectively as possible. They often rely on grassroots marketing and publicity techniques. Self-distributing filmmakers start with less expertise and fewer contacts, but they may be able to counterbalance these limitations through their passion and persistence.

NEW THEATRICAL OPTIONS

In the past most filmmakers interested in doing service deals faced a Catch-22. They had to commit several hundred thousand dollars to such a plan without any certainty about how their film would perform in theaters or how much of their initial outlay could be recouped through ticket sales. It was very difficult to convince investors to fund a service deal, because they couldn't be convinced that they would get their money back (with a premium) from theatrical and ancillary revenues. The costs were even higher if the filmmakers had produced their film digitally but had not yet made a print and had to raise an additional $30,000 to 50,000 to pay for a film transfer.

Today filmmakers interested in service deals or self-distribution have new options. The arrival of digital projection in a growing number of theaters has expanded opportunities, lowered costs, and increased flexibility. Before deciding on an approach to theatrical exhibition and committing a substantial amount of resources, filmmakers can test their film. If they can interest a theater in playing it, they can get a good sense of the potential theatrical audience. And if they find theaters able to create awareness for their film via the theaters' calendars and mailing lists, as well as free media (reviews and features rather than paid advertising), they may be able to test their film at very low cost. If these theaters have adequate video projection, a film print won't be necessary. As for a trailer, it is helpful but not essential.

If you cannot find a theater willing to book your movie, you can rent a theater and test your film. If the test bookings go well, it should be easier to make the case to potential investors who can fund a service deal. If the bookings go terribly, a theatrical release may not make sense. If the results of these initial bookings are inconclusive but the filmmakers are able to interest more theaters in playing their film, the next best step may be a limited release in five to ten additional markets.

There currently are at least forty cities where a film can be shown on video in theaters, and this number continues to grow. Landmark is planning to equip all of its theaters with digital projection. Many other exhibitors of independent films are moving in the same direction. The cost of a digital release is lower than the cost of a 35 mm release, which requires making and shipping prints (in addition to a transfer, if the film was shot digitally).

After playing additional cities, there should be sufficient information (box office results and press response) to determine whether a full 35 mm national release makes sense. If it does, there also may be enough evidence to convince potential investors to fund a service deal. If it does not, the options are to continue rolling out the film digitally or to end its theatrical release.

It is now possible to scale the resources spent on a theatrical release to the resulting revenues. Filmmakers able to test their movie in a limited number of theaters can make informed decisions about how much to spend based on projected box office. Previously, filmmakers and potential investors had to make their best guesses in a vacuum, before a film played a single theater.

Whether they are hiring a service deal company or working with an experienced booker, filmmakers should utilize the expertise and contacts of people with substantial distribution experience. These companies can provide legitimacy to exhibitors, can make the best deals, and can collect monies more effectively.

The primary goal of theatrical distribution for most independent films is to increase awareness and enhance ancillary revenues. Few independent films make money in theaters. But they can be considered a success if they break even or lose less than the amount by which they increase ancillary income.

VIDEO DEALS

Video is the ancillary with the greatest potential. This is the most important distribution route for independents to understand and master. When a video distributor offers to acquire an independent film, it will probably suggest a standard royalty deal with an 80 percent/20 percent (distributor/filmmaker) split in which the distributor covers expenses from its share. The split could be worse or better depending on the circumstances and leverage.

Video distributors will only make offers when they expect to cover their expenses and make a profit. The bulk of production and marketing expenses occur at the beginning of a release, and once these are covered the distributor is in a great position if it is receiving 80 percent of all revenues. If the retail price of a film is $25 and the wholesale price is $12.50, then the video distributor would receive $10 from each sale and the filmmaker would receive $2.50.

Filmmakers may be better off making other types of video deals. They could make a "distribution deal" in which the video distributor gets a distribution fee of 20 to 30 percent and the filmmaker receives 70 to 80 percent and covers all expenses. Another possible deal structure is one in which the video distributor and the filmmakers split revenues evenly after expenses are taken off the top.

Certain deals are better in certain circumstances. If video sales are small, a royalty deal is better for filmmakers because they will receive revenues from the first dollar of sales. If video sales are large, a distribution deal will be better, assuming expenses are capped. A fifty-fifty sharing of revenues may be best if sales are expected to be solid but not spectacular.

DIRECT VIDEO SALES

Filmmakers may be able to make a significant number of video sales themselves online. During the years they've been working on the film, they have had the opportunity to learn about and interact with the possible core audiences for their film. When making a deal with a video distributor, filmmakers should retain the right to sell their film online. There are several ways this can be structured. The filmmakers can create a window to sell a "preview" edition of the film on DVD before retail sales begin. This might be a plain vanilla DVD with just the film and none of the extras that will be on the retail DVD.

Filmmakers also can arrange to sell copies of the retail DVD online after retail sales begin. They can arrange either to make their own copies or to buy copies from the video distributor at cost plus some percentage. The video distributor will probably offer to sell them at wholesale minus 10 percent. The filmmakers will probably offer to buy them for cost plus 10 percent, and both parties will negotiate from there. The most a filmmaker should agree to pay is $5 per DVD.

The filmmakers will be able to target, reach, and sell to their core audience more effectively than any video distributor can. The video distributor should be able to reach and sell to a general audience through retail outlets more effectively than the filmmakers can. By supplementing what the video distributor does well, the filmmakers are expanding the pie. Because the filmmakers are doing all of the work to make these additional sales online, they should get the bulk of these extra revenues. The video distributor makes a profit on every DVD sold to the filmmaker (e.g., if the filmmaker pays $5 per DVD, the distributor makes approximately $4 profit). Video distributors also benefit from the increased retail sales resulting from the filmmakers' proactive online marketing.

The returns to filmmakers from direct online sales are much higher than returns from retail sales. Assuming a $25 retail price, a $12.50 wholesale price, and a 20 percent royalty, the filmmaker should eventually receive $2.50 from the video distributor for every DVD sold through retail. However, if the filmmaker sells the same DVD directly online, the returns could be eight times as much. If fulfillment and credit card charges can be covered by an additional shipping and handling charge, and if DVDs can be purchased from the video distributor for $5 apiece, the profit per sale could be $20 rather than $2.50. With direct sales, the money is coming directly to the filmmaker, without being diminished by accounting problems or delayed by the time it takes for cash to flow from consumer to retailer to wholesaler to distributor to filmmaker.

CORE AUDIENCES

A series of questions needs to be answered when formulating a distribution strategy for a film. One of the most critical questions is whether there is a sizeable core audience interested in buying tickets and/or purchasing the DVD. Varying types of core audiences exist. Some are defined by ethnicity, religion, or sexual orientation; others are linked by a subject they are passionately interested in, whether it is Tibet, college wrestling, or motorcycle racing. For the purposes of formulating a distribution strategy, a core audience must be identifiable and reachable, both of which have been made substantially easier and more affordable with the growth and diversification of the Internet.

Some films have an avid core audience (fan base) that can't wait to see a film and own it. Some films have multiple core audiences. Other films never find one. While researching, preparing, shooting, and posting a movie, filmmakers need to be exploring their film's core audience. How can these groups be reached online and offline? What are the key websites, Internet publications, discussion boards, and mailing lists? What organizations and clubs do they belong to? What special-interest publications do they read? What organized and ad hoc social gatherings do they frequent? Who are the leading figures in the field whose endorsements could be most influential?

During the filmmaking process, the filmmakers will have one to three years to learn how to best reach their core audience. They also will have time to create an effective Internet presence. This will enable them to build a valuable mailing list as they create awareness of their film within the target audience.

Reaching a general audience can be very expensive and inefficient, whereas connecting with a core audience can be less expensive and more efficient. In the past, many independent film campaigns targeted the general audience, assuming that the core audience would show up, which it often didn't do. For films with large and avid core audiences, filmmakers should make sure they can effectively reach the core audience first, then build on that base of support to cross their film over as widely as possible. *My Big Fat Greek Wedding, Monsoon Wedding, Y tu mamá también, The Passion of the Christ,* and *Fahrenheit 9/11* all attracted core audiences to theaters, enabling the films to stay on screens long enough to reach a general audience. Films with avid core audiences may be successful even if they don't cross over, if members of the core audience buy enough tickets and DVDs.

A PERSONAL AUDIENCE

Conceptually there are three audiences—the core audience, the general audience, and the filmmaker's personal audience. In the past, filmmakers had little knowledge of and few direct connections with their audience. However loyal were their regular viewers, the audience members were for the most part anonymous. Today's filmmakers have an unprecedented opportunity to build and nurture a personal audience. Thanks to the Internet, filmmakers can now have a much more direct connection with a personal audience made up of individuals with whom they can communicate.

This audience is built one name at a time. It includes everyone who e-mails you about your film, everyone who registers at your website, and everyone who buys a copy of a film from your site. This personal audience also should include everyone you meet while making and launching your film. At first this group's size may seem insignificant (in the tens or hundreds), but it may increase to thousands before long, and eventually, after several films, it could reach tens of thousands.

Each member of this audience can buy a ticket, encourage others to see your film in theaters, and later buy the DVD for themselves or their friends. Filmmakers sending out periodic updates to their personal audience should be able to create a sense of connection and loyalty; individual purchasers then see themselves as patrons of artists, not just consumers of products. Filmmakers may be able to carry much of this audience to their next projects. They also can benefit from direct feedback from this audience; for instance, reactions to the film in theaters may help filmmakers decide on the best extras for the DVD.

By skillfully using his website, Kevin Smith has built a formidable personal audience. The site, viewaskew.com, is unique, provocative, and very funny. Smith is ever present, through his postings and journal entries. He has built an extremely large fan base and has sold a significant amount of merchandise from his site. If Smith made a new film and chose not to utilize conventional distribution channels, he could easily sell enough DVDs and videos from his website alone to recoup a million-dollar budget.

A NEW ERA

Independent filmmakers now have unprecedented opportunities. Digital production is shifting the balance of power from financiers to filmmakers. Filmmakers who can make movies digitally, on lower budgets, are no longer dependent on financiers for the resources and permission to make their films. Likewise, new distribution models are freeing filmmakers from dependence on a traditional distribution system, which has been failing them. Powerful digital distribution tools—the DVD, digital projectors, and the Internet—are empowering independents to take their fate in their own hands and have a more direct relationship with their audiences. By effectively using these tools, filmmakers will be able to maximize the distribution opportunities for their current films as well as find investors for subsequent projects designed to reach core audiences. These tools also will enable an independent, digitally savvy filmmaker to build and nurture a personal audience, thus ensuring a long and fulfilling career.

The Desktop Studio

Mark Stolaroff

It is now possible for each of us to attempt to become a desktop Scorsese. Digital technologies are allowing filmmakers at all levels to create their own desktop "studios," which enable them to perform tasks critical to moviemaking at any budget level: capturing images and editing them. The new technologies also facilitate the creation of visual effects, ranging from traditional effects like dissolves and fades, to complex composites and computer graphic imaging.

There are many advantages to owning your own system rather than renting an expensive professional system such as an Avid. A typical rental for an Avid system is $1,000 to $2,000 per week, depending on the capabilities of the editing suite and the time of the day it is used. If the minimum amount of time to edit a feature is six weeks (and I would argue that for most features you will spend more like six months or more), then the minimum rental cost will be $6,000 to $12,000. For less than $6,000, you can purchase a standard-definition desktop studio (camera and editing system); for $12,000, you can purchase a high-definition desktop studio. And they will both be yours to make many more movies in the future.

One of the most expensive production elements on any feature is time. Owning your own system gives you loads of "free" time. It also allows for easy experimentation. If you are new to editing, it gives you the opportunity to learn and develop your skills. If your project isn't quite coming together, owning gives you the financial freedom to test alternative ideas and even reshoot scenes or shoot new material to ensure you are able to put your best project forward.

The components of a basic but powerful entry-level digital studio include[1]:

Digital video camera. High-quality, consumer digital cameras start at under $500 for a one-chip MiniDV model and go up to around $10,000 for the new generation of "prosumer" (professional/consumer) high-definition (HD) cameras. Many successful features have been made on standard definition DV cameras, from the award-winning 1998 feature *The Celebration,* shot with a tiny one-chip Sony PC7 to the 2002 box office hit *28 Days Later,* which was shot on a three-chip Canon XL1S MiniDV. Since it was introduced a few years ago, the revolutionary 24p MiniDV Panasonic DVX100 has been a popular choice for shooting indie feature films, including many shown at the last several Sundance film festivals.

With manufacturers like Sony (HVR-V1; HVR-Z1), JVC (GY-HD110; GY-HD250), Canon (XH-A1; XH-G1; XL-H1), and Panasonic (HVX-200) all

---

1. Average street prices, as of January 2007.

introducing low-cost HD cameras in the past couple of years, the move to affordable HD has been swift. Expect a host of features shot with these new cameras to turn up in festivals and theatrical venues in the coming year.

Desktop computer. Even the most basic computer editing systems today are powerful enough to edit MiniDV. Plug your camera into the FireWire port of just about any Apple laptop or desktop, even models several years old, and you can begin editing with iMovie, Apple's free and simple editing software, which comes standard on all Apple computers. The digital video and audio information is transferred from your camera's tape to your hard drive with no loss of quality.

Purchase a new computer and professional editing software for a faster and more powerful setup. An entry-level Apple iMac with Apple's Final Cut Express editing software is capable of storing around nine hours of DV or HD material on the standard 160 GB hard drive, leaving room for system files. The addition of a 500 GB drive would give you room for another thirty-eight hours of footage. An even more powerful system would be an Apple Mac Pro with dual monitors running Final Cut Pro 6. Fully featured, this editing system costs around $5,000, and with its speedy internal SATA hard drives it is capable of editing Panasonic's more robust HD codec, DVCPRO HD, found on its relatively inexpensive HVX200 and its top-of-the-line VariCam.

Standard-definition desktop studio

Panasonic DVX100B video camera (three-chip, MiniDV, 24p)	$ 2,700
Apple 17-inch iMac (2 GHz Core 2 Duo chip, 2GB RAM, 160 GB hard drive)	1,300
Additional hard drive (500 GB total)	200
Apple Final Cut Express HD (includes Soundtrack and LiveType)	100
TOTAL COST	$ 4,300

High-definition desktop studio

Panasonic HVX200 video camera; two 8 GB P2 cards (three-chip, HD)	$ 7,500
Apple Mac Pro (dual 2 GHz Xeon chips, 2 GB RAM, 1 TB hard drive)	3,100
Two 20-inch displays	540
Apple Final Cut Pro Studio 2 (Final Cut Pro 6, DVD Studio Pro 4, Motion 3, Soundtrack Pro 2)	1,300
TOTAL COST	$12,440

Shooting Film vs. Shooting Video

Mark Stolaroff

There are significant financial differences between shooting a movie on film and shooting on video. The following cost breakdown[2] compares shooting and preparing to edit one hour of 35 mm film, one hour of 16 mm film, and one hour of HD video (an affordable high definition video format):

Shooting 35 mm

Film stock (5,400 feet of new Kodak 5218 stock, at $0.595 per foot)	$3,213
Processing ($0.12 per foot)	648
Telecine ($200 per hour, 4:1 ratio)	800
Tape stock	70
TOTAL COST	$4,731

Shooting 16 mm

Film stock (2,160 feet of new Kodak 7218 stock, at $0.36 per foot)	$778
Processing ($0.12 per foot)	259
Telecine ($200 per hour, 4:1 ratio)	800
Tape stock	70
TOTAL COST	$1,907

Shooting high-definition video

Tape stock (shooting on high-quality tape)	$13

Note that although the workflow for getting film prepped for video editing is changing daily, it always includes processing (developing) and telecine (transfer to tape or file). I have assumed a common workflow above, transferring to DVCAM tape for ingestion into a typical Avid or Final Cut Pro editing system.

The lower the budget, the greater will be the financial impact of shooting on film rather than on video. This impact is illustrated by the table below, which shows relative stock costs as a percentage of the overall budget. In this case, twenty hours of raw footage is being shot for a ninety-minute feature (a 13.3:1 shooting ratio is typical of a very low budget film shot on film).

---

2. Line items are average figures and can vary depending on market conditions, workflow, and vendor deals

Stock Costs as a Percentage of Overall Budget

Total Budget	35 mm	16 mm	High-Definition Video
$10,000	946%	381%	3%
$50,000	189%	76%	1%
$250,000	38%	15%	0%
$500,000	19%	8%	0%
$1,000,000	9%	4%	0%

The table demonstrates how affordable it is to shoot high-definition video on a very low budget feature, and how prohibitively expensive it can be to shoot film on these budgets. Shooting twenty hours of footage on 35 mm or 16 mm would be extremely difficult in the $50,000 budget range—the stock costs alone when shooting 35 mm are nearly twice the budget!

Even on a $250,000 film, a filmmaker would be spending nearly 40 percent of the total budget of the project to capture the footage on 35 mm. When you consider the priorities of a typical independent film, such as story, performances, and the opportunity to experiment and make mistakes, it makes no sense to devote 40 percent of limited resources to film "resolution" and to a very specific film look.

If one were to shoot on high-definition video, the "film stock" costs, even on a $10,000 feature, would be almost nil. A filmmaker could even shoot twice the footage (forty hours) and still only spend 5 percent of the total budget on stock. Consider, too, that the Panasonic HVX200 doesn't use tape. After you've purchased the P2 flash memory cards, your stock costs are zero dollars, or zero percent of any budget—even for DVCPRO HD, a professional-grade, higher-quality format than prosumer high-definition video!

Of course, filmmakers like Michael Mann would never be satisfied with a 13:1 or 26:1 shooting ratio. Mann used a 93:1 shooting ratio on the $60 million *Collateral*. Nonetheless, even employing a Michael Mann shooting ratio on a $10,000 feature would still be possible in high definition video; that much tape stock would represent 24 percent of the total budget.

House Parties

Robert Greenwald

Like many good ideas, the concept of the house party as an alternative means of film distribution was born of both passion and desperation.

It was the fall of 2003, and although the second Iraq war was officially over ("mission accomplished"), the country was in the midst of a serious debate about the legitimacy of the invasion and our continuing military presence there. I had recently finished the first documentary I'd ever directed, *Uncovered: The War on Iraq,* which took just four and a half months from conception to completion. In the film, military and foreign policy experts persuasively debunk the reasons given by the Bush Administration for having invaded Iraq.

I wanted this film to be part of the debate, and I wanted it to reach a wide audience as soon as possible. I knew I could not rely on conventional means of distribution, which could take months or even years and which at best might only result in small audiences in a few art theaters around the country.

So my team started with screenings for opinion makers around the country, organized by the Center for American Progress, a wonderful progressive think tank in Washington, D.C. Simultaneously, the brilliant and adventurous folks at MoveOn.org—at the time a relatively new force in grassroots political organizing—agreed to offer the film on DVD to their more than two million members. The response from MoveOn members was overwhelming. We raised almost a million dollars by selling the DVD online. It was this enthusiastic response that led to the idea of house parties as a way to further expand the audience for the film. Quite simply, people would commit to showing the DVD in their homes to a group of friends and/or MoveOn members. I believe it was Eli Pariser, MoveOn.org's executive director, who first suggested that this form of distribution could widen our release and serve as an organizing and community-building tool for MoveOn by encouraging its members to connect face to face.

So, a few short weeks later, a miraculous map of the United States appeared on the MoveOn website. All across the map one could see dots where people were planning house parties. You could click on a dot and details of the house party appeared: location, how many people could be accommodated, potluck or not, and other relevant details. You could sign up online to join an existing party or offer to host your own.

I was fascinated as I scrolled through the tens, then hundreds, and finally thousands of house parties being planned. Here was a totally new combination of democracy, political organizing, and film distribution. I could see around the country—from yoga studio to bookstore to church to living room—the specifics of this event, scheduled to occur simultaneously on a certain date in early December.

The night of the house parties, I chose a random party to attend in Los Angeles. The MoveOn folks, using their amazing technological skills, arranged for me to welcome via speakerphone the participants at thousands of other house parties.

I have made over fifty films, but never before had I experienced the emotional satisfaction I did that night, knowing that thousands of people all over the country had come not just to see the film but also to stay afterward to discuss it, to ask questions, and most importantly, to decide what action to take! I was humbled to be part of one of the most important discussions of our time, through the medium I know best—film. And I was able to do it without spending months or years begging the traditional gatekeepers for entry.

Through the screenings, the Internet, and now the house parties, we did not need to ask anyone's permission. And although Universal and Warner Bros. aren't exactly quaking in their boots, the house party concept was and is a vital contribution to independent distribution, and an affirmation of my belief that "if you build it, they will come." They came, they saw, they took action. The experience inspired me to keep doing this work in this manner—to reach and affect and influence the important discussions of my country.

I recently set up Brave New Theaters to allow any filmmaker to easily organize house parties for his or her own film. It's free, and filmmakers can tap into the growing network of people who have hosted parties in the past. My hope is that over time this will become an important shared resource for all filmmakers. You can find out more at bravenewtheaters.com.

See you online or at a house party!

> "We all want to help one another,
> human beings are like that."
> —*Charlie Chaplin,* **The Great Dictator**

Addendum to House Party Sidebar

Peter Broderick

Within a few months after it played house parties across the country, Robert Greenwald's *Uncovered: The War on Iraq* had sold over 100,000 DVDs online and in stores. Then Robert added thirty minutes of new footage and created a theatrical version of *Uncovered,* which Cinema Libre released in a number of theaters. This version was then released on DVD, along with *Soldiers Pay,* a provocative short that Warner Bros. commissioned but refused to distribute because it was too "antiwar." *Uncovered* was subsequently broadcast on the Sundance Channel and ultimately sold around 150,000 DVDs.

MoveOn.org and the Center for American Progress helped finance *Uncovered,* which enabled MoveOn to raise about a million dollars for political work. Many peace groups around the country also used the film to raise funds for their activities. Robert was gratified that MoveOn and other groups were able to use the film so effectively for fund-raising.

Robert, along with the Center for American Progress and MoveOn.org, used the house party model again with *Outfoxed: Rupert Murdoch's War on Journalism,* a biting documentary critique of Fox News. Launched at over 3,500 house parties, *Outfoxed* sold over one hundred thousand DVDs in a few weeks and surpassed two hundred thousand sales during the following months. *Outfoxed* was shown theatrically in the United States, and the DVD was number one on Amazon for a few weeks. It also was shown on television around the world.

The interviews in *Uncovered* and *Outfoxed* used Creative Commons licenses. (See chapter 21.) An inspired hip-hop remix was done with some of the *Uncovered* interviews.

In the wake of the 2004 election and the spectacular success of *Outfoxed* and *Uncovered,* Robert founded Brave New Films, which created *Wal-Mart: The High Cost of Low Price,* Greenwald's hugely successful documentary that reached millions of people and forced the largest company in the world to become a better corporate citizen; distributed *The Big Buy: Tom Delay's Stolen Congress;* produced two television series; created Brave New Theaters; launched a nonprofit foundation; and created *Iraq For Sale: The War Profiteers*—a story of what happens to everyday Americans when corporations go to war. Using his website and e-mail list, Greenwald raised more than $350,000 in donations to make *Iraq For Sale*— over three thousand people contributed an average of $60 each.

9

INTERNET

HOW TO OPTIMIZE YOUR INTERNET PRESENCE FOR E-COMMERCE, OR, HOW TO GET PEOPLE TO YOUR WEB SITE AND TURN THEM INTO CUSTOMERS, SUBSCRIBERS, VOTERS, OR FANS . . . EVEN WHILE YOU SLEEP.

David Mathison

"He who feels punctured must once have been a bubble."
—*Lao Tzu*

If you own a business or run one, if you are an author, filmmaker, politician, community organizer, musician, public speaker, or person just testing the cyber waters, you may already have a website. However, you may not be maximizing it—pulling in as many people as you can or delivering your messages or wares to as many people as you can.

A virtual world awaits—once it knows you are there. Your Internet presence is a global business card that tells a complete stranger what you do. Because it becomes part of the Internet, it gives you global recognition. How much recognition? That depends on you.

The following suggestions—many, many suggestions—do not include how to start a site, because that is the easy part (see chapter 1), or how to wake up the teenager next door, offer $50, and have it done by the time you return with pizza. Instead, we will discuss how to use your website wisely and well so that it morphs into a highly visible Internet presence—for fun and games, for profit or not, or for saving the planet. Your choice.

PUT YOUR SITE ON AUTOPILOT

Computers are supposed to make your life easier, and they can, but only after you program them to handle your business whether you are at work or not. This chapter covers a lot of territory and is meant for a range of readers, from a nonprofit community group to a musician turned media mogul.

We look at it this way: After you have a central place where people can meet, you'll want to build an audience, then bigger and bigger audiences. Before they surf away, it makes sense to get ahold of and manage their contact information. And after you do that, you might as well—if you want to—earn some revenue from those visitors. If you offer something your audience can buy—whether it is a song, a film, a coffee mug for your Save the Redwoods organization, or your latest book—you better have plans in place to accept credit cards and to get the product to them.

As such, this chapter consists of ten sections, as follows:

1. The hardware and software required to create a successful Internet presence.

2. Domains and hosts for your site.

3. Some important content—online media room and privacy policy.

4. How to attract prospects with search engine optimization (SEO).

5. How to create an affiliate program to attract even more prospects.

6. How to maintain these prospects through e-mail list management.

7. How to earn passive revenue from Google's AdSense.

8. How to accept credit card payments.

9. Fulfillment services to get your products to customers.

10. Statistics and package tracking that can optimize your results.

Now, let's get started.

1. HARDWARE AND SOFTWARE REQUIREMENTS

You will need the following hardware: a computer (if I suggested specifications here, they would be outmoded by next week, so I'll leave the choice to you); a CD/DVD burner with software and/or external hard drive storage; a headset/microphone; a scanner; and a laser printer.

The importance of protection programs cannot be stressed enough. Back up your work and customer list! Use a CD/DVD drive and/or external hard drives. I back up every day and save my files both on-site and off-site in a safe-deposit box at my bank. External storage is inexpensive; here are some possibilities: Maxtor 100 MB wallet-size external hard drive ($79); Imation 4 GB flash drive ($79); Seagate 500 GB ($119); Western Digital 1 TB ($329).

Do you prefer Internet-based storage? Try ibackup.com ($9.95 per month for 5 GB).

In case of fire, flood, or theft, be sure to have computer insurance to cover equipment loss.

Buy and install software programs to protect your computer and work, including antivirus, firewall, and antispyware applications such as Symantec's Norton, or McAfee.

2. DOMAINS AND HOSTS

Pick a memorable domain name, one that not only is available but also is easy to remember and to spell. If you are an author, politician, or musician, try to register your name (e.g., mathison.com), the band's name, or the name of your book, album, or film.

You can register your domain and get your site built and hosted at locations listed below. They all have simple website creation tools that use templates with no technical knowledge required. For example, moonfruit.com is great for musicians—such as my nephew Scott who alerted me to it—or anyone. There is no requirement to learn any programming languages or code. Moonfruit offers a free website creation tool that allows anyone—even those with no previous Web technology experience—to create websites. It also provides a message board, a blog, a jukebox, and hosting. In exchange for the free site, Moonfruit runs ads on your site. Or, for just $5.99 per month, you don't have to include ads on your site. You have a six-person band? That's just $1 per month per band member.

Other hosts, such as 1and1.com, offer domain registration and free Web creation tools and templates (plans start at $2.99 per month). GoDaddy.com has 1.2 million active sites (plans start at $3.99/mo). Some other hosts include site2you.com ($59.95 per year), veryviphosting.com (start at $9.95 per month), homestead.com (start at $9.99 per month), dreamhost.com (start at $7.95 per month), freewebs.com, and register.com.

If you have a bit of technical expertise and want features that encourage user participation, check out the free, open source content management platforms mentioned in the We Media chapter. Platforms such as Plone or Drupal are favored by for-profits and nonprofits alike; more than fifty thousand sites are powered by Drupal alone. Or try Django (djangoproject.com), a favorite of online community newspapers.

For politicians, nonprofits, and civic groups, civicspacelabs.org offers powerful community-building tools, such as blogs, discussion forums, voting, and petitions, plus a central database to keep track of your contacts and interactions. It is a hosted service, so there is no software to install and no programming skills are required. All creation and administration is done from your browser.

3. ONLINE MEDIA ROOM AND PRIVACY POLICY

Let us say you want to push your new message or creation, whatever it is. Journalists and TV/radio show producers on deadline can't wait for you to respond to their requests for a quote or an appearance, so make everything available on your site.

Your online media room should be a virtual press kit, with samples of your writing, music, columns, or films. Producers want to hear how you sound on the radio and see what you will look like on TV. Sample clips on your website will give them the confidence to choose you as a guest. Include your biography and résumé; testimonials and endorsements from respected professionals in your field; any awards you have won; conferences you have spoken at or attended; interviews you have given to print, magazines, or on TV and radio; and articles or books you have written.

If you are an author, give viewers more information about your book, provide a sample chapter or two, and let surfers know how to purchase it. Musicians should highlight songs or albums. Include high- and low-resolution photos of you and your company, or book logos, album cover images, or film trailers.

If you don't have any video or audio, interview yourself and put it up as a sample. (See chapters 5 and 7.)

PRIVACY POLICY

If you want people to leave their contact information, it is time for another step: a privacy policy. Respect your customers' privacy at all times. Be sure to have a privacy policy on your site. Keep it simple, easy to read, understandable, and visible; for example, "We will never, ever share, sell, trade, or rent your e-mail address or contact information with any other person or organization—period." The Direct Marketing Association has a privacy policy generator at the-dma.org/privacy/creating.shtml, which creates a policy statement for you.

4. HOW TO ATTRACT PROSPECTS WITH SEARCH ENGINE OPTIMIZATION (SEO)

Now that you have a website, you'll want to bring people in, or as they say in cyber biz, "increase traffic." Eighty-five percent of Internet surfers will find your site through search engines. The top search engines include Google (about 35 percent of U.S. searches and 57 percent worldwide); Yahoo! (about 32 percent of U.S. searches and 21 percent worldwide); and MSN.com (about 15 percent of U.S. searches and 9 percent worldwide). Others include AltaVista, Excite, Lycos, iWon, search.aol.com, HotBot, LookSmart, ask.com, and the Open Directory Project at dmoz.com.

You know how it works. Surfers enter a term into search boxes (for instance, "independent media") and the engine produces a list of related sites, such as indymedia.org and various sites related to independent films, books, and bands.

As a website owner, you want to get more surfers. To find out how you are doing, enter into the top three search engines (Google, Yahoo!, and MSN) your name, company name, product names, or keywords related to your field. Where do you appear in the rankings? If you come up near the top, you can skip this section! If, on the other hand, you are buried below hundreds (or thousands) of results, use the following tips to improve your search engine ranking.

GOOGLE TOOLBAR AND PAGERANK

If you don't already have it, download and install the Google toolbar from toolbar.google.com. During installation, enable the Google PageRank (PR) feature, which will appear on top of your Web browser. PageRank rates websites on a scale of zero to ten, with a PageRank of ten (PR 10) being ranked "most important" and zero (PR 0) being ranked "least important."

According to Google, the search engine determines PageRank as follows: "Google interprets a link from page A to page B as a vote, by page A, for page B. But, Google looks at more than the sheer volume of votes, or links a page receives; it also analyzes the page that casts the vote. Votes cast by pages that are themselves 'important' weigh more heavily and help to make other pages 'important.' Important, high-quality sites receive a higher PageRank, which Google remembers each time it conducts a search."

OPTIMIZING YOUR PAGERANK

Your goal—assuming you want more people to come to your site—is to improve your site's Google PageRank. There are two ways to optimize your website: on-page and off-page. The on-page way is a little easier, so let's address that first.

ON-PAGE OPTIMIZATION

This is done by optimizing your site's title, keyword, and description meta tags; using proper keyword placement and keyword density; and using a site map.

What is a meta tag? In nontechnical terms, a meta tag is the data behind the scenes—the whispered cue to the actor. To the site visitor, it is invisible. The audience has no idea how important it is.

Meta tags are an element of HTML, a markup language used for creating Web pages. Meta tags are important because search engines such as Google "read" your Web page's title, keyword, and description meta tags first; then they read the rest of the text to make sure, in effect, that the story follows the headline.

To see your site's meta tags in your browser, surf to your website and choose "View" > "Source" on your browser's menu bar. As you can see in my example, the source HTML code for Be the Media's site might look like this:

```
<html><head>
<Title>BE THE MEDIA | Independent Media | Build Your Audience</title>
<meta name="keywords" content ="self-publish book, independent media, film, music,
podcast, blog">
<meta name="description" content="BE THE MEDIA teaches you the secrets of inde-
pendent media. We help independent publishers, authors, musicians, and filmmakers
```

find and grow an audience, build a platform, and keep more of the revenues.">
</head><body> Content of your pages goes here</body></html>

EIGHT TIPS FOR ON-PAGE OPTIMIZATION

Title. Use your top keyword search term in the title tag (e.g., "Be the Media"). A bad title would read "Welcome to my website." The fewer words there are in the title tag, the more weight Google gives to the keywords and the higher your site will rank. Don't repeat keywords (media, MEDIA, Media), which will only lower the weight of each.

Keywords. Create a ranked list of words and phrases that potential customers will search to find you and what are about (e.g., "self-publishing" or "independent media"). There are free keyword analysis programs you can use to target the keywords that customers might use to find you, such as inventory.overture.com, digitalpoint.com/tools/suggestion, and goodkeywords.com.

Description. Include a summary using your most important keywords. As you can see in my example, I used, "BE THE MEDIA teaches you the secrets of independent media."

Body. In the body, put your most important keyword within the <H1> tag, and your second most important term in the <H2> tag, which are between the <HEAD> and </HEAD> tags. Search engines will "spider" your site by reading from the top left side of each page down to the bottom right side. In the remaining body field, it is important to have relevant keywords (such as company name, products, and domain name) in the first few paragraphs (top left) and last paragraph (bottom right) of your page. Highlight keywords with bold, *italic,* or underline.

Keyword density. Keyword density is a measure of the number of times your keyword appears in relation to the total number of words in the body of the page. Don't overdo it and cram keywords—blatant overuse of keywords to trick search engines can get you banned from rankings. Check your keyword density with seochat.com/seo-tools/keyword-density.

Image tags. Use your keywords in the "alt" text for your images. For example <img src="BeTheMedia. jpg" alt="Be The Media logo">

Internal pages. Internal pages also are ranked according to your keywords and the anchor text, which describes incoming links. Use your keywords in the anchor text. Don't make the frequent mistake of using generic words like *home* or *click here* as anchor text; it means nothing to search engines. It would be like writing on a name tag that your name is Name.

Site maps. Site maps provide humans with a useful overview of the site's structure and navigation. Search engines also use site maps to crawl through every page in your site, so include on your home page a site map with links to every page on your site. For example, check out Apple's site map at apple.com/sitemap. Add a "no follow" tag on outbound links, so search engines don't leave your site.

OFF-PAGE OPTIMIZATION

When it comes to ranking, off-page optimization factors are much more important than on-page factors. And off-page optimization comprises just one thing: links—the quantity and quality of inbound, related, or highly ranked sites that link to you.

To check the quantity of the backlinks to your website, try out the free tool at tools.marketleap.com/siteindex/default.htm, or use Good Keywords. Its "link popularity meter" shows how many sites link to you.

To check the quality of backlinks and anchor text, try webconfs.com/anchor-text-analysis.php.

TEN TIPS FOR OFF-PAGE OPTIMIZATION: HOW TO GET MORE AND BETTER LINKS

Submit articles to directories. Public relations firm Britt & Associates of Mill Valley, California, successfully increased its client's ranking and built traffic to the client's website (proexhibits.com) by submitting how-to articles to ezine directories such as articlehub.com, ezinearticles.com, and impactarticles.com. You can do the same. Write an article based on your main topic or keyword, such as "Top Ten Podcast Tips." Include at the bottom of the article a link to your site. When Google spiders the article directories, it will index your article and the link to your site.

Syndicate articles. Syndicate (publish) your news, stories, articles, or blog posts to other sites, with links back to your site. Standard syndication protocols such as RSS or ATOM let you automate this process (to learn more, see chapter 10.)

Social bookmarks. Social bookmarks let people tag content to share, organize, and search Internet bookmarks, articles, news stories, photos, Web pages, blog posts, podcasts, audio, and video. Tags offer a new way of finding information online and create a people-powered search engine. In 1996 itlist.com popularized social bookmarking and was quickly followed by Blink, Hotlinks, Backflip, and Quiver.

Social news bookmark sites allow you to submit articles that are then read and voted on by viewers. Those articles with the most votes get moved up to the front page. Because the sites themselves have a high PageRank, the links improve your ranking. Try del.icio.us (PR 8), digg.com (PR 8), reddit.com (PR 7), simpy.com (PR 7), and blinklist.com (PR 7). You can find more sites at listible.com/list/social-bookmarking-sites.

Go to the social news site, create an account, and post the URL of your article, the anchor text, the title, a short description, and your tags (use your keywords). Want to easily post an article to many social news sites? Socializer from Ekstreme (ekstreme.com/socializer) lets you submit a link once and have it published on multiple social bookmarking sites.

Blogs and boards. Comment and participate on related blogs or on bulletin, message, and discussion boards. Your post should have a signature file with a link back to your site.

Reciprocal link exchange. Arrange to have related sites with a high Google PageRank link to your site. If you are a blues band, for instance, investigate link exchanges with blues-related websites and blogs. Using Google, search your main keywords to identify those sites with a Google PageRank higher than yours. PR 6 site links will get you indexed by Google within a few days; links from a PR 7 site will get you indexed in under twenty-four hours. Contact the webmistress or -master at those websites and see if they have a reciprocal link page. Etiquette suggests that you add their link to your site first, before asking them to link to you.

Open Directory Project. Google places a heavy emphasis on links from "authority sites" such as the Open Directory Project at dmoz.org (PR 8), which is the largest human-edited directory on the Internet. However, because editors at the Open Directory Project are all volunteers, it can take months to get your site listed.

Buy links. Text-link brokers and online marketplaces actually sell links. You may want to purchase a PR 7 link for a month for $100, so your site is indexed by Google within twenty-four hours. Try linkadage.com, text-link-ads.com, or textlinkbrokers.com.

Create a viral video. This is a great one for filmmakers and videobloggers. Prior to the 2004 U.S. presidential election, a Flash-based movie featuring an animated George Bush and John Kerry singing "This Land Is Your Land" resulted in more than eight million people per week visiting the video's creator at jibjab.com. Another viral video success story involved Scott Stratten, who attracted more than one million visitors to his website, thetimemovie.com, and seventy thousand subscribers to his newsletter. See chapter 7.

Badges and buttons. Create badges to automate the process of allowing people to link to your site. This way, you control the images, anchor text, and alt text. For example, check out (and use!) the badges from the Save the Internet coalition, a group that supports Net neutrality, at savethenet.com/=promote.

Anchor text. Search engines will rank you higher if your link's anchor text uses your target keywords and the name of your website, your company, or your product.

WHAT *NOT* TO DO

Be mindful about keyword density (cramming). Overuse of keywords will flag your site and completely exclude you from search engine rankings. Don't try to be tricky by hiding keywords (like using white text on a white background) or cramming them into your meta tags (the title, description, and alt image). Just because users can't see the keywords, doesn't mean the search engines are stupid!

It is generally a waste of time to submit your website to Google, Yahoo!, and other search engines via their online submission forms. It can take months for them to search your site. Search engines generally find new sites by going to a website in their index and then following ("crawling") through links on that site to get to another website. If you do choose to submit, there is no need to submit your site to ten thousand search engines. The top ten matter; eleven to one hundred are important but not critical; the rest are useless. Here is a tip: To get Yahoo! to index your site quickly, create a MyYahoo! page and add your site to it.

Don't use words that will flag you as a spammer, such as *online casino, Viagra, mortgage, Cialis, free,* and so forth.

DON'T SPAM. EVER.

Stay out of bad neighborhoods, like link farms, which spam a search engine index ("spamdexing"). Avoid penalized sites that have a gray bar where their Google PageRank should be. They have been banned, and could get your site banned, too.

5. HOW TO ATTRACT EVEN MORE PROSPECTS WITH AN AFFILIATE PROGRAM

Affiliate programs (also known as associate programs or reseller programs) are another way to drive traffic to your site or to sell your products. You enlist other people, groups, and sites to recruit subscribers and customers for you. These are pay-for-performance plans, an online version of paying a finder's fee. You only reward the finder (affiliate) if the introduction results in a lead or in a sale.

Many cite Amazon as having the first online affiliate program.[1] More than 50 percent of Amazon.com's sales come from its one million affiliates (or "associates"). To become an Amazon associate, an owner of a website, blog, or e-mail list displays books, CDs, and films to his or her readers, with a link back to Amazon's website. If the link results in a purchase, Amazon pays the affiliate up to 8.5 percent in commissions.

Be the Media has an affiliate program to help sell this book. Affiliates earn 20% commissions on referrals that result in sales of our books, products, consulting, and speeches at conferences and events. You can find out more about our affiliate program by visiting bethemedia.com/affiliates.htm. I use built-in affiliate software from 1shoppingcart.com to manage affiliates and their commission payouts. Using its interface, I created an affiliate toolkit so affiliates could sign up and start marketing and selling my book, with all the "creative" doodads they need be successful, such as banners, ads, links, buttons, and badges.

I started my affiliate campaign with small, local groups that support independent media, signing up Marin County, California-based Media Action Marin (which has hundreds of members),

---

1. Affiliate guru Shawn Collins clears up the history. Shawn says adult sites pioneered affiliate marketing, with Cyberotica likely being the first. CDNow began its BuyWeb program (created by Geoff Jackson and later called Cosmic Credit) in November 1994. Geffen Records was the first affiliate. This was followed by Flowers & Gifts in October 1994 and Autoweb in October 1995. Amazon's associates program started in July 1996.

Marin Peace and Justice Coalition, and San Francisco-based Media Alliance (which has thousands of members). They promoted a prepublication version of my book to their e-mail list and on their websites and blogs. Any sale that comes from their promotion earns them a 20 percent commission. This way, we support each other instead of giving money to giant media conglomerates, resellers, and distributors.

After testing the system on small, local groups, I opened up the affiliate program to larger regional and national groups such as CODEPINK, a peace group with 192,000 members who support peace and justice.

One of the benefits of self-publishing is that you keep more of the revenues, so you can reward like-minded allies. I was able to offer the book for a monthlong run at the low price of $19.95 for those who could not afford the normal price.

The 80/20 rule applies: 80 percent of your sales come from 20 percent of your affiliates. Expect to pay affiliates an average commission of just under 10 percent. To recruit the best affiliates, some sites pay up to 50 percent to reward top sellers. Good affiliates want to make money. High commissions motivate salespeople, but you have to base your commissions on your costs, which will be different for different products and services. The commision on eBooks and downloadable software can be as high as 50 percent, but print books and CDs/DVDs should be more like 5 to 10 percent commission.

Start out low and ease up. You might set up tiered commissions: unproven strangers get 5 percent, super affiliates get 7 to 10 percent, and VIP mega-affiliates get up to 15 percent or 25 percent. Another model, used by the online toy store eToys, pays a 12.5 percent commission to personal websites, and 25 percent to commercial sites.

According to Shawn Collins, CEO of Shawn Collins Consulting, an agency that manages affiliate programs, perhaps five or six out of his fifty affiliates are VIP level. "Of course, simply having an affiliate program doesn't guarantee sales. Successful programs take time, pay competitive commissions, and reward the best affiliates to keep them happy."

Test your banners and links before passing them to affiliates. Send your affiliates a regular newsletter, and maintain individual contact with your super and VIP affiliates. Be selective and screen out unscrupulous affiliates. To be safe, work with affiliates based in the United States, Canada, the UK, and Australia. Use caution and do some due diligence on all applications. You could get in trouble if they are spammers or violate Federal Trade Commission rules.

To create an affiliate agreement, check out agreements used by Commission Junction, PayLoadz, or the thousands of sites that have affiliate programs, and modify these to suit your needs. Even better, see Shawn Collins's book *Successful Affiliate Marketing for Merchants,* which has is a whole chapter on contracts, and attend his Affiliate Summit conference (visit affiliatesummit.com).

Once your program is running, notify affiliate directories, such as affiliateannouncement. com, which submits your announcement to over fifty affiliate directories. There are hundreds of affiliate directories, including associateprograms.com, affiliatematch.com, affiliatesdirectory. com, clickquick.com, and refer-it.com.

As your program evolves, consider hiring experienced, full-time staff to manage the program and affiliates.

CLICKBANK AND PAYLOADZ

If you sell digital-only products such as eBooks, you might consider joining hosted services such as the ClickBank and PayLoadz affiliate networks. The ClickBank network has over one hundred thousand affiliates selling products from over ten thousand vendors and costs $49.95 to register as a merchant. PayLoadz also lets you sell eBooks, music, podcasts, movies, digital art, manuals, articles, and files. PayLoadz's network is not as big as ClickBank's, but you get your money faster through them because PayLoadz uses PayPal.

The upside of hosted services? They handle administration, recruit new affiliates, have relationships with super affiliates, and operate under rules and regulations that weed out unscrupulous and nefarious affiliates (such as those with bad payment and credit history and violators of CAN-SPAM[2] rules), and they use solid, published privacy policies. The networks are free of negative affiliate relationships such as adult sites and illicit content.

The downside? They cost money to join and take a higher percentage of your royalties than if you manage the affiliates yourself. They also require that you meet monthly minimums to stay in the program and that you have creative (ad banners, text links, etc.), and it requires professional, full-time staff to manage your program. You really shouldn't attempt getting involved with a hosted service until you have a number of products with high margins, a creative grab bag, and a marketing plan.

OUT OF YOUR LEAGUE

When most people hear about affiliate programs, they think of LinkShare and Commission Junction (Be Free), which are by far the largest. These companies service well-established e-commerce companies and brands with lots of products. For example, LinkShare's clients include Buy.com, Overstock.com, and Dell, and Commission Junction has more than forty-one thousand partners, including Microsoft, Disney, ABC, and Oprah. The setup fee is thousands of dollars, and up to 30 percent of each dollar earned goes to commissions. Your products need really high margins to meet these expenses.

So, forget it, at least for now. LinkShare and Commission Junction are more than you need for selling a few books, CDs, DVDs, eBooks, or informational products.

---

2. The Federal Trade Commission's Controlling the Assault of Non-Solicited Pornography and Marketing (CAN-SPAM) Act of 2003 establishes requirements for those who send commercial e-mail.

6. E-MAIL LIST MANAGEMENT

It makes no sense to attract people to your site if you have no way of getting their contact information and managing the list of subscribers.

So repeat after me: "I am in the *list* business. I am in the *list* business." You may *think* you are in the music, book, or film industry, but even if you are a politician, a priest, a consumer advocate, an attorney, or a public speaker, you want to build and manage a large audience.

Your customer contact list is an incredibly important asset. If your office floods or burns today, and everything—even your subscriber list—is lost, you can still start all over again tomorrow if you have one thing: the *process* of building your list. So list-en up.

Most of us use e-mail from Microsoft (Outlook), AOL, EarthLink, Yahoo!, Hotmail, Juno, Google, or others. However, these tools don't automate the process of allowing surfers on your website or blog to subscribe to your services.

Imagine starting to send an e-mail to a thousand (or a million) people, and your e-mail program suddenly cuts out. Stops. Is your program smart enough to start where it left off, or will the first people on the list get multiple versions of the same e-mail? The more subscribers you have, the more important it is for you to outsource list management. It frees you up to do more important things.

List hosts are Internet-based companies that manage your subscribers and e-mail functions. For you, the content owner, list hosts offer fast, easy setup, with no special equipment or skills required; high bandwidth for massive e-mail campaigns; powerful capabilities (mail merge, headers, footers, etc.); and the ability to send from anywhere with just a Web browser and an Internet connection. The host also provides sample code so you can create and include subscription forms on your website or blog.

List hosts let your subscribers come to your website or blog, subscribe, and automatically get a confirmation of their subscription and a welcome e-mail message from you. If they ever want to unsubscribe, the list host handles this as well.

List providers also have arrangements with large domains and increasingly strict Internet service provider e-mail gateways like AOL and MSN, so that your messages get to subscribers without filtration and spam blocking, and abide by federal CAN-SPAM legislation.

A FEW GOOD LIST HOSTS

I use and recommend BIGLIST. President Omar Thameen and his team are knowledgeable and helpful. To see an example of a great newsletter, from header to footer, subscribe to the Be the Media *Update* at lists.bethemedia.com/sub.

Media Action Marin and other nonprofit and activist organizations use riseup.net. Dan Poynter uses Sparklist for his *PublishingPoynters* newsletter. *Democracy Now!* uses BIGLIST, and Holt Uncensored uses Topica. Also check out aweber.com, constantcontact.com, and lyris.com.

SET UP AND TEST!

Always let users know how to unsubscribe easily, usually by clicking on a spot in the footer. Give everyone an easy way to opt out of future e-mails. Fully test your system on close friends before e-blasting to your list of people who are not as close. Add yourself as a subscriber so you can see what messages look like—and that they even arrive.

It is frustrating to have your finely honed messages blocked by antispam filters and firewalls. ContentChecker from Lyris (lyris.com/resources/contentchecker) checks your message before you send it and reports on any words or phrases, such as *free, discount,* or *Viagra,* that might not make it past the spam filters.

HOW TO BUILD YOUR LIST

There is no secret to building your list. You build it in millions of little ways, one by one, step by step. Even simple things will gain you subscribers—for example, employing off-line publicity such as including your website URL on business cards, stickers, and labels; in advertising; on magnetic signs; on billboards; and on products, packaging, and direct mail pieces.

Then there are online methods to accelerating your list. Here are ten such techniques.

E-mail messages. Craft messages to attract ideal customers who will want to subscribe to your offer. An interesting subject line is vital. Try attention-getting, benefit-driven headlines, such as "Ten Tips to More Customers" or "Search Engine Secrets Revealed." Never say something generic such as "Subscribe to our Free Newsletter!"

Opt-in box. Opting in is when someone gives you the right to deliver them an e-mail. You must obtain permission to send e-mails to people, otherwise you are a spammer. The opt-in box is where people enter their e-mail address to subscribe to you. Place the opt-in box on the top right-hand side of every page on your website or blog. Don't use confusing phrases like "submit form"; use terms like "subscribe" or "sign me up now!" Make sure your privacy policy is accessible from the opt-in box and is clear.

Freebies. Offer something of value in exchange for the newcomer's name and e-mail address, such as an e-mail newsletter, course, tutorial, special report, excerpts/chapters, or audio and/or video tutorials. General Foods has a database with tens of millions of contacts that was created mostly from sweepstakes entries and premium and coupon redeemers.

Family, friends, and fans. Ask friends and family to recommend you to *their* friends. Most people purchase books, listen to music, and watch movies on the recommendation of trusted networks of friends and family. Come up with a list of one hundred people you know, and ask them to send a note on your behalf to ten of their friends. Include sign-up information at the bottom of each e-mail and newsletter.

Events. Attend events related to your topic or put on your own event. Go to conferences, take classes, and get business cards, or pass around a sign-up sheet.

Leverage other people's lists. Let large lists owners know that you have something of value for their subscribers. Have them send out a newsletter to people on *their* lists, which talks up your work and links to your site.

Survey. A survey is a way to engage and understand your audience better as well as to start a conversation. For example, Alex Mandossian's askdatabase.com is a search engine for survey data that allows you to discover what customers and prospects want to buy, so you can create new products and services that your customers want. Also try surveymonkey.com, keysurvey.com, ezquestionnaire.com.

Create a VIP Club. Airline frequent-flyer club members get discounts and membership reward points. Treat your preferred customers special, with discounts and personal e-mails. For example, Tom Antion has a Birthday Club that gives members 25 percent off all products all year, a free gift on your birthday, and 50 percent off all products for your entire birthday month. He makes you feel special and can promote things to you personally for an entire month.

Forums. Get active in related online forums and bulletin boards or professional organizations and associations where likely subscribers might be.

Thank you page. After subscribers opt-in to your list or make a purchase, send them to a dedicated Thank You page that lets subscribers enter their friends', families', or colleagues' e-mail addresses. Having a friend recommend you is the best form of advertising.

WHAT *NOT* TO DO

Don't spam or buy lists of millions of people and send out unsolicited e-mails to them. Never sign anyone up without permission. Don't use pop-up or pop-under boxes. Many marketers will tell you that these are great ways to get people to sign up, but most users see these as irritating annoyances—and have pop-up blockers.

THE LIST: A NUMBERS GAME

Always be increasing your list. If you have one hundred contacts, shoot for one thousand. Have one thousand already? Aim for ten thousand. If you have one hundred thousand people interested in your work, then when you release your new book, campaign, eBook, podcast, film, or music you will have a built-in audience interested in dealing directly with you. Cold calls to prospects usually return a meager 1 to 3 percent response rate, whereas response rates from existing customers can be as high as 20 to 50 percent. You want to keep your customers for life and maximize the lifetime customer value by upselling existing customers into higher-value, more profitable content as it becomes available.

For example, "Ezine Queen" Alexandria K. Brown has a list of thirty thousand subscribers. Publicist Joan "The Publicity Hound" Stewart has fifty thousand names, as does Dan Poynter's twenty-year-old newsletter, *PublishingPoynters.* It took electronic marketer Tom Antion over a decade to build his list of one hundred and thirty thousand people. E-mail list king Alex Mandossian has over two hundred fifty thousand names, which puts him on par with national organizations such as CODEPINK (two hundred thousand subscribers) and Common Cause (three hundred thousand members). The National Organization of Women has five hundred thousand members, and MoveOn.org has 3.3 million subscribers.

But remember that bigger is not always better. A small but responsive list is better than a big list with no sales. *Results* are what counts.

Which brings us to money—if that is what you want, that is.

7. HOW TO EARN PASSIVE REVENUE FROM GOOGLE'S ADSENSE

If you are a writer, blogger, musician, or podcaster looking for pocket change, or a politician or nonprofit seeking donations, then it is time to "pay" attention. Because you now have tons of visitors coming to your site, and a way for them to opt-in to your list, and a way for you to keep track of them, why not make some money from the traffic?

Craigslist has no ads, and it does just fine, thank you. Then there are the rest of us.

Just a few years ago, generating money from advertising was challenging and expensive. Thanks to Google, however, anyone with a blog or website can now monetize their audience by serving online ads. Google's AdSense automatically places contextual ads on your site with no maintenance, financial investment, or staff time on your part. In 2005, 20 percent of all online ad revenues in the United States were earned through ads sold by Google and its AdSense network. There are other contextual ad services (for example, Yahoo! Publisher Network, Kontera, and Chitika), but Google's AdSense is the king, so we'll focus on it.

AdSense can make you heaps of money if you know a few tips, tricks, and secrets. For example, plentyoffish.com, a personals site run by one person (Marcus Frind) earns more than $10,000 in AdSense revenue per day. Per day! In February 2006 Frind became the toast of the Internet world when he posted a photo of a Google AdSense check made out to Plentyoffish for $901,733.84.

Joel Comm, known as Dr. AdSense, was making just a few dollars a day from AdSense in 2002. In 2004 he increased his daily revenues by over 1,600 percent by applying new strategies. He saw his revenues jump from $30 per day to over $500 per day, with click-through rates exploding by over 300 percent. He is in the Google UPS Club—if you make over five figures, Google overnights your check via UPS. In one month Comm received a Google check for $25,983.02. Check out Comm's free report at adsense-secrets.com.

Apart from Google AdWords (which costs money), Google offers three free advertising vehicles for publishers of websites and blogs:

Google AdSense. AdSense automatically delivers ads related to your site's content, which translates to more click-throughs and more money in your pocket. The ads change as your site's content changes.

Google AdLink units. AdLink units are words related to the content in your site, and when clicked these links will bring the reader to a page of ads. When a user clicks on the ads on this page, you receive a payment.

Google AdSense for Search. An AdSense for Search box offers Google search right on your site, allowing users to search your website, blog, or the Internet. When a user clicks on the search results page and then clicks on these ads, Google pays you.

Google makes this all very simple. You sign up, copy-and-paste some code into your site, and start collecting money—that's it. AdSense automatically delivers ads onto your site. You decide where the ads are located, and their appearance.

SIX TIPS TO PROFITING FROM GOOGLE'S ADSENSE

Ad inventory. On your site, you can include up to three Google AdSense units, one Google AdLink unit, and two Google AdSense for Search boxes. You can filter and block ads from up to two hundred domains, to avoid having competitors advertise on your site. Opt-in to text, image, and video ads so advertisers have more ad options when serving your site.

Relevant content = targeted ads. Ads are targeted according to content. AdSense operates as an auction, and not all click-throughs are created equal. Some content won't earn you two cents, whereas other keywords (for example, "flat-screen HDTV") are worth dollars.

Placement. Web pages have "hot spots." Eye-tracking analysis shows that upper left is hotter than lower right. Place ads up top and close to the content, but don't aggravate users with annoying, intrusive ads. Try to blend the ads into your site.

Ad formats, sizes, and colors. Ad formats, sizes, and colors will make a big difference. The large rectangles and squares have a 300 percent higher click-through rate than do the smaller banner ads and the wide skyscrapers. Web surfers ignore banner ads. Don't distract readers—keep the color palette complementary to the pages on your site. Make the ad *not* look like an ad and it is more likely to be clicked on.

Test. Continually test your results, using all the variations above, until you find your balance. Google Channels allow you to track performance and see the how different combinations of ad format, placement, and color affect your click-through rates.

Statistics. Use the statistics packages Google provides to improve your revenues. Eliminate under-performing ads and increase the ads that are getting results.

WHAT *NOT* TO DO: DON'T GET BANNED!

Here are a few things to be careful of:

Terms of service. Break the rules of Google's terms of service and you can get banned for life—even if it is an innocent mistake.

Click fraud. Do not click on your own ads. Do not have your family, friends, coworkers, or colleagues click on your ads. Google checks IP addresses, and if you are caught in a click fraud scheme, Google will ban you for life.

Click fraud is another reason to check your statistics regularly. If someone wants to sabotage your income, they can commit click fraud on your site and you could be banned. Check in regularly and report any unusual events to Google.

Offensive content. X-rated websites or sites with hate speech will get you banned.

8. HOW TO ACCEPT PAYMENTS: PAYPAL AND SHOPPING CARTS

If you are selling an eBook, book, DVD, or CD, the majority of customers will want to pay with a credit card. Traditionally it has been hard for small or home-based businesses and start-ups, especially those with iffy credit ratings, to get a merchant account. Now the playing field is leveled, thanks to services like paypal.com and Google's Checkout (https://checkout.google.com), which allow individuals and companies to make and collect payments online. It costs nothing to set up and there is just a minimal per-transaction fee.

For example, with PayPal you get a business checking account at your bank. Once PayPal approves your account, you can begin placing PayPal buttons on your site and accepting and/or sending payments. You can withdraw funds from your PayPal account at any time by requesting an electronic funds transfer to your bank account, or by requesting that a check be sent to you via mail.

SHOPPING CARTS

Another option is to get a complete "shopping cart," which offers more features than just a payment mechanism. Shopping cart software automates payments, sales, and marketing functions. Like PayPal, shopping carts work while you are asleep, on vacation, or at a conference, but a fully integrated package creates a professional external appearance and a more efficient internal sales, marketing, and business process.

When shopping for your shopping cart, look for the ability to

- create online order forms for products;
- process major credit cards in real time;
- automatically deliver your eBook or newsletter;

- automate e-mail list management and mailings;

- use autoresponders to follow up with clients and prospects;

- create and manage affiliates;

- track visitors, sales, and conversions; and

- calculate sales tax and shipping (don't make your customers get a calculator or they may never come back!).

I use 1ShoppingCart.com, which has over ten thousand customers and offers a thirty-day test drive for $3.95. Its starter package is just $29.99 per month. I am in their affiliate program, so if you decide to use them and go through this link—1shoppingcart.com/app/?pr=1&id=98741—I get credit for the referral.

AUTORESPONDERS: SET AND FORGET

Experts say it takes about ten or more ad exposures before a prospective customer will purchase from you. Autoresponders are automatic responses to e-mails, making them the best way to communicate with your list, 24/7. You can vacation, work, and/or eat while the system sends sequential updates and different e-mails to different people and groups at set intervals. For example, a welcoming e-mail is sent upon registration, a training tips e-mail could go out on day two, and then a free e-mail seminar can be scheduled for delivery each day for seven days. 1shoppingcart.com has unlimited autoresponders built in.

Another good autoresponder provider is AWeber Communications (aweber.com), which offers a free thirty-day trial. The service has unlimited follow-up messages, campaigns, broadcasts, newsletters, and messages. Like major e-mail list managers, AWeber has relationships with major ISPs to ensure that your e-mail gets delivered to your customers through the ISP's firewall or spam filters.

9. FULFILLMENT

In the (semi) old days, fulfillment houses would not return the calls of small merchants doing under five thousand orders per month. Today, thanks to the Internet, there are many choices for fulfillment.

According to Jeff Rosen of Breakthrough Distribution (breakd.com), "Independent artists value reliability, timely shipments, excellent customer service, and minimal time to set up and manage account over price. Most content owners prefer to focus on developing and marketing *content,* not spending valuable time at the post office or answering e-mails about lost packages. However, a minimum limit on the number of daily orders often precludes independents from working with larger fulfillment centers targeting high-volume clients or clients with substantial short-run orders. Independents should look toward boutique fulfillment houses. Boutiques can be industry-specific, and tend to provide more personable service with their industry knowledge."

Boutique Fulfillment Houses

Here are a few boutique providers that specialize in your niche.

Authors, musicians, and filmmakers.

- Bookmasters.com offers fulfillment, storage, printing, binding, publishing, storage, and distribution.

- breakd.com: Breakthrough Distribution offers fulfillment services for film-makers, musicians, and authors.

- karolmedia.com: Karol provides media and fulfillment services such as video, CD, and DVD duplication and media packaging.

- thefulfillmenthouse.com: This company transfers VHS to DVD and does CD/DVD duplication.

- disk.com: Corporate Disk Company also does tape-to-DVD duplication.

Speakers and coaches. Speakerfulfillmentservices.com specializes in handling and delivering transcripts and CDs of seminars.

eBay, direct-response television, or catalogs. Atlastfulfillment.com.

BIG FULFILLMENT HOUSES

If you can move lots of product, here are three big shops:

Dart Entities (dartentities.com) has a 721,000-square-foot warehouse with 116 doors and parking for over three hundred trailers. Herb Duggan, who has worked for Dart for twenty-seven years, knows this business inside and out. Their major customers are Sears (a Dart customer for over sixty years), Lands' End, and no-money-down real estate entrepreneur Carlton Sheets.

eFulfillment Service (efulfillmentservice.com) has sixty-five thousand square feet of storage in two locations. It handles setup, storage, stocking, and programming, and it is ideal for start-ups because it has no fees for setup or receiving, and no minimum orders. You can start with as few as ten orders per month. According to a recent quote, eFulfillment charged around $2.30 per order based on shipping fewer than one thousand orders per month. Its storage fee for five thousand books would be $120 per month (a standard fee of $70 per month, plus $0.01 per book times five thousand books = $50). Returns cost $2.30 per item.

National Fulfillment Inc. (nationalfulfillment.com) ships over twenty million packages annually and has warehouses in Nashville and Los Angeles.

EXERCISE CAUTION!

One company, iFulfill.com, went out of business in July 2005, traumatizing customers who had stock in its warehouse and orders waiting to be shipped to customers. Merchants literally had to drive to the warehouse to retrieve their products.

10. STATISTICS AND TRACKING TO OPTIMIZE YOUR RESULTS

To increase traffic to your website, and to turn Internet visitors into purchasers (conversions), it's a good idea to analyze your surfers' grazing habits. Try Google's free analytics tool at google.com/analytics to see where your traffic is coming from. Or, try a free thirty-day trial from web-stat. com. No HTML knowledge is required, and the software installs on any website, MySpace, and most blogs. It offers site traffic reports, and alerts if it detects your site is down.

Other website statistics programs are found at visitorville.com, webtrends.com, and click-tracks.com.

In summary, having a website is not for hermits. It's a door to the world, or at least the world as defined by Internet users. How much of that world you want to invite in, and what you want the world to do when it gets there, is up to you.

"Only those who will risk going too far can possibly find out how far one can go."
—T.S. Eliot

10

SYNDICATION

ALL ABOUT SYNDICATION

David Mathison
Illustrations by Lloyd Dangle and Keith Knight

This chapter is available online as a downloadable eBook. Send an email to: info@bethemedia.com with the subject line "Syndication."

11

LICENSING

HOW TO LICENSE YOUR IDEAS WITHOUT SELLING YOUR SOUL[1]

David Mathison

> "To see things in the seed. That is genius."
> —*Lao Tzu*

In Southern California in 1960, a young surfer named Duke Boyd teamed up with Long Beach seamstress Doris Boeck to create shorts that would be durable enough to withstand the rigors of surfing. The logo for the company, Hang Ten, depicted the ultimate position in surfing: ten toes on the edge of a surfboard. By 1964, the company grossed $300,000, but net profits were low because of all the payments to contractors, salespeople, and accountants, and the cost of inventory and storage. Boyd and Boeck approached Richton Sportswear, their largest contractor, to become the first Hang Ten licensee. Richton would manage sales, manufacturing, and distribution, and would pay Boyd and Boeck a royalty. Today, Hang Ten has licensees in seventy-two countries with four hundred stores and $720 million in sales—without Hang Ten having to pay all that overhead.

ENTERTAINMENT LICENSING

Like Hang Ten, entertainment giants leverage their assets—logos, characters, films, cartoons, music, and books—as vehicles for lucrative licensing opportunities. Walt Disney and George

---

1. Thanks to Susan Harrow, author of *Sell Yourself Without Selling Your Soul* (Collins, 2002).

Lucas built their fortunes through the power of licensing. Disney Consumer Products is the world's largest licensor, with global retail sales of $23 billion for 2006. George Lucas made a fortune from the *Star Wars* franchise, and the officially licensed *Star Wars* material (outside of the films) even has its own umbrella term, Expanded Universe, which includes action figures, books, comics, and games.

One does not have to be Walt or George or Doris or Duke, though, to license original work. Anyone can do it. All you need is an idea.

WHAT IS LICENSING?

According to the late licensing guru Kenn Kerr,[2] "Licensing is the ultimate form of leverage. It's the fastest, simplest, and shortest distance between an idea in your head (or someone else's) and a lifetime stream of income in your mailbox. Think of it: no manufacturing, no setup costs, no inventory, no sales costs, no sales force, no distribution costs, no employees, no risk, no money, and little or no investment of time or energy."

Licensing is the leasing of a legally protected (trademarked or copyrighted) property—images, characters, ideas, or logos. According to the October 2007 issue of *License!*, it is now a $187.4 billion-a-year business, based on 2006 worldwide retail sales of licensed merchandise. Licensing multiplies resources, extends a brand, and diversifies revenue streams, giving the person with the original idea the free time and extra money to develop new ideas and do more creative work. Through licensing, a person or company gains access to new customers, markets, channels, and retailers. The main job of the licensor is to maintain quality control.

Before surfing into somewhat tricky waters, let us make sure we know a few basic terms. The licensor is the person who creates or owns the property (i.e., the Hang Ten feet), determines the products to be licensed (such as swimsuits or surf boards), creates awareness and demand for the products ("Hang Ten presents . . ."), and collects royalties from the licensee. The licensee (usually) manufactures, markets, and sells the product, and pays royalties to the licensor.

HISTORY

Licensing as we know it began in the early 1900s with newspaper cartoon characters like The Yellow Kid. In 1903 Beatrix Potter created a Peter Rabbit doll, and the Buster Brown comic strip image was licensed for a number of products. In 1913 President Theodore "Teddy" Roosevelt licensed his nickname for a Teddy bear; the royalties were used to establish a network of national parks. In the 1950s, with the advent of television, licensing exploded. Warner Brother's *Looney Tunes* characters and the *Howdy Doody Show* joined the fray, as did the *Davy Crockett* TV show,

---

2. Kenneth A. Kerr Jr. (1943–2004) created Woodsy Owl ("Give a Hoot, Don't Pollute") for the National Park Service in 1969 and the California Dancing Raisins for the California Raisin Board in 1986; worked on Epcot Center, Tokyo Disneyland, and Fantasyland as an executive with Walt Disney Imagineering; and licensed products as diverse as the Smurfs, Gummi Bears, Wuzzles, and Raggedy Ann and Andy.

which led Disney to license coonskin caps as well as lunchboxes and thermoses. Guitarist Les Paul licensed his name to Gibson's solid-body electric guitar. In the 1960s the James Bond movies led to licensed goods such as watches, toys, games, and comics. Television's *Sesame Street* begot Oscar, Ernie, and Big Bird dolls and toys.

By the 1970s, fashion licensing exploded with Pierre Cardin and Calvin Klein. Paramount Pictures made a fortune from licensed goods based on the TV shows *Happy Days, Star Trek,* and *Mork & Mindy.* In the 1980s myriad properties such as the TV's Smurfs, toys such as Cabbage Patch Dolls, sports (MLB, NCAA), action figures, and corporate entities such as the California Raisins and Budweiser's Spuds MacKenzie were for sale.

The next decade included licensing based on *South Park* (via Comedy Central), the first *Harry Potter* book (via Scholastic), and Pokémon (from Japan). In the early 2000s financially "safe" sequels re-emerged, including Spider-Man, The Hulk, Superman, and Batman. The movie *Spider-Man 2* generated over $750 million in licensed-product sales. TV shows with strong exposure, such as Nickelodeon's *Dora the Explorer* and *SpongeBob SquarePants,* also led to licensing lucre. Finally, celebrity licensing, which began with silent film star Charlie Chaplin in 1910, today includes Tiger Woods and Paris Hilton.

NO LOGO

As author Naomi Klein points out in her book *No Logo: Taking Aim at the Brand Bullies* (Knopf, 2000), brands have become ubiquitous (see Sidebar LogoLand). Studies show that U.S. children are brand-conscious by the age of three and that most children can recognize more than two hundred logos before beginning elementary school. "Liberated from the real-world burdens of stores and product manufacturing, these brands are free to soar, less as disseminators of goods or services than as collective hallucinations." Klein criticizes these moving billboards of "walking, talking, life-sized Tommy [Hilfiger] dolls, mummified in fully branded Tommy worlds."

LogoLand

Licensed goods are everywhere you look. You may have seen stores selling George W. Bush's face on toilet paper (I doubt he is collecting royalties). The Progressive Democrats of America (PDA) offer PDA-branded ImpeachMINTS ("for a fresher democracy"). Logos and characters can be found on action figures, apparel, backpacks, bed sheets, board games, book covers, bottles, bumper stickers, buttons, calendars, caps, casino slots, coffee mugs, collectibles, coloring books, comic books, costumes, cups, dolls, erasers, figurines, footwear, greeting cards, hats, interactive games, lunch boxes, office supplies, oral care, party goods, pencils, pens, pillow cases, planners, plates, plush, posters, school supplies, stationary, sweat shirts, tee-shirts, thermoses, ties, tote bags, toys, video games, video poker, watches, and wrapping paper. And much more. Just look around. Whenever you see a logo, someone is making some money.

CAUSE LICENSING AND NONPROFIT LICENSING

There are people and groups, however, implementing licensing programs with a social conscience. Royalty revenues from nonprofit product licensing totaled $40 million in 2003, up from $10 million in 1999. Nonprofit organizations leverage licensing to generate new income streams and to create awareness for their cause. Think of a tote bag from a public television station. Successful programs make an emotional connection with the audience. "This dovetails with an evolving consumer desire to express personal values externally—for example, the success of the Lance Armstrong Foundation's Live Strong bracelet," says Phoebe Campbell of Campbell Associates.

Some ventures are especially creative. Kids-Did-It! Properties represents illustrations by young art students, ages three to fourteen. The kids' illustrations adorn calendars, greeting cards, gift bags, postage stamps, and even real bank checks. The young artists also have provided images for Covenant House for homeless children, the Audubon Society, KPBS television, and San Diego Hospice, and they earn royalties for each licensed reproduction of their artwork. According to kidsdidit.com, the Kids-Did-It Designs collection of nearly five hundred images has rung up more than $5.5 million in retail sales to date. Several young artists have earned more than $2,500 in licensing royalties.

ESTATE: LONG LIVE THE KING

Licensing is the gift that keeps giving. Bob Marley, Marilyn Monroe, James Dean, and Jimi Hendrix are iconic personalities whose images have withstood the test of time and whose estates continue to earn royalties from their work and likenesses. According to Forbes's annual "Top-Earning Dead Celebrities" list, top dead earners in 2007 included Kurt Cobain, Elvis Presley—the King of licensing, Charles M. Schultz, John Lennon, and Albert Einstein. Kurt Cobain dethroned the King from the number one spot when Cobain's widow Courtney Love sold a 25 percent stake (worth an estimated $50 million) in Nirvana's catalog to Primary Wave Music Publishing. In the past, Love licensed Nirvana songs to the TV shows *Six Feet Under* and *CSI: Miami,* and the movie *Jarhead.* Forbes estimates that Elvis Presley Enterprises earned $42 million from licensing deals in 2005-2006, a forty-fold increase in revenue since Priscilla Presley became executor of his estate in 1979.

GETTING STARTED

It might seem that celebrities—living or dead—are a world apart from us here on earth, but remember, most started modestly. You can follow their early examples, and see where they lead.

Come up with your own idea. In 1928 Walt Disney traveled to New York City to negotiate a higher per-cartoon pay rate for his creation Oswald the Rabbit. He was getting $2,250 per cartoon and he wanted $2,500. Charles Mintz and distributor Universal actually owned the cartoon and secretly signed Disney's artists out from under him. Having lost his creation, Disney sketched Mickey Mouse on the long train ride home—and a multi-billion-dollar global business was born.

Find an existing business to leverage. Randolph W. Chan invented the plastic battery-case tester. By pressing the top and bottom of the battery in the plastic case, a consumer can be sure the batteries inside are fully charged before buying them. Instead of making batteries himself, Chan licensed the package design to Duracell, which has subsequently sold billions of batteries using Chan's new case.

Acquire the license to someone else's idea. Bill Gates did not invent DOS, nor does he manufacture computers. He paid another inventor $50,000 for the rights to the software and then licensed it to IBM for use in their personal computers. Gates didn't sell the software to IBM outright; he licensed it to them, and subsequently built one of the world's largest companies.

Use licensing to boost or extend a dormant business. Everlast, traditionally a supplier of boxing gear, has a licensing program that provides Everlast-branded nutritional supplements, deodorants, batteries, toys, treadmills, and swimwear, extending their brand from the ring to the pool.

Publicity rights. Publicity rights allow celebrities such as Tom Hanks, athletes such as Derek Jeter, and performers such as Bette Midler to control the use of their names, likenesses, signatures, and voices for commercial purposes. These rights can be extremely valuable. In 1988 the U.S. Court of Appeals awarded Bette Midler $400,000 after an advertising agency used a Midler look-alike to perform her version of the Bobby Freeman song "Do You Want to Dance?"

Do research. If you do not have your own idea, look for one. Read trade publications in any industry that interests you. The *Catalog of Catalogs* lists all catalogs in the United States, helpful for finding direct-mail catalogs that relate to music, book publishing, or film. Another resource is the *American Registry of Manufacturers,* which lists all manufacturers by subject, such as all companies that manufacture T-shirts. A good bookstore or library should be able to lead you to these publications and help you check on patents. If you then spot something worthwhile, contact the inventor and find out if he or she has sold the worldwide rights to the idea yet.

INSTANT LICENSING

If you have your own idea or image in your head, a number of different Web-based services let you personalize and brand your image onto T-shirts, hats, toys, umbrellas, pens, and key chains. Try spreadshirt.com, zazzle.com, branders.com, and customink.com.

If you want a virtual storefront to sell the goods, one of the most widely used services is Cafe-Press, started in August 1999 with an order for a T-shirt emblazoned with KILL POP RADIO! *Be the Media* has a CafePress storefront at cafepress.com/bethemedia. Buy! Buy!

We at *Be* are not alone. More than 2.5 million CafePress members have built 1.2 million virtual shops and made over thirty-five million unique products. CafePress manages everything—"storefront" development, website hosting, order management and fulfillment, secure payment processing, shipping, and customer service. There are no upfront costs and no inventory to store or manage. Just think of a catchy slogan (like the FREE MARTHA T-shirts, when Martha Stewart was in jail), upload the slogan or logo, and place it on more than seventy customizable products, from underwear to mouse pads to coffee mugs.

CafePress sets a baseline price for goods (say, $14.95 for a shirt) and lets you set your selling price (say, $19.95). You keep the difference ($5 per shirt).

Want to retain a higher percentage of the profits? Try Zazzle.com ("Capitalism done right"), which gives the creator 50 to 70 percent of the profits.

NEXT STEP: MORE PROFITS AND CONTROL

Eventually, you may start to feel limited by not having control over the raw materials or their origins, or not knowing whether socially responsible work practices or environmentally sustainable techniques were involved in making your T-shirts. You also may want higher margins than those offered by the places listed above or you may want to pursue off-line distribution capabilities, such as retail outlets or clubs. If so, it might be time to get serious about controlling your licensing program.

Keep in mind that you do not have to stick with T-shirts and coffee mugs. Maybe it is time to license something else you created, such as a book, magazine, song, film, or video.

Publishing. Let's start with, so to speak, the hard sell. It is hard for a book to become a licensed property. How many licensing opportunities are there for Mitch Albom's *Tuesdays with Morrie* or Thomas Friedman's *The World Is Flat*? Even good licensing candidates take time to mature. The authors of *Chicken Soup for the Soul* waited for four years and thirteen titles before they launched their licensing program, subsequently growing it to $100 million in retail revenue in five years. Today, *Soul* greeting cards are the number one license with American Greeting Cards. The book series was a perfect licensable product—moral, soul-stirring, heartwarming, people-centered stories with a great "American" cover image: red and blue letters on a white background, with a C in *Chicken* similar to the C in the Campbell's soup company's logo.

The authors' advice? Wait. According to one of *Soul's* authors, Mark Victor Hansen, you know you are ready to license your book when:

- you've sold a significant number of books and have reached best seller status. Awareness equals equity in your brand.

- your title has become a brand name. The mention of your brand should trigger a series of expectations or emotions in the audience.

- it is realistic that someone would pay you for the title of your book.

- you contact licensing agents and they show interest.

Another book that became licensable was the reissue of the classic children's story *Stuart Little*. Columbia Pictures' film and the toys from *Stuart Little* extended the Harper-Collins brand to a new generation that might not have read the original book.

All in all though, Stuart Little (and Harry Potter) notwithstanding, let's go to an easier arena than books: magazines.

Because the shelf life of an established publication is much longer than the short-term impact of advertising, many publications cash in on their cache as manufacturers tag along. *Cosmopolitan* has licensees for apparel, swimwear, lingerie, and bedding. *Food & Wine* has licensees for gourmet food products. Meredith's *Better Homes and Gardens* magazine extended its brand through licensing initiatives with Home Depot (in the form of books such as *Home Landscaping*) and Scotts' Miracle-Gro.

Music licensing. With concert and record sales down, musicians, bands, and labels are using licensing to generate additional income. Musicians license their music and ringtones via cell phones, on the Internet, and in video games, and license their images and graphics as wallpaper and screen savers or on posters and apparel. According to Lee Tepper, CEO of MerchDirect, "For many of our artists, merchandising is an important source of income, sometimes more so than record sales." MerchDirect designs and manufactures a band's branded gear, and then sells and ships the products to over one hundred retailers, including Hot Topic, Musicland, Urban Outfitters, Transworld, Alloy, and Old Glory.

Some companies specialize in bands on tour. BandMerch provides an entire tour package, even sturdy packing cases with product-display signage and credit card machines. Signatures Network, which licenses more than 125 artists and celebrities, gives artists an advance on projected merchandise sales—anywhere from $25,000 to $400,000, depending on the number of cities played and whether the band is the headliner or the opening act.

Musicians are extending even past these traditional licensing opportunities. U2 has a branded iPod with its signature red-and-black color scheme. Guitarist B.B. King signed an exclusive deal with Marketing On Demand as his licensing agency for furniture, apparel, and food. Signatures Network created a licensing program for apparel, accessories, dolls, paper goods, plush toys, stationery, and tea sets related to Madonna's children's book *The English Roses*. Signatures Network also represents rocker Sammy Hagar's tequila brand Cabo Wabo. In May 2008, 80 percent of Cabo Wabo was acquired for $80 million by Gruppo Campari/Skyy Spirits, making Sammy Hagar one very happy licensor.

Musicians and bands also need to consider the cell phone market in their licensing mix. As of this writing, there are more than 2 billion worldwide mobile phones, most are audio and video capable, and many fans are personalizing their devices with their favorite songs, ringtones, and wallpaper. Bling for your ring is available from many vendors, including FunMail, which helps content providers optimize ringtones and graphics. Ringtone Universe sells ringtones, animated graphics, logos, wallpaper, and screen savers from Snoopy to Superman and *South Park*. Airborne Entertainment helps its clients Deepak Chopra and *Maxim* magazine get their content onto mobile and wireless devices. Bango enables content providers to sell music, pictures, videos, and games directly to mobile users. Mforma, now Hands-On Mobile, resells ringtones, images, and wallpaper from well-known brands, including Marvel Comics, World Poker Tour, and Billboard (for more on music licensing, see chapter 4.)

Interactive. *Interactive* used to mean a stand-alone computer game, but today's film, music, and interactive gaming industries are colliding and intersecting. Increasingly, authors, designers, filmmakers, musicians, software developers, and graphic artists are collaborating. Interactive games based on movies like *The Matrix* can prolong the life of a film past the theatrical release and can widen its reach to a younger audience. TV-licensed properties are also going interactive, with games based on *24, CSI, ER, Law and Order,* and *South Park.*

Musicians and labels are getting into the "game" too. Video game publishers are giving gamers a variety of music choices, so they can personalize the music in their games. This offers musicians and bands a platform to expose their tunes to young players. For example, Electronic Arts partnered with artists from Sony Music Entertainment and Def Jam in EA's NFL Street game. Motown Records Group did a cross-promotional collaboration with Atari.

The basic caveat remains the same with games, though, as with anything else, including books: licensees, manufacturers, and retailers only want known products with low risk and the potential for high reward.

GETTING SERIOUS

As these examples demonstrate, licensing can be lucrative, but it usually requires a fully baked property, one that is distinct, widely recognized, well developed, and supported by product development, marketing, advertising, publicity, media, and promotion dollars. Licensees, manufacturers, and retailers are otherwise not interested.

Timing is a key, too. Will the property support an upcoming or ongoing TV show, movie, game, or book? Is it seasonal, for example—a toy during the holiday or a school supply for back to school? Do you need a prototype ready for industry trade shows, advertising, catalogs, or sales meetings?

Getting serious also means getting an attorney who specializes in trademarks and licensing. Permissions alone can be hard to track down. Say you want to use the images of a dozen Major League Baseball players for a calendar. You contact their agents and representatives, get the rights from twelve parties, and think you are covered. But for full clearance, you'll also need permission from their respective teams, the MLB Players Association, and the MLB itself. You will also need to make "split" royalty payments to each of these individuals and groups. Licensing requires serious due diligence, and specialist attorneys can make this phase easier, with less liability for you.

In most cases, an attorney would register your trademark in appropriate classes (more about trademarks and classes below). But I would recommend that anyone getting really serious to hire a licensing agent as well. A licensing agent is a deal-maker, marketer, and business development manager for your property. Licensing agents have extensive industry contacts and resources. They know, or should know, the business inside out. Some are strong in entertainment, corporate, and lifestyle properties (such as The Licensing Group Ltd.). Others, such as IMC Licensing, represent consumer brands such as Kraft and Planters. Some agents specialize in fashion, in sport and celebrity properties, in children's products, or in the toy industry.

To find an agent, read the trades (see Resources, below), where agents advertise and are quoted in articles. Contact the International Licensing Industry Merchandisers' Association (LIMA), attend trade shows in your area of interest, check directories, or ask for a referral. An agent's standard fee is one-third of the gross royalties, but some may take less commission for an early property. Some agents must be paid a retainer, some require a retainer plus commission, some take a straight commission (called brokering), and some are paid a flat fee for a project-based job. Agents are not to be confused with consultants, who represent manufacturers.

TRADEMARKS

A trademark is any word, logo, slogan, design, or symbol that serves as an indicator of its source or sponsorship. In the wonderful world of licensing, trademarks for goods and services are broken down into one of forty-five classes. For example, paper products are listed as Class 16 and toys and games are listed as Class 28. The cost for registration is $335 per class if registered online, and $375 per class if done by mail.

Let us assume you have a property, an audience, an interested licensee (see below, How to Choose and Monitor a Licensee), a lawyer, and possibly an agent. Now you need a license agreement.

To take a firmer example, your hot new band Bill Benjamin and the C-notes wants to license your album cover image *Hundred-Dollar Bill* for apparel and posters. A potential licensee forecasts that they will sell five hundred thousand T-shirts over three years, at an average price of $10 each, for $5 million in total revenues. They will pay you a 10 percent royalty rate over three years ($500,000) and a 10 percent advance ($50,000) on signing. You like this forecast. You ask your attorney to write up an agreement.

The following are the major deal points in the agreement:

- Product. The property's design, materials, and sizes, as determined by the licensor.

- Territory. The geographic region in which the licensee can sell the merchandise.

- Distribution channels. How the licensee will reach the customer—via retailers, mail order, Internet, concession stands, etc.

- Exclusivity. An "exclusive" deal would mean a single licensee gets all rights to use a property in a particular product category, territory, or distribution channel. This can be good for the licensee, but not the licensor. Licensors should use what are called nonexclusives, to minimize risk and to spread the wealth, exposure, and brand through different channels.

- Minimum guarantee. Usually based on anticipated and forecasted sales.

- Advance. Paid upon signing. Usually a portion of the guarantee, not an additional payment.

- Term. Agreement duration will depend on many factors. Usually two to three years to start.

- Royalties. Taken as a percentage of sales, rates range from 1 to 20 percent and average 8.4 percent. Royalties are generally paid as a percentage of the item's sale price. When Ken Kamen ("the father of modern licensing") was hired by Walt Disney in 1932, he paid licensees a commission of 5 percent, the percentage that traditional sales reps were paid. Today's industry-standard royalties run along category lines, such as designer (3 to 7 percent), celebrity (3 to 7 percent), corporate (5 to 8 percent), art (6 to 10 percent), sports (8 to 10 percent), character and entertainment (8 to 12 percent), toy (12 to 14 percent), and event (10 to 15 percent).

  Royalty rates can be complicated to negotiate. Factors include what to base the percentage on (e.g., gross versus net revenues), the payment schedule, advances, guarantees, and auditing. It is in the licensor's best interest to keep costs low and to incur as few expenses as possible; to base royalty rates on gross, not net, sales; and to require monthly or quarterly royalty payments and reports.

  To verify that the reports and financial calculations are accurate, it is wise to hire—yes—yet another person to conduct royalty compliance reviews. You need what is called a royalty audit. According to Sidney Blum, Partner at KPMG's Royalty Compliance Services group, 99 percent of licensees underreport royalties. Every audit he has ever undertaken has resulted in finding royalties owed to the licensor. So even after you have spelled out how royalties are to be calculated and records are to be kept, do not simply rely on your licensee's reporting. One-week audits with findings of over $1 million are common.

Moss-Adams LLP also does royalty compliance audits. Their clients include artists, producers, songwriters, music publishers, authors, and licensors, and they handle royalty audits for merchandising, recording, music publishing, motion picture, video, television, book publishing, and computer software.

- Termination. The most important clause in your agreement is the termination clause covering how to exit a bad deal. It is easy to write graceful exit strategies into the agreement. This agreement is terminated if the licensee fails to ship the goods by a particular date (such as before the C-notes have a big concert) or does not meet minimum sales requirements. It is typical to include a thirty-day notice for termination.

HOW TO CHOOSE AND MONITOR A LICENSEE

To find potential licensees, attend trade shows, see whom your competitors use, contact trade organizations, consult industry directories, or list or advertise your company name and property in category-specific trade publications, such as *License! Global* magazine, *KidScreen,* the *Toy Book, Gift & Stationery Business, Supermarket News, Adweek, Brandweek,* or *Advertising Age.*

It is typical for you, the licensor (creator/owner of the property) to make arrangements with multiple licensees (marketers of the property's logo on baseball caps, for example). But not all licensees are created equal. One or two productive licensees are better than many nonproductive ones who need constant monitoring and attention. A strong licensee will be able to generate revenues through their existing distribution channels. Be selective.

You might follow the example of Sesame Workshop (see Sesame Workshop Sidebar), which wanted licensees that loved children, were focused on education, did community outreach, and did not contribute to childhood obesity (even Cookie Monster declared that cookies are a "sometimes" food). Therefore, Sesame does not partner with fast food chains.

The National Wildlife Federation (see National Wildlife Federation Sidebar) only accepts licensees that are environmentally responsible and education-oriented. Scholastic's property Clifford the Big Red Dog has one hundred licensees. Scholastic prioritizes distribution in a licensee, since a great product may never reach the consumer if the manufacturer does not have access to retail shelves.

Sesame Workshop

Sherrie Westin

Sesame Workshop is the nonprofit organization of writers, artists, researchers, and educators behind *Sesame Street* and other educational programs for children. Founded in 1969, Sesame Workshop had as its original aim to give a head start to educationally disadvantaged preschoolers in the United States, using television as a tool to help them learn. Thirty-six years later, *Sesame Street* continues to bring the joy of learning to new generations of American children as well as children around the globe. Its mission is to maximize the educational power of media to make a difference in the lives of children everywhere.

The workshop recognized early on that licensing was a way to meet two key objectives: first, to extend the reach of the *Sesame Street* brand to support and enhance our on-air initiatives, and second, to generate additional revenue streams to support our programming and outreach efforts. Thanks in part to licensing revenue, Sesame Workshop programs and initiatives now reach children in over 120 countries through a variety of media, including television, radio, the Internet, film and home video, community outreach, books, and magazines.

Sesame Workshop's marketing relationships take a number of forms, depending upon the needs and objectives of both the workshop and its potential partner. In some cases, *Sesame Street* characters are licensed to established companies such as American Greetings, Fisher-Price, Gund, Random House, and Sony Wonder, which share the workshop's vision and values. Elmo and friends add to the appeal of products like party goods, plush toys, and apparel, and Sesame Workshop benefits in that the revenue it receives helps fund its mission-oriented activities in countries such as Bangladesh, Egypt, and Kosovo. Other workshop-licensed products conform more directly to the organization's mission—books and toothbrushes, for example—and the workshop receives the added benefit of extending the reach of its educational materials. No matter what the product, however, Sesame Workshop always strives to infuse it with positive messages in keeping with the *Sesame Street* brand and the workshop mission.

Sesame Workshop also seeks partnerships for initiatives targeting a specific need it has identified. One such initiative is "Healthy Habits for Life," developed in response to the growing crisis of childhood obesity in the United States and other parts of the world. The project involves a coalition of partners, many of whom are in the licensing industry, as well as an advisory board of health, nutrition, fitness, and education experts. Its goal is to develop and distribute age-appropriate multimedia content that will engage children with messages highlighting the importance of exercise and good nutrition.

From time to time, the workshop is approached by companies seeking its expertise and resources to address an issue of particular concern to them. Prudential enlisted the organization to help develop "*Sesame Street* Beginnings: Language to Literacy," an educational outreach initiative for children from birth to age three that helps lay the foundation for literacy during those critical, early years. And Merrill Lynch teamed up with the workshop on "Talking Cents," an initiative designed to foster good financial habits and encourage children to become fiscally responsible adults.

In each of these arrangements, Sesame Workshop's partners profit from their association with a beloved and trusted global brand, and the workshop receives funding to help sustain its educational activities around the world. But the ultimate beneficiaries are children, who, with the help of *Sesame Street* and other workshop programs, can learn and grow and strive to reach their highest potential.

National Wildlife Federation

Jaime Berman Matyas

National Wildlife Federation (NWF) is a nonprofit organization whose mission is to inspire Americans to protect wildlife for our children's future. National Wildlife Federation was created seventy-one years ago by President Theodore Roosevelt to bring together individuals, organizations, and agencies to restore and conserve our nation's wildlife resources. Today, NWF is recognized as America's largest conservation organization and benefits from the equity built from the respected reputation of its brand and kids' brands. National Wildlife Federation, Ranger Rick, Your Big Backyard, Wild Animal Baby, and other NWF properties have been successfully licensed for programs that generate revenue, extend NWF's brand, and raise awareness for wildlife conservation.

In the 1980s, NWF and Franklin Mint embarked on a licensing program around a wildlife-themed collectible plate series, bronze sculptures, and framed prints. Inspired by the success of this relationship, in 1994 NWF created an entire department dedicated to licensing and cause marketing programs, which now includes affinity marketing, sponsorship, licensed retail products, and promotions. NWF has since partnered with a number of high-profile, top-tier companies, such as the following.

In 2003, Green Mountain Coffee Roasters and NWF together introduced National Wildlife Blend and National Wildlife Decaf coffees to promote the benefits of shade-grown, certified organic Fair Trade coffee to U.S. consumers. This partnership, announced to coincide with International Migratory Bird Day in May, drew attention to the important link between shaded coffee habitat and the health and welfare of migratory birds. This coffee is sold in targeted markets through wholesale, online, and direct mail channels with the goal of expanding distribution based on demand.

Also in 2003, NWF entered into what might seem an unlikely partnership with outdoor power equipment engine manufacturer Briggs & Stratton to create a media campaign for "Mower Tune-Up Month." The organizations found common ground in promoting the benefits of tuning up lawn mowers, which include emissions reduction and improved fuel efficiency. The media was very receptive to the campaign, which reached over seventy-eight million Americans through multiple media channels. As a result, Briggs & Stratton enjoyed a three-fold increase in sales of lawn mower tune-up kits. The licensed media promotion was awarded a Cause Marketing Halo Award in the Best Environmental/Wildlife Campaign category in 2003.

More recently, NWF formed a partnership with leading "DIY" publisher Creative Homeowner to publish *Attracting Birds, Butterflies and Other Backyard Wildlife,* which teaches people how to restore habitat and attract wildlife to their backyards. The book's author, NWF's Naturalist David Mizejewski, took part in a national radio tour and book signings, and select television appearances including NBC's *Weekend Today Show* and *The Martha Stewart Show.* Other promotion included a press release and marketing in NWF's internal channels such as its magazine, website, and newsletters. To date, the book has sold almost forty thousand copies.

Leap Frog, another publishing partner, licenses the Ranger Rick brand for its Read-It-All series of high-interest, low-reading level books for struggling readers in grades three through five. The series of interactive books is used in classrooms to motivate these readers with high-interest nonfiction books. Because NWF is recognized as a leader in nature education, its licensed products can be marketed not only to parents and children, but also to educators and education publishers. The Leap Frog partnership is currently in year three of a ten-year contract. Since its inception, the program has grown 15 to 20 percent per year.

NWF also works directly with retailers. NWF and Home Depot developed a line of NWF-branded backyard products including birdhouses, birdseed, and other wildlife-friendly items. In addition, NWF volunteers held Backyard Wildlife Habitat clinics at selected store locations to educate consumers how to restore habitat and support wildlife at home. The program also included workshops for kids, where they learned how to build a birdhouse, among other fun projects.

Although the primary goal of licensing partnerships is to generate revenue, it's not the only goal. NWF sees tremendous value in its ability to extend its brand and conservation message. Licensing brings NWF into people's homes, whether through a line of personal checks or credit card program (NWF has each with Custom Direct, Inc., and Bank of America, respectively) or through a book or a toy, it literally puts the brand in people's hands. NWF knows its reputation can be enhanced or put at risk with each product or promotion; and therefore we evaluate every partnership very carefully to ensure a good fit. For information about NWF, please view our annual report at nwf.org/about/annualreport.cfm.

Here is a checklist of items to keep in mind when evaluating potential licensees (or retailers):

- Corporate information: Sales and marketing information, company history.

- Financial information and insurance certification.

- Manufacturing experience.

- Licensing experience: Past history, licenses currently held.

- Distribution channels and relationships with retailers: Can the company guarantee placement of your product? Does it control retail space?

- Advertising and marketing capabilities.

- Sample products: Can the company manufacture quickly and with quality if sales are hot?

- What product lines is the company successful in? Unsuccessful?

- What is the company's product rollout strategy? Time frame?

- Which retailers have committed to the company's properties?

- Does the company have its own sales force?

After you have signed your licensee or licensees, stay in constant communication with them. Strategize with them. Create a website for them that provides your latest product information, marketing and promotional materials, downloadable logos, and designs. Create a monthly newsletter to keep licensees and customers up to date. Visit licensees and their booths at trade shows.

RETAIL CONSOLIDATION

The process of retail consolidation only leaves room for a few new property placements each year. In the recent past, the top ten newly licensed products would get placement at retailers. In 2005 it was only the top five. Today, just the top three get decent placement at retailers.

Macy's Inc., one of the nation's biggest department store retailers, owns hundreds of stores, including May's Department Stores, Bloomingdales, and Marshall Fields. In June 2005, David Lieberman of *USA Today* reported that "After years of consolidation in retailing, including the recent merger of Kmart and Sears, it's harder than ever for studios, sports merchandisers, and other companies to find store managers who'll risk stocking up on toys, clothing, lunch boxes, backpacks, and other items plastered with images from movies or TV shows that might bomb." Another big trend in retailing is called private labeling, in which retailers create their own products, making it even harder for independents to break into retail.

Trying to get your newly licensed property into Macy's is like trying to get your new radio program on the airwaves of Clear Channel, or trying to get your band picked up by one of the few labels left, or trying to get your first novel signed by one of the few big publishers left, or trying to get an independent TV pilot picked up by one of the few major broadcast networks, or trying to get your first film bought by one of the few big studios. It ain't gonna happen.

The irony is that such a mind-set—that you're a failure if you're not with the behemoths—perpetuates the myth that you need to sell your soul to a major to be successful. The reality is, 99 percent of supplicants do not get a contract and the 1 percent who do are in a poor negotiating position. And they just perpetuate the consolidation juggernaut.

Depending on your product, you may be better off using underutilized distribution channels such as home improvement companies, discounters, supermarkets, department stores (not Macy's), drugstores, electronics retailers, or office supply stores.

Musicians and bands, for one example, should try licensing through Musicland, Urban Outfitters, Transworld, Alloy, or Old Glory. Hot Topic was founded in 1988 by Irv Madden, whose stores have helped promote the careers of alternative artists such as Korn, Linkin Park, and Good Charlotte. There are more than five hundred Hot Topic stores in the United States.

But some people will try to win the lottery. So, here is a list of large outlets to approach.

- Department stores: Macy's (U.S.); Harrods (UK)

- Specialty stores: Toys "R" Us, Lowe's Home Center, Hallmark, Gap

- Mid-Tier stores: JCPenney, Kohl's, Mervyn's

- Mass merchants: Wal-Mart, Kmart, Target

- Discounters: Loehmann's, T.J. Maxx

- Discount/warehouse clubs: Sam's Club, Costco

- Outlets: Nine West, Nautica, Ann Taylor

- Supermarkets/drug/grocery stores: Safeway, Publix, Albertsons, Walgreens, CVS

- Home shopping: QVC, Home Shopping Network

BAD IDEAS OF A DIFFERENT KIND

With all the millions of good ideas discovered and yet to be invented and licensed, do not lose track of the possibility that some are *really* bad. Among the (soundly rejected) ones I have heard of are a *Wizard of Oz* menorah and a Mrs. Fields line of young women's dresses (sizes from XL to XXL, I presume). Licensing consultant Gary Caplan tells of a woman who tried to license her own four-year-old boy, a man who claimed to be Jesus Christ's agent, and the Interplanetary Lizards of the Texas plains.

Somehow, none of these ideas flew.

> **"I advise you to go on living solely to enrage**
> **those who are paying your annuities."**
> *—Voltaire*

Resources

Licensing business directories: EPM, 212-941-0099; LIMA (Licensing Industry Merchandisers Association), 212-244-1962.

Print resources: The Licensing Book, 212-575-4510; Licensing for Dummies (free from licensemag.com); License! Global Magazine, 888-527-7008

Classes: University extension programs at UCLA and NYU

Conferences: Licensing Show (Advanstar and LIMA), American International Toy Fair, E3 (videogames) Comdex, ComicCon, Mipcom and Mip-TV (Reed Midem), National Association of Broadcasters (NAB), SHOPA (school, home and office products), JPMA (infant and baby licensing)

Trade Associations: Licensing has become such big business that specialist trade groups now service various segments of the market:
Licensing Industry Merchandiser's Association (LIMA): Trade association with a thousand members from over thirty-five countries; licensing.org
Association of Collegiate Licensing Administrators (ACLA): Licensing of university trademarks and logos
Music Publishers Association (MPA): Music licensing
Interactive Multimedia Association (IMA): Multimedia industry licensing

12

zines

BE A ZINESTER: HOW AND WHY TO PUBLISH YOUR OWN PERIODICAL

Anne Elizabeth Moore

"Reveal your simple self. Embrace your original nature."
—Lao Tzu

SELF-PUBLISHING BASICS

Forgetting about the exact terminology and the who-said-what-first of it all for a moment, the notion of controlling one's own voice has been around for as long as voice itself—or, for that matter, notions themselves. That is to say, the concerns that guide the credo of the self-publisher are not new, or secret, or hidden. They weren't invented in the 1970s, the 1930s, or 1517. Self-publishing and zinemaking are rooted in simple, timeless concepts. They grew from the desire of individuals to produce their own voice without interference from others. One needn't be a punk-rocker, poor, under the age of twenty-four, feel desperately misunderstood by one's peers, or live in the basement of a parent to desire to both speak and to control the conditions under which one will be heard. One must simply want to be understood clearly, and be willing to accrue and utilize the necessary resources—which will be detailed for you in a moment.

Note: At the request of the author, this piece was neither edited nor copyedited. At the requests of the editor and copyeditor, this notice is hereby posted.

HISTORY

That all being said, histories of self-publishing that trace the practice back to Benjamin Franklin, Siegel and Shuster, Ray Bradbury, or Aaron Cometbus not only create a false historical sanctity of zines, but give proof to the assumption that famous white men created everything interesting that has ever happened in the world. And this, really, is not true. Nor is it a helpful way of convincing people in general to make their own zines. Equally legitimate histories of zinemaking can be found in early American quilts, the lessons heard in church about reformation, written on the backs of old family photographs, crumbling in the alleyways of urban areas, the oral histories of conspiracy theorists, or made up in your own head during a long walk in the rain. Each of these potential histories have just as much to explain about who is granted power to speak in our culture and who is not; each of these potential histories provide models for exercising voice, even if the speaker hasn't been gifted it. The Underground Railroad produced coded maps in the form of bed-covers just as The Vageniuses popularize their appearance in town with wheat-pasted flyers. Both groups work against mainstream culture to bring their unique voice to people; both use whatever available means they can muster to do so.

Such unrecognized histories are extremely important to point out when discussing zines, because zines are currently one of the means by which hidden histories occasionally come to light. Zines are personal, small-scale paper ventures and tell the kinds of stories deliberately ignored, glossed over, or entirely forgotten by mainstream media. Zines are created by prisoners, young girls, people with emotional and physical disabilities, queers, geeks, non-native speakers of English, survivors of sexual assault, radical offspring of conservative politicians, homeschoolers, members of the military, Native Americans, sexworkers, and anyone else who has ever felt that the voices speaking for them in the larger culture weren't conveying their stories.

Fanzines

The term zine, however, has a specific history. It comes from the weird world of science fiction, a genre that grew as a hybrid of pure fantastical storytelling and a desire to geek out and show off to others how smart you were. When the genre first appeared in the 1920s, a group of people coalesced around it and something remarkable happened; either early science fiction was of such horrendous quality that it seemed instantly accessible to those who came across it, or it was an invention so late in coming that the audience's personal abilities had surpassed it already. Regardless, science fiction fans started creating their own science fictions almost immediately, photocopying them, mailing them throughout the country, trading them with each other, writing each other letters, printing those letters with addresses in subsequent issues, and, assumedly, dressing up like Storm Troopers on the weekends. Just kidding: This would not happen for another few decades. (But if you were not aware of it, it does happen, a lot. Even now.)

Geeks

The mimeographed fictions scifi fans created developed a name, identity, and following of their own. The word magazine wouldn't do. It was used to describe any kind of information or resource storage, and came to apply to both military ammunitions holdings and the esteemed collection of knowledge we think of as *People* today. Yet the term "magazine" connotes an officialness scifi fans wanted to buck. In no way legitimate magazine enterprises, merely fan-created magazines—with names like *The Comet, Time Traveler,* and *Alter Ego* (still publishing; see heroicpub.com/alterego/)—their early publications were called fanzines. This term was still used until the mid-1990s. For example, my first fanzine in 1994 was named *AnneZine* and was intended to support and popularize people named Anne, although this joke stopped making sense by 2000. To some degree, fanzines grew out of a passion for a form fans couldn't get enough of. But, they were also a legitimate testing ground for new directions in which to push a new genre, as well as a way for writers—and immediately, as comics came into the mix, artists too—to practice skills untaught in most schools.

The comic book was invented at around this same time and, many would say, by the same people—although comics themselves had been appearing in newspapers since the turn of the century, and crudely drawn packets of sex jokes called Tijuana Bibles had been passed around the pub circuit for about as long. By the 1960s, however, Joe Shuster and Jerry Siegel, the creators of Superman, and Biljo White, who edited and published *Batmania,* encouraged the union of words and pictures for popular consumption with their brightly colored, non-professionally produced tales of physically overdeveloped men.

If, however, comics and science fiction *were* taught in schools, it is unlikely they would have proceeded to develop as democratic institutions. Some histories, for example, indicate that early science fiction fandom was fairly gender equitable, and when fanzines were created, girls may have participated in even greater numbers than boys because they felt shut out from the traditional, masculine world of professional publishing. It is true that female writers came to take masculine-sounding names to publish their craft: Dale Messick, for example, creator of Brenda Starr. Interestingly, girls often purchased early comic books in greater numbers than boys—yet rarely were even the most talented then granted admission into the studios of the growing numbers of publishers who later became DC, Marvel, and Harvey Comics. Even Frederic Wertham in 1973—anti-comics activist, psychiatrist, and author of *Seduction of the Innocent* and *The World of Fanzines*—admits "the male-female proportion in fanzines is somewhat similar. . . . Among outstanding female fanzine editors and co-editors are Joanne Burger (*Pegasus*). Linda Bushyager (*Granfalloon*), Juanita Coulson (*Yandro*), Ethel Lindsay (*Haverings*), Pat Lupoff (*Xero;* a best-of book came out last year, available at tachyonpublications.com/book/Best_of_Xero.html?Session_ID=new&Reference_Page=/books.html), Lesleigh Luttrell (*Starling*), Karen Rockow (*Unicorn*), and Lisa Tuttle (*Mathom*)" (Wertham, 121). Clearly, the unprofessional natures of comics and science fiction fanzine publishing allowed for a great deal of flexibility in interpreting approaches to authorship, craft-honing, and audience: the high rate of participation by women, when compared to professional participation in comics and scifi publishing, was only one indication. Clearly, the democratic nature of fanzines was advanced by their status as outsider modes of communication—perhaps most exemplified by Valerie Solanas' *SCUM Manifesto,* which began to appear around New York in 1968, shortly before the author shot Andy Warhol.

Punks

Surely, the lines between various outsider and geek cultures are thin and malleable, so when punk culture got going in the 1970s, fanzines were adopted immediately by punk-rock music fans. Widely considered to be the first punk fanzine in England, *Sniffin' Glue* was edited by Mark Perry. Perry, however, had this to say about the distinction of his publication: " . . . All that stuff about *Sniffin' Glue* being the first fanzine is crap. Brian Hogg's *Bam Balam,* which was all about 1960s music, was in its fourth issue by then: it showed you could do a magazine and you didn't have to be glossy" (Savage, 1992). Other early punk fanzines included *Search and Destroy, Flipside,* and *Profane Existence* (profaneexistence.com).

As fanzines proliferated, the term describing them was shortened. First to 'zines, and then, simply, to zines. Zines and punk made a perfect match, for as Heath Row notes in "From Fandom to Feminism: An Analysis of the Zine Press" (zinebook.com/resource/heath.html), "The punk press demonstrates that not only clothes and music can be produced cheaply and immediately from limited resources and experience." The DIY ethic of punk culture, the bucking of mainstream acceptance, and the newly minted pejorative "selling out" all combined to grant zines the official voice of punk culture—or at least as official as it was going to get. Originally, too, this combination meant that the zine press developed a heavy reliance on music reviews, interviews with musicians, and talk of "shows," "gigs," and "sets."

Yet more importantly for a music non-fan such as myself, this infusion of print media into a culture focused on live performances opened up previously unexplored distribution options. Suddenly, going to see music often meant picking up three or four zines distributed for free at shows, dropped into bathrooms, or sold very cheaply at tables set up at music venues. Punk zinesters emulated scifi and comics fanzine creators directly: if you loved a certain musician, or a certain scifi writer, or a certain comic-book character, you wrote about them and networked with other people who would write about them for your zine. Thus, zine culture grew into a close-knit community. Obviously, however, zine culture developed beyond it's musical, scifi, and comics, origins. In fact, the hidden fourth antecedent of zines—porn—was just as influential. As a fast, sure way to shock the mainstream, graphic depictions of sex have never been bested. Tijuana Bibles—which displayed, for example, popular figures such as Popeye having sex with some young movie starlet (tijuanabibles.org)—and early photo-based pornographic magazines, pin-up collections, and erotic fiction that brought in the regular cashflow that allowed comic-book publishers to create *that* industry—these were all still prevalent in zine-making. Naked ladies, non-standard spelling, pop-culture commentary, street language, personal narratives: these came to mark the language of zinedom.

As zines moved away from music more and more, zine topics grew to focus on underground obsessions such as crappy jobs (*Dishwasher*), killing (*Murder Can Be Fun*), unique thrift-store purchases (*Thrift Score*), and zine-making (*Factsheet 5;* factsheet5.0rg/).

Post-Punk

Then, in the 1990s, a deliberately anti-media outgrowth of the post-punk music scene emerged in the Pacific Northwest called Riot Grrrl. While most histories of zine culture fold Riot Grrrl into punk, two distinct matters cause me to keep these discussions separate: 1) the media blackout mandated by the Riot Grrrl movement was a unique and thrilling invention that forced zine-making and personal experience to tell the entirety of the history, and 2) my personal involvement with Riot Grrrl zines profoundly influenced my education in the field of publishing.

"Riot Grrrl zines attempt to expand the boundaries of feminist conversation through discussion of editor's sexual exploits, the ins and outs of menstruation and feminine hygiene, and the danger of silverfish," Heath Row explains. "Like punk zines, Riot Grrrl zines exhibit the rough-edged, hand-written text, doodles in the margins, and third-generational photocopied photographs." Through collage, text, and comics, projects like Nomy Lamm's *I'm So Fucking Beautiful* radicalized the rejection of mainstream beauty images by sexualizing physical disabilities, fatness, queer desire, and masculine women. In 1992, mainstream press coverage began to distort the Riot Grrrl message and a media blackout was enacted. Interested parties were forced to turn to zines like *Girl Germs, Satan Wears a Bra, Girly Mag,* and *Quit Whining* for information; otherwise, newspaper reporters simply recounted tales of key Riot Grrrl figures refusing their phone calls. *Bitch* (bitchmagazine.com), *Bust* (bust.com), and *HipMama* (hipmama.com) all grew directly from the third-wave feminist/Riot Grrrl self-publishing ethos around this same time and are widely available on newsstands and in bookstores today. The expansion—and continuation—of punk relevance brought about by Riot Grrl also influenced the growth of two different zines, also widely available on newsstands and in bookstores, that remain influential: *Maximum Rock'n'Roll* (first published in 1982; maximumrocknroll.com) and *Punk Planet* (first published in 1994; punkplanet.com). Self-published comic books, now often called minicomics, have been launching pads for such contemporary artists as Tom Hart, Megan Kelso, David Lasky, and Jesse Reklaw. Their small, self-published comics are actively traded through the mail, sold at comic-book conventions, given away during social gatherings, and purchased through specialized distributors such as Global Hobo (slowwave.com/globalhobo), USS Catastrophe (usscatastrophe.com), and Cold Cut Comics Distribution (coldcut.com).

Yet even with this rich, profound, and slightly hidden but well-documented history, the word zine is not going to be found in most dictionaries. This is as important to note as the secret religious, quilt-related, and flyer-influenced histories of zinemaking, because it proves something very important about our culture: not everything that happens is granted space in our most widely available reference materials.

Mainstream Media

In fact, our most widely available reference materials, anathema as they are to self-publishing and anti-professionalism, frequently get it wrong when it comes to contemporary zines and comics. In 2004, *The Grand Rapids Press* described zines hilariously and nonsensically as "shaped from a blank piece of standard paper and folded into a pint-sized booklet . . . Some liken early books of the Bible to zine style" (Denton). Further trouble with relying on mainstream and professional press accounts of the history of zines—and the importance of seeking out alternative historical sources—is made clear by the fact that Wertham's Southern Illinois University Press-published book is considered one of the most important documents in zine history. While, granted, an excellent resource, few historians in the history of the world have ever been so clearly understood to be biased toward conservatism as Wertham was when *Seduction* was released in 1954, an act that lead to the creation of the Comics Code Authority (comics.dm.net/codetext.htm), widespread comics censorship, and the loss of entire comic-book lines and several publishers.

Getting Started

Nitpicking about the mainstream press, while a good idea *for* a zine, probably won't help you get started making one. To self-publish anything, one must have, at a minimum, significant quantities of the following:

- A medium (ink, paper, copier toner, sticker-paper, numerous crayons, a label-maker, etc.) and;

- A message (text, images, symbols, etc.).

- Also highly recommended for any successful self-publishing venture are: time, a distribution idea, plan, or network, some money you want to get rid of, and a desire to create something unique and *good*. These, however, are luxuries sometimes unaffordable to the soul burning already with both a medium and a message. The importance of having both a medium and a message cannot be overstated. Although you will find a way to overcome the lack of a medium if you already have a message, without a message there is no reason to make a zine.

The rest is actually easy. All of publishing concerns six major areas. If you make a zine, you deal with each of them—even if you don't want to. These major areas are:

- Concept Development

- Contribution Solicitation

- Editing

- Illustration and Design

- Production

- Marketing and Distribution

If you know how to do each of these, then you do not need to read any more of this chapter. Otherwise, below find further descriptions of each.

1. Concept Development. Decide what kind of zine you are going to publish. Consider your audience, your available resources, and what you want the final product to look like. Look at other zines at your local zine library or near the front of your local coffeeshop, bookstore, or rock club. Do sketches, drawings, or drafts—but not too many of them! Or you might get bored by your idea before you actually put out your first issue. Keep the page count and scope small at first because your zine will be cheaper to produce and, probably, easier to carry around with you and show off to other people.

After around eight years as a zinester—during which time I attempted to expand the idea of what books were with each new publication—I began making all my publications very small, fitting them into the 8 ½" X 11" 4-up format below. These fit easily into the back pocket of my pants, and I could slip them into sneaky distribution locations or pull them out when people asked what I'd been up to lately.

2. Contribution Solicitation. If you want other people to contribute, ask them early, ask them often, and give them a deadline. Most zinesters find that it's easy to find people at a coffee shop, club, or bar with good ideas that will fit into your zine, but that it's almost impossible to convince them to complete their projects for your zine. Many zinesters prefer to work alone, however, because other people rarely share a zinester's passion for certain subjects. Liz Mason of *Caboose* generally writes all of her own content, while her friend Christa Donner of *Ladyfriend* solicits contributions from all over the globe. If you do not take contributions, you will still need to gather materials for your zine. Set yourself a deadline and stick to it. This also applies to advertisements, if you decide to take them.

I sold ads in one issue of *AnneZine*—for the services of a psychiatrist named Anne Garden. When I was approached with the idea of running the ad, it was an easy decision to make: Her ad fit exactly within the extremely strict parameters of my project's scope. If you choose to accept ads, you may or may not eventually have to make some difficult choices about who to accept money from and for what. If you have been very clear with your mission, however, and you are clear with potential advertisers that their ads must also fit into your mission, it shouldn't take much extra thought.

3. Editing. Throw away all the stupid stuff you've received that you thought was cool at first and now turns out to suck. Even *Found* magazine, which relies exclusively on reader-submitted materials located through the course of one's day—though hard to still call a zine at this point—has an editorial process. If you receive contributions you didn't request, you have the luxury of being able to use only those you want to. If you have requested contributions from others, however, you are obligated to use them, even if they suck too. You are not, though, obligated to use them really big or anything, so get creative without ruining someone else's work. The last thing you want to do is make a contributor feel bad, because zines are all about keeping community growthful and thrivey. Making people feel bad doesn't help.

Also, make sure that you are spelling things the way you want them to be spelled, and forwarding ideas and concepts that you believe in. The punk publishing ethos, if such can be said to exist, demanded the inclusion of misspelled words and messy cross-outs. Language is, after all, supposed to be a living document of a culture, and if words aren't spelled the way you think they should be, change them! Your name is on your zine, so it will be taken as something you believe in, no matter what. For many people, this means not printing homophobic, racist, or sexist materials. For some, this means no capital letters and record must be spelled "rekkid." If you are using your zine as a way to branch into publishing so you will eventually go off to work at the *New York Times,* use a dictionary and adhere to their style guide, which can be found in bookstores. Otherwise, your zine is your chance to reinvent language and literature the way you want it to be. So make sure you're doing so thoughtfully.

4. Illustration and Design. Make your zine look as good as you can. Minicomics impresario Jordan Crane notes that everything you self publish should be thought of as the last thing on earth you may ever do. The cover should be brilliant, or people won't pick it up—but remember that brilliant doesn't mean that it has to look like *Jane* or *People.* Type the text, word-process it on computer, cut it out of *Newsweek*s, or handwrite it all out in your neat calligraphy. Retrace all your images, collage photographs, or redraw the entire story in comics format. While it really doesn't matter *what* the final product looks like, it does matter that *it looks the way you wanted it to look.* Be knowledgeable, but not scared, of copyright law (read Lawrence Lessig's *Free Culture* for more) or research alternative forms of authorship licensing such as a creative commons license. Use your zine to exercise talents you don't yet have or things you are already good at—but don't refuse to draw something, for example, just because you claim to be no good at art. Until a few minutes ago you were no good at self-publishing either, and now you're doing it anyway, so adhering to your own limitations is only going to limit your own work in the end. My friend Ruth created a pornographic coloring book despite that she doesn't consider herself good at drawing, whereas Jacinta Bunnell and Irit Reinheimer took images from other coloring books and recaptioned them to make their Girls Will Be Boys Coloring Book. Later, when Soft Skull Press republished their original zine, they had artists contribute drawings to the book.

5. Production. Several zine layouts are especially popular: quarter-page, 8-up, half-size, and half-legal. (I used this last for *AnneZine* because it is both the most square and the most humorously named of all the formats.) Besides the 8-up (see *How to Make This Very Zine* for instructions), the rest are permutations of the following:

Front

Back cover	Front cover
Page 5	Page 2

Back

Page 1	Page 6
Page 3	Page 4

If this is confusing, and you find yourself folding scrap bits of paper, numbering them, and refitting them together to work this out on your own, congratulations! You are already a zinester. I cannot teach you any more.

Other matters you may have forgotten about throughout this process include:

- **Getting a PO Box.** You will want to have both an e-mail and a mailing address listed in your zine so the widest swath of people can contact you when they find it, and PO Boxes are just safer.

- **A Table of Contents and Page Numbers.** Both can keep you and your zine more organized and legible, if you want these qualities. Biographical Information on Contributors. This can be helpful for contextualizing your project. The essay "I Am a Stark Raving Lunatic" has a very different meaning when coming from George, the crazed neighborhood vegan cat-herder than it does coming from George, the President of the United States of America.

- **Copyright information.** If you're freely ripping off other peoples' work, carefully consider whether or not copyrighting your own is meaningful. Other options popular with zinesters include simply *not* mentioning copyright ownership (and not caring who does what with your zine); uncopyrighting, or copylefting your work (specifically telling people to use whatever they want however they want to use it); or using a Creative Commons license (at creativecommons.org). In one anti-corporate zine, about and distributed inside a string of coffeeshops that was known to be very protective of its brand and logo, I attributed copyright of the entire zine directly to them, so as to allay any questions about who owned what. Regardless, copyright is the law on the books, whether or not you mark it our outline it in your zine, so anything you do outside of that will be a private agreement between you and your readers. This also means, however, that if worse comes to worse, and Coke used your anti-Coke screed to sell Coke, you could still mount a pretty good legal battle against them.

- **Barcodes.** You actually don't need to think about this until you decide to approach distributors, so more discussion of them appears below, but if you plan on using one, leave space in your cover design for it. Stores hate having the barcodes appear on the back!

Once you have created your "original," you will want to copy it. You can do this at a copy store (Kinko's used to be practically mandatory, but ever since they practically eliminated the extensive methods of scamming free copies, it's been significantly less popular), in an office, or by simply printing up multiple copies of whatever you create. I'd strongly suggest experimenting with hand-coloring, stenciling, screenprinting, mimeographing, or doing a series of charcoal-rubbings to create your zine. I frequently print up copies directly from my color printer for a slightly more appealing product as well.

6. Marketing and Distribution. Because the scope and resources for your zine are so small and limited entirely to your abilities, it is advisable to think of Marketing and distribution as exactly the same. Really, no one is going to *hear* of your zine without actually *coming across* your zine, so you may as well put all your energies into getting as many people to *see* your zine as you can.

One important factor in people seeing your zine is money. Zinesters should carefully weigh whether or not they will charge money for their wares. Because you will simply never make your financial investment back, it is advisable to consider the whole project a labor of love and not even charge the $1 or $2 you may be tempted to. Zines are an excellent means of disseminating a message, but charging for them limits your audience drastically and participates in the mainstream consumerist culture you may want to avoid by making a zine. In addition, charging any price means that an individual must be there for the exchange, which eliminates all kinds of creative distribution methods. *Gas Jockey,* in Oregon, was a zine for gas-station attendants and was distributed by rubber-banding the zine to the gas cap. State law disallows vehicle operators to dispense their own gas, so the distributors didn't even know they were delivering radical literature! Similarly, several zines have emulated train schedules, maps, and bus tickets, and are distributed in the public spaces where such pieces of information can usually be found. Zines providing consumer information about McDonalds and other megacorporations have been designed to emulate comment cards and fit into slots made for such things inside stores. If you want to reach a lot of people with your message, distributing it for free is the best means: Artists who work outside of or against the copyright system, for example, allowing their work to be downloaded from the Internet, have found that their messages and names became far more popular when they did not charge for their work. Even non-radical publications that work within the copyright system, such as *The 2nd Hand Reader,* alternative newsweeklies, and *Muse,* have found that their publications are ridiculously popular, primarily because they are available for free. Consider creating a non-financially based distribution method that will repay your time and energy in a non-monetary way. While it would be nice to earn a living doing what you love, alternative media is simply not prized enough in the US to support you, and your time—if you demand financial recompense—would be better spent writing a book proposal for Random House or St. Martin's Press.Even if you distribute your work in guerilla fashion, you may want to make it available to zine-reading audiences. Although several small distributors have already been mentioned, literally hundreds more exist, each catering to specific genres such as personal zines or perzines (Starfiend Distro, starfiend.com), queer zines (Xerox Revolutionaries Zine Distro, http://i.1asphost.com/xrdistro), grrrl zines (find several distrs listed at http://grrrlzines.net), politically radical zines (microcosm-publishing.com) and about every other kind of zine you can imagine. Several medium-scale distributors are known to not pay, therefore actually harming the viability of the independent press and killing off entire titles, who depend on such money for survival (Desert Moon, who will frequently sever connections with publishers *before* ceasing sale of their wares, is the most egregious). Therefore, for the sake of the community as a whole, it is advisable to avoid them entirely, or at least do careful research before working with them. While zinebook.com has a few links on distribution, most zinesters and publishers find distributors by looking in the front of their favorite magazines, most of which list distributors through which they are available. Or, you can e-mail another zinester. Distribution is not any kind of a secret club; most zinesters will share this information freely.

SELF-DISTRIBUTION

Far more radical and rewarding, however, is controlling distribution oneself. Most bookstores and newsstands will carry your publication, offer you better terms (a 50/50 or 60/40 split) and actually pay you if you just call them up and ask if they'll set up a direct account or carry your zine on consignment. In this case, walk your zine into every book (and music) store in town, and call independent retailers—Reading Frenzy in Portland, OR and Quimby's in Chicago, IL are by far the best in the country—throughout the US. Google "independent bookstores" for the most recent info—the market is too volatile to print an up-to-date list here.) Also remember to send your zine out for review to Punk Planet, Scram (scrammagazine.com), Broken Pencil (brokenpencil.com), Factsheet 5 (which plans a relaunch this year) and just about any other publication out there that might review your zine. And, donate copies to your local zine library: both will bring in orders for your zine.

LARGE DISTRIBUTORS

Larger distributors, such as Ingram and International Periodicals Distributor (IPD) do occasionally carry self-published materials, but are also controlled by large retail chains and their big media parent companies. Using them contributes to the idea that very soon, they will control all aspects of all media. This is sad, so why participate?

BARCODES

Much like worrying about distributors, you could worry about a barcode, but why? Barcodes are the digital tracking system stores use to mark product and pricing. In many zinesters opinion, stores that require them will print them on their own, they always mess up cover designs, and they're simply not necessary for print runs of 100–200—or even 500 (I wouldn't print any more than this for the first couple of issues). Also, bar codes are expensive and, like the big distributors, go against everything zine culture stands for. If you do need to, you can buy a bar code through a distributor or online. (Google "barcodes" or ask your distributor for the one they recommend) Again, however, eliminating the financial concerns of zine-making is one way of eliminating a whole series of ethical dilemmas you may just not want to face. Remember, you can be distributed in the bathroom or on free racks at every Borders within biking distance without a distributor or a bar code *as long as you don't charge for your zine.*

AS YOUR PROJECT CATCHES ON . . .

Eventually, however, bar codes and big distributors may become matters you will want to wrestle with. Generally, small distros will approach you and want to carry your project if it fits into theirs. Often, this will lead to greater demand, and your zine will grow organically for as long as you want to keep doing it. Zinesters like Joe Biel al have struggled with such issues for decades: is wider accessibility of your product through outfits like Borders, Amazon.com, and Barnes and Noble worth the trouble and loss of profit or does it label you a total sell-out, contributing directly to the financial resources of a humungous megacorporation with your independent project? These are questions you will have to answer on your own, but they do speak to the necessity of having a community of people to discuss these issues with. If you're struggling with a question, ask another zinester. E-mail or write them a letter, or join (or start) a listserv.

Cited Works

Denton, Kathy. "'Zine' trend catches on at school." *The Grand Rapids Press:* August 5, 2004.

Savage, Jon. *England's Dreaming.* New York: St. Martin's Press, 1992.

Wertham, Frederic. *The World of Fanzines.* Carbondale: Southern Illinois University Press, 1973.

"She who knows others is learned. She who knows herself is wise."

—Lao Tzu

- DRAW OR COPY YOUR IMAGE ON A PEICE OF PAPER
- GLUE THE PAPER ONTO A BIT OF CARD USING GOOD GLUE
- CUT STRAIGHT THROUGH THE DRAWING AND CARD AT THE SAME TIME USING A VERY SHARP KNIFE. SNAP OFF BLADES ARE BEST. THE SHARPER YOUR KNIFE THE BETTER YOUR STENCIL LOOKS.
- IDEAL CARD SHOULD BE ABOUT 1.5mm THICK MUCH FATTER AND ITS TOO DIFFICULT AND BORING TO CUT THROUGH. ANY THINNER AND IT GETS SLOPPY QUICK
- FIND AN UNASSUMING PEICE OF CARD AS A FOLDER TO HOLD YOUR STENCIL IN...
- GET A ROLL OF TAPE AND PRE-TEAR SMALL STRIPS READY TO ATTACH STENCIL TO THE WALL.
- SHAKE AND TEST CANS OF PAINT BEFORE YOU LEAVE, MATTE FINISH COMES OUT BEST + DRIES QUICKER
- APPLY PAINT SPARINGLY
- PACE YOURSELF AND REPEAT AS OFTEN AS YOU FEEL INADEQUATE...

PART II

THE COMMUNITY MEDIA RENAISSANCE

"All good people agree,
And all good people say,
All nice people, like Us, are We
And every one else is They."
—*Rudyard Kipling*

FOREWORD

THE OPPORTUNITY FOR RENAISSANCE

Douglas Rushkoff

"The future depends on what we do in the present."
—*Mahatma Gandhi*

I'm not sure whether to foreword or forewarn.

The good news—what this volume should be celebrating—is that the proliferation of interactive media holds within it the potential for a fundamental shift in the relationship of human beings to the values and authorities shaping their lives. In that sense, this moment is as big as the invention of text, the printing press, or radio transmission.

The bad news—what everyone reading this volume should also bear in mind while pondering the infinite capabilities of technology-fueled feedback and iteration—is that as profound as previous media renaissances may have been, they all have ultimately failed at delivering on their most essential promise: to give a majority of human beings a greater capacity to influence the world around them. Media and technology do a lot, but they haven't yet profoundly enhanced what philosophers refer to as "human agency."

I fear that like the participants of failed cultural eras before our own, we risk embracing the new technologies and literacies of our age without actually learning how they work, or how they work on us.

Consider the purported great leaps forward of the past.

The invention of the twenty-two-letter Hebrew alphabet may have inspired the writing down of Talmudic laws, but it did not ultimately lead to a society of literate Israelite readers. Instead, it led to a society of hearers who gathered to listen to the Torah scroll read to them by a priest. Likewise, the printing press and the television heralded not a society of writers and producers but a society of readers and viewers who were free to enjoy the creations of an elite who had access to the new tools of production. And as yet, today's relatively open computer networks have not led to a society of programmers but one of bloggers—free to write whatever they (or we) please but for the most part utterly unaware of the underlying biases of the interfaces and windows that have been programmed for us.

For example, a blog is a computer program that enables inexperienced users to write Web pages. Most bloggers are unaware, however, that the blogging interface only allows certain forms of Web page construction. The users' contribution is usually limited to the insertion of text into an existing page or format. Very rarely do bloggers consider the fact that their posts are listed in date order, that posts are presented as equally important members of a long list, that the expectation of daily contributions changes a blogger's relationship to his or her writing, that the use of advertising and view counters might influence the way they write, or that all of these decisions have been made by other people.

Most of us seem to remain one step behind the potential of each new media technology—embracing its lower capabilities while remaining either unwilling or unable to garner the kind of agency required to rebuild society itself. The powers that be remain the powers that be, our age-old beliefs and prejudices reassert themselves, and our new media simply become new avenues for varying forms of social control.

Renaissances offer us so much, but we tend to exploit them so little.

That is why historians, instead of studying revolutions to pinpoint regional and global power shifts, would do better to focus on renaissances. Revolutions, as the word suggests, are merely cycles. An oppressed group overturns the status quo and in many cases becomes the oppressor, itself.

Renaissances, on the other hand, are evolutionary in spirit and offer a much broader opportunity for social change. A "re-nascence" is the rebirth of old ideas in a new context. It's not a reaction to political oppression but a society-wide shift in perspective, literacies, and perceived relationship to power.

For example, the invention of the alphabet and agriculture in the Mediterranean region (a period of history between 800 and 200 BCE and frequently called the Axial Age) served as what we might call a renaissance moment. These innovations led quite directly to the developments of monotheism, ethics, and the rule of law. The invention of the printing press and perspective painting in the 1400s reintroduced the Greek notions of rationality and individuality, paving the way for everything from centralized currency and the Protestant Reformation to the concept of personal liberty and government by democracy.

Even more recently, the invention of computers and networking allowed for the revival of dormant systems of commerce, credit, collectivism, and cultural production. A renaissance offers a civilization the tools and motivation to increase its level of coordination, its self-awareness, and the agency it affords the individuals living within it.

So why do they always seem to go wrong? The failure of renaissances to deliver on their promise of enlightenment, democracy, autonomy, or even basic civility is so much more disturbing—and worthy of exploration—than the futility of revolutions. Bloody though they may be, revolutions are mere blips on the radar screen of history, moments when the face on the currency changes. Renaissances—though billed and experienced as grand evolutionary leaps forward—have proven instead to be long, slow-motion, quite voluntary descents into restriction and delusion. They offer us great possibilities, they make us think of new ways of interacting with one another and with the powers that be. But for some reason we don't seem to take advantage of the new possibilities they offer us.

To be sure, renaissances make us think and feel differently. The original Renaissance made people feel that their interpretations of religion, society, and politics mattered; today's renaissance makes us feel that our self-expression matters, too. It's not enough for us to have access to great works of literature or to pick whatever channel of programming we prefer. No, we want to be allowed to create the next great work of literature or television program ourselves, no matter what our former programmers may think of us. It's not enough for us to listen to what the politician or minister has to tell us about the way things are. No, we want our turn at the pulpit, too. And thanks to chat rooms, blogs, wikis, podcasts, videoblogs, instant messaging, and SMS buddy lists, we're getting that chance, at least partially.

But the real promise of interactivity, as I believe the essays in this volume will show, is less about making content than it is about gaining context. Less about writing a blog than about understanding the underlying biases of the blogging platform and changing them to suit our conception of how people might best express themselves and collaborate on solving the problems that are most important to them. Yes, it's important that each individual member of a digital society has the ability to create his or her own content. But if the intent behind all this content creation is simply to get picked up by a major media brand or to gain influence over an established political or social institution, then the ground rules remain unchallenged.

A renaissance serves as a moment of reframing. We step out of the frame as it is currently defined and see the whole picture in a new context. We can then play by new rules, and even more importantly, write new rules ourselves.

This progression of awareness and perspective is akin to the experience of a computer game player. At first, gamers will play a video or computer game by the rules. They'll read the manual, if necessary, then move through the various levels of the game. Mastery of the game at this stage means getting to the end: making it to the last level, surviving, becoming the most powerful character, or in the case of a simulation game, designing and maintaining a thriving family, city, or civilization. For many gamers, this is as far as it goes.

Some gamers, though—usually after they've mastered this level of play—will venture onto the Internet in search of other fans or user groups. They will gather "cheat codes" that can be used to acquire special abilities within the game, such as invisibility or an infinite supply of ammunition. When the gamer returns to the game with such codes, is he (or increasingly, she) still playing the game or is he or she cheating?

From a renaissance perspective, he or she is still playing the game, albeit a different one. The playing field has grown from the CD on which the game was shipped to the entire universe of computers, in which secret codes and abilities can be discussed and shared. Gamers no longer are playing the game but a metagame. The inner game world is still fun, but it is distanced by the gamer's new perspective, much as we are distanced from the play-within-a-play in one of Shakespeare's comedies or dramas.

After a gamer has moved through all the levels of the game in this fashion, she can either put the game down and find another, or she can take the next step outside the frame. This would mean going back online, learning from others how the game is programmed, and then creating new, personalized versions of the game. This is part of what made Doom so popular for so long: expert players became fledgling programmers who uploaded their own versions of the game for others to play.

These power users, we might argue, have stepped out of yet another frame into the latent sensibility of our current renaissance. They have deconstructed the content of the game, demystified the technology of its interface, and now feel ready to open the codes and turn the game into a do-it-yourself activity. Such gamers have moved from the position of receiving player to that of deconstructing user. They have assumed the position of author.

This leap to authorship is precisely the character and quality of the dimensional leap associated with today's renaissance—the ability of an individual to reflect or even affect the grand narrative. To write the game.

As game programmers instead of game players, as creators of testimony rather than believers in testament, we begin to become aware of just how much of our reality is up for discussion. So much of what seemed like impenetrable hardware is actually software—open source software—and ripe for reprogramming. The stories we use to understand the world begin to seem less like explanations and more like collaborations.

Such interactivity reduces our dependence on fixed narratives while also giving us the tools and courage to develop narratives together. We have witnessed together the wizard behind the curtain. We can all see, for this moment anyway, how so much of what we have perceived of as reality is in fact merely social construction. More importantly, we have gained the ability to enact wizardry ourselves.

This is the bright side of our saga. By the time the Internet became a household word, new forms of community had emerged that stressed the actual contributions of the participants rather than whatever prepackaged content they had in common. Indeed, the early interactive media space was a gift economy. People developed and shared new technologies with no expectation of financial return. It was gratifying enough just to see one's own e-mail program or bulletin board software spread to thousands of other users. The technologies in use on the Internet today, from browsers and POP e-mail programs to streaming video, all were developed by this shareware community of software engineers.

This style of collaboration offered up a new cultural narrative based in collective self-determination. Online communities sprang up seemingly from nowhere. On the West Coast in the late 1980s, one of Ken Kesey's Merry Pranksters, Stewart Brand (now cofounder of the prestigious Global Business Network), conceived and implemented an online bulletin board called The WELL (Whole Earth 'Lectronic Link). Within two years, thousands of users had joined the dial-in computer conferencing system and were sharing their deepest hopes and fears with one another. Famous scientists, authors, philosophers, and scores of journalists flocked to the site to develop their ideas collaboratively rather than alone. Meanwhile, as the Internet continued to develop, online discussions in a distributed system called Usenet began to proliferate. These were absolutely self-organizing discussions about thousands of different topics. They themselves spawned communities of scientists, activists, doctors, patients, and so many others, dedicated to tackling problems in collaboration across formerly prohibitive geographical and cultural divides.

It seemed as if the Internet's early developers realized that this was not a medium for broadcasting by a few but for expression by the many. People became the content. This shift had implications not only for the online community but also for society as a whole. The notion of a group of people working together for a shared goal rather than financial self-interest was, in sum, startling.

Yet share they did, as well as expand their thinking. After people are invited to participate in, say, the coding of an open source software program, they begin to question just how much of the rest of our world is open for discussion: our political processes, our allegiance to the almighty dollar, and even our belief in God. People realize that everything from the grid pattern of the city in which they live to the commodity-based energy industry on which they depend are social constructions with biases that favor certain parties and with rules that are not preexisting conditions at all but are subject to redesign.

Open source software has made the difference. People used to see software as an established and inviolable thing, something married to the computer, a given circumstance. With an open source awareness, though, they are free to discover that the codes of the software have been arranged by people who may have agendas that had not been apparent. One of the most widespread realizations accompanying the current renaissance is that a lot of what had been taken for granted as hardware is in fact software capable of being reprogrammed. And the people who realize this tend to begin to view everything that was formerly set in metaphorical stone—from medical practices to the Bible—as social constructions and subject to revision.

The birth of the Internet was interpreted by many as a revolution. Those of us in the counter-culture saw the Internet as an opportunity to topple the storytellers who had dominated our politics, economics, society, and religion—our very reality—and to replace their stories with those of our own. It was a beautiful and exciting sentiment, but one as based in a particular narrative as any other.

Revolutions simply replace one story with another. The capitalist narrative is replaced by that of the communist; the religious fundamentalist's is replaced by the agnostic's. The means may be different but the rewards are the same. So is the exclusivity of their distribution. That's why they're called revolutions—we're just going in a circle. The downside of "winning" is that someone else loses, and invariably the cycle begins again. Revolutions require faith, because movements generally involve killing and other nastiness that people will not normally commit to without some spirited motivation. Whereas revolutions revolve, however, renaissances evolve—and for the most part, peacefully. They are brief windows of opportunity when we have the ability to step out of the story altogether.

Nevertheless, despite the promise of an interactive media renaissance, I fear we are trading potential for more of the same, for receiving rather than creating. Even our high school and college classes in computing now value the teaching of software packages over the teaching of programming. Pupils are trained in the existing utility of these devices rather than in the potentials they offer. Children who peak behind the curtain are treated as threats to business, capable of breaking copyright or thwarting rightful business pursuits through their creation of unauthorized programs and extensions (except those who then sell such programs back to corporate America as new dot-com companies, of course). Anyone who stands a chance of resisting traditional programming is pathologized in one form or another. Children who have gained the ability to multitask and to resist the spell of advertising (whether with their remote controls or through their own obsession with creating flash animations) are labeled somehow deficient—even misdiagnosed as sufferers of attention deficit disorder.

The transparency of early computing interfaces encouraged a healthy hacker's sensibility for improvement and modification. Corporate software manufacturers, by contrast, have replaced these open interfaces with opaque ones that offer few or no opportunities to create changes beyond superficial appearance, or "skin." Microsoft Windows encourages users to install new programs by using a "wizard," as if to insist that these processes behind the curtain are simply too mysterious for the common mortal to undertake.

Corporations, meanwhile, continue to profit from all this activity, shifting the ways in which consumers are billed for entertainment hours. Instead of paying to watch a movie in the theater, we pay to make and upload our own movies online. Instead of paying a record company to listen to their artists' music on a CD player, we pay a computer company for the hardware, an Internet access company for the bandwidth, and a software company for the media player to do all this.

We are still creating content using expensive consumer technologies and are uploading the content to corporate-owned servers using corporate-owned conduits. More significantly, we are doing all of this with software made for us by corporations whose own interests are embedded in its very code.

Our activities are defined by the programs we use and the network ports to which we are granted access. iTunes monitors our use of music and video files as keenly as marketers monitor the goings-on at MySpace or Second Life for insights into consumer behavior. Microsoft's automated grammar editors sometimes change the pronouns we use for people from *who* to a dehumanizing *that,* and Verizon cripples the Bluetooth functionality of our cell phones, thereby forcing us to buy our ringtones from them instead of finding or making our own.

As I see it, the only way to make this renaissance different from all those before it is to both embrace the utility and self-expression offered by our new media technologies and to take the trouble to learn how those technologies actually work. We may be the media, but that means very little if we don't accept the responsibility that goes along with taking charge of a society's communications and collaboration capabilities. This doesn't mean promoting a particular politics, economics, or philosophy; rather, it means engaging with the underlying processes informing all of them.

If a book like this can take us a step toward this willful, informed, and conscious exploitation of the gifts now set before us, we may get the renaissance we've always deserved.

"Be really whole, and all things will come to you."
—Lao Tzu

INTRODUCTION
WE'RE ALL IN THIS TOGETHER

David Mathison

"Together we can be wiser than any of us can be alone."
—*Tom Atlee, author of* The Tao of Democracy, *founder of Co-Intelligence Institute*

We are living in a time unparalleled in the history of communication, a time that also means we face challenges and opportunities—all of possibly enormous consequence.

In the past, only a wealthy few had the resources to spread messages by publishing books, magazines, and newspapers, or by broadcasting radio and television shows, or by creating and distributing films. Today, inexpensive digital phones and computers—coupled with the Internet—have given rise to a wide, participatory renaissance among the global community. Today, almost anyone can create and distribute messages to people around the world, and can interact with them, too.

This new renaissance is comparable, in ways, to what the philosopher Karl Jaspers called the *Axial Age*, a period between 900 and 200 BCE. The incredible flourishing of human creativity in those years unleashed unprecedented changes in religion, thought, psychology, and philosophy. In four separate regions of the world, sages such as Gautama Buddha, Jeremiah, Muhammad, Confucius, Lao-tzu, and Socrates created religious traditions that continue to influence our spirituality today: Hinduism and Buddhism in India, monotheism in Israel, Confucianism and Daoism in China, and philosophical rationalism in Greece.

While the first axial age was considered a "renaissance of the individual," Karen Armstrong in *The Great Transformation* argues that currently the emphasis is changing back—or rather, forward—to a group effort.

> The old tribal ethic, which had developed a communal mentality to ensure the survival of the group, was being replaced by a new individualism. The sages demanded that every single person become self-conscious, aware of what he was doing.
>
> Today we are making another quantum leap forward. Our technology has created a global society, which is interconnected electronically, militarily, economically, and politically. **We now have to develop a global consciousness, because, whether we like it or not, we live in one world**. [emphasis added]

The individual who has taken the most stunning advantage of this renaissance of the community, as well as of the Internet's connective and collaborative power (and who understands why it must remain a public resource), is President Barack Obama. His presidential campaign was framed in terms of today's renaissance—we, the group; not me, the individual (*"Yes we can"* was his powerful mantra). He insisted that his candidacy was all about us, the American people, not about him, and he urged us to work beyond the divisiveness of "red" and "blue" states. This all-inclusiveness appealed to a global audience—including a global *wired-in* audience.

Obama engaged that wired-in audience through the Internet, just as Thomas Jefferson used newspapers to win the presidency in his time, F.D.R. used the radio, and J.F.K. mastered television. Millions of true fans visited Obama's website, social networks, and YouTube channel, then they virally accelerated his vision of unity and hope through their own networks and blogs and e-mails. The messaging was decentralized and participatory, versus the top-down, command-and-control style of his older adversaries (see Chapter 15, Social Networks).

His opponents, during both the Democratic primary and the general campaign, had neither the sophisticated tech-savvy staff nor the message that Obama's campaign, and the candidate himself, delivered: inclusion and participation. The concept of everyone working together is the touchstone of our current communal renaissance as well as of our shared history. Americans, despite the siren calls of "rugged individualism," have long united for common causes, such as the abolition of slavery, the advancement of civil rights, women's universal suffrage, and the protection of the environment. In the same way that our ancestors relied on family, friends, and neighbors to build barns, trails, roads, and schools, and to plant and harvest life-sustaining crops, so are many of us today—as you'll see in the following chapters—working together to build not only a more perfect union, but a more perfect *world*.

The Internet, *if* applied and used democratically (think "affordable, open, and ubiquitous broadband") and imaginatively, can do more than connect, inform, entertain, and support us. It can also cut down enormously on energy consumption and toxic greenhouse gases.

But note the word "if."

WHO CONTROLS THE RENAISSANCE?

Renaissances have a nasty tradition of being co-opted by powerful groups. As the Medicis controlled so much of the Italian art world, so do vast corporate interests in our time own and control the means of idea production and distribution. In virtually all aspects of media—newspapers, radio, television, and film—corporations dominate our spectrum. They create the messages, control the distribution infrastructure, and increasingly write the very rules of the game.

In the process, they privatize our communal rights to the public domain of knowledge. How? They freeload on our broadcast television and radio airwaves without paying rent, precisely like corporate welfare queens. They monopolize local rights of way for cable and phone access, in exchange for meager franchise fees. And now they are trying to get their mitts on the publicly funded Internet—the very heart and soul of our own Renaissance.

Herewith a few teeth-gnashing examples of the above. In 1994, despite the fact that the Internet was developed with billions of university, state, and federal tax dollars, the Federal Communications Commission spinelessly allowed the Internet backbone to be turned over to private companies. That same year, the FCC started auctioning off control of some of our airwaves—let me be precise, our *public* airwaves—to the highest bidder, putting valuable wireless spectrum in the hands of a few wealthy corporations.

Then consider the dastardly 1996 Telecommunications Act, the mother of all media deregulations. It lifted restrictions on media ownership and deregulated the Baby Bells and cable television. The result: unprecedented ownership consolidation. Today, we are still paying the price. Five conglomerates now control most major media (Time Warner, Disney, Bertelsmann, Viacom, and News Corp); in the telecommunications realm, Verizon, AT&T, and Qwest dominate; and two behemoths, Comcast and Time Warner, control over half the cable market.

Even more ominous, the phone and cable companies together control 98 percent of broadband Internet access. Game over! A single broadband provider can offer voice (telephone), video, and data (that is, high-speed Internet access)—a so-called "triple play" of services—to subscribers, all through one connection. Why is this ominous? For one example, acting entirely without legal authority, after 9/11 some of these "providers," at the government's behest, wiretapped millions of innocent Americans' phone calls and read their e-mails.

Feel that our renaissance is safe now? Need more ominous examples?

In 2000, corporations successfully lobbied Congress to extend copyright protection to works that had been created so long ago that they would naturally pass into the public domain. Congress obeyed, passing the Disney–heavily sponsored Sonny Bono Copyright Term Extension Act, derisively referred to as the "Mickey Mouse Protection Act." Not only does Disney own Mickey seemingly forever, but the rest of us cannot have access to works whose copyrights would have expired by now. Joichi Ito, the CEO of Creative Commons (more on it in Chapter 21), said, "What was once part of common knowledge is becoming the property of corporations."

In another dastardly example of top-down control, since 2005 cable and phone companies have spent millions of lobbying dollars to kill net neutrality—the "first amendment" of the Internet. Net neutrality would have guaranteed to consumers the right to gain access to the content, applications, or devices of their choice, without restrictions or limitations. The telecom behemoths want to replace the previous "common carrier" model, which was in place until 2005, with tiered pricing. That would eliminate the level playing field (beloved by most) in which pauper or zillionaire alike has the same access to the Internet. Instead, tiered pricing would alter the ability of independent musicians, authors, bloggers, filmmakers, small businesses, and yes, politicians, to compete with those who can afford to pay higher prices to the gatekeepers of the virtual on-ramps. Tiered pricing has been defeated so far, thanks to the efforts of some of the activists you'll read about in these pages, but the corporations have not given up. In 2006, after the Democrats swept Congress, the conglomerates redeployed their army of lobbyists to battle in state legislatures.

As a result, over a dozen states have laws on the books—drafted by phone and cable company lobbyists—restricting municipalities from erecting their own broadband systems. Other corporate-inspired legislation moved local—that is, community—control over cable franchise negotiations to the state level.

THE SCARY SIGNIFICANCE OF CORPORATE DOMINATION

One result? Our taxpayer-funded commonwealth has been redistributed (upwardly) to private companies. It's trickle-up economics, with a vengeance.

Another result is *redlining,* the same word used when banks redlined certain communities on a map…communities whose residents were not to be granted loans, typically for racial or "class" reasons. Today's modern version of redlining deploys broadband only to profitable areas, not to tens of millions of Americans who live in rural locations or areas of more modest income levels.

Voilà—a "digital divide," separating the interconnected "haves" from the isolated "have-nots."

The divide also *sub*divides people. Where broadband access does exist, download speeds are faster than uploads. Why? The corporations that control the flow see us as passive consumers of their products, not as creators, producers, and active participants in a democracy. Corporations hate competition, especially from the audience itself! Therefore they control the supply of bandwidth, products, and services to extract maximum profit. If you want to be ticked off even more, consider this: We American broadband subscribers get fewer choices at slower speeds and higher prices than do our counterparts in other Western nations.

My main point here, though, is that for our common global good, for our real and virtual community, for our very own renaissance, we must protect the infrastructure of the open Internet. To quote Eric Schmidt, CEO of Google, "Infrastructure is the foundation upon which wealth is created." This does not have to mean Google-istic wealth, but can simply mean making a living. The liberating technologies outlined in Part One—podcasts, blogs, websites, self-publishing—

mean little if our broadband provider limits or denies our ability to reach friends and fans across town or around the globe.

Internet infrastructure, after all, simply amounts to the latest kind of community infrastructure, one that everyone uses. Infrastructure means highways, levees, banking, courts, schools, hospitals, security, clean air and water. Infrastructure allows all people to be productive and prosperous, not merely those who already have achieved that condition. In today's world, according to the internetforeveryone.org coalition, broadband is a necessity, one that has fueled economic development, transformed communications, fostered free speech, unlocked new services and innovations, and engaged millions of people in civic participation.

It even helped elect a promising new Internet-savvy president.

The communications infrastructure, whatever big business says, is *not* a corporate birthright. It is ours. According to Federal Communications Commissioner Jonathan Adelstein, "We've forgotten that the airwaves belong to the public and not to special interests. Fewer and fewer companies are consolidating control of the means of creating and distributing ideas. Ownership is the key to getting yourself heard."

Fights for universal access to critical infrastructure included, in their times, the distribution of electricity, telephones, radio, television, and cable and satellite TV. Universal access to broadband is only the most recent of these battles, and is the infrastructure battle of our generation.

According to Robert McChesney in the *Monthly Review* (September 2008):

> At key moments in U.S. history, there had been considerable debate over how to structure the media system, and it was never a foregone conclusion that the system should be turned over to powerful commercial interests. But the policymaking process was corrupt and dominated by commercial interests. So the television system was gift-wrapped and hand-delivered to Wall Street and Madison Avenue without a shred of public awareness and participation. The same thing happened with FM radio and cable and satellite television.
>
> Millions of Americans understand that there is nothing natural about the media system and they have a right and a responsibility to participate in policy deliberations. Ultimately, the battle over media is about whether people or corporations, public interest or private profit, should rule the realm of communication.

As you'll see in Part Two, the battle for controlling broadband—and for doing really interesting things with it—is not actually about the infrastructure itself, but rather about that infrastructure's ability to offer people a platform to distribute their own messages in an alternative manner to that of the dominant commercial media.

As futurist R. Buckminster Fuller once said, "We humans must comprehend the giants' games and game-playing equipment, rules and scoring systems." Fortunately, as you will see in the following chapters, some of us do comprehend. Among our numbers are activists, educators, bloggers, consumer advocates, and increasingly, everyday people who have been (and still are) retaking some of our own turf back and making the tiny sliver of nonprofit, noncorporate media into something big, in its own little way.

In the following chapters, you will read about community newspapers and citizen journalists who enable the public, not corporations, to set the agenda for news coverage (see Chapters 13 and 14). You will find out how local, nonprofit radio, television, media centers, and news agencies provide people-powered broadcasting that is oriented to the community (see Chapters 16, 17, 18, and 20). You will thrill to learn how community broadband initiatives are cropping up around the country with ways to treat this vital infrastructure not like a private ATM but as a public utility, similar to the provision of gas, electricity, and water (see Chapter 19). And you will shout hosannas when you learn how "open source government" is enabling citizens to connect and engage with each other and their representatives, to solve problems collaboratively, to participate in government deliberations, and even to help shape legislation (see Chapters 22 and 23).

Their, or our, goal? To put decision-making processes and message-making power into the hands of the people, to ensure that this renaissance *of* and *for* the community will be controlled *by* the community.

How? Read on…and then get ready to participate!

Our destiny is not written for us, but by us.
—President Barack Obama

13

NEWSPAPERS

HOW TO CREATE A HIGH SCHOOL, COLLEGE, OR COMMUNITY NEWSPAPER

INTRODUCTION: DON'T STOP THE PRESSES. START THEM.

David Mathison

> "Were it left to me to decide whether we should have a government without
> newspapers or newspapers without a government,
> I should not hesitate a moment to prefer the latter."
> —*Thomas Jefferson*

Almost every major city's daily newspaper is the only daily newspaper that city has. In 1920 seven hundred cities had competing daily newspapers; by 1986 only twelve cities did. As a result, owners of the monopolistic dailies can exert undue leverage over content, suppliers, and consumers. More alarmingly, most owners are not individuals but corporations.

Independent ownership of daily newspapers, in fact, is at record lows. In 1945, 80 percent of daily newspapers were independently owned. By 1989 that number had fallen to just 20 percent. To save money on staff, newspapers increasingly use licensed content rather than original work, a move that gives syndicates and wire services incredible power. The top five syndicates in the United States control 96 percent of the distribution of features, cartoons, and columnists, and many news articles and photos are licensed from news agencies like the Associated Press and Reuters.

LOW CIRCULATION

Circulation is plunging as newspapers lose readers and advertisers to the Internet. According to the Audit Bureau of Circulations, during the six-month period ending in September 2007, circulation of 538 daily U.S. newspapers fell 2.5 percent, one of the largest declines on record. Overall, circulation has decreased every year for the past twenty years. Low circulation drives ad rates downward. According to the Newspaper Assoiation of America, total print ad revenue in 2007 experienced the most severe decline since the association started measuring ad expenditures in 1950.

Advertisers are migrating from print to online, where they can expose targeted ads to specific demographics. Websites like craigslist.com, monster.com, and eBay.com are taking over the newspapers' once-lucrative classifieds section, because they can offer advertisers precise messages targeted to niche audiences. In December 2004 Classified Intelligence LLC estimated that craigslist alone cost San Francisco Bay Area papers about $65 million in classified advertising revenues. In 2005 McKinsey & Company reported that the Internet's effect on help-wanted classifieds cost newspapers $1.9 billion in revenue from 1996 to 2004. Meanwhile, Yahoo! earned $672 million in ad revenue in the first quarter of 2005, a 50 percent increase over the first quarter of 2004. To see how some newspapers are making the successful leap to online, see the chapter on We Media: Participatory Media and Citizen Journalism.

HIGHER COSTS

Costs for ink, paper, and distribution are way up, in large part because of the increasing cost of oil and gas. In reaction, the *Wall Street Journal* reduced its page size, and the *New York Times* reduced its page size by 1.5 inches starting in April 2008. Many papers have eliminated the stock tables from the financial section to conserve the costs of paper, ink, labor, and expensive Wall Street data feeds. No one wants to wait a day to find stock and foreign exchange prices (and get black fingers) when online sites display market prices in nearly real time and enable you to track and chart your portfolio in depth—for free.

To meet the profit demands of Wall Street, corporate newspaper owners are maintaining margins by cutting costs, closing news bureaus, not investing in new plants and equipment, and laying off reporters. Reporting is labor intensive. Reporters are watchdogs that look out for the interest of the community, covering local governments, school boards, sports teams, hospitals, and emergency services issues. Yet in 2007, one hundred newsroom staffers were cut from the San Francisco Chronicle, and sixty got the axe at the Los Angeles Times. The Tribune Company cut nine hundred jobs in 2006 alone, and closed a plant, despite net operating profit margins of 20 percent. Knight-Ridder was sold in 2006 even though its thirty-two daily newspapers won eighty-four Pulitzer prizes and had a 16 percent operating profit margin—a much higher profit margin than hotel companies (11 percent) and grocers (4 percent). Indeed, the *Wall Street Jour-*

nal reported that publicly traded U.S. newspaper publishers recorded operating profit margins of 19 percent in 2005 and 21 percent in 2004, or as Molly Ivins said, "more than double the average operating margin of the Fortune 500."

The budget cuts in the newsroom have been even more dramatic; according to a 2002 study by the *American Journalism Review*, the number of reporters covering legislative news at state capitols had fallen to a level that they called "the lowest number we have seen." In his last column for *Editor and Publisher* in November 2003, former Senator and newspaper publisher Paul Simon (D-Ill.) wrote "Part of the diminished reporting of important news is caused by a reduction in the number of reporters . . . caused by mergers and the bookkeeping mentality of those who make big media decisions, people who are not news-oriented but dollar-oriented.

AN ALTERNATIVE: CREATE YOUR OWN NEWSPAPER

So what is an independent newspaper publisher to do? New newspapers can be extremely inexpensive to produce. In the not-so-distant past, it took five to ten years for a fledgling newspaper to post a profit. Start-up costs for a weekly with a circulation of between thirty thousand and fifty thousand hovered around $5 million. Dailies of the same size cost between $15 million and $20 million.

But these estimates included the multimillion-dollar costs of physical production and printing plants. Today, production costs have been slashed, thanks to inexpensive, high-quality desktop publishing technology, and the actual printing can be subcontracted to existing houses. Starting small and keeping costs low enables a publisher to gradually increase circulation, attract more advertisers, and generate enough revenues to expand and invest over time.

There also are nonprofit local newspapers of quality. These are maintained and run with minimal budgets and part-time staff at colleges, high schools, and religious organizations, or by local volunteers from the community (see the accompanying essays). With today's desktop computers, printers, and copiers, and with streamlined distribution, newspaper production is within the reach of most enterprising individuals and groups.

Don't stop the presses. Start them.

-30- [1]

---

1. The number -30- traditionally indicates the end of a wire service or newspaper story. In 1859, Western Union first adopted a numerical code (the "92 Code") to reduce bandwidth over telegraph lines. In several Superman stories, the failure of a *Daily Planet* newspaper employee to use this code usually revealed that a character was being impersonated, or indicated that the employee was subject to mind control.

Fault Lines: A Community Newspaper
The Fault Lines Collective

Fault Lines is the newspaper of the San Francisco Bay Area Independent Media Center (IMC). Our IMC is one branch of a global network dedicated to reclaiming media for the public by encouraging people to produce and distribute their own news. Before forming *Fault Lines,* the primary means of distributing content at our IMC was through the website indybay.org, the Web-based Enemy Combatant Radio, and the public-access show *Street Level TV.* As an alternative to corporate media, our goal is to tell the stories that don't get told or that get distorted by the corporate media, and to make the process of making media accessible to everyone.

Fault Lines grew out of the IMC's understanding that many people have no computer or Internet access, so any website, including our own, is limited in the audience it can reach and the community voices it can represent. In contrast, a newspaper could potentially reach anyone, if enough copies could be printed. This newspaper project, then, was seen as a way to reach a wider audience, to make alternative media more accessible to the community, and we hoped, to empower the people ignored by corporate media to tell their own stories.

Through word of mouth and a call for volunteers on the Indybay website, a small core of individuals who shared this vision gathered during the late spring of 2004. Some had experience with design and layout, some with writing and editorial, and others just had the desire to be part of the creation of independent media.

MISSION STATEMENT

During the early weekly meetings, one of the first tasks as a collective was to create a mission statement. This mission statement is now printed on the masthead of every issue:

> *Fault Lines,* the newspaper of the San Francisco Bay Area Independent Media Center, aims to give all communities the opportunity to actively participate in a collective process of media production and distribution. By operating with transparency, this newspaper hopes to achieve the goal of allowing the public, not corporate conglomerations, to set the agenda for news coverage. Our mission is to train and empower marginalized voices. This publication was created to be used as a tool for radical change in our communities by exposing the stories and raising the issues that the media plutocracy seeks to suppress. We are the people, we are the media and we are dissenting from the ground up.

ORGANIZATIONAL STRUCTURE

After more than two years, a fairly good structure is in place. The production of the newspaper has been divided into various working groups—design, editorial, and fund-raising—each with its own process for contributing to the production of every issue. In addition to the working groups, a task list includes everything required for each issue that doesn't necessarily fall under the purview of a working group. These tasks rotate among different individuals each month. They involve everything from putting together the calendar for our back page to dropping off the final product at the printer. Most importantly, we make it a priority to have open weekly meetings to draw in new volunteers and to keep all the existing members and working groups in close communication.

Although we set out to be an antiauthoritarian collective with a nonhierarchical structure, putting out a monthly paper is an extremely task-oriented process in which accountability is essential. The challenge of maintaining accountability for essential aspects of the paper, such as deadlines, while not having an editor-in-chief is a serious one, but it is not unsolvable. At *Fault Lines,* our modified production process, which includes structures such as a rotating coordinator for each issue, clearly defined task lists, and regular skills-sharing workshops, has helped promote a healthy division of labor and has ensured that multiple people are capable of producing the paper, instead of just a few core individuals.

The importance of organizational structure cannot be emphasized enough. The structure of an organization reflects the ideals embodied within it. The corporate media uses a strictly hierarchical structure in which the higher up you are on the ladder, the more decision-making power you have, and employees are expected to fill particular roles. This reflects the type of society the corporate media propagates. But for those of us who dream of and work toward another world, it is essential to break away from that structure.

Consensus decision- and compromise-making processes can be frustrating and will undoubtedly lead to long meetings. But the efforts are worth it, not only because we will be the change we would like to see but also because this alternate mode of operating will have an effect on our newspaper. Ensuring plurality and encouraging full, uninhibited participation means the content of the newspaper will organically reflect the process.

We have been adamant about *Fault Lines* being an all-volunteer collective from the very beginning. This is practical, in terms of keeping overhead costs down, but it also meshes with our nonhierarchical structure. Because everybody in the collective is doing work, we feel that paying members or contributors for certain tasks (but excluding others) would create de facto hierarchies and inevitably lead to ongoing intergroup conflicts.

Despite the lack of monetary rewards, we have rarely been short of volunteers willing to do the tasks necessary to produce and distribute the newspaper, from the creative work such as writing and designing to the "grunt" work such as mailing out subscriptions. We are conscious that the volunteer nature of our project creates an unfortunate exclusivity; a working, single parent probably doesn't have time to produce media. We have therefore attempted to structure the organization so that volunteers with very limited free time can still participate. For example, a few people help out right before we go to print by helping with proofreading. Also, as noted earlier, we encourage nonmembers of the collective to submit articles, which increases the diverse perspectives presented in *Fault Lines.*

It should be noted that no matter how solid the organizational structure, one key to keeping an organization such as ours alive is having a workspace that is conducive to the overall project. At *Fault Lines,* most activities take place in the San Francisco Bay Area Independent Media Center in a large converted post office, or in collective members' homes. Although the central location in the Mission District and the open-to-the-public nature of the IMC office is ideal, the space is very narrow and is not very comfortable for large meetings. Fortunately, several *Fault Lines* members live in the post office building that houses the IMC. Some members have rooms large enough to fit meetings and work gatherings of the entire *Fault Lines* collective. However, we've also had smaller work meetings in other members' apartments, as well as "retreat" meetings in members' backyards.

Although meeting in members' homes may be intimidating to newcomers (a problem we have experienced), it's unlikely that most low budget, do-it-yourself media projects can afford large office spaces, so we are forced to work with the resources at our disposal. Other IMC projects have been able to secure free meeting locations at local colleges and universities or through partnerships with local nonprofit groups. In short, it's a good idea for all of us to explore our communities for possible meeting and work spaces.

KNOWLEDGE SHARING

The *Fault Lines* collective has implemented "skill shares" to teach community members how to create a community newspaper. This inspires new folks to get more involved and creates a group that is more sustainable over time, because of the diversified skill sets within the collective. Some skill shares teach basic skills such as writing, editing, proofreading, and Photoshop techniques. For more complex tasks, such as designing page spreads, it might be more suitable to have a mentorship program in which experienced designers work one on one with new members. In our experience, *Fault Lines* has always had one or two members who are very knowledgeable and experienced designers. The entire collective as well as individual members have benefitted greatly by having such experienced, hands-on tutors.

EDITORIAL

On the cover of the first issue, we published an introduction to *Fault Lines.* It described our goals for the paper and our vision for the type of activist journalism that we were trying to promote: "Our agenda will not be cloaked behind the myth of 'professionalism.' In Independent Media, bias and integrity are not mutually exclusive. We do not consider our legitimacy to be compromised by promoting our values."

Fault Lines still stands by the goal of providing a media venue for community voices to tell their stories, but the combination of working with inexperienced writers and being a nonhierarchical collective can lead to some serious dilemmas, such as what to do about a rant or a press release presented as a news article.

Our practice is to have a group of members work as rotating editors. They try to meet at least once per week and to stay in close communication with one another when coordinating the content for each issue. Although the editors include a core group, we always encourage new members to become editors (which they usually do). We also encourage the core editors to take a break from editing one or two issues per year, in order to decrease the likelihood that a single member will unwittingly become too influential (which is nearly inevitable, given the dynamic of experienced editors working with journalistic newcomers). It is important to remember that the most important aspects of having a healthy editorial team are communication and reasonable goals. We learned to start small and work our way into more pages and longer articles, or we risk extreme stress and sleepless nights when deadlines come around.

Without a single, managing editor guiding the ideology of the paper, disputes among collective members over content can be a major obstacle. We use the consensus process to make sure everyone's concerns and suggestions for each article can be addressed, and we try to reach compromises regarding political differences. Compromises are often reached by agreeing to present multiple viewpoints from diverse sources in articles. This turned out to be a good idea, because readers then received more facts and perspectives on an issue.

PROCESS

Although our process is always evolving, there is a basic pattern for each issue. At the beginning of the month all the editors bring article ideas to a general meeting and the larger collective gathers to discuss what stories to cover and how to cover them for the upcoming issue. (The smaller details of articles are later discussed at editorial meetings). The following questions are considered:

- How long should this article be?
- How can we present a unique perspective on this issue that you wouldn't find in the mainstream?
- Is this a hard news story; a long, analytical feature; or an op-ed?
- Do we have any personal connections with people involved with this issue (who might be willing to write the article or contribute research)?
- Is this issue timely or will it be old news at print time?
- Will we be able to find original pictures or graphics to run with this article?

Many other questions help us reach agreement on how the final issue will look. We have learned that we constantly need to think ahead.

During this process, an editor or "bottom-liner" is assigned to each article. The bottom-liner is responsible for finding the writer, communicating with the rest of the editors on how the article is developing, and posting the text of the article onto our internal Web page by the deadline so the other editors can view the draft before final revisions are made. Another IMC newspaper, the (now-defunct) *Washington* [D.C.] *Spark,* had editors who were responsible for specific columns (e.g., health, music, and different geographical locations). There are many variations to consider when planning the editorial process.

Often, the most difficult task is finding an appropriate writer. *Fault Lines* is not worried about being biased, but we do want to portray issues accurately so readers know the entire story rather than just one perspective. For example, if the editors want to get someone to write an article about an environmentally devastating power plant, we might try to contact one of the activist groups organizing protests and information campaigns about the issue. Sometimes everything works out and a wonderful article full of direct quotes from multiple sources—including politicians, the police, corporate spokespeople, and right-wing pro-life groups—presenting all the updated facts about the issue gets sent to us by deadline. Often, though, we run into a few recurring problems:

- The article is a press release. These activists are often very busy, so it's easier for them to send a thinly veiled press release than to write an original article. A newspaper full of press releases is boring and one-sided.

- The article is a rant. People working for social justice are very passionate about their causes and usually are eager to write an article that will be published in the paper, but they also are prone to vent all their unfocused anger through their pen, resulting in an article that presents only one viewpoint and may scare away people who are unfamiliar with the topic.

Searching for articles long before the print deadline is a good way to cut down on stress. *Critical Moment,* the bimonthly print project of Michigan IMC, decides on a theme several months in advance and puts out calls for submissions in the paper and on other IMC websites.

Besides finding writers, another problem has been living up to our mission statement, which encourages people from marginalized communities to participate in media production. *Fault Lines* is meant to print stories directly from people being affected by injustice, not just the activists fighting it. There are several challenges inherent in this goal, because such people are often discriminated against in the educational system, meaning they lack the skills to produce media effectively. Also, many people are too busy struggling with day-to-day survival to come to a journalism workshop or to research and write a news article. As a result, members of the *Fault Lines* collective often end up writing the articles. We are still, however, working toward the goal of facilitating more community-based journalism.

One of the best solutions to all these problems is simply pursuing shorter articles. It's a lot less intimidating for readers to pick up a paper filled mostly with 500- to 900-word articles than one that's filled with huge blocks of tiny text. Many studies of newspaper reading habits confirm that most readers only skim the first few paragraphs of articles anyway, and information boxes can always augment what is in the article. It also is easier to modify a press release or a rant into something printable if it is kept short. Finally, if a writer flakes out and misses a deadline, it is easier to fill a one-quarter-page hole than a two-page one.

To ensure maximum communication and accountability at *Fault Lines,* two editors are assigned to each article. The first editor serves as the bottom-liner and the second is primarily responsible for copyediting. However, the second editor, like all other collective members, is free to offer suggestions or voice concerns regarding content, as long as they contact the bottom-liner before the predetermined final editorial deadline.

Once both editors have "signed off" or approved all the articles, but before the designers can begin, the editors meet to create a mock-up. The mock-up is basically a list or diagram of where everything (the articles, illustrations, ads, etc.) will be laid out in the paper. It is crucial when creating the mock-up to know how many words fit on each page and which articles have graphics, so each page is comfortably filled but not overstuffed. Balancing editorial concerns with space restrictions can be a delicate puzzle that requires much shifting and compromise.

The night before we are scheduled to go to print, there is always a lot of work left, so we gather for a monthly work party, which usually takes place at the former San Francisco post office space. Everyone brings his or her laptop, we set up a wireless network, and we proofread, make final design modifications, and—thanks in part to caffeine—finalize miscellaneous tasks and calendar updates.

DESIGN

We have found that graphic design can be the most technical and time-intensive step of publishing, and we also found a solution: using collectively created design templates saves significant time in laying out the articles. Putting the time into planning this aspect saves any group wasted energy, allowing it to focus on more pressing issues. Planning the design aspect of the publication can be split into two different categories: aesthetic considerations and technical considerations.

Aesthetic considerations. One of the first steps in designing a publication is to settle on what aesthetic is the most appropriate for the work being produced. On the one hand, a rougher cut-and-paste look can appeal to a do-it-yourself audience and convey a message of breaking out of mainstream culture, but it also can be alienating to some people. On the other hand, a more polished, clean, and computer-generated look can lend your publication an air of professionalism and integrity that may attract a wider audience, but it may turn off those from the zine-oriented DIY crowd. The choice of which aesthetic to use will depend not only on the mission of the specific publication but also on access to resources.

Technical considerations. A major decision is what kind of format to use to help you and your printer ensure the highest quality, the fastest turnaround, and the fewest complications. This format could range from a digital file created using industry-standard software such as Adobe InDesign (the software we use), QuarkXPress, or Adobe PDF files, to a stack of papers with your spreads printed out.

Another factor in designing a publication is access to technology. Although most companies in the major-publication industry own expensive software, it is not always practical for the independent publisher to spend the money to obtain such software. Anyone with scissors, glue, and paper can create a publication.

PRINTING

By far, printing costs are the largest expense for a volunteer-run paper. For us, as for any other volunteer organization, a budget, access to free or affordable printing options, and how many copies of each issue it makes sense to produce will determine how we choose to print the publication. We printed five thousand copies of our first twelve-page issue. Since we started, our circulation has doubled and our page count fluctuates between sixteen and twenty pages, depending on content and available volunteer time.

Although there are many ways publications are printed, the two most common options are either photocopying or offset printing.

Photocopying. Probably the best use of copy machines for producing publications is for those with a relatively small circulation. Individual photocopies are cheap, but the price per copy does not drop significantly with larger numbers of copies. Although some photocopiers can print directly from digital files, most of the time the originals are placed directly on the glass, which makes photocopying especially well suited for publications assembled by cutting and pasting by hand.

Offset printing. Because the process of making plates and films is time consuming and more expensive, offset printing is not practical for producing small numbers of publications, but it is perfect for those with large circulations, including most large newspapers and magazines. Offset printing works by creating films of the work to be printed, which in turn are used to create plates that ink is applied to and that will eventually end up on the paper.

Films are usually created from digital files produced on the computer, and they create the most professional-looking print jobs. It is possible to produce a cut-and-paste-style publication with offset printing, but it requires scanning the original handmade document into a computer file.

Printing costs can differ significantly around the country. Here are some examples of how much independent newspapers using offset printing pay:

- *Fault Lines* prints ten thousand copies per issue, black and white, sixteen pages, and we pay $800. For spot color we pay $1,100.

- *Critical Moment,* the newspaper of the Michigan IMC, pays $1,300 for six thousand copies on twenty-six-page tabloid, with full color front, back, and center spread.

- *Washington Spark* (D.C.) printed twenty thousand copies of a thirty-two-page paper; sixteen pages were in four-color. Their cost was $2,500 (including delivery).

- In Austin, Texas, *Issue* prints a sixteen-page paper with five thousand copies, color on the front, back, and center spread, for $600.

- *Confluence* in St. Louis prints ten thousand copies, twenty pages, with spot color on the cover, for $1,250.

- *The Indypendent* in New York City pays $1,285 to publish fifteen thousand copies of a sixteen-page paper with four-color on the front and back covers.

In our case, we called around to different printers in our area and found the most affordable printer that met all of our other needs. This printer is nonunion, which is very upsetting to some members of the collective. We think it is important to assess which printers are practicing socially and environmentally responsible business practices, such as using soy-based ink, recycled paper, and—we prefer—unionized labor and/or a cooperative business structure.

DISTRIBUTION

Starting a newspaper requires a large amount of human labor and organizational skill. Distribution focuses on placing the paper in strategic areas where it will find the people most interested in reading it. Do not neglect the details of the "distro" machine! Large stacks sitting around unread can be a huge anticlimax after the painstaking process of creating the paper in the first place. One fail-safe way to avoid the dreaded "stale stack": encourage as many people as possible to subscribe, both for financial reasons and to build a core group of regular readers.

One-on-one, in-person, street-level distribution at special public events is a way to find hundreds of like-minded new readers. At the recent Anarchist Book Fair in San Francisco, for example, *Fault Lines* volunteers connected with people who expressed their appreciation for the paper. Take advantage of as many tabling opportunities as possible—events where you can set up a table—focusing on events that represent the interests of your readers: environmental-justice street fairs, concerts featuring activist musicians, community meetings, etc.

Another channel of street-level distribution is major public transportation hubs such as train stations and bus stops, hand-distributing the paper to willing takers on their way to work in the morning.

When pursuing traditional distribution channels at local businesses and community organizations, seek permission from the management before leaving papers there for people to take. Check back with management from time to time to see whether they have read the paper and whether they have received feedback from patrons. In an effort to minimize wasted papers, avoid dropping more than twenty-five papers at a time in any new location for the first few months. It is better to check back weekly or biweekly to see whether any location needs a resupply than to risk leaving a tall stack in a location where they will barely be touched.

As a relatively new paper competing with hundreds of other small publications, *Fault Lines* has tried to focus on being consistent while also distributing the paper in as many different places as possible. This can mean being a little creative. Copies of *Fault Lines* have stowed away with friends and volunteers traveling throughout the country and overseas. Though the paper's focus is mainly local, we do cover national and international news . . . and you never know where your next subscriber will come from!

In addition to promoting paid subscriptions at tabling events and within the paper itself, *Fault Lines* provides complimentary subscriptions to writers, artists, and advertisers who have contributed or supported *Fault Lines,* as a way to say thank you and to keep the paper fresh in their minds. We seek to identify key activists in various fields and provide them with complimentary subscriptions as well. Every subscriber, paid or complimentary, will likely share the publication with a friend.

Occasional promotional offers, such as free gifts, can help boost subscriptions. Here's one example: A friend of the paper recently bought a block of tickets to a local production of the play *Guantánamo* and then donated the tickets to *Fault Lines* to offer to new subscribers. With this ticket fund-raiser and another for the San Francisco International Film Festival, we raised over $100, which we used to defray our printing costs!

SUBSCRIBER DATABASE

Fault Lines uses key resources—namely the most technical Web programming volunteer on the staff—to maintain online databases that track monthly distribution drop-off points and the current subscriber list. Both databases can be updated remotely by anyone in the collective. Using the distribution database, *Fault Lines* volunteers update the Indybay Web page with the number and location of recently distributed copies. In this way, the public can find the closest place to pick up a copy. The subscriber database also allows for convenient label printing during the mailing process. These tools have proven invaluable to streamlining the distribution process.

FINANCE

The least glamorous but most essential aspect of publishing is finance. You will have no periodical without it. This means you have to believe in what you are doing and be willing to ask for money to do it. It is important to address financial issues up front in the earliest conceptual stages of your publication. How much are printing costs for different types of print media, numbers of pages, and print runs? What should be charged for subscriptions and advertising? What other sources of revenue can be counted on? Will the costs and revenues balance out in a sustainable way over the long term?

As we learned, you can just jump into publishing with strong convictions, a core group of volunteers/staffers, and financing set for only the first issue, but it is not ideal. You should have at least one person—or better, more—willing to dedicate themselves to various financial ventures rather than getting fully tied up in the other time-consuming editorial and design aspects of publishing.

At *Fault Lines,* it was initially decided that advertising, subscriptions, donations, and benefit shows would be the primary financial cornerstones of our publication. In fact, a benefit show featuring local bands paid for most of the first issue. It was assumed that the rest of the needed monies would fall into place as time wore on. Fortunately, as an all-volunteer operation, *Fault Lines* has little overhead outside of its printing costs, and there have been a fair number of advertisers willing to buy space in our relatively radical paper. These ads subsidize most of the costs, although ad revenue has not quite become the reliable source of income we had hoped for. Subscriptions have varied, covering between 10 and 15 percent of the costs every month.

There also are occasional donations, institutional subscriptions, and orders for back issues. And more benefit shows, featuring other local bands, paid for many other issues. Benefit shows, though, are time consuming ventures to set up. Furthermore, we have found it difficult to find volunteers who have not only the time but also connections with talent and venues to do this work in a consistent manner.

Tabling events with donation jars and the selling of subscriptions and other items have paid for up to a third of various issues. We've learned, however, that there are far more of these events in the warmer summer months and a dearth of such events in the winter. Nonetheless, tabling events do include the benefit of making and maintaining connections and locating talent that benefits the group. For example, it has been to our great benefit that the San Francisco Bay Area IMC has video producers in our midst and ties to other IMCs that produce original documentaries, because they have donated copies to us, which we've sold at community events to generate income. Also, one of our volunteers silk-screened Defend Fallujah T-shirts just as U.S. forces were destroying that Iraqi town, and they sold like hotcakes.

New York City's IMC newspaper, *The Indypendent,* created poster maps of U.S. weapons of mass destruction, which they sold at antiwar demonstrations around the time the war broke out. The proceeds actually paid for more than an entire year of printing costs. Of course, these more edgy items would play differently in different parts of the country, but they show the importance of having the right thing to sell at the right time.

ADVERTISING

Before the publication of the first issue, several key decisions were made to accommodate *Fault Lines* members who were less comfortable with advertising and to be true to the larger collective's mission. No ads would be sold to chain stores or big box stores. *Fault Lines* advertising would rely entirely on the support of small businesses, nonprofits, and other community organizations. The largest advertisement we would carry would be one quarter page so that no single advertisement could dominate any section of the paper. The percentage of advertising to content in the newspaper as a whole would never exceed 20 percent, meaning there would be none of the giant "ad ghettos" found in numerous commercial publications.

Once it was determined what size our newspaper would be and some basic design principles were agreed to, it was possible to determine the specifications for advertisements. A one-page rate sheet was then created with graphical representations of the various sizes of advertising space *Fault Lines* would offer, the file types advertisers could use to submit their art, and the single-month ad rates, which we priced to allow us some financial cushion.

The first two advertisements in the first issue were freebies, given to thank those who helped get *Fault Lines* off the ground, such as Balazo 18 Art Gallery in San Francisco, the venue that hosted the first benefit show. We learned that advertising space can be valuable to offer in trade to those who have goods or services your publication needs but perhaps do not have funds to pay for space in your pages. When we started, the Post Carbon Institute owned the faultlines.org URL. They weren't using it, so we worked out a trade of the Internet address for advertising space.

Advertising kit. After an advertising working group was formed, one of the first orders of business was to expand the one-page rate sheet into a full advertising kit we could present when we approached potential advertisers. Our kit includes such things as a promo sheet that explains who we are as a newspaper, what our current print run and distribution methods are, our ethics regarding advertising, and above all, why we are a good place to advertise. It also includes copies of our last two or three issues. Many of the ideas for our kit, from specific items included to the language used, were borrowed from established players in the field whom we most admired, such as the *Indypendent* in New York.

Calling on sponsors. It is probably best to look at advertising as relationship building rather than a quick sell and disengagement. Advertisers need to have confidence in your publication and those who represent it. Besides the quality, reliability, and professionalism of the paper speaking for itself, spend the time to get to know the businesses and organizations you are soliciting, and have conversations with their respective representatives, before asking them to advertise with you.

Nurture long-term relationships with sponsors. For your publication's financial stability and for the advertisers' own brand awareness needs, as well as the value in their cost per ad, multimonth contracts are the best way to go. With every advertiser we approach or who approaches us, we start from the position of exploring the possibilities of a longer-term relationship without unreasonably overselling a potential client. Many times, though, an advertiser simply wants a one-month buy to hype a particular upcoming event they are sponsoring or has some other short-term goal for their advertising. Regardless, treat every advertiser with special appreciation and be certain to follow up regularly on their satisfaction with their ad and/or placement within your publication. You never know when opportunities for collaboration beyond the advertising relationship will arise.

AK Press in Oakland, for instance, includes copies of *Fault Lines* in hundreds of their mail orders every month, in exchange for large discounts on long-term advertising space. Even when AK Press is not advertising, they continue to send out copies of the paper as an added value to their customers. Likewise, historic City Lights Bookstore in San Francisco has become one of the paper's largest distribution points and, in turn, has chosen to advertise on several occasions. Like-minded businesses find a benefit in advertising in a publication they see is popular with their clientele. Communication and consistency have allowed for relationships like these to grow.

CONCLUSION

In closing, we would like to offer another quote from the cover article of our first issue, in order to reiterate why we started *Fault Lines,* and why we're still committed to it:

> Although we support "equality" and "freedom," we will not settle for paying homage to vague concepts and ideals. This publication is a tool for direct action. Knowledge is power, but facts alone will not dismantle the military-industrial complex, which profits from fabricated wars, the centralized clan of media executives who dictate our national discourse, or the political system that allows them to thrive. Each issue will provide access to a growing infrastructure of individuals and organizations that are engaging in a constant battle for immediate results.

**"A newspaper is not just for reporting news.
It is to get people mad enough to do something about it."**
—Mark Twain

How to Create a Great College Newspaper
Rachele Kanigel

Nearly every college or university has some kind of student newspaper. Whether it's a stapled sheaf of photocopied pages distributed every few weeks or a professional-looking daily broadsheet, a student paper plays a vital role on a college campus. In fact, a good student paper serves many roles:

- It's a chronicle of campus life, from scientific research and political discussions to championship basketball games and out-of-control fraternity parties.
- It's a watchdog that barks when the cafeteria is cited for health code violations or hale athletes drive around with handicapped parking placards.
- It's a community forum where students, faculty, administrators, and staff can debate issues of common concern.
- It's a voice for students in a world ruled by professors, residence advisers, and administrators.

In recent years, with advances in desktop publishing, college students have put out increasingly sophisticated-looking papers. Like professional publications, many have incorporated color photography, slick information graphics, and other visual devices to make them more appealing to readers.

Nonetheless, a disturbing number fail to provide the depth and breadth of content their readers deserve. Few take their watchdog roles seriously, and some wither from lack of dedication on the part of the staff. On many campuses, stacks of newspapers go straight into the recycling bin, unnoticed and unread.

How can you motivate a staff to dig deeper? How can you make a newspaper more in tune with its readers? How can you get student journalists to take their role as standard-bearers of the First Amendment seriously? And how can you get college students to turn off their iPods and pick up a newspaper?

Here are some tips for making your college paper more efficient, more relevant, and more essential to your campus community.

Recruit early and often. Student newspaper staffers come and go, and good editors know they need to be ever vigilant for potential recruits. Did the guy in your dorm just win a photography contest? Invite him to shoot Friday night's basketball game for the paper. Have you been moved to tears by the essays of a woman in your English composition class? Offer her a column or a chance to try out for a reporting spot. Even if you have set times for adding staff (the beginning of each school term, say), let students know your doors are always open to new contributors.

Train, train, train. Student newspaper staffers are by definition green. Even the journalism major who has taken five or six courses and the "veteran" who has worked on the paper since freshman year are still learning. Training is essential.

If your paper doesn't already have a comprehensive training program, create one. And if you already train your staff, add more training. Invite professionals from the local media as well as graphic design, photography, and writing teachers on campus to lead sessions. Incorporate team-building and leadership-training exercises. Most of all, make the training fun so students will come back for more.

Be accurate. From the time of an event to the spelling of a name to the precision of a quote, every fact in a newspaper should be correct. Even seemingly minor errors can erode a publication's credibility and integrity and cause readers to lose trust in it. Check and double-check everything, and make sure your paper's editorial production system includes fact checking, copyediting, and proofreading.

When you do make a mistake, admit it. If a reader rightly points out an error, run a correction. If your paper makes a significant ethical, factual, or judgment lapse, take responsibility by apologizing and explaining it in an editorial or editor's note.

Seek divergent views. A student newspaper isn't the creation of one or two student editors—at least it shouldn't be. A good newspaper staff is diverse in all ways—racially, culturally, religiously, politically. Recruit people of varying ethnic and racial backgrounds, but also reach out to older students, people of different political stripes, and other misrepresented minorities.

Be assertive in your news gathering. Don't wait for the news to come to you. Seek it out in the corners, where it hides. Read accreditation reports, audits, budgets, and other documents that will shed light on your campus. Look for the stories behind the numbers. Interview sources at every end of a story—janitors, secretaries, and student assistants as well as administrators, professors, and campus leaders.

Take a stand. Editorials, reviews, columns, and other opinion pieces are designed to express opinions. Be fair and tasteful, respecting your sources and your readers, but don't be timid. Back up your stance with facts to create a cogent and compelling argument.

Be fair. Don't take potshots at administrators, student government leaders, or others you don't agree with. Seek out a diverse range of sources and views and give each their say.

Promote your publication. Don't drop stacks of newspapers around campus and wait for people to pick it up. Hand it out in the quad. Encourage people in your classes, dorms, and social groups to read it. Find out what they'd like to read and encourage those kinds of stories.

Be aware of your power and use it wisely. A newspaper is a mighty tool. It has a wider audience and more impact than most other groups on campus and often is the only source of information about your institution. Use it wisely and you can change your corner of the world.

High School Journalism Matters
Katharine Swan

San Francisco's Mission High School, "the oldest comprehensive high school west of the Rockies," had seen better days by 1972. The students were economically disadvantaged, and they had difficulty making it to class regularly because they faced immense challenges in their home lives and in their neighborhoods.

At twenty-nine I had no journalism experience, but my year as a Volunteer in Service to America in Kansas City, Missouri, and my three years of teaching English in a small district high school that had just closed caught the eye of principal Ted Scourkes. I was asked to teach English and journalism and to jump-start a dying newspaper.

I began by giving lectures about the contents of newspapers to fourteen students, grades nine through twelve. Their ethnicities were as diverse as their classmates'—Latino, African American, Chinese American, Samoan, Italian American, Irish American. They quickly called my bluff, asking when they were going to begin work on the newspaper. So I rewrote my lessons and made all assignments goal oriented. That first year my students produced an amazing ten solid issues.

Toward the end of that year, the freshman editor in chief, Joseph Sprotti, rose to an unusual challenge. He and eight other high school editors had spent three days on a naval destroyer, interviewing sailors and taking part in a short seminar on photojournalism. Reporting on the experience, he carefully balanced the pros and cons of his voyage. However, the printer objected to the article and notified the principal, urging him to censor the story. When Scourkes refused, the printer notified a Navy recruiter, and two burly officers arrived at the school to try to intimidate the editor. While I was teaching a class, they spoke with Sprotti alone in the journalism office. He emerged thoroughly shaken but determined not to change his article. So the issue was printed just as it had been sent to press, students produced their final graduation issue in June, and we found a new printer.

Students continued to learn as they published an issue each month, and the paper grew stronger. However, challenges continued. Three years after the incident with the printer, Mission High's physical education department head sued two students and me for $350,000, charging libel. A student editor had written about funds being paid for nonexistent intramural sports at several San Francisco high schools; the article was illustrated with a cartoon of a man sneaking off with a bag of money. The article led to investigations into intramural funding, which the paper covered. Mission had no intramurals, and in September the principal named a new teacher to be physical education department head. Eventually the lawsuit was dropped. Good journalism is powerful.

Students write—and write well—when they have a vested interest in their paper. They develop this interest when their ideas regularly appear in print in a responsible, professional manner and when their newspaper and/or website reaches an appropriate audience that can offer feedback.

Good school papers are student driven. Story ideas come from students, who research, write, and rewrite these stories. Editors use these ideas to plan their pages and are responsible for developing and finishing them on deadline. The adviser is just that—an adviser. The key to success as an adviser is to listen carefully to students and to foster discussion. Good models are essential.

To write professional stories, students need to learn to contact expert sources and interview them thoughtfully and carefully. They need to learn both the ethical and legal boundaries of good journalism. And they need to interact with their peers both within their schools and within the student journalism and professional journalism communities. Attending state and national high school conventions and taking part in write-off competitions are excellent ways to achieve these goals.

This takes money, but far less than one might suspect. When students wanted to go to National Scholastic Press Association or the Columbia Scholastic Press Association conventions, they solicited and received donations from corporations. Indeed, at Mission High, $3,600 was enough to produce eight powerful eight-page papers every year. Advertisements covered two-thirds of these expenses.

I have found that journalism students are committed to producing good newspapers and to doing whatever they need to do to achieve excellence in reporting for their communities. Often, that requires long and serious discussions with fellow staff members, persistent phone calls, and many, many hours at a computer, but students are willing because they see a genuine payoff each month— and a long-term one when they apply to colleges and universities.

But times change. In 1995, after twenty-three years of working with three different principals at Mission, I met my match: Ted Alfaro. I was astonished at his first words to me: "You are $1,000 in debt." His next words were "I expect to read every issue of the paper before it goes to press." When I answered "I don't think so," his response was "I have case law on it."

Later that afternoon I received an unsolicited call from the school district lawyer, who said that Alfaro had been calling to ask for his "case law." The lawyer assured me that according to the California Education Code, no administrator had the right to prior review of a high school newspaper.

As for the "debt" . . . Each year $1,000 had been allocated for printing the paper. It was no debt, just an expense the principal wished to remove from the budget. Journalism students eventually persuaded him to agree to continue funding the paper at the traditional rate, and they continued to sell advertising to raise the remaining funds.

In September, after working with a new class of students for less than a month, we published the first issue. It was inoffensive. However, the principal objected to one editorial and demanded an opportunity to speak to the class, alone. Students rose to the occasion. Taking careful notes, they rebutted implications that they were being used and that I or anyone else was telling them what to write, and they had a powerful story ready for the October issue.

Each month students reported on the principal's actions. In November the issue centered on his argument with the city's first African American coach during a preseason basketball game, when Alfaro attempted to fire the coach on the spot because he felt Ernest McNealy was ineffective. The article headlined "Setting the Story Straight: Is Coach Ernest McNealy Really Back?" earned the reporter a $2,500 sportswriting scholarship.

January's issue covered three controversies: Alfaro bought basketball shoes for the boys' varsity and junior varsity teams; the girls got nothing. A teacher received a letter charging her with insubordination for holding a fund-raiser in her home. Teachers voted to overrule an administration attempt to close a faculty meeting to school newspaper staff members. February brought controversy when the community discovered that junior varsity basketball players were expected to repay the school for nine pairs of basketball shoes. The gift suddenly was no longer a gift after the shoes had been used.

In March, students won the first Edmund J. Sullivan award ever given by the Columbia Scholastic Press Association for consistent and responsible coverage of controversial subjects. A whirlwind of local and national publicity about the award brought in $17,000 in less than two weeks, and fourteen students were able to travel to New York City to be honored. Much to the administration's dismay, students set the priority for determining who would go, refused to use funds to enable a vice principal to accompany them, and handled all the television and print interviews. In addition, they completed the March issue two days before deadline so it would be ready for distribution when they returned.

But the year wasn't over. Administrators attempted prior review of the April issue, reading it when no one was in the journalism room. I got a call from John Quinn, a district assistant superintendent, who questioned me about one article and urged me not to allow it to go to press. Students ran the story, about a League of Women Voters' poll in which teachers rated each of the school administrators. Alfaro had received an F. His four assistant principals received a C, two Ds, and a second F. It was ironic that the issue also contained a letter of congratulations from Quinn and an associate superintendent, stating "Both of us are extremely proud of your accomplishment (The Sullivan Award) and want you to know that you have not only made a significant contribution to the field of journalism but have been a source of great pride for Mission High School and the San Francisco Unified School District."

The bigger irony was the fate of the school. Test scores had increased phenomenally the year before principal Alfaro arrived with his team to "turn the school around." He certainly did; at the end of the semester the school was reconstituted—a method of "improving" a school by firing all staff members, from the janitors to the principal. Everyone had to reapply for a job at the school, and I never worked there again because I knew that Alfaro would not rehire me.

For the next eight years I worked as a journalism adviser and English teacher at Lowell High School, which has been repeatedly named a California Distinguished School as well as a National Blue Ribbon School. At Lowell, students print a powerful, controversial student newspaper that the National Scholastic Press Association and the Columbia Scholastic Press Association consistently rank as one of the very best in the country. However, Mission no longer has journalism classes or a school newspaper. Students have lost their voice, and the school community is diminished by that loss.

WHY HIGH SCHOOL JOURNALISM MATTERS

Much of the learning in secondary schools is passive. Teachers lecture; students listen. Books are assigned, tests are administered, and grades are assigned. As classes have grown larger due to budget cutbacks, students write fewer and fewer papers and interact less and less with their instructors and their fellow classmates. Little in the education system fosters students' ability to understand concrete problems, create meaningful solutions, and act responsibly.

Student newspapers are an excellent antidote. By their very nature, good newspapers are a team effort, requiring committed reporters, photographers, graphic artists, and advertising managers; Internet-savvy staff members; and strong, creative, resourceful editors. Journalism courses challenge students to channel their energy responsibly so that their papers achieve respect and power. In my thirty-three years as a teacher and newspaper adviser, I have watched the magic of journalism transform students, and even entire schools. Students have the instincts to be powerful writers. They understand what is newsworthy, they have a desire to write responsibly, and they work hard to develop the power that comes from respect.

> **"Real education consists in drawing the best out of yourself."**
> *—Mahatma Gandhi*

14

WE MEDIA

PARTICIPATORY MEDIA, ONLINE COMMUNITY NEWSPAPERS, AND CITIZEN JOURNALISM

David Mathison

"Individual commitment to a group effort—that is what makes a team work, a company work, a society work, a civilization work."
—*Vince Lombardi*

Today, anyone with a cell phone camera can instantaneously share text, photos, and video with a global audience. One no longer needs an expensive printing press, satellite, or broadcast license to reach millions of people. The distinction between those who create the news and those who view it has blurred.

This became especially apparent to news organizations during the London subway bombing in July 2005. Camera phone video footage led the BBC's coverage, with eyewitnesses sending the BBC more than twenty thousand e-mails, one thousand photos, and twenty videos in the first twenty-four hours after the bombing.

"That had never happened before at the BBC," said Richard Sambrook, director of the BBC's Global News division. "This is not just a toe in the water. Even calling it a movement sells it a bit short. It's a fundamental realignment of the relations between big media and the public."[1]

---

1. "Citizens Media: Has It Reached a Tipping Point?," by Jan Schaffer, J-Lab Executive Director, Nieman Reports, Winter 2005. j-lab.org/nieman_article.shtml.

HISTORY OF PARTICIPATORY MEDIA

Participatory media is certainly not new, but it has accelerated dramatically over the last few decades. Some recent examples include the public access movement, which started in the early 1970s. (See chapter 18.) The WELL (Whole Earth 'Lectronic Link), Usenet (USEr NETwork), and bulletin board systems came about in the 1980s. In the late 1990s, content management systems made it easy for nontechnical people to author and publish Web-based content. In 1997 Hope College student Rob "CmdrTaco" Malda created slashdot.org, a participatory site featuring articles submitted by reader/contributors that now gets a half million visitors per day. In 1999 the first Independent Media Center was launched in Seattle, leading to the creation of IMCs in over two hundred cities. (See chapter 20.)

PARTICIPATORY MEDIA—IT'S ABOUT PEOPLE

Flickr is a great example of a successful participatory media venture.[2] The photo-sharing website has five hundred thousand registered subscribers and millions of users. Flickr built a platform that uses photos as a way to connect people. The success of the site says as much about the people and the community as it does about the photos themselves. Participants use tags to describe and organize their photos; this is a "folksonomy," a taxonomy created by users to organize information such as web sites, links, images, and photos, making them easier to search and discover. Organizing Flickr photos becomes a collaborative effort—you permit others (family, friends, even strangers) to organize, comment, notate, and tag your photos. It's the virtual equivalent of an ooh and aah when you share baby photos with friends, only without the grimy fingerprints.

In 2005, Yahoo! bought Flickr for an estimated $35 million. According to Bradley Horowitz of Yahoo!, "With less than ten people on the payroll, they had millions of users generating content, millions of users organizing that content for them, tens of thousands of users distributing that across the Internet, and thousands of people not on the payroll actually building the thing."

TRADITIONAL NEWSPAPERS WAKE UP

The newspaper industry could learn a lot from such online success stories.

While print newspapers struggle to survive (as I write this, the *San Francisco Chronicle* announced it is cutting 25 percent of its staff), their own online counterparts are attracting more readers. During the first half of 2006, more than 55.5 million unique visitors—or one in three Internet users—went to a newspaper website in a given month. That's a 31 percent increase over the same period a year ago.[3] Between 2005 and 2006, traffic to the blog pages of the top ten online newspapers grew 210 percent, according to Nielsen/NetRatings.

---

2. According to Flickr cofounder Stewart Butterfield: "*Participatory media*—that's actually a phrase I like more than, say, *user-generated content,* which I think completely gets it wrong."

3. "Newspaper Sites Continue Readership Gain" by Jennifer Saba, *Editor & Publisher,* October 4, 2006.

The good news, according to the Newspaper Association of America, is that "Ad spending on newspaper websites jumped 31.5 percent last year compared with the year before, to $2.7 billion." The bad news? Online spending represented only 5.4 percent of all newspaper ad expenditures in 2006."[4]

Actually, much of the "old media" sees "new media" as bad news. New media is a source of competition, especially for revenues from retail display ads and classifieds. Craigslist and eBay have much better profit margins than print newspapers, and they usually don't reinvest their profits into journalism. A study found that in the San Francisco Bay Area alone, where craigslist began, it is taking in more than $50 million a year in revenue at the expense of local newspapers, because classified ads make up more than 50 percent of newspaper ad revenues.

Large-circulation newspapers are slowly coming around, though, to incorporate new media into their daily regimen. *USA Today* has instituted MySpace-like social networking communities, letting users create profiles. The *Los Angeles Times* offers a personalization option that enables readers to pick and choose their favorite content. The *New York Times* encourages readers to submit "how we met" videos to its Weddings page announcements.

Online newspapers can, and are, learning a lot more from Indymedia, Slashdot, and Flickr than they can, or did, from the online versions of the *New York Times*. Today's successful online newspaper sites provide hyperlocal news and information at the neighborhood level by leveraging community correspondents and placebloggers, people who write about areas solely because they are passionate about the community (visit placeblogger.org).

But more importantly, the online newspapers' goal is not to lecture readers but to give people a platform where they can interact and to let them provide material that will inform and entertain themselves and one another.

ENCOURAGING PARTICIPATION

Some papers have used various creative ways to get people to participate. The following are some examples from J-Lab's Participatory Content page.[5] J-Lab is part of the Institute for Interactive Journalism based at the University of Maryland's Phillip Merrill College of Journalism.

AZcentral.com (an offshoot of the *Arizona Republic*) launched a Celebrity Look-Alike photo contest in July 2005. Readers contributed one hundred entries, resulting in 393,000 page views in one week. Viewers of the look-alike photos of celebrities such as Leonardo DiCaprio were given the option to select reactions ranging from "Wow! You're a dead ringer!" to "Oh please, dream on!"

---

4. "Drop in Ad Revenue Raises Tough Question for Newspapers," by Katharine Q. Seelye, *New York Times*, March 26, 2007. tinyurl.com/291t8n (quoting Newspaper Association of America).

5. Thanks to the J-Lab's Cool Stuff, Participatory Content pages for the following examples: Celebrity Look-Alike, South Florida Music Challenge, Create a Classic, and Average Joe. For these and more, check out j-lab.org/cool_participatory.shtml.

The *Miami Herald* invited area musicians to participate in the South Florida Music Challenge. Musicians submitted original music videos in three categories: high school, college, and semipro. In addition to recognition from Miami readers, first prize was a $500 gift certificate to a local music store.

The *Columbus Dispatch* site dispatch.com launched Create a Classic, in which *Dispatch* reporters and editors started novels and then had thirty-five volunteer writers submit succeeding chapters. The reporters and editors added endings. Readers then commented on the chapters and voted online for their favorite stories.

In 2004 the St. Paul *Pioneer Press* launched Average Joe Columnist, in which sixteen amateur columnists submitted sports articles in an *American Idol*-like competition. The program was so popular that over one hundred fifty columns were submitted in 2005.

START THE (VIRTUAL) PRESSES!

Interested? Would you like to start an online newspaper, one that happens to involve "virtually" your whole community? Do you have a few friends or colleagues who would join you? Possibly a source of revenue?

If the answer to any of the above is yes, the following shows how to create a successful participatory media venture (known, for our purposes, as an online newspaper).

Chances are it will stay small and local. Maybe, though, it will grow. And maybe—stay tuned—we can help you avoid the pitfalls.

EIGHT STEPS TO A SUCCESSFUL PARTICIPATORY MEDIA VENTURE

1. Create a mission statement. As with any new venture, it makes sense to think first, then act. Thinking leads you to a standard fact of life, these days: a mission statement. Your mission statement should reflect you and your community. Here are two to ponder, from already-successful online media ventures.

Launched in February 2003, ibrattleboro.com was one of the earliest participatory newspaper sites: "It's a local news source by and for the people of Brattleboro, Vermont, published continually. You can get involved in this experiment in citizen journalism by submitting meeting results, news, events, stories, reviews, how-tos, recipes, places to go, things to do, or anything else important to Brattleboro. Or, just drop by to see what others have contributed."

Another such virtual publication, blufftontoday.com, originating near Hilton Head, South Carolina, provides blogs, storage space, and community context. "This is a place for everyone in Bluffton to post news items, create a unified community calendar, and share photos, recipes, opinions."

2. Figure, and Get, Funding. You will need some start-up money, from roughly zero to hundreds of thousands of dollars; it is difficult to know exactly how much.

Figuring out if and how you want to make money is at least as important as figuring what you need in the first place. Examples vary widely. The following were showcased at J-Lab's 2005 Citizens Media Summit.

Voiceofsandiego.org was created by a former newspaper columnist and a private philanthropist who provided $350,000 in seed capital. The site also started a corporate sponsorship and a membership program, which brings in about $4,000 a week. Denver's yourhub.com teamed up with the Denver Broncos and the Colorado Avalanche for sponsorship opportunities. The revenue model of the blountcountyvoice.com in Marysville, Tennessee, is based on ads sold in the print edition, the *Daily Times,* which is sent free to ten thousand households weekly. The site turned a profit after just six months, and as of October 2005 it was making about $1,200 a month.[6]

You also can apply for grants. NewVoices (j-newvoices.org) helped fund thirty microlocal news projects with up to $17,000 in grants. New Voices is administered by J-Lab.

3. Staff creatively. For a nontraditional work of journalism, it makes sense to choose a staff made up of a mix of professional and nontraditional journalists. Newwest.net is one such hybrid of professional and nonprofessional journalism. It has enlisted twenty regular contributors comprising a mix of professional journalists, aspiring journalists, and outside experts. Some are paid positions.

Mary Lou Fulton of northwestvoice.com told J-Lab's 2005 Citizens Media Summit attendees, "Staff with people who are open to new journalism and are passionate about the community. People who you have to talk into participation and community journalism are not going to make good staff members."[7]

A J-Lab survey released in February 2007[8] found that "many citizen journalists felt they were 'a success' not because they had tons of readers, but because they had called attention to local problems overlooked by larger media outlets."[9]

4. Have a content plan. This is a brainstorming no-brainer: Decide what kind of content you want. Photos? Classifieds? Articles? Business listings? Personals? Some of them? All of them?

Flickr cofounder Stewart Butterfield suggests that "The key to success in participatory

---

6. As told to participants in J-Lab's 2005 Citizen's Media Summit: VoiceOfSanDiego's founding editor Barbara Bry (j-lab.org/postcmspane11.shtml#bry), Yourhub's Travis Henry (j-lab.org/postcmspane12.shtml#henry), and BlountCountyVoice's creator Catherine Shen (j-lab.org/postcmspane12.shtml#shen).

7. More at j-lab.org/postcmspane14.shtml#fulton.

8. "Citizen Media: Fad or the Future of News? The rise and prospects of hyperlocal journalism," by Jan Schaffer, February 2007.

9. "Tonight at 11, News by Neighbors," by Joe Garofoli, *San Francisco Chronicle,* February 11, 2007.

media is the people, not the photos or medium. The photos are just the 'locus' for people bringing people together."

Craigslist founder Craig Newmark turned local classifieds—traditionally boring commerce
transactions—into a successful, thriving, interactive, participatory community. Newmark put up
a platform, and people began dancing on it. They go to craigslist to meet, to post personals—and
oh, also to buy and sell things. It is successful because it is about people and relationships first,
classifieds second. Craigslist CEO Jim Buckmaster says, "The fact that our site is almost completely
self-service and community-moderated allows our tiny staff of nineteen to manage the seventh
largest website in the world."

You can get free content from citizens, nonprofits, religious organizations, and community
groups. Eighty percent of the online content for northwestvoice.com is submitted by the community—readers, organizations, churches, and schools. At voiceofsandiego.com, more than half the
content comes from "guest columnists" and "contributing voices" (citizen contributors).

Students at the University of Missouri in Columbia launched MyMissourian with the student-
run daily newspaper. MyMissourian's budget is nearly zero. It uses open source software and the
free labor of twenty student-editors from an online journalism class.

Try to attract as many people to work on your site as possible, said Mary Lou Fulton, founder
of northwestvoice.com, at J-Lab's Citizens Media Summit. "Contributors and columnists will
come and go because it is a volunteer effort. You need a large enough stable of people to make it
sustainable."[10]

5. Choose cohesive communities. If you want to start a local online newspaper, stay local. In a Vermont town of just twelve thousand people, iBrattleboro has 1,360 users who post stories and
comments; between 100 and 500 of them contribute regularly. The site averages 550 to 700 hits
per day.

Backfence.com launched sites in the upscale, wealthy communities of McLean and Reston,
Virginia, and Bethesda, Maryland. The site has user-contributed community guides, event calendars, local business reviews, yellow pages, and classifieds. Mark Potts, founder of Backfence,
told J-Lab's Citizens Media Summit attendees that "the person who's the hardware store owner
also tends to be the Little League coach and also tends to be a dad. And that person is a potential
advertiser, a potential contributor, and a potential reader."[11]

6. To edit or not to edit, and to post, or not to post. This step can keep the peace before any of your
(generally unpaid) contributors gets upset. Decide how your editor or editors will review any
contributed content. Obviously, editors will need to remove offensive, pornographic, libelous, or

---

10. More at j-lab.org/postcmspane14.shtml#fulton.

11. More at j-lab.org/postcmspane11.shtml#potts.

defamatory material. Not only is your reputation at stake but also you do not want to be sued for printing libelous or defamatory remarks.

On that note, you should definitely buy libel insurance (about $2,500 a year).

I would advise not using a profanity filter. Users work around the filter and use words that represent profanities. When there is no filter, the community usually self-moderates.

What about submissions that are not profane but also are not interesting, are poorly researched, or are terribly written? First, work out a policy such as the terms of service discussed next, which submitters can read before embarrassing themselves or getting angry at you for "censorship."

Some sites, like bakotopia.com, allow people to post anonymously. However, bakersfieldbands. com, which covers the Bakersfield, California, music scene, requires a valid e-mail address.

Another reason to require e-mail addresses is to handle "trolls" who annoy people and incite arguments. Although the community can identify trolls after a few posts, requiring a name and e-mail address for posts will winnow them out as well.

7. Figure out terms of service. Your site's terms of service should prohibit users from impersonating or attacking people and should stop them from posting content for which they don't own the rights, that is illegal, or that is in bad taste. Your terms of service should encourage users to tolerate diverse creeds, races, and national origins. Spam, racist remarks, pornography, profanity, or personal attacks should get a user TOSed (slang for being banned from a site due to a violation of the terms of service).

Now, a word for the person submitting content to an online publication: Be sure to check the site's terms of service before uploading any content. Posting a few pictures of your dog or posting a recipe is one thing, but make sure you will get compensated for any amazing photos or well-crafted articles before you submit them.

In other words, do not let corporate media co-opt or exploit your hard work. The terms of service for the BBC, for example, gives the Beeb the right to use your potentially valuable stories and images without paying you a dime. They get it all, royalty free, for perpetual use of the BBC. The flattery won't pay the rent, though.

8. Build it: Make the technology work. There is good news. Techies have done a lot of the technological work for you. Open source software platforms, including Plone, Drupal, and Django (djangoproject.com) make it easy—and free—to enable complex content-management and social-networking tasks that used to cost a fortune and require technical engineers and coders. These platforms let reader-participants contribute text, video, and photos without the need to know software code, and they make it simple for the staff to moderate and edit submissions.

For example, blufftontoday.com uses Drupal, an open source content management system that enables users to share their lives and experiences. Users create personal profiles, upload music and video, and post hundreds of thousands of photos of their pets, friends, and babies.

That's about all there is to starting a community-based online newspaper. And yet, there is a lot more to participatory journalism than uploading on Flickr, finding a job on craigslist, or even starting your on local online newspaper. Read on.

GETTING SERIOUS

According to the 2006 State of the News Media report by the Project for Excellence in Journalism, a research institute affiliated with Columbia University's Graduate School of Journalism, media is in an interregnum. The ability of professional print, radio, and television journalists to do their jobs properly and fearlessly is being reduced, but the promise of an egalitarian, online "citizen journalism" remains unfulfilled. As James Rainey of the *Los Angeles Times* wrote, "The worry is not the wondrous addition of citizen media but the decline of full-time professional monitoring of powerful institutions."[12]

"Serious journalism is labor-intensive and time-consuming and therefore requires large amounts of money and health benefits and pensions," wrote longtime journalist Sydney H. Schanberg in the *Village Voice,* in December 2006. At the National Conference on Media Reform in 2007, Bill Moyers agreed, saying, "Despite the profusion of new information platforms on cable, on the Internet, on radio, blogs, podcasts, YouTube, and MySpace, among others, the resources for solid, original journalistic work, both investigative and interpretative, are contracting rather than expanding."

ENTER "CITIZEN JOURNALISM"

Although the wide use of the term *citizen journalism* precludes me from calling this chapter anything else, I do not like this phrase. For one thing, the term is exclusionary. The word *citizen* leaves out tourists, expatriates, visitors, illegal aliens, and others. Only citizens need apply?

And capital J Journalists do not like nonpractitioners taking the mantle of journalism without training, credibility, and a swearing of allegiance to a higher calling, or at least to a code of conduct. Steve Safran, director of Digital Media for New England Cable News, summed it up by saying, "There isn't a citizen's medicine. There isn't a citizen's law. I am a little concerned."[13]

For their part, not all contributors necessarily aspire to be considered journalists. Most just want to be part of a conversation. Jonathan Weber, founder and editor of newwest.net, said the term *citizen journalist* "intimidated people who were not journalists." Now, citizen contributions to the site are simply labeled "unfiltered."[14]

A February 2007 We Media-Zogby nationwide survey of 5,384 adults found that most Ameri-

---

12. "More News Outlets, Fewer Stories: New Media 'Paradox'," by James Rainey, *Los Angeles Times,* March 13, 2006.

13. See j-lab.org/postcmspanel2.shtml#safran.

14. See j-lab.org/postcmspanel1.shtml#weber.

cans think citizen media is vital to the future of journalism. Almost 75 percent said they believed that amateur reporters would play a key role in the future of American journalism.

If citizens are becoming journalists, they should at least be familiar with some of the principles of journalism, including accuracy, independence, thoroughness, and transparency. According to journalism.org, "The central purpose of journalism is to provide citizens with accurate and reliable information they need to function in a free society."[15] Of the nine core principles of journalism, the first three are:

- Journalism's first obligation is to the truth.
- Its first loyalty is to citizens.
- Its essence is a discipline of verification.

Let us keep in mind throughout the debate, however, that communication is a fundamental *human* right.[16]

OHMYNEWS SETS THE BAR

With the rallying cry "Every citizen a reporter," South Korea's online publication ohmynews.com, which began on February 22, 2000, pioneered online participatory journalism and challenged conservative South Korean news organizations that were monopolizing coverage. Articles on the site supporting the South Korean political outsider Roh Moo Hyun were credited with helping him win the presidential election in 2002. (His first news conference after being elected was given, of course, to OhmyNews.)

OhmyNews started with 727 citizen reporters. Today there are over 36,000—students, professors, housewives, business owners, members of the military, police, and firemen. Ordinary people like thirty-four-year-old Lee Bong Ryul, who wrote around four hundred articles in four years, provide 70 percent of the news on the site. Citizen reporters receive $2 to $20 per story, based on merit, plus "gratuities" from readers. After columnist Kim Young Ok criticized the constitutional court of South Korea, readers gave him almost $30,000 in gratuities in one week—in increments of $10 or less. The site's hundreds of articles, stories, and reviews attract over one million daily visitors.

About 70 percent of OhmyNews's revenue comes from ad sales, 20 percent from syndication sales, and 10 percent from subscriptions. More than seventy employee and citizen reporters have landed book deals since the site was made available.

---

15. See journalism.org/resources/principles.

16. Article 19 of the Universal Declaration of Human Rights states that "everyone has the right to freedom of opinion and expression; that this right includes freedom to hold opinions without interference and to seek, receive and impart information and ideas through any media and regardless of frontiers." World Press Freedom Day (May 3) serves as an annual reminder of our human right to freedom of expression.

OhmyNews now has a professional staff of approximately fifty editors, copy editors, and reporters who check facts, style, grammar, punctuation, and spelling. They reject about one-third of submissions.

"It's participatory journalism," says OhmyNews Founder Oh Yeon Ho.

COMMUNITY CORRESPONDENTS LEARN THEIR CHOPS

OhmyNews has inspired some groups in this country to take participatory media to the next step: teaching untrained citizen journalists to become trained journalists. According to case studies from J-Lab's Knight Citizen News Network,[17] for example, community-supported KRFP radio in Moscow, Idaho, has eight to ten citizens contributing to the news. The volunteer journalists get trained in writing scripts and editing sound, and have produced stories on everything from politics to local zoning issues.

In Whitesburg, Kentucky, community radio station WMMT has a Community Correspondents Corps that teaches various aspects of journalism, from interviewing techniques to how to operate equipment such as digital recorders.

At the Citizen Journalism Academy[18] in Lawrence, Kansas, senior news managers from the daily paper and teachers from the University of Kansas journalism school teach seminars on news reporting. Training includes the basics of journalism and reporting, ethics, integrity, and the editorial process.

The Madison Commons[19] offers a six-week course that has so far trained sixty citizen journalists how to report on their own neighborhoods. And in Melrose, Massachusetts, almost one hundred people from the Milano Senior Center (dubbed the SilverStringers) have received training and practice "senior citizen journalism."

ENTER . . . CORPORATE CITIZEN JOURNALISM

Corporate media is getting in on the act, too. MSNBC's Citizen Journalists Report gives its readers "assignments" during or in advance of major news events. According to Howard Kurtz in the Washington Post, MSNBC's FirstPerson program has received 28,000 citizen submissions since its launch in April 2007. Launched in mid-2006, CNN's I-Reports lets viewers submit text, photos, graphics, audio, and video from computers, cell phones, or blogs. CNN has received more than 60,000 videos and pictures in just over one year. Reuters partnered with Yahoo! on

---

17. Thanks to J-Lab's Knight Citizen News Network for these examples, and many more here: kcnn.org/modules/training_citizen_journalists.

18. Organized by the World Company, publisher of the daily *Lawrence Journal-World,* and the William Allen White School of Journalism and Mass Communications at the University of Kansas.

19. Madisoncommons.org is a collaboration among neighborhood nonprofits and the University of Wisconsin-Madison School of Journalism & Mass Communication.

You Witness News, which lets users upload photos and video to be used on the Reuters.com or Yahoo! site.

New England Cable News supplements its news with contributed content from what it calls "citizen newsgatherers." In May 2006 the Merrimack River in Haverhill, Massachusetts, had its worst flooding in seventy years. Viewers with cell phones and video cameras contributed footage from places that NECN couldn't get to. Pappas Telecasting Company's TV stations have Community Correspondent areas where people upload photos, stories, and video, which are promoted on the stations' daily newscasts.[20]

JOURNALISM AS A DANGEROUS OCCUPATION

Amid all the upbeat, let's-communicate, we-are-the-world (or community), and general good feelings about "ordinary" people getting involved in media of various types, there is, however, a fact that must not be overlooked: Journalism—whether practiced by a citizen journalist, by a professional freelancer, or by someone connected with a new or old, online or mainstream news organization, and especially when practiced by an investigative journalist—can lead to trouble. Consider what happened to Sarah Olson.

In May 2006, thirty-one-year-old freelance writer and radio producer Sarah Olson interviewed U.S. Army First Lieutenant Ehren Watada, who felt he had a duty as an officer to evaluate the legality of his orders, and subsequently decided not to deploy to Iraq. He stated that the war was "manifestly illegal" and that his participation would make him a party to war crimes.

That was not the end of the story. Olson—who interviewed Watada on the radio—was subpoenaed to testify on behalf of the military prosecution. She faced a felony contempt charge that would result in jail time and/or a fine if she refused.

In January 2007 the U.S. government agreed to drop two charges against Watada, which exonerated Olson from having to appear and testify. Said Olson, "It is my job as a professional journalist to report the news, not to act as the eyes and ears of the government. I believe a journalist's duty is to the public and their right to know, not to the government."

Then there is twenty-four-year-old freelance video journalist and blogger Josh Wolf, who holds the unenviable record of being the journalist imprisoned longest for contempt in U.S. history; he was locked in the Federal Correction Institution in Dublin, California, for 226 days after refusing to testify and declining to cooperate with a grand jury investigation into a July 2005 San Francisco rally. Wolf's attorneys argued that granting the government the power to request unused recordings would turn journalists into an arm of the Justice Department, violating their First Amendment rights of free speech and assembly.

Wolf was freed on April 3, 2007, after prosecutors dropped the requirement for Wolf to testify in front of a grand jury, and after Wolf posted the unaired video online. Wolf said in a statement,

---

20. More from J-Lab at j-lab.org/coolstuff.shtml.

"Journalists absolutely have to remain independent of law enforcement. Otherwise, people will never trust journalists."[21]

Involvement in the story is more and more becoming part of the story. According to Adam Liptak of the *New York Times,* ten of nineteen witnesses in the trial of former vice presidential aide I. Lewis Libby were journalists, and "three of them played a central role in securing the conviction of Mr. Libby."

What about people who find themselves, and their cell phones or video cameras or reporter's notepad, at the center of a suddenly violent story, as happened during a pro-immigrant rally in Los Angeles? On May Day 2007 at least ten people, including seven professional journalists, were injured when members of the Los Angeles police department clubbed protesters and journalists in MacArthur Park. The police, dressed in riot gear, fired two hundred forty rounds of rubber and foam bullets and tear gas at the largely peaceful protesters.

Protestors and journalists generally do not have protective gear or bulletproof jackets when things go wrong. Nor do citizen journalists have another kind of protection: the backing of major news organizations.

REPORTING CAN BE FATAL

Sometimes, a journalist—of whatever stripe—deliberately puts him- or herself in harm's way by attempting to report accurately on a Colombian drug cartel, or on the fighting in Iraq or Mexico, or on the Mob.

Since the U.S.-led invasion of Iraq in March 2003, more than one hundred journalists have lost their lives there. It is the "deadliest conflict [the Committee to Protect Journalists] has documented."[22] Five employees of the Associated Press have been killed, and the news agency Reuters lost six employees in Iraq: five journalists including Cameramen Taras Protsyuk, 35; Mazen Dana, 41; Dhia Najim, 55; soundman and driver Waleed Khaled, 35; and photographer Namir Noor-Eldeen, 22; and a driver, Saeed Chmagh, 40. "They and their families have paid a terrible price for the pursuit of truth and we are deeply indebted to them for their sacrifice," said David Schlesinger, Reuters global managing editor.

Iraq, of course, is not the only lethal destination. According to a 2007 report by Reporters Without Borders, eighty-one journalists around the world were killed in 2006. Among them was thirty-six-year-old Bradley Roland Will from New York, who was murdered while videotaping unrest in Mexico's Oaxaca state. He not only videotaped but also wrote dispatches for indymedia.org. Protesters in Oaxaca accuse Governor Ulises Ruiz of electoral fraud.

---

21. Josh Wolf was the recipient of the 2006 Society of Professional Journalists Freedom of Information Journalist of the Year award, as well as the James Madison Freedom of Information award. See Wolf's first public statement at freejosh.pbwiki.com/My-First-Public-Statement-as-a-Free-Wolf.

22. Committee to Protect Journalists, cpj.org/killed/killed06.html.

There also are 134 journalists now jailed in twenty-four countries—an all-time high.

According to Lucie Morillon, Director of Reporters Without Borders, "There has never been a more dangerous time to be a journalist. But even more deplorable was the lack of interest, and sometimes even the failure, by democratic countries in defending everywhere the values they are supposed to incarnate."

A FREE PRESS? WHAT'S THAT?, OR "WE'RE NUMBER 53!"

In 2002 the United States was rated the seventeenth freest press in the world. As of this writing, the United States is ranked fifty-third, tied with Botswana, Croatia, and Tonga. Countries that have more press freedom than the United States include Bulgaria (thirty-fifth), Panama (thirty-ninth), and Mozambique (forty-fifth), according to the Reporters Without Borders fifth annual worldwide press freedom index.

In 2007 legendary broadcaster Bill Moyers accused the George W. Bush Administration of declaring war on journalism itself. "We're seeing unfold a contemporary example of the age-old ambition of power and ideology to squelch and punish journalists who tell the stories that make princes and priests uncomfortable," explained Moyers.[23] Laurie Levenson, a professor at Loyola Law School and a former federal prosecutor, agrees: "It's not a great time to be a reporter. Prosecutors have become much more aggressive in seeking information from the press. I think under the law, as it currently stands, the press has very little protection."

TWO SOLUTIONS TO HELP JOURNALISTS

A federal shield law. Whisleblowers won't speak out if they fear retaliation. Many important stories would not have been reported without the protection of confidential sources, such as Walter Reed Hospital's scandalous treatment of wounded Army veterans, the abuse of inmates at Iraq's Abu Ghraib prison, the National Security Agency's warrantless wiretapping of innocent Americans, and the scandals surrounding Watergate and Enron.

A strong federal shield law is needed to protect journalists and their sources in federal investigations. Forty-nine states and the District of Columbia recognize it, but the federal government does not. The U.S. federal government has no real protection for journalists.

In an op-ed for the *New York Times,* University of Chicago law professor Geoffrey R. Stone wrote, "Congress should expeditiously enact a federal journalist-source privilege law, which would protect journalists from compelled disclosure of their sources' confidential communications in the same way psychiatrists and lawyers are protected. . . . A strong and effective journalist source privilege is essential to a robust and independent press and to a well-functioning democratic society."[24]

23. "Bush's War on the Press," by John Nichols and Robert McChesney, FreePress.net, November 28, 2005.

24. "Half a Shield Is Better than None," by Geoffrey R. Stone, *New York Times,* February 21, 2007.

In October 2007, the U.S. House of Representatives overwhelmingly approved the "Free Flow of Information Act," the first-ever federal reporter shield law, by a vote of 398-21. President Bush has threatened a veto.

Newassignment.net. This organization was created by Professor Jay Rosen, a media critic and author. To paraphrase Rosen, media has traditionally been a one-way communication with one producer and many consumers. Now, there are many producers and more interaction between producers and their audiences. He sees a "producer revolution" highlighted by "pro-am" journalism comprising a few professionals working in tandem with many amateurs.

The system will solicit donations from individuals through the Internet to fund professional reporting on stories that they feel the traditional media are not covering. To find, fund, and develop real assignments, the initiative leverages open source methods, crowdsourcing (mass volunteers on call through the Internet, working on solving problems in their spare time for little or no compensation), and smartmobs (large groups of people who behave efficiently due to network connections with other people and information).

"The idea is to apply to journalism the same open source model of Web-enabled collaboration that produced the operating system Linux, the Web browser Mozilla, and the online encyclopedia Wikipedia. Assignment Zero will use custom software to create a virtual newsroom that enables collaboration on a discrete, but open-ended, topic from the very start," explained *New York Times* reporter David Carr in March 2007.

Newassignment.net is also collaborating with thirteen news organizations from around the United States and also with beatblogging.org, to help journalists use social networks to improve beat reporting.

These initiatives offer paid gigs to fledgling journalists who get a chance to practice the craft of reporting at a high level. Craig Newmark, founder of craigslist, contributed $10,000 to the venture. Reuters gave $100,000 to hire the first editor, who will start in early 2007. More than four hundred and fifty people have volunteered to be reporters.

It's a new beginning.

Resources

- Covering Communities: coveringcommunities.com. Gives insights and examples to help people report on issues in their towns and neighborhoods.

- J-Learning: j-learning.org. Helps schools and towns start community media projects. Offers training in website creation, audio, video, and animation.

- J-Lab: j-lab.org. Spotlights participatory journalism ideas, convenes citizen media practitioners, and rewards innovations in journalism.

- Knight Citizen News Network: kcnn.org. A portal to launch and operate community news sites. Hosts a database of 450 citizen media sites.

- News University: newsu.org. This project by the Poynter Institute offers interactive courses on journalism, such as reporting, writing, design, and editing.

- Society of Professional Journalists Training: spj.org/training.asp. Training and tutorials for editors and reporters.

- University of California-Berkeley: journalism.berkeley.edu/multimedia. Offers tips on multimedia reporting, as well as on shooting video and recording audio.

- Berkman Center for Internet and Society (http://cyber.law.harvard.edu): See their "Citizen Media Legal Guide," a free online guide to media law focusing on legal issues for online journalists.

- Center for Independent Media: (newjournalist.org)

- Center for Investigative Reporting: http://centerforinvestigativereporting.org

- NowPublic; Spot.us; ProPublica.org; Sunlight Foundation

"This is the moment freedom begins. The moment
you realize someone else has been writing your story,
and its time you took the pen from their hand and started writing it yourself."
—*Bill Moyers*

craigslist
Craig Newmark

Craigslist started back in 1995 as an e-mail list I sent out to a small group of friends. People called the e-mail list craigslist, and even when I wanted to change the name, people told me to keep it—personal and quirky.

In January 2005 craigslist received about 1.7 billion page views. We are now in nearly one hundred cities worldwide. One journalist said that our site has the "visual appeal of a pipe wrench," intended and taken as a compliment. Our offices are in an old Victorian in San Francisco and we have fewer than twenty employees. We think of ourselves as a family of community bulletin boards that help people connect with one another to get everyday stuff done. We give them a voice, and somehow, people do feel really connected.

My job title now is Customer Service Rep/Founder, and I work a very full week in the customer service department, dealing with bad situations such as, for example, naughty apartment brokers in Manhattan. A few years ago, I decided to be just an employee and I demoted myself from management. Jim Buckmaster has been CEO since then, and Eric Scheide is our CTO.

On craigslist we have a genuine culture of trust, maintained by the goodwill of people who use the site and helped by obsessive customer service. Personally, I like to give people a break, and people almost always want to do that for each other. People seem to be overwhelmingly trusting and trustworthy, and they are good at policing themselves. Our users are also great at helping and self-moderating one another, and we give them a lot of responsibility to do that.

Back in 1997 I was approached by Microsoft to run banner ads on the site. That didn't feel right, and we've chosen to avoid running distracting banner ads ever since. Since 1998 we've been charging people to post job ads in San Francisco. In 2004 we started charging job posters in Los Angeles and New York $25. These account for less than 1 percent of all our listings on the site. We'd had a lot of requests from users to charge for these job ads, as a way to improve quality, and their support was confirmed when we put it up for public discussion in our feedback forum before moving ahead.

The general feedback was that because businesses would be paying far more elsewhere for far less effective ads, we should charge for business ads. We don't make any big changes on the site without first discussing it in the forums. The bottom line is that there are many websites out there, and unless we're listening to our users, they will find another site that works better for them.

Wikis: Platforms for Participation
Adam Souzis and *David Mathison*

A wiki (pronounced "WICK-ee") is a unique website that allows anyone with a Web browser to create and edit pages quickly and easily or to share and cross-reference text, audio, video, and documents in real time. Internet users can create Web pages and even entire websites without having to know HTML code or worry about design. Any typist can change a page without a formal review process, like a community mural that everyone can work on.

Engage Your Audience and Partners

Wikis can be an essential part of a strategy for building and engaging an audience. Some authors have put entire books on their wiki, allowing readers to edit and rewrite them. For example, Cory Doctorow's best-selling *Down and Out in the Magic Kingdom* was made available free in the form of a wiki, and Lawrence Lessig allowed wiki users to cocreate a new edition of his influential book *Code.* Self-publishers can use a semiprivate or private wiki to collect feedback from editors, contributors, and reviewers. This project, *Be the Media,* used a wiki to review Richard Stallman's essay "Did You Say 'Intellectual Property'? It's a Seductive Mirage," giving the publisher, editor, and contributor an open platform that did not require the use of any proprietary, closed software from companies like Microsoft.

The Wiki Way

The first wiki was created in 1995 by Ward Cunningham in Portland, Oregon. He named it after the Hawaiian word for quick or superfast. Wikis are an example of open source publishing, which turns readers into writers, editors, and publishers. Wikis gained popularity among open source coders as a sly way to get their users to write technical documentation for them. Soon, scores of free implementations of wiki software were created. Writing and editing are completely transparent—anyone with Internet access can contribute or edit articles. However, wider adoption was limited; the Wiki philosophy of openness and simplicity created the skeptical perception of wikis as just toys.

Wikipedia

In January 2001, Wikipedia was created by Jimmy "Jimbo" Wales as a free, openly edited, noncommercial, decentralized, and collaborative encyclopedia. Because of its open nature, Wikipedia rapidly became the world's largest encyclopedia. As of March 2006 Wikipedia contained more than two million English-language articles as well as articles in one hundred twenty other languages, including Esperanto and Klingonese—spoken by the fictional Klingons from the TV show *Star Trek*. In contrast, *Encyclopaedia Britannica* has eighty thousand articles and Microsoft's Encarta has just forty-five hundred. In July 2006, Nielsen/NetRatings reported that Wikipedia had twenty-nine million unique visitors and an astounding 2.5 billion monthly page views.

The Demand Side Supplies Itself

How does Wikipedia maintain this growth with a staff of five and a $1.5 million annual budget? Simple. Thanks to the community-oriented read-write platform— the wiki—the demand side can supply itself. Wikipedia contributors form a pyramid. At its base are millions of grassroots, volunteer readers and writers. The next level includes hundreds of thousands of registered users who created an account with Wikipedia. They include people like Danny Wool (sixteen thousand contributions) and Bryan Derkson (forty thousand contributions and revisions).

At the next level are five hundred Wikipedia administrators who have the power to delete posts, protect articles from being edited, ban hackers, and block IP addresses. Above the administrators are the bureaucrats, and above them the stewards. At the top of the pyramid are about sixty developers who control the software and database that run the Wikipedia world. Jimbo sits at the top.

Wikipedia is a participatory community of people who post articles for social instead of monetary incentives. The reward instead is a sense of community, validation, recognition, and self-worth. Participants contribute to a virtuous circle of collaboration.

Quality and Version Control

At first the idea of allowing anyone to edit content may sound dangerous. If anyone can contribute to a wiki, how can accuracy be maintained? What about vandalism and spammers? The real key to understanding wikis' success is the fact wiki contributors are a self-selecting group: the most engaged participants are usually the most knowledgeable and tend to develop a commitment to maintaining the quality of their contributions. Attempts to spam or deface pages get fixed quickly, and inferior contributions are not accepted by the community. Consequently, vandals and spammers tend to lose interest in the wiki. In addition, most wiki software provides tools, such as banning certain users or IP addresses or locking down certain pages, for handling extraordinary problems. For example, some entries such as Albert Einstein, George W Bush, and Adolf Hitler are "protected" from editing, because of vandalism or disputes over the material.

Another reason wikis work is that reader expectations are different. Readers recognize that they are not reading a regular website (wiki pages generally look distinct from other Web pages), so they know the content of the page doesn't represent one "official" voice. They also recognize that the production quality of the content may be uneven.

Finally, every single change is tracked. This builds a universal body of knowledge and a group memory that makes it easy for administrators to maintain control of each version for review and examination of historical changes, and to revert an article to previous versions, if necessary.

Get a Wiki

Wikis are now becoming mainstream. Commercial vendors provide hosting and support; content management systems include wiki-like functionality, and the most popular wiki software has advanced features such as roles, permissions, and sophisticated word processor-style editing.

Even you can get a wiki up and running. If the server hosting your website can support some sort of dynamic pages (such as CGI or PHP)—and almost all do—there is free wiki software you can install.

Even easier is to use a free or commercial Wiki hosting service. Top vendors include Socialtext.com, pbwiki.com, wikia.com, and wikispaces.com.

So get yourself a wiki and try the Wiki way!

"A blog enables people to express their identity, while a wiki page de-emphasizes the individual and emphasizes the collective understanding of the group."
—*Ross Mayfield (Founder and CEO, Socialtext)*

15

SOCIAL NETWORKS

HOW TO STAY IN TOUCH WITH YOUR 1,000 TRUE FANS

David Mathison

"Love the world as your own self."
—Lao Tzu

As the saying goes, "If you haven't heard of MySpace, you're probably too old." MySpace.com, the world's largest social network, was launched on the Internet in September 2003. A year later it had three million members, who learned about it mostly by word of mouth, both real and virtual. By 2005 it had twenty million members. In 2006 the number had almost tripled, to fifty-six million. As of February 2008, MySpace had one hundred and fourteen million members. It signs up an astonishing hundreds of thousands of people, all over the world, each day.

Sometimes overlooked in the stupefying numbers of names is just one name: Rupert Murdoch. He owns MySpace. You might say YourSpace is HisSpace. We'll get back to what that means—and it means a lot—later.

WHAT IS A SOCIAL NETWORK?

Social relationships were traditionally based on proximity, kinship, education, and career—not to mention people brought together by religion, sports, or an endless range of common interests, from birding to bowling to backgammon to babies. It did take some effort; basically, you had to be there.

Now, you do not.

Virtual social networks are formed by common interests too, but they are unencumbered by physical barriers. Instead, electronic networks, leveraging technology that manages complex social behaviors, can optimize users' social, vocational, academic, and political lives, both online and, increasingly, offline. As members invite their friends into these online hangouts, their own inner circle expands, as does the overall network of potential fans, business partners, professors, students, teammates, family, and collaborators.

WE ARE ALL NETWORKS

Today, argues Mark Pesce in "The Telephone Repair Handbook,"[1] we are all networks. "Every individual harnesses their own social network to create their own media distribution network. Every single individual has become his or her own network. We hyperdistribute much which comes our way, forwarding e-mail, links to websites, podcasts, video clips, Flash animations, even 3-D games. We spend an ever-greater portion of our attention forwarding (i.e., publishing) relevant media to the relevant links in our social network. Occasionally we create the content in these networks, but far more often we pass content *through* our networks. This is the reason that eighty million people have forwarded links to JibJab's 'This Land' video."

WORD OF MOUSE

People are more likely to explore a new book, song, or film if it is based on a positive review from a friend or a familiar and trusted source. This "word of mouse" costs nothing; fans themselves create their own self-generating community. New tunes, new anythings, are discovered by fans, not by music industry executives, publishers, or focus groups. The fans spread the word through their personal networks—e-mail, feeds, blogs, and links—which have nothing to do with payola, corporate control over distribution, or a company's exclusive relationships with resellers and highly paid executives and lawyers. A fan's reward is not money, but the satisfaction of turning friends on to the hot new band, book, blog, or film.

According to MySpace President Tom Anderson, "Word of mouth is the way people find out about new music and MySpace enables this interaction on a massive scale."

HISTORY OF ONLINE SOCIAL NETWORKS

The first online social network, classmates.com, was launched in 1995 to help schoolmates stay

---

1. Mark Pesce, who coinvented the Virtual Reality Markup Language (VRML), is the author of five books on technology. He was a senior lecturer at the Australian Film Television and Radio School from 2004 to 2006. Excerpt from "The Telephone Repair Handbook," by Mark Pesce with Angus Fraser, December 14, 2005, at mindjack.com/feature/phone12142005.html.

in touch. It now has forty million members. Classmates was followed by SixDegrees in 1997 and Epinions in 1999.

Then, in 2002 came the real breakthrough when Friendster catapulted to the top of the social network heap. Within six months it had a million subscribers. The trouble was that Friendster's technology became its enemyster. It couldn't handle the unexpected load, frustrating users with long response times and loss of data. The company made tactical errors, such as deleting the profiles of commercial enterprises, bands, and musicians. Today, two-thirds of Friendster's thirty-one million subscribers reside outside the United States.

Inside the United States, sites like Orkut and MySpace were taking over the field. Orkut was launched in 2004 by Google employee Orkut Büyükkökten on a part-time basis. Within nine months it surpassed two million users. These two million were not simply hangers-on. They were all invitation-only, trusted friends. Although Orkut remains popular in spite of (or perhaps because of) its antipopulist strategy, there have been many issues with the service. The issues, well documented on Wikipedia, include concern over its relationship with Google, terrorist activity, fake profiles, hate groups, state censorship in Iran, speed, reliability, safety, and security. Three-quarters of Orkut's current users are from Brazil.

MYSPACE ASCENDANT

This brings us to the launch of MySpace in 2003, and the question of how—with limited publicity—it landed one hundred twenty million users in less than four years. Among those users, significantly, are five million artists and bands with MySpace profiles.

MySpace got things rolling by invoking the not-so-new maxim "sex sells." When they launched MySpace, its founders encouraged models in the Los Angeles/Hollywood and New York areas to submit suggestive and good-looking photos, thus making the site attractive and hip to the mostly sixteen- to twenty-five-year-old audience. It worked. The site also made it easy for users to "pimp their page" by adding photos, music, and video to their profiles—and to promote their favorite bands.

As the number of users grew, more bands joined the service to reach the growing audience, adding multimedia profiles with songs, videos, photos, lyrics, and tour dates. Now there was a community network of bands and fans, with content (music, photos, and videos) as the connective tissue among members—all the things a rabid fan desires. The bigger the band, the bigger the audience it brought to MySpace. With both fans and bands encouraging one another to join the system, "network effects" kicked in, meaning that the more people joining the network, the more powerful and useful the network becomes to its participants.

And the rest, as they say, is history.

MYSPACE = MYMANAGER/MYPROMOTER/MYPUBLICIST

For bands and fans, MySpace also solved some pretty big problems in the music industry. Today, risk-averse labels sign few new acts, preferring established bands or stars with large, built-in audiences that can move a half million CDs. Labels provide little or no money for promotion, marketing, and tour support. A few years ago it was impossible for an independent band to sustain a following of fewer than fifty thousand fans.

Artists who did "better" often were forced to enter into one-sided, unfair contracts and distribution deals with labels, studios, publishers, resellers, and distributors, all of whom grabbed a piece of the proceeds. It added up to the lion's share of the profits. After record company executives, lawyers, accountants—not to mention corrupt DJs, independent promoters, TV bookers, producers, and the rest—were finished feeding, the artists were last in line for dinner, and got the scraps.

MySpace let bands and fans connect directly, with no middlemen in the way. For singers, bands, and even for comedians, authors, filmmakers, and (gasp!) politicians, a MySpace profile provides an alternative to corporate media's choke hold on the audience, from marketing and promotion to distribution, sales, and fulfillment. Bands can sustain themselves without a huge fan base or major label contract. Instead of needing to move five hundred thousand CDs at $19.95 so that the major labels can recoup their ridiculously high expenses, musicians can actually make a living from a $0.99 song sold to ten thousand or twenty thousand "friends"— because the band keeps most of the profits. That math sure beats the pennies per CD they make in royalties. And because songs are digital, distribution costs are practically zero compared to the expense of reproducing and shipping books, tapes, and discs, and stocking them in retail outlets with limited shelf space.

Musicians use the site's tools and forums not only to sell their songs but also to promote their concerts and events directly to hungry fans. Touring bands can improve attendance at gigs by posting upcoming shows on the site's public calendars, blogs, and forums, or—before even scheduling a tour—by checking the zip codes of their friends to find out which cities would gather the most fans.

Fan profiles provide bands with demographic data that previously a direct marketer could only dream of. The band gets a real-time, direct look at what songs their friends like, what videos they watch, and what other sites and blogs they link to. Users spend an average of 72.7 minutes on the site each time they log in, connecting with friends and building multimedia profiles that showcase their tastes in music, film, books, photography, fashion, or sports. The fans promote the bands themselves—for free—through this word of mouse. Fans have listening parties, play games, and share photos, music, and video, freely promoting the bands, books, and films that they love.

AND THE BEAT GOES ON

In addition to hosting profiles for established acts like Beck, REM, the Black Eyed Peas, Nine Inch Nails, and Weezer, MySpace has helped launch the careers of a number of new bands, from Fall Out

Boy to Reliant K, a Christian pop-punk group that sold over five hundred thousand albums. My Chemical Romance grew a base of more than one hundred thousand MySpace friends. The bands kept production, promotion, and distribution costs low, provided a few free, downloadable songs in their online profile, and earned money from sales of licensed goods like T-shirts, hats, and posters.

Hawthorne Heights sold more than a half million copies of their debut album *The Silence in Black and White* without a major label, radio airplay, or extensive marketing and touring. They spent a modest $20,000 on a recording and $5,000 for a music video and then continuously posted new songs and updates on their blog, growing their base of friends from twenty thousand to two hundred thousand. And, of course, they leveraged access to their friends' profiles—the fans' ages, musical preferences, friends, genders, regions, and towns.

In 2005, to take further advantage of this musical career launchpad, MySpace joined with Universal Music Group's Fontana Distribution and Interscope Records to launch MySpace Records, a new label set up to sign and market artists discovered on the site. The label's first record was from Mickey Avalon, released on November 7, 2006. Hollywood Undead, whose fan base includes more than sixty-five thousand MySpace friends, expects to release a full-length record in 2007. The new business makes cents.

Really, really, really popular singers or bands on MySpace, however, do not even need a label of any kind, even one like Interscope Records. In a way, their own space has outgrown MySpace. Actress, blogger, model, and singer Tila Tequila (Tila Nguyen) is the most popular MySpace denizen, with over 1.7 million friends. Without a label, she released her single "I Love U" on iTunes in February 2007, for $0.99, and a sexually provocative Valentine's Day 2007 video on both her MySpace profile and on mobile phones. By March, her video was the number one downloaded video on iTunes, and her single charted there at number eighty-four.

Do the math. If her 1.7 million fan friends buy the tune for $0.99, minus no commission.

But MySpace is not just for musicians. Comedian Dane Cook's MySpace page led to a million friends, increased CD sales, a stint as host of *Saturday Night Live,* and a deal with HBO. Twenty-one-year-old amateur filmmaker David Lehre screened his short film *MySpace: The Movie,* a parody of the social networking site, which was subsequently viewed millions of times.

Presidential candidates, too, are busily building out their social networks to get in front of the hard-to-attract youth vote. Many have profiles on both MySpace and Facebook. As of February 2008, Barack Obama has three hundred thousand friends combined on the two sites, Hillary Clinton has one hundred and seventy thousand, and John Edwards has sixty-five thousand. They use blogging, e-mail, and videos to provide campaign updates, volunteer opportunities, and fund-raisers.

CALLING ALL DEMOGRAPHICS, OR THERE'S NO SUCH THING AS NOSPACE

Today, Internet-based social networks cover almost every demographic. The widest net is cast by online behemoths Microsoft (Windows Live Spaces) and Yahoo! (Yahoo! 360°). Niche networks cover activism (Meetup); teens (MySpace—of course!—Piczo, and Bebo, which was acquired by America Online for $850 million in March, 2008); academia (Facebook, CampusNetwork, Groupvine, SCHOOPY, mynoteIT); families (Famoodle); scrapbooks (SnapJot, OurStory, Tabblo); adults and personals/dating (Match.com, HotOrNot, FriendOfAFriend).

There are even dating networks that focus on specific religious and spiritual groups, such as BuddhistConnect.com, Muslima.com, CatholicSingles.com, JewCentral.com, and MeetChristianSingles.com.

We'll even be starting our own social network at bethemedia.com.

It is worth noting that the sites are not just for the people for whom they were originally targeted, but for anyone who wants to target that segment of the population. If an author writes a book about teens, he or she ought to have a site on MySpace, as well as on Piczo and Bebo. If a professor is looking for a job, a researcher, or a colleague, then he or she might join the undergrads on Facebook and CampusNetwork.

OUT OF ONE SITE, AND INTO ANOTHER

Meanwhile, friends/fans/users of Internet social networks are growing up. Just as pre-Internet kids of both sexes read such magazines as *Stone Soup* and boys went on to *Boys' Life,* then maybe to *GQ* (with a few stops—*Maxim,* anyone?—along the way), and girls went on to *Seventeen,* then to *Glamour* or *Self* (or lately, maybe *bitch*), so do today's tuned-in kids, on the way to becoming tuned-in adults, move from one site to another.

Teens who were on MySpace in high school and are now in college likely use Facebook as their primary online hangout. Facebook, created by Harvard University sophomore Mark Zuckerberg, is no longer just for students. As a social network, it now leads MySpace in popularity with 150 million members (MySpace has 120 million), and is the sixth most visited site in the U.S. According to TechCrunch, 85 percent of college students have Facebook accounts and 70 percent log in daily, spending 175 minutes a month on the site, versus 145 minutes a month on MySpace, and 9 minutes per month on LinkedIn. Students not using the service may be at a disadvantage, because the site's tools help organize classes, projects, extracurricular activities, and, yes, dates. Although early online learning sites were mostly focused on publishing content for students, social networks foster active connections, knowledge sharing, and group interactions.

On the negative side, some students have been stalked and harassed by others on the service. College instructors, counselors, and admissions staff also have access to the system, as do employers and recruiters, who increasingly use Facebook to check the profiles of potential employees. Facebook's investors are a concern too. In October 2007, Microsoft invested $240 million in Facebook for a 1.6% stake, valuing the start-up at an incredible $15 billion. Some members worry about Microsoft's influence on the direction of the company.

Facebook is not for forever, either. After Facebookers graduate from college and start a career, or at least a job, they will most likely move to the Internet's vocational social networks. Social net-

Get a (Second) Life

Another online social network alternative for bands, fans, authors, filmmakers, activists, and politicians is Second Life. Inspired by Neal Stephenson's science fiction novel *Snow Crash*, Second Life[1] is a virtual 3-D world created by its 1.5 million "residents." About ten thousand people are in the virtual world at a time, represented by online *avatars* that can interact, communicate, run businesses, play sports, listen to music, and watch movies. "Tenants" lease virtual "land" for $20 per month per acre, and companies such as BMG Music, Nissan, Sun Microsystems, and Toyota are spending upward of $195 per month for private islands and branded properties like hotels and nightclubs. It's like product placement in the movies, but, well, virtual. As much as $500,000 changes hands a day between inhabitants. Second Life's virtual currency can be converted into real U.S. dollars. The news agency Reuters even opened a virtual bureau, publishing news from the "real" world to members inside the virtual world, and news from Second Life to people in the "real" world. Users inside the virtual environment carry a mobile device to get news updates (secondlife.Reuters.com).

Second Life lets authors, filmmakers, and musicians perform for a global, live audience — all while sitting at their computers. No need to travel, or book expensive venues. Live music audio streams can be created and uploaded and played in Second Life for others to hear. Fans virtually mingle and chat, listening or watching videos as a community. Virtual avatars allow users to live out their online fantasies as a sexy woman or macho man, or do things impossible for humans in the physical world, such as fly like a bird or live under water. MTV even created Virtual Laguna Beach, an island where fans of the program can dress up like the show's characters and hang out in a similar environment. According to Linden Labs/Second Life CEO Phillip Rosedale, "When you are at Amazon.com you are actually there with 10,000 concurrent other people, but you cannot see them or talk to them. At Second Life, everything you experience is inherently experienced with others."

In 2004, Astrin Few was the first artist to perform virtually. Ben Folds promoted an album by "appearing" at a hotel by Starwood Hotels and Resorts and also at Sony BMG's Media Island, which has rooms devoted to stars like Justin Timberlake and DMX. Fans can virtually mingle, listen to tunes, or watch videos together. In 2006, Suzanne Vega did a live performance in Second Life, and author Kurt Vonnegut was interviewed on the program *Infinite Minds*.

So, if you don't have time, money, or resources to travel to remote cities to promote your song, film, or book, maybe it's time for you to get a (Second) life??

1. Other virtual sites include ActiveWorlds (started in 1997), Gaia (anime-style site created by comic book artists), IMVU, There, vSide, Wallop, Zwinky, and competitive fantasy game sites such as World of Warcraft.

works for business professionals include LinkedIn (the biggest, at 17 million members), Doostang, Ecademy, Go BIG Network, Ryze, Spoke, Xing, and EFactor.com, which connects entrepreneurs with angel investors, venture capitalists, and investment bankers. Users invite other professional friends into an inner circle and likewise are themselves invited into another user's "trusted" networks. The circle expands or contracts with one's online and offline reputation. According to Konstantin Guericke, Vice President of Marketing at LinkedIn, "No one should be picking a lawyer from the yellow pages. Recommendations based on personal connections are important."

Users post profiles (really, résumés) to network, recruit employees, seek jobs, and locate potential business partners. For example, in late 2004, perhaps anticipating inevitable layoffs, more than five thousand employees of PeopleSoft joined LinkedIn just before Oracle acquired PeopleSoft. LinkedIn now has nine million users across one hundred fifty different industries.

And so it goes. Just wait until retirement websites get as hot as MySpace.

HOW TO PIMP YOUR PAGE

It is so easy to put yourself on a social network—that is, to create a profile—that there is no need for a how-to lesson. If teens can do it, then you too can pimp your page. There are third-party sites (most built by other teens) that give you free HTML code to paste almost anything digital into a profile—from premade layouts and backgrounds to games, images, songs, videos, graphics, cursors, avatars (a virtual representation of the user, such as a cartoon, photo, or 3-D image), and emoticons ("emotional icons" like smiley faces written in ASCII text). A few of many such sites are pimpmyspace.org, myspacejunks.com, and myprofilepimp.com. Some sites that offer free code for music, videos, and trailers can be found at findvideos, videogroove, pcplanets, musicvideocodes.info, and music.com.

BEYOND PAGE PIMPING

MySpace made it easy for users to personalize their page with decorative photos, videos, and glittery text. Facebook took this concept further by allowing third-party developers to create entire applications. Known as "widgets," or, in Facebook parlance, the Social Network Application Platform (SNAP), these applications facilitate more-interesting and meaningful social interactions. For example, Facebook's Graffiti application enables friends to write messages or share music and video on a virtual wall. SuperPoke! lets members caress, hug, tickle, or lick each other. Naturally, the applications engage users, encouraging them to spend more time on Facebook.

In late 2007, Google trumped Facebook's SNAP platform with OpenSocial, which provides developers with a common set of APIs (Application Programming Interfaces) that enable the resulting application to run across dozens of OpenSocial-enabled partner sites. Developers no longer have to write unique code for each particular social network. And if users move to another site, they can simply take their network of friends with them. OpenSocial partners include Bebo, Flixster, Friendster, Hi5, LinkedIn, MySpace, Ning, Orkut, and SixApart . . . but not FaceBook.

Taking this to the next logical step, a few start-ups now enable anyone to create their own social networks to engage their audience, employees, family, and friends. Social networks have been created by the Portland Trailblazers basketball team, the University of South Carolina, and even U.S. presidential candidate Senator Barack Obama. Start-ups that provide these services include Netscape founder Mark Andreesen's Ning (which hosts ninety-seven thousand social networks), Crowd Factory, GraffitiWall, Kwiqq, and ConnectPlatform, which enables minorities to create their own free social networks.

REVEALING THE RISKS, AND THE RISKS OF REVEALING

The ease of use of the social networks means not only that it is easy to post a profile but also that it is easy for others to read it. According to the Pew Internet & American Life Project, "More than half of teenagers who use the Internet post profiles online. Of them, 82 percent use their first name in their profiles. Nearly 80 percent post photos of themselves, 61 percent disclose their hometown, and 49 percent give the name of their school. Two percent include their cell phone numbers."

There are obvious risks in revealing too much online. Your public profile is available to prying eyes: government agents from the IRS, FBI, and NSA; employers and fellow employees; hospitals, HMOs, and insurance agents; and parents and teachers, to name a few.

Imagine a few scenarios: A mortgage broker denies your loan based on the Facebook pictures of your college dorm room decorated with empty Budweiser cans. An employer doesn't hire you because of your circle of goth friends in MySpace. A life insurance agent raises your premium because you belong to the hang glider or ghost rider group on Yahoo! 360°.

It can, and does, get worse.

It is just as easy for pedophiles, crooks, and con artists to access user profiles. In response, some sites now track the crimes, pranks, and gimmicks used on social networks. One such site is mycrimespace.com, whose tagline is "A place for fiends," a play on MySpace's "A place for friends." A few of MyCrimeSpace's litany of horrors include:

- A fourteen-year-old girl sued MySpace and News Corporation, alleging she was sexually assaulted by a nineteen-year-old man she met through the service.

- A twenty-two-year-old woman was charged with sexually assaulting a four-teen-year-old boy she met through MySpace.

- Seven girls in Middletown, Connecticut, were sexually assaulted by men who contacted them through MySpace.

Due to complaints of negligent or lax security, MySpace limits access to people at least four-teen years old and has deleted over 250,000 profiles of children under the age of fourteen. Still, some users lie about their age.

Even worse, according to Brad Stone of the *New York Times*, "Some of the country's top law enforcement officials are charging that the online social network MySpace has discovered thousands of known sex offenders using its service but has failed to act on the information. Attorneys general from eight states said the company had not done enough to block sexual predators from the service and had failed to cooperate with the authorities."

"The fact that MySpace failed to come forward immediately with this information is really staggering," said Richard Blumenthal, attorney general of Connecticut.[2]

MURDOCHSPACE

When Rupert Murdoch's News Corporation acquired Intermix Media and MySpace for $580 million in cash in 2005, the site was number three in page views, behind online behemoths Yahoo! and MSN and ahead of giants Google and eBay. The acquisition doubled News Corporations's U.S. Internet traffic to more than fifty million unique visitors per month.

In 2005, six hundred million ads were displayed on MySpace in a single day. Google ogled, and signed a deal. It will pay News Corporation $900 million for the right to sell advertising on MySpace for three years.

One reason that Murdoch bought MySpace is that it costs virtually nothing to run, outside of bandwidth, technology, and support costs. Unlike film studios, broadcast, and cable networks, MySpace has no customer or content-acquisition costs for its millions of user profiles. The audience entertains and promotes itself. It is the bread dough that keeps rising, the loaves that keep multiplying, after the initial trickle of yeast was added. A stunning amount of demographic data is given up for free by users—without any coercion, trickery, sweepstakes, raffles, or redeemable coupons. MySpace user profiles are a direct-marketer's dream come true.

Adam Kenner, Director of Technology at Horace Mann, an independent college preparatory school in New York City, agrees. "It's a huge commercial enterprise. Talk about a haven for market research. You have fifty-seven million teenagers giving you their buying habits, and their likes and dislikes."

But, a marketer's dream could be a parent's or a child's nightmare. Murdoch's acquisition of MySpace means he and his News Corporation now have the keys to children's bedrooms: the posters on their walls, the songs on their iPods, the movies they watch, their hopes, dreams, and fears.

Rupert knows all.

PROTECTING PRIVACY—TIPS

Online privacy equals offline security. Parents should talk openly with children and teens about safe online habits and the dangers of exposing too much information. The Pew report shows that teens are wising up. It found that two-thirds of teenagers who use social networking sites keep their profiles private and only approve trusted friends. Furthermore, nearly half of them include false information.

---

2. "States Fault MySpace on Predator Issues," by Brad Stone, *New York Times,* May 15, 2007.

Here are tips for those users, children or adults, who have some wising up to do:

- Use a middle name or pseudonym instead of your real first name.
- Never post your last name, home address, phone number, passwords, or social security number.
- Delete any personal details, schedules, and photos that make it easy for strangers to find out where you live and where you are going.
- Report any crimes or violations to site administrators and local law enforcement officials.

KNOW YOUR RIGHTS: TERMS OF SERVICE

In the free-flowing world of social networks, there also lurks danger from the sites themselves. They just might own what you post. So, another warning:

Before posting your profile—not to mention your poem, your tune, your video, your chapter, your photograph—read each site's terms of service. Then, *before* you post that 3-CD compilation of songs you worked on for twelve years, you will know whether you are handing over your rights to the site! (For more on MySpace's TOS policy, see the Music chapter).

Some sites, like Yahoo! 360°, do not claim ownership of the content users place in private folders, but those users do grant Yahoo! a worldwide, royalty-free, and nonexclusive license for the content put in the publicly accessible areas of the service. This license expires when the user deletes the content from the public area.

For a good, artist-friendly terms of service agreement, check out the Internet Archive (archive.org) and its partner Ourmedia (ourmedia.org): "You own your own material. Ourmedia claims no intellectual property rights over the material you provide to our service."

For an example of a less friendly agreement, see collegehumor.com: "You hereby grant Connected Ventures and its successors a worldwide, perpetual, non-exclusive, irrevocable, royalty-free, sublicenseable (through multiple tiers), and transferable license (with a right to create derivative works) to use, copy, transmit, or otherwise distribute, perform, publicly perform, and display your submissions for any legal purposes whatsoever now known or hereinafter becomes known."

That is no joke.

"Every single individual has become his or her own network."
—Mark Pesce

16

COMMUNITY RADIO

PUT YOUR HANDS ON THE RADIO, PEOPLE![1]
A HANDS-ON GUIDE TO STARTING
A COMMUNITY RADIO STATION

Sakura Saunders, J. Zach Schiller, Pete triDish,
and the Prometheus Radio Project

A radio station should not just be a hole in the Universe for making money, or feeding an ego, or running the world. A radio station should be a live place for live people to sing and dance and talk: to talk their talk and walk their walk and know that they (and the rest of us) are not irretrievably dead. A visit to a typical radio station is like a visit to a morgue: all the good and joy and fun that can be COMMUNICATION has been turned into a corpse-run for money. We have tried to do KTAO differently. We have tried to find humans, who think and feel like humans; we have tried to give these humans a small speck of the air to let us all know of their liveness. We have tried to revive the body of American transmission.
    —*Lorenzo Milam, author of "Sex ... and Broadcasting,"*
is famous for helping communities start radio stations in the 1960's,
most notably KCHU, WAIF, WORT, KBOO, KDNA, KTAO, and KUSP.

---

1. "Please order your minions of Satan to leave my station alone stop you cannot expect the almighty to abide by your wave length nonsense stop when I offer my prayers to him I must fit into his wave reception stop open this station at once." —Aimee Semple McPherson, in a 1925 telegram to the Department of Commerce after they padlocked her radio station for frequency drift. As a faith healer, McPherson often entreated her listeners to put their hands on their radio receiver to "cure" them of their ailments.

HOW WE GOT HERE

. . . or how the pirates won back the airwaves for community radio.

Low power FM represents a renewal of radio in America. For years, licenses for community groups have been nearly impossible to obtain, especially if someone just wanted a little micropower station for their neighborhood association or small town. There's no real mystery about why licenses were so hard to get, why they suddenly became available in 2000, why they were then mostly taken away again, or why we stand poised to get them back. It's all politics.

The commercial radio broadcasting system in the United States crystallized into its current legal framework with the Communications Act of 1934, which established the Federal Communications Commission (FCC). The Act, the FCC, and Congress largely ignored proposals from educational broadcasters and social reformers to protect space on the dial for noncommercial broadcasters.[1] Some provisions for nonprofit educational broadcasters were added later, but in large measure radio has remained strictly commercial. Things only got worse as the decades wore on. Despite the emergence of Pacifica Radio in midcentury, followed by at least a hundred community radio stations over the years, real community radio stations are the exception rather than the rule in most towns.

Then along came pirate—radio that is. Illegal broadcasters have existed since the dawn of broadcasting, but by the 1980s a new type of politically charged pirate station emerged. The Kantako family's Black Liberation Radio (later Human Rights Radio) pioneered illegal community broadcasting from their apartment in a housing project in Springfield, Illinois. Their open defiance, remarkable staying power (close to twenty years), and unique form of public service broadcasting did not quite fit inside the National Public Radio box. The Kantakos were famous for rebroadcasting a police scanner with a running commentary, helping housing project residents avoid the wrath of overzealous police. Their station became the inspiration for thousands of low power broadcasters.

In the 1990s, Stephen Dunifer of Free Radio Berkeley was busted for his unlicensed station, but the bust led to a remarkable court case that lasted nearly four years. In it, attorneys for the National Lawyers Guild threw into doubt the legality of the FCC's licensing system (see the section on the origins of LPFM). They argued for microradio as a free speech right, calling into question the constitutionality of the licensing system that gave so many channels to corporations and so few to community groups. In the shadow of Dunifer's case, over a thousand unlicensed community radio stations rose up around the country. Though the case was ultimately lost on a technicality, microradio changed the reality of the radio dial.

With Dunifer's case closed, the FCC heightened its enforcement against microradio, shutting

---

1. For more on the early struggle to establish noncommercial broadcast protections, see *Telecommunications, Mass Media, and Democracy: The Battle for Control of U.S. Broadcasting, 1928–1935*, by Robert McChesney, and *Rebels on the Air: An Alternative History of Radio in America*, by Jesse Walker.

down over two hundred fifty stations in 1998 alone. These actions provoked more lawsuits, public demonstrations, and acts of civil disobedience, until the FCC realized that it must legalize a new form of community broadcasting.

One of the stations silenced by FCC enforcers was Philadelphia's Radio Mutiny. When that happened, the ex-pirates first got mad and then got organized. Reemerging in 1998 as the Prometheus Radio Project, they organized tours up and down the eastern seaboard to educate and inform whoever turned out to coffee shops, church basements, and campus classrooms about the need for greater community access to the radio dial. Pledging to start up ten new stations for every pirate station the FCC shut down, the Prometheans moved quickly to the front lines of the broadcast reform movement.

After a few high-profile protest actions in Washington to reclaim the airwaves, protesters got their message through. FCC Chairman William Kennard announced that he was spearheading a new class of radio station license. In January 2000, low power FM (LPFM) was born. Now an official license category exists for noncommercial, community-oriented broadcasting that has a power of 100 watts or less—the power of a lightbulb.

The main radio industry lobby, the National Association of Broadcasters, joined forces with National Public Radio and mobilized some bogus industry science to say that these little lightbulb stations were going to interfere with their 50,000-watt flamethrowers. In 1999, studies flew

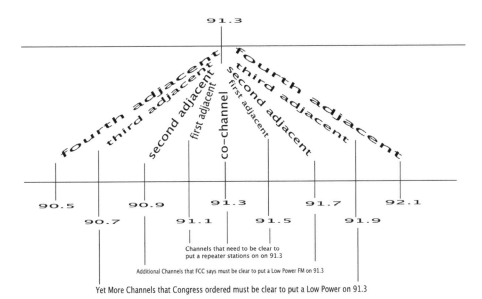

back and forth until Congress weighed in, slapping the FCC's new community radio stations down in favor of a scaled-back plan proposed by the big broadcasters.

Congress's Orwellian-titled Radio Broadcast Preservation Act of 2000 immediately clipped the wings of the LPFM service by requiring an excessive amount of space on the dial between existing full power stations and the newly licensed low power ones (see 3rd adjacent spacing diagram). The new law eliminated about 75 percent of potential stations, essentially keeping LPFM out of major cities. Despite the fact that a subsequent independent engineering study ordered by Congress confirmed the FCC's previous assessment that these spacing requirements were unnecessary, these restrictive "protections" have yet to be lifted.

Currently, about six hundred twenty LPFM stations are on the air in small towns and rural areas across the country. About four hundred more are still awaiting their construction permits. The LPFMs already on the air represent some of the best examples of community radio's potential, with stations run by farmworkers groups, civil rights organizations, schools, public access TV stations, neighborhood associations, and environmental groups.

The fight is not over. It is sad but true that community radio is not seen by the government as part of the basic fabric of democracy in the United States. People have to fight to get on the air at all. So the time to get your LPFM application together is now. We don't know when the FCC will next take applications, but it is best to be ready when they do.

Like we said, it's all politics, nothing more and nothing less. The corporate bigwigs and National Public Radio have their lobbyists in Washington, but we have people power. We've used it, and we need to keep using it to expand, preserve, and protect the airwaves we win back for our communities.

LAYING THE GROUNDWORK

Apply for a license. The application for a low power FM license can only be submitted to the FCC during one of its rare "filing windows." These are five-day windows of opportunity that occur when Jupiter lines up with the third transit of Pluto and the seventh rising of Antares in the belt of Orion . . . or whenever three of the five FCC commissioners decide it is more important for grassroots community groups to have an opportunity to build a radio station than to give away more airwaves to the corporations. You guess which is more common. Because the scheduling of filing windows is based on the whims of public officials rather than some regular interval, it is important to prepare your application ahead of time. The wait is excruciating, but if you are not planning to leave town, your chance to apply will eventually come.

Convene a board of directors. The board of directors is the group of people who are legally responsible for the radio station. There is no federally stated minimum number for boards of directors, though some states have minimums for incorporated organizations. The board of directors listed on the FCC form should match anything that your organization might have filed with the state in which you reside.

Location, location, location. A radio license is not like a driver's license: You can't just drive around town with it and put things up where you please. The transmitter can only be assigned to an exact geographic location, and you have to specify that location in your application, to make sure that it meets the FCC requirements. There are websites where you can go to find out your exact location in geographical coordinates by giving your street address (see, for example, prometheusradio. org/low_power_radio/faq's/street_address_from_coordinates.html).

After you know where you are, check out fcc.gov/mb/audio/lpfm/lpfm_channel_finder.html. This will tell you whether there are any frequencies available at that location. But be warned: The FCC frequency finder is not necessarily as accurate as some of the commercial services out there. It may miss some possible channels. Even if it says there are no channels available, you should double-check elsewhere.

A very powerful website that can be a big help is recnet.com. It is not guaranteed to be one hundred percent accurate, and it cannot be used in place of the FCC program or a professional engineering study, but it gives you an idea of other possibilities. A professional engineer will cost a few hundred dollars to do a frequency search, but it is the most reliable way of knowing that the frequency you choose is a good one.

It is cheapest and simplest to have your studio in the same location as your radio antenna, but the FCC does not care where your studio is—only the point of transmission. So do not worry if you have to put the studio someplace downtown. The transmitter needs to be somewhere up in the hills on the outside of town.

GET IT TOGETHER: COMMUNITY ORGANIZING TO BUILD A RADIO STATION

Mission (statements need not be) impossible! A concise mission statement is necessary to establish your station's core values and to identify who the station is meant to serve. A well-thought-out mission statement presents your station to the community and inspires volunteers and allies. Internally, mission statements can be used to establish programming priorities and to justify difficult programming decisions. For example, if a minority group comes to your station and is interested in producing a show, the station's mission statement can be used to justify displacing an incumbent programmer to make room for the new group. Similarly, you can remove a programmer from his or her show if that programmer airs material that runs counter to your mission (e.g., if it contains blatantly sexist, classist, or racist material).

One of the most important decisions you should make is whether your station is "community access" or is driven by a single interest or segment of the community. Stations thrive or die over such concerns, so precise language on this point is paramount. There is no FCC rule or other guideline that says you should be one or the other. As the licensee of a radio station, your group is allowed complete discretion in what you will or will not broadcast, as long as it is not obscene, libelous, and so forth. Your LPFM license is a noncommercial educational license, which means your group must have an educational mission. But it is entirely up to you to define what that mission is. It could be as narrow as "to educate the public that they will go to hell if they do not give my church money," or "to educate the public about the virtues of techno music." Think broadly—the FCC does not employ sociologists to evaluate one educational mission as more valid than another.

After you have drafted your mission statement, you should prepare to do some outreach. This should involve organizing community meetings, attending the meetings of other community organizations, and possibly creating a survey to gauge your community's aspirations for the radio station. For your own meetings, you should advertise in the local paper (preferably with a free article) and with well-placed fliers. Having a wide community base not only improves the diversity of programming but also increases the number of resources that are available to your community station. Some communities that you might be interested in reaching out to include minorities and immigrants, activists, youths, seniors, academics, community organizations, businesses, artists and musicians, local government, public health organizations, colleges and high schools, or organized labor.

HOW MUCH FOR THAT RADIO STATION IN THE WINDOW? THE LOWDOWN ON LOW BUDGETS

One of the absolutely beautiful things about low power radio is how cheap it is. A full studio can be put together with donated equipment or with used equipment bought cheaply. A cheap studio set-up using consumer grade audio stuff will cost you between zero and $2,000, depending on how much you scavenge and how picky you are. As you get to the high end of equipment and additional production studios, we have heard of people spending as much as $100,000, so you may need to keep your tech people on a strict leash to keep them from buying every gewgaw and whozawhatsit that they ever lusted after.

KRBS in Oroville, California (radiobirdstreet.org), raised $10,000, taking about $7,000 to get on the air; a good chunk of this money was spent on a quality transmitter and an antenna. Radio Conciencia in Immokalee, Florida, WCIW, got going for about $4,200, though they did receive a sweet mixing board donated from Tampa's awesome full-power community station, WMNF.

One (anonymous) LPFM does pay some staff, operating on a monthly budget of nearly $3,500, about 75 percent of which comes from grants; staff payroll, including taxes, amounts to about half the station's monthly expenses. Take away its grants (and staff!) and its monthly operating budget becomes $1,000.

Keep in mind that consumer-grade studio equipment is perfectly adequate, especially when you are starting out and short of cash. It is generally a little noisier, less convenient to use, and will break much quicker than good professional machinery, but if you are putting things together on

Thin Air's Mission Statement, kyrs.org

Thin Air Community Radio shall serve the Spokane area with progressive perspectives, filling needs that other media do not, providing programming to diverse communities and unserved or underserved groups.

Thin Air programming shall place an emphasis on providing a forum for non-corporate and neglected perspectives and discussions on important local, national and global issues, reflecting values of peace, social, economic and environmental justice, human rights, democracy, multiculturalism, freedom of expression and social change.

Thin Air's arts, cultural, and music programming shall cover a wide spectrum of expression from traditional to experimental and reflect the diverse cultures Thin Air serves. Thin Air shall strive for spontaneity and program excellence, both in content and technique.

Radio Mutiny Mission Statement (91.3 FM, until captured by the FCC)

Radio Mutiny is a broadcasting station for people who are denied a voice in the mainstream media. Our all-volunteer group operates a micro-powered FM transmitter, similar to hundreds of radio stations that have sprung up across the country in response to the ever-tightening control of public information by elite media corporations. Radio Mutiny does not promote useless products, vapid lifestyles, or the sound-bite, assembly line ideology that passes for news in this country. We use the public airwaves for news, music, performance, and for communicating with each other about our real daily lives and communities.

Radio Mutiny is rabidly non-hierarchical, decisively anti-authoritarian, avidly pro-feminist, staunchly anti-racist, and flamboyantly anti-homophobic. Our programming is anti-commercial, non-partisan, irreligious, and iconoclastic. Your radio dial was made for revolution!

a shoestring, the pro gear can wait. On the other hand, it is often easier to fund-raise for start-up expenses than for maintenance, so try to look at the skills of your volunteers and evaluate whether your group will be more skilled at fund-raising from listeners after you start up or at winning big grants before you start.

The transmitter and associated equipment usually costs between $4,500 and $8,000 unless you have a tower, which can range from "free if you get that damn thing my husband left there when he died" to $10,000, $20,000, or $30,000 for a fully installed tower. Check out these online resources to get the lowdown on all your equipment needs: prometheusradio.org/low_power_radio/faq's/start-up_equipment.html, prometheusradio.org/low_power_radio/faq's/understanding_radio.html, and prometheusradio.org/low_power_radio/faq's/station_schematic.html.

You may need to rent studio space—but it is often worth asking around to see about donated space. You may be able to get some local group to donate a room to you, at least for the first year or so. Having a radio station in its building is a big draw for a community center, public access TV station, or other institution that likes to have a lot of people coming through.

Many stations get by on volunteers exclusively. However, in many cases stations may want to hire part-time staff to keep the office running smoothly. This is largely a matter of your organization's operating philosophy. If paid staff are desired, figure out how much (or how little) they will work for and make this a part of your operating budget. Tasks that may require paid services include accounting, underwriting (should your station decide to pursue it), and just general paper shuffling—er—well-organized record keeping.

EVERYONE TALKS ABOUT COMMUNITY UNTIL IT IS TIME TO PAY THE BILLS: PARTICIPATORY FUND-RAISING

Fund-raising is the lifeblood of community radio. Here are a few tips on how everyone can help fund-raise to make the radio station a success.

- Set fiscal goals before the year starts.

- Appreciate the dedicated, always. You can't have radio without feedback to your volunteers, members, and donors.

- Keep a detailed record of all donations and the money used to solicit those donations so as to be able to accurately evaluate what works for your station and what doesn't—not to mention all the trouble you could get yourself into if you don't keep such records.

- Make fund-raising a group effort whenever possible.

- Think of fund-raising and publicity as birds of a feather.

- Be creative. Sometimes volunteered services and donated items are more valuable than money.

- Have a good database (and that means maintaining it!). This may be one of those skills to delegate to paid staff or to a foolproof, trustworthy workaholic who just loves organization. Seek Virgos or Cancers.

AND WITH YOUR FIFTY-DOLLAR PLEDGE, YOU CAN HAVE THIS SPECIAL TOTE BAG, *OR,* FUND DRIVES THAT DON'T SUCK

On-air fund drives are a crucial staple for staying on the air. Here are some ideas about how you can approach this sort of fund-raising.

Make recorded fund-raising pitches that are short and fun. Include information about where to send donations (and/or where to call) at least twice every break. Explain why you need the money and what it will be used for. Thank them for listening. These could be aired every day, especially if you don't have on-air fund-raising drives that begin and end on certain dates.

Plan the weeklong fund drive and preannounce it for at least a week; define a set goal and let listeners know periodically how close you are getting to it; invite guests and/or speakers to come in; and promote these events heavily—you can even tease listeners by not airing the conclusion to a talk until you get *X* number of new pledges!

Break down pledges into monthly or daily terms—"For pennies a day you can help us build our new tower!" Then you can print special bumper stickers for project-specific drives so people can proudly display that they helped raise the new tower, like KPFT in Houston, Texas, did in the early 1990s. Drawing connections between your radio station and the larger communities in which it participates is another great way to inspire pledges. Talk about how your station enriches the local music scene or mention its involvement in the greater independent media movement. Basically, remind your listeners of the value of community media.

Fund drives are also a great opportunity to utilize your station's connections both inside and outside of your community. Contact labels whose artists your radio station plays and ask them to donate their extra CDs to your fund drive. The same can be done for publishers and distributors of books, DVDs and videos, or whatever other product that your station can easily promote. This can be written off as a promotional expense for them and it makes a great premium for your listeners. Local businesses are also a great source of premium material. KDVS, a college radio station in Davis, California, offers everything from tattoos to dinners for two during their fund drives. They also get local restaurants to feed their volunteers during fund-raiser week in exchange for thank yous over the air.

Some programmers get creative. You might stage a dorky radio play, for example. WFMU in New York brings in musical group Yo La Tengo to play cover songs by request over the air during their fund drive. Programmers at KDVS often promise to do crazy things in order to inspire pledges, like getting the name of a donor tattooed on their butt cheek if that donor gives $500, or drinking a Red Bull for every $100 that comes in during their show.

IF A RADIO STATION PLAYED A GREAT SHOW IN THE FOREST AND NO ONE HEARD, WOULD IT MAKE A SOUND? *OR,* PROMOTING YOUR STATION IS ESSENTIAL

The best promotion is achieved by getting involved with local community organizations and by attending, promoting, or putting together local events. Get an ad in local newsletters from various organizations in return for mentioning their names and contact information on the air. This is great, especially in conjunction with a community events calendar. Your local antifluoridation chapter, as well as the Kiwanis Club and the Rotary Club, will appreciate you announcing their events as much as you will appreciate your call letters gracing their newsletters' pages.

Order up T-shirts, coffee mugs, key chains, and other stuff people will actually *want* with your station's name on it. Make these items available for sale in the studio, attach them as pledge premiums, and sell them at tables set up at community events or at station-sponsored fund-raising events.

Another great promotional idea is having a program guide. A simple guide will contain a program schedule along with vital information about the station (i.e., staff, mission, website, and contact information). More expansive guides can read like a magazine, containing articles, record reviews, and art by your programmers and DJs.

DON'T THEY GIVE OUT BIG GRANT MONEY FOR THIS?

Not really. Grants take loads of time and are very competitive. Just because you started a radio station does not mean that foundations are going to throw money at you. Take a number and wait in line with the zillion other people who want free money! As a rule, no foundation wants to go out on a limb and be your main funder. They want to see that you have community support in the form of pledge dollars, a healthy amount of merchandising and grassroots fund-raising, and some collaborations with other nonprofits that net you money for services that you provide. Unless you have a very special story to tell, you will not be able to rely on grants exclusively.

Grants are well worth the effort, however, for large-scale and expensive projects like equipment upgrades or studio/station remodeling. The Corporation for Public Broadcasting and the National Telecommunications and Information Administration have grants that can help you here if you are very, very ready. But they may be more trouble than they are worth. Be sure to read all the fine print!

Local foundations are best to pursue. Start looking at groups in the Funding Exchange network (fex.org) and try for a few grants under $5,000. You may need a fiscal sponsor (sometimes called a fiscal agent) to be able to accept tax-deductible donations and apply for grants.

WE'RE ON THE AIR, NOW WHAT?
Setting up a programming policy

Programming is usually the biggest source of drama at any radio station. Radio is notorious for its strong personalities, and managing these individuals into nonoverlapping time slots is inevitably challenging. To avoid the personal conflicts that limited time slots and strong personalities ensure, it is important to have a transparent decision-making process and a clear set of expectations for programmers.

You should get at least a skeleton of a process for programming decisions in place as quickly as possible. Many groups start without a process and then make one up the first time a new person comes in with something they do not like! By then, lots of people are already in and have different expectations about how their show will be reviewed, and everyone can write their own story about how it was unfair to them. Much better to have a process in place from the start. The process can change with time, as long as no one "got in on the ground floor" or feels like the rules of the station were made for other people and not for them.

Therefore, before any programming decisions are made, invent a process by which these decisions will be made. This largely just means that you have to find a person or committee to formulate this process (i.e., applications, interviews, scheduling, evaluations, FCC compliance, and communication with the programmers). Most of this stuff can be done by committee, but to avoid mixed messages it is often recommended that you only have one person in charge of making the schedule and/or communicating with the programmers.

Great advice from radio genius Elizabeth Robinson of KCSB, Santa Barbara, California:
**"A community station should make as few rules as possible.
But enforce the ones you make."**

Application Process

A show application is necessary for scheduling as well as setting expectations for program quality. A minimal program application should include the basics: a show description, personal information about the programmer (name, address, experience, etc.), availability, and an affidavit explaining that the programmer understands FCC and station policy. A more elaborate application may also include details about volunteer work that has been performed or is intended for the station and a short description of the radio station's process for assigning time slots. If the programmer is new to the station, it is also advised that you have an interview with that person before promising them a show. This process functions to get the programmer him/herself to set up the criteria by which the show will later be evaluated.

Program Criteria

As for programming criteria, you have to decide what rules, if any, you want to impose on your programmers. Here are some questions that you might want to consider: Do you want to require that music shows play no commercial music, or maybe just not the stuff heard on other radio stations? Do you want to require that programmers play a certain percentage of new or local music? Will there be established rules of on-air etiquette (e.g., keeping it positive, no discussion of station politics on the air, no making fun of callers)?

Outside of these rules, the basic tenets of programming quality are technical savvy, entertainment value, educational content, artistic content, and on-air presence. These rules in addition to the criteria set out by the programmer in their own application should determine how the program will be judged.

Programming Evaluations

It is a good idea to have a regular schedule for the reassignment of time slots and program evaluations. It is up to you to figure out how often this will occur and how elaborate the evaluations will be.

Preemption Policy

It is inevitable that there will be occasions when the station will need to halt its regularly scheduled programming for special programming (e.g., sports games, election coverage, breaking news, or Sun Ra marathons) and it is important that there be a clear procedure for this preemption.

There oughtta be a law—governing your community station

In addition to FCC regulations, stations can make up their own policies for keeping programmers in line. Stations often have rules regarding food, drugs and alcohol, handling equipment, on-air guests, on-air etiquette, subbing procedures, programming logs, and volunteer requirements. These rules should be accompanied by a procedure for grievances or reprimands. For example, a good policy could define both minor and major violations and lay out the consequences of each. There is no one way to govern. We have seen station styles ranging from benign dictatorships to anarchist collectives, and each has had strengths and weaknesses. Check out several stations whose sound you like and see how they make decisions.

I got a letter from the government: Knowing the FCC rules
Required Logs

Low power radio stations have significantly fewer logging requirements than full power noncommercial radio stations. Low power stations must keep engineering logs containing a date and description of transmitting-equipment failures, Emergency Alert System testing logs, and transmitter readings. They also must keep a political file, which contains every request for air time that is made by a candidate for public office. It is required by law that you give airtime to any candidate that requests it within seven days of airtime given to their opponent. It is also illegal for a radio station to endorse any candidate for public office.

Station Ids: It is required by law that you identify your radio station with its call letters, immediately followed by the name of the city in which you are licensed to broadcast, at the beginning of every hour.

Defamation: It is illegal for a programmer to attack the character of a public or private figure by making on-air statements that cannot be proven.

The FCC's Official Seven Dirty words: shit, tit, fuck, cunt, motherfucker, cocksucker, piss . . . or *any* variation of these words. (See FCC vs Pacifica Foundation, 1978.)

Obscenity vs. indecency: You cannot broadcast obscene material. The difference between obscene and indecent material is a tough distinction to make, because it is largely a matter of degree. Obscene material is sexually explicit material that lacks artistic, political, or scientific value. Any nonscientific description of excretory activities is also considered obscene. Indecent material, on the other hand, may use the nomenclature of these subjects but is far less descriptive (and offensive). A good rule of thumb for making this distinction is that indecent material can mention sex, but obscene material describes it. Indecent material can contain dirty words, but obscene material focuses on them. Indecent material can be broadcast during safe-harbor hours (10 p.m. to 6 a.m.); obscene material is prohibited at all times.

Calls to action: It is illegal for noncommercial programmers to issue any calls to action. These calls to action can be anything from ordering your listeners to riot for a political cause to telling them to go to the stores and buy your favorite album. Legally speaking, this law is generally enforced as it applies to sponsorship announcements.

Fighting words: Radio programmers cannot use language that is likely to cause listeners to react in a violent way. In light of this rule, radio hosts should be warned not to provoke on-air callers, as tempting as this might be.

Plugola: It is illegal for a radio programmer to promote their nonbroadcast business interests on the air, unless their interest is disclosed, in which case it is subject to the rules governing noncommercial sponsorship announcements. This includes accepting money to promote the business interests of others and playing one's own band during a radio show.

Payola is a form of promotion wherein a programmer accepts money for playing an artist's songs on the radio. This is not allowed.

Sponsorship announcements: Because all LPFMs are noncommercial, there are regulations about what can be broadcast in exchange for underwriting. Sponsorship announcements must only inform, avoiding qualitative statements that cannot be proven, such as "best pizza in town" or "great service," and so forth. For example, a typical sponsorship announcement will sound something like this: "KDRT thanks Company X for sponsoring this hour of KDRT programming, Company X provides XYZ services and is located at A Street in downtown Davis. For more information, Company X can be reached at 555-1234 or on the Internet at companyx.com."

TYPES OF PROGRAMS

Public service announcements (PSAs): Public service announcements can either be read live on the air or can be prerecorded. They can be used to announce community events, to promote community resources, or to distribute information of value to your audience. It is also a good idea to make prerecorded announcements promoting the various programs on your radio station.

Producing prerecorded programming such as public service announcements, station identifications, and news pieces has recently become easier for those without access to expensive recording equipment. Inexpensive, user-friendly sound-editing programs are available—and some are even free for download, such as Audacity (audacity.soundforge.net)—and digital recording equipment has never been less expensive or more portable. Minidisc recorders are popular but bewildering in variety; minidisc.org is a very helpful resource. From painful experience, we strongly recommend getting a quality microphone—it is the most important link in your production chain.

Music: Doing a good music show is pretty straightforward, but here is some advice from experience: Keep the air-breaks short and to the point, and announce the music starting from the last piece that your audience heard ("back-rapping"). Give out the phone number, call letters, and Internet address often. Be nice to on-air callers, but cut them off if they are boring. Promote your local music scene and take requests. Background music is always a good idea, as is background information. Themed shows (e.g., regional shows, historical shows, or shows centered around a certain topic) are also fun and interesting. Always remember that you are there to educate and entertain.

News: One of the beauties of low power radio is that it has a limited range. This enables stations to broadcast material that might be irrelevant to a larger audience. Your news department (if you have the resources to have one) should take advantage of this situation, covering local issues and giving a voice to those who usually do not make the news. This news should also, if possible, do more than simply bringing color to the stories already covered by the local press. Your news department should aspire to be investigative, following up on reports of community injustice, researching campaign contributions of local politicians, and highlighting the accomplishments of community groups.

Recording daily headlines, to be played several times throughout the day, is a cheap and easy way to provide a valuable service to your listeners. You can create guidelines, like having X number of local, regional, national, or international stories, and have your news staff summarize and record these stories at the beginning of every day. It is best to have these headlines read by alternating voices because it makes them easier to listen to and easier to record, and because you only have to read one story at a time. For national and international news, there are many quality syndicated shows that are available to LPFMs either for free or really inexpensively.

Resources for Syndicated Content

- pacifica.org (Pacifica Radio)
- fsrn.org (Free Speech Radio News)
- democracynow.org
- prx.org (Public Radio Exchange)
- radio4all.net (Radio for All)
- transom.org

Public Affairs: Public affairs shows aim to educate the community. They can be shows about gardening, bike culture and repair, politics, philosophy, health, hobbies, psychology, literature, or legal advice . . . just to name a few. WCIW, a station for farm laborers in Immokalee, Florida, has shows devoted to workers rights and news from workers' home countries.

Every public affairs show can benefit from theme music. You should also keep music on the side to interject between talking segments. Cohosts are good for dividing up the talking load, which is necessary because radio listeners tend to tune out after hearing the same voice for too long.

For political talk shows, it is often best to have more than one point of view presented, unless someone is sharing a personal experience. Otherwise, you are likely to turn off anyone who doesn't already agree with you. Also, when you interview others be sure to listen to what they have to say, rather than asking what they think about your political views. A good rule of thumb is to ask questions that start out with the five Ws—who, what, when, where, and why . . . as well as how—rather than questions that start with a verb ("Do you think . . . ?"). Speak as you would in the context where your listener is located, if perhaps not quite as informally. Remember that your listeners can't see you, so body language won't help; your words have to be descriptive so they can paint pictures in their minds.

FINAL TRANSMISSION

For more on the history of the struggle to reclaim our airwaves, on ways to get involved in the campaign to get LPFM in our cities, or on getting your own LPFM application together, take a gander at the website of the Prometheus Radio Project, prometheusradio.org. There, you can learn more about how to start your own legal low power FM station. Your community needs you!

Civil Disobedience, Legal Defense, and the origin of Low Power FM

Peter Franck, Esq.

In 1988 the National Lawyers Guild Committee on Democratic Communications, based in San Francisco, received a call from a professor at Sagamon State College in southern Illinois. "My friend is in trouble with the FCC," the caller said. "Can the Lawyers Guild help him?"

An unemployed blind man, later known as Mbanna Kantako, had been broadcasting with a small one-watt radio kit to his housing project in Springfield, Illinois. Virtually the whole black population of Springfield lived in this housing project and was completely unserved by the existing commercial media in the area. Kantako was filling that need, but the Federal Communications Commission notified him that he was being fined for broadcasting without a license.

The Lawyers Guild went to work. We researched the ban on low power radio and concluded that the FCC's refusal to consider licenses for low power and low cost radio stations violated the First Amendment of the U.S. Constitution and the right to communicate guaranteed under international law. A 110-page brief was written, and we were ready to defend Kantako's little Springfield station. In the end, the case did not go to court. Kantako successfully defied the FCC for many years.

A couple of years later, in 1993, in part inspired by Springfield and by the distorted information reported in the U.S. media about the first Gulf War, Free Radio Berkeley was born. Free Radio Berkeley started its life in engineer Stephen Dunifer's backpack. Every Sunday evening he would climb the hills behind the University of California's Berkeley campus and broadcast with a few watts of power to the campus and the surrounding Berkeley community for several hours. Dunifer also used the Internet (then a new and somewhat geeky medium) to find information from all over the world about events in the Gulf, including massive opposition abroad to what the United States was doing.

Soon the government went to federal court seeking an injunction to order Free Radio Berkeley off the air because it was broadcasting without a government license. The Lawyers Guild was ready. Its Kantako brief quickly became the Free Radio Berkeley brief. We convinced Judge Claudia Wilken that there were serious First Amendment issues involved in the ban of low power radio. Judge Wilken denied the government's request for an injunction, citing our First Amendment arguments. The court sent the case back to the FCC on January 30, 1995, for further consideration in light of changed technology and the free speech issues.

Buoyed by this judicial victory and the court's recognition that the low power ban threatened First Amendment rights, dozens and then hundreds of unlicensed low power stations came on the air. Recognition by the court changed the name of this movement of unlicensed stations from "pirate radio" (with its intimation of illegitimacy) to "microradio." Within a few years, there were as many as one thousand unlicensed low power FM stations on the air in the United States.

This was the essence of civil disobedience. The FCC, recognizing that it could not shut down such a massive civil disobedience movement, started the process of legalizing microradio, and ultimately it adopted regulations authorizing low power FM.

The Lawyers Guild has always believed that it can be successful in court only when it is supporting a movement that is in the streets, or in this case, on the air. The early legal victory gave this free speech movement a legitimacy and breathing space to grow and become successful.

A new kind of radio was created out of thin air.

"How you choose to be makes a difference for everyone."
—*Stephen Gaskin, Monday Night Class*

17

PUBLIC ACCESS

HOW TO CREATE A PUBLIC ACCESS TV SHOW

David Mathison
Dedicated to Dirk Koning[1]

*"The way of life is to do nothing through acting.
The way of life is to do everything through being."*
—*Lao Tzu*

Michael Essany of Valparaiso, Indiana, hosted his own weekly cable access television show from the time he was fifteen years old. Valparaiso's public access station management—at first leery of a teenager having his own TV show—wanted to see three sample episodes before committing to Essany, so he sent out five hundred requests for celebrity interviews. Finally, three agreed to fly to Valparaiso and come on the show—two talk show pros (Ed McMahon and Leeza Gibbons) and actor Timothy Dalton.

Valparaiso committed, and Essany's audience grew from twenty-four thousand to two hundred thousand viewers in less than one year. His "set"—wallpaper of a NYC skyline—cost $49. He taped from his parents' living room in Valparaiso, with his mother as camerawoman, sound engineer, wardrobe designer—and cook for the guests.

---

1. Dirk Koning (1957–2005) was founder of the Grand Rapids Community Media Center in Grand Rapids, Michigan. He wrote: "The Latin origin for the words community and communication is the same: to share. The idea of community media is to establish radio, television, print and Internet of, by and for the people. In other words, citizen-controlled media for non-commercial and social development purposes."

The Michael Essany Show ultimately aired on local, national, and international television and was broadcast for two seasons on E! Entertainment Television—all before Essany's twenty-first birthday. Leeza Gibbons herself went from being guest to producer. His E! program featured guests Ray Romano, Kevin Bacon, Walter Cronkite, Jewel, and Jay Leno, among others.

If a teenager in Valparaiso, Indiana, can do it, so can you. And according to federal law, you certainly are allowed to.

According to Douglas Kellner, writing for the Museum of Broadcast Communications (museum.tv), "The rationale for public access television was that, as mandated by the Federal Communications Act of 1934, the airwaves belong to the people, that in a democratic society it is useful to multiply public participation in political discussion, and that mainstream television severely limited the range of views and opinion. Public access television, then, would open television to the public, it would make possible community participation, and thus would be in the public interest of strengthening democracy."

One goal of public access television is to give people the ability to program and distribute local, noncommercial programming that addresses the needs and concerns of their community. Each local municipality negotiates a cable franchise agreement with cable companies, and some agreements—but not all—include provisions for public, educational, and government (PEG) equipment, facilities, and programming.

There are hundreds of PEG facilities in communities throughout the United States, including Access SF in San Francisco, California; Cambridge Community Television in Cambridge, Massachusetts; Chicago Access Network Television in Chicago, Illinois; and Manhattan Neighborhood Network in New York City.

Because each site is as unique as the community it serves, each has its own rules and regulations. Check out openchannel.se/cat/linksus.htm and ourchannels.org/alpha.htm to find an access center near you and to inquire about their hours, operations, and regulations.

GETTING YOUR MESSAGE OUT

Access centers constantly need programming to fill airtime. If there is an access facility available in your community, there usually are several ways you can express yourself and get your message out. For example, you may post noncommercial messages on what is called a community billboard. If you want to air a video program, you can sponsor a program that has already been produced (such as the award-winning *Democracy Now!*), you can create your own program outside the facility, or you can use the facility to create your own noncommercial program.

What Is Local Origination Programming?

Local origination programming is produced by cable company employees or contractors. For example, The Marin Report (now the North Bay Report) in California is an award-winning neighborhood newsmagazine that provides in-depth coverage of local issues of concern to over four hundred thousand homes in the north San Francisco Bay Area. The producer, director, and editor is Marin-born and raised Gary Wasley, who has been producing community programming for almost twenty-seven years. One of his many innovative programs included *Opportunity for Independence,* for people with developmental disabilities.

The Marin Report won "Best Multi-Part Series" from the Radio and Television News Directors Association (RTNDA) for coverage of the Mount Vision fire, as well as a Western Access Video Excellence Award (WAVE) for "Community News Program" from the Alliance for Community Media.

Whichever option you choose, there are regulations that must be obeyed. Again, check your local facility. Usually,

- producers and crew must be volunteers;

- programs cannot be sold or rented;

- the content and reuse cannot promote for-profit products, services, or trades;

- the program must be noncommercial, with no advertisements, and must follow FCC guidelines;

- grants are okay, but only to cover the costs of production (such as videotape);

- the sponsors' logos, addresses, and phone numbers cannot be displayed; and

- your show cannot be defamatory, libelous, obscene, or infringe on any copyright.

Although your program must be noncommercial, that does not mean it can't contain valuable content—quite the opposite. An auditor can produce a show on identity theft. A family therapist can produce shows on helping unwed mothers deal with unplanned pregnancies, or can assist families with teenage runaways. For example, Dr. Sheri Meyers Gantman produces a weekly television talk show, *Straight from the Heart,* on Time-Warner channel 98 in the Los Angeles area, where she interviews leading experts in psychology, relationships, health, and personal growth.

As long as you do not include advertisements or directly promote any product or service, you can create a show on just about anything.

MINIMUM TECHNICAL REQUIREMENTS

Whether you are creating your own program or submitting someone else's, there are minimum technical requirements. Again, this varies from facility to facility, but in general the show must

- be recorded at normal speed, with stable audio and video;

- be saved on VHS, SVHS, three-quarter-inch tape, DVD, or as a digital file;

- be labeled with the title of the program, the producer's (or sponsor's) name and phone number, both on the tape/DVD and on the outside of the box containing the tape/DVD; and

- include a minimum of thirty seconds of unbroken color bars or black slate leading into the beginning and following the end of the program.

1. SPONSORING AN EXISTING PROGRAM

Sponsoring an existing program would seem to be the simplest route for people to become involved in public access TV, but sometimes it is not. A case in point:

In early 2004, community media advocates from Media Action Marin in Marin County, California, wanted to sponsor *Democracy Now!,* a daily, award-winning, independent news program that already airs on more than seven hundred public access stations in North America. After being put through many hoops, Media Action Marin member Steve Fein found that satellite was the preferred method for delivering the program to other cable franchises in the area.

However, Free Speech TV and the satellite provider EchoStar could not make the program available because Comcast was broadcasting commercial programming on the channel, making it ineligible to receive the noncommercial *Democracy Now!* program. In a subsequent report commissioned by the Marin Telecommunications Agency in March 2005, CBG Communications, an independent research firm, found that Comcast was in violation of numerous terms of Comcast's cable franchise agreement with Marin, specifically regarding the provision of community programming.[2]

On August 1, 2005, after almost a year and a half of activism by Media Action Marin, *Democracy Now!* finally aired on Comcast channel 26. Media Action Marin members continue to sponsor the show, which airs each weekday morning at 9 a.m.

In view of how unreasonably long this process took, it became crystal clear to community media advocates that channel 26 was in fact Comcast-owned and -operated and was not truly a Public, Education, and Government channel. Media Action Marin members eventually succeeded in lobbying the Marin Telecommunications Agency to negotiate $2.5 million from Com-

---

2. See CBG Communications, Inc., "Report on Cable-Related Needs and Interests, Technical Audit Results and Franchise Past Performance Issues Within the Member Jurisdictions of the Marin Telecommunications Agency," March 2, 2005, pp. 26–28, 126–128.

POSITIVE SPIN
Bill McCarthy

In September 1998 I produced the first *Positive Spin* television show in San Francisco. The program presented positive, innovative, and solutions-oriented news that promoted a better world for both present and future generations.

I called my local cable access television station (Access SF,[1] channel 29 in San Francisco) and was told that anyone who lived in San Francisco was eligible to produce and air a television show on its station. The only requirement was to fill out a one-page application form, describing the program and verifying that the applicant lived in San Francisco.

Since our associates, Dirksen Molloy Productions, have video production and editing facilities in the same building as our Unity Foundation's office, we did not need to use the production facilities of channel 29. Because the show was self-produced by a professional production company, we were not required to take any production classes.

The first *Positive Spin* television program aired in September 1998. The program included a three-segment format, with introductions from a host. The host stood in front of a backdrop of a map of the world and introduced local and national news stories. The host then introduced Kim Weichel, the show's UN and Foreign Affairs Correspondent, who covered international stories while standing in front of a green screen, which allowed her to be projected in front of images of different locations.

The first show's segments featured a presentation on nuclear disarmament; a theatrical performance by students from the Robert Muller School in Texas, founded by Dr. Robert Muller, former Assistant Secretary General of the United Nations and Chancellor Emeritus of the University For Peace; and a poetry performance by Pulitzer Prize Nominated poet Ron Jones.

Since that first show, *Positive Spin* now airs ten times each month on Free Speech TV, the Dish satellite network, and on public access stations in San Francisco, Marin County, San Jose, Petaluma, Los Angeles, and New York City.

---

1. According to Access SF Executive Director Zane Blaney, "With 225 regular shows, and from five to seven thousand hours of programming a year, Access San Francisco has more locally based programming than all of the broadcast TV stations in the state of California put together."

cast to fund the creation of an independent, nonprofit community media center that would run Marin's Public, Education, and Government channels. (See chapter 18 for more about the negotiation and resolution.)

2. PRODUCING A PROGRAM OUTSIDE THE FACILITY

To produce a show outside the facility and air it from the station, the program must meet the station's guidelines, and the sponsor usually signs a programming channel agreement and a copyright law acknowledgment statement. (See Positive Spin Sidebar.)

3. PRODUCING A PROGRAM AT THE FACILITY

When producing a program at the facility, you will first need to get a program proposal approved by staff. These are considered on a first-come, first-served basis, details your intentions (e.g., single program or series pilot; thirty minutes or sixty minutes long) and your technical requirements (studio, field, or mobile equipment). Single programs are easier to schedule than the multiple production dates required for a series. Use your single production as the pilot, to fine tune a show idea's set design, format, crew, and talent.

Studio productions are just that: They use in-house equipment for multicamera productions, which can be live or taped. Daytime studio hours are usually more available and therefore easier to schedule than evening and weekend hours because most producers have full-time jobs and can only come to the facility after 5 p.m. or on weekends.

A field production means the filming (or taping) is done on location—at a site outside the studio—and is edited later. Unlike in the studio, where everything is available, a field producer needs to book the cameras and tripods, lights, microphones and audio equipment, cables, extension cords, and power strips. Some facilities have mobile equipment in vans or trucks, with a mobile control room, generator, cameras, and equipment. Mobile units make on-location work a lot easier.

Next, you will need to take classes to get certified to use the facility's equipment. Most facilities offer production classes, either free of charge or at minimum cost. For example, Access Sacramento charges a minimal amount to get certified on equipment, and the fees go to keeping the access facility operational. Classes may be offered to use the following equipment, if it is available:

- In the studio: Cameras, character generator, lights, and microphones.
- Out of the studio (or in the field): Audio, lighting, and mobile cameras.
- Editing (postproduction work): Facilities usually offer both linear (SVHS, VHS) and nonlinear (Avid, Final Cut, and Toaster) editing packages. For example, Access Sacramento offers nonlinear editing with iMacs running iMovie software.

After the classes are completed, creators sign a programming channel agreement to accept responsibility for the program, and a copyright law acknowledgment statement, indicating the creators' understanding that copyright clearance is required and that the creator needs to pay royalties on copyrighted material. For more information, see *Copyright and You,* published by the National Federation of Local Cable Programmers, and the chapter in this book on Creative Commons, for a less restrictive alternative to copyright. Many locations supply CDs of public domain sounds and music. For example, the studio in Marin County, California has over forty CDs of music clips that can be played legally and royalty-free.

Once you've completed the certification classes, you'll need to get some hands-on experience, and gather a team of experienced volunteers. A great way to get started in TV production is to volunteer to help others. If you are a skilled and eager volunteer, you will be in high demand. But even unskilled volunteers are needed. Producing a video program usually requires a lot of work, and at least a handful of studio-certified people. Even "simple" productions such as talk shows require a host, guests, a writer, camera operators, a sound engineer, a graphics designer, technicians, and a director. Production is a team effort, so invite your family, friends, or colleagues from school, your religious organization, your baseball team, or your Girl Scout troop to join you. If you are not technically trained, volunteer to answer phones or clean the studio. You will absorb lessons just by being there and watching.

For example, *Homefront* is a public affairs series taped monthly before a studio audience at the Andy Warhol museum in Pittsburgh. It is produced by the nonprofit Pittsburgh Educational Television. According to Dr. Jerold Starr, the host of the show, "in all, some twenty-eight individuals are directly involved in producing the series, all but six under the age of thirty, several still enrolled in school. They volunteer to book guests, promote programs, operate cameras, floor manage, house manage, and whatever else is needed. Volunteers come from Duquesne University, Robert Morris University, the Art Institute of Pittsburgh, the Andy Warhol Museum, Pittsburgh Community Television (PCTV 21), and the Thomas Merton Center for Peace and Justice."

In January 2005 I interviewed Gail Connolly as she produced a live show featuring guest Curt Hayden, who himself was a former producer of *The Marin Athlete.* Connolly was directing seven volunteers, including three camera operators in the studio (one doubling as the floor director) and four people in the control room: an audio board operator, a technical director, a director, and an operator of the character generator—the machine that, for example, puts the name of the person on the screen while the person talks. Each volunteer had completed a few hour-long sessions of training, weeks in advance.

The better your program and reputation, the easier it will be for you to attract volunteers to your show. And it doesn't hurt to be a good cook. One advantage of volunteering is that it is customary for the producer to feed the crew and for all to have a meal together. Sure enough, on the day I observed, Connolly brought in a hot, home-cooked meal for everyone involved in the production.

If you are a student, see if the facility has an internship program. Since 1979, Marin's internship program has provided students with hands-on video production experience, including videotape machine and character generator operation, floor directing, editing, and camera and audio operation. Previous interns have gone on to attend the USC Film School and to work as professionals at commercial stations KRON and KTSF in San Francisco.

If your local access channel has no such intern program, suggest they start one!

Another tip is to keep an eye out for experienced mentors. Watch the public access channel in your community and make a list of your favorite shows. At the studio, search out the people whose shows you respect and admire, especially the producers. They are the heart of the production. Follow them around, do their bidding (within reason), and learn what you can from them. Even professionals realize the importance of mentorship:

MENTORS by Robert Kubey

Learning story structure and television writing can take time, experience, and, often, a good mentor. Matt Groening, who only had experience telling the shortest stories in his syndicated comic strip *Life in Hell*, tells how he had to learn the discipline of longer storytelling from James L Brooks, his co-creator on *The Simpsons*.

Susan Harris worked on Garry Marshall's *Love, American Style*, *The Odd Couple*, *Barefoot in the Park*, and *The Partridge Family*, and Norman Lear's *All in the Family* and *Maude*. She went on to create *Soap*, where she was executive producer and wrote all episodes, and then created *Benson* and *Golden Girls*. For Harris, Garry Marshall was a key mentor, as was Norman Lear.

Writing for television often involves collaboration. Larry David's fondest memory from his *Seinfeld* years is of the hours spent alone in a room with Jerry Seinfeld, making one another laugh.

All of these writer-producers have worked with a key partner or mentor.[3]

Production. After your program proposal has been approved, you've been certified to use the equipment, you've gained some hands-on experience, and you've got some eager volunteers or interns, let's get on with the show. You need to be realistic, but it is ok to be idealistic too. Community programming is not supposed to compete with professional broadcasting. It is supposed to help build community with neighbors and to alert them to issues you might not see on the nightly news or commercial TV—upcoming speeches, council meetings, local high school or col-

3. *Creating Television: Conversations with the People Behind 50 Years of American TV*, by Robert Kubey. Lawrence Erlbaum Associates, 2004, p. 125.

lege events, lectures, and religious functions. Shows contribute a valuable local service or are a medium for personal expression.

PREPLANNING A PROGRAM

Planning is everything. It is said that beginners point and shoot; professionals plan and shoot. Solicit input from experienced producers, wherever you can find them. Preplan your program by creating a script and/or storyboard listing all the planned shots. Be as organized as possible. You need to manage people, equipment, time, and events consistently and coherently.

Define your audience and why they should watch the show. You have to think about what message you wish to communicate to your intended audience. Are you trying to inform, amuse, enlighten, or persuade? Do you want them to vote, laugh, cry, think?

Once you know your target audience, the purpose of your program, and the desired result, the planning begins.

In the studio. Before you set foot in the studio, plan everything in detail. A production sometimes requires up to two to three months prior to the shoot. The producer needs to consider booking guests, layout, set design, lighting, crew, music, copyrights, permissions, props, backdrops, graphics, roll-ins, training, and must schedule the recording equipment, editing systems, and sessions.

Organize your thoughts by scripting dialogue or interview questions. The script is also the blueprint for the entire production, with directions for the stage manager and talent, shot sheets for the camera people and equipment operators, and sound cues for the audio and video engineers. By minimizing misunderstandings, you don't waste time in the studio, maximizing efficiency.

In the field. If you are going to shoot in the field, you should make a checklist to ensure you have the following: camera, tripod, plenty of tapes, a fully charged battery, spare fully charged batteries, a power supply and cord, extension cord, microphones, audio equipment, lights and stands, pens, log sheets, bottled water, sunglasses, penlight (for night shots or concerts/venues where you need to see your equipment or change tapes but don't want to disturb the performance).

And, pack this paradox: At the shoot, despite all your planning, try to keep things loose and let the action unfold on its own. Others may have interesting ideas, the weather may change, the water may part and the planets collide, or things may just not work out according to plan—that is art! Don't lock everything into unnecessary boxes—leave some space for divine intervention.

PROGRAM FORMATS

The format of the program determines the set, talent, music, and more. Here are a few to consider:

Public meetings/sports. Straight footage of public meetings and sporting events, without narration, is the easiest production. TV, however, is much better when you add context, so try a "wrap-around" in which the host wraps a local introduction and ending around the event.

Speeches. Speeches are also easy to broadcast. Locate the camera in a spot that gets you a straight-on shot or three-quarter frontal shot. It is best to be in the front of the room, so you have a close-up shot and people don't walk in front of the camera. Keep camera movements to a minimum. Start wide to show the scene, then zoom in to the speaker's bust (basically, head to heart), and don't move the camera. Watch how C-SPAN zooms in at the beginning and out at the end.

Sometimes speeches become history. For example, on January 21, 2004, on a houseboat owned by the Cruising Club in Sausalito, CA, I was the sole videographer at a speech by University of California-Berkeley cognitive linguist George Lakoff, founder of the Rockridge Institute. The text of his extemporaneous speech, "Framing 101: How to Take Back Public Discourse" became the book *Don't Think of an Elephant!* which was quickly published by Chelsea Green prior to the 2004 US presidential elections.

Interviews. For interviews, the best camera angle is the over-the-shoulder style—a three-quarter frontal shot of the interviewee. The interviewer sits next to the camera and the interviewee responds to the interviewer—not the lens. Use a wide establishing shot when asking questions, and have the cameraperson zoom in when the interviewee responds. Watch Charlie Rose, Larry King, *60 Minutes,* or Amy Goodman of *Democracy Now!* for examples.

Homefront uses three cameras—one in the back of the room for establishing shots, and one each to the left and the right of the stage for medium shots and close-ups. After the presentations, they open the show to audience participation. For this, they turn one camera around to record questions and reactions. Some of the reactions are inserted into the program during the editing phase.

For interviews, be prepared. Know your subject. Have a list of questions but build in flexibility. Often, the best next question is based on the subject's previous answer. Start out with broad, open-ended questions and then narrow down. Avoid questions that evoke a yes or no answer.

For *Homefront* interviews and panel discussions, Starr seeks diversity in both background (e.g., race, ethnicity, and gender) and profession. A show on the war on drugs includes a policy analyst, a human rights attorney, a black community activist, and a Colombian educator. A show on nuclear weapons includes a medical doctor, a physicist, a mass communications analyst, and a military advisor. And a show on media monopoly includes a TV/radio personality, a director member of the American Federation of Television and Radio Artists, a TV station owner, a communications scholar, and an FCC attorney.

Starr asks the guests to emphasize what they consider most important for the audience to know, negotiating the questions in advance. He interviews each of them in turn for seven minutes, asking between two and four questions. Members of the audience then are invited to make short statements and ask questions to advance the analysis.

Sometimes, just being there early is enough. Before the 2004 U.S. Presidential elections, I interviewed Representative Dennis Kucinich (D-Ohio) about his stance on media reform at a music and dance community center called Ashkenaz in Berkeley, California. After getting there early to set up my camera and microphone, a surprise guest, Sean Penn, walked right to my microphone and began talking directly into it, announcing that he was endorsing Dennis Kucinich for president in 2004. Two days later, when Penn won the best actor Oscar for the movie *Mystic River,* the Kucinich campaign chased me down, because I had exclusive high-quality audio and video footage of Penn's endorsement.

Music and drama. Have multiple cameras for these events. If you only have a single camera, tape the production from several angles—center, right, left, as well as up close and from the back. Try to get all the performers and all the angles. You'll spend more time editing and syncing sound later, but the end result will be much stronger if you shoot it "film style" rather than using a straight shot as you would with a speech.

Unlike in other formats, camera movement here adds to the drama and excitement. Consider using a handheld camera to get close-ups and action shots to intersperse with the main footage. Try a shot with the camera as low to the ground as possible, pointed up. I did this for a contemporary worship service at my local church, and it made the performers look both larger than life and reverential.

During instrumental solos, begin with a close-up of the musician's mouth, face, or instrument, and then zoom out to show the whole band. It's a nice effect when a performer starts out singing alone and then is joined by the entire band for the chorus.

Live call-in shows. Slightly more challenging to produce, but popular, is a call-in show. You need phone lines connected to the sound board and someone to answer, screen, prioritize, and route the calls to the host. The callers and the host effectively engage viewers and provide immediate feedback regarding the success of the show. You might invite a guest from a local sports shop, or a therapist, local celebrity, politician, etc.

THE TECHNICAL SIDE

Directing. The subject here is not film-style directing but directing from the studio's control room. Here the director coordinates various production elements, such as the talent, cameras, audio, remote feeds, studio engineers, character generator operator, and audio operators, all while keeping an eye on the script and the control room clock. In TV production, split-second timing is critical. Even if the show is not live but is taped for later broadcast, TV stations rely on shows and breaks starting and stopping on cue.

Directing includes basic but specific words and nonverbal cues that everyone on the crew should understand. For example, a director's cues to the studio camera operator might include

"Pan up," "Pan down," "Pan left," or "Pan right," meaning move the camera up, down, left, or right, and "Zoom in" or "Zoom out," meaning get a tighter or looser shot.

Director's cues to the studio control room operator might include "Ready two—take two" which means the operator of camera two should be sure to steady it before the director cuts to it. Director's cues to the character generator operator might be "ready effects" or "wipe effects." Audio cues would include "Ready music—music" which means (surprise!) to start the music.

Lighting. Lighting will differ according to your surroundings—you may be filming outdoors with sunshine or with clouds; indoors with sun coming from windows; under fluorescent lights, house lights, desk lamps, or candlelight. Wherever you are, make sure you have enough light to activate the camera's sensor, giving you clean, bright pictures with good color.

The viewer's eye will naturally gravitate toward the brightest area, so refine the brightness and placement of lights. Cinematographers use light to create mood and ambience, to emphasize detail, or to subtly give the audience messages and clues about situations and characters. For example, soft light gives a "sexy" look that hides detail and blemishes, whereas hard light accentuates texture and creates sharp, well-defined detail.

Classic portrait lighting, called three-point lighting, uses three lights placed in strategic locations. The primary, or *key* light, is the subject's main illumination, and it creates shadows, texture, and depth. Place the key light slightly to the side of the subject, at approximately face level. A second, softer, and less bright *fill* light is placed opposite the key, making the subject more visible and serving to fill in any shadows. The third light, called a *back* or *rim* light, is placed above and behind the subject, shining a light on the subject's hair and shoulders. This makes the subject stand out from the background, providing definition and highlights that create a three-dimensional look.

You may also want to include set lights that illuminate the set or background. The background should always be darker than the subject, so that the subject is the focus of attention.

Microphones. Sound quality is one of the most important aspects of your production. People will forgive jerky, grainy video, but if the audio quality is poor, most people will change the channel or tune out. Your choice of microphones will depend on your program; an interview, a town council meeting, a play, or a high school basketball game all will have different audio requirements.

Handheld mics are great for interviews because they are versatile, inexpensive, and easy to use. Lapel or lavalier mics are more portable and personal and can be clipped onto a shirt or jacket. They provide excellent, consistent sound reproduction with minimal noise. A boom mic (a microphone placed on an extended, sometimes telescopic arm) can be held above the speaker by a boom operator so that the mic is out of the camera frame. Wireless mics send radio waves to a receiver that records the sound and have the advantage of freeing the participants from the physical limitations of audio cables.

Using the built-in camera mic should be a last resort. It is unlikely to produce the quality sound required for a professional production.

You can find decent mics at Radio Shack or online. If you are doing a studio interview, try the Studio Projects B1 ($79) or the Shure SM-57 ($90) and SM-58 ($100) models. Quality, moderately priced mics include the Shure KSM-27 ($300), the Sennheiser 421 ($350), and the KSM-32 ($500). High-quality, expensive mics include the Neumann TLM-103 ($900) and the Neumann U-87 ($2,600).

Music. Music sets the mood and theme of a show and enhances the production value. You'll usually want to open and close the show with a theme song. If you have friends or family members who play an instrument or are in a band, this would be a good way to give them some publicity. If not, try some public domain content from the CDs provided by your access center; the new label Magnatune (magnatune.com), which offers Creative Commons-licensed content; or search the audio section of the Creative Commons website (creativecommons.org). Another option is to pay a royalty fee to BMI or ASCAP for the rights to rebroadcast copyrighted material. You are liable for royalty payments to the artists, their labels, etc.

Local talent is your best bet—promote the people in your own community!

What (Not) to Wear. Be careful with wardrobe, especially colors, on anyone who will appear on camera, particularly in the studio. Solid colors are best. Avoid stripes, checks, herringbone, and busy patterns. Good colors for TV include earth tones such as brown and green, pastels, and gray. Avoid vibrant colors such as purple and pink. If you will be doing an interview, wear something that will be easy to clip a microphone onto—strapless dresses and turtleneck sweaters leave little choice for attaching microphones. Women should avoid necklaces, earrings, and other jewelry that can distract, cause reflections, and/or be noisy. No bells!

POSTPRODUCTION: LINEAR AND NONLINEAR DIGITAL VIDEO EDITING

The editing suite is where movie magic is made. Organizing your many media assets (e.g., your film footage, CD music, voice-overs, and files) is critical. Here you will review and select shots; create an edit decision list; edit; add transitions, effects, and titles; and finally, export the finished work from your computer to tape or DVD.

Add voice-overs as narration and use cutaways when the interviewee is answering. For example, if the interviewee is the mayor, you can edit in a cutaway of the town hall while his voice-over is answering the question. If he is talking about cuts to the hospital budget, edit in a shot of the hospital, or of ambulances, doctors, nurses, and patients.

For editing, you will need to learn a lot more than there is room to teach here.

BROADCASTING, SCREENING, DISTRIBUTION, AND PROMOTION

Once your show is complete, and you have an air date, get moving! Let people know which channel your show will be on, what day and time it will air, the subject, and why they should watch. Create a one-page press release that you can send to your local media or post on a website, and send to your contacts via e-mail. Create a website or a blog (see chapters 1 and 9), or get the word out through newsletters, flyers, and posters in libraries and coffee shops. Your local radio stations may air public service announcements for free. Put the information on the electronic community billboard and in print and electronic TV guide listings. Get the word out—however you can—to like-minded community organizations such as religious, political, and affinity groups, seniors, and youth.

Then, when your air date arrives, pop the champagne and sit back with your friends at home and watch your program on your local cable channel. You are now a broadcast producer!

Then, get to work again. Widen your distribution wherever you can. Screen your creation at town hall and city council meetings, festivals, demonstrations, public libraries, schools, community centers, or private groups of friends, family, colleagues, and coworkers.

Send copies to festivals, competitions, and contests such as the Alliance for Community Media's Hometown Video Awards. According to their website (acmhometown.org), "The Hometown Video Awards honors and promotes community media and local cable programs that are first distributed on Public, Educational, and Governmental access cable television channels. Awards are presented to creative programs that address community needs, develop diverse community involvement, challenge conventional commercial television formats, and move viewers to experience television in a different way."

If your program has regional, national, or global relevance, consider wider distribution, like *Positive Spin* or *Homefront*. *Positive Spin* has sponsors in both San Francisco and west of Los Angeles, and the program has national exposure, thanks to a distribution arrangement with Free Speech TV on the DISH Satellite Network.

Homefront is carried on Pittsburgh Community Television, reaching up to seven hundred thousand people, and on Comcast channel 20, reaching another two hundred thousand. Nationally, *Homefront* airs on the Free Speech TV Network of the DISH Network (nine million viewers) as well as on about fifty public access stations across the country and on PBS station KOCE in Orange County, California.

Then, start all over again. You didn't want to stop at just one program, did you? Just think of Michael Essany of Valparaiso, Indiana.

"I think I am a verb."
—R Buckminster Fuller

18

COMMUNITY MEDIA CENTERS

HOW TO CREATE A MEDIA CENTER FOR YOUR OWN COMMUNITY
David Mathison, with thanks to Media Action Marin[1]

Dedicated to Val Schaaf[2]

"Creating the world we want is a much more subtle but powerful
mode of operation than destroying the one we don't want."
—*Marianne Williamson*

Your town may look peaceful on the surface, but it has become a battlefield. Powerful cable and telephone companies are engaged in turf warfare, competing to deliver their own so-called "triple play" bundles of phone, video, and Internet access all through a single high-speed broadband connection to you and your neighbors.

The prize, with a huge profit potential, is your local cable franchise agreement.

Historically, locally elected leaders controlled valuable "rights-of-way" cable access to homes and businesses by negotiating video franchise agreements. During the negotiation process, local leaders and residents attempted to ensure that the supplicant cable company met the community's telecommunications needs. That involved, for example, advocates often battling the cable

---

1. Media Action Marin (MAM) is a media advocacy group in Marin County, California, whose active members include Bruce Baum, Regina Carey, Norman Carlin, Vera Falk, Steve Fein, Peter Franck, Christian Heath, David Mathison, Juan Ortega, Evelyn Schaaf, June Swan, and Barbara Sykes. Thanks also to the Marin Peace and Justice Coalition, whose members supported Media Action Marin's work, especially Barbara Bogard, Jim Geraghty, Craig Slater, and Zhenya Spake.

2. Val Schaaf (February 5, 1920–January 8, 2007) was instrumental in creating the nonprofit Community Media Center of Marin and winning the passage of the Marin County Living Wage Ordinance. He chaired the Social Justice Center of Marin and was a board member of the Prison Law Office. In April 2007, the county's Board of Supervisors posthumously honored Schaaf by adopting a resolution commemorating his life of activism.

company to make sure it included, protected, and expanded the government-mandated Public, Education, and Government (PEG) channels in the franchise agreements.

Even though communities have a legal right to these Public, Education, and Government channels, advocates worked to make sure that that right was being applied.

Their concern was, and is, legitimate. From a cable company's viewpoint, Public, Education, and Government channels have consumed, and still consume, highly valuable commercial channel space on the TV dial.

The turf war, furthermore, is far from over. Across the country, local control, community input, and public access, all of which are modern aspects of exercising rights guaranteed us citizens by the First Amendment to the Constitution, find themselves in jeopardy, because the mega-businesses are upping the ante. The stakes, in many senses, are huge.

THE BATTLE OF THE BEHEMOTHS, OR, "WHEN ELEPHANTS FIGHT, THE GRASS LOSES"

Their basic plan is this: The phone companies want to speed their entry into the video delivery business to compete with cable and satellite operators before those companies capture too much of the digital phone and Internet business and leave the phone companies behind eating their dust. However, instead of playing by the existing rules, which let any provider deliver one or more of these digital services, AT&T (to choose just one example) wants to fast-track its installations. How is it going about this? By lobbying to rewrite current laws.

Phone company-sponsored bills propose to strip municipalities of their local franchising authority in favor of state or federal authority, thus making it easier and more efficient for phone company lobbyists to successfully complete their rounds. The change directly threatens the future of local public access to the broadcast communications spectrum. The revised rules would allow the new provider to cherry-pick the most profitable areas to implement video services (known as "redlining"), leaving less-affluent parts of most communities on the wrong side of the digital divide. Much of the same happened in the 1930s with electrification of farms and so forth, until the federal government stepped in to enforce more-equitable practices for rural areas.

Community leaders also fear that the state will take local franchise fees: that is, the monies charged by cable companies, but paid by their customers, in exchange for rights-of-way access to homes and businesses. According to Rick Tucker, executive director of Novato (California) Public Access, "This will affect more than just public-access TV. This was a pretty good revenue source for each local city government."

The behemoths are well-funded, inventive, and arrogant. Consider AT&T's new Project Lightspeed (aka U-Verse), identified by the company as an "IP Video Network." SBC/AT&T decided it wanted to base its new product in San Jose, California. But because phone companies, including AT&T, are exempted from cable franchise-type rules, AT&T also decided it should not have to acquire the comparable special permits required for that right.

So, in a letter sent to the City of San Jose, AT&T said it was not constructing a "cable" system, but instead laying a fiber backbone, over which IP video was one of many new services. Therefore, it would not need to obtain a local cable franchise. AT&T wrote it had the "right to use the public rights of way throughout California to install and operate its facilities without having to obtain a local franchise or pay franchise fees," and that it was against the law for San Jose to deny AT&T the permits required.

Another ploy is a plea. Phone companies say the video franchise process is cumbersome and is therefore slowing the broadband rollout. AT&T says it might have to negotiate more than thirty thousand local franchises across the country. Currently, it holds just twenty-four cable video franchise agreements and has only twenty thousand video customers.

Negotiation was no obstacle for Verizon, however. Verizon obtained local video franchise agreements in three hundred municipalities and is working on another four hundred. At the end of March 2007, Verizon reported that its digital video service, FiOS TV, had 348,000 customers.

According to Ron Cooper, executive director of Access Sacramento, "In truth, AT&T has never tried the process." FCC Commissioner Jonathan Adelstein suggested that instead of trying to subvert and overturn the local franchise process, AT&T should direct its resources into negotiating local agreements.

Cable companies agree. Because they have been negotiating local franchises for forty years (and incurring unrecoverable costs to do so), they understandably feel that the phone companies should not get special treatment.

In most cases, the slowness of the franchise negotiation is caused by the cable companies themselves, not by local municipalities. Comcast, for example, balked on its agreement with Oakland, California, after the city passed a labor rights ordinance to help facilitate union organizing, then it sued Oakland over the ordinance and voided the agreement, all following more than three years of negotiation.

According to Lori Panzino-Tillery, division chief for San Bernardino County, California, and president of the National Association of Telecommunications Officers and Advisors (NATOA), "I have cities that have said they've sat at the table for only four hours over a six-month period."

One quality some big players in the turf war lack is—wait for it—patience.

THE (SCARY) MOVEMENT FROM LOCAL TO NATIONAL AND STATE FRANCHISES

In early 2006, Senator Ted Stevens (R-Alaska) introduced the COPE Act (Communications Opportunity, Protection, and Enhancement Act,[3] or HR 5252), an attempt to create national franchises for video providers. This act would give the providers "opportunity, protection and enhancement" for their businesses by funneling the collected franchise fees into the federal

---

3. Naming a proposed law with positive-sounding words may shield its actual intent and details.

budget. That is, the fees would not go to local communities where the rights of way exist, by law, in the first place.

The legislation proposed one single process for every community in America, and not surprisingly it included minimal requirements to prevent redlining, as well as weak consumer protections and marginal support for Public, Education, and Government channels. The phone companies, which obviously supported Stevens's COPE Act, bolstered their public relations efforts through "Astroturf," or fake grassroots, campaigns designed to mislead both lawmakers and the public.[4]

After the Democratic takeover of Congress in November 2006, the communications behemoths realized that they would have a hard time getting their federal legislation passed, and so they aggressively moved to state legislatures. In California, State Assembly bill AB 2987 proposed to strip local towns and cities of their regulatory authority and then move video franchising to the state level, in Sacramento, the capital.

A legislative hearing on June 27, 2006, revealed the writing on the wall. According to Ron Cooper of Access Sacramento, who attended the California Senate Energy, Utilities, and Communications Committee hearing on AB2987, "Out of approximately 150+ speakers, at least 40 spoke in support of PEG access in their communities and against the bill unless amended to protect PEG. The Chair, Senator Martha Escutia (D-30th Assembly District, Calif.), finally insisted that she had heard enough about 'PEG' and stopped all further references."

Marin County Supervisor Susan Adams also attended the AB 2987 hearing, and encountered Escutia, too, writing to her Marin Telecommunications Agency (MTA) colleagues and concerned residents via e-mail on June 28, 2006: "Overall, a very disappointing show for democracy. The telecom and cable suits all had seats in the hearing room . . . the rest of us were jammed outside in the hallways and in distant locations to listen to and watch on TV. I had an opportunity to testify . . . but Senator Escutia was cutting people off right and left."

The phone companies spent lavishly on lobbying for their bill. According to *San Francisco Chronicle* reporter Matthew Yi, "State lobbying reports show that in April, May, and June, AT&T and Verizon spent almost $19.7 million to influence the vote on AB2987, an amount that astounds Capitol veterans. AT&T led the way by spending nearly $18 million on lobbyists, television, radio and newspaper advertising. Some lobbying efforts seemed to be well targeted, such as $1,238 AT&T spent on Lakers basketball tickets and refreshments for Sen. Martha Escutia."[5]

On June 30, 2006, despite strong opposition by local governments and community advocates,

4. See "Wolves in Sheep's Clothing: Telecom Industry Front Groups and Astroturf," Common Cause, March 2006. Common Cause reported that phone companies were using "underhanded tactics . . . creating front groups that try to mimic true grassroots, but they are all about corporate power, not citizen power," with campaigns designed to "deliberately mislead citizens and they deliberately mislead our lawmakers."

5. "Big Business Lobbies Hard for Video Licensing Bill," by Matthew Yi, *San Francisco Chronicle,* August 28, 2006.

the California Legislature approved AB 2987, the video franchise "reform" bill. In September 2006, Governor Arnold Schwarzenegger signed it into law.

California thus became the thirteenth state to move local video franchising to the state level.[6]

Throughout the country, local residents, who want locally run cable stations to run locally produced programming, face daunting and hungry opponents. Just like the pliant legislators who depend on their campaign contributions, the carriers seem to prefer that people stay home, shut up, watch only the programming the behemoths provide, and pay for that programming without a peep of complaint.

If you live in one of the thirty-seven states not yet gagged and bound by the behemoths, my advice to you and your community is to fight to get what you can while you can, before the corporations get the politicians to change the rules on you, too.

Here's how one group of California community media advocates and their leaders did that, and just in time.

But first, a little background . . .

A BRIEF HISTORY OF PUBLIC ACCESS (AND OF PUBLIC, EDUCATION, AND GOVERNMENT CHANNELS)

By law, communities have the right to control their own local cable channels, facilities, and equipment. This is a right that some say starts with the First Amendment.

The nationwide battle for free speech via cable access began in the late 1960s to early '70s in Manhattan, when cable companies bid to operate the lucrative franchises there. Community advocates felt that, in exchange for their valuable rights-of-way, such as digging up local streets to lay cable, residents deserved access to the means of cable TV production and transmission. Because the federal government required over-the-air broadcasters to provide time for programs in the public interest, it extended a minimum public-access provision to cable companies as well.

In 1972, FCC member Nicholas Johnson helped craft provisions for Public, Education and Government access channels, meaning that cable companies had to supply free local airtime to citizens and also help fund facilities for media production. Subsequent federal laws, such as the Cable Acts of 1984 and 1992, updated earlier rules and further defined PEG access requirements.

Manhattan granted its first cable franchise in August 1970. Shortly thereafter, New York City franchise authorities were the first in the nation to require channels for PEG. In 1971, Red Burns and George Stoney created one of the first public access centers in Manhattan. The two went on to cofound the Alternate Media Center in 1972, which trained citizens in the tools of video production for public access TV. Stoney believed that public access centers should stand alongside public schools and libraries to support learning and education.

Let's hear it for public access, the forerunner of participatory media. It allows everyone to be a

6. The thirteen states are California, Florida, Georgia, Indiana, Iowa, Kansas, Michigan, Missouri, New Jersey, North Carolina, South Carolina, Texas, and Virginia.

provider as well as a recipient of content. (See chapter 14.) Public access moves people from being passive observers and consumers or targets for advertisers, to being active producers of media messages, while participating in community arts, politics, news, sports, activism, and culture. Public access programs are not necessarily meant to compete with CNN or ESPN, or to promote products, or even always to entertain, but rather to allow space for the expression of views, ideas, and creations outside the dominant commercial media marketplace. Ethnic groups, for example, can use public access programs to promote cultural integrity and cohesion and to correct inaccurate or demeaning images propagated by corporate media. (See chapter 17.)

According to Barbara Popovic, executive director of Chicago Access Network Television, "CAN TV is not about creating a television station—it is about facilitating communication." Improved civic communication results in stronger communities, with "community" defined not only as the physical territory covered by the franchise, but also as wider, virtual "communities of interest." For example, DeeDee Halleck and the New York City-based Paper Tiger TV collective drove a wider definition of community by bringing together like-minded collections of people and groups, such as pro-peace, nonprofit, and ecological organizations.

Representing more than three thousand such public access organizations is the Alliance for Community Media (ACM), a nonprofit organization. According to its website, alliancecm.org, member stations are supported by more than 1.2 million volunteers and a quarter million community groups. The volunteers at access stations "produce more than 20,000 hours of new local programming each week. That's more than all the local programming produced by NBC, CBS, ABC, FOX and PBS combined!"

Public, Education, and Government channels offer a world of possibilities, including:

- **Public:** A public channel could be used to broadcast local talent, musicians, artists, street fairs, events, parades, and content created by, for, and about local community nonprofits, as well as religious, ethnic, minority, and linguistic groups.

- **Education:** This channel could provide distance learning programs, university courses on-demand, high school sports, and class assignments that connect students, parents, and teachers.

- **Government:** This channel might include information about health, human services, security, emergency services, disaster alerts, public safety, fire, police, town council meetings, city-sponsored events, and interviews with local leaders.

COMMUNITY MEDIA CENTERS: MORE THAN JUST CABLE ACCESS

Because most media, including text, voice, video, and audio, is now digital and therefore can be delivered over the Internet, many facilities are evolving beyond cable access into full-fledged community media centers. These centers can provide a wide range of training opportunities, including teaching people how to operate studio cameras, design sets, arrange lighting, manage postproduction and editing, and improve media literacy skills, both in and out of studios. Indeed, content no longer need always be produced in a studio, as we see from the popularity of YouTube and other Internet video distributors. (See chapter 7.)

Each center strives to reflect the character and requirements of the individual community. While small centers are the norm, some large, notable ones include the Grand Rapids (Michigan) Community Media Center, which has a 1,000 watt radio station, WYCE 88.1, and offers Internet access, computer training labs, mobile vans, a recording studio, and a three-hundred-seat historic theater. The Manhattan Neighborhood Network (MNN) in New York City owns its three-story building and streams programs on the Internet. Chicago Access Network Television, or CAN-TV, has five channels that reach over one million viewers.

HOW TO ESTABLISH A COMMUNITY MEDIA CENTER: A CASE STUDY

In Marin County, California, just over the Golden Gate Bridge from San Francisco, what began as a plea by one individual for both a community-friendly cable franchise agreement and a quality local media production facility has become part of the public access movement, to say nothing of a national example and a cautionary tale.

Self-described "ordinary housewife" Natica ("Tica") Lyons, who was concerned about Marin's cable franchise renewal process and terms, started attending monthly meetings of the Marin Telecommunications Agency (MTA) around the time it was founded as a Joint Powers Authority in 1998.

Prior to MTA's formation, cable companies negotiated with each Marin city, as well as the county, for the unincorporated areas. This resulted in variable services, quality, and cost. The goal of forming the MTA was to bring uniform, high-quality cable service to the entire county through the power of collective bargaining by several jurisdictions, including Marin County itself, together with the incorporated cities of Belvedere, Corte Madera, Fairfax, Larkspur, Mill Valley, Ross, San Anselmo, San Rafael, Sausalito, and Tiburon.

At the MTA meetings, Lyons was usually the lone voice representing the public interest. She was not impressed with the new entity. The MTA staff promised reports and audits of cable company operations, but failed to produce them. The MTA staff did not properly transcribe public comment, either, nor did it appear to act on those comments. The staff assured the public that everything would be on its website, but until 2005 neither the agenda nor the minutes of previous monthly Board meetings were available online.

Lyons thought that MTA's staff stacked the agenda, intentionally leaving little time for public participation. When she did speak, she was routinely cut off and interrupted. Meanwhile, she learned that nearby towns had successfully negotiated cable franchise terms much more favorable to their communities. She became concerned about the possible misuse of public funds. So, in the great American tradition, she hired an attorney.

Lyons and the MTA faced an intertwined foe. By 1998, media mergers and consolidation resulted in AT&T Broadband Internet (AT&TBI) owning most of Marin's cable franchises. In early 2001, Marin's proposed franchise agreement with AT&T included a strong commitment to public access. Some 5 percent of franchise fees, meaning fees collected by the cable company from its customers, plus $12 million in allowances within the cable company's budget over the life of the fifteen-year contract, would fund public access. Simply put, the terms meant that AT&T would agree to fund both the facility, as required by law, and the ongoing annual operations of the media center.

At the end of 2001, however, Comcast acquired AT&TBI, and subsequently refused to agree to the terms in the proposed Marin/AT&T franchise agreement.

Three years of negotiation went out the window.

Around the same time, the MTA created a nine-member citizen group to advise the MTA on PEG issues. The group was called the Media Access Advisory Committee, or MAAC.[7] After months spent researching and studying the situation, it recommended in February 2002 that a nonprofit organization—not the entrenched operator, Comcast—operate Marin's public access channel.[8]

INTRODUCING MEDIA ACTION MARIN

The MAAC made the right recommendation, but needed backup from the community to show the MTA that there was support for the notion. Enter the Social Justice Center of Marin, of which Tica Lyons was a member, and which already had a media task force. Intrigued by her passion about the uses (or misuses) of cable and her deep understanding of the cable franchise renewal process, the task force founded Media Action Marin, or MAM, and decided to take on cable as an issue. In July 2002, Media Action Marin, consisting of a diverse group of people united by the belief that people should control the means and methods of communication, held its first meeting.

Media Action Marin was concerned that the distant corporation, Comcast, which is based in faraway Philadelphia, owned and operated Marin's sole "public" channel, channel 26, instead of the community. Activists were also concerned that Comcast's access facility had outdated equipment, failed to provide channels for educational and governmental information, and was located in an industrial park. The location was convenient for Comcast's service trucks, but difficult to reach for seniors, youth, and the disabled, the very voices that public access is designed to serve.

Lastly, under the control of Comcast, channel 26 aired only public access, noncommercial

---

7. According to MAAC member Craig McAllister, "The most vocal and experienced citizens available were selected for the MAAC, which under the Brown Act, were no longer permitted to release public comment outside of MTA proceedings. To some, this finesse by the MTA throttled expert public commentary rather than capitalizing on it. To this day, although the MAAC meetings are open to public attendance, few know when or where the meetings are held, public comment is strictly limited, and meeting minutes are controlled by the MTA."

8. "Community Media Center Organization Recommendations," Media Access Advisory Committee, February 5, 2002.

content five hours per day, Monday through Friday. The programming for the remaining nine-teen hours per weekday and all twenty-four hours on weekends was determined by Comcast, which inserted commercial programs for its own benefit.

Media Action Marin believed the community had a legal right to more.

With negotiations now starting from scratch, Media Action Marin members, including Lyons, started attending and speaking out at MTA meetings and taking advantage of the Brown Act, a California law that allows for public comment after each agendized item. They also met with town council representatives, built community support, and generated publicity for the issue.

Media Action Marin members, in learning about the often complex issues surrounding cable franchising and PEG, devoted more time to this issue than did some members of MTA itself. Of eleven MTA representatives and one staff member, only a few supported the MAAC and Media Action Marin's vision of community access. Allies included Marin County Supervisor Susan Adams, San Anselmo Mayor Barbara Thornton, and Fairfax Town Council Member Larry Bragman.

Media Action Marin members also visited ACM's site at alliancecm.org and received a briefing from James Horwood, ACM's legal affairs attorney, who educated them on public access, PEG, and franchise negotiation law. They became familiar with local, state, and federal cable law, and reviewed copies of important documents that can be found online and in local government offices:

- *The Cable Communications Policy Act of 1984* (Section 626), which specifically addresses the renewal procedure, as precisely defined in federal law

- The *Enabling Ordinance*, which sets the ground rules and minimum standards for service between a community and the cable operator

- The *Cable Franchise Agreement*, which sets out the contractual relationship between a community and the cable service provider

DEMOCRACY NOW! (OR MAYBE LATER)

For months in early 2004, MAM member Steve Fein had been trying to get the *Democracy Now!* program onto channel 26. The program is a noncommercial, national, daily, independent, award-winning news show airing on more than 700 public access TV stations across North America. It is broadcast on Pacifica Radio, National Public Radio, community and college radio stations, PBS, and satellite television, as well as streamed over the Internet—but *not* on Comcast-Marin's "public" access channel, channel 26.

MAM members reasoned that it would be easy to get this award-winning program on Marin's public TV channel. They reasoned wrong. Many of the MTA members had never even heard of the popular program. Subsequently, Fein surveyed nearby access stations, found that satellite was the preferred method of delivery, and then presented his spreadsheet and findings to the MTA. Fein still had no success getting Comcast channel 26 to air the show.

In April 2004, members of Media Action Marin met at Book Passage, a local independent bookstore in the town of Corte Madera, where *Democracy Now!* host Amy Goodman was promoting her new book, *The Exception to the Rulers*. MAM members, led by Norman Carlin, collected more than three hundred petitions from the overflow crowd that supported having the MTA request that Comcast air the program on its local channel. The petitions were presented to the MTA at the next monthly meeting.

Fast forward seven more months. Still no *Democracy Now!*, or even *democracy now*.

At the November 10, 2004, MTA meeting,[9] concerned that the MTA staff would stack the agenda against the public yet again, two Media Action Marin members, Tica Lyons and I, David Mathison, videotaped the session. Lyons booked a time slot on channel 26 to broadcast the meeting afterward. The very act of videotaping public meetings usually encourages local officials to act appropriately, and some did.

At the start of the meeting, County Supervisor Susan Adams, recently elected as vice chair of the MTA, requested an open public session, citing her concern about "favoritism and special treatment regarding items to be agendized." Her move ensured that the increasingly vocal local folks would have a chance to speak during the public comment period.

MTA Director Bragman reported that *Democracy Now!* was still unavailable on channel 26. According to the MTA minutes, "The satellite provider, *Echo Star*, refused to deliver the program because Channel 26 is not a public access channel." The distributor, *Free Speech TV,* could not sign an affiliate agreement because Comcast was broadcasting commercial content over channel 26, in violation of the local franchise agreement.

Bragman concluded, "That is why we have to have public access."

Media Action Marin Chair Peter Franck, a local entertainment and intellectual property attorney, knew that, during the long period of public comment that followed, Comcast was required by law to take its commercial content off the channel, in order to get the noncommercial *Democracy Now!* on the air. Franck requested that the MTA pass a resolution requiring that Comcast immediately dedicate channel 26 to strictly noncommercial PEG-only uses, to honor the existing franchise agreement.

After listening to comment from Franck and many members of the public, the MTA board, however, again failed to act, police, or enforce its own PEG contract terms.

Comcast went about its business as if nothing had happened.

But the tide was changing.

THE CABLE CONSULTANT: MR. ROBINSON'S NEIGHBORHOOD

To accelerate negotiations with Comcast, in late 2004 the MTA board engaged professional help. It hired CBG Communications, experienced consultants familiar with local cable franchise

---

9. See Marin Telecommunications Agency, Regular Meeting Minutes, November 10, 2004.

negotiations. CBG Executive Vice President Thomas G. Robinson reviewed local documents relating to the cable franchise, town codes, the enabling ordinance, and past performance reviews. He met with MTA counsel and staff, town council members, the public, nonprofit organizations, and community leaders. He conducted a telephone survey, which Media Action Marin members Regina Carey and Juan Ortega translated into Spanish, since a high percentage of the population in the service area is Latino.

THE PUBLIC ACCESS WORKSHOP

With the help of the consultant, the MTA planned a public access workshop for December 10, 2004. Enthusiastically received by the standing-room-only audience, the workshop included presentations from Ron Cooper, executive director of Access Sacramento; Lisa Morowitz from the Communications Workers of America, a union; and Comcast's Vice President of Government Affairs for Comcast Johnny Giles, who openly admitted that an inherent conflict existed between public access users and a Comcast-owned facility.

The workshop did what it was supposed to: It educated city staff, elected officials, community leaders, and the public alike about channel capacity, analog-to-digital delivery migration, services offered, infrastructure, facilities, equipment, personnel, and funding sources for both startup and ongoing operations.

KEEP THE PRESS INVOLVED AND INFORMED

Up to this point, the major newspaper, radio, and TV outlets had shown no interest in the issue, perhaps because Comcast is a major advertiser. Now, the local daily newspaper, the *Marin Independent Journal,* invited Media Action Marin Chairman Peter Franck to write an op-ed article outlining the benefits of public access TV. Media Action Marin members, in particular Bruce Baum, wrote letters to editors and fed information to local journalists. This work paid off in December 2004, when Peter Seidman wrote an engaging, informative article on the Marin franchise possibilities in the *Pacific Sun:*

> A more spectacular vision for Marin . . . includes a system of public access channels. . . . The system could connect cities, schools, libraries and nonprofits across the county, all of which could produce programming for the new system. Not to mention the artists, writers, filmmakers and videographers who would be able to gain access to a new distribution system.[10]

COMCAST LOVES MARIN—*NOT*

Comcast clearly was not trying to win Marin's hearts and minds. In the middle of negotiations, on Valentine's Day in 2005, Comcast unilaterally and arbitrarily halted part of its popular public

---

10. "The Long and Winding Road," by Peter Seidman. *Pacific Sun,* December 16–21, 2004, pp. 8–11.

service: FM broadcasting via Marin cable TV, a service that had continued uninterrupted for nineteen years. Due to Marin's hilly terrain, cable is the only way some residents are able to receive FM radio signals.

Comcast's move attracted negative, front-page coverage of this action by the cable company, and outraged the community.

In immediate response, Media Action Marin leveraged its mailing list and newsletter and, assisted by Bruce Baum's frequent updates to the website, it helped organize a coalition of civic organizations, schools, religious groups, the disabled, nonprofit groups, and seniors, including *Seniors For Peace* member Vera Falk, to protest the move.

Media Action Marin's public advocacy efforts peaked at the March 9, 2005, MTA meeting, when a standing-room-only crowd of angry cable subscribers filled the San Rafael city hall, demanding that the MTA have Comcast restore carriage of the FM signal. County Supervisor and MTA Vice Chair Susan Adams remarked, "It is extremely unusual for this many people to show up at an evening meeting," and encouraged Comcast VP Giles to "urge the people to whom he reports to reconsider their decision."

The MTA board directed the staff to draft a resolution requesting that California State Senator Carole Migden craft legislation requiring Comcast to carry FM again. Senator Migden helped get all parties back to the table for FM carriage over cable, suggesting that Comcast needed to find a way to get FM stations back on cable, or she would find a way to legislate it.

As for the continuing *Democracy Now!* saga, Director Bragman commented, "[Channel 26] is a public asset, like a park, or open space. This is our property to the extent that that property is usurped for private use. We should take a stand to protect this asset."

In a unanimous vote, the MTA finally directed its General Counsel to draft a letter to Comcast, requesting that Comcast end all commercial broadcasts on channel 26 and begin broadcasting *Democracy Now!* as of June 2005.

For the next two months, though, Comcast continued to drag its feet, without receiving any penalty from the MTA for noncompliance. Comcast, in fact, refused to provide a satellite dish to receive the program. The dish was ultimately provided by *Democracy Now!* at Free Speech TV's expense.

The tide had finally turned. Comcast could no longer prevent true public access in Marin.

On August 1, 2005, after a year and a half battle, *Democracy Now!* started broadcasting on channel 26. Media Action Marin members now sponsor the show's daily 9 a.m. time slot. It is now the most watched program on channel 26 in Marin County.

But we are getting ahead of the story . . .

THE COMMUNITY FINALLY GETS AN UPDATED NEEDS ASSESSMENT

In March 2005, after Comcast's Valentine's Day "gift" to Marin, and upon Tica Lyon's relentless prodding, the MTA requested that CBG Communications submit an expanded Needs Assessment report to bring the 1998 Needs Assessment up-to-date. Knowing it would be hard to get the area's cities and towns to pay for the update, Marin County Supervisor Susan Adams successfully requested that her colleagues on the Board of Supervisors allow the release of funds to pay for the consultant's revised assessment. The Needs Assessment identifies a community's current and future communications needs, and could strengthen its negotiating posture vis-à-vis the service providers. It can be conducted at any time, even before a franchise is in place.

A thorough Needs Assessment consists of representative focus groups, numerous public workshops, at least one telephone or mail survey taken from each major demographic group, technical community communications planning, a detailed current and future technology assessment, review of the current PEG facility and operations, and a great many public hearings.

Robinson's report found that, at 4 percent, channel 26 had a "significant level of viewership" for a cable access channel. For example, the February 9, 2005, issue of CableFAX's *Cableworld* reported that during the week CBG's study was conducted, the top watched cable program was the Screen Actors Guild Awards with 3 percent of cable households watching, and the second highest rated program, *Law and Order,* had a 2.7 percent share.

The CBG report said: "Only a handful of the 300 cable networks have viewership that exceeds 1% share of the audience. Even the seemingly popular cable network, ESPN, rarely has 1% of the total television audience watching. By comparison, one can see that the 4% of households that report watching more than five (5) hours of community programming a week in Marin County indicates a strong interest in Channel 26."[11]

The updated Needs Assessment also confirmed that Comcast had done a consistently poor job of providing adequate facilities, equipment, and technology to support Marin public access.

THE PAST PERFORMANCE REVIEW OF THE CABLE OPERATOR

Robinson then conducted a Past Performance Review of Comcast. The report criticized Comcast for numerous violations of the franchise agreement, specifically regarding community programming, as follows:

- "Comcast appears to be in violation of the Franchise concerning a number of parameters related to the provision of community programming."[12]

---

11. CBG Communications, Inc. "Report on Cable-Related Needs and Interests, Technical Audit Results and Franchise Past Performance Issues Within the Member Jurisdictions of the Marin Telecommunications Agency." Thomas G. Robinson, EVP. March 2, 2005, p. 26.

12. Ibid., Section E, "Franchise Requirement Past Performance Review." March 2, 2005, p. 123.

- **"Comcast appears to be providing commercial programming over (Channel 26) in violation of the 'non-commercial purposes' indicated in the franchise."[13]** (Emphasis is from the CBG report.)

Other violations he and his staff found were in the areas of annual reporting, senior and low-income discounts, customer service, basic service drops, and liquidated damages. Comcast also refused to acknowledge that it owed Marin franchise fees of $112,000 from a 2003 audit. The MTA did not conduct audits for other years.

In conclusion, CBG reported, "We believe that the MTA should move forward . . . to quickly determine the extent of the violation and require immediate improvements, including a separate non-commercial channel for Community Access."[14]

COMCAST—THE "WAL-MART OF TELECOM"?

Comcast's corporate antisocial behavior is not unique to Marin County or even California. Comcast was dubbed the "*Wal-Mart of Telecom*" by the American Right to Work Foundation, and was recently removed from mutual funds specializing in "socially responsible" corporations, such as the Domini 400 Social Index and the Calvert Social Index. And, according to the May 2002 American Customer Satisfaction Index (ACSI), Comcast's customer satisfaction rating is lower than that of the IRS.

Comcast can certainly afford to meet the needs of local communities. The Communications Workers of America union says that in 2005 Comcast increased revenues 10.7 percent to $20.3 billion, generated nearly $2 billion of cash flow, and broke ground on a new fifty-seven-story, $435 million Philadelphia headquarters building. *Forbes* adds that Comcast CEO Brian Roberts earned $14.3 million in 2005 and $26.5 million in 2006 ($2.5 million of that in salary).

According to the FCC, overall cable TV fees increased 93 percent from 1995 to 2005, with basic cable rates jumping from $22.37 to $43.04. The operating margin of a typical U.S. company is 12 percent, while the typical cable franchise boasts operating margins of over 45 percent.

And things will only get better, but for cable companies, *not* subscribers. Kagan Research estimates cable's average monthly revenue per residential subscriber will climb from $79.65 in 2005 to $140.49 by 2015 as cable ramps up its triple-play subscribers.

Meanwhile, back in Marin County . . .

WHAT TO ASK FOR—FEATURES AND KEY PROVISIONS

Knowing how profitable the exclusive cable provider was getting, and knowing the results of the Needs Assessment, Past Performance Review, and Public Access Workshop, the Marin community was now in a much stronger negotiating position.

---

13. Ibid, p. 127.

14. Ibid, p. 132.

While each town's needs are unique, the key areas of negotiation in a franchise renewal include maintaining local authority over franchises and fees (still, alas, the most important elements of the franchise terms from the town's perspective, not public service), preservation and expansion of PEG channels, capacity, services, and capital cost funding for the facility, equipment, and upgrades; remedies for enforcement of franchise violations; universal service (no redlining, or eliminating poorer neighborhoods from coverage); customer service standards; an institutional network (or "I-NET," a high-speed, fiber optic, multichannel, bidirectional interactive network for schools, libraries, and government buildings); and, finally, a community media center.

DRAFTING A RESOLUTION FOR A NONPROFIT COMMUNITY MEDIA CENTER

Based on the experience in Marin County alone, my advice is this: Don't wait for your cable provider, or your city council or MTA, to draft a proposal. They probably won't. It is becoming clear that neither corporate America nor many governments that depend on corporate interests (such as campaign donations, franchise fees, or special I-Net superconnectivity between government offices) have public interest issues in mind.

So, write your own proposal.

By doing this, you set the terms of the debate. During public comment at an MTA meeting in June 2005, Media Action Marin member Steve Fein urged the board to guarantee through a resolution that the public access facility be run by a nonprofit. Fein had conducted a survey of sixteen northern California cities, and found that all but one was operated by a nonprofit, thereby bolstering the MAAC's findings that independent, nonprofit management is the broadly accepted and most successful model for community media centers.

It should be noted that the real need is for *local* management, regardless of actual corporate structure. There are thousands of for-profit local cooperative organizations that successfully manage equally complex operations, power utilities, educational systems, food management operations, and so forth.

In Marin, the best proposal soon followed. In September 2005, 85-year-old Media Action Marin member Val Schaaf submitted the only community-generated proposal for an independent media center. The proposal included a "Designated Access Provider" (DAP) clause to enable the transfer of the Comcast-owned public channel to a community-based nonprofit.

To gain support for Schaaf's proposal, Media Action Marin members again met with local leaders, including Democratic Congresswoman Lynn Woolsey. She subsequently wrote to the MTA in support of Media Action Marin's proposal for a local nonprofit community media center that would operate Marin's Public, Education, and Government channels.

Schaff's proposal lucidly listed the benefits of a community-run nonprofit over a corporate-run facility:

- Protects the interests of the community, not those of the cable company

- Ensures that a board of directors is locally elected and representative of the community

- Encourages the participation of ethnic, linguistic, and cultural minorities

- Enables nonprofits to approach additional potential sources of funding

- Guarantees that the media center stays in the community long after the cable company leaves, and that the center remains independent of the vagaries of Wall Street and the interlocking financial and legislative system

REVENUE SOURCES: FRANCHISE FEES (OR, KEEP CONTROL OF YOUR OWN MONEY)

The most critical part of any self-sustaining business is calculating how to cover all the capital and operational costs. Cable companies, for example, are required to fund a local media center's capital costs for equipment, upgrades, and the facility itself, but are not required to fund ongoing operations.

Cable companies collect revenues from subscribers plus a premium to forward to local government as the franchise fee, which typically is 5 percent or less, as compensation for leasing the public's rights-of-way and digging up streets, conduits, or highways to lay cable. Some local governments use their franchise fees to cover the annual operating costs of public access.[15] For example, the city of Anoka, Minnesota, gives all of its 5 percent franchise fee, $435,000 annually, to fund public access. The media center in Ann Arbor, Michigan, is 100 percent funded through the city's franchise fee. Access Sacramento gets 80 percent of its operating funds from franchise fees. And the California county of Napa collects more than $600,000 in annual cable franchise fees, of which one quarter goes to fund media access operations.

But nearby Marin County, California, is not so fortunate.

Representatives on the Marin Telecommunications Agency so far have refused to allocate any of the 5 percent franchise fees to fund PEG operations. Instead, they send all the franchise fees, about $2.5 million per year, to the general funds of their towns and the county, which in turn have come to rely on them. The largest municipality, San Rafael, gets about $600,000 a year, as does Marin County.

---

15. According to the Alliance for Community Media, a 2006 survey conducted for NATOA found that 94 percent of local government cable offices reported that their community collects a franchise fee from cable operators; 87 percent collect a franchise fee of 5 percent of gross revenues. "More than half of the fees are used by local governments to support their general fund, which funds police, fire, schools, transportation, and other vital public services provided by local governments. Some 17 percent of the fees are used for oversight of cable franchising and for public access channels; 20 percent are used for a combination of general fund and cable oversight; and 11 percent of fees are used solely for public access channels."

REVENUE SOURCES: PASS-THROUGH FEES

Knowing that Marin could not count on franchise fees to sustain operations, Val Schaff's proposal agreed with CBG consultant Robinson's Needs Assessment: that annual operational costs for the community media center could easily be funded through implementing a fee of $0.57 on each monthly cable bill. This fee is known as a "pass-through" fee and subscribers can "opt out" of paying it.

CBG's Needs Assessment reported that *"Local Access programming is of considerable importance in the MTA area* [emphasis in the original] with almost half of all subscribers indicating it was important that a portion of their bill should go to fund local community use of the channel,"[16] and "Forty-three percent (43%) of all subscribers indicated a willingness to financially support local access programming."[17]

Yet, despite a willingness by subscribers to support their own local media, Comcast resisted including a clause requiring the fee provision in the franchise agreement, and the MTA did not push for it. However, many communities use a pass-through mechanism to support PEG operations. In Allen, Texas, the City Council passed an ordinance establishing a "Pass-Through Fund" to support ACTV-15 (Allen City Television) with a fee of $0.35 per cable subscriber each month. Other Texas cities have pass-through fees that are more supportive, such as Dallas ($0.39) and Fort Worth ($1).

Another option is a combination of franchise and pass-through fees. For example, Salinas, Kansas, gets 40 percent of the city's 5 percent franchise fees and a $0.70 pass-through charge on the cable bill. Evanston, Illinois, gets a total of $448,000 per year from 3 percent of the city's 5 percent franchise fees and a $0.35 pass-through.

REVENUE SOURCES: *DIVERSIFY!*

It is best for any enterprise, including media centers, to diversify funding as widely as possible, and not merely rely on one or two sources, which could dry up. Revenue opportunities can come from training classes, contract production, fund-raising, grants, membership dues, equipment rental, fees for administering channels, fund drives, auctions, concerts, and even garage sales of used audio/video equipment (hey, some people like that stuff)!

The best solution is to plan for the long haul. For example, in Grand Rapids, Michigan, the local media board decided early on that they wanted its media center to be a solid, debt-free, long-term, community institution. The board managed to raise three grants totaling nearly $300,000. Twenty-one corporate donors contributed an average of $10,000 each, the city of Grand Rapids contributed $70,000, and MCI donated use of a high-speed telecommunications line for three years. $10,000 came from individual contributions, and $300,000 more came from Michigan's capital improvement budget.

---

16. "Report on Cable-Related Needs and Interests." March 2, 2005, p. 35.

17. Ibid, p. 28.

MARIN'S COMMUNITY MEDIA CENTER—ALIVE AND KICKING, AFTER ALL

Astonishingly, on May 16, 2006, after negotiating for almost eight exhausting years, mostly due to the cable company's intransigence, Marin County's new ten-year video franchise agreement was signed with Comcast. It included the Designated Access Provider provision, which would allow the county to create an independent community media center, along with $3 million in start-up funds from cable subscribers. One million dollars more was included for a high-speed fiber-optic Institutional Network (I-Net), to interconnect thirty-one Marin public agencies, schools, and libraries capable of TV broadcasts of city council meetings, emergency alerts, and the like.

Advocates thought the contract could have been better. After all, Comcast wasn't *giving* Marin anything. The county's 62,000 cable subscribers will each pay a $0.60 increase in their monthly cable bills throughout the ten-year franchise to repay Comcast's upfront "loan" of $3 million. Other sticking points included weak low-income discounts, wage and consumer protections, and liquidated damages, the latter being fixed-dollar-amount penalties paid by the provider for violations or noncompliance with agreement terms. Carriage of FM radio signals was not guaranteed in the agreement, but a side letter requires Comcast to give notice if it intends to drop FM again.

Still, this agreement can be viewed as a monumental achievement for media advocates. In a comment to the FCC's Notice of Proposed Rulemaking (NPRM) for video franchising, Media Action Marin wrote, "The experience of this community demonstrates the importance of preserving local franchising. This provides an opportunity for voluntary citizen organizations to participate actively in the process. That opportunity is lost if all policy is made in Washington, or even Sacramento."[18]

If the state had passed AB 2987 earlier, the bill that basically would have allowed Sacramento to dictate the local cable landscape of California's communities, there was no way that the Media Action Marin contingent, consisting largely of seniors, minorities, the disabled, and your humble bike-riding author, would have been able to travel a hundred miles to the capital to hold corporations responsible and to fight for free speech via public access.

The Marin-Comcast pact may have been the last franchise agreement negotiated in California under the old guidelines. Thirteen states have laws on the books—co-sponsored by cable and phone companies—that restrict municipalities from creating their own broadband systems. But the media and communications turf of thirty-seven other states remains up for grabs. Therefore, let the above saga be a message to community organizers and free speech advocates: *Get what you can, while you can, before the elephants trample all the grass in your town.*

> **"All things in the world come from being. And being comes from non-being."**
> —*Lao Tzu*

---

18. In 2005, Tica Lyons received the "Activist of the Year" award from the Social Justice Center of Marin.

How to Create an Award-Winning Public Access Station
Susan Fleischmann[19]

Cambridge Community Television is the nationally recognized public access television station and computer center serving Cambridge, Massachusetts. CCTV provides training in video production and computer applications, access to equipment and facilities, and operates three community cable channels, a studio, art gallery, and a computer lab. In 2006, for the sixth time since we opened in 1988, CCTV was awarded the Overall Excellence in Public Access Programming award by the national Alliance for Community Media. This is the highest honor in our field.

BACKGROUND

CCTV, like most public access centers, was established as the result of the cable-franchising process. In order to use the public rights-of-way cable companies must enter into agreements with local municipalities. As part of this franchising process, federal law permits municipalities to require cable companies to provide channels for noncommercial community use, as well as facilities and/or capital monies and ongoing annual operating support of up to 5 percent of the cable company's gross revenues. The thinking behind this is that as streets and sidewalks are public space, and use by a private corporation to make a profit should result in financial and other benefit to the community.

Activist note 1: A high priority of telecommunications corporations is to pass legislation that wrests control of public rights-of-way from local municipalities and makes control regional or even national. This drastic change in regulation would result in the loss of funding for local programming, production training, and facilities, and loss of municipal control over how and when their public space is used or altered.

Many communities choose to use their franchise revenues to set up public, educational, and governmental (PEG) access operations. In Cambridge, for example, CCTV receives a portion of the franchise revenue to provide public access to the cable system. The balance of the revenue supports educational and governmental access. However, each community is unique, and franchise agreements differ. Sometimes the same organization will provide a combination of public, educational, and governmental access, and some municipalities use franchise fees for other purposes entirely.

19. Thanks to Ginny Berkowitz, John Donovan, and Ellen Grabiner.

Activist note 2: It is critical to educate local officials and members of the community about the importance of using franchise fees and other means to fund PEG access. There is no other mechanism in place to ensure that the interests of the community are truly represented among the cable channels.

STRUCTURE

CCTV is a nonprofit corporation and is subject to all state and federal laws governing such entities. In some cities, public access facilities are operated by the cable company, but establishing a separate nonprofit organization ensures that there is no conflict of interest between the two. The original board of directors of CCTV was appointed by the city manager. Now, the membership of CCTV elects the board and the members advisory committee, which serves as liaison to the staff and board.

Any Cambridge resident or member of a Cambridge organization may become a CCTV Access Member. Access Members may vote in elections, use the equipment and facilities to produce programming for CCTV's channels (at no charge), and enroll in any workshop.

Anyone from any community may become an Affiliate Member of CCTV. Affiliates may enroll in educational seminars, show programming on the community channels (with a Cambridge resident as sponsor), and use the computer lab at no charge.

CCTV strives to have all of our constituents—including our membership, our staff, our board, our member advisory committee, and our viewers—reflect the full diversity of our community. To ensure that no one is excluded due to financial hardship, CCTV charges only nominal membership fees and provides volunteer opportunities for those who seek a reduced fee.

Mission

CCTV's mission statement says, "Cambridge Community Television is a public forum for all Cambridge residents, businesses, and organizations. CCTV provides the training and access to telecommunications technology so that all may become active participants in electronic media. CCTV strives to involve the diverse population of Cambridge as producers and viewers, and to strengthen its efforts through collaborations with a wide variety of community institutions."

Activist note 3: The process of formulating a mission statement is an important one. Invite representation from all constituencies to ensure that each issue is explored from many points of view. The mission statement will serve as a blueprint in developing the range of services and programs that will be offered, and constituent buy-in will only come if they have been involved in its creation.

PROGRAMMING, OR "CAN YOU REALLY DO THAT ON TV?"

Public access channels are noncommercial. Aside from the obvious benefit of not having to sit through endless assaults on our senses, a noncommercial channel also provides the opportunity to "narrowcast"—target a small subset of viewers. Commercial sponsors, for example, would be unlikely to support a program in a language other than English, because the audience would be too small. And programs featuring the local Little League would face the same issue. But because public access channels do not rely on commercial sponsors, they are able to showcase local, niche programming. That is one of their major strengths.

One of the most difficult concepts for people to grasp is that public access channels are not subject to the same content regulation as broadcast channels. Anything that is considered protected speech under the First Amendment may be shown—which is very difficult to explain to an irate viewer who has just seen nudity or heard offensive language. In fact, public access channels are required by law to be content neutral, ensuring that each and every programmer's First Amendment rights are protected.

Activist note 4: Educate the public and local elected officials about the First Amendment *before* a crisis. Provide elected officials with talking points so that they have the tools to respond when someone complains about your programming. (It's also not a bad idea to invite candidates into your studio during election season to make sure that they see the positive role that public access can play in placing local issues—like their campaigns—before the community.) CCTV produces channel "explainers" that run between regular programming and that describe how access channels are different from broadcast channels.

DIVERSIFY, DIVERSIFY, DIVERSIFY

Funding. Franchise fees or other cable/municipal support may be substantial; however, no healthy organization is one hundred percent reliant on one source of revenue. CCTV has developed other revenue streams that together account for 25 to 30 percent of our budget. These include rental of equipment and facilities, for-hire production services, membership and workshop fees, grants, channel or program sponsorships, fund-raising events, product sales, and an individual donor campaign, Friends of CCTV.

Programs and services. Access centers have become more than just a place to make television programs. The more the center can offer, the more people can be served. For example, CCTV opened its computer lab, computerCENTRAL, in 1996 to provide access to computers and the Internet for those who could not otherwise afford it. The lab has attracted constituencies who would probably not otherwise participate:

homeless people, recent immigrants and others with low-level English proficiency, and seniors. Another example of a service that appeals to a different constituency is the Drive-by Gallery, which offers exhibition space for Cambridge artists.

Constituencies. One of the traditional cornerstones of the public access movement is the concept of first come, first served—everyone is treated the same and has equal access to resources. But the idea, regardless of its benign intent, is flawed at its core. Everyone *does not* have equal access, due to barriers of race, class, language, and sense of self in the greater society, for example.

Activist note 5: Identify key leaders and organizations that serve your targeted constituencies. Talk to them about the needs of their communities and how the access center and channels can address those needs. Do some homework so you will be prepared when people respond. Be willing to tailor programs to meet their needs. Think about how to deepen the connection to their community. And make sure that from the moment anyone walks through the door, they feel welcomed, valued, and respected.

Getting started is the hardest part. Small, well-planned pilot projects are very useful. This provides an opportunity to see if what was intended worked or if the program design needs tweaking to meet the need of the targeted group better. After the program is successful, others will be more likely to see the center as a resource and a place where they are welcome.

Finally, use every means possible to deepen the connection between the organization and your constituents. Distribute participants' work, include them in the advisory/decision-making process of the organization, highlight their involvement in the newsletter or other public events, and most importantly, shepherd them through the complex world of making media at the facility, encouraging them to try new ways to get their message out.

This is a brief introduction to public access, from the perspective of one community. Access centers share a common purpose in the spectrum of media in this country—a purpose that no other television media serves, and all face many of the same challenges. However, no two access centers will be the same, nor should they be, because no two communities are the same. The strength of each center lies in its ability to define, project, and organize itself around its mission, and to become integral to the life of the community that it serves.

As Greg Epler Wood and Lauren-Glen Davitian wrote in *Community Media Review* (Spring, 2004), "We are living in a time in United States history when the mass media can no longer be counted on to provide a free and independent voice in a political debate, or to be a countervailing force against large corporate commercial interests. Two important independent communication systems thankfully still exist—the Internet and PEG access—and it is vitally important that we all work to make certain that both continue to thrive, unencumbered by the threats that would chip away at their foundations, and with them, our basic democratic freedoms."

For more resources, see bethemedia.com/resources.htm.

"It's never too late to be who you might have been."
—*George Eliot*

19

COMMUNITY BROADBAND

HOW TO OFFER YOUR COMMUNITY THE "TRIPLE PLAY" OF VOICE, VIDEO, AND INTERNET ACCESS

David Mathison

"The sea is king of a thousand streams, because it lies beneath them."
—Lao Tzu

Universal, high-speed, broadband Internet access is becoming an essential public service, similar to the provision of gas and electricity. It is critical for economic development, education, and public safety. In April 2004 President George Bush called for "universal, affordable access for broadband technology by the year 2007." The United States, for its part, is not doing very well at making it accessible at all. The International Telecommunications Union claims that, since 2001, the United States has fallen from fourth place to sixteenth place globally in supplying broadband to its population. As of December 2006, 60 percent of U.S. households do not subscribe to broadband because it is either unavailable or unaffordable.

Americans who are connected to broadband get slow Internet speeds at high prices. In June 2007 the Communication Workers of America union reported that the median real-time download speed in the country is 1.9 Mbps, compared to 61 Mbps in Japan, 45 Mbps in Korea, and 17 Mbps in France.[1] According to the Organisation for Economic Co-operation and Development, Americans pay ten times more for speeds that are ten to one hundred times slower than those of subscribers in other countries. In Japan, 100 Mbps fiber access is almost ubiquitous, whereas

---

1. A megabit per second (Mbps) is a unit that measures data transfer rates. It is equal to 1,000,000 bits per second, or 1,000 kilobits per second (kbps). A "bit" is short for "binary digit," and can hold only one of two values, 0 or 1.

"slower" 25 Mbps connections are just $20 per month. In South Korea, users get speeds in excess of 100 Mbps for both uploads and downloads. Meanwhile, U.S. broadband providers offer 1 to 4 Mbps (download speed only; upload speeds are significantly slower) for between $20 and $60 per month.[2]

According to the OECD, subscribers in Japan, Sweden, Korea, Finland, and France pay the least per megabit per second (Mbps) of connectivity:

- Japan: $0.22

- Sweden: $0.35

- South Korea: $0.42

- Finland: $0.59

- France: $0.82

- U.S.: $10 per Mbps (3 Mbps DSL); $7.50 per Mbps (6 Mbps cable)[3]

In the United States, 98 percent of all high-speed broadband connections are provided by the incumbent phone or cable companies, which can now deliver all media—voice, video, and data (the so-called triple play)—via one broadband pipe. Other alternatives, like satellite and cellular phones with broadband, are more expensive and slower than cable modem and DSL. There is no meaningful competition for the "duopoly" of cable and phone companies, especially in rural areas. A recent study by the Pew Charitable Trust found that 29 percent of rural Internet users have only one provider available to them, most often a satellite provider. Not surprisingly, rural populations subscribe to broadband service at roughly half the rate of urban and suburban areas. Low-income communities also are priced out of the market. Millions of American households are stranded on the wrong side of the digital divide.

Facing the prospect of being denied the benefits of true high-speed broadband Internet access, many communities rightly fear job loss, declining educational opportunities, barriers to first-class public safety systems, and a loss of civic vitality. They are looking for new technologies to bring broadband to their homes and businesses, and seeking new business models that will provide competition, lower prices, and better service that reaches everyone in their community.

Broadband can also lower carbon monoxide emissions and reduce energy consumption. How? Emissions can be cut by telecommuting and teleconferencing instead of driving. Soon,

2. The FCC considers 200 kbps to be a "high-speed" connection. According to S. Derek Turner, research director at freepress.net, 200 kbps "was barely enough to surf in 1999 but is far below what's needed to enjoy streaming video, VoIP, flash animation, or other common Internet applications." In this chapter, the concept of high-speed broadband assumes connection speeds of at least 2 Mbps downstream and 1 Mbps upstream.

3. Testimony of Ben Scott, Policy Director, freepress.net, April 24, 2007, before the U.S. Senate Committee on Commerce, Science, and Transportation.

almost everyone and everything will be connected to the Internet—cell phones, thermostats, refrigerators, air conditioners, even cars. Modernizing our century-old electricity system with an adaptive, Internet-connected "smart grid" would enable remote monitoring of electricity use, and promote more efficient uses of energy. A 2008 study by the American Consumer Institute concluded that "the wide adoption and use of broadband applications can achieve a net reduction of 1 billion tons of greenhouse gas over 10 years, which, if converted into energy saved, would constitute 11% of annual US oil imports."

Local governments, businesses, neighborhoods, schools, and community groups are realizing the importance of controlling their telecommunications destiny and bringing the benefits of broadband service to their neighborhoods. For an overview of these benefits, see freepress.net/communityinternet/=benefits.

In recent years, communities have found solutions and have taken matters into their own hands. We call these solutions "community broadband." New community broadband networks and municipal broadband projects are cropping up across the country every day. Traditionally, a carrier-centered model dominated, with phone and cable companies building, owning, and operating the infrastructure. But this is by no means the only model. Many businesses, universities, and local governments own their fiber backbone, and benefit from the advantages of owning rather than renting.

Fiber is the fastest, most robust, and best solution for the long term. In Utah, for example, a consortium of fourteen cities is deploying and operating a fiber-optic network called the Utah Telecommunication Open Infrastructure Agency (UTOPIA). Because existing service providers were not delivering high-speed services in their areas, these communities joined together to create a 100 percent fiber-optic network with 100 to 1,000 Mbps capacity capable of providing 15 to 20 Mbps symmetric-connection service packages for just $40 per month.

Lafayette, Louisiana, is building a municipally owned fiber network that will be operated by its utilities system, despite the efforts of incumbent providers Cox and Bell South to stop it. The city of Kutztown, Pennsylvania, already owns a fiber network that competes with private companies to offer Internet access, video, and phone service. Burlington Telecom in Vermont deployed a fiber backbone providing phone, cable tv, and high speed Internet to over 3,000 residents. The network has positive cash flow and was financed by private investors, without any taxpayer money. Revenues from subscribers are recycled back to local government and Main Street, instead of being exported to remote corporations and Wall Street. The fiber infrastructure, jobs, and revenues stay in the community.

However, fiber is an expensive solution to deploy; it requires digging up streets to get the fiber to each home and business.

Another alternative is a wireless network, which uses inexpensive, easily installed antennas that do not require digging up streets. Sophisticated software makes these antennas highly intelligent, ensuring that connections between the nodes (also known as transmitters) of the network are reliable and efficient. They do not require investment in large towers or expensive broadcasting equipment. What's more, when additional users, businesses, and public institutions join the network, it becomes less expensive and more robust. Wireless networks are rarely substitutes for a triple-play service offered by cable and telephone companies. But they are a low-cost, high-speed Internet connection offered to communities that previously have not been connected.

For example, in Lamberton, Minnesota, the Meadowland Farmers Cooperative joined with the local high school to provide the town and surrounding areas with wireless Internet access. The height of their fourteen silos helps to distribute the wireless signal widely.

In rural Iowa and Illinois, Prairie iNet placed direct line-of-sight transmitters on top of grain elevators, which transmit signals across the plains to towns miles away.

In San Diego County, California, Tribal Digital Village took matters into its own hands and created a 45 Mbps high-speed network, using solar-powered antennae to link fourteen remote Indian reservations over two hundred fifty square miles.

In April 2006, MuniWireless released a summary of city and county municipal projects, which reported that one hundred and eighty communities had or were planning public broadband access projects. As of this writing there were at least four hundred such projects, including:

- Regional and city networks, like Chaska, Minnesota. In St. Cloud, Florida, the city paid for a wireless network providing free access to residents.

- City hot zones, including Los Angeles; Washington, D.C.; and Urbana, Illinois.

- Public safety and municipal use projects, such as San Diego; Las Vegas; and New Orleans.

- City- and countywide projects, such as Phoenix; Mountain View, California; and Philadelphia.

- Cities and counties considering wireless, such as New Haven and St. Paul, where a portion of the revenue will go toward funding community technology projects.

A COMMUNITY BROADBAND HOW-TO

Community projects are being deployed for different reasons, and they use various technologies, ownership structures, and business models. You can determine the best solution for your community by following these three steps.

1. Conduct a Community Broadband Needs Assessment

A community broadband needs assessment should be undertaken, with a plan for digital inclusion to ensure that everyone will benefit. According to Media Alliance's advocacy toolkit (tinyurl.com/2o7nbe), digital inclusion consists of four elements:

A DIY Wireless Solution — CUWiN[1]

Sascha Meinrath

If, after evaluating your options, you decide to go wireless, you might want to look into using the free CUWiN system. CUWiN (Champaign-Urbana Community Wireless Network, cuwin.net) is a coalition of wireless developers and community volunteers committed to providing low-cost, do-it-yourself, community-controlled alternatives to contemporary broadband models. They offer a free wireless networking system that any municipality, company, or group of neighbors can easily set up themselves. Following in the footsteps of the open-source software programs Linux and Firefox, CUWiN's wireless networking software is, and always will be, available for free.

To set up a wireless network, all users need to do is burn a CD with CUWiN's software, put the CD into a desktop computer equipped with a supported wireless card (which comes with most new computers and can be purchased at any computer supply store), and turn the computer on. Once the computer boots from the CD, the rest of the setup is completely automated: from loading the networking operating system and software, to sending out beacons to nearby nodes (such as other computers), to negotiating network connectivity, to assimilating into the network. All the complicated technical setup is taken care of automatically, and needs to be done only once. Unlike most broadband systems, CUWiN's software builds a local intranet as well as providing Internet connectivity to the world at large. Thus, a town that uses CUWiN's system is also creating a communitywide local area network over which streaming audio and video, voice services, and the like can be sent.

---

1. Thanks to Sascha Meinrath, executive director, Champaign-Urbana Community Wireless Network (CUWiN.net).

The first element is basic access. Everyone in the community has the right to broadband access. The second element is hardware and software. Everyone should have access to inexpensive or free devices to connect to the proposed high-speed broadband network. After all, such a network is useless if people lack equipment to access it. Consider programs that collect, refurbish, and distribute used computers to underserved constituents, or provide low-interest loans for new computer purchases. The third element is training and technical support services. A technology fair or a traveling "techmobile" (similar to a library's bookmobile) can address this issue in low-income neighborhoods. Finally, offer tools and resources for media production so that users can project their content and voice into the system.

2. Create a Proposal

Be sure to give input to your town's request for information and subsequent request for proposal (an RFP) that will be sent to businesses to bid on the project. Or better yet, submit a proposal of your own. Community media advocates at Media Action Marin in Marin County, California, submitted a community broadband proposal to the Marin Telecommunications Agency in 2008 after allowing members of the community to participate in the discussion. Once complete, submit the proposal to ethostoolkit.net, which serves as a clearinghouse for information on community broadband initiatives.

Your proposal might include the following:

- Competition: Your community Internet could create competitive alternatives that encourage lower prices, faster speeds, and better service.

- Technology leadership: High-speed broadband service will attract and maintain high-tech businesses, entrepreneurs, and investment capital to your community (think Silicon Valley in California, or college towns and campuses).

- Cost savings: Your town can save on telecommunications costs it would normally pay to broadband providers.

- Public safety: A high-speed Internet will enhance public safety and security. Some of the most successful projects in the United States and abroad involve municipal departments, such as the police, deploying a key application for public safety, with a clear return on investment.

- Universal access: A community-initiated, publicly owned network can provide universal access, just as publicly owned road, water, and sewer networks are accessible to everyone without discrimination.

3. Identify Structure

This step consists of identifying the community broadband's ownership, management, and business structure, and will vary from town to town, depending on unique local requirements.

Ownership: The system could be owned by a public/private partnership, a community or private nonprofit, a joint powers authority, a commercial entity, a public utility, or a private/internal governmental network, among other possible entities.

Management: Define who will run and manage day-to-day operation of the system, and who will provide training and technical support.

Business model: What is the business model for your community? For example, you might give away free 300 kbps access to low-income residents and schools, a $20-per-month 1 Mbps connection to residences, and a faster connection at a higher cost to businesses. You'll also need to determine the length of the contract and how to handle complaints.

Security and privacy: Users must be able to protect their security, privacy, and identities, and must control their own personal data. A user's online activity and registration information is not the property of the provider, whether it be a private company or a municipal government, and providers should agree to not sell or track personal user information.

By going through these three steps, you will be better able to address the broadband needs of your town from the perspective of your local community up, instead of the government down, or viewing those needs through the myopic business lens of a remote, profit-driven corporation.

COMMUNITY BROADBAND: BARRIERS TO ENTRY

The major barrier to establishing community broadband is not technological or economic. It's political.

Throughout 2005 big telephone and cable companies used their lobbying clout in Congress and in state legislatures to try to outlaw municipal broadband systems, to prevent competition, and to undercut local control. Thanks to the thousands of activists, dedicated communities, local governments, and the successes of community broadband projects, these efforts were largely defeated in state after state. The successful defense of community broadband in 2005 was a startling example of how people can beat corporate lobbyist influence over state and federal policies that affect our lives.

Going forward, Congress may take steps to protect from any further interference the authority of communities to offer broadband service. Meanwhile, the very same companies that opposed municipal broadband are now bidding to partner with local governments on community broadband projects!

TOWARD A NATIONAL BROADBAND STRATEGY

In the nineteenth century the United States adopted policies to create canals and railroads to facilitate transportation. In the twentieth century the United States created policies to deploy universal telephone access in order to enhance communication. Today, the United States needs a national broadband strategy to deliver universal high-speed broadband access to all citizens.

By unlicensing or "opening" access to the airwaves, new technologies would enable everyone to broadcast his or her own media. Currently, our airwaves are bought and sold to the highest bidder. The public airwaves ("spectrum") are regulated by rules that license their use to various parties for specific purposes. Radio, television, cellular phone service, garage door openers, and remote controls are all allocated or licensed to specific frequencies by the FCC. For years, regulators have assumed that the airwaves were scarce and that only a limited amount of space was available. Regulation, then, served to prevent interference among those who used the airwaves.

That was then. Today, new technologies are making it possible for many more parties to fit onto the public airwaves, if not share exactly the same airwave space outright. This is perhaps the biggest conceptual shift to occur in media policy in decades. The airwaves could become more akin to a public park, sidewalk, or thoroughfare than to the gated community they are now . . . if policy makers open the gates.

As these new possibilities become apparent, big media interests are working to prevent new rules from opening the spectrum and to take the public airwaves out of the hands of people altogether. Corporate lobbyists are advancing proposals that would give the biggest conglomerates permanent property rights over the public airwaves they now use, shutting ordinary people out for good and leaving the once-public airwaves completely at the whim of the biggest communications corporations.

According to Timothy Karr of FreePress.net, "Forcing public broadband networks to ask permission from Verizon before offering service is akin to forcing public libraries to ask permission from Borders before checking out books."

With open spectrum and new technologies, the public airwaves are no longer scarce—there's room for everyone. By unlicensing them, innovation can flourish and communities can truly be given a voice over their own media. (See sidebars.)

TAKE ACTION! FILE A COMMENT WITH THE FCC

Broadband is no longer a luxury, it is a public necessity. Freepress.net and the Media Access Project offer a convenient way to contact the FCC regarding the policies and regulations that affect community broadband. Visit freepress.net/communityinternet for more information and join internetforeveryone.com to help.

Let's connect!

Open Spectrum

"The assumptions underlying the dominant paradigm for spectrum management no longer hold. Today's digital technologies are smart enough to distinguish between signals, allowing users to share the airwaves without exclusive licensing. Instead of treating spectrum as a scarce physical resource, we could make it available to all as a commons, an approach known as 'open spectrum.'

Open spectrum would allow for more efficient and creative use of the precious resource of the airwaves. It could enable innovative services, reduce prices, foster competitions, create new business opportunities and bring our communications policies in line with our democratic ideals."

—*Open Spectrum: The New Wireless Paradigm*, by Kevin Werbach. New America Foundation, Spectrum Series Working Paper #6. October 2002.

Digital Television Spectrum (White Spaces)

"Existing Wi-Fi networks operate in 'junk bands' cluttered with signal from cordless phones, microwave ovens, baby monitors and other consumer devices. At lower frequencies—like in the television band—signals travel farther and can go through walls, trees and mountains. Opening up some of this spectrum would make Community Internet systems much faster and cheaper to deploy." —*Let There Be Wi-Fi*, by Robert McChesney and John Podesta. *Washington Monthly*, January 1, 2006.

On November 4, 2008, the FCC approved unlicensed use of the 700-MHz spectrum that now sits vacant between TV channels two and fifty-one (also known as "white space.") The FCC had previously protected these empty airwaves to prevent transmission interference. This protection resulted in more than three-quarters of the broadcast spectrum in US markets sitting idle. With the migration of television signals from analog to digital transmission in February 2009, interference is no longer an issue. These prime airwaves can now be put into practical use. Unlicensed use of the white space will bring Internet service to millions of Americans who are caught on the wrong side of the digital divide, and provide them with an alternative to the cable and phone duopoly control over Internet access.

Resources

*Broadband Reality Check II: The Truth Behind America's Digital Decline,"*by S. Derek Turner, Research Director, FreePress.net; Consumers Union; Consumer Federation of America. August 2006.

Broadband Reality Check: The FCC Ignores America's Digital Divide, by S. Derek Turner, Research Fellow, FreePress.net; Consumers Union; Consumer Federation of America. August 2005.

Connecting the Public: The Truth About Municipal Broadband, by Ben Scott (FreePress.net), Harold Feld and Gregory Rose (Media Access Project), and Mark Cooper (Consumer Federation of America). April 2005.

Radio Revolution: The Coming Age of Unlicensed Wireless, by Kevin Werbach, New America Foundation; Public Knowledge. December 2003.

For more resources and websites to visit, see bethemedia.com/resources.htm.

"Like our national parks, the airwaves are a public trust."

—Representavie Diane Watson (D-Calif.)

20

((i))ndymedia

THE GLOBAL INDEPENDENT MEDIA CENTER NETWORK

Dorothy Kidd

Dedicated to the memory of Brad Will

"Don't hate the media, become the media."
—Jello Biafra

The Independent Media Center network (IMC) is perhaps the best-known example of the power of do-it-yourself media represented in this book. Birthed during demonstrations in Seattle against the World Trade Organization (WTO) in late 1999, five hundred independent and alternative media activists helped expose the blatant commercial exploitation of many of the world's peoples and resources at the hands of a few rich people and corporations. Operating from a storefront that cofounder Jeff Perlstein described as a "community-based people's newsroom" they produced up-to-the minute text and photo accounts for the Web, as well as low power FM and community radio reports, a newspaper, and a video series.

The IMC outperformed the corporate media. It drew 1.5 million visitors to its site and broke stories that had been largely unreported in the corporate U.S. media. Since then, this collabora-tive experiment in radical democracy and networked communications has grown to a worldwide network involving approximately five thousand people in one hundred fifty groups in fifty countries. Just as importantly, activists covering social justice issues around the world have since replicated the IMC model. They also have provided a model for the recent explosion of sites based on user-generated multimedia content.

The IMC pioneered many of the technologies and software that are now part of the Web 2.0 menu. The people involved developed a multimedia networked system that allows anyone with access to the Internet to upload content. The system also fully utilizes the Internet's digital capacity to operate simultaneously at local, regional, and international levels, with links to a multitude of sites.

However, the success of Indymedia is not its technological wizardry. If there is magic afoot, it is a result of the committed volunteer crews, who combine their collective intelligence and experience with a new organizational structure and common set of social justice values. Not without growing pains, which are discussed below, the IMC remains committed to adapting to the multiple interests of their member sites and the movements to which they belong.

Indymedia's philosophical DNA of participatory democracy informs every aspect of the network, from the horizontal links among autonomously operated local sites and special teams to the consensus-based forms of decision making and the dynamism of the open publishing, archiving, and collaboration software. From the initial focus on protests against the agenda of capitalist globalization orchestrated by the WTO and other transnational bodies,[1] the global IMC now provides reports from a wide diversity of social justice movements. The mission statement notes:

> The Independent Media Center is a grassroots organization committed to using media production and distribution as a tool for promoting social and economic justice. It is our goal to further the self-determination of people underrepresented in media production and content, and to illuminate and analyse local and global issues that impact ecosystems, communities and individuals. We seek to generate alternatives to the biases inherent in the corporate media controlled by profit, and to identify and create positive models for a sustainable and equitable society.

BECOME THE MEDIA

The IMC became the model for a new kind of grassroots global media that is autonomous of both the old corporate and state systems. Mixing and mashing from the principles and practices of radical media, social justice organizing, and the open source software movement, the IMC prefigured current experiments in citizen journalism. Instead of being driven by the profit motive

---

1. Transnational bodies include institutions such as the World Bank, the International Monetary Fund, and the Internet Corporation on Names and Numbers. They are not directly responsible to national governments, which would be "international." Instead, they combine national governments, global bureaucracy, and private partnerships with transnational corporations.

of capitalist media or the narrow framing of citizens' interests in reporting from national capitals, produced by public broadcasters such as National Public Radio or the BBC, IMC volunteers combine accuracy with "radical" opinion and "passionate tellings of the truth," bringing direct witness from their special vantage points within local, national, and transnational social change movements. There are no IMC stars, and very few talking "experts" in their videos. Not satisfied with armchair critiques of big media, the IMC approach is instead encapsulated in an early banner of IMC Italy: DON'T HATE THE MEDIA—BECOME THE MEDIA.

Committed to enacting the participatory communications that government and so-called public stations only preach, the IMC champions values of solidarity, cooperation, and openness. Many of the centers share servers and operating code, systems of content management, and the basic Web page logo and layout. The decentralized networked structure is designed so that each center manages itself after signing a common agreement based on the IMC's Principles of Unity (https://docs.indymedia.org/view/global/principlesofunity). As the network has grown, IMC teams have developed new ways to promote local and transnational cooperation both on- and off-line, including easier translation functions and more participatory forms of collaboration in production and discussion.

In the beginning, the principles of openness were extended to everyone within reach of the Internet. Indymedia's open publishing, initially developed by techies from Australia and Colorado, provides a 24/7 forum to directly represent oneself through audio, video, or print reports. (See Matthew Arnison's sidebar on Open Publishing.) All site visitors are encouraged to comment, to add translations of articles on the site, and to post notices of upcoming events. The hyperlinked design encourages visitors to select content from among the extensive range of news, commentary, resource links, or discussion opportunities. In addition, in those areas of the world where access to the Internet and to other kinds of media production is limited, IMC groups provide media and journalism production training for community members and sponsor off-line forums for local people to watch and discuss media presentations.

THE NEXT GENERATION

The IMC was not the first media movement to encourage the stories of those excluded by the dominant media and society or to emphasize participatory democracy. Nor was it even the first global network to focus on challenging capitalist globalization, or as Indymedia South Africa puts it, to "encourage a world where globalization is not about homogeneity and exploitation, but rather, about diversity and cooperation." The radical and tactical grassroots media projects this book outlines are only the latest generation in their long history. The IMC represents a new convergence of networks, of global social justice movements, of radical media makers, and of free and open source software, whose stories start at least two decades earlier.

Beginning in the late 1970s, social justice movements began to mobilize against what we now call the Washington or neoliberal agenda.[2] The livelihoods of ordinary people were shattered as multilateral organizations such as the World Bank and the International Monetary Fund encouraged national elites to cut social programes and to privatize and deregulate public institutions, and instead to spend state budgets on weapons and exorbitant loans with high interest rates. Beginning in the hardest-hit countries of the southern hemisphere, social movements and nongovernmental organizations began organizing across national borders, exchanging information via the existing technologies of linked computer newslists, faxes, and phone lines as well as through face-to-face meetings. Gradually, they built what radical political economist Harry Cleaver calls "an electronic fabric of struggle," most famously in the transnational solidarity campaign in support of the Zapatistas' resistance to the North American Free Trade Agreement, in Chiapas, Mexico.

The Zapatistas were an inspiration to the emerging grassroots antiglobalization movement around the world, and especially to activists involved in communications change. Several IMC founders were especially influenced by the link the Zapatistas made between radical democracy, internationalism, and the importance of media networks, and had either participated in meetings in Chiapas, had heard Subcomandante Marcos at an independent media network meeting in New York City in 1997, or had read or watched a video of his communiqué of 1996: "We have a choice: We can have a cynical attitude in the face of media . . . (or) we can ignore it and go about our lives. But there is a third option . . . (and) that is to construct a different way—to show the world what is really happening—to have a critical worldview and to become interested in the truth of what happens to the people who inhabit every corner of this world."

The Zapatistas were one node in a growing network of activism against neoliberalism, which relied on the Internet and combined older media with participatory practices. In 1997, South Korean labour and student movements experimented with on-the-spot broadband-Internet-based reporting during demonstrations against the International Monetary Fund, forming two powerful broadband news cooperatives, NodongNet and JinboNet. During the June 18, 1999, Reclaim the Streets demonstrations in London, European activists utilized some of these community-activist technologies, which were then adopted in Seattle.

The Seattle IMC represented a leap forward in both scope and scale for this new political media movement. In the home of Microsoft and other software giants, and under the glare of the global mainstream media, the Seattle IMC brought together older and younger radical media activists and artists from the open source software movement, micro- and community radio, independent video and public access television, zine makers and the independent press, and the punk music world.

---

2. Neoliberalism was first popularized by the Ronald Reagan and Margaret Thatcher governments in the United States and the UK. Both leaders argued that there is little need for government because free markets can, and should, self-regulate society. They implemented a drastic set of national and international changes, the most publicized of which were their efforts to privatize public institutions and remove most regulations governing corporate behaviour. From the perspective of media justice advocates, these and other measures contributed to the unfettered growth of media monopolies and the end of the Fairness Doctrine.

While the corporate media repeatedly showed shots of the smashing of a Starbuck's window, the IMC presented images of police in full riot gear teargassing largely peaceful demonstrators, myself included, among the giant puppets of turtles (and other animals threatened with extinction), the costumed dancers, the drum-and-bugle bands, the trade unionists, and other people of all ages.[3] Just as importantly, the IMC provided context, making available interviews and commentary from a wide range of people from the United States and elsewhere about the costs of World Trade Organization policies and the values represented by corporate neoliberalism. The new website was so successful, that it received over 1.5 million hits from around the world, and mainstream publications such as the *Christian Science Monitor,* the *New York Times,* and the *Washington Post* began to cite its content.

The IMC turned the tables on the dominant media's model of news making and of organization. They rejected the commercial media, in which information is packaged as a commodity to be sold to audiences via subscriptions or within the tight frames of advertising and product placement. They also rejected the professional spin of nongovernmental organizations, whose spokespeople tended to stick to the narrow talking points of reform. In contrast, the IMC presented a do-it-yourself approach for both media producers and audiences. Their open publishing format and volunteer production teams bypassed the professional gatekeepers of media organizations and nongovernmental organizations. They wanted not only to circulate counterinformation but also to create a very different kind of synergy between producers and audiences.

This interactive approach to citizen journalism was made possible partly by the creativity and resourcefulness of the technical crew. The crew brought with them a common ethos of collaborative problem solving derived from the open source software movement. They built a digital environment featuring free software and open source code, which in large measure spurred the network's rapid growth. Centers everywhere could quickly share and adapt the resource to their own local needs. The global technical crew remains indispensable, supporting and improving via cyberspace and on-site visits both local sites and the network as a whole.

GROWING PAINS

The astonishing pace of the IMC network's development from one center to over one hundred fifty has not been without growing pains. Like many of the precursor radical media, the IMC network continually deals with problems of sustainability, uneven and unequal distribution of resources among people around the globe, attacks from hostile governments and individuals, and the difficulties inherent in sustaining a more democratic communications model in an increasingly enclosed corporate media environment. Although IMC strives to be transparent, there are nonetheless technological, economic, and social barriers to entry and full participation.

---

3. For an extensive discussion of the media in Seattle and other global protests, see *Representing Resistance: Media, Civil Disobedience and the Global Justice Movement,* a volume edited by Andy Opel and Donnalyn Pompper. Praeger, 2003.

For example, although there are significant numbers of centers and projects in the southern hemisphere, the network is still dominated by young, white, male, professional-class North Americans and Europeans. In its Principles of Unity the IMC has committed itself to working toward nonhierarchical and antiauthoritarian relationships. However, a study by Lisa Brooten and Gabriele Hadl, based on discussions with IMC women and men, suggests there is still a lot of work to be done.

Nevertheless, what is remarkable is the way the IMC has tried to attend to all of these issues. Its strength has been the pragmatic and imaginative way participants use the network structure to create connective tissues of solidarity. The network is run by several different working groups that cooperate through knowledge-sharing newslists and wikis, which are open to new members and can be accessed on the website. There are also several transnational, regional, and subregional working groups as well as issues forums and ongoing discussion links among groups of women and indigenous peoples.

The global technical team continues to support centers around the world, online and sometimes in person. There have also been several solidarity initiatives to assist developing sites in centers of global conflict, such as Palestine and Iraq, or in regions with fewer resources, such as Africa and Latin America. Intraregional projects such as newsreels enable collaboration across national borders. Newer projects, such as Indymedia Estrecho and the Oceania hub site, defy older colonial definitions of regional borders. Indymedia Estrecho combines collectives from Spain, the Canary Islands, and Morocco, providing links of solidarity across one of the oldest migration routes between Africa and Europe. The Oceania Indymedia website brings together contributions such as columns, articles, political cartoons, and photos, from the Southeast Asia and Pacific region. Member centers also are collaborating on a video project.

EDITORS OR LIBRARIANS?

The IMC also has revised its initial ideas and policies about how best to encourage participatory communications. Partly in response to racist, sexist, and hate-filled commentaries, and partly through a reevaluation of what free speech really means, local centers and the network as a whole have revised their policies and their content-selection and editing practices. Many IMCs have realized that in a world where media power is so unevenly distributed, the barriers to democratic communication go well beyond simple questions of access and require complex policies and practices to facilitate, support, and prioritize participation by specific marginalized groups and individual voices.

Not without controversy, most sites have set up new kinds of editorial controls. One team selects, translates, and publishes stories from around the world on the center column of the main indymedia site, which helps to increase global diversity and to counterbalance the U.S. and Eurocentric perspectives of the mainstream global news services. Another team, the global newswire working group, clears duplicate posts and commercial messages, and hides spam and objectionable posts on the very back pages of the site. Most local sites also publish a policy statement, which explains the guidelines for using the open newswire. Some sites, such as IMC Germany, have created an extra step for anyone using the open newswire; rather than automatically feeding to the front page, news posts are published on a special page and then filtered by an editorial team for racist, fascist, sexist, and anti-Semitic content, as well as for newness or originality of analysis.

Each of these modifications has elicited a great deal of controversy. Many have argued against any new gatekeeping protocols. "Who sets the ideological filters? Who applies them? How is this process accountable to the volunteers who are giving their labour to Indymedia working groups, let alone the casual reader?" writes Luther Blisset in an October 2004 post. On the other side of the argument, some groups like San Francisco Indymedia would like a much heavier editorial role for Indymedia collectives. "The network at large needs to be less about small clubs of friends running a Web log and must tackle the challenges of being a global, noncommercial media network."

Others, such as Matthew Arnison from Sydney, Australia, one of the original code programmers, argue that the whole idea of editing should be reconceived so as to "involve a new wave of people in media democracy." He envisions developing new software that would enable users to find stories without hours of searching. As Graham Meikle has discussed, the trend toward selection and ranking of content could lead to a professionalisation of news writing and editing and/or to a much more peer-to-peer network, in which audiences are actively enlisted in ranking and curating stories. The question posed by Sheri Herndon of the original Seattle IMC is whether the IMC crews should be editors or librarians.

GROWING LOCALLY

Most IMC sites began as the result of a specific event, such as the series of antiglobalization protests in the early 2000s or the more recent peace campaigns. The heady excitement of organizing is often enough to inspire small, closely knit teams to work all out for several months. However, this carnivalesque pace of production and dependence on individual volunteers often leads to individual burnout and collective disarray. Now, after the first years of rapid, ad hoc growth, the network requires new IMC centers to proceed formally through an application process, to develop a "local mission statement, adopt a specific consensual decision-making process, satisfy requirements for openness and transparency in their editorial policies, and agree to hold open meetings, among a number of other provisions." (See also docs.indymedia.org/view/Global/WebHomeWG#New_IMC.)

Individual centers have experimented with different ways of reaching into their own communities and using their own particular traditions of media and social justice movement organizing. The IMC group in Bristol, England, cooperates with other local, national, and international alternative media groups, but it also emphasizes localness: "Please refrain from posting articles which are not directly related to Bristol or the southwest." In June 2003 the Bristol IMC jointly produced a Community Media Day as a platform for debate and skill sharing. In Urbana-Champaign, Illinois, the IMC has over three hundred volunteers, whose accomplishments include creating a multimedia center in the local post office, starting a free monthly paper funded by local labour groups, producing news segments for community radio, and starting a new radio station.

The tremendous power of the convergent and networked architecture of the Internet and of information and communication technologies has shrunk the battles over resources but has by no means eliminated them. Telephone lines, computers, Internet access, and volunteer expertise and time remain unequally distributed between rich and poor countries and individuals. As Luz Ruiz of Chiapas Media puts it, "Most people in Chiapas don't have access to water, let alone the Internet." Nor do most poor people, and especially women, have the free time to volunteer.

In many centers in poorer countries where there are very few phones, let alone Internet hook-ups, IMC activists work with the existing circuits of social-movement communications. In Chiapas, the birthplace of the Zapatista movement, whose approach to radical grassroots democracy has inspired so many IMCistas, mainstream communications means word of mouth. The Chiapas center uses the Internet mostly as a distribution conduit. Local production of programs is primarily via audiotape and radio.

In Brazil, the national website links several different centers and production teams. The teams also work primarily off-line, through existing networks of community radio and video; through news sheets printed for distribution in schools, workplaces, and neighbourhoods; or through short-term video screenings in poor neighbourhoods or central plazas.

In Ecuador, the IMC has organized three independent film festivals of social documentaries from Latin America. It also encourages website visitors to link to other alternative media, such as the *National Confederation of Indigenous Nationalities of Ecuador* in Ecuador, *Aporrea* in Venezuela, *Znet* in the United States, or the French daily *Red Voltaire*. The Pueblos Originarios, or indigenous peoples team, in Argentina encourages everyone to think of him- or herself as a reporter and a distributor of news, suggesting that visitors distribute IMC content to their friends and workmates.

Begun during protests against the Free Trade Area of the Americas, the Buenos Aires IMC took off during the massive civil disobedience in Argentina against the national government and the International Monetary Fund, in late December 2001. Argentina was once the darling of free-market fundamentalism, with a large and well-educated urban population. However, after more than a decade of IMF-imposed structural adjustment programs, half of the Argentine population lives below the poverty line.

Despite three decades of state and military repression, Argentinians have nonetheless maintained a strong tradition of social-movement organizing, radical journalism, and media making. The younger generation now involved with Argentina Indymedia draws from these traditions. Their philosophy, that every person is a reporter, was first articulated by Rodolfo Walsh, a famous Argentinian journalist who was killed by the military junta in 1977. The IMC team also has adapted the practices of the radical filmmakers of the 1970s, whose work encouraged dialogue between workers and neighbourhood militants, intellectuals, and journalists.

The new generation of Argentinian IMC media makers facilitates unemployed workers, youth, neighbourhood activists, and the Mapuche, an aboriginal group, in documenting their lives and struggles on video. Supporting the voice of the voiceless has become all the more crucial as the Argentinian state has regrouped and begun a campaign of divide and rule, vilifying and marginalizing the most militant of the social movements that had protested against them. In June 2005 a journalist with Indymedia Rosario was attacked, and his camera stolen, by groups supportive of President Nestor Kirchner. Rosario had been reporting on a protest by the unemployed and by human rights organizations.

THE THREAT OF A GOOD EXAMPLE

It is not just in Argentina where the authorities have taken exception to what Noam Chomsky calls "the threat of a good example." The IMC has been consistently raided by national and international security agencies in the United States, Canada, Italy, the United Kingdom, and Spain. Several sites, especially the global IMC Israel and Palestine IMC, have been systematically attacked. In 2002, in advance of the European Union meetings in Barcelona, the Spanish police announced they were tracking the IMC and other alternative information networks. In October 2004, just before a European Social Forum meeting on communications rights, the FBI seized the hard drives of the Ahimsa servers in the United States and the United Kingdom, claiming that the action was part of an "international terrorism investigation." The servers linked twenty IMC sites and several Internet radio streams. After an international solidarity campaign, in which the Electronic Frontier Foundation provided legal support, the servers were returned and the IMC discovered that the Italian government had prompted the actions.

The IMC's tactical media innovations also make the sites vulnerable. For example, the innovative text messaging and Internet reports during the New York protests against the Republican National Convention provided both demonstrators and police with easily accessible, up-to-the-minute reports. The same week, the Justice Department demanded that the IMC service provider hand over records listing names of Republican delegates. Despite the intimidation, IMC editor Gupta told *Democracy Now!* reporter Jeremy Scahill that it was a significant step forward in tactical resistance. Gupta also told Scahill that "Technology can't substitute for good organizing."

Finally, IMC activists face the same threat of violence that increasingly is faced by journalists around the world. On October 27, 2006, New York City-based IMCista Brad Will was killed when progovernment attackers opened fire on protesters in Oaxaca, Mexico. Brad, a documentary filmmaker, died with his video camera in his arms. In response to his death, the New York City IMC published this statement: "[Brad Will] was part of this movement of independent journalists who go where the corporate media do not or stay long after they have gone. Perhaps Brad's death would have been prevented if Mexican, international, and U.S. media corporations had told the stories of the Oaxacan people."

CREATING THE FUTURE IN THE PRESENT

As the neoliberal project has fostered the extension of corporate media worldwide, it has also created conditions of radical possibility. In a short time, the IMC has grown into a worldwide communications network that provides a vital resource for social justice movements amid the encroaching global corporate enclosure of media. It represents a qualitative shift from a scattering of media "alternatives" to an autonomous multimedia network that is independent of the ownership of global corporations and governments and of the logics and languages of the mainstream "stenographers to power."

The activists in the IMC network and in sister networks such as the ones mentioned in this book are providing insights into what a truly democratic and participatory media environment could look like. Many are also realizing the need to challenge the global corporate lords of media directly and to link with national and transnational efforts to take back our common communications resources.

In January 2007, as I write this, several IMC members are in Nairobi, Kenya to support an Indymedia convergence during the seventh annual World Social Forum. The intention of the convergence is to provide a local communications space for reports on the conference, training workshops, and support for developing the local Kenya IMC. The global IMC also will link other sites that are taking up the issues from the Forum.

In addition, IMCs and their allies from Europe, North America, and Latin America have been involved in the World Summit on the Information Society, a UN-sponsored forum about the future of global media and communications, which was held in Geneva in 2003 and in Tunisia in 2004. And in the United States, members of local IMCs have participated in a number of different national media reform and media justice conferences, including those sponsored by Free Press, Action Coalition for Media Education, and the Grassroots Radio Conference.

Building a new global system of communications that is responsive to, representative of, and accountable to people all over the world presents no end of challenges. Removing the first lines of electronic gates is only the beginning; the deep divisions among us—of class, gender, race, and colonial history—continue both on- and off-line. What is remarkable is how much the IMC continues to morph and change, to find collective solutions to problems, and to develop new kinds of collaboration.

> **"Until the lions can tell their own story,**
> **tales of the hunt will always glorify the hunter."**
> *—African proverb*

Open Publishing in a Nutshell

Matthew Arnison

It was 1999, one week before the protests in Seattle, and the first Indymedia website was almost ready.

Seattle was buzzing, with tens of thousands of global justice protestors converging on a key meeting of the World Trade Organisation. The Independent Media Center was expecting five hundred media activists, who would report daily using their own daily newspaper, radio and video broadcasts, and the Internet.

I was working from Sydney, Australia, on software running on a computer in Colorado[4], which would publish and broadcast news from the IMC in Seattle.

In 1999 the word *blog* had only just been coined, and blogging software wasn't easy to find. So we adapted our own software from an earlier event,[5] which collected text, audio, and video reports. The software automatically published each report on the front page of the website.

Before we switched on the website, however, we had a question to answer: How could we control access to publishing on the IMC website? How could we protect ourselves against potential spammers and other saboteurs?

We could set a password on the publish button. But how would we get that password to five hundred media activists? Could we even modify the software quickly enough to add password support before the protests started?

Then, we wondered, what would happen if we had no password? Maybe the audience could make its own decision to publish? The IMC collective took the plunge and decided to forego a password and to trust the audience. Later, we coined a name for that experiment in trust: open publishing.[6]

The results were breathtaking. The website exploded with stories reflecting the amazing events of that week in Seattle.

As we had hoped, the decision to go with open publishing on the website helped IMC volunteers keep the front page up to date with breaking news. For example, the corporate media reported as fact a claim by the Seattle police that no rubber bullets had been fired. Within hours, digital photos of rubber bullets

---

4. Free Speech TV (freespeech.org) was a vital collaborator on the first IMC website.

5. The software was called Active (active.org.au), and was written by Community Activist Technology (cat.org.au).

6. M. Arnison, "Open publishing is the same as free software," purplebark.net/maffew/cat/openpub.html, March 2001.

that the police had fired appeared on Indymedia. The corporate media had to change its story.[7]

But open publishing also allowed something we didn't expect: Reports began appearing from people outside the IMC. Witnesses from the blockades were writing their own stories on the Indymedia website. Reading those stories from Sydney, I could feel the diversity and passion of those involved. It was a brilliant contrast to the cold, patronising, and narrow view of the same events relayed by the Sydney media.

After Seattle, there were plenty of people keen to repeat the experiment. In April 2000 the global justice movement arrived in Washington, D.C., to protest at a meeting of the International Monetary Fund and the World Bank. A Bolivian consultant for the World Bank was walking to work and happened to pass by one of the protest groups. Just at that moment, the police swept up everyone on the block: protestors, journalists, passersby, and the consultant. They were all detained for a day.

Before this happened, the consultant hadn't really understood the protests. But afterward he wrote a fascinating story about what had happened to him and how it changed his views about the activists and what the World Bank does. He published his story on the D.C. Indymedia website.

Open publishing certainly helps Indymedia gather more stories, both good and bad. But beyond the sheer number of stories lies a more important trend. I think open publishing allows Indymedia to find and promote completely different kinds of stories—stories from unexpected people, or people with a vital mix of energy and first-person insight.

There are some stories we only hear when we trust the audience to tell them. Those are the stories of open publishing.

For more of my rants, see my home page, purplebark.net/maffew.
You may copy and distribute this article as long as you include the Internet address of the original (purplebark.net/maffew/cat/openpub-summary.html) in a way that the whole audience can see. Please let me know if you do reproduce it somewhere, especially if you make changes to it.

"A riot is the language of the unheard."
—Martin Luther King, Jr.

---

7. G. Hyde, "Independent Media Centers: Cyber-Subversion and the Alternative Press" firstmonday.org/issues/issue7_4/hyde/, First Monday, 7:4, April 2002.

21

CREATIVE COMMONS

SPEAKING ABOUT YOUR CREATIVITY LEGALLY: COPYRIGHT, COPYLEFT, AND CREATIVE COMMONS

Mia Garlick

"The sage does not hoard. The more she helps others,
the more she benefits herself."
—Lao Tzu

Artists, musicians, filmmakers, animators, writers, and all creators do what comes naturally to them—they get inspired by their surroundings and experiences, experiment with different forms of artistic expression, learn from collegial feedback, and thrive on audience appreciation. For many, the fact that nearly every creative step they take has legal ramifications is learned only in hindsight, after something has gone wrong: A creator receives a threatening letter from a lawyer or feels ripped off by a verbal business deal that goes sour, or a creator has signed a contract that requires a transfer of all rights in their work to another person or entity, but then later wants greater control over how their work is exploited.

To avoid or at least minimize the chances of something going wrong, knowledge about the law that most applies to your work—copyright law—can go a long way toward helping you understand your options. An understanding of the impact of copyright law on creativity is particularly important in the digital age. Digital technologies offer incredible and unique opportunities to create, produce, and distribute your creativity in new and different ways, and to an international audience. Knowing your legal rights and options lets you take advantage of these benefits whilst minimizing the potential downsides.

COPYRIGHT LAW: THE LAW THAT APPLIES TO MOST CREATIVITY

Copyright law has two main purposes. On the one hand, it grants creators exclusive rights to their own works as a reward and incentive to them to create. On the other hand, it is intended to encourage the dissemination of those works. The inherent tension is apparent: More people may create if given strong legal rights, but stringent legal protections may interfere with the works' dissemination. Similarly, if works are protected less stringently, they might be shared more readily throughout society but people may be discouraged from creating the works in the first place. Much of the copyright debate has been about how to achieve the proper balance between these competing interests.

WHAT IS COPYRIGHT?

Copyright is best described as a bundle of exclusive rights. In the United States, these rights control the following activities: copying a work, making derivative works or adaptations of a work, distributing a work, publicly displaying a work, and publicly performing or transmitting a work over the Internet. There are several exceptions to copyright, the most important of which, under U.S. law, is known as fair use (see sidebar "More About Fair Use").

Here are some examples: I wrote this article and therefore, thanks to copyright law, I can control who may photocopy or publish it. If a band makes a recording of one of its songs, band members can rely on copyright law to stop someone from posting it to a website for others to download without their permission. A scriptwriter or novelist has control, under copyright law, over who may make a film of the script or novel. Similarly, a painter can prevent a gallery from publicly exhibiting his or her work without permission and can stop someone from making postcards of their art.

There also are some activities not covered by copyright. I may, for example, read your book at the bookstore or at my friend's house without violating your copyright. Once I have bought a movie, I can lend it to a friend to watch. We can also play a band's music at a private party—all without touching on any of copyright's exclusive rights.

WHAT IS PROTECTED BY COPYRIGHT?

According to the U.S. Copyright Act, copyright applies to "original works of authorship that are fixed in a tangible form" and that come within specific categories of protected works. These include writings, such as books, articles, blogs, and software; artwork, such as paintings, drawings, graphs, and sculptures; movies, video games, and other audiovisual materials; lyrics and musical compositions; plays and choreography; sound recordings; and architectural works.

More About "Fair Use"

What's called "fair use" is an important exception to U.S. copyright protection. But it can be difficult to identify in advance whether something is a "fair use." Four fair use factors serve as guidelines to help U.S. courts determine whether something is a fair use:

- The purpose and character of the use, including whether the use is of a commercial nature or is for nonprofit educational purposes
- The nature of the copyrighted work (i.e., is the work highly creative and so close to the core of copyright protection, deserving of a high level of protection, or is it highly factual in nature?)
- The amount and substantiality of the portion used in relation to the original work as a whole
- How the "fair use" might affect the market value of the original copyrighted work

Applying these factors, courts have ruled it is a "fair use" to make personal copies of TV programs for later viewing, or to provide a search engine that generates thumbnails of others' photographs that people could download and print. Courts have ruled it is not "fair use," however, for the online music service Napster to enable users to share music files or for another early digital music provider — MP3.com — to offer "digital locker" services.

In the art world, Barbie dolls were the focus of another "fair use" case. The manufacturer Mattel took on "artsurdist" Tom Forsythe for selling photographs of Barbie dolls juxtaposed against various kitchen appliances in threatening poses. Forsythe said he wanted to "critique the objectification of women associated with Barbie, and to lambaste the conventional beauty myth and the societal acceptance of women as objects because this is what Barbie embodies." The court held that Forsythe made a "fair use" of Barbie because he completely transformed her meanings.

By way of contrast, Jeff Koons's three-dimensional sculpture of Garfield's friend "Odie" was held *not* to be a "fair use" because the court found that Koons was providing social comment on how the mass production of both commodities and media images has caused a deterioration of the quality of society; he was not commenting on "Odie" itself.

Because "fair use" can be difficult to identify in advance and can often involve lawyers, many people speak of the "chilling effect" it has on people of modest means who may otherwise be prepared to wade into the boundaries of "fair use."

For a work to have copyright protection, there are two important preconditions. First, the work must be original or creative. The telephone white pages, for example, have been held to not meet that criterion because the alphabetical ordering of names and addresses was considered too obvious to merit copyright protection. Second, the work must be not only original but also tangible. A conversation or even an impromptu, unwritten speech will not be eligible for copyright protection. Also not copyrightable, most likely because of its lack of tangible form, is anti-object artist Le Ann Wilchusky's performance piece in which colored streamers were dropped from an airplane to "call attention to the higher spirit of mankind" by "sculpting in space."

Original works that meet the two preconditions of originality and tangibility are automatically protected by "all rights reserved" copyright, meaning that unless a copyright owner signals otherwise, persons encountering a copyrighted work must assume that they have only very limited rights to use the work—for example, under "fair use."

HOW TO GET A COPYRIGHT

After your work is created, you don't have to do a thing to get a copyright. Copyright protection attaches automatically whenever you commit pen to paper—or the modern-day equivalents. For U.S. creators, however, it may be advisable to register your copyright with the U.S. Copyright Office, so that you can properly enforce your rights. For information, check out the Copyright Office's website at copyright.gov.

A copyright can protect even the tiniest bit of your work. In a recent case, a two-second sample was taken from the song "Get Off Your Ass and Jam" by George Clinton Jr. and the Funkadelics. The sample was then looped to create a seven-second segment and was used five times (for a total of thirty-five seconds) in the song "100 Miles and Running," which was included on the sound track for the movie *I Got the Hook Up*. The court held that the sample was an infringement of copyright. The judge said, "Get a license or do not sample."

WHEN YOU MAY NOT BE THE FIRST OWNER OF COPYRIGHT:
WORK FOR HIRE AND TRANSFERS OF OWNERSHIP

The creator is the first owner of copyright of his or her own work, with two exceptions. The first exception involves what is known in the United States as a work for hire. There are two situations in which a copyrighted work may be considered a work for hire: when a copyrighted work is made by an employee within the scope of employment; and when a work comes within one of nine specifically identified categories in the U.S. Copyright Act, the creator has been specially commissioned to create the work, and the creator has agreed in writing that the work is a work for hire. The categories of works for hire mentioned in the statute include motion pictures, atlases, translations, test questions and answers, compilations, and instructional works. For both employee-created works and specially commissioned works, copyright law operates automatically

Copyright and the "Digital Threat"

Because notions of copyright are largely overlooked by the general public (how many people read the copyright notice on a CD or a book or in film credits?), most people equate the scope of their permitted use of a copyrighted item with the scope of what they can do with that product. Today people are remixing, mashing-up, resyncing, and sharing as never before. This often clashes with the business interests of copyright-based industries.

The initial reaction to what the U.S. Congress termed a "unique digital threat" by big media players was to bring a variety of infringement actions to prove that existing laws applied with equal force to the online space. In fact, lawsuits were brought not only against various providers such as Napster and Grokster, all of whom provided services that enabled the public to share music online, but also against hundreds of individual file sharers.

At the same time as existing laws were rigorously applied to the digital world, the content industry has successfuly sought new copyright laws that grant additional protection to protect copyrighted works online, from hackers. New laws were introduced to protect the digital locks (called "digital rights management") that copyright owners wanted to use to protect access to their works and also to enforce their copyright in the online world. This made it illegal, for example, to hack iTunes' technology that prevents users from playing iTunes tracks on anything other than an iPod or, for example, to hack DVD encryption so that they can play a DVD on a Linux-run computer.

Around the time that these new copyright laws took effect, the term of copyright protection in the United States was also extended by twenty years. In effect, the term of protection for most works was raised from life of the author plus fifty years, to life of the author plus seventy years. If we assume that the average life expectancy of an U.S. citizen is around seventy-five years, this takes the term of copyright protection to between one hundred forty-five and one hundred sixty-five years. In addition, works for hire or anonymous or pseudonymous works (which had been published) had their copyright term extended from seventy-five years to ninety-five years. The extension was deemed necessary to keep U.S. law in line with the copyright protections given in Europe. As a result, countless works that would have fallen into the public domain (and provided a resource for creative reuse and remixing) remain under copyright.

In summary, whether these technological and legal developments are a boon or a curse depends on the kind of artist you are. For artists and creators with wholly new and unique ideas and forms of expression and for those artists who like to maximize control of their works, copyright law is being expanded to grant them greater protection. But for artists and creators who borrow, reinterpret, collaborate, and share by using other people's creative expression as a source of inspiration for their own works, the process has potentially become more complex and fraught with legal risk.

to render the employer or the person who commissioned the work, not the employee or the person who created the work, the first owner of copyright.

The second exception to the general rule occurs when a creator agrees in writing to transfer ownership of work to someone else—for example, when a creator agrees to sign an assignment of copyright. Transfers of ownership must be in writing and must be signed by the creator to be effective.

WHAT DOES COPYRIGHT LAW MEAN FOR CREATORS TODAY?

In brief, it means a contradiction. On the one hand, digital technologies enable creativity at a level of professionalism never experienced before. On the other hand, the increasingly rigorous enforcement and expansion of copyright law (See Sidebar "Copyright and the "Digital Threat") raises serious legal issues for those who seek to take advantage of these technologies. A classic example of the clash involves members of the public using new digital photography technology but then being stopped from having prints made by photo shops, because the photograph looked too professional, too "copyrighted," and the photo shop was worried about getting sued by the professional photographer who presumably took the photos.

Established industry practices have not been developed to take into account individual creators owning and utilizing the means of production. Adobe's Photoshop and Apple's GarageBand and Final Cut Studio enable us all to manipulate images, sounds, and video in new and different ways, to express ourselves creatively by ever more varied and highly professional means. We may get in trouble, though, if we use the new technology to remix, mash up, or comment on existing cultural content.

A TOOL TO ASSIST IN SPREADING CREATIVITY: CREATIVE COMMONS

Creative Commons is a nonprofit organization that offers creators simple legal and technical tools to publish their content more flexibly than is allowed by "all rights reserved" copyright protection. The tools can be utilized to create a public good—content that is freer to access, share, and remix.

THE LICENSES

Creative Commons has devised a system of licenses that lets creators decide what rights they want to reserve or share with the public—in other words, "some rights reserved" as opposed to the default "all rights reserved" level of copyright protection. By giving the option of "some rights reserved" licensing, Creative Commons is working to enable the growth of a pool of precleared content that can be legally ripped, mixed, mashed up, and shared. It allows a breathing space for a participatory culture, as opposed to a wholly permissions-based culture in which people must assume that they have to ask for permission to do anything other than passively receive content,

About Copyleft

Obviously a play on *copyright,* the word *copyleft* is most famously associated with Richard Stallman and his development of the GNU General Public License (GNU GPL), which he drafted sometime in 1984 to render software "free." The term *GNU* is a recursive acronym for "GNU's Not Unix." Unix is a computer operating system originally developed in the 1960s and 1970s by a group of AT&T employees at Bell Labs. The freedom that GNU GPL seeks is the freedom for people to run, copy, distribute, study, change, and improve the software.

As the Free Software Foundation explains, the specific freedoms that the GNU GPL seeks to provide members of the public are:

- The freedom to run the program, for any purpose.
- The freedom to study how the program works and adapt it to a user's needs. Access to the source code is a precondition for this.
- The freedom to redistribute copies so that users can help their neighbor.
- The freedom to improve the program, and to release the user's improvements to the public, so that the entire community benefits. Access to the source code is a precondition for this.

The Free Software Foundation (FSF) is a nonprofit corporation founded in October 1985 by Richard Stallman to support the free software movement, and in particular the GNU project. Of the concept of copyleft the FSF explains:

"*Copyleft* is a general method for making a program or other work free, and requiring all modified and extended versions of the program to be free as well."[1]

In essence, the term *copyleft* describes one particular condition of the GNU-GPL and similar licenses. That is, any derivatives or modifications of the original software must be distributed under the same license terms. This requirement is designed to ensure that "free" software (in the sense of freedom to tinker, not as in price) remains free. The rationale for this provision is that if software were simply made available without any license terms (i.e., dedicated to the public domain), that software could easily be taken by a less ideologically committed person or company and adapted to create a new program that was proprietary, or, in other words, was closed source. The consequence of this is that, while the public would continue to have the benefit of the free original project, it would not have the benefits of any improvements. By requiring that derivatives are relicensed as free software, existing projects are capable of being adapted, rather than having those adaptations "fork" into proprietary licensing systems that are made available on terms that do not recognize the four freedoms above.

---

1. See "What Is Copyleft?" (available at gnu.org/copyleft/copyleft.html).

Legally, however, despite inferences that may be able to be drawn from its name, the copy*left* licensing schema relies on copy*right* law for its enforcement.

Given its background and context, it is not surprising that the terms of the GPL are highly software-specific, in particular because of its requirements relating to source code. Nevertheless, the idea of using a contractual mechanism that relies on copyright law to promote a greater "freedom" than is permitted under default copyright law has been transposed to other, nonsoftware copyrighted works. One of these efforts is Creative Commons.

even if they have the technical tools to do more. The Creative Commons licenses seek to allow content to be used more flexibly, similar to the way free and open source software licenses have worked for software. (See Sidebar "About Copyleft?" on previous page.)

The Creative Commons's core licensing suite comprises six licenses that permit members of the public to use Creative Commons-licensed content on certain terms. All Creative Commons licenses require attribution as specified by the author or licensor. When creators come to the Creative Commons' license generator (creativecommons.org/license), they also can choose from three additional license conditions:

- noncommercial: meaning, feel free to use my work, but please don't make money from it;

- no derivatives: meaning, feel free to use my work, but do not change or adapt it; and

- share alike: meaning, feel free to make derivatives or adapt the work, but if you publish the derivatives, those derivatives must be under the same license as the original work.

These license options produce six different licenses. The least restrictive is the attribution license, which authorizes both verbatim and derivative use for commercial and noncommercial purposes and places no requirements on the licensing of derivatives, provided attribution is given. The most restrictive is the attribution/noncommercial/no derivatives license, which permits only verbatim reproduction and distribution for noncommercial purposes, provided that attribution is given—essentially, noncommercial file sharing.

Once a license is chosen, it is available in three different formats, to ensure that it is easy for the non-legally trained to understand and is capable of harnessing the benefits of search technologies. The three different formats are:

- the human-readable commons deed, which contains a summary of the key license conditions and intuitive icons that symbolize these conditions;

- the lawyer-readable legal code, which is the actual license, designed to be enforced in a court of law; and

- the machine-readable resource description framework, which is metadata that describes the key license terms and allows Creative Commons-licensed content to be searched by license conditions.

These three different formats are then summed up in a "some rights reserved" license button and brief license notice statement (e.g., "This image is licensed to the public under a Creative Commons attribution license"), together with a linkback to the applicable license. The license generator gives the creator the resource description framework metadata that can be cut and pasted and included in a creator's Web page; this generates the "some rights reserved" button and license statement.

EXPERIENCE WITH CREATIVE COMMONS LICENSE ADOPTION TO DATE

Since the release of the core licensing suite in December 2002, the number of LinkBacks[1] to Creative Commons licenses has been steadily increasing. Within a year, there were over one million LinkBacks to Creative Commons licenses. At a year and a half, that number was over 1.8 million. After two years, in December 2004, the number was just about 5 million. As of December 2005 there were over 45 million LinkBacks to Creative Commons licenses, and by December 2006 that number rose to 145 million LinkBacks.

Of the over 145 million Creative Commons licenses that have been applied to content to date, more than two-thirds permit the making of derivative works. This means that a pool of remixable content now exists, thanks to Creative Commons licensing. This remixable content pool would not have been possible in a world in which "all rights reserved" was the only option for creators.

Publishing tools. Creative Commons also has released various publishing tools to help creators take advantage of the cheaper and more accessible digital technologies. For example,

- ccPublisher is a desktop application that enables the drag-and-drop marking of files with Creative Commons licenses, and the uploading of those marked files to the Internet Archive, which offers free hosting to any Creative Commons content.

---

1. Linkbacks provide a useful, though imperfect, measure of identifying the number of Creative Commons-licensed works in existence, because the recommended method for applying a Creative Commons license to an online work is by including an HTML link to the applicable license, together with a human-readable license notification and the metadata on the relevant work. This measure does not, however, measure the total number of license adopters (because the same person may apply a Creative Commons license to more than one work) or of all copyrighted works under a Creative Commons license (because a license may be applied to a variety of works on, say, one website, and because a license may be applied to an off-line work).

- ccMixter.org is a site that enables musicians to upload their tracks and to list any other songs they have remixed or sampled as part of such tracks. Other musicians visiting the site can then refer to this track if they, in turn, sample from or remix it. In this way, everyone can see the relationships and history among the sampled tracks, thereby allowing people to trace the history and referencing among music and encouraging further remixing and reuse.

- In June 2006 Microsoft released a Creative Commons plug-in for its Office applications Word, PowerPoint, and Excel. You can download the plug-in and then, when you next open your Word, PowerPoint, or Excel application, you will have the option to apply the Creative Commons license of your choosing to your document. Once applied, the document will contain both the relevant license metadata and the human-readable license notice and will link to the Commons deed.

- Find tools. Both Yahoo! and Google have incorporated a Creative Commons-specific search as part of their Advanced Search pages. This means a user can search for, say, pictures of the Empire State Building that are available to be adapted and remixed, and the engine will gather images filtered according to that restriction, making it easier to find Creative Commons-licensed works.

For examples of creators who have used one of the Creative Commons licenses, see the examples for "CC Music," "CC Books," "CC Film," and "CC Video" below.

CC MUSIC

From ccMixter to YouTube: In 2004, musician Lisa Debendictis uploaded the vocals for an existing track, "Brilliant Day,"[2] to ccMixter under an Attribution-NonCommercial license. In July 2005, a remix called "Brilliant Daze (days are confused),"[3] also under Attribution-NonCommercial, was posted by a frequent ccMixter remixer who goes by the name of Pat Chilla the Beat Gorilla.

The "Brilliant Daze" remix was picked up and included in the lonelygirl115[4] videos, which posted to YouTube.[5] In keeping with the Attribution requirement, the video included full credits and links to Pat at ccMixter and Lisa's website.[6] The lonelygirl15 video was downloaded

---

2. ccmixter.org/media/files/lisadb/65.

3. ccmixter.org/media/files/beatgorilla/1838.

4. en.wikipedia.org/wiki/Lonelygirl15.

5. youtube.com/watch?v=iR04JP81HPo.

6. Id., click "More" on the information box about the video.

over 450,000 times and became an Internet sensation. Recently the inventors of lonelygir115, respecting the NonCommercial clause of the license, have been in touch with musicians Lisa and Pat to work out payments for use of the work in a commercial setting.[7]

Philharmonia Baroque Orchestra: In mid-2006, the Philharmonia Baroque Orchestra[8] decided to eschew traditional music distribution methods and release its performance of Handel's 1736 opera *Atalanta* exclusively through the Internet record label Magnatune.[9] Magnatune releases all its artists' music online in both streaming and MP3 format under a Creative Commons Attribution-NonCommercial-ShareAlike license and sells albums. The orchestra's decision was prompted by disappointing CD sales; now the music can be enjoyed by streaming at no cost, or by download, or as a CD-on-demand. The *Wall Street Journal* quotes Music Director Nicholas McGegan as saying that the Internet "has potentially given the industry a tremendous shot in the arm" by enabling orchestras to reach "new audiences, including ones that are unlikely to hear you in person."[10]

CC BOOKS

Kembrew McLeod,[11] an assistant professor at the University of Iowa's Department of Communication Studies, wrote a book, *Freedom of Expression,* that was released online in PDF format under a Creative Commons Attribution-NonCommercial-ShareAlike 2.0 license[12] and made available for sale under an "All Rights Reserved" copyright in hardcopy.[13]

Because McLeod's book was physically available only in the United States and Japan, he benefited from his work's being freely available in a PDF version that virtually anybody could read or even print, using Adobe's free Reader software. McLeod received feedback from someone at a UN office in Switzerland, who shared his research interests, as well as from others from various European, Asian, and African countries. Because of the new global interest, soon after the book was released, Professor McLeod was invited to speak at an event in Budapest, called: "RE:activism: Re-drawing the boundaries of activism in a new media environment."[14]

---

7. lisadebenedictis.com/?p=101.

8. philharmonia.org.

9. magnatune.com.

10. philharmonia.org/WSJ.pdf.

11. kembrew.com.

12. kembrew.com/books/index.html.

13. tinyurl.com/3bbsb8.

14. creativecommons.org/text/kembrewmcleod.

CC FILM

CC Film: The Documentary *Teach*—In 1999, Creative Commons Director Davis Guggenheim (who recently directed Al Gore's the Academy Award-nominated film *An Inconvenient Truth*) and producer Julia Schachter undertook an ambitious project: documenting the experiences of teachers in the Los Angeles Unified School District. In examining the trials and rewards that come with educating children, the filmmakers created two powerful documentaries: the Peabody Award-winning *The First Year* and *Teach,* a short film created to attract talented and passionate people to the teaching profession.

In February 2006, Guggenheim and Schachter made *Teach* available under a Creative Commons Attribution-NonCommercial-NoDerivatives license and offered the film online to the public, free.[15] The filmmakers explained that the CC license was the perfect tool for artists looking to have their work be more freely available to the general public. In addition, they noted that the availability of a NoDerivatives option enabled them to preserve the integrity of the film subjects' stories.

CC VIDEO

CC Video: *The Lonely Island Trio*—Andy Samberg, Jorma Taccone, and Akiva Schaffer are three actors/writers who comprise The Lonely Island,[16] a Los Angeles-based comedy collective. The three released the majority of their music and video shorts online under a Creative Commons Attribution-NonCommercial-ShareAlike license. In early 2005, the trio shot a TV pilot for Fox, but the network rejected the show. So, the group posted the full video on their CC-licensed site. The video became a viral hit and eventually landed all three performers jobs on *Saturday Night Live* (where they went on to create such fan favorites as "Lazy Sunday" and "Young Chuck Norris"). You can read more about CC and the ascent of *The Lonely Island* in *Wired.*[17]

NOW, GO FORTH AND CREATE

By understanding the nature of copyright law, the trends of technological and legal developments, and your options, you can minimize your legal exposure while ensuring that the law will help rather than hinder you.

> **"All creation is a mine, and every man a miner."**
> —*Abraham Lincoln (1860)*

---

15. creativecommons.org/teach.

16. thelonelyisland.com.

17. wired.com/news/culture/0,69042-0.html.

Did You Say "Intellectual Property"?
It's a Seductive Mirage

Richard M. Stallman

It has become fashionable to toss copyright, patents, and trademarks—three separate and different entities involving three separate and different sets of laws—into one pot and call it "intellectual property." The distorting and confusing term did not arise by accident. Companies that gain from the confusion promoted it. The clearest way out of the confusion is to reject the term entirely.

According to Professor Mark Lemley, now of the Stanford Law School, the widespread use of the term *intellectual property* is a fad that followed the 1967 founding of the World Intellectual Property Organization and only became really common in recent years. (WIPO is formally a UN organization, but in fact it represents the interests of the holders of copyrights, patents, and trademarks.)

The term carries a bias that is not hard to see: It suggests thinking about copyright, patents, and trademarks by analogy with property rights for physical objects. In fact, this analogy is at odds with the legal philosophies of copyright law, of patent law, and of trademark law, but only specialists know that. These laws actually are not much like physical property law, but use of this term leads legislators to change the laws to be more so. Because that is the change desired by the companies that exercise copyright, patent, and trademark powers, the bias of *intellectual property* suits them.

The bias is enough reason to reject the term, and people have often asked me to propose some other name for the overall category—or have proposed their own alternatives (often humorous). Suggestions include IMPs, for imposed monopoly privileges, and GOLEMs, for government-originated legally enforced monopolies. Some speak of "exclusive rights regimes," but referring to restrictions as rights is doublethink too.

Some of these alternative names would be an improvement, but it is a mistake to replace *intellectual property* with any other term. A different name will not address the term's deeper problem: overgeneralization. There is no such unified thing as intellectual property—it is a mirage. The only reason people think it makes sense as a coherent category is that widespread use of the term gives that impression.

The term *intellectual property* is at best a catchall to lump together disparate laws. Nonlawyers who hear one term applied to these various laws tend to assume they are based on a common principle, and function similarly. Nothing could be further from the case. These laws originated separately, evolved differently, cover different activities, have different rules, and raise different public policy issues.

Copyright law was designed to promote authorship and art, and it covers the details of expression of a work. Patent law was intended to promote the publication of useful ideas, at the price of giving the one who publishes an idea a temporary monopoly over it—a price that may be worth paying in some fields and not in others. Trademark law, by contrast, was not intended to promote any particular way of acting but simply to enable buyers to know what they are buying. Legislators, under the influence of "intellectual property," however, have turned it into a scheme that provides incentives for advertising.

Because these laws developed independently, they are different in every detail as well as in their basic purposes and methods. Thus, if you learn some fact about copyright law, you'd be wise to assume that patent law is different—you'll rarely go wrong!

People often say intellectual property when they really mean some larger or smaller category. For instance, rich countries often impose unjust laws on poor countries to squeeze money out of them. Some of these laws are intellectual property laws, and others are not; nonetheless, critics of the practice often grab for that label because it has become familiar to them. By using it, they misrepresent the nature of the issue. It would be better to use an accurate term, such as *legislative colonization,* that gets to the heart of the matter.

Laypeople are not alone in being confused by this term. Even law professors who teach these laws are lured and distracted by the seductiveness of the term *intellectual property* and make general statements that conflict with facts they know. For example, one professor wrote in 2006, "Unlike their descendants who now work the floor at WIPO, the framers of the U.S. Constitution had a principled, procompetitive attitude to intellectual property. They knew rights might be necessary, but . . . they tied Congress's hands, restricting its power in multiple ways."

That statement refers to article 1, section 8, clause 8 in the U.S. Constitution, which authorizes copyright law and patent law. That clause, though, has nothing to do with trademark law. The term *intellectual property* led that professor into a false generalization.

The term *intellectual property* also leads to simplistic thinking. It leads people to focus on the meager commonality in form of these disparate laws—that they create artificial privileges for certain parties—and to disregard the details that form their substance: the specific restrictions each law places on the public and the consequences that result. This simplistic focus on the form encourages what we might call an economistic approach to all these issues.

Economics operates here, as it often does, as a vehicle for unexamined values (such as that amount of production matters, whereas freedom and way of life do not) and factual assumptions that are mostly false (such as that copyright on music supports musicians, or that patents on drugs support lifesaving research).

Another problem is that, at the broad scale of "intellectual property," the specific issues raised by the various laws become nearly invisible. These issues arise from the specifics of each law—precisely what the term *intellectual property* encourages people to ignore. For instance, one issue relating to copyright law is the question of whether music sharing should be allowed. Patent law has nothing to do with this. Patent law raises issues such as whether poor countries should be allowed to produce lifesaving drugs and then sell them inexpensively to save lives. Copyright law has nothing to do with such matters.

Neither of these issues is solely economic in nature, and their noneconomic aspects are very different; using the shallow economic overgeneralization as the basis for considering them means ignoring the differences. Putting the two laws in the "intellectual property" pot obstructs clear thinking about each one.

Thus, any opinions about the issue of intellectual property, and any generalizations about this supposed category, are almost surely foolish. If you think all those laws cover one issue, you will tend to choose your opinions from a selection of sweeping overgeneralizations, none of which is any good.

If you want to think clearly about the issues raised by patents, copyrights, or trademarks, the first step is to forget the idea of lumping them together and to treat them as separate topics. The second step is to reject the narrow perspectives and simplistic picture that the term *intellectual property* suggests. Consider each of these issues separately, in its fullness, and you have a chance of considering them well.

And when it comes to reforming WIPO, among other things, let's call for changing its name.

"If there is to be any peace, it will come through being, not having."
—*Henry Miller*

22

POLICY

MAKING MEDIA POLICY PUBLIC

Ben Scott, Jeff Perlstein, and David Mathison

"The hand that rules the press, the radio, the screen
and the far spread magazine, rules the country."
—*Judge Learned Hand, Memorial service for Justice Brandeis, December 21, 1942*

A small handful of huge corporations dominates American media—in both production and distribution.

We are going to show you why this is an extremely bad situation, and then tell you what all of us can do about it.

When Ben Bagdikian published the first edition of *The Media Monopoly* in 1983, the United States had fifty dominant media corporations. When the fifth edition of his book was published in 1997, that number had shrunk to ten. As of this writing, only six corporations control most major media in the United States. They are General Electric, Time Warner Inc., The Walt Disney Company, Viacom, CBS, and The News Corporation, the latter headquartered in Australia. According to Bagdikian, these corporations "decide what most citizens will or will not learn."[1]

Worse than the change in corporate media ownership concentration is the change in motivation, for private profit has eclipsed public service. Today's media system is set up to maximize profit for a handful of large companies, and does so extraordinarily well. The system, however, is a disaster for the communication requirements of a healthy society.

---

1. *The New Media Monopoly,* by Ben Bagdikian. Beacon Press, 2004. P. 14.

In other words, corporate inbreeding is not only pervasive and exclusionary, but antidemocratic.

The problem is not personal; it is systemic. Even if Rupert Murdoch and Sumner Redstone were to retire tomorrow, the operations of their companies, News Corporation and Viacom respectively, would not change significantly. Whoever replaced the two men would follow the same cues, with more or less the same results, because the primary catalysts of the system would remain intact.

To change the motivations of those who control the media, we have to transform the media system itself. We have to rewrite the rules that govern the system and then put the system to work for the people.

The first step in doing this is to understand how the iron-clad system was forged.

HOW WAS OUR MEDIA SYSTEM CREATED?

Conventional wisdom would have us believe that our media system is the result of competition between entrepreneurs fighting it out in the free market.

Wrong.

In reality, each of the giant media dominating firms is the recipient of massive corporate welfare. Explicit government policies, regulations, and subsidies have paved the avenue down which they have strolled to their gargantuan financial success.

We citizens, through our elected representatives, our lobbyists, and our own lack of watchfulness, have authorized our government to lease our public resources to media companies, such as monopoly licenses to the public airwaves for radio, television, and the wireless spectrum. We have allowed rights-of-way franchises to dig up our streets to build out cable and telecommunications infrastructure, okayed direct benefits to private interests from publicly financed technologies like the Internet, and permitted nearly unlimited copyright protection that has stifled creativity . . . all these actions being performed for the profits of a few companies.

When the government provides a firm with one or more of these services, it is virtually a license to print money.

PUBLIC INTEREST OBLIGATIONS

In exchange for the license to earn billions of dollars from the public's resources, broadcasters formerly were required to meet a number of public interest obligations. The Communications Act of 1934, for one, required commercial broadcasters "to operate in the public interest and to afford reasonable opportunity for the discussion of conflicting views of issues of public importance." The goal was to promote localism, diversity, democratic deliberation, and public accountability.

Therefore, as part of their license renewal process, every three years broadcasters had to demonstrate in community hearings how they had served the public interest. These hearings dealt with programs about public affairs, children's education, and election coverage.

Although this did not result in what some think was a mythical "golden age of media," thanks to these mechanisms media outlets certainly became a great deal more accountable to their local communities than they might have been otherwise.

Fast forward to today. Over the past three decades, media conglomerates have gradually lobbied our government to do away with these basic requirements. Broadcasters renew their licenses once every eight years (not three), simply by mailing a "postcard" to the FCC. There are no community hearings to judge how well the broadcasters have served the public. Nor are broadcasters any longer required to cover public affairs, or to give free airtime to qualified political candidates in the weeks preceding elections.

Moreover, the broadcasters are increasingly bending the few rules that have survived. To meet requirements that stations broadcast three hours of children's educational programming each week, they have aired such programs as *NFL Under the Helmet* and *Miracle Pets*.

SELF-SERVING POLICYMAKING

The process of making policies that control the media has, in recent decades, been among the most corrupt in Congress. Decisions that determine the structure of our media system, and indirectly its content, are made by a handful of legislators, regulators, and industry lobbyists.

A report by the Center for Public Integrity documents more than $1.1 billion spent by the communications industries to lobby Congress and influence elections between 1998 and 2004. This figure is more than double the amount spent by lobbyists for the much larger oil and gas industry.[2]

The result? Governmental policies that serve the needs of a tiny group of big commercial interests. Most Americans have no idea that these policies have been made in their name and without their informed consent, because indeed they are not informed. After all, the companies charged with doing the informing are the same ones that sought the policy changes. Typically, these policies, if covered at all, are covered in the corporate-owned press, and are treated as business stories of importance to owners, managers, and shareholders, not as political stories of vital interest and concern to participants in a democracy.

Here's an example.

In passing the Telecommunications Act of 1996 during the Clinton Administration, the Republican-controlled Congress removed the limit on how many radio stations a single company could own. A provision in the Act to remove the limits was written by radio industry lobbyists, was tacked onto the bill by a pliant legislator, and sailed through Congress without an iota of discussion or press coverage.

As a consequence of this single provision in the Act, a wave of ownership consolidation swept over the land, and radio became the province of a small number of giant firms. Clear Channel

---

2. John Dunbar, Daniel Lathrop, and Robert Morlino, "Networks of Influence: The political power of the communications industry," openairwaves.com/telecom/report.aspx?aid=405, October 28, 2004.

alone grew to own over twelve hundred stations, up from the legal limit of forty stations before the passage of the 1996 law; the previous cap was twenty FM and twenty AM stations. In addition, competition has declined, local radio news and programming have been decimated, music playlists have been homogenized often from afar, and the amount of advertising has skyrocketed, from eleven to twelve minutes per hour in the early 1990s to seventeen to nineteen minutes per hour after the Act was passed.

Bagdikian called this 1996 Act a "major accomplishment" for media corporations. The law they crafted increased their power and abolished long-standing regulations. "In the process, the power of media firms, along with all corporate power in general, has diminished the place of individual citizens."[3]

A little bit of legislation can go a long way, no matter who is in the White House.

MEDIA MONOPOLY PROTECTION RACKETS

Corporations are increasingly crafting and pushing legislation to protect their own cartels, a combination of commercial enterprises created to limit competition and fix prices. Here are just a few examples:

- Media companies pushed laws in fifteen states prohibiting towns from building, owning, or operating their own municipal broadband networks. (See chapter 19.)

- In 2000, the National Association of Broadcasters (NAB), representing the radio industry, argued that the new low-power FM (LPFM) stations the FCC was finally proposing to allow, which, at 100 watts, were the equivalent power of a light bulb, would interfere with huge stations with 50,000 watt flamethrowers. "Ridiculous," argued some of us. Nonetheless, the Democratic Congress passed a law that limited low-power FM to small towns. A subsequent $2 million taxpayer-supported study known as MITRE found there to be no interference. Now a bill pending in Congress, the Local Community Radio Act of 2007, would allow these stations, at least in midsized towns. (See chapter 16.)

- Phone and cable companies are waging war against community control over video franchising. In California alone, telecommunications companies spent $20 million pushing legislation that would usurp power from local authorities. (See chapter 18.)

- The Recording Industry Association of America (RIAA), Soundscan, and the Copyright Royalty Board all want exorbitant royalty rates for Internet radio stations, potentially destroying this diverse programming outlet for independent music. (See chapter 6.)

---

3. *The New Media Monopoly*, p. 9.

- In 2007, the Postal Regulatory Commission approved magazine postage increases based on a rate structure proposed by Time Warner, publisher of *Time* and *People* magazines. The plan gives discounts to large publishers while increasing postage rates for small magazines, thus threatening their survival.

- In 2006, telephone and cable companies spent more than $175 million trying to defeat Net Neutrality, nicknamed the "First Amendment" of the Internet (see more on that battle, below).

SOLUTION: A THREE-PRONGED APPROACH

Changing the media structure as it now exists requires a broad-based movement that can take on "organized money" with "organized people" and that can curtail the media corporations' governmental proxies. Historically, building such a movement has focused on harnessing the leadership and wisdom within local communities, in tandem with national policy experts and coalitions. At the same time, such movements as civil rights, women's suffrage, and anti-Apartheid have addressed the race, gender, and class inequalities within their own group as well as within the larger society. This approach establishes the integrity that draws people in greater and greater numbers to mobilize around strategic initiatives at both local and national levels.

A movement to change the current media structure involves three interrelated components:

- **Expanding Independent Media:** Expanding independent media widens the body of news and information available to the public. You are encouraged to support, watch/listen, and participate in local community media initiatives. To make your own media, see the related chapters in this book, and visit bethemedia.com/resources.htm to find independent media sources.

- **Increasing Media Literacy and Education:** It is critical for participants in any media reform movement to understand, analyze, and evaluate the content and structure of today's media. Among the general public, acquiring media literacy is one of the best ways to combat the power of corporate media. Critical thinking changes the way people perceive media, content, and its creators' motivations. Again, check out bethemedia.com/resources.htm.

- **Making Media Policy Public:** To change the media system, we, whether we are full-time activists or outraged citizens with limited time, need to open up the media policymaking process to public scrutiny, and then provide a forum for public participation and opportunities for meaningful action. For example, citizens can contact their local leaders or Congressional representatives, start a local media reform organization, or write focused and persuasive letters to the editor. For more ideas, keep reading . . .

THE RISE IN PUBLIC PARTICIPATION IN MEDIA POLICYMAKING

Historically, media activism has seen some notable upsurges, sporadic mass organizing, and a few populist victories and near wins, such as the battle between public and private interests during the early days of radio; for more on the latter, see Robert W. McChesney's book *Telecommunications, Mass Media, and Democracy: The Battle for the Control of U.S. Broadcasting, 1928–1935.*

Over the last few decades, media policy has increasingly been forged behind the scenes and inside the Washington Beltway by the media industry in league with their armies of lobbyists. In 2002, however, widespread public outrage over proposed media ownership rules favoring more consolidation brought together millions of people from across the political spectrum, from Senators Ted Kennedy (D-Mass.) and Trent Lott (R-Miss.) and CNN's liberal founder Ted Turner to conservative media mogul Barry Diller, along with scores of local and national organizations as diverse as NOW and the NRA. The importance of the situation gradually sank in, as these people and allied forces realized that failure to reform the media system threatened the ability of *all* of us to advance social reforms in any other sector.

Their outrage galvanized the burgeoning media reform movement, unified broad-based political goals, and laid the building blocks of a social movement. Longtime activists and organizers expanded their membership, held public hearings, staged demonstrations, and planned new strategies to link up with policy advocates in statehouses around the land and in Washington, D.C. The coalition that formed, one driven by grassroots energy and channeled into action by experienced advocates, proved exceptionally potent and enduring.

It also led to a historic victory.

PROMETHEUS RADIO VS. THE FEDERAL COMMUNICATIONS COMMISSION

In 2003, pro-business regulators at the Federal Communication Commission, with Michael Powell as its chair, were busily drafting rules to allow even greater concentration of ownership and further reduce public interest limits on ownership of media outlets. Against all odds, the newly fortified coalition of public interest and activist groups banded together in a remarkable campaign to stop the proposed rule changes.

With the help of Common Cause, the Center for Digital Democracy, MoveOn, Free Press, and others, including the NRA, more than two million people contacted the FCC and Congress in opposition to Chairman Powell's push. A large group of plaintiffs, represented by the Media Access Project, took the FCC to court over the rule changes. The plaintiffs included the Prometheus Radio Project, a small but influential nonprofit organization that helps communities build Low Power FM radio stations (for more on Prometheus, see chapter 16). On September 3, 2003, in Philadelphia, the Third Circuit Court of Appeals found in favor of Prometheus, staying, not changing, the rules on ownership.

Thankfully, the media ownership rules today, flawed though they are, stand almost exactly as they were in June 2003 when the FCC tried to wipe them off the books.

Success like this would have been unthinkable only a year or two earlier.

This is not to say the media moguls have been resting, or that Congress has been anticonglomerate. In a compromise vote in 2004, and as a sop to Rupert Murdoch of News Corporation, Congress limited the number of television stations that one company could own to those serving a maximum of 39 percent of the national audience. Murdoch thus did not have to sell off any stations, but could not buy any more, either.

THE POSSIBILITIES FOR CHANGE

This grassroots upsurge, provided it remains vibrant, points to new possibilities for a massive change in the way policy is made. On July 2, 2003, in his dissenting statement to the FCC's Biennial Regulatory Review, Democratic FCC Commissioner Michael Copps wrote: "The Commission's drive to loosen the rules and its reluctance to share its proposals with the people before we voted awoke a sleeping giant. . . . The obscurity of this issue that many have relied upon in the past, where only a few dozen inside-the-Beltway lobbyists understood this issue, is gone forever."

His prediction, if true, will mean a sea change in the way media politics, and possibly politics overall, is conducted in Washington.

Copps was soon proved right in his metaphor of a sleeping giant waking up.

Today, community-based advocates are taking action on the local level and rippling the effects up to the national. One example involves renewals of local TV and radio station licenses, which occur every eight years. When some licenses were up for renewal, a number of awakening giants were limbering up. In 2004, Media Alliance and the Youth Media Council filed "Petitions to Deny" radio station license renewals to Clear Channel in the San Francisco Bay Area. In December of that year, Bill Huston of NY/PA Media Action and the Binghamton, New York, Independent Media Center filed eleven "Petitions to Deny" radio license renewals for every station in town held by Citadel or Clear Channel. Chicago Media Action, Third Coast Press, and the Wisconsin Democracy Campaign filed license renewal challenges against Chicago and Milwaukee commercial television stations.

While all the license renewals were ultimately approved, the actions of local activists did put pressure on broadcasters to serve the public interest in the local community.

And activists can take local action in a number of additional areas.

One is cable TV franchises, which are negotiated every ten to fifteen years. In Marin County, California, Media Action Marin lobbied local officials to get $3 million from the county's franchise renewal with Comcast. The money will be used to create a nonprofit, independent community media center, administered by a locally elected board of directors instead of by Comcast. (See chapter 18.)

Another opportunity ripe for local policy organizing is the issue of municipal broadband, which you can read more about in chapter 19.

And in July 2007, in a real-world civics lesson on the legislative process, Senator Dick Durbin

(D-Ill.) went online to solicit comments and suggestions for the drafting of legislative language to set out America's very first national broadband strategy. According to Durbin, "We need more public participation and transparency in the way Congress crafts significant legislation. If we're successful, it could become a model for the way legislation on health care, foreign policy, and education is drafted in the future."

WHAT'S NEXT?

Those who want a democratic media system are focusing their efforts these days on two main policy areas: media ownership and net neutrality.

1. Media Ownership

After the Prometheus victory, media advocates moved from defense to offense.

Instead of blocking the broadcasting industry's efforts to grant the expansion of media giants, the challenge now is to create ownership structures that support independent, diverse, local, and truly *competitive* media. Increasing diversity and localism in ownership will produce more choice, as well as more owners who are responsive to their communities.

The goal is not less speech, but more.

This is unquestionably an uphill struggle. Even though the public airwaves are owned by the people and are not a corporate birthright, three recent reports demonstrate that the majority of the U.S. population is systemically excluded from the broadcast airwaves:

- **"Out of the Picture"** (October 2006): This report found that though women represent 51 percent of the U.S. population, they own just 4.97 percent of full-power commercial television stations. And while minorities, particularly African Americans, Latinos, and Asians, represent 33 percent of the total U.S. population, they own just 3.26 percent of these TV stations.[4]

- **"Off the Dial"** (June 2007): This report found that, despite their majority percentage of the population, women own just 6 percent of all U.S. full-power commercial radio stations and minorities own just 7.7 percent of such stations.[5]

- **"The Structural Imbalance of Political Talk Radio"** (June 2007): This report revealed that 91 percent of total weekday talk radio programming is conservative, and a mere 9 percent is progressive. The report found that "Ownership diversity is perhaps the single most important variable contributing to the structural imbalance. Quantitative analysis conducted by Free Press of all 10,506 licensed

4. "Out of the Picture: Minority and Female TV Station Ownership in the United States," by S. Derek Turner (FreePress.net) and Mark Cooper. October 2006.

5. "Off the Dial: Female and Minority Radio Station Ownership in the United States: How FCC Policy and Media Consolidation Diminished Diversity on the Public Airwaves," by S. Derek Turner, FreePress.net. June 2007.

commercial radio stations reveals that stations owned by women, minorities, or local owners are statistically *less* likely to air conservative hosts or shows." The report concluded, "The gap between conservative and progressive talk radio is the result of multiple structural problems in the U.S. regulatory system, particularly the complete breakdown of the public trustee concept of broadcast, the elimination of clear public interest requirements for broadcasting, and the relaxation of ownership rules including the requirement of local participation in management."[6]

Visit stopbigmedia.com and media-democracy.net for more information and to learn how you can participate in the debate.

2. Net Neutrality

The term Net Neutrality, which was coined by Columbia University Law School Professor Tim Wu, means simply that all Internet data should be treated alike.

From its birth to its coming of age and constituting the primary conduit for information as well as an essential component of our modern economy, the Internet was open to all users on equal terms, that is, a "common carrier"[7] . . . until 2005. Until then, Net Neutrality prevented cable and telephone companies from discriminating as to content based on its source, ownership, or destination. Since then, however, the big telecommunications and cable companies began a $175 million lobbying campaign in Congress to destroy Net Neutrality and throw it on the ash heap of history.

Why is this important?

Every website has the potential to become a TV or radio station.

Virtually all digital media, whether text, video, pictures, music, or voice, can be delivered by means of broadband Internet, thus breaking the corporate stranglehold over distribution. The Internet allows *everyone* to reach a global audience. Artists can be judged by their talent, with no "help" from major labels, studios, publishers, distributors, or resellers. The audience can decide which artists succeed and which fail, not a corporate media executive paid to flack for certain artists.

But today, cable and phone companies, which control services to nearly 99 percent of all residential broadband customers, are trying to privatize the Internet to their benefit by removing the long-standing principle of Internet (or Net) Neutrality.

Free Press put the situation clearly in a public Issue Brief: "When we log onto the Internet, we take lots of things for granted. We assume that we'll be able to access whatever website we want,

---

6. "The Structural Imbalance of Political Talk Radio" by FreePress (Ben Scott, Josh Silver, and S. Derek Turner) and the Center for American Progress (John Halpin, James Heidbreder, Mark Lloyd, and Paul Woodhull), June 22, 2007.

7. Common carriers, such as U.S. highways, railways, and the phone system, cannot discriminate. Any person with a license can drive on any highway, or ride a train with a valid ticket. The phone system cannot discriminate or censor conversations/speech—but rather, it carries all voice traffic regardless of content, ownership, origin, or destination.

when we want to. We assume that we can use any feature we like, anytime we choose—watching online video, listening to podcasts, searching, e-mailing, and instant messaging. We assume that we can attach devices to make our online experience better—things like wireless routers, game controllers, or extra hard drives. What we are assuming is called 'network neutrality,' the principle at the core of the Internet's DNA. The idea is that the Internet should be open and free, unrestricted by anyone.

But that could all change.

The network giants believe they should be able to charge website operators, application providers, and device manufacturers for the right to use the network. Those who don't make a deal and pay the network giant will experience discrimination. Their sites won't load as quickly as those who pay up, and their applications and devices won't work as well as do those of people who pay up. Without legal protection, consumers could find that a network operator has blocked the website of a competitor, or slowed it down so much that it's unusable, effectively crushing it.

We'll have first and second class citizens on the Internet.

This flies in the face of the fundamental idea behind the open Internet—that every website, every feature, every service, and every user is treated exactly the same. That's how bloggers can compete with CNN and *USA Today* for readers. That's how up-and-coming musicians can build vast underground audiences before they get their first top 40 single and start raking in the bucks.

If the gatekeepers have their way, the ability for independent writers, directors, bloggers, politicians, producers, and musicians to reach millions through the Internet will be restricted and controlled. The carriers would have the power to pick and choose which artists get distribution, as well as to set the quality and cost of that distribution. Exclusive deals between phone and cable companies could give the fast-lane option to preferred content providers such as big record labels or movie studios, which can afford to pay bribes. Smaller sites get kicked to the virtual curb.

The Future of Music Coalition writes, "What would happen if Sony paid Comcast so that sonymusic.com would run faster than iTunes or, more important, faster than cdbaby.com, where over 135,000 indie artists sell their music? Would a new form of Internet payola emerge? Would it shut down the burgeoning new economy and replace it with one that looks a lot like our closed media market?"[8]

Professor Wu wrote in agreement, "It's just too close to the Tony Soprano vision of networking: Use your position to make threats and extract payments. This is similar to the outlawed, but still common, 'payola' schemes in the radio world."

More ominously, the gatekeepers of online media pose a threat to free speech. On August 5, 2007, during its webcast from the Lollapalooza festival in Chicago, AT&T censored Pearl Jam when lead singer Eddie Vedder sang, "George Bush, leave this world alone."

8. "Indie-Rock Revolution, Fueled by Net Neutrality," by Jenny Toomey and Michael Bracy (Future of Music Coalition). TheHill.com, June 13, 2006.

In September 2007, Verizon Wireless denied text messages from Naral Pro-Choice America, a reproductive rights group, to subscribers who had already signed up to receive the messages. Verizon issued an apology after a *New York Times* editorial that opined that "The Verizon policy was textbook censorship. Any government that tried it would be rightly labeled authoritarian. If Verizon had attempted it on normal phone lines, it would have been violating common carrier laws that bar interference with voice transmissions. Unfortunately, those laws do not apply to text messaging."

What can be done? The SaveTheInternet.com coalition, which is coordinated by Free Press, brought together representatives of more than eight hundred organizations from across the political spectrum, and through them collected more than one and a half million petitions supporting the doctrine of Net Neutrality. Among the petitioners were hundreds of individual citizens, librarians, journalists, and bloggers, who coordinated with their neighbors and met with their Congress members. YouTubers such as AskaNinja.com even created minivideos with their unique take on why Net Neutrality matters.

Opposition was powerful, and rich—really, really rich. As mentioned earlier, companies including AT&T, Verizon, and Comcast spent more than $175 million on advertising, campaign contributions, lobbying, slanted research, and "Astroturf" (fake grassroots) groups to defeat Net Neutrality.

But grassroots participation proved more powerful than money and lobbying.

In a *Democracy Now!* radio interview on May 8, 2006, Free Press cofounder Robert McChesney said, "I think what we're seeing is this across-the-board outrage at the corruption of the process in which powerful special interests sneak through these privileges that benefit only them."

WebProNews Jason Lee Miller included the SaveTheInternet.com coalition in his year-end list of *Internet Heroes of 2006*, writing, "The SavetheInternet.com Coalition took on the most powerful players around to drum up support for Net Neutrality. What's happened in the last year has been nothing short of amazing, and those heroics should be recognized."

SLOUCHING TOWARD WIRELESS NET NEUTRALITY

For a dystopian vision of an Internet without Net Neutrality, simply think about your own experience freely browsing online around the globe and then compare today's open, standards-based Internet with the closed, proprietary world of wireless in the United States.

In Europe and Asia, you can use just about any phone on any telephone network. Consumers there buy phones, then pack them with applications, games, and music from a variety of providers. They can even switch carriers, without having to toss their device into a toxic landfill.

Not in the U.S. wireless world.

Just four main U.S. wireless carriers—Verizon, AT&T, Sprint Nextel, and T-Mobile USA—exert tremendous control over the applications, features, and functionality of devices, thereby crushing innovation and limiting consumer choice. Verizon and AT&T alone control 51 percent of the wireless market in the United States.

Columbia Law Professor Tim Wu says that equipment makers "have used that power to force equipment developers to omit or cripple many consumer-friendly features," such as Wi-Fi, Bluetooth, GPS, SMS, browsers, photo and sound file transfers, and e-mail clients. In the pathetic words of one mobile phone developer, "There is really no way to write applications for these things." Another called the development environment "a tarpit of misery, pain and destruction."[9]

The current U.S. wireless market, as led by the carriers, is similar to the control exercised by the AT&T monopoly over landline customers, circa 1950. Back then, consumers could have any phone they wanted, as long as it was rotary-dial and black (and owned by Ma Bell). In the absence of competition, long distance rates were high, and innovations few. AT&T considered the pink "Princess Phone" (basically, a pastel version of its standard phone) to be an innovation.

The FCC's landmark "Carterfone" ruling in 1968 changed all that. The ruling permitted consumers to attach any safe device to their phone line through a standard jack, as long as it did no harm to the network. The ruling created an explosion of true innovations in phone products and services, such as answering machines, cordless phones, fax machines, headsets, and modems. And long distance rates dropped, thanks to healthy competition.

Today, pondering the U.S. wireless market is like taking a trip down Monopoly Memory Lane. Poor policies are nurturing a noncompetitive wireless industry that is dominated by a few companies. Their power allows them to maintain a stranglehold over developers, products, artists, services, and consumers, thereby stifling innovation and limiting service and choice.

A good example is the first generation Apple iPhone, considered by some to be a bellwether for the future of the mobile Internet.

The iPhone is "locked," meaning it only works with one carrier, AT&T. As Professor Wu said during House testimony, "Imagine buying a television that stopped working if you decide to switch to satellite. Or a toaster that died if you switched from Potomac Power to Con Ed. You'd be outraged."[10]

The iPhone also "blocks" certain applications and features, since carriers do not permit applications they do not approve of or sell. For example, the phone has Wi-Fi access, but you cannot use its Wi-Fi connection to make phone calls, or use VOIP applications like Skype or Vonage, or grab ringtones from your computer, or even access music from Apple's iTunes directory. And top speed is a painfully slow 200 kbps. As the New York Times' David Pogue writes, "You almost ache for a dial-up modem."

---

9. "Wireless Net Neutrality: Cellular Carterfone and Consumer Choice in Mobile Broadband," by Tim Wu, Columbia University School of Law. New America Foundation, Wireless Future Program, Working Paper No. 17. February 15, 2007.

10. "Why Apple's new cell phone isn't really revolutionary," by Tim Wu. Slate.com. June 29, 2007.

Carriers force consumers to use their slow networks to access so-called *walled gardens* where they sell "preferred" content like Verizon's V CAST for music downloads, or to use carrier-operated photo-sharing sites where users can upload photos from their phone to an online album (such as Sprint's Picture Mail). And all for a fee, of course.

They get away with this because there is no real competition.

You may think you have a lot of options, but you are just dreaming. The carrier's platforms are closed, proprietary systems that benefit them and them alone.

In a Network Neutral world, consumers should be able to use any device they wish on any network, and choose any application or content that they prefer. A "Carterfone for Wireless" ruling by the FCC (which, after all, is owned by the taxpayer) would trigger a virtual explosion in wireless innovation, equipment, applications, products, and services.

A CHANGE IS IN THE AIR: OPEN ACCESS

In January 2008, the FCC auctioned off high-quality public broadcast spectrum in the 700 megahertz band, as broadcasters transition from analog to digital television signals in February 2009. The 700 MHz frequency band is especially valuable because its signals can travel long distances and penetrate thick walls.

These airwaves, and not only the 700 MHz band, are owned by the public. Broadcasters lease access to this spectrum by entering the highest bid at auction. The proceeds go to the U.S. Treasury. Normally, the few wealthy incumbents would have an enormous incentive to overbid for the rights to the spectrum, thereby pricing new entrants and competitors out of the auction.

This time around, though, in advance of the auction, Free Press helped more than a quarter of a million Americans contact the FCC and Congress to file comments supporting four "open access" provisions. The plan was to get all four provisions accepted as terms on which the auction would be conducted. They include:

- **Open Devices:** This is a "no-locking" requirement that lets consumers attach any device to the network, so long as it does no harm. The principle essentially imports the "Carterfone" decision to the wireless broadband market. Just as consumers do not need to buy a new TV if they switch from Comcast to Time Warner, Apple iPhone owners should not be required to buy a new cell phone if they switch from AT&T to Verizon.

- **Open Applications:** This is a "no-blocking" requirement, allowing wireless broadband users to download and enjoy any and all content, services, and applications installed on their devices, without fear of a network carrier blocking the downloads or services. This principle allows the use of Skype for Internet phone calls, Wi-Fi, and Apple's iTunes without interference, thus promoting consumer choice and creating incentives for innovation.

- **Open Services:** This requirement mandates licensees to make their network interfaces available to wholesale customers and third-party application providers. Competition must not end at the edge of the wireless network. If a consumer can take a device from one network to another, but each time faces a new "gatekeeper" that limits access to the broader network, the advantages of the two open devices and open applications rules listed above are lost.

- **Open Networks:** Most importantly, open access requires that the 700 MHz licensees provide wholesale network capacity to service providers without discriminating among them. The licensee would be required to resell its bandwidth at a wholesale rate to any entity that wishes to provide broadband wireless services at the retail level. Therefore, parties not affiliated with the licensee, be they start-up companies, governmental entities, or nonprofit organizations, will be able to gain access to the valuable spectrum at a reasonable price and enter the broadband wireless market on their own. Only this final condition can provide iron-clad assurance that one or more independent broadband providers will emerge from the auction, either directly as a licensee or indirectly through leasing wholesale access after the auction. Anything less than this wholesale competition is not truly "open access."

A wide spectrum of activists hoped that the fourth provision (open networks) at auction would result in a "third-pipe" wireless broadband service that would compete with the duopoly of DSL and cable, and would provide an alternative to the four wireless carriers. This would give consumers more choice, lower prices, better services, and innovative products.

They hoped wrong.

The first two provisions, open devices and open applications, were indeed accepted for the auction rules. Unfortunately, however, the third and fourth provisions (open services and wholesale open networks) were *not* accepted, denying American consumers a golden opportunity to have a truly open, competitive wireless market.

Overall, the outcome of the open access battle can be characterized as a minor victory. Still, it is part of a long-term field campaign for media reform activists. Our future successes will be determined by how many people get involved, and that includes you, our readers.

The auction is important, but it is far from the only battle.

CONCLUSION

Americans stand at a crucial moment of transition in the history of media, communications, and the politics that affects both. We need to put media to work for everyone, instead of just for the handful of corporations that are privatizing our valuable public resources and marginalizing the voices of the many to serve the interests of a wealthy few.

A democratic media system requires more voices and choices, not fewer. A democratic media infrastructure should decentralize ownership, encourage participation, represent all people, use common assets to serve the public interest, and make new technology available as a public utility, not a private commodity.

Arguably, there has never been a more important time to increase public involvement in media policy-making and grassroots organizing for a better media system.

You can help by participating. Visit bethemedia.com/resources.htm for more information and links to resources and organizations, among a wealth of material.

> "But of a good leader, when his work is done,
> they will all say, "We did this ourselves."
> —*Lao Tzu*

23

OPEN SOURCE
MAKING A NEW WORLD

Doc Searls

"The source is within you. And this whole world is springing up from it."
—*Rumi*

If designing and building the Internet had been left up to the usual suspects, it never would have happened. Networking would still be a private affair, a grace of large vendors, each operating its own separate and barely interoperable networks.

For an example of what that would be like, consider instant messaging. IM is a network service that never found its way into the Internet suite (unlike, say, hypertext, file transfer protocol, e-mail, and domain names). The situation for IM is not much different today than it was back in the 1980s, when online services like CompuServe, AOL, and Prodigy each had their own, incompatible e-mail systems. Today Yahoo!, Microsoft, AOL, and Apple all remain committed to closed, proprietary IM systems that run *on* the Internet but are not *of* the Internet. In other words, they contribute nothing to the Internet's open, free, shared, and ubiquitous infrastructure. They are platforms supporting closed silos that trap and hold dependent inhabitants.

This chapter originally appeared in *Open Sources 2.0,* by Danese Cooper, Chris DiBona, and Mark Stone. 2006. Used with permission of O'Reilly Media.

The platform-and-silo systems are as old as computing, and they won't go away quickly, if ever. But as a defining model for the software business, they are being replaced by a growing assortment of open standards and open source tools and building materials that together support far more business than they replace. Linux and its familiar LAMP suite (Linux, Apache, MySQL, PHP, Perl, Python, PostgreSQL, etc.) are the most obvious ones. SourceForge lists another 136,000, with dozens more tools added every day.

Nearly all of these tools and building materials were created by the demand side of the marketplace, to solve practical problems, and to provide useful infrastructural support for similar activities. The free and open way they contribute to the world is good for business. Whole businesses and business categories, old and new, are sited on bedrock comprising open standards and open source components. These businesses and categories do not depend on vendors and their platforms; their environment is the wide world of the Internet, not the inside of some vendor's silo. In fact, all platforms and silos in the computer business now find themselves in a subordinate position to the Internet. To survive, they have to operate in the wide new world of the Internet.

That goes even for Microsoft, which built the largest and most widely used platforms and silos in computing history, with a monopoly in the most ubiquitous product category of all: personal computing.

Yet, even Microsoft finds its vast monopoly, and all of its platforms and silos, forced to live in a new and larger world that:

- Nobody owns

- Everybody can use

- Anybody can improve

One current example of the new and larger world is podcasting. The term first appeared in August 2004. When I wrote about it in IT Garage (an online sister to *Linux Journal*) in September 2004, a search for *podcasts* brought up twenty-four results on Google. Now the same search gets thirty-five million results.

Podcasts are audio files distributed to subscribers' audio players (mostly iPods) via Really Simple Syndication (RSS), an XML dialect designed to serve as a syndication format for weblogs. Two prime movers behind podcasting are Adam Curry and Dave Winer. Curry is a veteran broadcast personality (best known as an early MTV veejay) and a serial entrepreneur. Winer is a programmer, writer, and businessman whose fingerprints are on XML-RPC, SOAP, OPML, outlining, blogging, and other useful innovations, including RSS 2.0. RSS 2.0 supports enclosure of media and other files—creating a natural stepping-stone from blogging to podcasting—and its use grew rapidly after Adam created iPodder, a script that automatically routes podcast feeds into subscribing iPods and other MP3 players, via computers.

As a distribution system for audio (or any kind of media) files, iPodder and its relatives form an infrastructural foundation for a whole new industry—one in which anybody can participate. And by providing a limitless supply of talent, material, and low-cost any-to-any distribution, podcasting also offers boundless new opportunities for broadcasting, cable, satellite TV and radio, the record business, and lots of other industries, as well as to noncommercial institutions ranging from churches and civic organizations to public broadcasting and government.

Note that podcasting became a hot category without the help of a large company. Instead, it began with the demand side supplying itself. Now, watch for big companies to jump in and for businesses of all sizes to start making money. And watch for most of that money to be made *because of* podcasting's open standards and open source components, instead of *with* them.

It will eventually become clear to everybody that far more money is being made *because of* open source than *with* open source. This is what we have to remember every time somebody asks, "How can you make money with [open source product]?" The answer is, "You don't make money *with* it. You make money *because of* it."

The *because of* principle is old hat in mature business categories, but it's new to the software business. Too many of us still want to see business models for all kinds of goods that don't belong on the income side of the balance sheet. Would you ask your telephone what its business model is? How about your front porch? Your driveway? Your clothes? Those things may *help us* make money but they are not *how* we make money.

Well, the same goes for open source products. They are a means to an end. You make money *because of* them, not *with* them.

It's also easy to forget that the most original sources in this new world are not technologies but talented and productive human beings. We all know that reputation is tremendously important in hacker culture and that open source is required, literally, to substantiate reputations. It is less obvious that the same is true for every other talent that operates on the Internet. Reputation grows fastest when the goods and services of creative minds are open to inspection, improvement, adoption, and reuse.

Reputation matters. Authority matters. Google (perhaps the world's biggest example of how to make money *because of* open source) sorts search results by the PageRank system, which the company explains in this way:

> PageRank relies on the uniquely democratic nature of the Web by using its vast link structure as an indicator of an individual page's value. In essence, Google interprets a link from page A to page B as a vote, by page A, for page B. But Google looks at more than the sheer volume of votes, or links a page receives; it also analyzes the page that casts the vote. Votes cast by pages that are themselves "important" weigh more heavily and help to make other pages "important."

That importance is what Cory Doctorow, in his book *Down and Out in the Magic Kingdom* (Tor 2003), called Whuffie. By whatever name we call it—reputation, authority, brand value, Whuffie—we don't acquire it alone. Its value is bestowed by others. In fact, the same might be said for its substance.

Several years ago, I was talking with Tim O'Reilly about the discomfort we both felt about treating information as a commodity. It seemed to us that information is something more than, and quite different from, the communicable form of knowledge. It is not a commodity, exactly, and it is insulted by the generality we call "content."[1]

Information, we observed, is derived from the verb *inform,* which is related to the verb *form.* To inform is not to "deliver information," but rather to *form* the other party. If you tell me something I didn't know before, I am changed by that. If I believe you and value what you say, I have granted you *authority,* meaning I have given you the right to *author* what I know. Therefore, *we are all authors of each other.* This is a profoundly human condition in any case, but it is an especially important aspect of the open source value system. By forming each other, as we also form useful software, we are not merely changing the world, but making it.

"The sage puts himself last, and finds himself in the foremost place."
—Lao Tzu

---

1. I had the same kind of trouble when I first started hearing everything one could communicate referred to as "content." I was a writer for most of my adult life, and suddenly I was a "content provider." This seemed ludicrous to me. No writer was ever motivated by the thought that they were "producing content." Their products were articles, books, essays, columns, or (if we needed to be a bit more general) editorial. "I didn't start hearing about 'content' until the container business felt threatened," John Perry Barlow said.

AUTHOR BIOGRAPHIES

BARRY BERGMAN: Veteran manager, music publisher, speaker and consultant Barry Bergman is the founder and president of the Music Managers Forum in the United States. Barry has published more than 150 songs recorded by various artists including Michael Bolton, Cher, Kiss, Joan Jett and others. See bethemedia.com for full bio.

PETER BRODERICK is President of *Paradigm Consulting*, which provides consulting services to filmmakers and media companies. He was founder and President of *Next Wave Films*, a company of the *Independent Film Channel*, which supplied finishing funds to filmmakers. Broderick played a key role in the growth of the ultra-low budget feature movement, and has given presentations on digital production at Cannes, Sundance, Toronto, Berlin and many other festivals. A graduate of *Brown University*, *Cambridge University*, and *Yale Law School*, he practiced law in Washington, DC. See bethemedia.com for full bio.

LLOYD DANGLE is a writer, artist, illustrator, cartoonist, and political satirist. Dangle is the author and animator of the syndicated weekly comic strip *Troubletown*, which debuted in 1988 and now appears in newspapers, magazines, weeklies, and on websites such as the *Austin Chronicle, FAIR! Extra, Funny Times, Honolulu Weekly,* and *Tuscon Weekly*, among others. Dangle's work has appeared in over 100 publications, including *Cosmopolitan,* the *New York Times, Time Magazine, Village Voice, Weirdo,* and *Wired.* Dangle served as National President and Northern California Chapter President of the Graphic Artists Guild. Dangle earned a BFA in 1983 from the University of Michigan School of Art. See bethemedia.com for full bio.

JAY DEDMAN is the co-author of *Extreme Tech: Videoblogging* (John Wiley & Sons). Jay has practiced journalism at every level - from CNN International in Atlanta, Manhattan Neighborhood Network (MNN) in NYC, and even as a freelance journalist in the war-torn Congo. In 2004, Jay and the original vlog pioneers formed an online community where they taught people around the world how to videoblog for free at freevlog.org. They created a tool called FireAnt.tv that lets users find, subscribe, watch, and share videoblogs. See bethemedia.com for full bio.

THE FAULT LINES COLLECTIVE: *Fault Lines* is the newspaper of the San Francisco Bay Area Independent Media Center (SF Bay IMC). We aim to give all communities the opportunity to actively participate in a collective process of media production and distribution. Our mission is to train and empower marginalized voices. This newspaper was created to be used as a tool for radical change in our communities by exposing the stories and raising the issues that the media plutocracy seeks to suppress. We are the people, we are the media and we are dissenting from the ground up. See bethemedia.com for full bio.

SUSAN FLEISCHMANN has been with *Cambridge Community Television* (CCTV) since it opened in 1988, serving first as Access Manager. Executive Director since 1993, Susan is responsible for the day-to-day operations of CCTV, and developing a long-range vision for the organization. CCTV won the *Overall Excellence in Public Access Programming* award in the Hometown Video Festival for 7 years in a row. See bethemedia.com for full bio.

PETER FRANCK is an attorney specializing in intellectual property, and Chairman of Media Action Marin. In the 1960's, Mr. Franck served as a legal advisor to Mario Savio. He organized legal defense for Cesar Chavez's Union Farm Workers. He was President of the Pacifica Foundation from 1980-1984, and Treasurer of the National Lawyers Guild from 1992-1993. In 1993, Mr. Franck filed an *amicus curiae* brief with the Ninth Circuit Appeal Court in *Dugan v. FCC*, arguing for the constitutional right to micro-broadcasting. In 1994, Mr. Franck was Amicus Counsel in the *US v. Dunifer* case, a key legal test of the first amendment rights of LPFM broadcasters. Mr. Franck earned his *J.D.* from the *Columbia University School of Law,* and received a B.A. from the *University of California at Berkeley.* See bethemedia.com for full bio.

MIA GARLICK was most recently General Counsel for the Creative Commons. Prior to the Creative Commons, Ms. Garlick worked in the Silicon Valley office of the law firm *Simpson Thatcher and Bartlett.* Mia worked as an IP associate in the Sydney office of *Gilbert & Tobin Lawyers.* Mia received a Bachelor of Arts and a Bachelor of Laws from the *University of New South Wales* in 1998 and her Masters of Law from *Stanford Law School* in 2003. See bethemedia.com for full bio.

ROBERT GREENWALD is the director/producer of documentaries including *WAL-MART* (2005); *Outfoxed* (2004); *Unconstitutional* (2004); *Uncovered: The Iraq War* (2003); and *Unprecedented: The 2000 Presidential Election* (2002). Greenwald produced and directed *Steal This Movie*, a feature film about 60's radical Abbie Hoffman. Greenwald has produced and/or directed more than 50 television movies, miniseries and feature films. Greenwald's films have garnered 25 Emmy nominations, four cable ACE Award nominations, two Golden Globe nominations, the Peabody Award, the Robert Wood Johnson Award, and eight Awards of Excellence from the Film Advisory Board. See bethemedia.com for full bio.

RACHELE KANIGEL is an assistant professor of journalism at *San Francisco State University* and a freelance writer and editor. She teaches newspaper and magazine classes and advises the *Golden Gate [X]press*. Rachele is author of *The Student Newspaper Survival Guide*. Rachele was a newspaper reporter for 15 years, working at *The Oakland Tribune, the Contra Costa Times*, and *The Raleigh News and Observer*. She was also a freelance correspondent for *TIME*. Rachele holds a master's degree in journalism from *Columbia University's Graduate School of Journalism* and a bachelor's degree in journalism from *San Francisco State University*. See bethemedia.com for full bio.

DOUG KAYE: In June 2003 Doug launched *IT Conversations*, a network of high-end tech talk-radio interviews, discussions, and presentations from major conferences delivered live and on-demand via the Internet. Doug is author of the books *Loosely Coupled—The Missing Pieces of Web Services* and *Strategies for Web Hosting and Managed Services*. See bethemedia.com for full bio.

KEVIN KELLY is Senior Maverick and Editor-at-Large for *Wired* magazine. He helped launch *Wired* in 1993. He is editor and publisher of the Cool Tools website, which gets 1 million visitors per month. From 1984–1990 Kelly was publisher and editor of the *Whole Earth Review*, and published four versions of the *Whole Earth Catalogs*. Over a million *Whole Earth Catalogs* have been sold. See bethemedia.com for full bio.

DOROTHY KIDD is Chair and Associate Professor in the Department of Media Studies at the University of San Francisco. She received her Ph.D. in Communication from Simon Fraser University. Professor Kidd has published in the area of political economy of media, media and social change and community media. She has also worked extensively in community radio production. Her areas of interest include democratic and participatory communications, media and globalization. See bethemedia.com for full bio.

KEITH KNIGHT'S work appears in various publications, including *Salon.com*, *The L.A. Weekly*, *The Funny Times*, *PULSE!* magazine, and *MH-18*. In 2007, Knight won the prestigious *Harvey Award*, the comic book industry's oldest and most respected award, for *Best Syndicated Strip or Panel*. Keith's daily strip, "*The Knight Life*," syndicated by United Features Syndicate, debuted on Monday May 5, 2008. Keith serves on the Board of the Cartoon Art Museum in San Francisco, CA. His semi-conscious hip-hop band, the *Marginal Prophets*, won the California Music Award for their disc, *Bohemian Rap CD!* See bethemedia.com for full bio.

ROBERT KUBEY is Director of the Center for Media Studies and Professor of Journalism & Media Studies at Rutgers University in New Brunswick, New Jersey. Professor Kubey has authored three books, Creating Television: Conversations with the People Behind 50 Years of American TV; Television and the Quality of Life; and Media Literacy in the Information Age.

ROBERT LAUGHLIN has taught more people to play the piano, face to face, than any other human being alive (over 30,000). He is the author of some 15 books and audio programs. As a performer he has either backed up or opened for such artists as the Ventures, Fabian, Wolfman Jack, Bobby McFerrin, Sawyer Brown, and the Diamonds. He has an undergraduate degree in anthropology from UC Berkeley. He's an avid skier and scuba diver and has earned a black belt in karate. He lives in Chico, California with his wife Pam, who is also a musician. See bethemedia.com for full bio.

ALEX MANDOSSIAN, since 1991, has hosted teleseminars with many of the world's top thought leaders such as Mark Victor Hansen, Jack Canfield, Stephen Covey, Les Brown, Brian Tracy, David Bach, and many others. He has generated over $233 million in sales and profits for his clients and partners via "electronic marketing" media. He is the CEO of Heritage House Publishing, Inc. See bethemedia.com for full bio.

DAVID MATHISON is a new media consultant, speaker, entrepreneur, and publisher. From 1998-2002 he was founder and CEO of the Kinecta Corporation (now part of Oracle), whose customers included Reuters, the *Financial Times,* the *Economist*, and Fidelity Investments, among others. From 1994-1999, Mathison was Vice President with Reuters, where he pioneered standards-based online syndication. Mathison earned a Masters degree in International Affairs from Columbia University in 1995, and a B.A. from SUNY Brockport in 1984. See bethemedia.com for full bio.

JAIME BERMAN MATYAS is the Executive Vice President and Chief Operating Officer of the *National Wildlife Federation* (NWF). Ms. Matyas is responsible for their branding, educational outreach, corporate and internet marketing, and strategic partnerships. Jaime serves on the board of directors of *eNature.com*. Prior to joining NWF, she held marketing and communications positions at Hanna-Barbera Productions and International Marketing Group, Inc. Jaime holds bachelors degrees in Communications and Psychology from the University of Pennsylvania. See bethemedia.com for full bio.

BILL MCCARTHY is the producer and host of the *Positive Spin* television show. Mr. McCarthy is the founder and president of *Unity Foundation*, a non-profit organization with a 29 year history of promoting world peace, cooperation and unity. Over one million people have attended the foundation's special events; and more than five hundred million people have been reached through the organization's media campaigns and television programming. See bethemedia.com for full bio.

SASCHA MEINRATH is an expert on Community Wireless Networks (CWNs) and Municipal Broadband. He is the co-founder and Project Coordinator of the *Champaign-Urbana Community Wireless Network* (CUWiN). Sascha is a policy analyst for *Free Press*, a Washington, DC-based think-tank. In 2004, Sascha organized the *First National Summit for Community Wireless Networks*. Sascha completed his undergraduate degree at Yale University and his Masters degree in Psychology at the University of Illinois, Urbana-Champaign, where he recently finished his PhD. See bethemedia.com for full bio.

JEFF MERSMAN is co-founder of OMMHD. He earned his Bachelors of Science degree in health care finance. Mersman worked for 3 years in private practice, and over 10 years with a major corporate healthcare provider. See bethemedia.com for full bio.

ANNE ELIZABETH MOORE (Best American Comics; Punk Planet) has seen her work in print since the age of 15. She is the author of *Hey Kidz, Buy This Book!* and *Unmarketable* (The New Press, 2007). Her work has appeared in The Progressive, Bitch, and Tin House, among many others. Moore's writing and editorial projects have been acclaimed by *Entertainment Weekly, Time, USA Today, Time Out New York, Kids, The Boston Globe, In These Times,* and others. See bethemedia.com for full bio.

CRAIG NEWMARK is a senior Web-oriented software engineer, with around twenty-five years of experience (including 18 years at IBM). Craig has become a leader in online community by virtue of his efforts at craigslist. In 1995, he started craigslist which serves as a non-commercial community bulletin board with classifieds and discussion forums. See bethemedia.com for full bio.

MERLIN OWENS is co-founder of OMMHD. He worked for Boeing Engineering in the late 1970s. In 1981 he joined Stevie Wonder's production group, The MYX, at Wonderland Studios in Los Angeles, where he collaborated with some of the brightest stars in entertainment, music and technology. See bethemedia.com for full bio.

EDITOR: ALISON OWINGS is the author of *Hey, Waitress! The USA from the Other Side of the Tray* (University of California Press, 2002), and *Frauen - German Women Recall the Third Reich* - a *New York Times* "Notable" Book of the Year (Rutgers University Press, 1993; UK Penguin, 1995; Mursia-Italy, 1997; Ullstein-Germany, 1999). Ms. Owings co-wrote 28 of the 50 *America 24/7* state books. In 2002, she co-wrote *Vertical Frontier, a* documentary about rock climbing in Yosemite National Park. From 1977-1999, Alison wrote freelance television news for the *The CBS Evening News with Dan Rather, Sunday Morning with Charles Kuralt, NBC Nightly News with Tom Brokaw,* and for *KTVU* and *KPIX* in the San Francisco area. From 1973-1977, Ms. Owings wrote exclusively for CBS-TV network news broadcasts, including *The Evening News with Walter Cronkite, the Weekend News with Dan Rather, Bob Schieffer, Ed Bradley,* and *The CBS Morning News with Hughes Rudd.* She is currently writing *Listening to Native Americans.* See bethemedia.com for full bio.

JEFF PERLSTEIN was recently the Executive Director of *Media Alliance*, a thirty year old media resource, training, and advocacy center in San Francisco. Jeff is a co-founder of the *Media Justice Network* as well as the initial *Independent Media Center* (IMC) in Seattle and the website Indymedia.org, which now links hundreds of IMC's in more than 40 countries. See bethemedia.com for full bio.

DOUGLAS RUSHKOFF is an author, teacher, and documentarian. His ten best-selling books on media and popular culture have been translated to over thirty languages. His book *Coercion* won the Marshall Mcluhan Award for best media book. Rushkoff founded the *Narrative Lab* at *NYU's Interactive Telecommunications Program*. Rushkoff graduated magna cum laude from *Princeton University*, received an MFA in Directing from *California Institute of the Arts*, a post-graduate fellowship (MFA) from *The American Film Institute*. See bethemedia.com for full bio.

SAKURA SAUNDERS served as program director and office coordinator of *KDVS*, a college/community radio station in Davis, CA, and has been an active member on the working group that established *KDRT-LP*, also in Davis. Ms. Saunders sits on the board of directors of *Prometheus Radio Project*. See bethemedia.com for full bio.

J. ZACH SCHILLER is Assistant Professor of Sociology at Kent State University, Stark Campus. He received his *Ph.D. in Sociology* from the *University of California, Davis*. He has been an itinerant college/community radio volunteer and programmer since 1995. Professor Schiller's essay, *"On Becoming the Media: Low Power FM and Alternative Public Spheres"* appears in *Media and Public Spheres* (2007). See bethemedia.com for full bio.

BEN SCOTT is the Policy Director for *Free Press*. His work monitors ongoing legislative and regulatory debates in Congress and at the FCC. He helps to facilitate collaborative efforts with other public policy organizations and grassroots groups to open up media policy debates to public participation. Ben is in the final stages of his doctoral degree in communications from the University of Illinois. He holds a bachelors degree from Northwestern University and a masters from the University of Sussex (UK). See bethemedia.com for full bio.

DOC SEARLS is a writer, speaker and consultant on topics that arise where technology and business meet. He is the Senior Editor of *Linux Journal*. He is co-author of *The Cluetrain Manifesto: The End of Business as Usual*, a *New York Times*, *Wall Street Journal, Business Week, Borders Books* and an *Amazon.com* bestseller. A former radio personality, Doc has appeared on many networks, stations, and podcasts. Doc's marketing background dates from 1978, when he co-founded Hodskins Simone and Searls, one of Silicon Valley' leading advertising and public relations agencies. HS&S was sold to *Publicis Technology* in early 1998. See bethemedia.com for full bio.

ADAM SOUZIS is the co-founder of StyleMob, a community for street fashion inspiration. Adam is also the creator of the *Rhizome project* (liminalzone.org). Mr. Souzis was co-founder and CTO of content distribution software company *Kinecta Corporation*, now part of Oracle. Adam previously worked for startups including General Magic, NetObjects, and Stellent. See bethemedia.com for full bio.

RICHARD M. STALLMAN is the founder and President of the *Free Software Foundation* and the *GNU Project*, launched in 1984 to develop the free software operating system GNU. There are estimated to be some 20 million users of *GNU/Linux systems* today. Richard Stallman is the principal author of the *GNU Compiler Collection*, a portable optimizing compiler which supports over 30 different architectures and 7 programming languages. Stallman graduated from *Harvard University* in 1974 with a BA in physics.

JEROLD M. STARR is Executive Director of the *Center for Social Studies Education* (CSSE), and founder of the *Citizens for Independent Public Broadcasting* and *Pittsburgh Educational Television*. PET's "Homefront" program reaches millions through public access cable and satellite channel distribution across the nation. A *Brandeis Ph.D.*, Starr taught for 30 years at the *University of Pennsylvania* and *West Virginia University*. He currently teaches winter term in the Communications Department of the *University of California at San Diego*.

MARK STOLAROFF is an independent producer and a founding partner of Antic Pictures. Stolaroff was formerly a principal of Next Wave Films, a company of The Independent Film Channel that provided finishing funds to exceptional, low budget films. Next Wave took seven films to Sundance and five to Toronto. Stolaroff is the founder of No Budget Film School, a unique series of classes specifically designed for the micro-budget filmmaker. A native Texan, Stolaroff received his BBA from the prestigious Business Honors Program at the University of Texas in Austin and minored in Film Production. See bethemedia.com for full bio.

KATHARINE SWAN recently retired from teaching English and journalism in San Francisco. For 25 years she taught at *Mission High*, an under-performing inner-city school. She moved to *Lowell High*, one of the top performing schools in the country. Her students have earned the *National Scholastic Press Association Pacemaker Awards* in 2001, 2002, and 2003; the *Columbia Scholastic Press Association Gold Crown Awards* in 1999, 2000, and 2003; and the *National Scholastic Press Association Hall of Fame Award* in 2001. See bethemedia.com for full bio.

PETE TRIDISH works with the *Prometheus Radio Project*, a non-profit organization created by radio activists to facilitate the growth of the Free Radio Movement. He was a member of the founding collective of *Radio Mutiny*, 91.3 FM in Philadelphia. He actively participated in the rulemaking that led up to the adoption of LPFM. Tridish has helped to build a number of low power radio stations, and provided advice to hundreds. He holds a BA in Appropriate Technology from Antioch College. See bethemedia.com for full bio.

SHERRY WESTIN is the Executive Vice President and Chief Marketing Officer for *Sesame Workshop*, the non-profit educational organization that produces *Sesame Street*. Westin currently serves on the Board of Directors of Communities in Schools, the Board of Directors of the United States Fund for UNICEF, the Board of Advisors of the National Committee on United States-China Relations, and the Advisory Board of the Association to Benefit Children. Westin received a B.A. in Communications from the University of Virginia. See bethemedia.com for full bio.

CREDITS AND PERMISSIONS

Grateful acknowledgement is made to the following for granting permission to reprint their material:

In Memoriam: "Thanatopsis" excerpt reprinted from Yale Book of American Verse. Ed. Thomas R. Lounsbury. New Haven: Yale University Press, 1912.

Introduction to Part One, Chapters 1, 2, 3 (sidebar: guitar), 4, 5, 6, 7, 9, 10, 11, 15 © 2009 copyright David Mathison and natural E creative group, LLC. All rights reserved.

Who Should Use This Book: BE-DO-HAVE reprinted with permission of Bob Baker.

Page 3: 1,000 True Fans. Reprinted with permission of Kevin Kelly. www.kk.org.

Page 17: Illustration: Product Pricing Curve and Author Publishing Model © 2006 Janet Switzer All Rights Reserved. Reprinted with permission.

Page 63: Teleseminar Secrets reprinted with permission of Alex Mandossian.

Page 67: Making Music. Reprinted with permission of Robert Laughlin.

Page 84: "There Is Power in a Union." Words and Music by Billy Bragg. Copyright ©1986 Chrysalis Music. All rights reserved. Used by permission.

Page 95: An Interview with Barry Bergman. Reprinted with permission of Bob Grossweiner and Jane Cohen, from an interview in Celebrity Access/Encore (March 14, 2003).

Page 113: Illustration: Dividing up the Ringtone Pie. Used by permission, MasurLaw 2007, 2009. Copyright © All rights reserved. www.masurlaw.com.

Page 117: Home HD Studio: From Hobby to Small Business. Reprinted with permission of Jeff Mersman and Merlin Owens.

Page 139: Lessons Learned from IT Conversations. Reprinted with permission of Doug Kaye.

Page 177: How to Videoblog: Eleven Steps to Your First Vlog. Reprinted with permission of Jay Dedman.

Page 189: How to Produce and Distribute Your Ultra-Low Budget Digital Film. Reprinted with permission of Peter Broderick.

Page 202: The Desktop Studio. Reprinted with permission of Mark Stolaroff.

Page 204: Shooting Film vs Shooting Video. Reprinted with permission of Mark Stolaroff.

Page 206: House Parties. Reprinted with permission of Robert Greenwald.

Page 208: Addendum to House Party sidebar. Reprinted with permission of Peter Broderick.

Page 246: Sesame Workshop. Reprinted with permission of Sherrie Westin.

Page 248: National Wildlife Federation. Reprinted with permission of Jaime Berman Matyas.

Page 255: Be a zinester: How and Why to Publish Your Own Periodical. By Anne Elizabeth Moore. Licensed under Creative Commons. Some rights reserved. 2009. Reprinted with permission.

Page 268: Existencilism: Painting With Stencils. By Banksy. All rights reserved.

Introduction to Part Two, Introduction to chapter 13, chapters 14, 17, 18, 19, are licensed under creative commons. Some rights reserved. 2009. David Mathison and natural E creative group, LLC. Reprinted with permission.

Page 273: The Opportunity For Renaissance. Reprinted with permission of Douglas Rushkoff.

Page 292: Fault Lines: A Community Newspaper. Reprinted with permission of the Fault Lines Collective.

Page 304: How to Create a Great College Newspaper. Reprinted with permission of Rachele Kanigel.

DISCLAIMER

The information provided in this book is to educate and entertain only. This book should be used solely as a general guide. The information provided herein is not designed to be up-to-date or all-inclusive, and can only commit to being current up to the print date. All attempts have been made to verify information, individuals, companies, organizations, and websites provided in this publication. There may be mistakes.

Author and publisher make no guarantees or warranties as to the accuracy of the material included in this book. **Neither author nor publisher assumes any responsibility for errors, omissions, or contrary interpretation of the subject matter herein.**

Author and publisher are not legal, accounting, or financial experts, nor are we engaged in rendering legal, accounting, or financial advice. Any decisions or activities undertaken based on the information herein should be done only with the advice of qualified legal counsel and/or other business experts. This publication is by no means a get-rich-quick scheme. There is no guarantee for potential or implied earnings using the techniques and ideas outlined in this book. Readers should be aware that some techniques in this book may require substantial investments in time, effort, and money. Reader's results may vary, and as with any other business opportunity, success depends on the time devoted to applying these strategies; on the reader's personal finances; and on knowledge, connections, skills, and talent. Since these attributes vary from person to person, we cannot guarantee a reader's success or potential income.

Author and publisher stress that the information contained herein may be subject to local, state, federal, and international laws or regulations. Adherence to applicable laws and regulations governing professional business practices is the sole responsibility of the reader. Author and publisher disclaim any and all responsibility for any activity undertaken by any reader—legal, illegal, or otherwise—relating to the use of information contained in this book.

The author and publisher of this book hereby disclaim any responsibility whatsoever for losses, liabilities, or damages caused, or alleged to have been caused, directly or indirectly, by the use or misuse of the information contained in this book by any reader of these materials. Reader assumes full responsibility for any risk, damages, injuries, or losses that they may incur from participating in the activities mentioned herein. Reader agrees to waive, release, discharge, and hold harmless David Mathison; his heirs, executors, and administrators; and natural E creative group LLC, its owners, board of directors, officers, representatives, and all individual members thereof, from any and all right, claim, demand, cause of action, or liability for damages of any kind or nature whatsoever, whether or not well founded, that might result or arise out of reader's direct or indirect participation in any activity, lesson, suggestion, or strategy described herein.

If you do not wish to be bound by the statements on this page, you may return the book to the publisher within thirty days of purchase for a refund of the purchase price, minus shipping and handling charges. Shipping and handling is the responsibility of the customer.

ACKNOWLEDGMENTS

"When you are grateful, fear disappears and abundance appears."
—*Anthony Robbins*

First I want to acknowledge those who give birth to an idea, a song, a book, a film, a business; to a new way of seeing. Thanks to the dreamers, the creators, the lovers, fathers and mothers, brothers and sisters, midwives, doctors, and nurses.

Any creative endeavor, this book included, is a group effort and a family affair. Thanks to my own family for your encouragement, advice, support—and especially your patience—with me and this project. They include these people:

Carolyn Mathison, my mother, who never hesitates to support our family and me.

My sister, Dianne Mathison-Ronan, and brother-in-law Michael Ronan, who selflessly took me into their hearts and home over the last year and a half of this project. Dianne and Michael were always there to help me, without me having to ask. Thank you both from the bottom of my heart.

My brother Eric Mathison and my sister-in-law Margaret. Eric was one of the first Coast Guard volunteers to go by boat to Ground Zero on 9/11 to support relief efforts. Thanks to my nieces Melissa and Kimberly for letting me draw the book's cover concept in chalk on their driveway.

Special thanks go to my brother, Peter Mathison, and his wife, Suzanne. While it has been said many times that "This book would not have been possible without . . . ," in fact this book would absolutely *not* have been possible without Peter. He has been my promoter, BEA booth buddy, advisor, financier, banker, consigliere, confidant, therapist, mover, landlord, back-up editor, copyeditor, page-proofer, and best friend. Peter believed in me and this project from the very beginning, and has been my most ardent supporter.

And it's not just me. He gives of himself for everyone, both inside and outside the family. Peter gives life to his company's slogan, "Like a Good Neighbor, State Farm Is There." If you need insurance in New York, call (516) 354-4949, or send an e-mail to pete@petemathison.net.

Thanks to Pete's son, my nephew, and all-around great guy Scott Mathison, for interning with me, for manning the booth with me, for getting awesome photos of me with Slash, Larry Lessig, Phil Donahue, Bill Moyers, Robert Kiyosaki, and Garrison Keillor. Yes! Thanks also to my nephew Daniel and niece Nicole.

To my extended family, my thanks for helping this baby grow to be a healthy and responsible adult. If *Be the Media* turns out to be great, it will be because of contributions from all the people involved—*you*, dear reader, included. Where it may not be so great, the fault lies entirely with me. Thanks to friends and neighbors, peers, teachers, librarians, and students, mentors, and protégés. If I tried to mention everyone, I would surely leave out some, and I don't want to be responsible for that! So thank you, everyone. You know who you are. A few people deserve special mention:

- Contributors: Thanks to the more than fifty people and organizations that contributed pieces to this book's puzzle, as well as the countless peer reviewers, such as Jenny Toomey, Barry Bergman, Sarah Sostiak at Six Apart, Shawn Chang, and S. Derek Turner, among many, many others.

- Endorsers: Thanks to everyone, especially Phil Donahue. Special thanks to Robert McChesney and his FreePress.net for shining a light of hope in otherwise dark times.

- Editor: Alison Owings. www.alisonowings.com. The brilliant, insightful, and beautiful Alison took very complicated material from each individual expert contributor, and skillfully made each piece intelligible and easy to read for the layperson. Then she proficiently wove the disparate chapters into a unified whole, giving the book one authoritative voice. And she did it all with her characteristic enthusiasm, grace, good humor, and love. Thanks, Alison, for making me look like a writer; I am eternally grateful.

- Copyeditor: Mark Woodworth. www.editcetera.com.

- Interior design and composition: Dorie McClelland. www.springbookdesign.com.

- Interior design: Liz Tufte. www.folio-bookworks.com.

- Cover design: Kathi Dunn. www.dunn-design.com.

- Cover copy: Graham Van Dixhorn. www.writetoyourmarket.com.

- Index: Nancy Humphries. www.wordmapsindexing.com.

- Graphics: Kathleen White. www.ferociousdesign.com.

- Steve Piersanti: For believing in this from day one. www.bkconnection.com.

- Alex Mandossian: Thanks for the stronger subtitle! www.alexmandossian.com.

- Dan Poynter: For being there when I called. www.parapublishing.com.

- Author photo: Stephanie Mohan. www.creativeportraiture.com.

- Hair: Jubilee Stanton. www.jubileehairstudio.com.

- FCC Commissioners Michael Copps and Jonathan Adelstein. http://fcc.gov.

I also am deeply indebted to many financial supporters who made this book possible. You would not be holding this book in your hands without the help of the following people:

PATRONS

- Peter Broderick: In October of 2003, Peter was one of the first people I approached about the book. He is one of the smartest, most helpful, nicest people I ever met, and I am so grateful for his friendship and advice. www.peterbroderick.com.

- Stephen Sillari: A great friend and supporter. Board of Directors, Cambridge Community Television; Community Arts Center. www.cctvcambridge.org.

- David Rubinson: He bought hundreds of galley proofs of the book and gave them to people who needed them most. http://thedrant.blogspot.com.

- Bill Densmore: A bundle of positive vibes. Thanks for being supportive of my work, and for building a bridge to the future of journalism. www.mediagiraffe.org.

- Alexandra Zburova: She didn't like it when I would run on empty, but did enjoy it when I put the truck in neutral and coasted from the top of the rainbow tunnel down to

Seminary Drive! Thanks also for courageously blazing a trail with me during the New Year's blizzard at Northstar. Thank you for your trust and your support.

SUPERPATRONS

- Jim Dietz: Board of Directors, Bank of Marin. Trustee, Dominican College. www/jdeitz.com.

- Phil Kranenburg: Trustee, College of Marin. Founder, Kranenburg Funds. www.kranenburgfunds.com.

- Brian Lantier: Elder, Westminster Presbyterian Church (Tiburon, California). Thanks to Brian and Carla for their unwavering support, friendship, and brunches atop Tiburon.

- Emanuel Stern: My main mensch, the ultimate son, brother, husband, father, friend, and Columbia University uptown local buddy. www.hartzmountain.com.

- EFactor: www.EFactor.com: Thanks to EFactor, I requested and rapidly received a small business loan. EFactor.com is a community network with 643,000 members and over 150 investors from 127 different countries, representing more than 80 different industries. Thanks especially to founders Marion Freijsen, Adrie Reinders, and Roeland Reinders for their support and patience.

- My Twitter angel, Ruth Ann Harnisch of the Harnisch Foundation, who purchased 5,004 books, all through one Twitter connection. We will be giving the books to worthy causes. Thanks to Ruth Ann for listening, and for coming through for me at the perfect time. Support her great work: www.thehf.org.

Special thanks to those of you who did not constantly pester me with "When will the book be out?" and to my wonderful neighbor Charlene Fisher, who patiently reminded me that "Books write themselves" (present company excluded, of course).

Which reminds me to thank Lao Tzu, the Tao, harmony, selflessness, water, flow, *wu wei*, and "creative quietude."

Finally, thanks to the tireless peacemakers, the first responders, the men and women in uniform, community organizers, and those who struggle for human rights, social justice, and media justice.

"We are all artists creating every single second of our lives."
—Bethany Jane Andrews Hoey

INDEX

"About the Author" resource box, leveraging, 54

Abraham, Jay, 16

Access Sacramento, 366, 379, 382, 387

Access SF, 362

AC/DC, 113

acoustics in rooms, 122. *See also* soundproof enclosures

Action Coalition for Media Education, 422

ActiveWorlds, 337n1

activists: creating public access TV stations, 395–399; filing comments with the FCC, 408; getting a message out via public access TV shows, 362–363; getting the press involved and informed, 387; making a living, 3–8; media policymaking, 448; radio programs, 149, 150; and telecommunications companies, 377–381; website hosts, 213

Adams, Susan, 380, 385, 386, 388, 389

ADAT audio optical protocol, 119

Adelstein, Jonathan, 87, 285, 379

AdiBooks, 50

administration agreements, 110

Adobe Audition, 134, 150

Adobe Flash, 179

AdSense. *See* Google AdSense

advanced book information (ABI), 48

advances: to musicians, 88–89; to songwriters, 110

advance sales of books, 49–50

advertising: ads on your radio show, 159; click-through ads, 226; community newspapers, 301, 302–303; licensing venues, 111; mean annual blog revenues, 35; newspaper website, 313; "per-inquiry" ads, 161; on radio shows, 161–166; revenues for videos, 184; superstar acts fees for, 110; via podcasts, 137; in zines, 261–262. *See also* classified ads; Google AdSense; promotion

advertising kits, 302

Aerosmith: fan club, 20

affiliate agreements, 220

affiliateannouncement, 220

affiliatematch, 221

affiliate programs, 219–222. *See also* relationship-building

affiliatesdirectory, 221

affiliate stations, 145, 156–161

affiliatesummit, 220

affliates, 55

agents. *See* fiscal agents; licensing agents; literary agents

aggregators, 32n2; audio, 128n2; publishing podcasts via, 136–137; ringtone market share, 113, 114; selling music via, 107–108; vlog (videoblog), 177

agreements. *See* contracts

Airborne Entertainment, 242

AK Press, 303

Albini, Steve, "The Problem with Music," 88

album costs and financing, 21

Alien (movie), 57

"All About Syndication" (David Mathison), 233

Allaire, Jeremy, 184

All for U (Janet Jackson), 113

Alliance for Community Media, 382, 392n15, 395; Hometown Video Awards, 374; WAVE (Western Access Video Excellence) Award, 363

Alliance of Motion Picture and Television Producers (AMPTP), 172

Alloy, 251

"all rights reserved" copyright, 430

Alter Ego, 257

Alternate Media Center, 381

Amazon, 58; affiliate programs, 219; BookSurge, 43; CreateSpace, 43; selling books via, 61–62; selling music via, 108

American Association for Independent Music, 87

American Dream, The, 11–12; expropriated idea of, 12–14, 22–23; rebooting, 15–16, 23

American Greeting Cards, 240

American Idol (TV show), 11, 12–14, 22–23, 109

American Society of Indexers (ASI), 49

AMPTP. *See* Alliance of Motion Picture and Television Producers (AMPTP)

anchors for text on web pages, 216, 217, 218
1and1, 213
Andreesen, Mark, 339
AnneZine, 257, 261
anonymous copyrighted works, 431
anonymous posts online, 317
Antion, Tom, 53, 225
AOL, 459
Apple, 459; suit against Think Secret, 28. *See also* iPods
apple.com/sitemap, 216
Apple Final Cut Express, 203
Apple Final Cut Pro, 204
Apple iLife, 133
Apple iPhone, 454
Apple iTunes, 32n2, 53; monitoring of music use, 279; podcast directory, 136
Apple iTunes directory, 179–180
Apple iTunes store: making a living via, 19; podcasts, 56; selling digital songs on, 107–108
Apple Loops, 134
Apple QuickTime, 173
Arcade Fire, 94, 116
archive.org, 136
Argentina Indymedia, 420–421
Arizona Republic, 313
Armstrong, Heather B., 28
Armstrong, Karen, 282
Arnison, Matthew, 419; "Open Publishing in a Nutshell," 423–425
article99, 56
articlehub, 217
articles: awards for newspaper articles, 308; for community newspapers, 295–296, 297; how-to, 217; participatory sites for, 312; publishing for free, 56; on sports, 314; using for Internet presence promotion, 217
artists. *See* design and designers
"Artist Services Model," 22, 94, 95, 116
ArtistShare, 102
artwork. *See* products
ASI (American Society of Indexers), 49
AskaNinja, 453
askdatabase, 63, 224

assets of your business, 51
Assignment Zero, 324
Associated Press, 182, 322
Associated Production Music (apmmusic), 112
associateprograms, 221
associate programs. *See* affiliate programs
Association of Author's Representatives, 41n2
Atari, 242
atlastfulfillment, 229
Atom feeds, 136
ATO record label, 100
Atrios, 36
AT&T, 378, 380, 452, 453
AT&T Broadband Internet (AT&TB1), 384
Audacity, 114, 133, 134, 135, 140, 150, 356
Audible, 53
audiences: active ranking of news stories by, 419; control over videos, 173; digital video (DV) feature films, 200–201; podcasts, 129; videos on mobile devices, 185. *See also* fans; patrons
audience shares and ad costs, 166
Audio-blogger, 34
audiobooks, 53, 56; backing up and saving files for, 135; podcasts, 130. *See also* CD audio series
audio file formats, 134. *See also* MP3 files
Audio Hijack Pro, 134
Audio Lite (cmx.gigavox.com), 135
Audio Publishers Association, 53
Audio Renaissance, 56
AuthorHouse, 43
authority and reputation, 461
Author Link, 41n2
author royalties, 41
authors. *See* writers
authors of each other, 462
autoharps, 71
autoresponders, 228
Avalon, Mickey, 335
avatars, 337
Avid editing system, 204
aweber, 222, 228
Axial Age, 281
AZcentral, 313
azchords, 82

Babolat, Sebastien, 129
Bach, David, 57, 58
backfence, 316
Backflip, 217
Back in Black (AC/DC), 113
backlink checking, 217
badges and code to share links, 218
Bagdikian, Ben, 443, 446
bakersfieldbands, 317
Baker & Taylor, 59
bakotopia, 317
Balazo 18 Art Gallery, 302
Bam Balam (Brian Hogg), 258
BandMerch, 241
bands: "tabs" for songs by, 82
Bango, 242
barcodes, 264; books, 49; music CDs, 108; zines, 266–267
Barenaked Ladies, 90, 109, 113, 114
Barrett, Dave, 85
Batmania, 257
Batterson, Mark, 129
Baum, Bruce, 388
BBC (British Broadcasting Corporation), 311, 415; terms of service, 317
BEA (Book Expo America), 59
beatblogging.org, 324
"Be a Zinester: How and Why to Publish Your Own Periodical" (Anne Elizabeth Moore), 255–267
Bebo, 338
Beck, 334
benefit concerts, 22, 301
Berger, Joanne, 257
Bergman, Barry, 14, 87, 96, 111, 463; "What's Going on Here? The Artist Services Model," 95
berkleeshares, 84
Berkowitz, Ginny, 395n19
Berkson, Bryan, 328
Berrett-Koehler Publishers, 47
Berry, Chuck, 103
best-seller lists, 62. *See also* blockbuster hits
bethemedia: affiliate program, 219; blog hosting consultation service, 30; blogtalkradio.com, 147; CafePress storefront, 239; eBook, "All About Syndication," 233; ommstudio.htm, 122; resources.htm, 399, 457; sending feedback to, 23; social network, 58, 336; YouTube channel, 179
Be The Media (David Mathison): cover, 47; designer, 48; editor, 46; layout designers, 48; use of a wiki, 327
Be The Media *Update* (lists.bethemedia.com/sub), 223
Better Homes and Gardens, 241
Biel, Joel, 267
Bierne, Dan, 116
Big Buy, The: Tom Delay's Stolen Congress, 208
BIGLIST, 222
Big List of Blog Search Engines, 33
Big Monday (Michael Rehfield), 192
Billboard, 242
biographical information on contributors, 264
BitBoard, 57
Bitch, 259
BitTorrent, 174–175, 181
Black, Duncan ("Eschaton" at atrios.blogspot), 27
Black Eyed Peas, 334
Black Liberation Radio, 344
Blair, Richard, 50
Blair Witch Project, The, 171
Blanchard, Ken, 44
Blast My Music, 106
Blink, 217
blinklist, 217
BlipTV, 177
Blisset, Luther, 419
blockbuster hits, 5, 14; picked by fans, 15. *See also American Idol* (TV show); best-seller lists; superstar acts
blog ad placement companies, 36
Blogads, 36
blog applications, 30
blog contests, 29
blogcritics.org, 56
Blogdex, 34
blog etiquette, 31
Blogger, 31, 33, 34, 136, 177
bloggers: for music PR, 116; and technology, 274, 275; 1,000 True Fans business model, 3–8

blogging: getting links connected to your blog, 34; getting more visitors to your blog, 32–34; getting started, 30; main goal, 31; moderating reader comments, 32; revenue opportunities, 35–36; why start, 29. *See also* moblogging; RSS feeds

blog hosts, 30–31

Bloglines, 34

blogosphere: automatically monitoring, 28; size, 26

BlogPulse, 34

blogrolling, 34

blogrolls, 34

blogs: care in use, 28; code for embedding Internet TV into, 182; comments, 32; compared with other Web and print media, 25; compared with wiki pages, 329; directories of, 33; employee best practices, 28; growth in numbers, 26; history, 26; personal diary, 26–27; posting on, 31–32; promoting your website via posts, 217; reader demographics, 36; for writers, 56. *See also* business-based blogs; citizen journalism; flogs; political blogging; splogs

blo.gs, 33

Blogsearchengine, 34

blog search engines, 33, 34

Blogstreet, 34

BlogTalkRadio, 132, 147

blooks, 36–37

Blosxom, 30

blountcountyvoice, 315

bluesrevue, 85

Bluetooth, 279

blufftontoday, 317

Blum, Sidney, 244

BMG Music, 337

board game products, 18

board of directors, 346–347

Body Brilliance (Alan Davidson), 58

Boeck, Doris, 235

Boehlert, Eric, 87

BoingBoing, 36, 52

Bolles, Nelson, *What Color Is Your Parachute,* 44

Bondage Records, 101

book-blog, 56

bookcatcher, 56

book clubs, 50

bookcrossing, 61

book discussion groups, 58

book distributors, 60

Book Expo America (BEA), 59

book fairs, 299

Book Locker, 54

bookmasters, 229

Book Passage, 386

book promotion, 52–54; best-seller lists, 61–62; bookstore appearances, 59, 60–61; licensing subsidiary products, 240–241; via book reviews and reviewers, 59. *See also* book tours; book trailers

book publishing: book "deals," 40–42; eBook market share, 54; finding a publisher, 41n2; four basic choices, 40; making a living, 6–7, 17. *See also* blooks; contracts; rights; self-publishing; traditional book publishing

book reviews and reviewers, 52, 56, 59

books: covers, 47–48; Creative Commons licensing, 437; design and designers, 47–48; indexes and indexers, 49; layout, 48; licensing, 240–241; pricing, 49; printing, 50–51; proposals, 44, 46; selling via Amazon, 61–62; spines, 47–48; titles, 45; on wikis, 327. *See also* audiobooks; eBooks; podcasts

Books in Print (R.R. Bowker), 48

Book Slut, 56

Booksmith (Brookline, MA), 107

BookSpan, 50

BookSurge, 43

BookTour, 58

book tours, 58, 59–60

book trailers, 58. *See also* video trailers

boredom, 15

boutique fulfillment houses, 228–229

Bowker, R.R., 48

Boxes, 190

Boyd, Duke, 235

Brack, Brandon, 80

Bracy, Michael, 87, 97n1

Bragg, Billy, 104; "There is Power in a Union," 83–84

Bragman, Larry, 385, 386, 388

Brand, Stewart, 277
branders, 239
brand vallue, 461
Braun, Christo, 121
Brave New Films, 208
Brave New Theaters, 207, 208
Braxton, Toni, 89
Breakthrough Distribution (breakd), 228, 299
Brenda Starr, 257
Brightcove, 184
Bright Eyes, 94
"Brilliant Day" and "Brilliant Daze (days are confused)", 436–437
Britt & Associates, 217
broadband: connection providers, 401–402; environmental potentials, 402–403; resources for, 410; toward a national strategy, 408, 450. *See also* community broadband
broadband news cooperatives in South Korea, 416
broadcasting: people-powered, 286
Broderick, Peter, 14, 15, 21, 463; consulting services, 22; "House Parties," 208; "The Revolution in Digital Movie Production and Distribution," 189–201
Brooks, James L., 368
Brooten, Lisa, 418
Brothers McMullen, The (Ed Burns), 191
Brown, Alexandria "Ali," 18, 19, 225
Brown Act (California), 385
Bry, Barbara, 315n6
Bryne, David, 20
Buckmaster, Jim, 316, 326
Buenos Aires Independent Media Center (IMC), 420
bulk sales of books, 50
bulletin boards, 312, 326; promoting your website via posts, 217; radio, 57
Burns, Ed, 191
Burns, Red, 381
Bush, George, 401
Bushyager, Linda, 257
business-based blogs, 27–28; intracompany blogs, 30–31
business-based podcasts, 130

business-based social networks, 337, 338
businesses with social network sites, 339
business models, 461; affiliates, 220; *Be the Media's* three basic step model, 16, 23; community broadband, 407; grassroots global media, 414–415, 422; self-publishing, 54–55; Street Performer Protocol, 6–7; syndication and aggregation, 127n1; tip jar revolution, 101–102. *See also* 1,000 True Fans business model
businesspersons: Internet presence via websites, 211–212; making a living providing services to creative people, 5; slogans or memes, 240, 243. *See also* affiliate programs; post office boxes; relationship-building
Bust, 259
Butterfield, Stewart, 312n2, 315–316
Büyükkökten, Orkut, 333
BuyWeb program, 219n1
BuzzMachine, 29, 36
BYOAudio, 132
Byrne, David, 96, 98, 99, 109, 116

Cable Acts of 1984 and 1992, 381
cable companies, 377–381; franchise fees, 392; lobbying by, 446; local origination programming by employees, 363; opposition to net neutrality, 283–284, 447, 451–453. *See also* Comcast; IPTV (Internet Protocol Television)
cable franchise fees, 395–396
cable franchises, 378–379, 381; franchising process, 395–399; important documents, 385
cable modems, 402
cables, electronic, 121–122
cable TV merchandise licensing, 236, 237
Cabo Wabo, 241
CafePress, 43, 240
California Brown Act, 385
California legislation on video franchising, 380–381, 394
Cambridge Community Television, 362, 395–399
camera mics, 373
camera phones, 171
Candy Hill, 102
Canfield, Jack *(The Success Principles)*, 16

Caplan, Gary, 251

Carey, Regina, 387

Carlin, Norman, 386

cartoonists. *See* comic books and cartoons

Cashflow (Robert Kiyosaki), 18

Catalog of Catalogs, 239

catalogs: books, 48, 50; song rights, 112

cause licensing, 238, 248

CBG Communications, 386–387, 389

CBS. *See* Viacom/CBS

ccMixter.org, 436

ccPublisher.org, 435

CCTV. *See* Cambridge Community Television

CD audio series, 18. *See also* audiobooks

CD Baby, 108

CDNow, 219n1

CDs: demo radio show, 150, 156; of public domain
    sounds, 367; recording seminars onto, 140; and
    transcripts of seminars, 229. *See also* music CDs

Celebration, The, 202

celebrities: *American Idol,* 12–14; book deals for, 41;
    book endorsements by, 46; celebrity authors, 41;
    estate licensing by, 238; licensing by, 236, 237,
    239; radio show vignettes, 144; use by participa-
    tory media, 313. *See also* microcelebrities

Celestine Prophecy, The (James Redfield), 44

cellfest.ca, 186

cellfixfestival.ca, 186

cellphone/mobile users: broadband speeds, 402;
    licensing merchandise to, 241–242; licensing
    music to, 112–113; Verizon, 279. *See also* mobile
    device videos; mobile podcasting; moblogging;
    ringtones

censorship: comic books and cartoons, 260; by pub-
    lic school administrators, 307–309. *See also* free-
    dom of the press

Center for American Progress, 206, 208

Center for Digital Democracy, 448

Center for Public Integrity, 445

Center of the World (Wayne Wang), 190

certificate of performance, 162, 165

chain bookstores, 59

Chan, Randolph W., 239

Chaplin, Charlie, 237

characters: licensing television show, 236–237; Walt
    Disney's, 238–239

Chicago Access Network Television, 362, 382, 383

Chicago Media Action, 449

Chicken Soup for Teacher's Soul, 59

Chicken Soup for the Soul (Mark Victor Hansen), 16,
    41n2, 46, 47; licensing by, 240

Chitika, 225

Choosing a Book Distribution System (John
    Kremer), 60

Chopra, Deepak, 242

chordfind.com, 83

chords. *See* musical chords

Citadel Broadcasting, 160

citizen journalism, 318–321, 413–415, 417; blogs,
    28–29; corporate media use of, 321–322. *See also*
    reporters

Citizen Journalism Academy, 320

"Citizen Media: Fad or the Future of News?", 315n8

"Citizens Media: Has It Reached a Tipping Point?"
    (Jan Schaffer), 311n1

City by the Light Divided, A (Thursday), 104–105

City Lights Bookstore, 303

civicspacelabs.org, 213

"Civil Disobedience, Legal Defense, and the origin
    of Low Power FM" (Peter Franck), 358–359

Clap Your Hands, Say Yeah, 116

Clarkson, Kelly, 12

classified ads, 290; for jobs, 326

Clear Channel Communications, 90–91, 92, 159–
    160, 445–446, 449

Cleaver, Harry, 416

Clerks (Kevin Smith), 191

ClickBank, 221

clickcaster, 132, 137

click fraud, 227

clickquick, 221

click-through ads, 226

clicktracks, 230

Clinton, George Jr., 430

Clinton, Hillary, 335

CNN I-Reports, 320

coaches. *See* speakers

Cobain, Kurt, 238

CODEPINK, 220, 225

Cohen, Bram, 174

Cohen, Cindy, 80

Cohen, Jane, 95

Cold Cut Comics Distribution, 259

Coldplay, 113

collaborative media, 277

Collateral (Michael Mann), 205

college appearances, 59

collegehumor, 183, 341

college newspapers, 304–305, 316

college radio stations, 149, 351

Collins, Shawn, 219n1, 220

color printing, 51

Columbia Scholastic Press Association, 307, 308, 309

Columbus Dispatch, 314

Comcast, 384; cable franchise agreement with Marin County, CA, 364, 387–390, 391–392, 393–394, 449; channel 30, 374; lawsuit against City of Oakland, 379; opposition to file sharing, 181–182; opposition to net neutrality, 453

comedians, 433; use of MySpace, 334, 335

Comet, The, 257

comic books and cartoons, 257, 337n1, 368, 429; censorship, 260; licensing, 236, 242. *See also* characters; zines

Comics Code Authority, 260

Comm, Joel "Dr. Adsense," 225

commercial radio stations, 114, 343–346; consolidation, 445–446; FCC required airtime for independent artists, 93; ownership diversity, 160; resources for, 357; women and minority ownership, 450. *See also* community radio stations; low power FM radio stations

commercial television stations, 449–450. *See also* public access TV stations

Commission Junction, 220, 221

Committee to Protect Journalists, 322–323

common carriers, 451n7

Common Cause, 225, 448

Communications Act of 1934, 344, 444–445

Communications Workers of America, 387, 390, 401

Community Activist Technology, 423n5

community and communities: encouraging participation, 276–278, 336; global, 282–286; involving in PEG facility management, 366; organizing, 398; radio station community outreach, 348; virtual, 337–338. *See also* participatory media; social networks

community-based journalism: obstacles, 296

community broadband, 404–407, 449–450; resources, 410. *See also* wireless networks

community broadband initiatives, 286

community media centers, 382–383; drafting a resolution for a nonprofit, 391–392; how to establish, 383–384; programs and services, 397–398; revenue sources, 392–393. *See also* Independent Media Centers (IMCs)

community needs assessment, 405

community newspapers: advertising, 301, 302–303; creating and structuring, 291–294; distribution, 299–300; editorial process, 294–297; financing, 300–301; mission statements, 292; production, 292–293, 297–299; website hosts, 213. *See also* local online newspapers; zines

community radio stations: broadcast content policies, 348; community access or spcialized, 347–348; costs, 348–349; equipment, 356; FCC regulations, 353, 354–355; financing, 350–352; mission statements, 347–348; and newspapers, 292; programming policies, 348, 352–355; promotion, 352; show application, 353; studios, 348, 350; types of programs, 355–357; use of citizen journalists, 320. *See also* radio shows

companies. *See* business-based blogs

computers: hard drive RAID arrays, 120; Mac *vs.* PC, 118, 141, 203; mobile workstations, 121; peripherals, 212–213; for radio show production, 150; saving and backing up files, 135, 150, 212–213. *See also* equipment

concept development for creative projects, 261

Concert in the Garden (Maria Schneider), 102

concerts: admission passes, 21; ticket prices, 91. *See also* tours

conference appearances, 59

conference call recording, 141

Confluence, 299

Congdon, Amanda, 176

Congress' media policy, 445–446

ConnectPlatform, 339

Connolly, Gail, 367

consensus decision- and compromise-making process, 293

constantcontact, 222

consultants: for activists, 386–387; difference from licensing agents, 243; engaging, 19, 22; for musicians, 116; VIP consulting, 54–55

consumers: and long tail of publishing, 3–8; passivity of, 284; *vs.* patrons, 15

ContentChecker, 223

contracts: with affiliate radio stations, 159; "cross-collateralized," 89; entertainment industry, 88–90; options for songwriters, 110; public access TV show, 366; traditional publishers boilerplate, 52; with traditional publishers/producers, 13; why use, 427. *See also* affiliate agreements; licensing agreements; rights; royalties

Cook, Dane, 335

Cool Edit Pro, 134

Cooper, Ron, 379, 380, 387

COPE Act, 379–380

Copeland, Henry, 36

Copps, Michael, 87, 449

copublishing agreements, 110

copyeditors, 47

copying artists' works, 15

copyleft, 433

copyright, 57; copublishing agreements, 110; defined, 428; "digital threat" to, 431; how to get, 430; impact of media conglomerates on, 283; impact on creativity in digital age, 427–428; and Internet Radio, 147–148; and lead sheets or "fake books," 79; for musicians, 102–103; problems caused by digital technologies, 431–432; relation to copyleft, 434; to songs, 90; and "tabs," 84; transfers of ownership, 430, 432; who is protected by, 428–430; and zines, 264. *See also* Creative Commons licenses

Copyright and You, 367

copyright law acknowledgment statements, 367

copyright protected products, 236

Copyright Royalty Board, 446

core audiences, 200

Corporation for Public Broadcasting, 352

corporations. *See* business-based blogs; media conglomerates

Cosmic Credit, 219n1

Costolo, Dick, 128

Coulton, Jonathan, 100, 105, 114

countrytabs, 82

Cowell, Simon, 11, 13. *See also American Idol* (TV show)

Cox News Service, 13

CPP (cost per point), 166

craigslist, 225, 290, 313, 316, 326; for book promotion, 58

cramming, 218

Creative Commons, 283; publishing tools, 435–436

Creative Commons licenses, 52, 432, 433–435; example, 267; for films, 208; for musicians, 103; sites that use, 84

Creative Homeowner, 249

credit card payment mechanisms online, 227–228

Creedence Clearwater Revival, 103

Critical Moment, 296, 299

Crooke, Robert, *Sunrise,* 43

Crooks and Liars, 36

Crowd Factory, 339

C-SPAN, 370

Cuban, Mark, 117, 138

cultural renaissance, 15–16

Curb Records, 90

Current, 156

Curry, Adam, 128, 131, 137, 139, 460

Curtis, Drew, 31

customers: author's lack of information about own, 42; finding out who yours are, 108; tracking online, 228. *See also* fans; patrons

customlink, 239

CUWIN (Champaign-Urbana Community Wireless Network), 405

Cyberotica, 219n1

Daily Kos, 27, 36

Daily Source Code (Adam Curry), 128

Dancer in the Dark (Lars Von Trier), 190

Dancing Barefoot (Wil Wheaton), 37

Dangle, Lloyd, 463

Dart Entities, 229

David, Larry, 368

Davidson, Alan, *Body Brilliance,* 58

Davitian, Lauren-Glen, 398–399

Debendicitis, Lisa, 436, 437

Dedman, Jay, 175–176, 463; "How to Videoblog," 177–178

defamation, 354

DeFilippo, Michele, 51

Def Jam artists, 112, 242

del.icio.us, 217

Democracy Now!, 222, 362, 385–386, 388

democracynow.org, 357

Densmore, John, 113

Denton, Kathy, 260, 267

design and designers: aesthetic and technical considerations for publications, 47–48; books, 47–48; cover art for podcasts, 135; games, 7; licensing of works, 236; making a living, 3–8; trademarking designs, logos, slogans or symbols, 243; zines, 262–263. *See also* illustrators and illustration; layout

desktop publishing, 304–305

"Desktop Studio, The" (Mark Stolaroff), 202–203

Diamond Comic Distributors, 60

Diaryland, 37

Diary of a Flight Attendant, 28

"Did You Say 'Intellectual Property'?" (Richard M. Stallman), 439–441

digg, 36, 217

Digidesign's ProTools, 101

digital artwork for music, 19

digital divide, 378, 401–402

"digital locker" services, 429, 431

Digital Millenium Copyright Act, 1998, 84, 147

digital movies. *See* digital video (DV) feature films

digital music: performance fees, 147–148; singles, 102. *See also* audio file formats; songs

Digital Music Marketing, 108

digital printing of books, 50

Digital Rights Agency, 108

digital television spectrum (white spaces), 409

digital video cameras, 202–203

digital video (DV) feature film production: costs, 203, 204, 205; economics, 192–193; rules for keeping budget low, 193–194; scripting, 192, 193; shooting video *vs.* shooting film, 204–205; studios, 202–203

digital video (DV) feature films, 191; advantages to making, 191–193; costs to make, 190, 191, 203; distribution, 195–196, 196–200; financing, 190–191, 193–194; lab tests, 194; promotion with house parties, 206–208; rights, 196. *See also* filming; filmmakers

digital video editing, 373

directing public access TV shows, 371–372

directories: affiliate programs, 220–221; Apple iTunes, 179–180; blog software, 33; ezines, 217; free articles, 56; licensing business, 252; podcasts, 56, 128, 129, 131, 133; publishing podcasts via, 136–137; using for Internet presence promotion, 217

Dirksen Molloy Productions, 365

discussion boards, 20

Dishwasher, 259

disk, 229

Disney, 443; licensing of merchandise, 237

Disney, Walt, 238–289, 244

distribution: books, 41, 59–61; comics, 258, 259; community newspapers, 299–300; digital video (DV) feature films, 195–200, 206–208; music, 94, 98–114; podcasts, 136–137, 179–180; public access TV shows, 374; punk rock zines, 258; of radio shows to affiliate stations, 160–161; ringtones, 113–114; traditional media, 12; videos, 169, 171, 172, 183; vlogs (videoblogs), 178, 179–180; zines, 258, 259, 265–267. *See also* fulfillment; promotion

distribution channels, 244, 251

DIY Wireless Solution-CUWIN (Sascha Meinrath), 405

Django (djangoproject), 213, 317

DMX (hip hop artist), 112

DMX (music licensor), 112

Doctorow, Corey, 462; *Down and Out in the Magic Kingdom,* 52, 327

Dolby, Thomas, 107

dollarshort.org, 28

domain names, 213

donations, 20–21, 301; publishing products serially, 6–7; via Google AdSense, 226. *See also* tip jars

Donovan, John, 395n19

"Don't Stop the Presses, Start Them" (David Mathison), 289–292

Don't Think of an Elephant (George Lakoff), 25

dooce, 27, 28

Doostang, 338

DopplerRadio (dopplerradio.net), 131

Down and Out in the Magic Kingdom (Corey Doctorow), 52, 327, 462

Downhill Battle, 87

downloads. *See* file sharing

dramas, broadcasting, 372

dreamhost, 213

drummers, recording live, 118, 120–121

Drupal, 213, 317

DSL, 402

Duane, Diane, 7

Dubansky, Mindall, 36

Duggan, Herb, 229

Dunifer, Stephen, 344, 358

Dunn, Kathi (Dunn Associates), 47, 48

Durbin, Dick, 449–450

DV cameras, 202–203

DVDs: compared with Internet downloads, 171; direct online sales, 199–200; learning to play music from, 76; monetary value of, 17. *See also* digital video (DV) feature films

Eagle Publishing, 41–42

Earl, Jack, 85

EarthCore (Scott Sigler), 56

eBay, 290, 313; acquisition of Skype, 146

eBooks, 49, 54, 58, 60; affiliate commissions, 220; "All About Syndication" (David Mathison), 233; distribution, 221

Ecademy, 338

e-chords.com, 82

EchoStar, 364, 386

echoStreet, 114

Eckstein, Warren, 144

Economics, 441

Edge, Bryce, 100

Edison, Thomas Alva, 68–69

Editcetera, 46, 47

editing: books, 46–47; sound, 141; zines, 262

Editor and Publisher, 46

editorial: community radio station broadcast content policies, 348; finding editors, 46; online newpaper content policies, 316–317; policy statements of IMCs, 418–419; student newspapers, 305, 306; teams and content in community newspapers, 294–296, 297; using wikis for, 327

educational podcasts, 129

Edwards, John, 335

E! Entertainment Television, 362

EFactor.com 338

E-filtrate, 55–56

eFulfillment Service, 229

Einstein, Albert, 238

Einstuerzende Neubauten, 20

eLance, 46, 55

electrodelicious, 27

Electronic Arts, 112, 242

electronic cables, 121–122

Electronic Frontier Foundation, 421

elevator pitch, 57

El Mariachi (Robert Rodriguez), 191

Elvis Presley Enterprises, 238

email address collection, 18, 222–225; by filmmakers, 201; by musicians, 100, 105; via widgets, 105

email address lists, finding owners of big lists, 61

e-mail message writing, 223

e-mail *vs.* RSS feeds, 33

EMI records, 92, 99

eMusic, 107–108, 108

Enemy Combatant Radio, 292

England's Dreaming (Jon Savage), 267

Enja record label, 102

entertainers: making a living, 3–8; sychronization (synch) fees, 110–111 entertainment industry contracts, 88–90

ephemeral materials, 256

Epic (Sony BMG), 91

ePodcast Creator, 134

equipment: classes on using television station, 366–367; for community broadband access, 406; community radio stations, 348, 350, 356; for creating public access TV shows, 364; for digital filming, 202–203; filmmaking, 202–203; home HD studio, 118–124; needed to be a broadcaster, 174; podcast recording, 133, 135, 139–141; radio show production, 150–151. *See also* computers; headphones; microphones; software; studios

eReader, 54

erotic fiction, 258

Eschaton (atrios.blogspot), 27

Escutia, Martha, 380

Essany, Michael, 361–362

ethostoolkit.net, 406

Eventful, 58, 106

"Evolution of Dance" (Judson Laipply), 170

exclusive deals, 244

Ex Libris Book Reviews, 56

Expanded Universe, 236

expertarticles, 56

ezinearticles, 56, 217

ezine directories, 217

"Ezine Queen," 225

ezinetrendz, 56

Facebook, 336, 338; Graffiti, 338; SuperPoke!, 338

Fahrenheit 9/11, 200

fair use, 429

"fake books." *See* lead sheets

Falk, Vera, 388

Fall Out Boy, 103, 112, 334–335

"Famous Last Words" (My Chemical Romance), 170

fan clubs. *See* musician fan clubs; street teams

Fancorps, 114

fans: building and selling to a core audience, 103–105; building your relationship with, 16; code for embedding Internet TV into blogs, 182; helpful roles they play, 15, 114–115, 300; interest in live interaction with artists, 20; rewards

for supporting artists, 15, 23. *See also* audiences; customers; musician fan clubs; 1,000 True Fans business model; patrons; personal audiences

Fantasy Records, 103

fanzines, 256–257, 258

fark, 31

fashion licensing, 109, 235, 237

Fault Lines Collective, 463; *Fault Lines,* 299–303

FCC (Federal Communications Commission), 87; "Carterfone" ruling in 1968, 454, 455; control of frequencies, 408, 409; frequency finder, 347; licensing renewals, 449–450; and microradio, 344–346, 348–349, 358; regulations for community radio stations, 353, 354–355; required radio station airtime for independent artists, 93; ruling on Comcast Internet download interference, 181; *vs.* Prometheus Radio, 448–449

Federated Media, 36

FeedBurner, 33, 128, 136, 178

feedforall, 133

feeds. *See* RSS feeds

Feedster, 34

Fein, Steve, 385, 391

Feingold, Russ, 87

feminist zines, 258, 259

festivalpocketfilms.fr, 186

Few, Astrin, 337

fiber-optic access to Internet, 403

fiber-optic Institutional Network (I-Net), 394

Fictionwise, 54

field production, 366, 369, 370–371

Figgis, Mike, 190

fighting words, 355

file compression, 177

file formats, 298. *See also* audio file formats; MP3 files

file sharing, 18, 21, 429, 441; download speeds in U.S. *vs.* other countries, 401–402; impact of media conglomerates on, 181–182; lawsuits, 431; of music, 99–100; the video revolution, 173–175

film: shooting video *vs.* shooting film, 204–205; using for printing, 298

film blogs, 30

film festivals for mobile and handheld device videos, 186

filming: equipment for digital, 202–203; on location, 192, 366, 369, 370–371; for mobile and handheld devices, 185; production process, 192. *See also* digital video (DV) feature films

filmmakers: adoption of digital technology, 189–190; boutique fullfilment houses for, 229; Creative Commons licensing, 438; making a living, 17, 22; product pricing and fundraising, 21–22; promotion of Internet presence, 218; resource assesments, 191, 193; service companies, 196–197; types of video deals, 198–199; use of MySpace, 334, 335. *See also* digital video (DV) feature films; independent films

film review podcasting, 135

film studios: licensing of movie merchandise, 236, 237, 242

film trailers, 198. *See also* video trailers

finslippy.typepad, 27

FireAnt, 32n2, 176, 178

Firedoglake, 27

First Year, The, 438

fiscal agents, 352

Fit to Cook (Jerry Jenkins), 50

flashkit.com/loops, 134

Fleischmann, Susan, 463; "How to Create an Award-Winning Public Accees Station," 395–399

Flickr, 312, 313

Flipside, 258

Flixster, 338

flogs, 35

Fluxblog.org, 116

Fogarty, Mignon, 56

Fogerty, John, 103

Folds, Ben, 337

Folio Bookworks, 48

folksonomies, 312

Forsythe, Tom, 429

Forthcoming Books in Print (R.R. Bowker), 48

Fotolog Inc., 35

Franck, Peter, 386, 387, 464; "Civil Disobedience, Legal Defense, and the origin of Low Power FM," 358–359

freebies: complimentary newspaper subscriptions, 200; craigslist, 326; by traditional book

publishers, 42; using to build your email list, 223; widgets, 106. *See also* giveaways

free blog hosts, 31

FreeConference, 53

free content for news stories, 316

Freed, Alan, 91n4

Freedom of Expression (Kembrew McLeod), 437

freedom of opinion and expression, 319n16

freedom of the press, 67, 323–324; high school newspapers, 307–309. *See also* censorship

"Free Flow of information Act of 2007," 324

free hosts for podcasts, 136

Freemantle Media, 13

free meeting locations, 294

free music downloads, 99–100

free online video-sharing sites, 183

free phone podcasting, 132

Free Press, 422, 448, 451, 453, 455

freepress.net, 97, 408

Free Radio Berkeley, 344, 358

Free Software Foundation, 433

free speech: FCC regulations, 355; PEG facilities, 381–382; rights for microradio, 344–346

Free Speech Radio News, 357

Free Speech TV, 364, 383, 388, 423n4

free video-sharing sites, 179

freevlog.org, 177

freewebs, 213

free zines, advantages, 267

Friendster, 333, 338

Frishman, Rick, 44, 46

"From Fandom to Feminism: An Analysis of the Zine Press" (Heath Row), 258

From Under the Cork Tree (Fall Out Boy), 103

fruitcast, 137

fulfillment: books, 51. *See also* distribution

fulfillment houses, 228–230

Fuller, Simon, 12, 13

Fulton, Mary Lou, 315, 316

Fundable, 7

Funding Exchange network (fex.org), 352

Funkadelics, 430

futureofmusic, 148

Future of Music Coalition, 87–88, 90, 97, 148, 452

Gaia, 337n1

games: board games, 18; designers, 7; licensing, 237; virtual fantasy, 337n1. *See also* videogames

"Gannon, Jeff" (James Guckert), 29

Gantman, Sheri, 363

GarageBand, 134, 135

Garcia, Jerry, 109

Garfield, Steve, 175, 176

Garlick, Mia, 464; "Speaking About Your Creativity Legally," 427–438

Garofoli, Joe, 56, 180, 315n9

Gates, Bill, 239

Geffen Records, 219n1

General Electric, 443

general managers, 158

General Mills, 223

Geoghegan, Michael, 335

Ghosts (Trent Reznor), 99

ghostwriters, 46

Gibbons, Leeza, 361, 362

Gigavox, 135, 141

GigFinder, 106

Gilbert, Randy, 61

Giles, Johnny, 387, 388

"Girlfriend" (Avril Lavigne), 170

Girl Germs, 259

Girls and Boys (Ingrid Michaelson), 104

Girly Mag, 259

giveaways, 18; books on air, 57. *See also* freebies

Glaser, Rob, 173

global consciousness, 282–286

Global Hobo, *259*

"Global Independent Media Center Network, The" (Dorothy Kidd), 413–422

Global Voices Online (blogger network), 29

Go BIG Network, 338

Good Charlotte, 251

Good Clean Fun (Bonnie Hayes), 89

Good Keywords, 217

Goodman, Amy, 370, 386

Good Reads, 58

Goodwin, Kathleen, 50

Google, 284; deal with News Corporation and MySpace, 340; OpenSocial, 338

Google AdLink units, 226

Google AdSense, 35, 225–227

Google AdWords, 225

Google Channels, 226

Google Checkout, 227

google.com/base, 137

Google free analytics tool, 230

Google PageRank feature, 215, 461; gray bar, 219

Google Toolbar (toolbar.google.com), 215

Google UPS Club, 225

Gordon, Peter, 87

gorillavsbear.blogspot, 116

Grabiner, Ellen, 395n19

Graffiti Wall, 339

Grand Rapids Community Center, 383, 393

Granfalloon, 257

grants: for community radio studios, 352; newspapers and news projects, 315

grassroots campaigns (Astroturf or fake), 380

Grassroots Radio Conference, 422

Gray V, 112

GreatTeleseminars, 53

Great Transformation, The (Karen Armstrong), 282

GreenCine, 30

Greenwald, Glenn, *How Would a Patriot Act?,* 56

Greenwald, Robert, 21, 208, 464; "House Parties," 206–207

Grey Eye Glances, 101

Groening, Matt, 368

Grokster, 431

Grossweiner, Bob, 95

Guckert, James, 29

Guerilla Marketing guides, 46

GuerrillaPR, 116

Guggenheim, Davis, 438

Guide to Book Editors, Publishers, and Literary Agents (Jeff Herman), 41n2

guitaretab, 82

guitar playing, 77, 80–84

Gunn, Moira, 139

Gydget, 106

hackingnetflix, 28

Hadl, Gabriele, 418

Hagar, Sammy, 241

Hail to the Thief (Radiohead), 99

Halleck, DeeDee, 382

Hal Leonard Publications (halleonard), 79

Hammer, MC, 96

Hammersley, Ben, 128

handheld devices. *See* mobile device videos; mobile podcasting

Hands-on-Mobile, 242

Hang Ten, 235

Hang Up (Madonna), 113

Hanks, Tom, 239

Hansen, Mark Victor, 60, 240; *Chicken Soup for the Soul,* 16, 41n2, 46, 47; Mega Book Marketing conferences, 48

harmonicacountry, 85

harmonica playing, 80

harmony, 70, 75. *See also* musical chords, 70

harpinanawhinin, 85

Harris, Allan, 102

Harris, Susan, 368

Harrow, Susan *Sell Yourself Without Selling Your Soul,* 236n1

Harry Potter series, 241241

Hausman, Michael, 109

Haverings, 257

Hawthorne Heights, *The Silence in Black and White,* 94, 335

Hayden, Curt, 367

Hayes, Bonnie, 20, 87, 89, 101

HD (high definition) audio and video home studios, 117–124, 202–203

HDNet, 117

headphones, 135

Henley, Don, 87, 92

Henry, Travis, 315n6

Here it Goes Again (OKGo), 115

Herman, Jeff: *Guide to Book Editors, Publishers, and Literary Agents,* 41n2; *Write the Perfect Book Proposal,* 44

Hey, Waitress! The USA from the Other Side of the Tray (Alison Owings), 49

"High School Journalism Matters" (Katharine Swan), 306–309

Hightower, Jim, 149, 150

Hilton, Paris, 130, 237

HipMama, 259

history: famous white man theory of, 256; as study of revolutions, 274, 278

Ho, Rodney, 13

Hodson, Ryanne, 176, 177

Hogg, Brian, 258

Hollywood studio system. *See* studio systems

Hollywood Undead, 335

Holt Uncensored, 222

Home Depot, 241

Homefront, 367, 374

"Home HD Studio, The" (Mersman and Owens), 117–124

homestead, 213

Hooka, 105

Horwood, James, 385

Hotlinks, 217

Hot Topic, 251

Houghton, Sarah, 29

House Carpenter's Daughter (Natalie Merchant), 98

house concerts, 21

"How to Create a Community Media Center" (David Mathison), 377–394

"How to Create a Great College Newspaper" (Rachele Kanigel), 304–305

"How to Create an Award-Winning Public Accees Station" (Susan Fleischmann), 395–399

"How to Create and Promote Your Podcast" (David Mathison), 127–139

"How to Create and Self-syndicate Your Radio Show" (David Mathison), 143–166

"How to Create a Public Access TV Show" (David Mathison), 361–364, 365–374

"How to License Your Ideas Without Selling Your Soul": Mathison, David, 235–246, 250–252

"How to Make Music with Just Three Chords and the Truth," 67–86

How to Make Your Book an Amazon Bestseller in 38 Days at Almost No Cost (Gilbert and McColl), 61

How To Offer Your Community the Triple Play of Voice Video, and Internet Access" (David Mathison), 401–404, 406–410

"How to Optimize Your Internet Presence for E-Commerce" (David Mathison), 211–230

"How to Play Guitar and Harmonica--the Easy Way" (David Mathison), 80–85

"How to Self-Publish Your Book (and Promote the Hell Out of It)" (David Mathison), 39–62

How to Self-Publish Your Book (Dan Poynter), 43

"How to Stay in Touch With Your 1,000 True Fans" (David Mathison), 331–341

"How to Videoblog" (Jay Dedman), 177–178

How to Write a Book Proposal (Michael Larson), 44

How Would a Patriot Act? (Glenn Greenwald), 56

Huffingtonpost, 32

Human Rights Radio, 344

Humphreys, Nancy, 49

Husker Du, 111–112

Huston, Bill, 449

Hyatt, Ariel, 116

Hype Machine (hype.nonstandard.net), 116

ibackup, 213

ibiblio.org/jimmy/folkdenwp, 84

IBM, 239

iBrattleboro, 316

Icecast (icecast.org), 147, 148

Icerocket, 34

ID3tag, 135

iFulfill, 230

iLike, 106

illustrators and illustration, 236, 262, 268–269. *See also* characters; comic books and cartoons

"I Love You" (Tila Tequila), 335

image tags on web sites, 216

IMC Licensing., 243

impactarticles, 217

I'm So Fucking Beautiful (Nomy Lamm), 259

Imus, Don, 160

IMVU, 337n1

income streams from multiple products, 17–18

independent broadband providers, 456

Independent Film Channel, 190

independent films: costs, 170, 189–190, 203–205; distribution, 194; on film *vs.* video, 204–205; new opportunities, 201; synchronization (synch) fees, 110; video distributor deals, 198–199. *See also* filming; filmmakers

Independent Media Centers (IMCs): about, 413–415; first, 312; global development, 417–418; Israel and Palestine, 421; local structures, 419–421; Michigan, 296; model for grassroots global media, 414–415, 422; New York City, 301, 421; predecessors, 415–417; Principles of Unity, 415; printing costs for community newspapers, 299; San Francisco Bay Area, 292, 294, 301; Seattle, 312, 416, 424. *See also* community media centers; Indymedia

Independent ONline Distribution Alliance (IODA), 108

Ind-E-Pubs, 58

indexes and indexers, 49

InDigEnt, 190

indirect sales methods: for musicians, 20

indybay.org, 292

Indymedia, 313

Indymedia Estrecho, 418

indymedia.org, 322

Indymedia Rosario, 421

Indymedia South Africa, 415

Indypendent, 299, 302

Infinite Minds, 337

info kits for radio show marketing, 156, 158

information folksonomies, 312

infrastructure, 284–285

Ingram, 59, 60, 266; Lightning Source, 50

inner circle programs, 19

In Rainbows (Radiohead), 94, 99, 100

Instant Income series (Janet Switzer), 16

instant messaging (IM), 459

Instant Piano method, 79

Institute for Interactive Journalism, 313

intangibles, 17

interactive media: citizen journalism, 417; licensing, 242; potentials, 273, 277. *See also* wikis

Interactiveness of blogs, 25–26

interactive software products, 18

Intermix Media, 340

International Licensing Industry Merchandisers' Association (LIMA), 243

International Monetary Fund, 416

International Periodicals Distributor (IPD), 266

International Telecommunications Union, 401

Internet: early communities, 277; impact of media conglomerates on speed, 181–182; potentials for global community, 282–286; preserving openness, 284–285; proposed fees for network providers, 97; reputation or authority on, 461–462. *See also* broadband; net neutrality; Web 2.0

Internet access, 283

Internet Archive (archive.org), 341

Internet Archive/OurMedia, 177, 183–184

internetforeveryone, 285, 408

Internet Radio, 147–148; market shares, 147

Internet Radio Equality Act of 2007, 148

Internet radio stations, 115

Internet search engines. *See* blog search engines; search engines

Internet services "redlining," 284, 378, 380

Internet traffic BitTorrent market share, 174

Internet TV, 179; ad revenues from, 184; compared with broadcast and cable TV, 181–182; difference from IPTV (Internet Protocol Television), 180–181; making video clips for, 182; self-service platform for video production for, 184; series, 171. *See also* videos; YouTube

Interpol, 94

Interscope Records, 99, 335

interviews: broadcasting, 370; community radio stations, 357; microphones for, 372; podcasting, 139–140, 141; for radio shows, 145

iPodder, 128, 137, 460

iPods, 128, 179–180

IPTV (Internet Protocol Television), 180–181

Iraq for Sale (Robert Greenwald), 21, 208

Isalee, 103

ISBN numbers, 43, 48

ISBN.org, 49

Island Records, 170

isnare, 56

Issue, 299

IT Conversations, 137

itlist, 217

Ito, Joicho, 283

iTunes. *See* Apple iTunes

"iTunes of licensing," 112

iUniverse, 43

Ivins, Molly, 291

Jackson, Geoff, 219n1

Jackson, Janet, 113

Jackson, Michael, 96

Jambase, 106

Jam Packs, 134

Janal, Dan, 53

Jarvis, Jeff, 29, 36

Jaspers, Karl, 281

Javablogs, 33

Jen, Mark, 28

Jenkins, Jerry (The Jenkins Group), 50

Jenner, Peter and Mushi, 87

Jib Jab animation *This Land Is Your Land,* 174, 218

Jiggerbug, 53

JillsNextRecord, 20

J-Lab: Citizen's Media Summit, 2005, 315n6, 316; Knight Citizen News Network, 320; NewVoices (j-newvoices.org), 315; Participatory Content page, 313

Joel, Billy, 22

Johnson, Nicholas, 381

Johnson, Spencer, 44

jollyblogger.typepad, 56

Jordan, Eason, 29

journalism: core principles, 319; as a dangerous occupation, 321–323; high school, 307–309; resources, 325; serious, 318. *See also* freedom of the press; reporters

Juice, 32n2, 128, 131

Julie and Julia: 365 Days, 524 Recipes, 1 Tiny Apartment Kitchen, 36

Just a Geek *(Wil Wheaton),* 107

Kaltschnee, Mike, 28

Kamen, Ken, 244

Kanigel, Rachele, 464; "How to Create a Great College Newspaper," 304–305

Kantako, Mbanna, 358

karolmedia, 229

Karr, Timothy, 408

katrinacheck-in.org, 28

Kaye, Doug, 135, 464; "Lessons Learned from IT Conversations," 139–141

Kazaa, 146

KDVS radio, 351

Kellner, Douglas, 362

Kelly, Kevin, 464; "One Thousand True Fans," 3–8, 14

Kelsey, John, 6

Kennard, William, 345

Kennedy, Ted, 448

Kenner, Adam, 340

Kerr, Kenneth A., Jr., 236

Kerry, John, 42

keywords on websites, 215, 216, 218; not to use, 219. *See also* meta tags

Kid A (Radiohead), 99, 100

Kidd, Dorothy, 464–465; "The Global Independent Media Center Network," 413–422

KillerTracks.com, 112

Kim Youn Ok, 319

Kinberg, Josh, 176

King, B.B., 241

King, Larry, 370

Kiyosaki, Robert, 18

Kiyosaki, Robert, *Rich Dad, Poor Dad* series, 53

Klein, Howie, 90

Klein, Naomi, *The Shock Doctrine,* 58

Knight, Peter, 465

Knight Citizen News Network, 182

Knight-Ridder, 290

Knowitallvideo, 183

knowledge sharing: within organizations, 294; on social networks, 336

KOCE (PBS station), 374

Koning, Dirk, 361n1

Kontera, 225

Koons, Jeff, 429

Korn, 96, 113, 251

KPFA (Berkeley, California), 129

KPFT radio, 351

KPMG Royalty Compliance Services group, 244

KRBS (radiobirdstreet.org), 348

Kremer, John, 60

KTAO radio, 343

Kubey, Robert, 465; "Mentors," 368

Kucinich, Dennis, 371

Kulash, Damian, 97

Kuo, Sam (kuodesign), 30, 48

Kwiqq, 339

KYOU Radio (San Francisco, California), 129

kyte.tv, 185

LaChance, Gordie, 107

Laipply, Judson, 170

Lakoff, George, 25, 370

Lamm, Nomy, 259

Landmark movie theaters, 198

Lao-tzu, 281

Largehearted Boy (blog.largeheartedboy), 116

Larson, Michael, 41; *How to Write a Book Proposal,* 44

Last Broadcast, The, 190

Laughlin, Robert, 465; "The Medium Is the Music: Feel the Power of Creating Your Own," 67–79

Lavigne, Avril, 170

layout: books, 48; community newspapers, 297; zines, 263

LCCN (Library of Congress Catalog Number), 49

lead sheets for piano, 73–76; how to find, 79. *See also* tabs

Lead Us Not Into Temptation (David Byrne), 96, 98

Leap Frog, 249

Lear, Norman, 368

Lee, Sharon, 7

Lee Bong Ryul, 319

Leeds, Jeff, 112

legal advice about book publishing, 45

Lehre, David, 335

Lennon, John, 238

Leonhard, Gerd, 14

Lesser Fans, 4. *See also* 1,000 True Fans business model

Lessig, Lawrence, 327

"Lessons Learned from IT Conversations" (Doug Kaye), 139–141

Levelator (gigavox), 141

Levenson, Laurie, 323
Levinson, Jay Conrad, 46
Levy, Alain, 92
Libby, I Lewis, 322
libel insurance, 317
Librarian in Black blogger, 29
library appearances, 59
library market share of publishing, 59
Library of Congress Catalog Number (LCCN), 49
Library Thing, 58
libsyn, 136
license deals with record companies, 96
licenses for LPFM stations, 346
licensing: about, 236–237; business aspects, 242–245; celebrity, 236, 237, 239; choosing and monitoring a licensee, 245, 250; controlling your licensing program, 240–242; copyleft, 433; doing research for, 239; estate, 238; getting started, 238–239; instant, 239–240; interactive media, 242; merchandise and clothing, 109, 235, 237, 249; music, 103, 111–114; music subsidiary products, 109–110, 241–242; to other artists or corporations, 20; public airwaves, 408; resources, 252; subsidiary products, 235–236; video clips, 177. See also Creative Commons licenses; virtual storefronts
licensing agents, 243
licensing agreements, 243–245
Licensing Group, Ltd., 243
licensing local TV and radio stations, 449–450
licensing of public airwaves, 409, 444–445, 455–456
licensors and licensees, 236
Lieberman, David, 250
lighting for television shows, 372
Limbaugh, Rush, 161
Linden Labs, 337
Lindsay, Ethel, 257
Line, Lorrie, 101
linkadage, 218
link buying, 218
LinkedIn, 338
link exchanges, 218
Linkin Park, 251
LinkShare, 221

links on your web page, 216, 217
links to your web page, 217; Google AdLink units, 226
Linux users: podcatchers, 131; vlog aggregator, 178
list hosts, 222
listible.com/list/social-bookmarking-sites, 217
listservs for book promotion, 58
literacy, 68–69
literary agents, 41; finding, 41n2
Literary Market Place, 46
Little, Brown and Company, 36
Little Voodoo, A (Grey Eye Glances), 101
live365, 147, 148
live call-in shows, 371
LiveJournal, 28, 31
Live Nation, 96
live training events, 18
Local Community Radio Act of 2007, 446
local control of telecommunications, 403
local intranets, 405
local online newspapers, 316
local origination programming, 363
local public access to the broadcast spectrum, 378, 444–445
local sponsors: for radio shows, 162–163
LOC.gov, 49
logos: licensing, 237; trademarking, 243
lonelygirl15 video, 436, 437
Lonely Island comedy collective, 438
long tail of publishing, 3
Lopez, Jennifer, 91
Lorrie Line Music, 101
Los Angeles Times, 290, 313
Lott, Trent, 448
Love, Courtney, 89, 93, 238
low power FM radio stations, 446; board of directors, 346; coalition of activist groups to preserve, 448–449; license application, 346; location for, 347; mission statements, 349; number of, 346; origins, 343–346, 358–359; required logs, 354; studios, 347; transmitters, 349, 350. See also community radio stations
Lucas, George, 236
Lulu, 42, 43

Lupoff, Pat, 257

Luttrell, Lesleigh, 257

Lutz, Robert A., 27

Lydon, Christopher, 139

Lyons, Natica ("Tica"), 383, 386, 389, 394n18

lyris, 222, 223

MacKinnon, Rebecca, 29

macropatrons, 21. *See also* superpatrons

Madden, Irv, 251

Madison Commons (madisoncommons.org), 320

Madonna, 109, 113; children's books, 241; recording contract, 96

magazine licensing, 241, 245

magazines. *See* trade publications; zines

Magnatune, 103, 373, 437

"Make Internet TV," 182

Making a New World" (Doc Searls), 459–462

"Making Media Policy Public" (Scott, Perlstein, Mathison), 443–457

making money. *See* moneymaking

Malda, Rob "CmdrTaco," 312

Mandossian, Alex, 53, 224, 225, 465; "Teleseminar Secrets," 63–64

Manhattan Neighborhood Network, 362, 383

Manila, 30

Manley, Lorne, 92

Mann, Aimee, 109

Mann, Michael, 205

manufacturing and distribution deals, 98

Marantz recorders, 140

Marin Athlete, The, 367

Marin Community Media Center, 394

Marin County Free Library blog, 29

Marin Peace and Justice Coalition, 220

Marin Report, 363

Marin Telecommunications Agency (MTA), 383–384, 389, 392

market channels for writers, 50, 55–62

marketing: "bypass," 60; to libraries and schools, 59; for more income and more impact, 16–22; old and new methods, 39–40; of radio shows to affiliate stations, 150, 156–159; of radio shows to sponsors, 162–164; via family, friends, and fans, 223; via house parties, 206–208; via relationships and partnerships, 246–247, 248–249; viral marketing widgets, 106; viral social networks, 332; zines, 265–266. *See also* affiliate programs; market research; promotion

"marketing intimacy," 63

Marketing On Demand, 241

market research: source of demographic data, 334, 340; teleseminars, 63; tools for tracking your products, 183

Marlowe, Frogg, 104

Marshall, Garry, 368

Marshall, Joshua Micah, 27

Marysville, Tennessee *Daily Times,* 315

Matchwriters, 46

Mathison, David, 465; "All About Syndication," 233; "Don't Stop the Presses, Start Them," 289–292; "How to Create a Community Media Center" (David Mathison), 377–394; "How to Create and Promote Your Blog," 25–37; "How to Create and Promote Your Podcast," 127–139; "How to Create and Self-syndicate Your Radio Show," 143–166; "How to Create a Public Access TV Show," 361–364, 365–374; "How to License Your Ideas Without Selling Your Soul," 235–246, 250–252; How To Offer Your Community the Triple Play of Voice Video, and Internet Access", 401–404, 406–410; "How to Optimize Your Internet Presence for E-Commerce," 211–230; "How to Play Guitar and Harmonica--the Easy Way," 80–85; "How to Self-Publish Your Book (and Promote the Hell Out of It)", 39–62; "How to Stay in Touch With Your 1,000 True Fans," 331–341; interview of Dennis Kucinich, 371; "Making Media Policy Public," 443–457; "Participatory Media, Online Community Newspapers, and Citizen Journalism, 311–325; "Rebooting the American Dream," 11–23; 1ShoppingCart link, 228; "The New Way to Promote and Sell Your Music," 87–94, 96–116; "Video Revolution, The," 169–176, 179–186; "We're All In This Together," 281–286; "Wikis: Platforms for Participation," 327–329. *See also* Be The Media

Mathom, 257

Matthews, Dave, 100

Matyas, Jaime Berman, 465; "National Wildlife Federation," 248–249

Maxim, 242

Maximum Rock'nRoll, 259

Maybellene (Chuck Berry), 103

McAllister, Craig, 384n7

McBride, Terry, 113

McCarthy, Bill, 466; "Positive Spin," 365

McChesney, Robert, 285, 409, 453; *Telecommunications, Mass Media, and Democracy,* 344n1, 448

McClelland, Dorie, 48

McColl, Peggy, 61

McEwan, Ian, *On Chesil Beach,* 58

McGegan, Nicholas, 437

McGuinn, Roger, 84

MCI, 393

McLeod, Kembrew, 437

McMahon, Ed, 361

McPherson, Aimee Semple, 343n1

mechanical royalties, 111

media: battle over who controls, 285; deregulation, 416n2; infrastructure, 284–285; interaction between old and new, 25–26, 27, 28–29; "old *versus* new," 313; policies that control, 445–446; and technology, 273; women and minority ownership, 450–451. *See also* media conglomerates; participatory media

Media Access Advisory Committee (MAAC), 384

Media Access Project, 448

Media Action Marin (MAM), 222, 364, 377n1, 384, 391, 405, 449

Media Alliance, 46, 220, 449; advocacy toolkit, 404

media conglomerates, 14, 416n2; control of publishing, 40–42; control over media, 283–286; impact on Internet upload and download speeds, 181–182; and IPTV (Internet Protocol Television), 180; monopoly protection, 446–447; origins, 443–446; possibility of changing, 449–450; and public airwaves, 408; selling out to, 267; that control book publishing, 40; three-pronged approach to changing, 447–449. *See also* chain bookstores; commercial radio stations; commercial television stations; newspapers; radio conglomerates; traditional media

media-democracy.net, 451

Media Monopoly, The, 443

Meetup, 58

Mefeedia, 32n2, 178

Mega Book Marketing conferences, 48, 59

Megatrax, 112

Meikle, Graham, 419

Meinrath, Sascha, 405, 466

"Mentors" (Robert Kubey), 368

merchandise, 21; branded, 19, 109; community radio stations, 352; financing volunteer activities with, 301; licensing, 109, 235–236, 237, 249; and retail industry consolidation, 250–251; types licensed, 237

Merchant, Natalie, 98

merchant account alternatives, 227

MerchDirect, 241

Mercury Nashville, 91

Mersman, Jeff, 117–124, 466

Messick, Dale, 257

metadata, 175, 183, 435. *See also* tags

meta tags, 215

Method Man, 112

Mforma, 242

Miami Herald, 314

Michael Essany Show, 362

Michaelson, Ingrid, 104

Michigan Independent Media Center (IMC), 296

Mickey Mouse, 239

"Mickey Mouse Protection Act," 283

microcelebrities, 6

micropatronage, 7. *See also* patrons

microphones, 139, 150–151; for interviews, 372; for television shows, 372–372

microradio, 344; legalization of, 358–359

Microsoft, 459; Creative Commons plug-in for Office, 436; influence on Facebook, 336

Microsoft banner ads, 326

Microsoft Video for Windows, 173

Microsoft Windows, 278

MIcrosoft Windows Media DRM protection, 106

Midler, Bette, 239

Migden, Carole, 388

Miller, Jason Lee, 453

Miller, Steve, 7

Million Ways, A (OKGo), 115

Mills, Mike, 90

minidisc.org, 356

Mintz, Charles, 238–239

Miro (getmiro), 178

mission statements: Cambridge Community Television, 396; community newspapers, 292; community radio stations, 347–348; global IMC, 414; low power FM radio stations, 349; online newspapers, 314

Mizejewski, David, 249

mobifest.ca, 186

mobile carriers, 455; ringtone market share, 113, 114. *See also* cellphone/mobile users; phone companies

mobile device videos, 185–186; promotion, 186

mobile podcasting, 140

mobile podcatchers, 131

mobiles. *See* cellphone/mobile users

mobile workstations, 121

moblogging, 34–35

Moderati, 114

moneymaking: difficulties under traditional media systems, 11–23; Google statistics packages, 226; steps involved in, 16; teleseminars, 53; using long tail business model, 3–8. *See also* success; types of creatives, e.g., musicians, videographers, writers, etc.

Monsoon Wedding, 200

monster, 290

Moore, Anne Elizabeth, 466; "Be a Zinester: How and Why to Publish Your Own Periodical," 255–267

Moore, Neil, 80

Morillon, Lucie, 323

Morrison, Shana, 87

Morrowitz, Lisa, 387

Moss-Adams LLP, 245

Motown Records Group, 242

Mould, Bob, 111

Movable Type, 28, 30

MoveOn.org, 206–207, 208, 225, 448

moviemaking. *See* filming; film studios

movies. *See* digital video (DV) feature films

Moyers, Bill, 318, 323, 325

MP3.com, 429

MP3 files: monetary value of multiple copies, 17; of podcasts, 132; saving podcasts onto, 134, 139, 141; uses, 19

MP3 players. *See* iPods; widgets

MSNBC Citizen Journalists Report, 320

MTA. *See* Marin Telecommunications Agency (MTA)

MTV television show, 114, 115

multimedia products, 18

municipally owned fiber networks, 394, 402, 446. *See also* community broadband

Muni Wireless, 404

Murder Can Be Fun, 259

Murdoch, Rupert, 13, 331, 444. *See also* News Corporation

music: broadcasting, 371; community radio shows, 356; Creative Commons licensed, 436; how it works, 70; learning, 69–70; learning, by ear, 72–74; learning, by reading musical notation, 75–76; learning, from music CDs, 76; local online newspapers that cover, 317; making, without musical notation, 68–69; rough tracks and album outtakes, 21; for television shows, 373. *See also* lead sheets; MP3 files; recordings of music; songs; tabs

musical chords, 70, 71, 72, 75–76; for guitar, 81; popular music, 76–77

musical instruments, 70–71

musical literacy, 68–69

musical perfection, 76

Musicane, 106

music business. *See* music industry

music CDs: advance copies, 21; costs and profits of independent sales of, 108; death of, 92; distribution, 108; having fans sing on, 21; prices, 93; relying on, for income, 19; royalties, 89; sales, 99–100; tracking record sales, 108. *See also* audiobooks; CDs; recordings of music; songs

music distribution. *See* record labels; self-distribution of music

music downloads. *See* file sharing

music.for-robots, 116

musician fan clubs, 20, 21, 114. *See also* street teams; zines musicians: bloggers who publicize, 116; boutique fullfilment houses for, 229; first on MySpace, 104; licensing of names and images, 237; making a living, 3–8, 6–7, 7, 17, 89, 98–100, 109–115; new options, 94–100; online communities for, 115–116; pension plans for, 109; performances on Second Life, 337; product pricing and fundraising, 19–21; publicists, 116; touring, 106–107; traditional options, 88–94; use of MySpace, 334–335; websites by, 214; websites for, 213. *See also* music publishers; podcasting; punk rock zines; recordings of music; record labels; studios

music industry, 92, 93. *See also* commercial radio stations; music publishers; record labels; royalties

MusicIP, 106

Musicland, 251

music library royalties, 111–112

music loops for podcasts, 134

music-makers.org, 80

music notation, 68–69, 75–76. *See also* lead sheets; tabs

music promotion, 114–116; licensing subsidiary products, 241–242

music publishers, 110–114

music recordings. *See* recordings of music; record labels

music retailers, 92–94, 241–242

music sampling, 430, 436

music videos, 114

Muzak, 112

My Big Fat Greek Wedding, 197, 200

My Chemical Romance, 112, 170, 335

mycrimespace, 339

My Ding-A-Ling (Chuck Berry), 103

MyFreeTeleconference, 53

myprofilepimp, 338

Myrick, Dan, 171

MySpace, 333–336, 338; about, 331; acquisition by News Corporation, 340; widgets, 105–106

MySpace: The Movie (David Lehre), 335

myspacejunks, 338

MySpace Records, 335

My Yahoo!, 32n2

NAFTA. *See* North American Free Trade Agreement (NAFTA)

Napster, 99–100, 108, 173–175, 431; Napster 2.0, 174

National Association of Broadcasters, 345–346, 446

National Conference on Media Reform in 2007, 318

National Federation of Local Cable Programmers, 367

National Fulfillment Inc., 229

National Lawyers Guild, 344; Committee on Democratic Communications, 358–359

National Organization of Women, 225

National Public Radio, 345–346, 415; podcast broadcasters, 129

National Scholastic Press Association, 309

National Telecommunications and Information Administration, 352

National Wildlife Federation, 245

"National Wildlife Federation" (Jaime Berman Matyas), 248–249

Nelson, Bethany, 80

neoliberalism, 416n2

net neutrality, 97, 451–453; cable and telephone companies' opposition, 447

newassignment.net, 324

New England Cable News, 318

New Friend Request (Gym Class Heroes), 115

Newmark, Craig, 316, 324, 466; "craigslist," 326

New Radio Star, 57

News Corporation, 104, 340, 443, 449. *See also* Murdoch, Rupert

news coverage, control of agenda, 286, 419

newspapers: about, 289; big daily, 312–313; blog pages of major dailies, 312; circulation and revenue, 290; costs for large dailies, 290–291; creating your own, 291. *See also* college newspapers; community newspapers; journalism; online newspapers

newsreaders, 32n3, 33, 34

news shows on community radio stations, 356–357

"New Way to Promote and Sell Your Music, The" (David Mathison), 87–94, 96–116

newwest.net, 318

New York City Independent Media Center (IMC), 301, 421

New York Times, 313; blogs, 29

Next Wave Films, 194

Nimbit OMT, 105

NiMIQ (nimiq.nl), 131

Nine Inch Nails, 20, 98, 99, 334

911tabs, 82

19 Group, 12

99zeros, 28

Ning, 338, 339

Nirvana, 238

nongovernmental organizations, 417

nonprofit community resource centers, 391–392

nonprofit licensing, 238

nonprofit newspapers, 291

North American Free Trade Agreement (NAFTA), 416

North Mississippi Allstars band, 114

northwestvoice, 315, 316

Novato (California) Public Access, 378

NPG, 98

n-Track Studio, 141

Nutri-Books, 60

Obama, Barack, 22, 282, 335, 339

Oberholzer-Gee Felix, 99–100

O'Brien, Danny, 6

obscenity *vs.* indecency, 355

Obscuresound.org, 116

Oceania Indymedia, 418

Odeo, 56, 137, 178

Odeo Studio (studio.odeo), 132–133

offset printing, 50–51, 298

ohmynews, 319–320

Oh Yeon Ho, 320

OK Go, 97, 115, 170

Old Glory, 251

Olson, Eric, *Slaves of Celebrity,* 12

Olson, Sarah, 321

OMM HD, 117

on-air fund drives, 351

On Chesil Beach (Ian McEwan), 58

1106 Design, 51

One Long Year (Todd Rundgren), 101

One Minute Manager, The (Blanchard and Johnson), 44

$100,000 per year, making, 4

one sheets for radio shows, 156, 157.158

1shoppingcart, 219, 228

1,000 True Fans business model, 3–8; for bands and other groups, 5; for bloggers or book publishers, 5–6; 5,000 passionate fans, 14; True Fans and Lesser Fans defined, 4; variations according to type of media, 6

1001 Ways to Market Your Books (John Kremer), 60

online ads, 225

online catalogs of song rights, 112

online communities, 18; for musicians, 115–116. *See also* social networks

online databases, 300

online fulfillment services, 51

online newspapers, 313; financing, 314–315; mission statements, 314; staffing and content plan, 315–316; starting, 314. *See also* community newspapers; local online newspapers

Online Success Blueprint (Ali Brown), 18

open access broadcasting provisions, 455–457

OpenAds, 36

Open Directory Project (dmoz.com), 214, 218

Open Media Network (omn.org), 183–184

open publishing, 415, 423–424

open source adserver sofware and advertisers, 36

open source government, 286

open source Internet radio station, 147

open source journalism, 324

open source software, 276, 277, 278, 459–462; for free wireless networking, 405; platforms for online news publishing, 317

open spectrum, 409

operations managers, 158

Opportunity for Renaissance, The" (Douglas Rushkoff), 273–279

Oprah's Book Club, 58

Oprah (TV show), 14

opt-in boxes, 223

Opus1 Music Library (opus1musiclibrary), 112

O'Reilly, Bill, 160

Orkut, 333, 338

Ortega, Juan, 387

ourmedia.org, 136, 183–184, 341

Outfoxed: Rupert Murdoch's War on Journalism, 208

outtakes and rough music tracks, 21

Owens, Merlin, 117–124, 466; "The Home HD Studio," 117–124

Owings, Alison, 46, 49, 466

Pacifica Radio, 344, 355, 357

"Painting With Stencils" (Banksy), 268–269

Pandora, 101, 115, 147, 148

Panic! At the Disco, 170

Panzino-Tillery, Lori, 379

Paparow, Ari, 33

paperfrigate.blogspot, 56

Paper Tiger TV collective, 382

Pappas Telecasting Company TV stations, 321

Participatory Culture Foundation, 182

participatory democracy, 414, 448

participatory media, 311–314, 326–329; resources, 325. *See also* community newspapers; community radio; Independent Media Centers (IMCs); public access TV shows

"Participatory Media, Online Community Newspapers, and Citizen Journalism (David Mathison), 311–325

participatory media communications, 418–419

partnerships. *See* relationship-building

Passion of the Christ, The, 197, 200

pass-through fees, 395

Pat Chilla the Beat Gorilla, 436, 437

patent law, 439–441

Patronet, 101

patrons, 15; macropatrons, 21; micropatronage, 7; and products they will buy, 17; superpatrons, 19, 22. *See also* fans; sponsors

Paul, Les, 109, 237

PayLoadz, 220, 221

payola, 91, 92, 355; Internet, 452

PayPal, 227–228

pbwiki, 329

PCN (Preassigned Control Number), 49

PDA-branded ImpeachMINTS, 237

PDF files, 49

Pearl Jam, 452

peer reviews of your book, 47

Pegasus, 257

PEG (public, educational and government) facilities, 362, 364, 366, 378, 381–382, 396

PenguinTV (penguintv.sourceforge.net), 178

Penn, Sean, 371

PeopleSoft, 338

performance art, copyrighting, 430

Performance Rights Societies (PROs), 111; ringtone market share, 113

performance royalties, 111

Perlstein, Jeff, 413, 467; "Making Media Policy Public," 443–457

permalinks, 31

Perry, Mark, 258

personal audiences, 201

personalized program products, 19

Pesce, Mark, 174, 332

Philharmonic Baroque Orchestra, 437

phone companies, 377–378; lobbying by, 446; opposition to municipally owned fiber networks, 402; opposition to net neutrality, 283–284, 444, 451–453. *See also* IPTV (Internet Protocol Television); mobile carriers

photocopying of print publications, 298

photo sharing websites, 312, 455

piano playing, 71–77; Instant Piano method, 70

Pieces of April, 190

Piersanti, Steve, 47

pimpmyspace.org, 338

Ping-O-Matic, 33

pirate radio, 344, 349. *See also* low power FM radio

Pittsburgh Educational Television, 367

placeblogger.org, 313

Planned Television Arts (PTA), 57

Platinum Mastermind (Ali Brown), 19

Playnetwork, 112

plentyoffish, 225

Plone, 213, 317

Pluck, 32n2

plugola, 355

Pneuma Books, 48

POD. *See* Print on Demand (POD) publishing

podcastalley, 56, 129, 136

podcast distribution, 136–137

podcasting, 460–461; ads, 137; advantages, 131; beginnings, 127–128; hosts, 136; making a living by, 3–8, 138; origin of the name, 128; validating your feeds, 136. *See also* videos

podcastingnews, 137

podcasting studios, 139–141

podcast.net, 56, 136

podcastpickle, 137

podcast promotion, 136–137

podcast recording: audio file formats, 134; equipment, 139–141; including music, 134; listening to your podcast, 135; naming your podcasts, 135; posting and tagging your podcast, 136; recording equipment, 133, 135; saving and backing up voice and music files, 135; software recording tools, 133–134; via phone, 132, 141

podcast reviews, 131

podcasts: of audiobooks, 130; cover art, 135; defined, 127; directories, 56, 128, 129, 131, 133; distribution, 179–180; finding, 130; getting ready to be on, 132; growth of subscribers, 128; marketing of books via, 56; program formats, 129–130; revenue opportunities, 137–138; similarity with vlogs (videoblogs), 175; subscribing to, 130–131; types of subjects, 129–130; who podcasts, 129

podcasts.yahoo, 137

podcast syndication, 136

podcatchers, 32n2, 131

Podesta, 409

podfeed.net, 137

podfinder.podshow, 131

podnova, 137

podshow, 137

Pogue, David, 454

Point Reyes Visions (Blair and Goodwin), 50

political activists. *See* activists

political blogging, 27, 36

politicians: use of MySpace, 334, 335

Popovic, Barbara, 382

popular music, 73, 76–77, 80

pornography zines, 258–259

Positive Spin, 374

"Positive Spin" (Bill McCarthy), 365

Postal Regulatory Commission, 447

Post Carbon Institute, 302

post office boxes, 264

postproduction, 192, 194

PostSecret, 36

Potter, Beatrix, 236

Potts, Mark, 316

Powell, Julie, 36

Powell, Michael, 448

Power and Soul (Ali Brown), 18

PowerUploads, 183

Poynter, Dan, 222, 225; *How to Self-Publish Your Book,* 43

Pozner, Jennifer, 172

Prairie iNet, 404

Preassigned Control Number (PCN), 49

Premiere Radio Networks, 90–91, 160

presidential campaign of 2008, 22

Presley, Priscilla, 238

press kits, 214

pricing: books, 49; eBooks, 54; your products, 16–22

primary rights, 57–58

Prince, 89–90, 98

Prine, John, 84

printers and printing: books, 50–51; community newspapers, 298–299, 301; green companies, 299; printing costs of community newspapers, 299; working with, 306

Print on Demand (POD) publishing, 40, 42–43, 50. *See also* self-publishing; traditional book publishing; vanity publishing

print royalties for sheet music, 111

privacy policies, 223; community broadband, 407

privacy tips, 340–341

private labeling by retailers, 250

prleap, 56

"Problem with Music, The" (Steve Albini), 88

producers: *American Idol* (TV show), 12–13

production: community media production resources, 406; community newspaper, 292–293; community newspapers, 292–293, 297–299;

filmmaking, 192; public access TV shows, 366–369, 373; of video for mobile and handheld devices, 185; zine layouts, 263

product placement: of music via ringtones on television shows, 110; in vlog (videoblog) series, 176

Product Pricing Curve (Janet Switzer), 16–22

products: controlling your own, 16; how to make money with, 17–23; making a living from online, 3–8; marketing to retailers, 250–251; monetary value of multiple copies of, 17; multimedia, 18; others' live interaction with you, 20; subsidiary rights, 52; tools for tracking distribution, 183. *See also* repurposing your own work; serial products; subsidiary products

Profane Existence, 258

profanity filters, 317

profit-sharing deals, 96

program clocks, 153–155

program directors, 158

program guides, 352

programming channel agreements, 366

Progressive Democracts of America (PDA), 237

Project for Excellence in Journalism, 318

Project Opus Folio, 106

Prometheus Radio Project, 151, 345; equipment pages, 350; "Put Your Hands on the Radio, People," 343–357; *vs.* the Federal Communications Commission, 448–449; website (prometheusradio.org), 357

PromoteABook, 61

promotion: books, 52–54, 58; campus newspapers, 305; community newspapers, 299, 300; community radio stations, 352; do-it-yourself, 39; hiring others to do, 22; illegal means, 355; mobile device videos, 186; music, 114–116; newspapers, 313, 314–315; podcasts, 136–137; public access TV shows, 374; traditional media, 12; via MySpace, 334; via your own website, 213–214; videos and video series, 182; vlogs (videoblogs), 178; of websites online, 217–219; "word-of-mouse," 94. *See also* distribution; licensing; marketing; publicity

Propaganda, 134

proposals (RFPs), 406

PROs. *See* Performance Rights Societies (PROs)

Pro Tools, 150

prweb, 56

PTA (Planned Television Arts), 57

Pub-Forum.net, 58

public access TV shows, 292; directing, 371–372; equipment for creating, 364; getting a message on, 362–363; internship programs, 368; lighting for shows, 372; microphones for, 372–373; music for, 373; *Positive Spin* (San Francisco), 365; post-production and digital video editing, 373; production, 366–369; program formats, 369–371; program planning, 369; promotion and distribution, 374; sponsoring an existing show, 364, 366; what not to wear, 373; who can create, 361–362. *See also* PEG (public, educational and government) facilities

public access TV stations, 181, 362, 395–399. *See also* commercial television stations

public airwave auctions, 455

public interest obligations, 444–445

publicity: affiliateannouncement, 220; publicists for musicians, 116; radio, 57. *See also* promotion

publicity rights, 239

Public Radio Exchange, 357

public service announcements (PSAs), 355–356

Publisher's Weekly magazine, 41n2

publishing: long tail, 3; old and new methods, 39–40; sheet music and lyrics, 110–114. *See also* book publishing; podcasting; serial products

Publishing Mavericks series (Janet Switzer), 16

publishing policies: community newspapers, 295–296, 297

PublishingPoynters, 222, 225

Publish-L, 58

PumpAudio, 112

Punk Planet, 259

punk rock zines, 258–259

Purinton, Mark, 85

purplebark.net/maffrew, 424

Purpose Driven Life, The (Rick Warren), 53

Pussycat Dolls, 96

Putting the Can in Cancer, 42

"Put Your Hands on the Radio People" (Saunders, Schiller, Pete triDish), 343–357

QDNow (Quick and Dirty Tips), 56

qik, 185

Quiltmakers Gift, The (Don Tubesing), 60

Quirk, Tim, 114

Quit Whining, 259

Quiver, 217

R. Buckminster Fuller, 285

Radio and Television News Directors Association (RTNDA), 363

radio appearances, 57. *See also* interviews

Radio Broadcast Preservation Act of 2000, 346

radio bulletin boards, 57

Radio Conciencia (WCIW), 348

radio conglomerates, 90–92, 159–160; and copyright, 148; market shares, 90–92; market shares for satellite, Internet and terrestrial radio, 149. *See also* commercial radio stations

Radio for All, 357

Radiohead, 94, 98, 99, 100, 105

Radio Ink, 156

Radio Mutiny, 345, 349

radio show marketing: to affiliate stations, 150, 156–158; to sponsors, 162–164

radio show production: equipment, 150–151; in-home studios, 151; making a living from, 161–166; planning your show, 151–155

radio shows: ads, 159; beginning your own, 143–144; buying air time, 158–159; contracts with affiliate stations, 159–160; ideas and topics for, 144–145; keeping extra shows on hand, 161; making a living from, 3–8; naming your show, 149; options for broadcasting, 146–151; podcasts of, 130; start-up costs, 150–151; talk radio, 160; themed, 356; time needed to prepare, 145, 146; timing of segments, 153–155; vignettes for, 144. *See also* affiliate stations; community radio stations; podcasts; radio show marketing

Rainey, James, 318

Rather, Dan, 29

Really Simple Syndication (RSS). *See* RSS feeds

RealNetworks RealAudio and RealVideo, 173

recnet, 347

Recording Industry Association of America, 99–100, 148, 173, 446

recordings of music: album costs and financing, 21, 101–102; home HD studios, 117–124; for learning to play by ear, 68–69; learning to play from, 77–79; market shares of major and independent labels, 88; mixing and mastering, 119. *See also* songs

recording studios. *See* studios

record labels, 88–90; battle against file sharing, 173–174; contracts, 88–90; decline, 93; with new kinds of contracts, 103; types of record "deals," 94, 96, 98

record stores, 93

reddit, 217

"Redefining Television" (Mark Pesce), 174

Redfield, James, *The Celestine Prophecy,* 44

Redstone, Sumner, 444

reelreviewsradio, 135

refer-it, 221

register, 213

Regnery Publishing, 41–42

Rehfield, Michael, 192

relationship-building: for marketing and licensing deals, 246–249, 250; steps involved, 16

Reliant K, 335

religious podcasts "godcasts," 129

REM, 90, 334

renaissances, 274, 278, 283–286

Renshaw, Simon, 92

reporters: college newspaper, 304; dangers faced by, 321–323; federal shield law for, 323–324; financing news stories by, 324; high school, 307–308; at major newspapers, 290–291, 312. *See also* citizen journalism; journalism

Reporters Without Borders, 322, 323

Reprise Records, 90

repurposing your own work: books, 52–53; musicians, 109–110; podcasts, 137; radio shows, 161; types of products from, 63; why do it, 16. *See also* licensing; Product Pricing Curve (Janet Switzer); subsidiary products

reputation, 461

reseller programs. *See* affiliate programs

retailers for licensed merchandise, 240–241, 250–251

retail licensors of music, 112

Reuters, 320–321, 324, 337

ReverbNation, 106, 114

"reverse shoplifting," 60–61

"Revolution in Digital Movie Production and Distribution, The" (Peter Broderick), 189–201

Reznor, Trent, 20, 98, 99

Rhapsody, 108, 114

RIAA. *See* Recording Industry Association of America

Ribler, Marc, 111

Rich, Robert, 19

Rich Dad, Poor Dad series, 18, 53

Richton Sportswear, 235

rights: book, 51; books, 42; for content posted on social networks, 341; for content submitted online, 317; digital video (DV) features, 195–196; if you don't write your own book, 46; registration of digital recording, 105–106; songwriters, 110; splitting up and selling various, 21–22, 196; under traditional publishing, 42. *See also* contracts; copyright; Creative Commons licenses; terms of service

rights and royalties: traditional media, 12; why control your own, 16. *See also* contracts

Rimes, LeAnn, 90

ringtones, 19, 20; distributors and market shares, 113–114; licensing, 241–242; selling music via, 113; and Verizon cellphones, 279

Ringtone Universe, 241

Rio-Reviewers, 52

Riot Grrl zines, 259

riseup.net, 222

Roberts, Brian, 390

Robertson, Ed, 90

Robinson, Thomas G., 387, 389–390

Rocketboom, 176

Rockow, Karen, 257

Rock the Net Neutrality, 97

Rodriguez, Robert, 191

Roger McGuinns' Folk Den, 84

Roh Moo Hyun, 319

Rolling Stone, 114

Roosevelt, Theodore "Teddy," 236

Rose, Charlie, 370

Rose, Don, 87

Rosedale, Phillip, 337

Rosen, Jay, 324

Rosen, Jeff, 228

Row, Heath, 258, 259

Roxio Inc., 174

royalties: audits, 244–245; author, 41; deals for filmmakers, 198–199; for Internet radio stations, 446; licensing, 244; for music CDs, 89; for music for TV shows, 373; for musicians, music publishers, and songwriters, 111; music library, 110; to performers broadcasting on Internet stations, 147–148; publisher's share of songs, 110. *See also* contracts; rights

royalty free sound effects, 150

RSS feeds, 32–33, 139; 2.0, 460; and Adobe Flash format, 179; for podcasting, 127; RSS 2.0, 178

Rubinson, David, 87, 110

Rumblefish, 112

Rundgren, Todd, 101

Rushkoff, Douglas, 467; "The Opportunity for Renaissance," 273–279

Ryze, 338

Saba, Jennifer, 312n3

Safran, Steve, 318

Saidthegramaphone, 116

sales: advance sales of books, 49–50; bulk sales of books, 50; to core audiences, 103–105; direct sales of digital video (DV) feature films, 199–200; eBooks, 54; 80/20 rule, 220; music, 98–100; music digital singles, 102; of music via aggregators, 107–108; Soundscan service for record sales, 108; via affiliates, 55; via online sales letter, 63; via widgets, 105–106. *See also* indirect sales methods; promotion; upsells

Samberg, Andy, 438

Sambrook, Richard, 311

San Francisco Bay Area Independent Media Center (IMC), 292, 294, 301

San Francisco Chronicle, 290, 312

San Francisco Indymedia, 419

San Francisco Unified School District: Lowell High School, 309; Mission High School, 306–309

SAN (Standard Address Number), 49

Satan Wears a Bra, 259

satellite companies, 402. *See also* IPTV (Internet Protocol Television)

Satellite Radio, 149

Saunders, Sakura, 151, 467

Savage, Jon, 267

Savage, Steve, 101

Save the Internet coalition (savetheinternet.org), 97, 218, 453

savenetradio.org, 148

Scarface, 112

Schaaf, Val, 377n2, 391

Schachter, Julia, 438

Schaffer, Akiva, 433

Schaffer, Jan, 311, 315n8

Schanberg, Sydney H., 318

Scheide, Eric, 326

Schiller, A. Zach, 467

Schmidt, Eric, 284

Schneider, Maria, 20, 102

Schneier, Bruce, 6

Scholastic, 245

schools as book markets, 59

Schwarzenegger, Arnold, 381

science fiction zines, 256–257

Scoble, Robert, 27

Scott, Ben, 402n3, 410, 467; "Making Media Policy Public," 443–457

screen grabs, 177

SCUM Manifesto (Valerie Solanas), 258

Search and Destroy, 258

search boxes on your website, 226

search engine optimization, 214–219

search engines: Creative Commons find tools, 436; keeping them on your website, 216; market shares, 214; online submission forms for websites, 218–219; rankings of video by, 183; on websites, 55. *See also* blog search engines

Searls, Doc, 467; Making a New World", 459–462

Seattle Independent Media Center (IMC), 312, 416, 424

Second Life, 337; musicians on, 104

Secrets of Videoblogging (Verdi and Hodson), 177

Seduction of the Innocent (Frederic Wertham), 257, 260

Seifer, Adam, 35

Seinfeld, 368

self-distribution of digital video (DV) feature films, 197

self-distribution of music, 94, 98–100; controlling your rights, 102–103; costs and financing, 101–102; direct selling to core audience, 103–105; distribution channels, 251; online sales channels, 107–108; repurposing and licensing your music, 109–114; selling via widgets, 105–106; ways to let fans find your music, 106–107

self-distribution of zines, 258, 266

self-expression, 275

self-publishing, 39, 40, 43–46; benefits, 220; business model, 54–55; process, 46–53; by writers and others, 19. *See also* book promotion; books; Print on Demand (POD) publishing; traditional book publishing; vanity publishing; zines

Self-Publishing Manual, The, 47

Sell Yourself Without Selling Your Soul (Susan Harrow), 236n1

serial products: best-sellers, 16, 18; books, 46; Internet TV series, 171; making an Internet TV series, 182; Marin Report awards, 363; public access TV shows, 367; publishing via donations, 6–7; radio shows, 161; vlogs (videoblogs), 176. *See also* repurposing your own work; subsidiary products

"Sesame Workshop" (Sherry, Westin), 246–248

"Sex, Drugs and Updating Your Blog" (Clive Thompson), 100

sexual predators online, 339, 340

Shane, Scott, 27

Shelfari, 58

Shen, Catherine, 315n6

shipping. *See* distribution; fulfillment

Shlain, Tiffany, 180
"Shooting Film *vs.* Shooting Video" (Mark Stolaroff), 204–205
shopping carts, 227–228
shoutcast, 147, 148
Shuster, Joe, 257
Siegel, Jerry, 257
Sigler, Scott *EarthCore,* 56
Signatures Network, 241
Silence in Black and While, The (Hawthorne Heights), 94
Silver MasterMind (Ali Brown), 19
Simon, Paul, 291
Simonetti, Ellen, 28
SimplyAudiobooks, 53
simplymusic.com, 80
simpy, 217
Sin City, 190
Sirius, 149
site maps on websites, 216
site2you, 213
sivertongue1, 28
Six Apart, 28, 30, 33, 338
Sixeyes, 116
60 Minutes, 370
Skype, 454, 455; Skypecasts, 53, 146
slashdot.org, 312, 313
Slaves of Celebrity (Eric Olsen), 12
Sling Media, 173
slogans or memes, 240; trademarking, 243
SmartMobs, 36
Smartypants, Mimi, 37
smartypants.diaryland, 27
Smith, Kevin, 21, 191, 201
SNAP. *See* Social Network Application Platform (SNAP)
Sniffin' Glue (Mark Perry), 258
SNOCAP, 105–106
Snow Crash (Neal Stephenson), 337
Soap, 368
Sobule, Jill, 7, 20–21
social bookmarks, 217
Socializer (ekstreme.com/socializer), 217

Social Justice Center of Marin, 384, 394n18
social justice movements, 414
Social Network Application Platform (SNAP), 338
social networks: about, 331–332; bethemedia, 336; book promotion on, 58; for every demographic, 335–336, 339; finding, 115–116; history of, 332–333; open source platforms for, 317; page personalization (pimping), 338–339; risks of revealing on, 336, 339–340; terms of service, 341; use by journalists, 324; use by musicians, 104, 334–335. *See also* Facebook; MySpace
Socialtext, 329
software: BitTorrent free client, 175; copyleft, 433; from corporate manufacturers, 278–279; developer APIs from Google, 338; for film editing, 203, 204; influence on blog writing, 274, 275; podcast recording, 133–134; for print publication design, 298; programming of, 276, 278–279; to promote information access, 419; radio show production, 150; that track changes in writing, 329; for validating feeds, 136; for vlogs (videoblogs), 177; wiki, 328–329. *See also* open source software
Solanas, Valerie, 258
Soldiers Pay, 208
SomaFM, 147
"some rights reserved" copyright, 432
songs: monetary value of one-off, 17; song "deals," 111–112; writing for individual fans, 21. *See also* digital music; MP3 files
songwriters publishing and promotion agreements, 110
Sonny Bono Copyright Term Extension Act, 283
Sony BMG, 93. *See also* Epic (Sony BMG)
Sony Music Entertainment, 242
sound bites, 57
sound clips, 214
sound effects in radio shows, 150, 151–152
sound files, 134
SoundForge, 141
sound in videos for mobile and handheld devices, 185
soundproof enclosures, 121, 151
Soundscan, 108, 446

SoundsGood, 53

Souzis, Adam, 467; "Wikis: Platforms for Participation," 327–329

spam and spamdexing, 219, 224; CAN-SPAM Act of 2003, 221. *See also* splogs

spam filters, 55–56, 222

Sparklist, 222

speakerfulfillmentservices, 229

speakers: broadcasting speeches by, 370; impact of Creative Commons licenses, 438; making a living, 17; podcasts, 129. *See also* teleseminars

"Speaking About Your Creativity Legally" (Mia Garlick), 427–438

Speed of Sound (Coldplay), 113

Spitzer, Eliot, 91

Splog Reporter, 35

splogs, 35

SplogSpot, 35

Spoke, 338

sponsors: community newspapers, 302–303; community radio stations, 352; mobile film festivals, 186; for radio shows, 162–165; sponsor kits, 162, 164. *See also* affiliate programs; patrons

sponsorship announcements, 355

Sportsblogs, 35

spreadsheet, 239

Spring Book Design, 48

Springsteen, Bruce, 22

Sprint Music Store, 112

Sprint Nextel, 453–454

Sproutbuilder, 106

Spy Kids movies, 190

St. Paul *Pioneer Press,* 314

Stallman, Richard M., 433, 467–468; "Did You Say 'Intellectual Property'?", 327, 439–441

Standard Address Number (SAN), 49

standard distribution deals, 96

Stand by Me (movie), 107

Starling, 257

Starr, Jerold, 367, 370, 468

Starring Amanda Congdon, 176

Start Late, Finish Rich (David Bach), 57

startup costs prefinancing, 6, 7

Star Wars: subsidiary product licensing, 236

Steadman, Carl, 6

Stefani, Gwen, 112–113

Steisel, Mark, 46

Stephenson, Neal *Snow Crash,* 337

Stereogum, 116

Stevens, Ted, 379

Stewart, Joan "The Publicity Hound," 225

Stolaroff, Mark, 468; "Shooting Film *vs.* Shooting Video," 204–205; "The Desktop Studio," 202–203

Stolze, Greg, 7

Stone, Brad, 340

Stone, Geoffrey R., 323

Stoney, George, 381

stopbigmedia, 451

Straight from the Heart, 363

Strand, The: Venice, CA, 171

Stratton, Scott, 58, 218

Straus, David, 180

streaming video from/to cell phones, 185–186

street-level distribution, 299–300

Street Level TV, 292

Street performer Protocol, 6–7

street teams, 114

Strumpf, Koleman, 100

Stuart Little, 241

studio productions, 366.369

studios: community radio stations, 348, 350; digital video (DV) feature film production, 202–203; home HD video and audio, 117–124; in-home radio program, 151; low power FM radio stations, 347; podcasting, 139–141; recording, 101

studio systems: movie costs, 170. *See also* traditional media

subscribers, 224–225; database for, 351; varying products for, 18; 100,000 video, 171

subscriptions as products, 18

subscription services for music, 108

subsidiary products: from books, 46, 51; funneling, 54–55; licensing, 434; from other artist's works, 435; rights to your, 42. *See also* eBooks; licensing; repurposing your own work; serial products

subsidiary rights, 52, 57–58

success: downside to "winning," 278; as getting a book "deal," 40; idea anyone can be a, 11–12; as a writer, 40–42. *See also* moneymaking

Successful Affiliate Marketing for Merchants (Shawn Collins), 220

Success Principles, The (Jack Canfield), 16

Suck, 6

Sullivan Award, 308

Sundance Channel, 208

Sun Microsystems, 27

Sunrise (Robert Crooke), 43

Superman comics, 257

superpatrons, 19, 22. *See also* macropatrons

superstar acts, 88; advertising income, 110

surveys on websites, 224

Survivor Movie, The, 58

Svensson, Peter, 181

Swan, Katharine, 468; "High School Journalism Matters," 306–309

Switzer, Janet, 14; Product Pricing Curve, 16–17

sychronization (synch) fees, 110–111

syndication, 233; of articles online, 217; blog post feeds, 32–33; content syndication protocol, 127; newspaper articles, 289; podcasts, 136; radio shows, 161–166

syndication sales firms, 162

tabs, 80, 81, 83, 85. *See also* lead sheets for piano

tab site takedown notices, 84

Taccone, Jorma, 438

Tadpole, 190

tags, 217. *See also* metadata

Talking Heads, 96

Talking Points Memo, 27

talk radio, 160, 451–452

TalkShoe, 141

talkshoe, 132

talk shows on community radio stations, 357

targeted ads, 226

Tatum, Art, 77

Taylor, Brian, 48

Teach, 438

techmobiles, 406

Tech Nation, 139

technology: copyright problems caused by, 431–432; impact on media and society, 274; learning how it really works, 279; for making a living online, 5. *See also* Creative Commons; equipment; social networks; software; studios

Technorati, 33, 34

"Teenagers" (My Chemical Romance), 170

Telecommunications, Mass Media, and Democracy (Robert McChesney), 448

Telecommunications Act of 1996, 90, 159–160, 283, 445

telecommunications industry lobbying, 445

"Telephone Repair Handbook" (Mark Pesce), 332

teleseminars, 53; "Teleseminar Secrets" (Alex Mandossian), 63–64

television appearances, 57–58; getting via affiliate partnerships, 249

television commercials, 111

television shows: costs, 170–172; licensing of characters and shows, 236–237, 242, 245, 246–247; and music library royalties, 111–112; podcasts, 130; "prime time," 173; programing for mobile minicasts, 185; ringtone product placement, 110; synchronization (synch) fees, 110; "two-minute TV," 185. *See also* digital video (DV) feature films; fanzines; Independent Film Channel; public access TV shows; Sundance Channel

Tepper, Lee, 241

Tequila, Tila (Tial Nguyen), 335

terms of service: caveat for videographers, 183–184; Google's, 227; online newspapers, 317; social networks, 341. *See also* rights

Terra Naomi, 170

text-link-ads, 218

textlinkbrokers, 218

text messaging: contests, 113; for selling music, 112

Thameen, Omar, 222

thank you pages on websites, 224

theaterchurch, 129

theatrical distribution of films, 195, 197–198, 207

"The Audience Takes Control" (Mark Pesce), 174

thefulfillmenthouse, 229

"The Medium Is the Music: Feel the Power of Creating Your Own" (Robert Laughlin), 67–79

theopenpress, 56

the Orchard, 108

thepetshow, 144

The Purpose Driven Life (Rick Warren), 53

There (comic book artist), 337n1

"There is Power in a Union" (Billy Bragg), 83–84

The Shock Doctrine, The (Naomi Klein), 58

The Silence in Black and White (Hawthorne Heights), 335

thetabworld, 82

thetimemovie, 218

Thin Air Community Radio (kyrs.org), 349

Think Secret, 28

Think to Grow Rich (Ali Brown), 18

Third Coast Press, 449

This Land Is Your Land (Jib Jab animation), 174, 218

Thompson, Clive, "Sex, Drugs and Updating Your Blog," 100

Thomson, Kristin, 87

Thornton, Barbara, 385

360 (or equity) deals, 94, 96

Thrift Score, 259

Thumbplay, 114

Thursday, 104–105

Tijuana Bibles, 258

Tiki Bar TV, 176

Timberlake, Justin, 337

Time Code (Mike Figgis), 190

time-shifting devices, 173

Time Travelers, 257

Time Warner, 443, 447; channel 98, 363

tip jars: new model for music marketing, 101–102; at tabling events, 301

titles of websites, 216. *See also* slogans or memes

TLC, 96

T-Mobile USA, 453–454

Tofu Hut (tofuhut.blogspot), 116

Toomey, Jenny, 14, 87–88, 97n1, 107

Topica, 222

TOSed, 317

tours: music touring, 106–107. *See also* book tours; concerts

Tower Records, 92

Towse, Ruth, 8

trade association licensing, 252

trademarks and trademark licensing law, 236, 243, 439–441

trade publications, 245

traditional book publishing, 40–42. *See also* Print on Demand (POD) publishing; self-publishing; vanity publishing

traditional media, 12, 13. *See also* media conglomerates

Traffic-geyser, 183

transnational bodies, 414n1

transom.org, 357

Transworld, 251

"Treadmill Dance" (OKGo), 170

Tribal Digital Village, 404

Tribe, The (Tiffany Shlain), 180

Tribune Company, The, 290

triDish, Pete, 468

"triple play" telecommunications bundles, 377; alternatives, 401–410

Trott, Mena, 28

True Fans, 4. *See also* 1,000 True Fans business model

Truffaut, Francois, 186

Tubemogul, 183

Tubesing, Don, *The Quiltmakers Gift,* 60

Tucker, Rick, 378

Tufte, Liz, 48

Tune Core, 108

TuneWidget, 106

Turner, Ted, 448

Tuttle, Lisa, 257

TV networks: diminished need for, 173; pilot shows, 172

Twain, Shania, 91

28 Days Later, 202

Twersky, Lori. *See Bitch*

"two-minute TV," 185

TypePad, 28, 31, 34, 136, 177

U2, 96, 241

ultimate-guitar, 82

Uncovered: The War on Iraq (Robert Greenwald), 21, 206–207, 208

underground magazines, 256, 259–260

Unfit for Command (Regnery Publishing), 41–42

Unicorn, 257

United States Copyright Royalty Board, 147–148

United States rank among world countries: freedom of the press, 323; supplying broadband to citizens, 401–402

Unity Foundation, 365

Universal, 238

Universal Declaration of Human Rights, 319n16

Universal Product Code (barcode), 108

Universal records, 89

upcoming.yahoo.com, 106

upsells, 21

Urban Outfitters, 251

Usenet (USEr NETwork), 312

USS Catastrophe, 259

Ustream.tv, 182

Utah Telecommunication Open Infrastructure Agency (UTOPIA), 403

validator software, 136

Van Dijck, Peter, 175, 176

Van Dixhorn, Graham, 47

vanity publishing, 40, 42, 49. *See also* Print on Demand (POD) publishing; self-publishing; traditional book publishing

Vantage Press, 42

Vedder, Eddie, 452

Vega, Suzanne, 337

Verdi, Michael, 176, 177

Verizon, 279, 379

Verizon FiOS, 180

Verizon V CAST music store, 112, 455

Verizon Wireless, 453

veryviphosting, 213

VHS recorders for podcasting, 140

Viacom/CBS, 159, 160, 443

video appearances, 58

Videoblogging (Jay Dedman), 175

videoblogs. *See* vlogs (videoblogs)

video clips: metadata, 175; for mobile and handheld devices, 185–186; by music fans, 114; sending from cell phones, 185; spoofs, 115. *See also* podcasting; vlogs (videoblogs)

video franchise agreements, 377

videogames, 20; licensing of, 242; music in, 112; playing *vs.* writing, 275–276. *See also* games; interactive media

videographers: making a living, 17, 171, 179–180; promotion of Internet presence, 218; terms of service caveat for, 183–184. *See also* filmmakers; studios

"Video Revolution, The" (David Mathison), 169–176, 179–186

videos: Creative Commons licensing, 438; distribution, 169, 171, 172, 183; historical markers, 173–176; making a living by creating, 184; for mobile and handheld devices, 185–186; numbers viewed online, 172; production platform for Internet TV, 184; promotion, 182; uses, 172–173; video recording devices, 171; viral, 218. *See also* digital video (DV) feature films; Internet TV; video clips; videographers; vlogs (videoblogs)

video-sharing sites, 179

video trailers, 21. *See also* book trailers

viewaskew, 201

VIP clubs on websites, 224

viral social networks, 332

viral videos, 218

virtual collaborative networks for making music, 118

Virtual Reality Modeling Language (VRML), 174

virtual reality sites, 337

virtual storefronts, 239–240

visitorville, 230

vlogs (videoblogs), 175–176; advantages over Internet TV free sites, 170; creating your first one, 177–178; distribution, 178, 179–180; finding a host, 177–178; by founding vloggers, 176; promotion, 178; series, 176; tool for sharing, 176. *See also* Internet TV; video clips

vocal booths, 122

voiceamerica, 148

voiceofsandiego.org, 315

volunteers: all volunteer organizations, 293; for public access TV shows, 367–368

Vonage, 454

Vonnegut, Kurt, 337

Von Triers, Lars, 190

Voo Doo Babies, 111

Vox, 28, 31

VRML. *See* Virtual Reality Modeling Language (VRML)

vSide, 337n1

Wagner, Paul, 192

Walker, Jesse, 344

walled gardens, 455

Wallop, 337n1

Wall Street Journal, 290–291; approved sites for books, 62

Wal-Mart: The High Cost of Low Price, 208

Walsh, Rudolfo, 420–421

Wang, Wayne, 190

wannabegirl.org, 27

Warner Bros., 208

Warner Music Group, 96

Warner records, 89, 93

Warren, Frank, 36

Warren, Rick, 53, 60

Washington (D.C.) *Spark,* 296, 299

Wasley, Gary, 363

Watt-Evans, Lawrence, 6

Watts, Duncan J., 91

WAVE (Western Access Video Excellence) Award, 363

WCIW radio, 357

Web 2.0, 414

webconfs.com/anchor-text-analysis.php, 217

Weber, Jonathan, 318

weblogs, 33

websites: domain names and hosts for, 213; equipment and software for creating content, 212–213; hot spots on web pages, 226; marketing with, 55–56; offensive content, 227; privacy policies, 214; rankings, 215; source code example, 215–216; statistics packages for, 226, 227, 230; superiority over ringtone sales, 114; tools and templates for creation, 213; using wikis to design, 329; why you need, 104, 211; as your online media room, 213–214. *See also* virtual storefronts

web-stat, 230

webtrends, 230

Ween, Dean and Gene (ween.com), 101

Weezer, 334

Weichel, Kim, 365

WELL (Whole Earth 'Lectronic Link), 277, 312

We Media-Zogby, 318

"We're All In This Together" (David Mathison), 281–286

Wertham, Frederic, 257, 260, 267

Westergren, Tim, 101, 115–116, 148

Westin, Sherry, 468; "Sesame Workshop," 246–248

Westwood One Inc., 160

WFMU radio station, 351

What Color Is Your Parachute (Nelson Bolles), 44

"What's Going on Here? The Artist Services Model" (Barry Bergman), 95

Wheaton, Wil, 37, 107

White, Biljo, 257

Whitney, Brian Austin, 14

Whole Foods Markets, 60

wholesale book distributors, 59, 60

widgets, 105–106, 338

Wikipedia, 327–328; for book promotion, 58

wikis, 327–329

wikispaces, 329

Wilchusky, Le Ann, 430

Wiliams, Robbie, 96

Will, Bradley Roland, 322, 421

wilwheaton.net, 36

Windhorse (Paul Wagner), 192

"Wind It Up" (Barenaked Ladies), 114

Winer, Dave, 127, 129, 138, 139, 460

Wired, 94, 99

wireless networks, 403–404, 405, 453–455

wireless phone store music catalogs, 112

WireTap Pro, 134

Wisconsin Democracy Campaign, 449

Withoutabox, 180

WMMT radio, 320

WMNF radio, 348

Wolf, Josh, 321–322

Women in Media and News, 172

Wood, Greg Epler, 398–399

Woods, Tiger, 237

Woodworth, Mark, 47

Wool, Danny, 328

Woolsey, Lynn, 391

wordcast.audible, 137

"word of mouse," 332

Word of Mouth Marketing Association (womma.org), 116

WordPress, 30, 31

work. *See* products

works for hire, 430, 431, 432

World According to Mimi Smartypants, The, 37

World Bank, 416

World Intellectual Property Organization (WIPO), 439–440

World of Fanzines, The (Frederic Wertham), 257, 267

World of Warcraft, 337n1

World Social Forum, 422

World Summit on the Information Society, 422

World Trade Organization demonstrations in Seattle, 413–414, 417, 423

writers: book "deals," 40–42; boutique fullfilment houses for, 229; for community newspapers, 296; "content" vs reputation, 462; Creative Commons tools, 436; of digital video (DV) features, 191; freelance, 55; ghostwriters, 46; influence of technology, 274, 275; interviews on Second Life, 337; licensing by, 240–241; licensing of images from books, 236, 237; making a living, 3–8, 41, 44, 55; market channels, 55–62; product pricing and fundraising, 18–19; promotion of Internet presence, 217; revenue opportunities for blog writers, 35; use of focus groups, 47; use of MySpace, 334; use of wikis, 327; websites by, 214. *See also* articles; songwriters

Writers Guild of America, 13, 172

Write the Perfect Book Proposal (Jeff Herman), 44

Write to Your Market, 47

WSJ. See Wall Street Journal

Wu, Tim, 452, 453

Xero, 257

Xing, 338

Xingtone, 114

Xlibris, 43

XL Recordings, 100

XM Satellite Radio (xmradio), 149

Yahoo!, 459; classified ad revenue, 290; purchase of Flickr, 312; You Witness News, 321

Yahoo! Music, 147

Yahoo! Publisher Network, 225

Yahoo videoblog group, 175

Yandro, 257

Yo La Tengo, 351

Yorke, Thom, 99

yourhub, 315

Youth Media Council, 449

YouTube, 58; "comments" feature, 181; music fan videos, 114–115; similar sites, 179; videos, 170. *See also* Internet TV

Y tu mamá también, 200

Zaentz, Saul, 103

Zapatistas, 416

zazzle, 239, 240

Zelinsky, Susan, 87

ziePod, 131

zine distribution, 258, 259, 265–267

zine-making, 260–269; zines on, 259

zines: about, 255; charging for, 267; feminist, 258, 259; financing, 261–262; origin of the word, 257; porn, 258–259; punk rock fanzines, 258–259; science fiction fanzines, 256–257; topical, 259. *See also* comic books and cartoons; community newspapers

zinesters, 256, 257–258

"Zine trend catches on at school" (Denton, Kathy), 267

Zingy, 114

Zisk, Brian, 87

zoiefilms.com/cellularcinema.html, 186

Zuckerberg, Mark, 336

Zwinky, 337n1

"Be the change you want to see in the world."
—*Mahatma Gandhi*